Handbook of Research on Complex Dynamic Process Management:
Techniques for Adaptability in Turbulent Environments

Minhong Wang
University of Hong Kong, Hong Kong

Zhaohao Sun
University Of Ballarat, Australia

BUSINESS SCIENCE REFERENCE

Hershey · New York

Director of Editorial Content:	Kristin Klinger
Senior Managing Editor:	Jamie Snavely
Assistant Managing Editor:	Michael Brehm
Publishing Assistant:	Sean Woznicki
Typesetter:	Daniel Custer, Carole Coulson, Ryan Cohick, Daniel Wilson
Cover Design:	Lisa Tosheff
Printed at:	Yurchak Printing Inc.

Published in the United States of America by
Business Science Reference (an imprint of IGI Global)
701 E. Chocolate Avenue
Hershey PA 17033
Tel: 717-533-8845
Fax: 717-533-8661
E-mail: cust@igi-global.com
Web site: http://www.igi-global.com/reference

Library of Congress Cataloging-in-Publication Data

Handbook of research on complex dynamic process management : techniques for
adaptability in turbulent environments / Minhong Wang, Zhaohao Sun, editors.
     p. cm.
   Includes bibliographical references and index.
   Summary: "This book combines both a managerial and technical view of
business process management, providing advanced analysis and concrete
approaches for relevant problems, as well as the implications for further
studies and practices"--Provided by publisher.
   ISBN 978-1-60566-669-3 (hardcover) -- ISBN 978-1-60566-670-9 (ebook) 1.
Workflow--Management. 2. Management information systems. 3. Industrial
management. I. Wang, Minhong, 1969- II. Sun, Zhaohao. III. Title.

   HD62.17.H36 2010
   658.5'1--dc22
                              2009006916

British Cataloguing in Publication Data
A Cataloguing in Publication record for this book is available from the British Library.

All work contributed to this book is new, previously-unpublished material. The views expressed in this book are those of the authors, but not necessarily of the publisher.

List of Contributors

Table of Contents

Section 1
Conceptual Modeling for Business Process Management

Section 2
Adaptive Technologies for Business Process Management

Section 3
Collaborative Business Process Management

Section 4
Practical Issues in BPM Technology Development

Section 5
Business Process Management in Practice

Detailed Table of Contents

Section 1
Conceptual Modeling for Business Process Management

This chapter analyzes the complexity of business processes and the technologies for modeling and constructing complex BPM systems. Based on the complexity of business processes and modular theory for complex systems, the DCAR architecture is presented for complex process management, which includes decomposition of complex processes (D); coordination of interactive activities (C); awareness of dynamic environment (A); and resource selection and coordination (R). On the other hand, modular computing technologies, such as Object-Oriented Programming; Component-Based Development; Agent-Oriented Computing; and Service-Oriented Architecture; have been widely applied in developing complex systems. However, there is considerable ambiguity in differentiating between these overlapping technologies and their use in developing BPM systems. No explicit linkage has been established between the requirement of BPM and the supporting technologies. This study uses the DCAR architecture as the foundation to identify the BPM requirements for employing technologies in developing BPM systems. Based on an examination of both sides (BPM requirements and supporting technologies), this study presents a clear picture of business process complexity with a systemic approach for designing and developing complex BPM systems by using appropriate computing technologies.

Chapter 2

This chapter describes an approach for enterprises to use their own domain concepts to model their business processes. Conventional BPM tools often provide a standardized business process modeling language and implementation technology. This makes the tools inflexible and difficult to use for individual enterprises. This chapter provides a tool-based framework that allows an enterprise to customize BPM languages and tools to its specific needs instead of developing them from scratch. It applies the basic model driven development principles for direct representation and automation of BPM tools through a tool experiment in Danske Bank. BPM tools are developed to capture Danske Bank's specific modeling concepts and use of technology, and automate the generation of the code. The empirical evaluation has revealed the remarkable advantage of the approach in development productivity and code quality.

Claudio Petti, Scuola Superiore ISUFI, Università del Salento, Italy
Mark Klein, Massachusetts Institute of Technology, USA

This chapter presents a methodology for redesigning and inventing new business processes that relies on a handbook of process models. It focuses on a practical approach for dealing with business process changes by connecting IT experts with business people. The methodology is the fruit of a decade-long MIT research effort known as the Process Handbook project. It is based on acquiring an abstract model of core activities and dependencies in the existing process, and then engaging in a structured and systematic exploration of process alternatives, where a large repository of best-practice business process models, that is, a Process Handbook, can be used for inspiration. The chapter uses the case of a real-life risk management process to illustrate the steps of the methodology and demonstrates how its concepts such as inheritance and exception handling can be used to design more effective and robust IT-based processes by enabling easier and more structured gathering of software requirements; in this way reducing the possibility of misunderstandings between IT experts and business people, and reducing software bugs.

Ilia Bider, IbisSoft AB, Sweden
Erik Perjons, Stockholm University/Royal Institute of Technology, Sweden

This chapter discusses the selection of an appropriate approach for business process modeling by means of a simplified classification of business process modeling approaches. To ensure the "right" choice of modeling approach, three factors are addressed for consideration: (a) properties of the object to be modeled; (b) characteristics of the environment in which the model is being built; and (c) intended use of the model. This study analyzes the factors involved in the domain of business process modeling. It lists the most essential properties of business processes, classifies modeling environments, and discusses practical tasks where a business process model can be used. Based on the analysis, practical recommendations on what modeling approach to choose are given dependent on the type of the process under consideration, the task at hand, and the environment in which the model is being built and verified.

Section 2
Adaptive Technologies for Business Process Management

Michael Adams, Queensland University of Technology, Australia
Arthur ter Hofstede, Queensland University of Technology, Australia
Nick Russell, Eindhoven University of Technology, The Netherlands
Wil van der Aalst, Eindhoven University of Technology, The Netherlands

This chapter provides a comprehensive examination of the principles that underpin business process technologies in order to derive a novel approach that moves beyond the traditional assembly-line metaphor. The study provides an overview of approaches to exception handling and flexibility in Process-Aware Information Systems, investigates theoretical foundations of process adaptation, and proposes a comprehensive framework for exception handling in work practices. Using a set of principles derived from Activity Theory, a system Worklet Service has been implemented, using a Service Oriented Architecture that provides support for dynamic and extensible flexibility, evolution, and exception handling in business processes.

Manfred Reichert, University of Ulm, Germany
Thomas Bauer, Daimler AG, Germany
Peter Dadam, University of Ulm, Germany

This chapter presents the concepts and techniques for adaptive process management during run-time and in distributed systems. The focus is placed on minimizing the communication costs among workflow servers, while ensuring correct execution behavior as well as correctness of ad-hoc workflow changes. To achieve this, it is crucial to identify the workflow servers that are involved in the synchronization of an ad-hoc change. These active servers need to know the schema and state of a changed workflow instance in order to correctly control its execution. In addition, it should be decided whether, when, and how a changed workflow instance schema has to be transmitted to other workflow servers.

Mair Allen-Williams, University of Southampton, UK
Nicholas R. Jennings, University of Southampton, UK

This chapter addresses two challenges to computing technology in complex distributed systems: decision making in uncertain and partially-observable environments, and coordination with other agents in such environments. The authors have developed an approach to this problem using a Bayesian learning mechanism, extending previous work on learning models of other agents, and have demonstrated its effectiveness in a scenario from the disaster response domain. The novelties in this work lie in an extension of online model-based learning techniques into partially observable domains using finite automata.

Chapter 8

This chapter introduces a Workflow-based Information Integration (WII) approach for dynamic and adaptive workflow management in inter-organizational business collaboration and service provision. The implementation framework comprises five layers: semantic, application, workflow, service, and message. The chapter focuses on the workflow layer for providing adaptiveness based on various types of flows such as control-flows, data-flows, security-flows, exception-flows, and semantic-flows. The issues of data-integration, semantic-referencing, and exception-handling assertions are discussed in order to achieve dynamic and adaptive workflow-based information integration.

Chapter 9

This chapter presents a flexible approach to ad-hoc exception handling by using forward stepping, backtracking, and alternative paths. The author provides an analysis of a workflow model based on which, backtracking and forward stepping can be evaluated and implemented. The algorithms for alternative route identification and forward stepping are proposed to allow dynamic modifications to workflows at design time or run time. The meta-process, that is, the mechanism for automatic activation of the proposed algorithms, is demonstrated, which includes functional block detection; alternative paths detection; process parameter analysis; and exception handler construction.

This chapter describes an approach to exception handling in BPM by using a multiple-step backtracking mechanism. This study aims to maintain a tradeoff between re-planning and rigid backtracking for exception handling and recovery. The concept of the BDI (belief, desire and intention) agent is applied to model and construct the BPM system to inherit its advantages of adaptability and flexibility. Then, the flexible backtracking approach is introduced by utilizing the beneficial features of event-driven and means-end reasoning of BDI agents. Finally, the study incorporates an open nested transaction model to encapsulate plan execution and backtracking to gain the system level support of concurrency control and automatic recovery. With the ability to reason about task characteristics, this approach enables the system to find and commence a suitable plan prior to or in parallel with a compensation process when a failure occurs.

Section 3
Collaborative Business Process Management

The chapter presents a rule-based approach for collaboration development and management of business processes. The proposed approach allows organizations to capture the requirements for their business collaborations in an explicit, manageable, and uniform manner in the form of rules. These rules can then be used to drive and constrain the development and management of needed collaboration models. In this way, collaborative business process design becomes a runtime activity, where the business collaboration shapes itself to its specific circumstances by applying the appropriate rules. The feasibility of the approach is demonstrated in the context of a complex insurance claim scenario using prototype tooling.

The chapter introduces a service oriented relative workflow model to help organisations create flexible and privacy-safe virtual organisation alliances. An organisation centred design method and a visibility mechanism are proposed to deal with the challenges of temporary partnership and low trustiness between collaborating organisations. Contracts are not only used to define and regulate business service collaborations, but also to assist developing the visibility constraints for the business process integration. A visibility control mechanism is applied to remove potential authority violation, and guarantee the safety on privacy between collaborating organisations.

The chapter provides a specific account of inter-workflow in logistic processes. A logistic process is considered as a combined process that manages the flow of materials among the partners. It consists of multiple sub processes, each of which is managed by a single partner. This study proposes a set of inter-workflow patterns that represent the relations among the separate processes in logistic environments. Based on the patterns, ECA (Event-Condition-Action) rules are generated to control the execution of the logistic process by the rule engine.

Trust is an important issue in collaborative business process management. The chapter discusses intelligent techniques for trust management in electronic commerce. The chapter examines the engineering of experience-based trust in e-commerce systems, as well as the interrelationships among experience-based, knowledge-based and inference-based trust. A knowledge-based model of trust management in e-commerce, together with a multi-agent system architecture for experience-based trust engineering in e-commerce are presented.

Chapter 15

This chapter discusses Process Harmonization in global businesses. Process Harmonization is a complex initiative carried out by large companies seeking to standardize the process variants being executed by different business units across several countries or regions. Motivations for this exercise include: cost pressures; mergers and acquisitions; customer satisfaction; the need for agile and flexible processes; and risk reduction in outsourcing processes. The complexity of this exercise is inherent as it involves multiple regions with special needs and characteristics, existing process and IT systems evolved over time, and organizational dynamics around different business groups. This chapter examines the drivers of Process Harmonization, identifies the challenges and constraints associated with the initiatives, and finally proposes a methodology to execute process harmonization initiatives.

Chapter 16

The chapter focuses on composition oriented architecture for establishing extended, connected, adaptive, and on-demand business processes. As next-generation IT is presumed to thrive on spontaneous and seamless collaboration among systems, services, and servers by sending messages as well as sharing a wider variety of connected and empowered resources, there arises a distinct identity and value for progressive composites. The author discusses how rapidly and smoothly services enable business-aligned and process-centric composition, with respect to composition paradigms; patterns, platforms; processes; practices; products; perspectives; problems; and potentials.

Section 4
Practical Issues in BPM Technology Development

Chapter 17

Jon Espen Ingvaldsen, The Norwegian University of Science and Technology, Norway
Jon Atle Gulla, The Norwegian University of Science and Technology, Norway

The chapter introduces semantic business process mining of SAP transaction logs. SAP is the most widely used Enterprise Resource Planning (ERP) system, which contains transaction logs linked to large amounts of structured data. However, the core of SAP systems was not originally designed from the business process management perspective. The business process layer was added later without full rearrangement of the system. As a result, system logs produced by SAP are not process-based, and can not be directly used for process mining. This chapter shows how data available in SAP systems can enrich process instance logs with ontologically structured concepts. The authors introduce and valuate three techniques for mapping executed transactions with the standard business process hierarchies in SAP.

Chapter 18

Semih Cetin, Cybersoft Information Technologies, Turkey
N. Ilker Altintas, Cybersoft Information Technologies, Turkey
Ozgur Tufekci, Cybersoft Information Technologies, Turkey

The chapter addresses the issue that traditional techniques for modeling and executing business processes are too generic to support diverse business environments. Most BPM tools are not scalable enough for typical business cases, lack architectural coverage to manage the tradeoffs between dynamism and other business quality issues, are insufficient to support integration with legacy business processes, and are without a balanced guidance between "primary" and "supportive" processes. This chapter aims to refrain from using generic approaches and techniques for process modeling by partitioning the big picture into domain specific parts. The authors use the "Domain Specific Kit" for abstraction and composition of primary and supportive processes in an organization. This approach has been put into action for the implementation of central operations management of a mid-scale bank in Turkey.

Chapter 19

Hajo A. Reijers, Eindhoven University of Technology, The Netherlands

This chapter presents an approach that is opposite to the direction of most developments in the workflow field: lightweight workflow. Lightweight workflow management systems are workflow management systems that only provide the most basic functionalities and are characterized by a relatively small and non-intrusive effort to implement and adopt them. The underlying idea is that in many situations, especially when flexibility and application integration are not big issues, a "lighter" workflow system provides a better proposition to arrive at a successful and satisfactory workflow implementation. This chapter introduces the essential features of lightweight workflow, and reflects on the application of lightweight workflow in practice.

Chapter 20

Krishnendu Kunti, Infosys Technologies Limited, India
Bijoy Majumdar, Infosys Technologies Limited, India
Terance Bernard Dias, Infosys Technologies Limited, India

This chapter draws attention to the testing of business process management systems. One of the aspects of managing complex and dynamic business processes is to make sure that the process delivers what is required of it at all times. The authors identify the aspects of business processes that need to be tested and the capabilities that the testing tool should have in order to perform such testing. V-model, a commonly used software testing methodology is applied to BPM for provisioning of structured mechanism for business process systems development and testing.

Chapter 21

Jian-Xun Liu, Hunan University of Science and Technology, China
Yiping Wen, Hunan University of Science and Technology, China

The chapter discusses the issue of batch processing in workflow in order to dynamically improve the execution efficiency of business processes. The employment of batch processing in workflow is to model and enact the batch processing logic for multiple cases of a workflow to optimize business processes execution. Inspired by workflow mining and functional dependency inference, this chapter proposes a method for mining batch processing patterns in workflows from process dataflow logs. According to batch dependency discovered by techniques, the activities that merit batch processing and their batch processing features are identified. Based on batch processing features, the batch processing areas in workflow are recognized for process optimization.

Section 5
Business Process Management in Practice

Chapter 22

Arla Juntunen, Helsinki School of Economics, Finland

This chapter presents a case study on business process management in a Finnish telecommunication company from 1990 to 2007. This study focuses on the R&D process development and changes from in-house development to a multi-partner R&D network, with respect to the company's competitive advantage; organizational structure; and product and service portfolio. It discusses how a competitive advantage in mobile and multimedia business has been created by efficient process changes and network management capabilities, during which Information and Communication Technology (ICT) acts as a strategic catalyst and enabler of business process reengineering (BPR).

Chapter 23

Diana Heckl, Frankfurt School of Finance & Management, Germany
Jürgen Moormann, Frankfurt School of Finance & Management, Germany

The chapter analyzes the challenges of operational process management for banks and insurance companies. The financial services industry faces significant competitive pressures as a result of economic and political influences, incessant regulation, and fast changing markets. Banks and insurance companies are forced to permanently improve their performance, and raising process performance represents one of the biggest levers for success. The involvement of customers in service processes of financial institutions make final processes not as easy to be managed as production processes. In response to the challenges, a general framework for operational management of service processes is required. This chapter presents a framework for structuring service processes which allows the combination of operational process management with customer influences.

Chapter 24

Rajiv Khosla, La Trobe University, Australia
Mei-Tai Chu, La Trobe University, Australia
Shinichi Doi, NEC Corporation, Japan
Keiji Yamada, NEC Corporation, Japan
Toyoaki Nishida, Kyoto University, Japan

The chapter discusses business process management in the context of knowledge flow network (KFN) and communities of practice (CoPs). It focuses on knowledge flow that occurs between knowledge workers and transcends business functions and organizational boundaries. Knowledge flow is dynamic phenomena; a dynamic model for analysing knowledge flow activities like knowledge sharing, knowledge discovery, and knowledge creation is thus needed. This chapter develops a CoPs Centered KFN model in a multinational organization context, by taking into account four organization performance evaluation dimensions and sixteen criteria. Fuzzy multi-criteria decision making and cluster analysis techniques are employed for evaluation of the model.

Chapter 25

Carl L. Oros, Lt.Col., Naval Postgraduate School, USA
Mark E. Nissen, Naval Postgraduate School, USA

The chapter discusses Edge, an organizational form receiving considerable attention for designing organizations as complex adaptive systems in dynamic environment. The Edge distributes knowledge and power to the "edges" of organizations, and enables organizational members and units to self-organize and self-synchronize their activities. However, the dynamics of such self-organization and self-synchronization are extremely complex, and balancing the flexibility and adaptability inherent in the Edge with sufficient control to avoid chaos is very challenging. This chapter informs the understanding of complex organizational design and management. The state-of-the-art POWer environment is employed for dynamic organizational representation and emulation to develop and experiment with models of competing organizational forms.

Foreword

The concept of *business process* goes back to Adam Smith and the origins of economic theories. However, the concept was adopted and exploited in areas outside manufacturing only in the past 20 years, thanks to the rise of a cluster of IT-based technologies that could support business process automation, optimization and reengineering.

Today, business processes constitute the centerpiece around which organizations structure their operations, measure their performance, and base their competitiveness. Business processes have also become a core concept for organizational information systems in the sense that they define the operational environment and many of the requirements for such systems.

The organizational world is evolving at an ever-faster pace to meet global challenges such as the environment, increased regulatory control, and global competition. In this context, business processes have to adapt as well, along with the information systems that support their operations, in order to continue to fulfill their mission. Business process adaptation, and the mechanisms by which it can be supported, constitute today a major research challenge for researchers spanning the Management/Technology landscape.

The edited collection herein constitutes a timely and welcome edition to the literature on business processes. The volume offers a comprehensive, interdisciplinary state-of-the-art overview of research on the topic, covering the research of leading groups around the world. I look forward to reading it!

John Mylopoulos
University of Trento
Trento, Italy

March 29, 2009

Preface

INTRODUCTION

Businesses around the world are paying more attention to process management and process automation to improve organizational efficiency and effectiveness. *This has led to business process management being increasingly recognised as a critical factor in business success.* Business Process Management (BPM) refers to activities performed by organizations to design, implement, operate, manage, and improve their business processes by using a combination of methods, techniques, and tools. Most approaches to BPM use information technologies to support or automate business processes, in whole or in part, through building process-oriented information systems. These technology-based solutions help coordinate and streamline business transactions, reduce operational costs, and promote real-time visibility in business performance.

Traditional approaches to building and implementing BPM systems have used workflow technologies to design and control the business process. Workflow-based systems follow highly structured and predefined workflow models; they are well suited to applications with standard inputs, processes, and outputs. In recent years, business environments have been changing from centralized-and-closed to distributed-and-open. Business processes are becoming increasingly complex and dynamic as they seek to cope with a wide range of internal and external interactions and changes. Real-world processes are often much messier than the input-transformation-output view might suggest. The processes usually evolve and change over time due to complex interactions, resource competition, breakdowns and abnormal events, and other sources of uncertainty. A business process displays complexity as a result of multiple interactions of its internal components and interaction between the process and its environment. Traditional approaches and technologies for process management are often inadequate for complex and dynamic situations due to lack of flexibility and adaptability.

Against this background, business process flexibility and adaptability at an operational and strategic level has shown its significance. Given the limitation of traditional approaches, organizations are facing the challenge of managing complex dynamic business processes in the following aspects ways:

1. Dealing with increased changes and interactions arising from turbulent environments: current research is attempting to support the continuously changing nature of business processes by developing flexible BPM solutions using various technologies and tools. Design and development of adaptive systems for dynamic process management have become the focus of a great deal of research in recent years.

2. Creating and maintaining a fit between the requirements and supporting technologies for process management: most studies on technology development for flexible process management are experience-driven and ad-hoc; they often lack a systematic analysis of the rationale for the technology

support. Little work has been done on examining the roots of the complexity of business processes, the need for effective approaches for flexible process management, and how this need affects the requirements and technology solutions of process management.

3. Integrating technological, organizational, and managerial perspectives into process management: given that business processes operate in an organizational context, it is important to pay more attention to organizational and managerial aspects of business processes, such as business requirement, organizational structure, worker autonomy, decision making, business strategies, knowledge management, and human involvement, which have been oversimplified in current BPM solutions. This may be linked to soft thinking of business process management, that is, how a process management system can be strategically designed, not only to execute the logic of workflow, but also to satisfy organizational and managerial needs.

4. Managing complex and interactive processes across multiple organizations: the rise of Internet-mediated businesses has given rise to the era of quickly connected global business relationships. A business process can be dynamically established at run-time by connecting services from different organizations through alliances, partnerships, or joint ventures. In this context, attention to business processes should go beyond task and procedure and take other elements into consideration such as resources discovery, selection, integration, and coordination.

This book aims to address these challenges by providing an in-depth understanding of business processes and investigating advanced solutions to complex process management. The book has been prepared in close cooperation with active scholars and experts from the area of business process/workflow management and other related areas including business management, finance, and marketing, as well as from various industrial sectors such as banking, insurance, manufacturing, logistics, and telecommunication. It is a compilation of contributed chapters from 33 universities and nine companies over 20 countries or regions. Recent findings on complex dynamic process management have been collected, including observations, analyses, perspectives, strategies, architectures, models, methodologies, techniques, tools, and case studies.

This book combines both a managerial and a technical view of business process management, providing advanced analysis and concrete approaches for relevant problems, as well as implications for further studies and practices. It may benefit professionals, researchers, and practitioners working in business process and workflow management from various disciplines, including information technology, industrial engineering, management information systems, organizational management, business administration, supply chains, customer relationship management, and so forth. The book will introduce the reader to various issues, trends, and problems faced by researchers and practitioners in business process management, together with principles, approaches, and tools for solving the problems.

BOOK ORGANIZATION

This book is organized into five sections comprising 25 chapters: the first section includes four chapters discussing approaches and tools for conceptual modeling of business processes or process management systems in complex situations; the second section consists of six chapters presenting technologies and solutions for adaptive process management in turbulent environments; the third section comprises six chapters focusing on collaboration issues in business process management; the fourth section contains five chapters addressing a number of practical issues in developing BPM systems; and finally, the fifth section includes four chapters discussing the application of business process management to practical situations, together with the challenges involved.

Section 1. Conceptual Modeling for Business Process Management

Conceptual modeling is the fundamental issue of business process management. In Chapter 1, Minhong Wang and Kuldeep Kumar analyze the complexity of business processes and the technologies for modeling and constructing complex BPM systems. Based on the complexity of business processes and modular theory for complex systems, the chapter presents the DCAR architecture for complex process management, which includes decomposition of complex processes (D); coordination of interactive activities (C); awareness of dynamic environments? (A); and resource selection and coordination (R). On the other hand, modular computing technologies, such as object-oriented programming, component-based development, agent-oriented computing, and service-oriented architecture have been widely applied in developing complex systems. However, there is considerable ambiguity involved in differentiating between these overlapping technologies and their use in developing BPM systems. No explicit linkage has been established between the requirement of BPM and the supporting technologies. This study uses the DCAR architecture as the foundation to identify the BPM requirements for employing technologies in developing BPM systems. Based on an examination of both sides (BPM requirements and supporting technologies), the study presents a clear picture of business process complexity with a systemic approach for designing and developing complex BPM systems by using appropriate computing technologies.

In Chapter 2, Steen Brahe describes an approach for enterprises to use their own domain concepts to model their business processes. Conventional BPM tools often provide a standardized business process modeling language and implementation technology. This makes the tools inflexible and difficult to use for individual enterprises. This chapter provides a tool-based framework that allows an enterprise to customize BPM languages and tools to its specific needs instead of developing them from scratch. It applies the basic model driven development principles for direct representation and automation of BPM tools through a tool experiment in Danske Bank. BPM tools are developed to capture Danske Bank's specific modeling concepts and use of technology, and automate the generation of the code. The empirical evaluation has revealed the remarkable advantage of the approach in development productivity and code quality.

Chapter 3, by Claudio Petti and Mark Klein, presents a methodology for redesigning and inventing new business processes that relies on a handbook of process models. It focuses on a practical approach for dealing with business process changes by connecting IT experts with business people. The methodology is the fruit of a decade-long MIT research effort known as the Process Handbook project. It is based on acquiring an abstract model of core activities and dependencies in the existing process, and then engaging in a structured and systematic exploration of process alternatives, where a large repository of best-practice business process models, that is, a Process Handbook, can be used for inspiration. The chapter uses the case of a real-life risk management process to illustrate the steps of the methodology and demonstrates how its concepts such as inheritance and exception handling can be used to design more effective and robust IT-based processes by enabling easier and more structured gathering of software requirements; in this way reducing the possibility of misunderstandings between IT experts and business people, and reducing software bugs.

In Chapter 4, Ilia Bider and Erik Perjons turn their attention to the selection of an appropriate approach for business process modeling by means of a simplified classification of business process modeling approaches. To ensure the "right" choice of modeling approach, three factors are addressed for consideration: (a) properties of the object to be modeled; (b) characteristics of the environment in which the model is being built; and (c) intended use of the model. Their study analyzes the factors involved in the domain of business process modeling. It lists the most essential properties of business processes, classifies modeling environments, and discusses practical tasks where a business process model can be used. Based on the analysis, practical recommendations on what modeling approach to choose are given, dependent on the type of the process under consideration, the task at hand, and the environment in which the model is being built and verified.

Section 2. Adaptive Technologies for Business Process Management

In Chapter 5, Michael Adams, Arthur ter Hofstede, Nick Russell, and Wil Van Der Aalst provide a comprehensive examination of the principles that underpin business process technologies in order to derive a novel approach that moves beyond the traditional assembly-line metaphor. Their study provides an overview of approaches to exception handling and flexibility in process-aware information systems, investigates theoretical foundations of process adaptation, and proposes a comprehensive framework for exception handling in work practices. Using a set of principles derived from activity theory, a system Worklet Service has been implemented, using a service oriented architecture that provides support for dynamic and extensible flexibility, evolution, and exception handling in business processes.

Chapter 6 enters into a specific but critical aspect of adaptive process management during run-time and in distributed systems. Manfred Reichert, Thomas Bauer, and Peter Dadam present the concepts and techniques for enabling ad-hoc workflow changes in distributed workflow execution. The focus is placed on minimizing the communication costs among workflow servers, while ensuring correct execution behavior as well as correctness of ad-hoc workflow changes. To achieve this, it is crucial to identify the workflow servers that are involved in the synchronization of an ad-hoc change. These active servers need to know the schema and state of a changed workflow instance in order to correctly control its execution. In addition, it should be decided whether, when, and how a changed workflow instance schema has to be transmitted to other workflow servers.

In Chapter 7, Mair Allen-Williams and Nicholas R. Jennings address two challenges to computing technology in complex distributed systems: decision making in uncertain and partially-observable environments, and coordination with other agents in such environments. The authors have developed an approach to this problem using a Bayesian learning mechanism, extending previous work on learning models of other agents, and have demonstrated its effectiveness in a scenario from the disaster response domain. The novelties in this work lie in an extension of online model-based learning techniques into partially observable domains using finite automata.

Chapter 8, by Dickson K.W. Chiu, Thomas Trojer, Hua Hu, Haiyang Hu, Yi Zhuang, and Patrick C.K. Hung, describes a Workflow-based Information Integration (WII) approach for dynamic and adaptive workflow management in inter-organizational business collaboration and service provision. The implementation framework comprises five layers: semantic, application, workflow, service, and message. The chapter focuses on the workflow layer for providing adaptiveness based on various types of flows such as control-flows, data-flows, security-flows, exception-flows, and semantic-flows. The issues of data-integration, semantic-referencing, and exception-handling assertions are discussed in order to achieve dynamic and adaptive workflow-based information integration.

In Chapter 9, Mati Golani presents a flexible approach to ad-hoc exception handling by using forward stepping, backtracking, and alternative paths. The chapter provides an analysis of a workflow model based on which, backtracking and forward stepping can be evaluated and implemented. The algorithms for alternative route identification and forward stepping are proposed to allow dynamic modifications to workflows at design time or run time. The meta-process, that is, the mechanism for automatic activation of the proposed algorithms, is demonstrated, which includes: functional block detection; alternative paths detection; process parameter analysis; and exception handler construction.

Chapter 10, by Mingzhong Wang, Jinjun Chen, Kotagiri Ramamohanarao, and Amy Unruh, describes another specific approach to exception handling in BPM by using a multiple-step backtracking mechanism. This study aims to maintain a tradeoff between re-planning and rigid backtracking for exception handling and recovery. The concept of the BDI (belief, desire and intention) agent is applied to model and construct the BPM system to inherit its advantages of adaptability and flexibility. Then, the flexible backtracking approach is introduced by utilizing the beneficial features of event-driven and means-end reasoning of BDI agents. Finally, the study incorporates an open nested transaction model to encapsulate plan execution and backtracking to gain the system level support of concurrency control and automatic recovery. With the ability to reason about task characteristics, this approach enables the system to find and commence a suitable plan prior to, or in parallel with, a compensation process when a failure occurs.

Section 3. Collaborative Business Process Management

In recent years, business environments have been changing from centralized-and-closed to distributed-and-open. More attention should be paid to situations where dynamic collaboration and soft-connection between business partners is playing an increasingly important role in BPM. Chapter 11, by Bart Orriens and Jian Yang, presents a rule-based approach for collaboration development and management of business processes. The proposed approach allows organizations to capture the requirements for their business collaborations in an explicit, manageable, and uniform manner in the form of rules. These rules can then be used to drive and constrain the development and management of needed collaboration models. In this way, collaborative business process design becomes a runtime activity, where the business collaboration shapes itself to its specific circumstances by applying the appropriate rules. The feasibility of the approach is demonstrated in the context of a complex insurance claim scenario using prototype tooling.

In Chapter 12, Xiaohui Zhao and Chengfei Liu introduce a service oriented relative workflow model to help organisations create flexible and privacy-safe virtual organisation alliances. An organisation centred design method and a visibility mechanism are proposed to deal with the challenges of temporary partnership and low trustiness between collaborating organisations. Contracts are not only used to define and regulate business service collaborations, but also to assist developing the visibility constraints for the business process integration. A visibility control mechanism is applied to remove potential authority violation, and guarantee the safety of privacy between collaborating organisations.

Chapter 13, by Hyerim Bae, provides a specific account of inter-workflow in logistic processes. A logistic process is considered as a combined process that manages the flow of materials among the partners. It consists of multiple sub processes, each of which is managed by a single partner. This study proposes a set of inter-workflow patterns that represent the relations among the separate processes in logistic environments. Based on the patterns, ECA (Event-Condition-Action) rules are generated to control the execution of the logistic process by the rule engine.

Trust is an important issue in collaborative business process management. In Chapter 14, Zhaohao Sun, Jun Han, Dong Dong, and Shuliang Zhao discuss intelligent techniques for trust management in electronic commerce. The chapter examines the engineering of experience-based trust in e-commerce systems, as well as the interrelationships among experience-based, knowledge-based and inference-based trust. A knowledge-based model of trust management in e-commerce, together with a multi-agent system architecture for experience-based trust engineering in e-commerce are presented.

In Chapter 15, Jude Fernandez and Jyoti Bhat discuss the specific issue of process harmonization in global businesses. Process Harmonization is a complex initiative carried out by large companies seeking to standardize the process variants being executed by different business units across several countries or regions. Motivations for this exercise include cost pressures, mergers and acquisitions, customer satisfaction, the need for agile and flexible processes, and risk reduction in outsourcing processes. The complexity of this exercise is inherent as it involves multiple regions with special needs and characteristics, existing process and IT systems evolved over time, and organizational dynamics around different business groups. This chapter examines the drivers of process harmonization, identifies the challenges and constraints associated with the initiatives, and finally proposes a methodology to execute process harmonization initiatives.

Chapter 16, by Pethuru Raj, focuses on composition oriented architecture for establishing extended, connected, adaptive, and on-demand business processes. As next-generation IT is presumed to thrive on spontaneous and seamless collaboration among systems, services, and servers by sending messages as well as sharing a wider variety of connected and empowered resources, there arises a distinct identity and value for progressive composites. This chapter discusses how rapidly and smoothly services enable business-aligned and process-centric composition, with respect to composition paradigms, patterns, platforms, processes, practices, products, perspectives, problems, and potentials.

Section 4. Practical Issues in BPM Technology Development

Chapter 17, by Jon Espen Ingvaldsen and Jon Atle Gulla, introduces semantic business process mining of SAP transaction logs. SAP is the most widely used Enterprise Resource Planning (ERP) system, which contains transaction logs linked to large amounts of structured data. However, the core of SAP systems was not originally designed from the business process management perspective. The business process layer was added later without full rearrangement of the system. As a result, system logs produced by SAP are not process-based, and cannot be directly used for process mining. This chapter shows how data available in SAP systems can enrich process instance logs with ontologically structured concepts. The authors introduce and valuate three techniques for mapping executed transactions with the standard business process hierarchies in SAP.

In Chapter 18, Semih Cetin, N. Ilker Altintas, and Ozgur Tufekci address the problem that traditional techniques for modeling and executing business processes are too generic to support diverse business environments. Most BPM tools are not scalable enough for typical business cases, lack architectural coverage to manage the tradeoffs between dynamism and other business quality issues, are insufficient to support integration with legacy business processes, and are without a balanced guidance between "primary" and "supportive" processes. This chapter aims to refrain from using generic approaches and techniques for process modeling by partitioning the big picture into domain specific parts. The authors use the "Domain Specific Kit" for abstraction and composition of primary and supportive processes in an organization. This approach has been put into action for the implementation of central operations management of a mid-scale bank in Turkey.

In Chapter 19, Hajo A. Reijers presents an approach that is opposite to the direction of most developments in the workflow field: lightweight workflow. Lightweight workflow management systems are workflow management systems that only provide the most basic functionalities and are characterized by a relatively small and non-intrusive effort to implement and adopt them. The underlying idea is that in many situations, especially when flexibility and application integration are not big issues, a "lighter" workflow system provides a better proposition to arrive at a successful and satisfactory workflow implementation. This chapter introduces the essential features of lightweight workflow, and reflects on the application of lightweight workflow in practice.

Chapter 20, by Krishnendu Kunti, Bijoy Majumdar, and Terance Bernard Dias, draws attention to the testing of business process management systems. One of the aspects of managing complex and dynamic business processes is to make sure that the process delivers what is required of it at all times. This chapter identifies the aspects of business processes that need to be tested and the capabilities that the testing tool should have in order to perform such testing. V-model, a commonly used software testing methodology is applied to BPM for provisioning of structured mechanism for business process systems development and testing.

In Chapter 21, Jian-Xun Liu and Yiping Wen discuss the issue of batch processing in workflow in order to dynamically improve the execution efficiency of business processes. The employment of batch processing in workflow is to model and enact the batch processing logic for multiple cases of a workflow to optimize business processes execution. Inspired by workflow mining and functional dependency inference, this chapter proposes a method for mining batch processing patterns in workflows from process dataflow logs. According to batch dependency discovered by techniques, the activities that merit batch processing and their batch processing features are identified. Based on batch processing features, the batch processing areas in workflow are recognized for process optimization.

Section 5. Business Process Management in Practice

Chapter 22, by Arla Juntunen, presents a case study on business process management in a Finnish telecommunication company from 1990 to 2007. This study focuses on the R&D process development and changes from in-house development to a multi-partner R&D network, with respect to the company's competitive advantage; organizational structure; and product and service portfolio. It discusses how a competitive advantage in mobile and multimedia business has been created by efficient process changes and network management capabilities, during which information and communication technology (ICT) acts as a strategic catalyst and enabler of business process reengineering (BPR).

In Chapter 23, Diana Heckl and Jürgen Moormann analyze the challenges of operational process management for banks and insurance companies. The financial services industry faces significant competitive pressures as a result of economic and political influences, incessant regulation, and fast changing markets. Banks and insurance companies are forced to permanently improve their performance, and raising process performance represents one of the biggest levers for success. The involvement of customers in service processes of financial institutions make final processes not as easy to be managed as production processes. In response to the challenges, a general framework for operational management of service processes is required. This chapter presents a framework for structuring service processes which allows the combination of operational process management with influences by the customers.

In Chapter 24, Rajiv Khosla, Mei-Tai Chu, Shinichi Doi, Keiji Yamada, and Toyoaki Nishida discuss business process management in the context of knowledge flow network (KFN) and communities of practice (CoPs). This chapter focuses on knowledge flow that occurs between knowledge workers and transcends business functions and organizational boundaries. Knowledge flow is dynamic phenomena; a dynamic model for analysing knowledge flow activities like knowledge sharing, knowledge discovery, and knowledge creation is thus needed. This chapter develops a CoPs Centered KFN model in a multinational organization context, by taking into account four organization performance evaluation dimensions and sixteen criteria. Fuzzy multi-criteria decision making and cluster analysis techniques are employed for evaluation of the model.

Finally, Chapter 25, by LtCol Carl L. Oros and Mark E. Nissen, discusses Edge, an organizational form receiving considerable attention for designing organizations as complex adaptive systems in dynamic environment. The Edge distributes knowledge and power to the "edges" of organizations, and enables organizational members and units to self-organize and self-synchronize their activities. However, the dynamics of such self-organization and self-synchronization are extremely complex, and balancing the flexibility and adaptability inherent in the Edge with sufficient control to avoid chaos is very challenging. This chapter informs the understanding of complex organizational design and management. The state-of-the-art POWer environment is employed for dynamic organizational representation and emulation to develop and experiment with models of competing organizational forms.

Minhong Wang
Zhaohao Sun
January 18, 2009

Acknowledgment

This book could not have been completed without the help, support, patience, and encouragement of many people. One "Big Thank You" is to my husband Haijing, who initially put forth the idea of editing this book. The book is the result of his great inspiration, constant encouragement, and unfailing support. Another "Big Thank You" is to Professor Douglas Vogel and Kuldeep Kumar, who provided deep intellectual insights into the research of business process management.

I would extend my special gratitude to Professor John Mylopoulos for taking the time from his very busy schedule to write the foreword for this book.

The book has been prepared in close cooperation with active scholars and experts from 33 universities and 9 companies over 20 countries or regions. I would like to thank the editorial advisory board for their valuable guidance and expert advice on the creation of the book. Thanks also go to all chapter authors for their efforts in preparing the manuscripts and their insights and excellent contributions to this book.

Most of the authors included in this handbook also served as referees for chapters written by other authors. I would like to thank all reviewers who provided constructive and comprehensive comments for improving the quality of this book.

Special thanks to IGI Global, whose contributes throughout the whole process from inception of the initial idea to final publication have been invaluable; in particular, to Christine Bufton and Rebecca Beistline, who continuously prodded via e-mail to keep the project on schedule.

Last, but not least, I thank the Research Grants Council (RGC) of Hong Kong and The University of Hong Kong. The book is supported by the General Research Funds of RGC (No. 716907 and No.717708) and the Seed Fundings for Basic Research (No.200611159216 and No.200711159052) of the university.

Minhong Wang
The University of Hong Kong
Hong Kong
March 30, 2009

Section I
Conceptual Modeling for Business Process Management

Chapter 1
Challenges and Solutions for Complex Business Process Management

Minhong Wang
The University of Hong Kong, Hong Kong

Kuldeep Kumar
Florida International University, USA

ABSTRACT

A business process displays complexity as a result of multiple interactions of its internal components and interaction between the process and its environment. To manage complexity and foster flexibility of business process management (BPM), we present the DCAR architecture for developing complex BPM systems, which includes decomposition of complex processes (D); coordination of interactive activities (C); awareness of dynamic environments (A); and resource selection and coordination (R). On the other hand, computing technologies, such as object-oriented programming, component-based development, agent-oriented computing, and service-oriented architecture have been applied in modeling and developing complex systems. However, there is considerable ambiguity involved in differentiating between these overlapping technologies and their use in developing BPM systems. No explicit linkage has been established between the requirement of complex BPM and the supporting technologies. In this study, we use the DCAR architecture as the foundation to identify the BPM requirements for employing technologies in developing BPM systems. Based on an examination of the both sides (BPM requirements and supporting technologies), we present a clear picture of business process complexity with a systemic approach for developing complex BPM systems by using appropriate computing technologies.

INTRODUCTION

Businesses around the world are paying more attention to process management and process automation to improve organizational efficiency and effectiveness. It is increasingly common to describe organizations as sets of business processes that can be improved by business process management (BPM). Most

DOI: 10.4018/978-1-60566-669-3.ch001

approaches to BPM have used information technologies to support or automate business processes, in whole or in part, by providing computer-based systems support. These technology-based systems help coordinate and streamline business transactions, reduce operational costs, and promote real-time visibility in business performance.

Traditional approaches to building and implementing BPM systems use workflow technologies to design and control the business process. Workflow-based systems follow highly structured and pre-defined workflow models, and are well suited to applications with stable inputs, processes, and outputs. Contemporary business processes are becoming increasingly complex and dynamic as they seek to cope with a wide range of internal and external interactions and changes. To provide sufficient flexibility and adaptability in BPM, a number of researchers have been investigating the approaches and techniques for developing BPM systems for an increasingly turbulent environment (Casati et al., 1999; Chiu et al., 1999; Weske, 2001; Wang et al., 2002, 2005a; K. Kumar et al., 2006). Most studies have focused on present process structures and provide rapid response to changes that lead to temporary and short term fluctuations in the organization's activities.

In this study, we view business process as a complex system that adapts to continuously changing and unpredictable environments in order to survive. A business process displays complexity because of multiple interactions of its internal components and interaction between the process and its environment. To manage complexity and foster flexibility of complex systems, modularity is the key to the solution (Baldwin et al., 1997; Simon, 1981). Modularity in BPM requires decomposing a complex BPM system into a number of interacting components that perform the processes. Based on the investigation of business process complexity and modularity theory, we present the DCAR architecture for developing complex BPM systems, which include decomposition of complex processes (D); coordination of interactive activities (C); awareness of dynamic environments (A); and resource selection and coordination (R).

On the other hand, various modular computing technologies, such as Object-Oriented Programming (OOP); Component-Based Development (CBD); Agent-Oriented Computing (AOC); and Service-Oriented Architecture (SOA); have emerged to model and develop complex systems. There has been a proliferation of studies about the application of these modular technologies in developing BPM systems (Weske, 1998; Kammer et al., 2000; Jennings et al., 2002; Wang et al., 2005b; Leymann et al., 2002). As the modular computing paradigms and technologies become popular, researchers often attempt to employ and integrate them in creating business process management solutions. However, there is considerable ambiguity involved in differentiating between these overlapping terminologies and consequently their use for BPM systems development. The fundamental questions about the use of these technologies, i.e., why we need to use them for solutions of BPM, how we apply them, and how we integrate them with other solutions, remain unexamined. Most research on technology support for BPM is experience-driven, ad-hoc, and often lacks a systematic analysis of the rationale for the technology support (Wang et al., 2008a). Little work has examined the root of complexity of business processes, the need for effective approaches to BPM, and how this need affects the technology solutions for process management (K. Kumar et al., 2006). In this study, we analyze the differences and relationships between these overlapping terminologies and techniques, and match them to BPM requirements. The DCAR architecture we proposed for complex BPM is used as the foundation to identify the BPM requirements for employing these modular computing technologies in developing BPM systems. Based on an examination of both sides (BPM requirements and supporting technologies), we present a clear picture of business process complexity with a systemic approach on how these technologies can be applied and integrated in developing systems for complex process management.

RESEARCH BACKGROUND

Business Process

A business process can be simply defined as a collection of activities that create value by transforming inputs into more valuable outputs (Hammer et al., 1993). These activities consist of a series of steps performed by actors to produce a product or service for the customer. In more details, a business process is typically a coordinated and logically sequenced set of work activities and associated resources that produce something of value to a customer (El Sawy, 2001). Each process has an identified customer; it is initiated by a process trigger or a business event (usually a request for product or service arriving from the process customer); and it produces a process outcome (the product or a service requested by the customer) as its deliverable to the process customer. Given the scope and variety of actions that are needed to produce the product or service, the process is differentiated (sub-divided) into a set of tasks or activities. These tasks are assigned to and performed by actors (either machines or humans), using resources such as work-stations; machines; raw materials; and supplies that are available to the actors.

Business Process Management

Business Process Management (BPM) refers to activities performed by organizations to design (capture processes and document their design in terms of process maps), model (define business processes in a computer language), execute (develop software that enables the process), monitor (track individual processes for performance measurement), and optimize (retrieve process performance for improvement) operational business processes by using a combination of models, methods, techniques, and tools (van der Aalst et al., 2002; Melão et al., 2000). Process design in turn includes the differentiation or subdivision of the process into underlying tasks or activities, process-configuration (arranging the process tasks into a logical sequence to produce the process outcome), and selection and allocation of specific actors and resources to particular process-tasks. The monitoring and control phases can be an extension to provide feedback into the continuing design, implementation, and execution cycle. Among various approaches or methods for BPM, this study focused on the use of information technologies to support or automate business processes, in whole or in part, by providing computer-based systems support. These technology-based systems help coordinate and streamline business transactions, reduce operational costs, and promote real-time visibility in business performance.

Traditional approaches to building and implementing BPM systems use workflow technologies to design and control the business process (van der Aalst et al., 2002). Workflow-based systems follow highly structured and predefined workflow models, and are well suited to applications with stable inputs, processes, and outputs. Contemporary business processes are complex and dynamic. They evolve and change over time as a result of complex interactions, resource competition, breakdowns and abnormal events, and other sources of uncertainty. Realizing the need to provide sufficient flexibility and adaptability in BPM, many researchers are investigating the approaches and techniques for developing BPM systems for an increasingly turbulent environment. In perusing this, most studies have focused on the capabilities that are based on present process structures of an organization and provide rapid response to changes that lead to temporary and short term fluctuations in the organization's activities. Efforts to improve flexibility in business processes can be found in numerous studies on adaptive workflow/process modeling, workflow/process monitoring, and exception management (Casati et al., 1999; Chiu et al., 1999; Weske, 2001; Wang et al., 2002, 2005a; K. Kumar et al., 2006). On the other hand, while faced with revolutionary changes, an organization needs more flexibility to rearrange its internal or intra-organizational structures and processes. Efforts can be found in research on business process analysis and redesign, and business process reconstruction or reengineering, which enable new forms of working and collaborating within an organization or in cross-border businesses (Hammer et al., 1993). With the recent growth of electronic services, a business process can be dynamically established by connecting or composing appropriate services based on market demand (A. Kumar et al., 2002; Petrie et al., 2003; K. Kumar et al., 2007). A worldwide network of organizations can be formed through process composition over the Internet (Casati et al., 2001).

CHALLENGES OF BUSINESS PROCESS MANAGEMENT

Business Requirement

To business, dealing with changes is a fact of everyday life that must be exploited. Real-world processes are often much messier than what the typical input-transformation-output view suggests. Business processes are best viewed as networks, in which a number of actors collaborate and interact to achieve a business goal. A business process displays complexity because of multiple interactions of its internal components and interaction between the process and its environment (Melão et al., 2000). In recent years, business environments have been changing from centralized-and-closed to distributed-and-open. Business processes are becoming increasingly complex and dynamic as they seek to cope with a wide range of internal and external interactions and changes. In this situation, BPM should be able to manage a number of components and their complex interactions in business processes, in particular in continuously changing and interplayed environment (Wang et al., 2006a; K. Kumar et al., 2006). Furthermore, attention should be paid to situations where dynamic collaboration and soft-connection between business partners is playing an increasingly important role (K. Kumar, 2001; Wang et al., 2008b). This needs both information technologies and managerial capabilities to adapt the organization structure and its decision-making and communication processes in order to facilitate cross-hierarchical, cross-functional, cross-product/service, and cross-market capability development.

In this context, we need to shift from the mechanistic view of workflow paradigm which focuses on static and structure features of business process. Instead, business processes can be viewed as complex dynamic systems that adapt to continuously changing and unpredictable environments in order to survive. This requires the integration of organizational, managerial, and technological issues in understanding and managing business processes. In addition to a set of logically related tasks, more aspects need to be taken into account such as environment awareness; knowledge for process management; flexible resource coordination; and so on.

Technology Support

To deal with a complex system like business process management, software technologies have been on constant evolution. Structured or function-oriented analysis was used in 1970s for functional decomposition of more stable systems, concealing the details of an algorithm in a function. To deal with constant changes related to data structure, *object-oriented programming (OOP)* was addressed to separate data from the applications, where data and its corresponding operations were encapsulated within an object. Based on this method, traditional workflow systems have been developed by taking processes or workflows out of the applications to improve the control and change of business processes (Weske, 1998). More recently, to deal with more complex and frequent changes of business processes, new computing technologies have emerged in BPM, such as Component-Based Development (CBD) in Kammer et al. (2000); Agent-Oriented Computing (AOC) in Jennings et al. (2002) and Wang et al. (2005b); and Service-Oriented Architecture (SOA) in Leymann et al. (2002).

However, the fundamental questions about the use of these technologies, i.e., why we need to use them for solutions of BPM, how we apply them, and how we integrate them with other solutions, remain unexamined. Most research on technology support for BPM is experience-driven, ad-hoc, and often lacks a systematic analysis of the rationale for the technology support (Wang et al., 2008a). There is only minimal work that examines the root of complexity of business processes, the need for effective approaches to BPM, and how this need affects the technology solutions for process management (K. Kumar et al., 2006).

MODULARIZATION FOR COMPLEX SYSTEMS

As discussed, business processes display complexity due to interactions of their internal components and interaction of the process with its environment. Business processes are complex systems that are made up of a number of interacting objects with dynamic behavior. Alexander and Simon addressed the theories about how we design complex systems; to design a complex structure, one powerful technique is to decompose it into semi-independent and interrelated components, which in turn have their own components in (Simon, 1981). Though they did not use the word "modularity", the concept was central to their thinking. Baldwin and Clark (1997) addressed modularity as a particular design structure, which refers to development of a complex product or process from smaller subsystems that can be designed independently. It is possible for us to view all entities – social, biological, technological, or otherwise – as hierarchically nested system. Modularity is the key to managing complexity and fostering flexibility of complex systems (Baldwin et al., 1997; Simon, 1981). It ensures easy maintenance and updates of complex systems by reducing the interactions among the components. A complex system can be managed by separating the high-frequency intra-module linkages from the low-frequency inter-module linkages, and limiting the scope of interactions between modules by hiding the intra-module relations inside a module box. A module in a complex system is a unit whose structural elements are powerfully connected among themselves and relatively weakly connected to elements in other units. The guiding principle for decomposition is that intra-module cohesion is generally stronger than inter-module coupling. This fact can be used to distinguish diverse interactions, and deal with them by encapsulating the intra-module interactions inside a module box (Wolters, 2002). Using modularization, a complex structure can be decomposed into sub-functions, sub-processes, sub-areas, and in other ways. Alternative decompositions correspond to different ways of dividing the responsibilities.

While pursuing modularization, choosing right granularity of the component is an important issue in decomposing complex systems. The identity of any unit as the module is not fixed, but determined by the level of analysis we choose (Schilling, 2003). Granularity is the size of the unit under consideration. It refers to the degree to which a system can be separated and reorganized. For example, a company is generally divided into departments, the departments into groups, and the groups into employees. Systems of large components are called coarse-grained, and systems of small components are called fine-grained. Granularity is a relative concept that can be precisely defined only in a specific context (Elfatatry, 2007). For instance, if a component implements all functions of a banking system, then it can be considered coarse grained; if it supports just credit-balance checking, it is considered fine-grained. The greater the granularity, the more the flexibility, but the greater the overheads of synchronization and communication. To maximize the performance of modularization, a complex system must be analyzed and implemented by choosing right granularity of the components. A tradeoff between modularity and integrity should be considered to ensure overall system performance (Garud et al., 2003).

With respect to business process management, modularity supports two things. First, modularity increases the range of "manageable" complexity. It does this by limiting the scope of interactions between various components by encapsulating some components (such as data, resources, knowledge, and responsibility of a specific task) and their interactions inside the task module, thereby reducing the amount and range of interweaving that occurs in an interconnected process. Second, modularity accommodates uncertainty. Through modularity, components are partitioned into those that are visible and those that are hidden. Hidden components lying inside a black box (the task module) are isolated from other parts and are allowed to vary without changing much in other parts. This provides flexible process structures by permitting uncertainty as well as accommodating changes.

DCAR ARCHITECTURE FOR COMPLEX PROCESS MANAGEMENT

Based on the above investigation of BPM challenges (3rd section) and the modularity theory for managing complexity (4th section), we propose the DCAR architecture for developing BPM systems, which includes decomposition of complex processes (D); coordination of interactive activities (C); awareness of dynamic environments (A); and resource selection and coordination (R).

Decomposition of Complex Processes (D)

According to the modular architecture, a business process can be decomposed into tasks, task into sub-tasks, and so on. Interactions between sub-tasks within a task are often encapsulated within the task; interactions between tasks are encapsulated within their higher-level process or task. This raises the issue on how we decompose complex processes. Traditional workflow approaches have selected "task" as the basic module for building process management systems. A business process can be decomposed into a number of semi-dependent and interrelated tasks. These tasks are then linked to each other in a pre-established and usually sequential inter-relationship or dependency. With the extension of business processes from intra-organizational to inter-organizational scope, we need to deal with interactions within an organization as well as interactions across organizations. Moreover, the complexity of BPM is increased by interweaving of inter- and intra-organizational interactions.

To manage the complexity, we need to distinguish between inter- and intra-organizational interactions and deal with them by isolating one type from another. We propose "service" as a high level view of the building block of a process, where a process is composed of a set of services. Each service is provided by a corresponding actor (organization, individual, or computer program), and can be further decomposed into sub-tasks. For example, a complex supply chain management process can be decomposed into "customer order service", "procurement service", "manufacturing service", and "transportation service";

Figure 1. Decomposition of a supply chain process

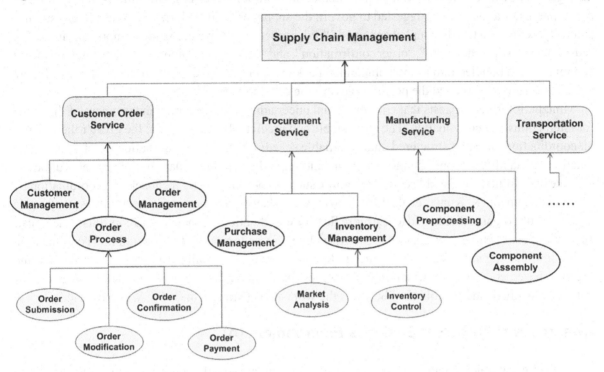

each service can be provided by a corresponding organizational actor, and can be further decomposed throughout several layers as shown in Figure 1.

Coordination of Interactive Activities (C)

To manage complex interactions in complex processes, multiple actors, activities, resources, and goals need to be coordinated. Every organized human activity gives rise to two fundamental requirements: 1) differentiation, or the division of work into tasks to be performed by various actors; and 2) integration, that is, the coordination of these tasks to accomplish the goals of the activity (Mintzberg, 1979). After decomposing a complex process into a number of task components, we need to coordinate various interactions between the components at different levels in a network hierarchy. In the context of a hierarchy, a component can be involved in vertical interactions with its subordinates and super-ordinates, and in horizontal interactions with its peers. A component in a complex system, no matter how large or small, may interact with a limited set of superiors, inferiors and coordinate peers (Simon, 1981).

In a complex system, the components interact, represented as coupling or dependency between the components. Based on degree of strength of dependency, the components in a complex system are loosely or tightly coupled (Simon, 1977). Based on the relationship between the components in their interactions, the components in a complex system can be centrally or de-centrally coordinated. Take the example of supply chain management in Figure 1. In a loosely coupled context of "supply chain management", the participating components include "customer order service", "procurement service", "manufacturing service", and "transportation service". Each service is regarded as an autonomous entity, managing its own activities as well as the interaction with other services. Decentralized coordination or mutual negotiation can be suggested to govern the supply chain if no formal centralized governance authority exists. In a tightly coupled context of "order process", the participating components including "customer login", "order input", "order confirmation", and "order submission" are highly interdependent and mixed, and bundled into a single integrated package. Centralized coordination can be used if there is a central authority granted the power to govern the order process.

Mintzberg further suggests that environmental uncertainty is an important determinant of the mode for interactions and coordination. The more stable and predictable the situation, the greater the reliance on coordination based on structured and specifiable schedules, such as coordination by plan and coordination by standardization. The more variable and unpredictable the situation, the greater will be the reliance on informal and flexible communication, such as coordination by feedback and coordination by mutual adjustment (K. Kumar et al., 1996, 2007). When faced with increased uncertainties in dynamic environments, organizations need to use more flexible coordination mechanisms to coordinate their business activities. Flexible coordination is portrayed by more bottom-up initiatives and less centralization of decision-making in the top. This requires flatter hierarchies, decentralized autonomy-based units, and decision-based coordination, which in turn reduces direct hierarchical control and encourages greater mutual adjustment and coordination between the work-units (Mintzberg, 1979; Volberda, 1999).

Awareness of Turbulent Business Environment (A)

As a result of complex interactions, resource competition, abnormal events, and other sources of uncertainty, business processes continuously evolve and change over time. A complex process is usually semi-structured or unstructured to the extent that there is an absence of routine procedures for dealing with it. In such situations, BPM solutions do not depend on providing the computer system with exact details about how to accomplish a process; but provide the system with guidelines to help it determine how to deal with the process. In other words, problem solving is regarded as an interaction between the behaving organism and the environment under the guidance of a control system. Information and data are input to this system, represented in its memory as declarative knowledge, and then used in problem solving following algorithmic or heuristic steps (Wang et al., 2006a).

A complex system interacts with and adapts to its environment for survival, in addition to interactions of internal components. Any adaptive system must develop correlations between goals and actions in the world of process. This requires continuous translation between the state and process and discovery of a sequence of processes that will produce the goal state from an initial state based on means-ends analysis (Holland, 1995; Simon, 2003). A basic idea underlying is the control of complex dynamic systems or situations based on situation awareness. Awareness, according to biological psychology, is a human's or an animal's perception and cognitive reaction to a condition or event. Situation awareness is the perception and understanding of objects, events, people, system states, interactions, environmental conditions, and other situation-specific factors in complex and dynamic environments (Endsley, 1995). Situation awareness underpins real-time reactions to environmental changes. In terms of cognitive psychology, situation awareness refers to the active content of a decision-maker's mental model; its purpose is to enable rapid and appropriate decisions and effective actions.

In a dynamic business process environment, an exact execution order of activities is impractical; the interaction or relationship between the environment and activities is more appropriate in determining how to manage and coordinate activities (Wang et al., 2006a). The dynamicism therefore requires spontaneous decisions and coordination of processes based on situation awareness. In this context, BPM should be able to coordinate the processes by sensing and comprehending the situation, determining responses to it, while at the same time, taking actions to work towards business goals. In other words, the question of which task to execute and when to execute it is dependent on the current environment and underlying business rules rather than a static process schema. To achieve this, knowledge or rules for process management has become important foundation for BPM in dynamic environment. The modular system architecture can greatly improve the ability to identify and leverage knowledge for coordination in business processes (Sanchez et al., 2003). Through modularization, the knowledge becomes embodied in specific BPM components, which helps an organization to discover and focus on opportunities for organizational learning and capability development in BPM.

Resource Selection and Coordination (R)

Business processes require actors and resources to perform the tasks. These actors and their associated resources may reside either within the organization, or in the case of inter-organizational processes, across a network of multiple organizations. In some situations, more than one actor may be qualified and available for performing a task; while in some others, more than one task requires the same actor and resource. Resource management is an important and complicated issue to the efficiency and effectiveness of business processes or workflows. In addition to task, structure, and procedure, the resource aspects of business process should be taken into account. However the traditional process model or definition does not include the resource concept. Though some common principles for resource allocation in workflow management (e.g., first-in first out, shortest processing time, and earliest due date) have been recommended (van der Aalst et al., 2002), the research on resource management, in particular on process flexibility through resource selection and coordination in business processes is far from sufficiency.

In today's business environment, business networks of resources and actors can be temporarily assembled, integrated, and driven by demands that emerge and operate for the lifespan of the market opportunity (K. Kumar, 2001). In this conception, a firm is not considered as a black box guided by the strategist, but as a bundle of firm-specific resources of use for specific tasks. Along with this, new business models have accordingly come into view, such as demand chain; virtual enterprise; and electronic marketplace. They allow companies to operate in dynamically changing environments by quickly and accurately evaluating new market opportunities or new products. The companies may coordinate with potential partners in demand-driven and resource-based soft connections that are made for the duration of the market opportunity.

As a result, a business process can be dynamically established at run-time by connecting or composing several services together from different organizations through alliances, partnerships, or joint ventures. In this situation, attention on business processes should go beyond task and procedure, and extend to other elements, which include resources discovery; selection; integration; and coordination.

What is new in this business process model is reliance on the idea of separating resource requirements from concrete satisfiers (Mowshowitz, 1997). This separation allows for crafting process structures that enable switching between different resources options for implementing a process, as shown in Figure 2. It creates an environment in which the means for reaching a goal are evaluated and selected for optimized performance. The success of the model is highly dependent on the match between the requirements and satisfiers that deliver the services. One way to ensure this balance is to model the integration or composition of business processes as a management problem which involves: 1) the separation of

Figure 2. Resource selection and coordination in business processes

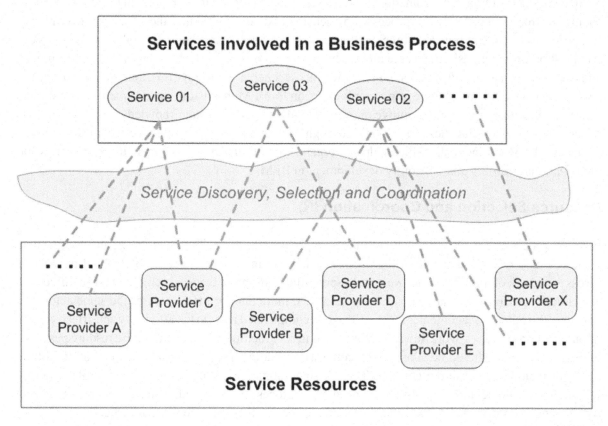

requirements from the means for realization, and 2) the dynamic selection and allocation of available resources to requirements.

INVESTIGATION OF MODULAR COMPUTING TECHNOLOGIES

There has been a proliferation of studies about the application of agent, service, component, and object oriented computing technologies to BPM (Jennings et al., 2002; Wang et al., 2005b; Leymann et al., 2002; Kammer et al., 2000; Weske, 1998). The aspiration of these modular computing technologies have facilitated the modeling of process architecture by modular software architectures (object, component, Web service, and software agent), thereby creating analogs of the business process in software. Each paradigm represents a philosophy of perception, abstraction, and decomposition of complex systems in order to deal with changes. As the modular computing paradigms and technologies become popular, researchers often attempt to employ and integrate them in creating business process management solutions.

However, different modular technologies have different philosophical beliefs with respect to how a complex system should be decomposed in order to tackle changes (Elfatatry, 2007). These technologies are usually applied in BPM without identifying the real rationale for their use in BPM scenarios. At present there is considerable ambiguity in differentiating between these overlapping terminologies and consequently their use for BPM systems development. For example, we often hear people discussing their proposed solutions as agent-based systems whereas they may just be simply using object abstraction. Furthermore, the common-sense understanding of these concepts and technologies does not easily map onto each other. Unless we have clarity on these terminologies and the way how to use them, the application and integration of these techniques is likely be problematic.

In this section we outline the four concepts: Agents and Agent-Oriented Computing; Services and Services-Oriented Architecture; Objects and Object-Oriented Programming; and Components and Component-Based Development. The purpose is not to re-define these concepts and approaches, but to clarify their similarities and differences, in particular towards their abstraction and decomposition techniques, and to make explicit some of the underlying assumptions inherent in the use of the terminology.

Object-Oriented Programming (OOP)

Object-Oriented Programming (OOP) is a software engineering paradigm that uses "objects" and their interactions to design applications and computer programs (Rumbaugh, 1991). A program is seen as a collection of cooperating objects, as opposed to a traditional view in which a program is seen as a list of instructions to the computer. The OOP paradigm addressed issues of reuse and maintenance by encapsulating data and its corresponding operations within an object class. To change a data structure, it is often necessary to change all the functions related to the data structure. OOP was deployed as an attempt to promote greater flexibility and maintainability, since the concepts of objects in the problem domain has a higher chance of being stable than functions and data structures.

Component-Based Development (CBD)

Component-Based Development (CBD) is another branch of the software engineering discipline, with an emphasis on decomposition of the engineered systems into functional or logical components with well-defined interfaces used for communication across the components. CBD includes a component model and an interface model. The component model specifies for each component how the component behaves in an arbitrary environment, and the interface model specifies for each component how the component interacts with its environment (Szyperski, 2002).

OOP vs. CBD. A component is a small group of objects working together to provide a system function. It can be viewed as a black box at the level of a large system function. At a fine level of granularity, we use objects to hide behavior and data. At a coarser level of granularity, we use components to do the same. OOP focuses on the encapsulation of both data and behavior of an object. CBD goes further by supporting public interfaces used for communication across the components.

Object-Oriented (OO) technologies provide rich models to describe problem domains, however it is not enough to adapt to changing requirements of real-world software systems (Elfatatry, 2007). OOP assumes that it is possible to identify and solve almost all problems before coding, while CBD and later SOA and AOC adopt a more pragmatic approach that believes business system development is an incremental process and changes are an inescapable aspect of software design. Specifically, objects were too fine-grained and did not make a clear separation between computational and compositional aspects. Components were then proposed to encapsulate the computational details of a set of objects. Using CBD, software development can be improved since applications can be quickly assembled from a large collection of prefabricated and interoperable software components.

Components inherit much of the characteristics of objects in the OO paradigm. But the component notion goes further by separating the interface from the component model. OO reuse usually means reuse of class libraries in a particular OO programming language or environment. For example, to be able to reuse a SmallTalk or Java class in OO, you have to be conversant with SmallTalk or Java language. A component, by using public interface, can be reused without even knowing which programming language or platform it uses internally.

Service-Oriented Architecture (SOA)

A *service* is defined as an act or performance that one party can offer to another that is essentially intangible and does not result in the ownership of anything. Its production may or may not be tied to a physical product.

A *Web Service,* defined by W3C (World Wide Web Consortium), a software application identified by a URI (Uniform Resource Identifier), whose interfaces and bindings are capable of being defined, described, and discovered by XML, and which supports direct interactions with other software applications using XML-based messages via Internet-based protocols. Web services are self-contained and modular business applications based on open standards (Leymann et al., 2002). They can share information using standardized communication protocols and ask each other to do something, i.e., ask for service.

Service-Oriented Architecture (SOA) utilizes Web services as fundamental elements for developing applications. It is an emerging paradigm for architecting and implementing business collaborations within and across organizational boundaries. SOA enables seamless and flexible integration of Web services or applications over the Internet. It supports universal interoperability and location transparency. SOA reduces complexity of business applications in large-scale and open environments by providing flexibility through service-based abstraction of organizational applications.

SOA vs. CBD. Compared with a component, a service is relatively *coarse-grained* which should able to encapsulate more details. SOA is an extension of earlier OOP and CBD concepts. CBD supports more close system architecture where the exact source of the required functionality and communication is predetermined. Propriety standards and implementation dependent specification of components have hindered CBD from achieving its primary goal facilitating reuse. The point in SOA is the service specification rather than the implementation. SOA focuses on the user's view of a computing object or application, i.e., the services that are provided and the metadata that define how the services behave. In SOA, a service has a published network-addressable interface. A published interface is exposed to the network and may not be changed so easily, because the clients of the published interface are not known. The difference between component and service in the interface is analogous to an intranet-based site only accessible by employees of the company and an Internet site accessible by anyone.

A service does not define any structural constraints for *loose coupling* of services over the Internet. CBD architectures, on the other hand, represent a case of *tight coupling*. For example, in CORBA, there is a tight coupling between the client and the server as both must share the same interface with a stub on the client-side and the corresponding skeleton on the server side. Composing a system from a number of components is relatively controlled compared to dynamic service composition. Moreover, CBD assumes *early binding* of components, i.e., the caller unit knows exactly which component to contact before runtime. SOA adopts a more flexible approach where the binding is deferred to runtime, enabling the change of source of provision each time.

Most significantly, the idea of the service model differs from CBD by the fact that SOA supports the logical separation of service need from service fulfillment. Delivering software as a service brings about new business models and opportunities of software development and service provision in demand-driven dynamic environment.

Agent-Oriented Computing (AOC)

Recently the Agent-Oriented Computing paradigm has gained popularity among researchers who attempt to develop complex systems for business process management (Jennings et al., 2002; Wang et al., 2005b). Terms such as "autonomous agent" and "agency" are now commonly used in computer science literature. On the other hand, a rich body of literature on the concept of Agency and the role of agents already exists in the institutional economics and business field. We attempt to reconcile the various terms from the two research traditions.

Actor is someone who performs an act, i.e., does something. An actor may be a person, an organizational unit, or a computer program. An actor may be completely autonomous, that is, it acts of its own volition. If the actor is authorized to do something on behalf of someone else, the actor is an "agent" of the other party.

Agent is an actor (performer) who acts on the behalf of a principal by performing a service. The agent provides the service when it receives a request for service from the principal. The principal-agent relationship is found in most employer-employee relationships. A classic example of agency relationship occurs when stockholders hire top executives to run the corporation on their behalf. To manage the relationship between a principle and an agent of the principle, agency theory is concerned with various mechanisms used for aligning the interests of the agent with those of the principal such as piece rates/commissions and profit sharing (Eisenhardt, 1989).

Broker is a special type of agent that acts on behalf of two symmetrical parties or principals – the buyer and seller. A broker mediates between the buyer (service requesting party) and the seller (service providing party). Acting as an intermediary between two or more parties in negotiating agreements, brokers use appropriate mediating techniques or processes to improve the dialogue between the parties, aiming to help them reach an agreement. Normally, all parties must view the mediator as neutral or impartial.

Autonomy is the power or right of self-government. It refers to the capacity of a rational individual to make an informed, uncoerced decision. "Autonomous" means that the actor is independent, i.e., the actor can decide what to do and how to do it. An autonomous agent therefore is a system situated in, and part of, an environment, which senses the environment, and acts on it, over time, in pursuit of its agenda as derived from its principal. As an agent acts on behalf of the principal, the agent cannot be fully autonomous. The principal may give the agent different levels of choice in performing the task. For example, the principal can tell the agent what to do, but leave it to the agent to decide as to how to do it.

Software Agent. In computer science, the term "agent" is used to describe a piece of software or code that acts on behalf of a human user or another program in a relationship of agency. It may denote a software-based entity that could enjoy the some properties of autonomy (agents operate without the direct intervention of its principal humans), social ability (agents communicate with other agents), reactivity (agents perceive their environment and respond to changes in a timely fashion), and pro-activity (agents do not simply act in response to their environment, but are able to exhibit goal-directed behavior by taking some initiative) (Jennings et al., 2002). The agent-based computing paradigm is devised to help computers know what to do, solve problems on behalf of human beings, and support co-operative working. The behavior of software agents is empowered by human and implemented by software.

Agent-Oriented Computing (AOC) is based on the idea of delegating tasks and responsibility of a complex problem to a group of software agents. It emphasizes autonomy and mutual co-operation of agents in performing tasks in open and complex environments. A complex system can be viewed as a network of agents acting concurrently, each finding itself in an environment produced by its interactions with the other agents in the system. AOC is used to model and implement intelligent solutions to semi- or ill-structured problems, which are too complex to be completely characterized and precisely described. AOC offers a natural way to view and describe systems as individual problem-solving agents pursuing high-level goals defined by their principals. It represents an emerging computing paradigm that helps understand and model complex real-world problems and systems, by concentrating on high-level abstractions of autonomous entities (Wooldridge et al., 1999).

AOC vs. OOP. From a software engineering point of view, Object-Oriented methodologies provide a solid foundation for Agent-Oriented modeling. AOC can be viewed as a specialization of OOP. OOP proposes viewing a computational system as made up of modules that are able to communicate with one another. AOC specializes the framework by representing the mental states and rich interactions of the modules (agents). While objects emphasize passive behavior (i.e., they are invoked in response to a message), agents support more autonomous behavior, which can be achieved by specifying a number of rules for interpreting the environmental states and knowledge for governing multiple degrees of freedom of activities. In relation to this, mechanisms of knowledge acquisition, modeling, and maintenance have become important foundation for building of autonomous agents.

AOC vs. SOA. Software agent is a software-based entity that enjoys the properties of autonomy, social ability, reactivity, and pro-activity. Web service is a software application in the Web based on open standards. Though both of them are computer applications that perform tasks on behalf of principals (human beings or other programs), the focus of software agents is on their autonomous properties for solving complex problems, while Web services are characterized by their open access standards and protocols over the Internet. While a Web service may only know about itself, agents often have awareness of other agents and their capabilities as interactions occur among the agents. Agents are inherently communicative, whereas Web services are passive until invoked. Agents cooperate autonomously and flexibly, and by forming teams and coalitions can assemble higher-level and more comprehensive services. However, current standards or languages for Web services do not provide for flexible composing functionalities, such as brokering and negotiation in e-marketplaces (Huhns, 2002). Web services are inherently less autonomous and independent than software agents.

Against this background, there is a movement towards combining the concept of Web services with software agents. W3C introduced a concept, where software agents are to be treated as the foundation for Web services architecture - "A Web service is an abstract notion that must be implemented by a concrete agent". AOC may take SOA into new dimensions to model autonomous and heterogeneous components in uncertain and dynamic environments. The integration of Web services with software agents can function as computational mechanism in their own right, thus significantly enhancing the ability to model and construct complex software systems. It will be a promising computing paradigm for efficient enterprise service selection and integration.

Reconciling OOP, CBD, SOA, and AOC

From OOP and CBD to SOA and AOC, the practice of software programming has evolved through different development paradigms. At the conceptual level, these concepts and approaches are complementary and built upon each other; all have a role to play in designing and managing software systems. Each method shift came about in part to deal with greater levels of software complexity. In all cases, the way to manage complexity is by decomposing a complex system or process into smaller modules that can be designed independently, i.e., modularization. Modularization ensures easy maintenance and updates of complex systems by separating the high-frequency intra-module linkages from the low-frequency inter-module linkages, limiting the scope of interactions between the modules by hiding the intra-module relations inside a module box. Based on the idea of modularity, constructs such as objects, components, software agents, and Web services have been continuously invented and evolved for developing software applications.

OOP provides a foundation for software engineering that uses objects and their interactions to design applications and computer programs. CBD provides a coarser grained construct for larger systems, and separates interface from the behavior of the construct for supporting public communication between the components which know about each other before runtime. SOA goes further by using XML-based and network-addressable interface as well as XML-based messages and standard protocols for open communication among all software applications in Internet. Different from OOP, CBD, and SOA, AOC is used to model and implement solutions to semi- or ill-structured problems, which are too complex to be completely characterized and precisely described. Agent is used to perform more autonomous activities in solving complex problems. To achieve this, knowledge or rules for governing the behavior of an agent are separated from the behavior of the agent.

In computer science, the terms object, component, software agent, and Web service describe a piece of software that performs some action on behalf of human beings, like an agent or actor. In addition to an actor, the agent can also be a broker, which mediates between the service requesting party and the service providing party. In terms of broker, software agent can be used to search appropriate applications to perform requested services. This special type of agent works as an intermediary between service requesters and service providers, coordinating on behalf of the two parties by taking into account of service requirements, qualities, costs, constraints, and so on.

APPLYING MODULAR COMPUTING TECHNOLOGIES IN COMPLEX BPM

In the 5th section we propose the DCAR architecture for developing complex process management systems, which includes decomposition of complex processes (D); task coordination (C); awareness of environmental changes (A); and resource selection and coordination (R). This provides the foundation to identify the BPM requirements for employing appropriate technologies in developing flexible BPM systems. In the 6th section we clarify and explicitly define the similarities and differences between the four modular technologies: OOP, CBD, SOA, and AOC. In this section we will show how these technologies can be used to implement the proposed BPM architecture.

Decomposition of Complex Processes (D)

Business processes display complexity as a result of interactions of their internal components and interaction of the process with its environment. A process can be decomposed into a set of tasks, task into sub-tasks, and so on, through several layers in a network hierarchy. Tasks or sub-task components can be delegated to software objects, components, agents, and services, as actors of the tasks, which interact and communicate in performing the process.

To deal with interactions across different organizations, SOA proposes "service" as a high level view of the building block of a process. A process is composed of a set of services, each of which is provided by an individual organization. By using SOA, the inter-service interactions are separated from intra-service interactions; the complexity of both is maintained at different layers. Moreover, we can take advantage of reusability, inter-operability, and extensibility of Web services on the basis of open standards to cater for business process integration and interoperation over the Web.

The highly dynamic and unpredictable nature of business processes makes agent-based approach appealing. AOC assigns business applications' main activities to autonomous agents. Such agents are flexible problem solvers that have specific goals to achieve and interact with one another to manage their autonomy and interdependency in business processes. AOC is well suited for complex process situations that are not all known a priori, cannot be assumed to be fully controllable in their behaviors, and must interact on a sophisticated level of communication and coordination (Wang et al., 2005b).

Flexible Task Coordination (C)

A business processes is made up of a number of task components that interact with dynamic behavior. OOP uses objects to hide behavior and data, supporting communications among small objects, e.g., functions of tasks. CBD extends OOP by supporting interaction among components (e.g., tasks), i.e., coarser grained constructs, using public communication interface. SOC goes further by using XML-based and network-addressable interface as well as XML-based messages and standard protocols for open communication among BPM applications over the Internet.

While OOP, OBD, and SOA mainly support structured communications among tasks or task components, AOC are able to support ill-structured interactions. To coordinate the interactions in dynamic situations, flatter hierarchies, decentralized autonomous units, and decision-based coordination mechanisms are required, where AOC is directly applicable. AOC supports decentralized control and asynchronous operations by a group of autonomous software entities, which are able to perform decision-based coordination of their activities.

In AOC, after decomposing a complex process into a number of loosely coupled tasks in a flat hierarchy, we may delegate the tasks to a number of autonomous agents, each working both autonomously and collaboratively throughout the whole process. In complex process management, it is impossible to predefine all activities and interactions at design time. Instead, we define the goal or role of each agent, and specify a set of rules for governing the behavior of the agent. Agents operate asynchronously and in parallel. This results in an increase in overall speed and robustness in BPM. The failure of one agent does not necessarily make the overall system useless, where other agents may adjust and coordinate their behavior reactively and proactively to the change.

Figure 3. Agent-based Process Management in Dynamic Environment

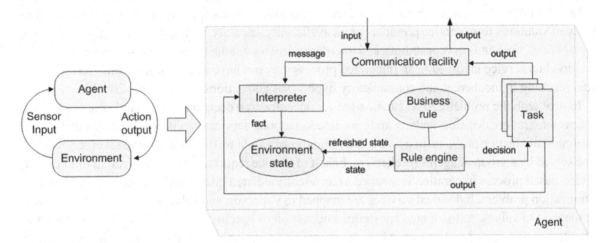

Awareness of Dynamic Environments (A)

The complexity of business processes comes not only from interactions of their internal components, but also from interaction of the process with its environment. To manage business processes in a dynamic environment, we need to be able to continuously perceive the environment, and make real-time decisions on the process. Objects, components, and services are normally unable to behave in dynamic environments. Agent-based software entity is able to sense and recognize the situation and determine appropriate actions upon the situations.

Unlike the ECA (event-condition-action) rules in workflow systems that enable reaction to certain events, AOC goes further by incorporating all environmental information into a mental state that watches over the whole environment. Individual events are put together for a comprehensive understanding; ambiguous information is understood after appropriate interpretation and reasoning (Wang et al., 2006a). As shown in Figure 3, information about the environment (e.g., events, activities, and resources) is sensed and interpreted by the agent on the basis of predefined scheme and rules. In case that information is unanticipated or comes as a complete and total surprise, it will be sent to human manager for manual processing. Moreover, AOC supports prediction of future state of the environment for purpose of proactive actions. Different from passive response to current events, proactive behavior has an orientation to the future, anticipating problems and taking affirmative steps to deal with them rather than reacting after a situation has already occurred. It refers to the exhibition of goal-oriented behaviors by taking initiatives.

Flexible Resource Coordination (R)

As discussed, the rise of Internet-mediated e-Business brings the era of demand-driven and resource-based soft connections of business organizations. A business process can be dynamically established by connecting or composing services provided by different organizations. SOA provides a real platform for resource selection and allocation in order to implement seamless and flexible integration of business processes over the Internet.

However, it is a complex problem to search appropriated services from a large number of resources as well as schedule and coordinate them under various constraints. The complexity arises from the unpredictability of solutions from service providers (e.g., availability, capacity, and price), the constraints on the services (e.g., time and cost constraint), and interdependencies among the services. A service solution to an individual service involved in an integrated process may not have a view of the whole service, very often resulting in incoherent and contradictory hypotheses and actions (Wang et al., 2006b).

To deal with the problem, AOC can be used for decentralized decision making and coordination. In process integration, decision-making and coordination among services can be modeled as a distributed constraint satisfaction problem, in which solutions and constraints are distributed into a set of services and to be solved by a group of agents (brokers) on behalf of service requesters and providers. In this context, service-based process integration is mapped as an agent-mediated distributed constraint satisfaction or optimization problem. Individual services are mapped to variables, and solutions of individual services are mapped to values. A distributed constraint satisfaction or optimization problem consists of a set of variables, each assigned to an agent, where the values of the variables are taken from finite and discrete domains. Finding a global solution to an integrated process requires that all agents find the solutions that satisfy not only their own constraints but also inter-agent constraints (Wang et al., 2008b).

CONCLUSION

In this paper, we have investigated the challenges and solution for complex BPM. Based on the analysis of business process complexity and the modularity theory for complex systems, we present the DCAR architecture for developing BPM systems in turbulent environment. On the other hand, we investigated relevant modular programming technologies that can be used to model and develop complex systems. We analyze the overlapping technical concepts and techniques as well as clarify the differences and relationships between these terminologies and techniques in the context of BPM. Based on the examination of 1) the requirements of complex BPM based on the DCAR architecture and 2) the supporting technologies for complex systems, we have made a clear picture with a systemic approach on how these technologies can be applied and integrated in developing systems for complex process management. This work will benefit professionals, researchers, and practitioners by advanced analysis and theoretical investigations of problems and solutions in developing solutions for complex BPM.

ACKNOWLEDGEMENT

This research is supported by a General Research Fund (No. RGC/HKU7169/07E) from the Hong Kong SAR Government, and a Seed Funding for Basic Research (200611159216) from The University of Hong Kong.

REFERENCES

Baldwin, C. Y., & Clark, K. B. (1997). Managing in an age of modularity. *Harvard Business Review*, *75*(5), 84–93.

Casati, F., Ceri, S., Paraboschi, S., & Pozzi, G. (1999). Specification and implementation of exceptions in workflow management systems. *ACM Transactions on Database Systems, 24*(3), 405–451. doi:10.1145/328939.328996

Casati, F., & Shan, M. (2001). Dynamic and adaptive composition of e-services. *Information Systems, 26*(3), 143–163. doi:10.1016/S0306-4379(01)00014-X

Chiu, D. K. W., Li, Q., & Karlapalem, K. (1999). A meta modeling approach for workflow management system supporting exception handling. *Information Systems, 24*(2), 159–184. doi:10.1016/S0306-4379(99)00010-1

Eisenhardt, M. K. (1989). Agency theory: An assessment and review. *Academy of Management Review, 14*(1), 57–74. doi:10.2307/258191

El Sawy, O. A. (2001). *Redesigning enterprise processes for e-business*. Boston: Irwin/McGraw-Hill

Elfatatry, A. (2007). Dealing with changes: Components versus services. *Communications of the ACM, 50*(8), 35–39. doi:10.1145/1278201.1278203

Endsley, M. R. (1995). Toward a theory of situation awareness in dynamic systems. *Human Factors, 37*(1), 32–64. doi:10.1518/001872095779049543

Garud, R., & Kumaraswamy, A. (2003). Technological and organizational design for realizing economies of substitution. In R. Garud, A. Kumaraswamy, & R.N. Langlois (Eds.), *Managing in the modular age: Architectures, networks, and organizations* (pp. 45-77). Blackwell Publishing Limited.

Hammer, M., & Champy, J. (1993). *Reengineering the corporation: A manifesto for business revolution*. London: Brealey.

Holland, J. (1995). *Hidden order: How adaptation builds complexity*. Cambridge, MA: Perseus.

Huhns, M. N. (2002). Agents as Web services. *IEEE Internet Computing, 6*(4), 93–95. doi:10.1109/MIC.2002.1020332

Jennings, N. R., Faratin, P., Norman, T. J., O'Brien, P., & Odgers, B. (2002). Autonomous agents for business process management. *International Journal of Applied Artificial Intelligence, 14*(2), 145–189.

Kammer, P. J., Bolcer, G. A., Taylor, R. N., Hitomi, A. S., & Bergman, M. (2000). Techniques for supporting dynamic and adaptive workflow. *Computer Supported Cooperative Work, 9*(3-4), 269–292. doi:10.1023/A:1008747109146

Kumar, A., & Zhao, J. L. (2002). Workflow support for electronic commerce applications. *Decision Support Systems, 32*(3), 265–278. doi:10.1016/S0167-9236(01)00114-2

Kumar, K. (2001). Technology for supporting supply chain management: Introduction. *Communications of the ACM, 44*(6), 58–61. doi:10.1145/376134.376165

Kumar, K., & Narasipuram, M. M. (2006). Defining requirements for business process flexibility. In *Seventh Workshop on Business Process Modeling, Development, and Support*. CAiSE

Kumar, K., & van Dissel, H. (1996). Sustainable collaboration: Managing conflict and cooperation in interorganizational systems. *MIS Quarterly*, *20*(3), 279–300. doi:10.2307/249657

Kumar, K., van Fenema, P. C., & von Glinow, M. A. (2007). Offshoring and the global distribution of work: Implications for task interdependence theory and practice. In *First Annual Research Conference and Workshop on Offshoring*. North Carolina

Leymann, F., Roller, D., & Schmidt, M. T. (2002). Web services and business process management. *IBM Systems Journal*, *41*(2), 198–211.

Melão, N., & Pidd, M. (2000). A conceptual framework for understanding business processes and business process modeling. *Information Systems Journal*, *10*(2), 105–129. doi:10.1046/j.1365-2575.2000.00075.x

Mintzberg, H. (1979). *The structuring of organizations*. NJ: Prentice Hall.

Mowshowitz, A. (1997). Virtual organization. *Communications of the ACM*, *40*(9), 30–37. doi:10.1145/260750.260759

Petrie, C. J., & Bussler, C. (2003). Service agents and virtual enterprises: A survey. *IEEE Internet Computing*, *4*, 68–78. doi:10.1109/MIC.2003.1215662

Rumbaugh, J. (1991). *Object-oriented modeling and design*. Englewood Cliffs, N.J.: Prentice Hall

Sanchez, R., & Mahoney, J. T. (2003). Modularity, flexibility, and knowledge management in product and organization design. In R. Garud, A. Kumaraswamy, & R.N. Langlois (Eds), *Managing in the modular age: Architectures, networks, and organizations* (pp. 362-389). Blackwell Publishing Limited.

Schilling, M. A. (2003). Towards general modular systems theory and its application to interfirm product modularity. In R Garud, A. Kumaraswamy, & R.N. Langlois (Eds.), *Managing in the modular age: Architectures, networks, and organizations* (pp. 172-216). Blackwell Publishing Limited.

Simon, H. A. (1977). *The new science of management decision*. Englewood Cliffs, N.J.: Prentice-Hall

Simon, H. A. (1981). *The sciences of the artificial*. Cambridge, MA: MIT Press.

Simon, H. A. (2003). The architecture of complexity. In R Garud, A. Kumaraswamy, & R.N. Langlois (Eds), *Managing in the modular age: Architectures, networks, and organizations* (pp. 15-44). Blackwell Publishing Limited.

Szyperski, C. (2002). *Component software: Beyond object-oriented programming*. Bosoton: Addison-Wesley Professional.

van der Aalst, W. M. P., & van Hee, K. M. (2002). *Workflow management: Models, methods, and systems*. Cambridge, MA: MIT Press.

Volberda, H. W. (1999). *Building the flexible firm: How to remain competitive*. Oxford University Press

Wang, M., Cheung, W. K., Liu, J., Xie, X., & Lou, Z. (2006b). E-Service/process composition through multi-agent constraint management. *International Conference on Business Process Management (BPM 2006)* (LNCS 4102, pp. 274-289).

Wang, M., & Kumar, K. (2008a). Developing flexible business process management systems using modular computing technologies. In *Proceedings of Eighth Global Conference on Flexible Systems Management (GlOGIFT-08)*. Hoboken, NJ.

Wang, M., Liu, J., Wang, H., Cheung, W., & Xie, X. (2008b). On-demand e-supply chain integration: A multi-agent constraint-based approach. *Expert Systems with Applications, 34*(4), 2683–2692. doi:10.1016/j.eswa.2007.05.041

Wang, M., & Wang, H. (2002). Intelligent agents supported flexible workflow monitoring system. In *Proceedings of the14th International Conference on Advanced Information Systems Engineering (CAiSE'02)* (LNCS 2348, pp. 787-791).

Wang, M., & Wang, H. (2005b). Intelligent agent supported business process management. In *Proceedings of 38th Hawaii International Conference on System Sciences (HICSS-38)*. IEEE Computer Society Press.

Wang, M., & Wang, H. (2006a). From process logic to business logic - A cognitive approach to business process management. *Information & Management, 43*(2), 179–193. doi:10.1016/j.im.2005.06.001

Wang, M., Wang, H., & Xu, D. (2005a). The design of intelligent workflow monitoring with agent technology. *Knowledge-Based Systems, 18*(6), 257–266. doi:10.1016/j.knosys.2004.04.012

Weske, M. (1998). Object-oriented design of a flexible workflow management system. *2nd East-European Symposium on Advances in Databases and Information Systems* (LNCS 1475, pp. 119-130).

Weske, M. (2001). Formal foundation and conceptual design of dynamic adaptations in a workflow management system. In *Proc. HICSS-34*. Maui, Hawaii

Wolters, N. J. (2002). *The business of modularity and the modularity of business*. PhD Thesis, Erasmus Research Institute of Management, Rotterdam

Wooldridge, M., & Jennings, N. R. (1999). software engineering with agents: Pitfalls and pratfalls. *IEEE Internet Computing, 3*(3), 20–27. doi:10.1109/4236.769419

KEY TERMS AND DEFINITIONS

Agent-Oriented Computing: Agent Oriented Computing (AOC) is based on the idea of delegating tasks and responsibility of a complex problem to software agents. It emphasizes autonomy and mutual co-operation of agents in performing tasks in open and complex environments.

Business Process: A business process can be simply defined as a collection of activities that create value by transforming inputs into more valuable outputs. These activities consist of a series of steps performed by actors to produce a product or service for the customer.

Business Process Management: Business Process Management (BPM) refers to activities performed by organizations to design (capture processes and document their design in terms of process maps), model (define business processes in a computer language), execute (develop software that enables the process), monitor (track individual processes for performance measurement), and optimize (retrieve process performance for improvement) operational business processes by using a combination of models, methods, techniques, and tools

Component-Based Development: Component-Based Development (CBD) is software engineering discipline, with an emphasis on decomposition of the engineered systems into functional or logical components with well-defined interfaces used for communication across the components.

Modularity: Modularity refers to a particular design structure, which refers to development of a complex product or process from smaller subsystems that can be designed independently.

Object-Oriented Programming: Object-oriented Programming (OOP) is a software engineering paradigm that uses "objects" and their interactions to design applications and computer programs

Situation Awareness: Situation awareness is the perception and understanding of objects, events, people, system states, interactions, environmental conditions, and other situation-specific factors in complex and dynamic environments

Service-Oriented Architecture: Service-Oriented Architecture (SOA) utilizes Web services as fundamental elements for developing applications. It is an emerging paradigm for architecting and implementing business collaborations within and across organizational boundaries.

Chapter 2
Enterprise Specific BPM Languages and Tools

Steen Brahe
Danske Bank, Denmark

ABSTRACT

Many enterprises use their own domain concepts when they model business processes. They may also use technology in specialized ways when they implement the business processes in a Business Process Management (BPM) system. In contrast, BPM tools often provide a standard business process modeling language, a standard implementation technology and a fixed transformation that may generate the implementation from the model. This makes the tools inflexible and difficult to use. This chapter presents another approach. It applies the basic model driven development principles of direct representation and automation to BPM tools through a tool experiment in Danske Bank. We develop BPM tools that capture Danske Banks specific modeling concepts and use of technology and which automate the generation of code. An empirical evaluation reveals remarkable improvements in development productivity and code quality. We conclude that BPM tools should provide flexibility to allow customization to the specific needs of an enterprise.

INTRODUCTION

Business Process Management (BPM) is currently receiving much focus from the industry. Top management demands to understand and control their business processes and agility to adjust them when market conditions change. This can be achieved through Process Aware Information Systems (Dumas et al.,2005). A BPM system (Jablonski and Bussler,1996; Leymann and Roller, 2000) is one example of such a system. It allows execution and automation of a business process that can be described explicitly as an executable workflow.

DOI: 10.4018/978-1-60566-669-3.ch002

Although the hype about BPM and process automation is high, previous work has shown that it is relatively complex to understand, model and implement a business process as an executable workflow (Brahe, 2007). First the process must be understood, second it must be formalized and modeled at a highly conceptual and logical level, and third the process design must be transferred to technology. Many software vendors have complete BPM tool suites for modeling and implementing business processes. Such tools are mostly based on a predefined process modeling language like the Business Process Modeling Notation (BPMN) (White, 2006) for capturing the business process at the conceptual level and one technology like the Business Process Execution language (BPEL) (BPEL, 2003) for implementing the process. These tools also assume a fixed development process where only two models exist, i.e. the conceptual business process and the implementation.

Using such tools causes two challenges for an enterprise that has specific requirements to its development process, uses its own modeling concepts and uses technology in specialized ways; First, a standardized modeling notation does not allow users to use domain concepts and may contain too many modeling constructs which makes the tool difficult to use. The models may also be difficult to understand and use as a communication media. Second, transformation of a model into implementation must be done manually as the enterprise may use a variety of technologies to implement the process and not only e.g. BPEL as many state-of-the-art tools support today. Even if one technology as e.g. BPEL is used, the enterprise may be using its own implementation patterns which cannot be generated because the transformations are hard-coded into the BPM tools.

The approach behind current BPM tools is similar to the extinct Computer Aided Software Engineering (CASE) tools from the 90es. They also often used a standard modeling language, one implementation technology and a standardized transformation. Their limited flexibility in supporting enterprise specific standards was one of the reasons why they were never accepted (Windsor, 1986; Flynn et al., 1995).

This chapter takes another approach than state-of-the-art BPM tools. In order to avoid the CASE trap we must come up with an approach that allows an enterprise to use its own modeling notations and specific use of technology. Our hypothesis is that this can be achieved through applying the basic model driven development (Stahl et al., 2006) principles of direct representation and automation (Booch et al., 2004) to BPM tools; An enterprise should be able to model its business processes directly in enterprise specific concepts, decide on a target platform and write transformations that encapsulate its specific use of technology, and that automate the generation of code.

This leads us to the research question which we will answer through this chapter: Does an enterprise specific BPM tool improve the efficiency and quality of modeling and implementing business processes, how difficult is it to create, and is it worth the effort?.

We use a design research approach to answer this question; We will implement above hypothesis though an experiment where we develop BPM languages, tools and transformations for a specific enterprise. Successively, these will be empirically evaluated to show the validity of the hypothesis. We use Danske Bank, the second largest financial institute in northern Europe, as a case study. In lack of sufficient industrial standards, Danske Bank has defined its own development process and uses a number of different tools to support it. This has caused several challenges as described by Brahe (2007).

A prototype tool was developed to show that it provide value to develop BPM tools fitted for the needs of a specific enterprise. The prototype illustrates that it is possible to do model driven development of a business process with nearly 100% code generation. The prototype is fitted specially for Danske Banks development process and consists of three different Domain Specific Languages (DSLs) (Mernik et al., 2005) and corresponding editors that are used to model a business process and related information. Furthermore, the tool provides transformations between the DSLs and a transformation to BPEL. These transformations capture implementation patterns specific for Danske Banks modeling standards and use of the implementation technology. Manual changes can be introduced into the generated BPEL code by a persistence utility feature.

We use a fictitious Project called Customer Quick Loan throughout the chapter. First, we illustrate the current development process in Danske Bank and the observed challenges of using current BPM tools. Second, we show how the prototype tool eliminates these challenges. We conclude that BPM tools customized to a specific enterprise potentially have a huge effect on the efficiency of a project team and will result in implementations with fewer errors.

However, we also conclude that developing BPM tools from scratch requires high expertise and much effort and is a strategic decision that many enterprises will not take. What we need is a tool based framework that allows the enterprise to customize languages, transformations and tools to their specific needs instead of develop them from scratch.

The rest of the chapter is organized as follows. Section 2 introduces Danske Bank and related work. Section 3 introduces the fictitious Customer Quick Loan project. Section 4 discusses challenges regarding the development process and used modeling tools. Section 5 abstracts the development process into metamodels and algorithms for transforming models into code. Based on this abstraction, the developed BPM tools are described in section 6. Section 7 describes an empirical evaluation of the tool. Section 8 discusses the results and section 9 summarizes the chapter and outlines future work.

BACKGROUND

This section introduces Danske Bank and presents related work.

Danske Bank

Danske Bank has grown to become the largest financial group in Denmark - and one of the largest in northern Europe. It comprises a variety of financial services such as banking, mortgage credit, insurance, pension, capital management, leasing and real estate agency.

Support for executing and automating business processes is achieved through different process execution engines. One of them is batch execution of process implementations in PL1 and COBOL. Another one is a BPM system from IBM, where the business processes are implemented in BPEL. The BPM system has been extended in areas where business requirements were not fulfilled. For example, the enterprise has created its own Human Task Manager to handle and distribute human tasks that are part of an executable workflow and its own task portal where process participants claim and execute human tasks. Furthermore, it has specific uses of BPEL fault handlers and has defined specific strategies of capturing business and technical faults during process execution.

Danske Bank has defined its own development process as no standardized development process as e.g. the Rational Unified Process (Kroll and Kruchten, 2003) was sufficient to fulfill their requirements. Business and IT solutions are developed as one for any business problem. This is in contrast to most development methodologies which focus on producing software solutions. It is based on service oriented principles (Erl, 2005) where business requirements are mapped into required business services and processes. All important stakeholders are represented at a project team to ensure that different issues are addressed. This includes defining efficient business processes and specifying and developing IT systems that may support them. A project team includes business process participants, business analysts, solution architects, system developers and test specialists. Most requirements and design decisions are captured in models. They are used for documentation and communicative purposes and as blueprints for the implementation. The development process includes specialized modeling notations and creation of different modeling artifacts.

Related Work

Only limited work has previously been reported on customizing business process modeling notations and corresponding tools to a specific domain and enterprise. In general, most modeling languages like Petri nets (Murata,1989), Event-driven Process Chains (EPC) and the Business Process Modeling Notation (BPMN) (White, 2006) only have one notation which all domains have to follow. An exception is UML activity diagrams that can be extended by a profile for a specific domain. UML Activity diagrams are used by both academia and industry for its extensibility and available tool support in form of general UML modeling tools. Dumas and Hofstede (2001) argue based on workflow patterns (van der Aalst et al., 2003) that the expressiveness of activity diagrams as a workflow language is large and Guntama et al. (2003) have extended activity diagrams to enable flexible business workflow modeling. There are also various UML profiles for business process modeling, e.g. List and Korherr (2005) who consider both the business process flow as well as the business process context.

Brahe and Østerbye (2006) use UML activity diagrams as the semantic base for creating domain specific modeling languages for business process modeling based on UML profiles. They suggest that many enterprises need their own modeling notations and present a prototype tools that allows metamodeling of domain-specific workflow-based languages and automatically generation of domain-specific tool support in form of editors. Jablonski and Götz (2007) have a similar approach. They present a flexible and extensible metamodel and the concept of perspective oriented business process visualization that allows multiple visual presentations of a business process model.

Model Driven Development (Stahl et al., 2006) and the Model Driven Architecture (Frankel, 2003) have been used extensively in transforming business process models to implementations, particularly from UML activity diagrams to service composition languages e.g. Bézivin et al. (2004); Bordbar and Staikopoulos (2004a,b); Skogan et al. (2004); Koehler et al. (2003, 2005). Common for all approaches is the use of a fixed modeling notation and a fixed transformation. In contrast, Brahe and Bordbar (2006) present a transformation framework that builds upon the use of domain specific business process modeling languages and customized transformations. They also introduce a prototype implementation that allows definition and execution of customized and pattern-based transformations for a domain specific modeling language.

Fowler (2005) talks about Language Workbenches as tools that allow definition and usage of Domain Specific Languages, editors and transformation between languages. Several of such workbenches exist such as MetaEdit+ (Tolvanen & Rossi, 2003), GME (Ledeczi et al., 2001), Microsoft DSL tools, and many others. The Eclipse projects used to build Danske Bank Workbench can also be considered as a language workbench. The research presented in this chapter follows cutting edge trends in language workbenches; models should be constructed in domain or enterprise specific concepts and transformed into an implementation. The experiment presented in this chapter has been documented in details in a technical report (Brahe (2008)).

EXAMPLE: CUSTOMER QUICK LOAN

The fictitious project "Customer Quick Loan" will be used for illustrative purposes throughout the rest of the chapter.

Changes in consumer patterns have required immediate action for introducing a new type of customer loans. The new loans can be requested from email and mobile phones with possible immediately approval and transfer of the requested amount to the customers account. A project team is established which includes a loan specialist, a business analyst, a solution architect, system developers and a project manager. They name the project Customer Quick Loan.

In the following we will see how the project team follows Danske Banks development process to model business events, design the solution, specify the physical design and implement it as an executable workflow.

Business Events

The business analyst defines all possible business events that may occur for a given business case. A business event is defined as an occurrence that influences a business area and which initiates a well defined business process in this area. The events are described in a model called an event map.

For the Customer Quick Loan the primary events are ApplyForLoan, which occurs when a customer requests a loan, and PayoffLoan, which occurs each month after a loan has been created. The event map is defined as a UML class diagram in Rational Software Modeler (Swithinbank et al., 2005) (Figure 1). Additional information about the events is specified in MS Word documents. An event is classified as external if it is invoked by an actor as e.g. a customer for another department in the enterprise. It is classified as timedependent if the event is occurring at a certain point in time. The ApplyForLoan event is external as it is invoked by a customer while the Payoff loan is time dependent as it is invoked once a month.

Solution Process Flow

When a business event takes place it will involve execution of some business logic. For each business event, the business analyst together with a solution architect and possible a system developer will model such business logic as a Solution Process Flow (SPF), which is a technology independent or logical business process model. Each task in the Solution Process Flow must either be of type Automatic, which means handled automatically by a service invocation, Manual as e.g. moving papers from a table to an archive or UserExperiance as e.g. creating a loan using an application user interface. The IBM Websphere Business Modeler is used to define these models.

The Solution Process Flow for the primary business event, ApplyForLoan, is illustrated in Figure 2. It consists of four logical tasks; the automatic ApproveLoan task will make a risk calculation of the customer. If the risk is high, the loan request is rejected; a process participant will be notified by the Reject task of type UserExperience, and will have to send a rejection message to the customer using an application interface. If the risk is low, the loan, or possible several loans applied for at once, will be created by the automatic CreateLoans tasks, and a confirmation will be sent to the customer by the Confirm task.

Figure 1. Business events for the Customer Quick Loan project modelled as a UML class diagram in Rational Software Modeler.

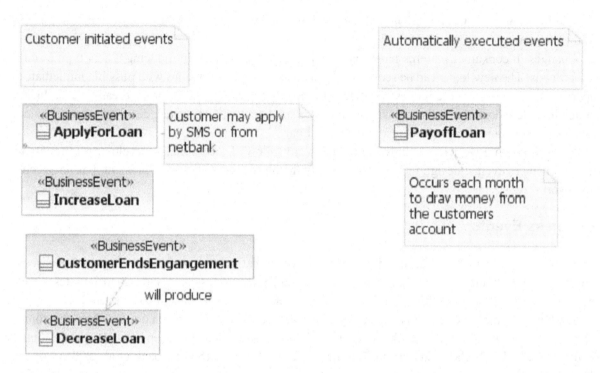

The project team has examined the local service repository for existing services and has found that two existing service operations called in a sequence will fulfill the requirement for a Confirm task in the Solution Process Flow. Therefore, the Confirm task is further broken down and modeled in a separate sub process as illustrated in Figure 3. First, a service operation is invoked to create the content of the confirm message, and second, a service operation is invoked to send the message by SMS, email or letter.

Figure 2. Solution Process Flow for the ApplyForLoan business event modeled in Websphere Business Modeler.

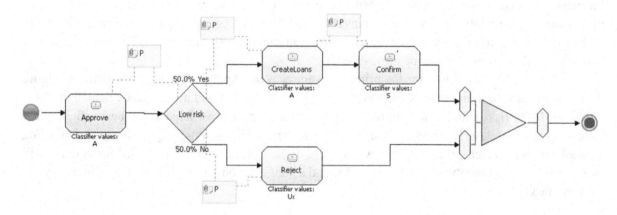

Figure 3. The Confirm task modeled as a sub process.

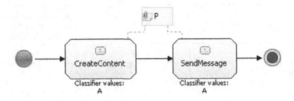

Physical Design

Some business processes may be implemented in BPEL, others may be implemented in PL1 or COBOL for batch execution, and finally some may not be implemented by IT at all. The project team decides to automate the execution of the ApplyForLoan process by implementing it in BPEL. Two kind of physical specifications now have to be made: BPEL process design, also called Control Flow Behavior, and a Workflow Specification, which contains additional information required to implement the Solution Process Flow and all its tasks in the BPM system.

Control Flow Behavior

The Solution Process Flow is the starting point for the Control Flow Behavior, a model of the physical implementation in BPEL which is also created using Websphere Business Modeler. Three physical design decisions make them different. This is described in the following three sections.

Separate vs. Inlined Subprocess

It must be decided if the Solution Process Flow should be implemented as one BPEL process, or if it should be broken down into several. Extracting parts of the process into sub processes has advantages:

Figure 4. Control Flow Behavior of the ApplyForLoan SPF.

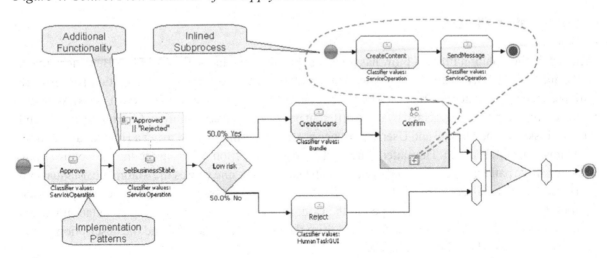

Table 1. Solution Process Flow tasks mapped into Control Flow Behavior.

Task	Implementation pattern
AssessRisk	ServiceOperation
CreateLoans	Bundle
CreateContent	ServiceOperation
SendMessage	ServiceOperation
Reject	HumanTaskGUI

More than one developer can simultaneously work on the construction, it is easier to make a change and deploy a small sub process compared to change and deploy the main process, and a sub process can be reused by other processes. Though, extensively use of sub processes has the disadvantages of maintaining and operating several processes instead of one main process. This causes an overhead and introduces complexity regarding change management. The developer decides to implement the Confirm sub process as an inlined sub process in the ApplyForLoan BPEL process. This is illustrated in Figure 4. The developer could also have implemented the sub process as a separate BPEL process.

Technology Dependent Functionality

Functionality needed for the implementation in a specific technology should not be modeled in the Solution Process Flow. Using BPEL, this could be complex data transformations inside in a BPEL process that are externalized as separate service invocations, it could be synchronization of data between different systems that make up the extended BPM system in Danske Bank, or it could be a specific service invocation that updates the business state for the specific process instance, a feature of Danske Banks extended BPM system.

An additional service invocation has to be inserted in the Control Flow Behavior for the ApplyForLoan process after the AssessRisk service invocation. It updates the business state of the process instance to either "Approved" or "Rejected". This information can be viewed by employees in the Danske Bank through the Human Task Portal. The additional functionality is not required if the Solution Process Flow was implemented using another technology like COBOL (see Figure 4).

Implementation Patterns

Each task in the Solution Process Flow has to be mapped to a task in the Control Flow Behavior. A task can be implemented by different implementation patters. In this context implementation patterns are patterns, or code templates and rule used by Danske Bank to implement tasks of different types. An Automatic task type can be implemented by three different patterns; ServiceOperation, MultipleInstances and Bundle. Tasks of type Manual and UserExperience are always implemented using a HumanTaskManual or a HumanTaskGUI pattern. The patterns are explained a later section. When modeling the Control Flow Behavior, these pattern names are used to classify all tasks in the same way as the Automatic, Manual and UserExperience classifiers were used in the SPF model. Table 1 lists how tasks from the ApplyForLoan Solution Process Flow have been mapped to the Control Flow Behaviour. The implementation pattern to be used in the physical design is determined from the task type in the SPF and the description of the task in the corresponding System Use Case.

Table 2. Danske Bank specific BPEL implementation patterns. The dots are replaced with information from the Control Flow Behavior and the Workflow Specification documents.

Pattern name	BPEL template

ServiceOperation	```<assign name=. .>. .</assign>```
	```<invoke name=..>```
	```<catch faultName=TechFault . .>```
	```. .```
	```</catch>```
	```</invoke>```

MultipleInstances	```<assign name=. .>. .</assign>```
	```<while name=. .>```
	```<assign name=. .>```
	```<invoke name=..>```
	```<catch faultName=TechFault>```
	```. .```
	```</catch>```
	```</invoke>```
	```</while>```

Bundle	```<assign name=. .>. .</ assign>```
	```<while name=. .>```
	```<assign name=. .>```
	```<invoke name=..>```
	```<catch faultName=TechFault>```
	```. .```
	```</catch>```
	```</ invoke>```
	```</while>```
	```<receive name=..>. .</receive>```

HumanTask	```<assign name=. .>. .</assign>```
	```<invoke name=SetTaskInQueue>```
	```<catch faultName=TechFault>```
	```. .```
	```</catch>```
	```</ invoke>```

Workflow Specific Information

Much information has to be specified to implement the Control Flow Behavior in the BPM system. For a ServiceOperation task this includes information about which service operations to invoke, input and output data structures, exception handling and escalation of errors, if the task must be restarted in case of failures during service invocation etc.

A task of type HumanTaskManual or HumanTaskGUI is a task handled by humans. Process participants will be able to list, claim and execute such a task from a task portal. For both type of tasks following information is needed; groups allowed to claim and execute a task are defined as Allocation Rules, labels, descriptions and data values in three to five different languages must be described to be presented to the process participants in the task portal, and rules about earliest start of the task and a possible deadline and several others also has to be specified. The HumanTaskGUI task further has a link to an existing application interface where the process participant has to handle the task. It must also be specified which data values from within the running BPEL process instance the link should transfer to the business system. For the process itself, additional information also has to be specified. This includes input data for the process, allocation rules, and description in several languages for presentation in the task portal.

All information for one task is specified in a MS Word document and is called a Workflow Task Specification. A Word template is available for each task type which describes required information. Six task specification documents are created for the ApplyForLoan process.

BPEL Construction

All required information and design decisions are now available, and the BPEL process can be constructed after the Control Flow Behavior and Workflow Specification have been completed.

A system developer now maps the Control Flow Behavior into a BPEL process. From the Workflow Specification he is able to specify input/output data, set attributes about the process as e.g. when it is valid from, if it is a long running process etc. Also other systems as e.g. Danske Banks proprietary Human Task Manager can be populated with allocation rules specified in this document. Each task in the Control Flow Behavior is mapped to the BPEL implementation based on the developer's knowledge of BPEL implementation patterns in Danske Bank. Each task type introduced in previous section has a certain BPEL template and an algorithm for how to implement it. The pattern names and corresponding BPEL templates are illustrated in Table 2.

The Service Operation pattern invokes a service operation and incorporates specific way of using logging and fault handling. All service operations in Danske Bank throw a Technical Fault, which is caught by the fault handler for the Invoke node. The fault handler forces the invoke node into stopped state.

The MultipleInstances pattern is a loop containing a service invocation as implemented by the Service Operation pattern. It is similar to the workflow pattern "Multiple instances without priori runtime knowledge" (van der Aalst et al., 2003).

The service operation invoked in the loop may initiate another process or thread that runs concurrently. For some business scenarios the main business process is not allowed to continue before all initiated processes behind these service invocations have finished. Danske Bank has extended the BPM system with infrastructure functionality that allows such a mechanism. In the BPEL process it is called the Bundle pattern and is implemented as the MultipleInstances pattern followed by an event. At runtime after invoking the service operation a number of times, the main process will wait until all the initiated concurrently running processes have finished. The BPM infrastructure extension will be notified about the state change and will fire the event that will cause the BPEL process to continue executing.

The HumanTaskManual and GUI patterns are implemented by invoking a specific service operation exposed by Danske Banks Human Task Manager followed by an event node. The translation of a task and its related information is purely manual, even though it is the same patterns that are implemented multiple times.

Above descriptions only show a subset of the implementation steps that the developer has to go through when implementing the tasks from the Control Flow Behavior. Common for all patterns is that data mappings also have to be specified before invoking a service operation. Control flow logic also has to be specified by the developer. This is described at the edges that connect the tasks in the Control Flow Behavior model.

Figure 5. Current development process with main modeling artifacts and decision points. The clouds indicate that decisions are not documented, and the rounded boxes indicate that no metamodels are used.

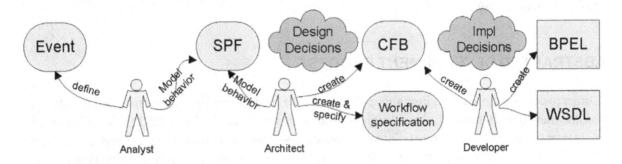

A NEED FOR CUSTOMIZED TOOLS

The development team faces several challenges in using the described BPM tools and development process:

Difficult to use domain concepts. Danske Bank has defined its own concepts for modeling business processes, but it is not possible to create models by directly using these concepts. Tools have been twisted and tweaked to force them to behave as desired. The usability is low and it is hard to use the models for communicative means.

Difficult to comprehend information. A number of different tools are used to describe and specify how a business process should be implemented. The developer and the architect therefore need to look into several different tools and models to find relevant information.

Missing traceability and consistency. It is difficult to find relevant models because traceability between models is handled by textual descriptions. Furthermore, a model created in one tool cannot refer to models created in other tools. Consistency between models must therefore be handled manually.

Imprecise data definitions. The data definitions can only be interpreted by humans. For instance, the name and version of the service operation is specified in the MS Word Workflow Specification document.

Because of above challenges, transformation of models and information from specification and physical design into physical artifacts as e.g. BPEL have to be done purely manually. The system developer needs to open models in Rational Software Modeler and Websphere Business Modeler and retrieve information manually, and he/she must open many MS Word documents to get detailed information about design decisions. Although model driven development is the goal of the development process, the result is mere a document driven development process.

For the simple example of the ApplyForLoan business process, the number of models and documents get high even for a simple example with only four tasks. One RSM model, two WBM models and about 10 word documents make up the specification. It is quite difficult to comprehend the large amount of distributed information required for constructing the BPEL code. Further, the construction process is inefficient and error-prone as much of the information from the specification has to be manually reentered into the physical artifacts.

The core of the problem is that the commercial tools used presume one development process defined by the software vendor, a fixed set of modeling languages and a specific way to use the implementation technology. This is in deep contrast to the requirements from Danske Bank who found the standard development process and standard notations insufficient for their needs. They need to build their own development process into the tools, to use their own modeling notations and artifacts and to define their own use of technology.

ABSTRACTED DEVELOPMENT PROCESS

In order to develop tools that address above challenges, we need a formal description of required information and transformational algorithms. In this section we therefore use the Customer Quick Loan example to abstract the development process into metamodels and transformations. First, we give an overview of the current development process and describe requirements to a model driven development process. Second, we introduce the abstracted development process, which uses the metamodels and transformations that we will develop in this section. Last, we define these metamodels and describe algorithms of how to carry out the transformations. The metamodels and transformation algorithms form the basis for the prototype tool described in next section, which has been developed specific for Danske Bank.

Current Development Process

Figure 5 gives an overview of the development process described in previous section, and illustrates the created artifacts as well as design decisions.

The artifacts are depictured with rounded boxes to indicate they are not precisely modeled, and the clouds indicate decisions that are not documented but instead put directly into models or code. Much of the information required through the development process is described as plain text. A human must read and interpret it to be able to construct the implementation. The cloud between the Solution Process Flow and the Control Flow Behavior illustrates that decisions about how the physical design are taken by the architect or developer; First, for each sub process modeled in the SPF it must be decided if it should be implemented as an inlined flow or as a separate process. Second, additional functionality must be specified. By defining the Control Flow Behavior from scratch, but inspired by the Solution Process Flow, the possibility to have tool based consistency check between them is lost. The Control Flow Behavior model needs to be manually updated each time the Solution Process Flow changes. The cloud between the Control Flow Behavior model and the BPEL code indicates decisions taken by the developer about BPEL specific information as e.g. the name of the project where the code is being developed, default package name, target namespace to use in the BPEL process, if generated WSDL files are kept in separate directories, etc.

Requirements to a Model Driven Development Process

One of the main ideas behind model driven development is to have tools that can transform platform independent models to platform specific models, and then generate the implementation code. In our example this means transformation of a Solution Process Flow into a Control Flow Behavior from which the BPEL implementation and related documents can be generated. In general, three basic requirements must be fulfilled to enable an efficient model driven development process:

Figure 6. New development process with metamodels and transformations. Information is specified precisely by using the Eventmap, SPF, WFSpec, BPELCodeGen and ModelInjections metamodels.

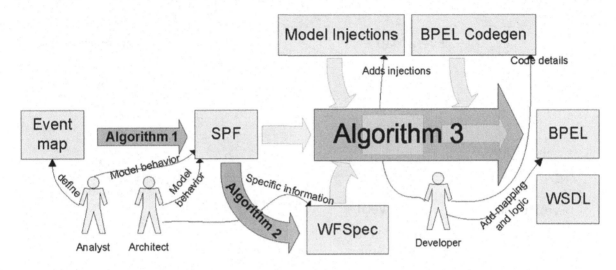

Information and design decisions must be specified precisely in models.

Transformation between models must be formally described.

Information added to generated models or code must survive future transformations.

Creating precise models requires availability of languages or metamodels that support modeling standards and which allow modeling of all required information in a precise manner. As Danske Bank has created its own notations and use technology in specific ways, they need to be able to express this in their models.

Abstracted Development Process

Figure 6 illustrates the model driven development process that we will describe through the rest of this section. It uses metamodels, called Eventmap, SPF and WFSpec, for modeling event maps, Solution Process Flows and Workflow Specifications.

It further uses a ModelInjection metamodel, and a BPELCodeGen metamodel. They are used to capture decisions currently taken in the "clouds". The metamodels form the basis for algorithms that can generate models and code. The BPELCodeGen metamodel is used to describe specific BPEL implementation decisions, while the WFSpec metamodel and the ModelInjection metamodel are used to describe the three differences between the Solution Process Flow and the Control Flow Behavior described in a previous section.

Decisions about how to implement sub processes modeled as part of the Solution Process Flow is captured by the WFSpec metamodel. It also specifies workflow specific information for each task in the Solution Process Flow.

Additional technical functionality is modeled as separate process fragments, also called model injections as it is to be injected at a specific point in the Solution Process Flow to generate the Control Flow

Figure 7. Event map (EventMap) metamodel. An event can either be external or timedependent and consists of a number of scenarios.

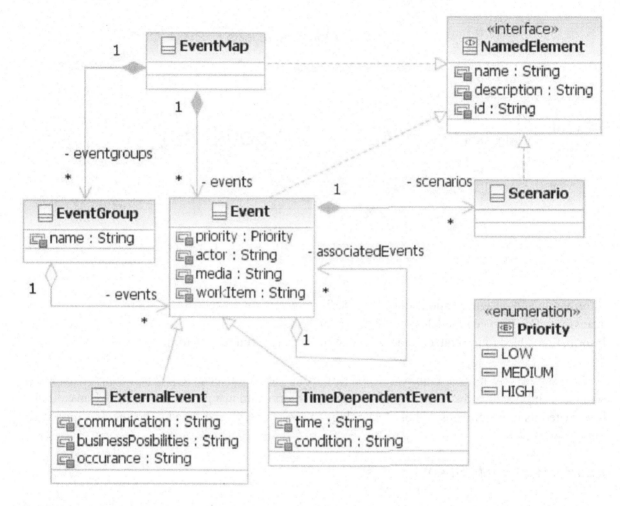

Behavior. Process fragments are modeled using the Solution Process Flow metamodel. The relation between a process fragment and where to inject it is captured by a ModelInjection metamodel.

The implementation patterns to be used for implementing tasks in the Solution Process Flow are documented by the WFSpec metamodel, for instance that an *Automatic* task is implemented by the *ServiceOperation* or the *Bundle* implementation pattern.

The Control Flow Behavior model has disappeared as it is indirectly generated from the Solution Process Flow, the WFSpec model and theModelInjection model. The development process illustrated in Figure 6 has been implemented in the prototype tool described in next section that uses the meta-models to capture information precisely and transformations to automate the generation of the BPEL implementation.

Figure 8. Solution Process Flow (SPF) metamodel. Tasks are modeled by the Automatic, Manual, User-Experience and SubProcess tasks types and connected in a control flow by using edges of type Process, Dialog or ProcessDialog.

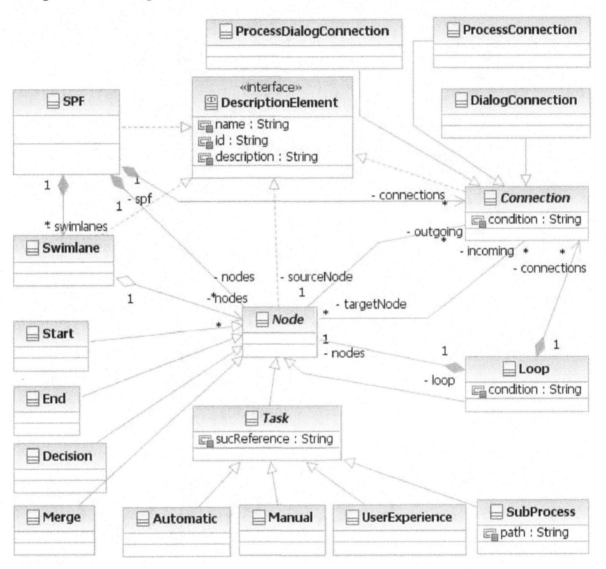

Metamodels

The five metamodels introduced above will now be described. They have been developed by analyzing the current development process. This includes discussions with development teams, enterprise architects and examination of educational material.

Figure 9. Workflow specification (WFSpec) metamodel. The SPF4WFM metaclass refers to a Solution Process Flow and contain a number of TaskSpecifications. A task specification refers to a task in a Solution Process Flow and can be of type Manual, UX, Automatic or SubProcess

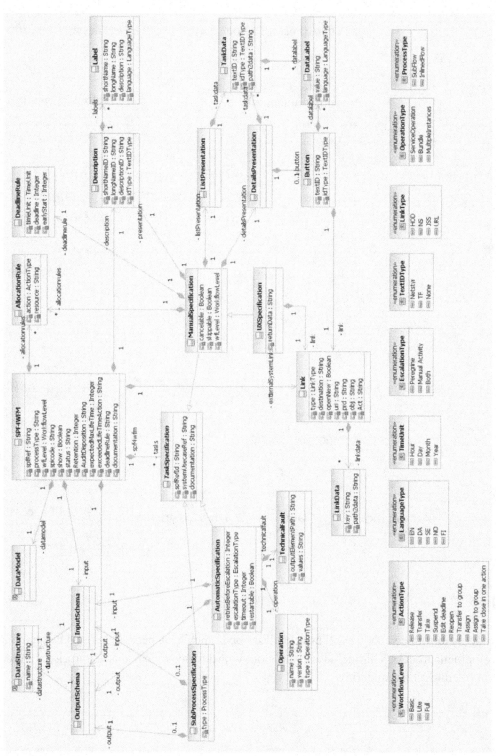

Eventmap Metamodel

The Eventmap metamodel, depictured in Figure 7, expresses how events can be modeled and related. The metamodel has incorporated all information that previously was described as plain text in MS Word documents. Inheritance has been used to define the External and Timedependent event types and requirement for different information. An abstract *Event* metaclass contains attributes for information common for both types of events while the *TimedependentEvent* and the *ExternalEvent* subclasses contain specific attributes, which were previously described in MS Word documents.

Solution Process Flow Metamodel

A Solution Process Flow is constructed for each event modeled in the event map. The SPF metamodel is illustrated in Figure 8. It is a simple flow based metamodel that reminds much of a UML activity diagram. The difference is the use of the domain specific task types, i.e. *Automatic*, *Manual* and *UserExperience*, and the domain specific edges, i.e. *ProcessConnection*, *DialogConnection* and *ProcessDialogConnection*.

Workflow Specification Metamodel

The Workflow Specification (WFSpec) metamodel, illustrated in Figure 9 is a formalization of the Workflow Specification previously defined in MS Word documents. A WFSpec model refers directly to a Solution Process Flow model instead of referring to a Control Flow Behavior model, as this is not explicitly modeled after the introduction of the Model Injection concept in previous section. Much information is required by the WFSpec metamodel, therefore only selected parts of it are described here. The *SPF4WFM* metaclass is the main element. It refers to a Solution Process Flow model and has several attributes specifying information required for implementing the BPEL process, e.g. a deadline rule, process lifetime information, allocation rules about process responsibility, department owner, process type etc. Many of these attributes are specific for Danske Bank as a BPEL process implemented in the BPM system is a part of a larger proprietary case system that extends the commercial BPM system with additional functionality.

   The *SPF4WFM* metaclass contains a number of Task- Specification elements. A TaskSpecification can either be an *AutomaticSpecification*, *ManualSpecification*, *UserExperienceSpecification* or a *SubProcessSpecification*. An Element of one of these metaclasses refer to a task of type *Automatic*, *Manual*, *UserExperience* and *SubProcess* respectively. A TaskSpecification specifies required additional information for the implementation in BPEL and which implementation pattern to use. Previously, information about the implementation pattern was stored directly in the Control Flow Behavior while additional information was stored in MS Word documents.

Addtional Metamodels

Two more metamodels have been defined to capture additional information in the development process. The BPEL code generation (BPELCodeGen) metamodel is used to store decisions of how to implement a physical design in BPEL. It refers to a Solution Process Flow and specifies target namespace to use for the BPEL process, name of the project that should contain the BPEL process, base package name

Figure 10. Overview of Danske Bank Workbench and its dependencies of other Eclipse projects.

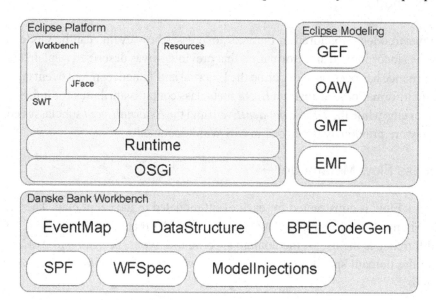

to define the BPEL process in, if WSDL files should be located in the separate folders, and the name of the base WDSL folder name. In previous section it was described how the Control Flow Behavior could be generated based on the Solution Process Flow model and model injections. The ModelInjection metamodel keeps track of all process fragments to inject and where to inject them in a Solution Process Flow model.

Transformations

Now, when all information required during the development process can be stored precisely in models, we are able to explicitly define the transformation algorithms illustrated in Figure 6 that depictured the abstracted development process. Here, we only give a short description of the algorithms. Detailed descriptions in pseudo code can be found in Brahe (2008).

From Event to Solution Process Flow

One Solution Process Flow model has to be created for each event in the eventmap. Algorithm 1 in Figure 6 creates an empty Solution Process Flow model. It is named and stored according to Danske Banks standards. The analyst and the architect model the behavior of the business process inside the generated model.

From SPF to Workflow Specification

Algorithm 2 in Figure 6 generates the Workflow Specification (WFSpec) model based on the Solution Process Flow model. It is named and stored according to Danske Banks standards. A TaskSpecification class is generated and added to the WFSpec model for each task in the Solution Process Flow. The

Figure 11. Event map editor with events for the CustomerQuickLoan project. External and Timedependent events can be modeled directly from the tool palette and required information can be specified as properties.

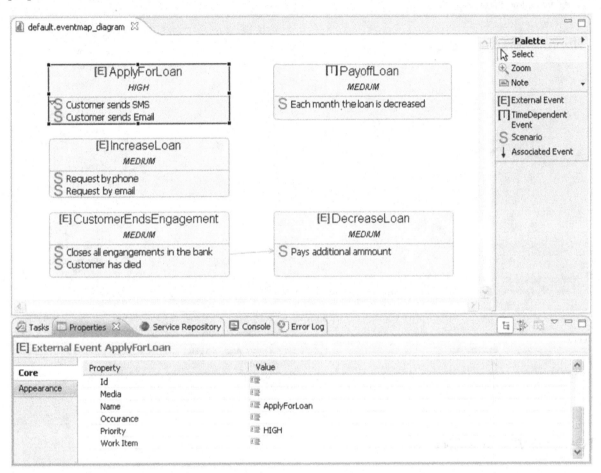

WFSpec model contains all required information, but all attributes contain default values. Successively the architect therefore fills it with correct information.

Generation of the BPEL implementation

The BPEL implementation can be generated by Algorithm 3 in Figure 6. All required information has been specified; information about each task is stored in the WFSpec model, process fragments has been modeled and the ModelInjection model created, and BPEL specific attributes have been defined in the BPELCodeGen model. Algorithm 3 merges information from these three models with information from the Solution Process Flow model and generates BPEL code and related artifacts. Only control flow logic and data mappings have not been generated.

Figure 12. Solution Process Flow editor. The ApplyForLoan process is modeled. Task and connection types are available from the tool palette. The concrete syntax is customized for tasks as well as edges.

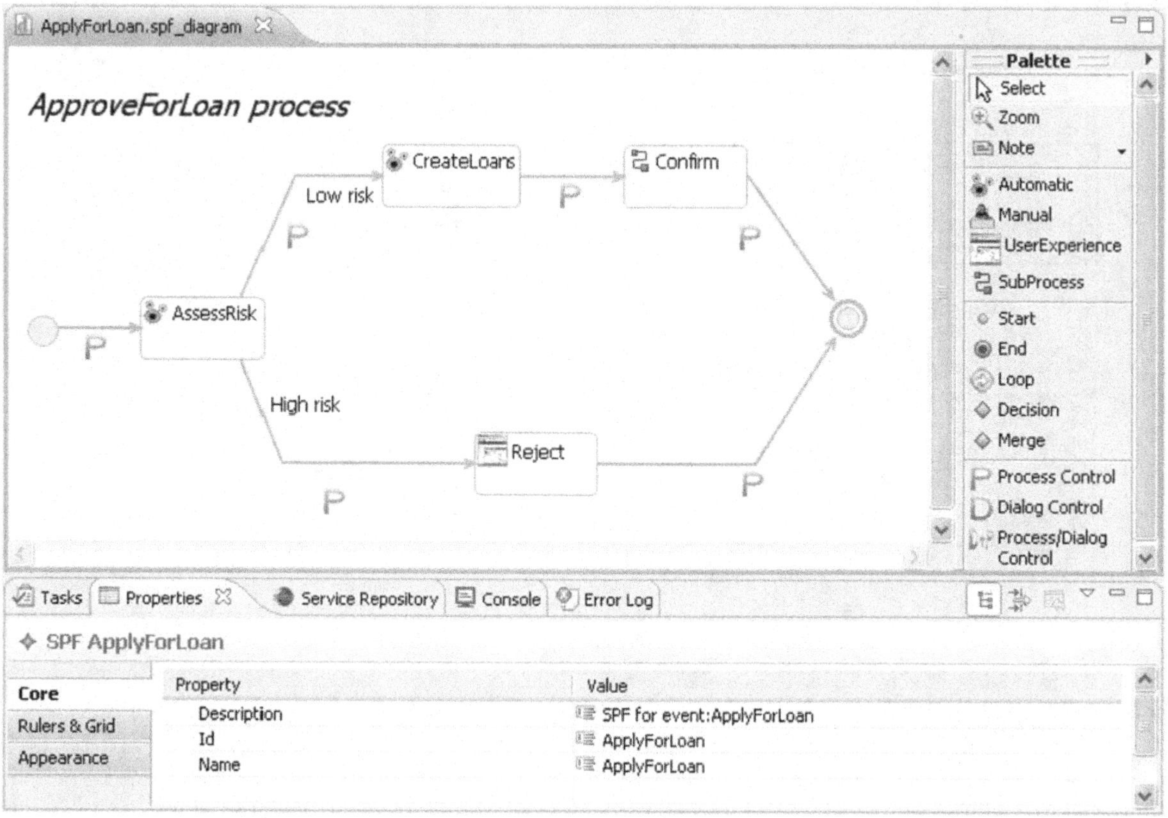

TOOL DEVELOPMENT

In this section we describe a tool called Danske Bank Workbench (DBW) that was developed as part of this research. It implements the metamodels and transformations described in last section. Hence, it directly supports Danske Banks development methodology, modeling concepts and use of technology.

Tool Architecture

Danske Bank Workbench is built on Eclipse platform (Eclipse, 2008) and various Eclipse open source projects. The Eclipse Modeling Framework (EMF) (Budinsky et al., 2003) has been used for defining the abstract syntax, or metamodels of the DSLs, that have been implemented. The concrete syntax of the DSLs and editor support have been implemented by using the Graphical Modeling Framework (GMF, 2008), while openArchitectureWare (oAW) (oAW, 2007) has been used to implement the semantics of the DSLs as model-to-model and model-to-text transformations.

Danske Bank Workbench consists of several independent tools for developing the different artifacts in the development process. These are depictured in Figure 10, which also illustrates dependencies to other Eclipse projects. The names of the projects conform to the names of the metamodels previously described.

Figure 13. WFSpec editor with task specifications for the ApplyForLoan process. Information can be modeled precisely for Automatic, Manual and UserExperience tasks.

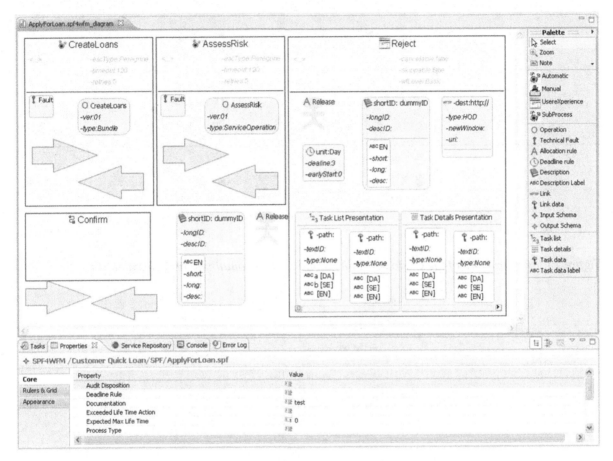

Metamodels and Editors

All metamodels have been modeled in Rational Software Architect as UML class diagrams. Each of these were exported as an XMI representation of UML and imported into Eclipse by using the EMF model creation wizard which comes as a part of the EMF project. The GMF editors were created based on the EMF metamodels. Figure 11, Figure 12 and Figure 13 illustrate the GMF based Eventmap, SPF and Workflow Specification (WFSpec) editors in action.

Transformations

The three transformation algorithms described previously have been implemented in oAW. Algorithm 1 and 2 has been implemented as model-to-model transformations using the Xtend language. Algorithm 3, which is supposed to generate BPEL code, has been implemented as a model-to-text transformation using the Xpand language. The implementation is quite complex. It is implemented as a graph transformation that recursively runs through the SPF control flow starting with the initial node. When a model injection or a sub process is detected, the corresponding process fragment or sub process is be

Figure 14. Workflow for using tools through the customized development process. Letter tags refer to screen dumps in Figure 16. A thick arrow indicates a tool utility while a thin arrow indi

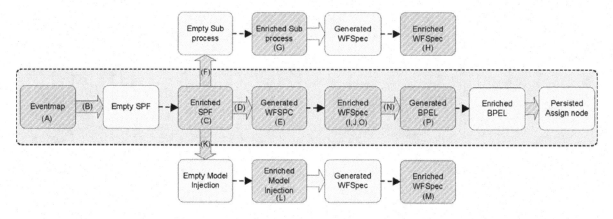

Figure 15. File structure of the Customer Quick Loan project containing all generated files.

Figure 16. Using Danske Bank Workbench

(a) Event map model. Events are modeled as External or Timedependent events and contain scenarios

(b) Tool utility to generate a Solution Process Flow. The modeler has right-clicked at the ApplyForLoan event.

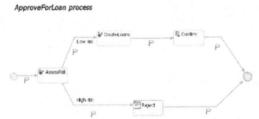

(c) Solution Process Flow for the ApplyForLoan event. The business analyst or solution architect has completed the generated model

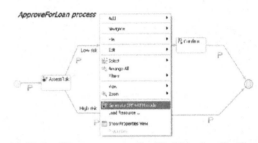

(d) Tool utility to generate the Workflow Specification model for the ApplyForLoan Solution Process Flow. The modeler has right-clicked at the canvas

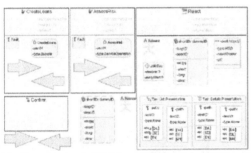

(e) The generated Workflow Specification (WFSpec) model for the ApplyForLoan Solution Process Flow

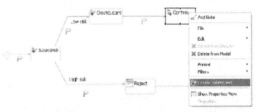

(f) Tool utility to create an empty sub process. The modeler has right-clicked at a SubProcess task in the Solution Process Flow

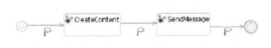

(g) The Confirm subprocess as modeled by a business analyst or a solution architect

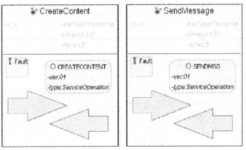

(h) Generated Workflow Specification for the Confirm subprocess

Figure 17. Using Danske Bank Workbench (cont'd)

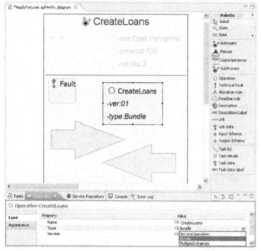

(i) Setting the CreateLoans task to be implemented by the Bundle pattern

(j) Setting the confirm subprocess to be implemented in the ApplyForLoan process as in inlined flow

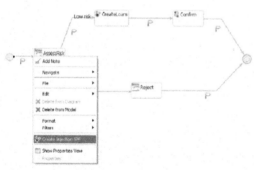

(k) Tool utility to create an empty process fragment for a model injection. The modeler has selected at the connection between the start node and the AssessRisk task as injection point by right-clicking on it

(l) Process fragment to be used as injection. The solution architect has modeled it.

(m) Generated Workflow Specification (WFSpec) model for the injection process fragment

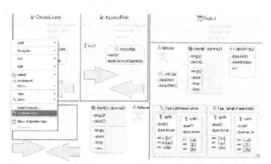

(n) Utility tool to generate BPEL implementation. The modeler has right-clicked at the canvas

interpreted and BPEL code generated, which must then be merged into the partly generated BPEL code. It requires much book keeping handling the associations between models as four different models, i.e. SPF, WFSpec, ModelInjection and BPELCodeGen are used as input to the transformation. A number of utility functions have been written in Xtend and in Java to support this.

Figure 18. Using Danske Bank Workbench (cont'd)

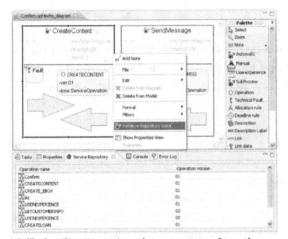

(o) Tool utility to retrieve data structures from the enterprise Service Repository into the WFSpec model. The modeler has right-clicked at an AutomaticSpecification element

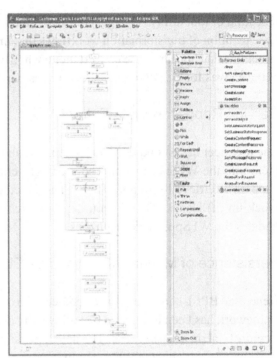

(p) BPEL code generated from the Solution Process Flow model, the WFSpec model, the ModelInjections model and the BPELCodeGen model

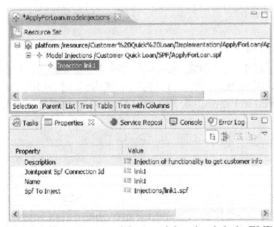

(q) ModelInjections model viewed by the default EMF editor

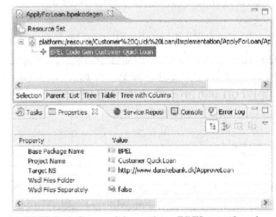

(r) BPELCodeGen model specifying BPEL specific values for the implementation

Tool Utilities

Several tool utilities have been developed to enhance usability of Danske Bank Workbench and to smoothen the use of the different tools. The users of the tools are guided from one step in the development process to the next by using these utilities.

Transformation Execution

One kind of tool utility is the generation of "the next" development artifact in the development process, i.e. execution of transformation workflows that implement Algorithm 1, 2 and 3. They are implemented as actions that appear on the context menu when the user right-clicks on an event in an Eventmap model, at the canvas for an SPF model and at the canvas for a WFSpec model.

Service Repository Data Extract

The architect has to find definitions of input and output data structures for service operations and put them into the WFSpec model. The user right-clicks on a task specification for an *Automatic* task and chooses "Retrieve Repository Data". The executed action looks up the defined service operation in (a mock up of) Danske Banks centralized service repository, retrieve definitions of data structures and updates the WFSpec model with these.

Persistence of Manually Changed BPEL Code

Generated BPEL code needs to be updated with data mapping and control flow logic. A small persistence framework has been developed that allows the developer to persist logic from within an assign node or a control link in a separate file. The developer simply right-clicks on the assign node or control link and chooses "Persist element". The action creates a separate file where the assign or control flow logic is persisted. Next time the transformation that implements Algorithm 3 is executed, the changed BPEL code is overridden, but successively, the persisted changes are copied into the newly generated BPEL code.

Customer Quick Loan Retooled

Danske Bank Workbench will now be illustrated by applying it at the example. Figure 14 illustrates a workflow of the development process with the artifacts that are created and the transformations between them. The letter tags in the figure refer to screen dumps of tool utilities and artifacts developed for the ApplyForLoan process. After Figure 15 they are depictured in Figure 16, Figure 17, and Figure 18 which can be found in the end of the chapter.

Eventmap

First, a business analyst creates a new Eventmap. All business events are now modeled as either *external* or *timedependent*, and scenarios are added to each event (Figure 16a). The editor provides direct support for these concepts from the tool palette. The analyst simply drags and drops events and scenarios to the canvas. The property view reflects properties for the selected event type, where e.g. priority can be

Table 3. Questions and answers for the empirical evaluation. The ratings were: 1 is "Much worse", 2 is "worse", 3 is "a little worse", 4 is "a little better", 5 is "better" and 6 is "much better"

	Question	Mean Value
1	How is the Danske Bank specific syntax to work with compared to Websphere Business Modeler?	5.5
2	How is it to work with the WFSpec editor compared to MS Word?	5.6
3	Is the information easier to comprehend and access?	5.2
4	How is it to comprehend the number of modeling artefacts and locate where they are?	5.4
5	Are the tool utilities helpful and support the developement process?	5.4
6	Is the code generation to prefer over manual translation?	5.0
7	Do you believe in model driven development as the right direction to go in?	5.0
8	How is the quality of generated code compared to manually written code?	3.8
9	Do you prefer to model and generate the solution instead of manually implement it?	5.0
10	Does the tool eliminate tedious work?	5.0
11	Will the tool influence on the development productivity?	5.0
12	Will the tool decrease the number of errors in implemented code?	4.8

selected as low, medium or high and business possibilities can be described. Event types and properties directly reflect the defined Eventmap metamodel.

Solution Process Flow

After finishing the event map, the business analyst has to create a Solution Process Flow for each event. The analyst simply right-clicks on the event, for instance the ApplyForLoan event, in the Eventmap editor and chooses "Generate SPF" (Figure 16b). An empty Solution Process Flow is now generated in a subfolder named "SPF" and is given the same name as the business event. It is then modeled by either the business analyst or the solution architect. Tasks may now be modeled directly as *Automatic*, *Manual* or *UserExperience* (as defined by the SPF metamodel) by dragging them directly onto the canvas from the tooling palette. Connections of type *Process*, *Dialog* or *ProcessDialog* are also directly available.

Workflow Specification

The architect right-clicks at the Solution Process Flow when it is complete (Figure 16c) and chooses "Generate WFSpec model" (Figure 16d). A WFSpec model is now generated under the Implementation folder and a subfolder named after the Solution Process Flow. It contains task specifications for all tasks and has been populated with default data. The task specifications and all objects inside them conform directly to the WFSpec metamodel.

Now, information has to be entered into the specification. For example, the architect defines that the CreateLoans task must be implemented by the Bundle pattern; he or she selects the Operation object in the CreateLoans task specification and in the properties view changes the type from *ServiceOperation* to *Bundle* (Figure 16i).

Subprocess

The Confirm task is modeled as a SubProcess task type in the Solution Process Flow. The architect chooses that it must be implemented as an inlined flow in the BPEL process by selecting the Confirm task specification in the WFSpec model and sets the *Type* property to *InlinedFlow* (Figure 16j). The subprocess to which the Confirm task refer is generated by right clicking on it and choose "Generate SubProcess". An empty sub process is created and opened automatically. It is named accordingly to the name of the Confirm task and optionally put in a sub directory if the *path* property at the Confirm task has a value. The subprocess is now modeled as a sequence of two automatic activities (Figure 16g), and its Workflow Specification can be generated (Figure 16h).

Model Injection

The architect and the developer recognize that an additional task is needed in the physical implementation. The task should set the business state of the process instance to either "Approved" or "Rejected" depending of the outcome of the AssessRisk task.

They right click on the control link in the Solution Process Flow that connects the AssessRisk task with the CreateLoans, and the Reject task and choose "Create Injection". An empty model is created under the Injections folder and is automatically opened in an SPF editor. The developer models the process fragment as one automatic activity (Figure 16l) and generates the Workflow Specification for it (Figure 16m).

The book keeping of Model injections are handled by the ModelInjection model. This model is illustrated in Figure 16q. It contains one injection that has two important properties; the injection point in the Solution Process Flow, which is the ID of the control link, and the process fragment to inject (SPF to Inject) at the injection point.

Before having the WFSpec metamodel and editor, all the design decisions were modeled in the Control Flow Behavior without any reuse of the Solution Process Flow, and required additional information was defined in textural documents. Now, the project team has modeled three processes; one SPF, one subprocess and one process fragment. They are all modeled in the same language and have each a corresponding WFSpec model.

Synchronizing Data

All automatic task specifications must be synchronized with the centralized Service Repository to obtain correct input and output data definitions. Figure 16o shows the selected CreateContent task specification in the WFSpec model for the Confirm subprocess. The modeler has right-clicked on it and selected "Retrieve Repository Data". The operation name for the CreateContent specification has been set to CREATECONTENT. The same operation name exists in the service repository, which can also be seen in the figure. The action now retrieves data definitions from the repository and populates the WFSpec model with these. Subsequently, the BPEL code generator can use these data structures to create a correct WSDL document for the service operation. Without this import utility, the developer had to find data definitions and create XSD schemas manually.

Code Generation

The developer sets parameters for the code generation in a BPELCodeGen model before executing the BPEL code generation. Previously, these design decisions were not documented. Figure 16r illustrates that the developer has selected default values for the code generation; The BPEL code will be generated in the same project as where the models are, and WSDL files will be located in the same directory as the BPEL file. The developer generates the BPEL code by right-clicking on the WFSpec model and chooses "Generate BPEL" (Figure 16n).

Figure 15 shows the Customer Quick Loan project and all files generated through the development process and Figure 16p shows the generated BPEL code opened in the Eclipse open source BPEL editor. Only the event map has been created manually. The rest of the artifacts have been created by tool utilities supporting the enterprise specific development process. Hence, the file structure follows specified standards, and the traceability between models can be ensured. Without Danske Bank Workbench these artifacts and all the information bookkeeping are handled manually by the project team.

EVALUATION

The tool was evaluated through an empirical test which involved five people employed at Danske Bank. They have all worked as workflow developers. Two of them have experiences from working as - or closely together with - a business analyst, and one of them is a solution architect. They used Danske Bank Workbench to model an event map, a Solution Process Flow and a Workflow Specification and generate the BPEL code. The business scenario was the same as presented in this chapter. They got a one-page description of how to use the tool. From the description they used about 30-40 minutes to complete the exercise. They filled out questionnaires with 12 questions and were interviewed about their experiences with the tool. Each question asked about the experience of using the tool compared to current practice in Danske Bank. The questions and their ratings can be found in Table 3.

The developers found that the tool would improve their productivity significantly and it would be easier to work with. Especially, they were happy with the Danske Bank specific modeling capabilities. It was much easier and intuitive to work with domain specific modeling. Further, it was easier to comprehend the workflow specific information that had to be specified for the Solution Process Flow (question 1-5). Some of the developers suggested that validation rules would improve the development process as a modeler would be caught if required information was not specified.

In general, they found that model driven development would help improving their daily work. This is reflected in question 6, 7, 9, 10 and 11. They all got an average score at 5 out of 6, which is equal "Better". One of the developers suggested that data and control link logic should also be modeled to allow 100% code generation. Some of the developers were quite skeptical about the quality of the generated code as they suspected that manually written code would perform better than generated one (question 8). However, they thought that the number of errors would be lower in generated code compared to manually written code (question 12).

The evaluation has several limitations; The number of participants could be increased and include a more diverse population of people, the case could be extended to a realistic business scenario, and the questions could be accomplished with measurements of the number of errors in-, and the efficiency of the code. Further, a control group of developers could use the current method and tools in Danske Bank at the business scenario, and the results from the two groups could be compared.

However, making a realistic evaluation of a prototype tool in an industrial setting is extremely difficult. It is hard to get permission to use time from the right people, the tool is not mature enough for large scale testing, and the tool requires more development to model a realistic business scenario. Despite these limitations, the evaluation of the tool shows that it provides significant improvements over the current use of commercial tools in Danske Bank.

DISCUSSION

We have used Danske Bank Workbench for modeling and implementing the ApplyForLoan business process. The exemplification of the tool and the empirical evaluation has shown that the development process becomes more efficient as the different experts are supported directly in their work. They are able to use familiar domain concepts directly in the modeling tools, they are guided to provide correct information, and execution of the transformation algorithms has been automated. We have shown that it is possible to define and utilize a number of DSLs and tools to effectively support an enterprise specific development process for business process modeling and implementation.

Danske Bank Workbench is a prototype, and therefore it has a number of limitations and points for improvements;

Consistency checking. We have not defined methods, nor implemented tools to check consistency between different models.

Validation and modeling constraints. Validation rules and constraints on how a model can be constructed should be specified by the team responsible for defining the metamodels. These rules and constraints should be handled by the modeling tool to avoid creation of invalid models.

Controlflow. Several controlflow structures cannot be handled by the transformation such as cyclic behavior and loop constructs.

Data mapping. It might improve the prototype and the development process to abstract the definition of data mappings to either the WFSpec model or to a generated Java class which would be responsible for the data mapping.

Restrictions on the SPF. The prototype only supports a one-to-one relationship between a Solution Process Flow and a BPEL implementation. In reality there are often cases where an SPF might be divided to several BPEL processes or several SPF's may be merged into one BPEL implementation.

Implementing above items in Danske Bank Workbench is a demanding task; First, it requires further analysis of requirements in Danske Bank. Second, it requires design and implementation of several advanced tool utilities. Especially, the last item may show up to be very hard to specify and implement.

SUMMARY AND FUTURE WORK

In the introduction of the chapter we postulated that general purpose business process modeling and implementation tool suites are not feasible for many enterprises. Using the case study of Danske Bank and an example we showed that a development team faces many challenges when they use standard modeling languages and tools but have to use enterprise specific modeling notations, follow an enterprise specific development process and use technology in specialized ways.

We abstracted the development process into metamodels and transformational algorithms and developed a tool called Danske Bank Workbench, fitted specially for Danske Bank. The tool implemented the model driven development principles of direct representation and automation as it allowed creating models directly in Danske Bank specific concepts and it automated the generation of lower level models and code.

We saw through the example that it is possible to achieve an efficient model driven development process where a project team collaborate to create different modeling abstractions of a business process with tool based transformations and ensured synchronicity between the different modeling abstractions. Using the tool, information only has to be defined once, and it is easy to comprehend. Knowledge of implementation patterns is reused by automated transformations. Several tool utilities support the development process which makes Danske Bank Workbench very efficient to work with. An empirical evaluation of the tool confirmed this. Hence, we have confirmed the hypothesis that was set up in the introduction, which stated that applying the basic model driven development principles of direct representation and automation to BPM tools would solve many of the experienced challenges.

Danske Bank Workbench was not difficult to build as many language workbenches exist for building metamodels, editors and transformations (though it did require deep insight in various Eclipse technologies and MDD concepts). However, it has several limitations, and it only addresses a small subset of business processes that may be modeled. It requires much more effort to make it a production ready tool that can be used by the organization. Despite a promising prototype, our guess is that only a very limited number of enterprises will go the way and implement their own tools. While it may be economical beneficial to develop ones own tools, there might be political reasons not to do so. To answer the research question set up in the introduction we can now say,

"Defining and developing a model driven development tool to support an enterprise specific business process development process seems promising. It will heighten the productivity of development teams and probably cause fewer errors in implementations. However, it requires a high degree of expertise in model driven development methodology and technology to develop such a tool. It will probably be unachievable for most enterprises"

Although language workbenches provide huge support in development of model driven development tools, it should be much easier to customize ones own BPM languages and tools. For future research we therefore suggest to work on tool-based frameworks that feature extensions of predefined BPM languages, editors and visualizations to a specific enterprise. It would require less investment and it would be easer for an enterprise without experienced tool developers to *customize* BPM tools instead of *develop* them from scratch.

REFERENCES

Bézivin, J., Hammoudi, S., Lopes, D., & Jouault, F. (2004). *An experiment in mapping Web services to implementation platforms* (Tech. Rep. LINA, University of Nantes).

Booch, G., Brown, A., Iyengar, S., Rumbaugh, J., & Selic, B. (2004). An MDA Manifesto. *Business Process Trends - MDA Journal*. Retrieved from http://www.bptrends.com/publicationfiles/05-04%20 COL%20IBM%20Manifesto%20-%20Frankel%20-3.pdf

Bordbar, B., & Staikopoulos, A. (2004a). Modelling and transforming the behavioural aspects of web services. In *Third Workshop in Software Model Engineering (WiSME2004) at UML, Lisbon, Portugal.*

Bordbar, B., & Staikopoulos, A. (2004b). on behavioural model transformation in Web services. In *Conceptual Modelling for Advanced Application Domain (eCOMO)* (pp. 667-678). Shanghai, China.

BPEL. (2003). *Business process execution language for Web services (BPEL4WS). Version 1.1.*Retrieved from http://www-128.ibm.com/developerworks/library/specification/wsbpel

Brahe, S. (2007). BPM on top of SOA: Experiences from the financial industry. In G. Alonso, P. Dadam, & M. Rosemann (Eds.), *BPM2007* (LNCS 4714, pp. 96-111).

Brahe, S. (2008). *An experiment on creating enterprise specific BPM languages and tools* (Tech. Rep. ITU-TR-2008-102). IT University of Copenhagen.

Brahe, S., & Bordbar, B. (2006). A pattern-based approach to business process modeling and implementation in Web services. In D. Georgakopoulos (Ed.), *ICSOC 2006* (LNCS 4652, pp. 161-172).

Brahe, S., & Østerbye, K. (2006). Business process modeling: Defining domain specific modeling languages by use of UML profiles. In A. Rensink & J. Warmer (Eds.), ECMDA-FA 2006 (LNCS 4066, pp. 241-255).

Budinsky, F., Steinberg, D., Merks, E., Ellersick, R., & Grose, T. J. (2003). Eclipse Modeling Framework: A Developer's Guide. Addison Wesley.

Dumas, M., & Hofstede, A. H. M. (2001). UML activity diagrams as a workflow specification language. In *UML 2001* (LNCS 2185, pp. 76-90).

Dumas, M., van der Aalst, W., & Hofstede, A. (2005). Process-aware information systems: bridging people and software through process technology. John Wiley & Sons, Inc.

Eclipse (2008). *The Eclipse project.* Retrieved from http://www.eclipse.org

Erl, T. (2005). Service oriented architecture: Concepts, technology and design. Prentice Hall.

Flynn, D., Vagner, J., & Vecchio, O. D. (1995). Is CASE technology improving quality and productivity in software development? *Logistics Information Management, 8*(2), 8–21. doi:10.1108/09576059510084966

Fowler, M. (2005). *Language workbenches: The killer-app for domain specific languages?* Retrieved from http://martinfowler.com/articles/languageWorkbench.html.

Frankel, D. S. (2003). Model driven architecture: Applying MDA to enterprise computing. OMG Press.

GMF. (2008). *Graphical Modeling Framework project.* Retrieved from http://www.eclipse.org/gmf.

Guntama, E., Chang, E., Jayaratna, N., & Pudhota, L. (2003). Extension of activity diagrams for flexible business workflow modeling. *International Journal of Computer Systems Science & Engineering, 18*(3), 137–152.

Jablonski, S., & Bussler, C. (1996). *Workflow management - Modeling concepts, architecture and implementation.* London: Intl. Thomson Computer Press.

Jablonski, S., & Götz, M. (2007). Perspective oriented business process visualization. In 3rd International Workshop on Business Process Design (BPD) in conjunction with the 5th International Conference on Business Process Management (BPM 2007). Brisbane, Australia.

Koehler, J., Hauser, R., Kapoor, S., Wu, F. Y., & Kumaran, S. (2003). A Model-driven transformation method. In *7th International Enterprise Distributed Object Computing Conference (EDOC 2003)* (pp. 186-197).

Koehler, J., Hauser, R., Sendall, S., & Wahler, M. (2005). Declarative techniques for model-driven business process integration. *IBM Systems Journal, 44*(1), 47–65.

Kroll, P., & Kruchten, P. (2003). The rational unified process made easy. In *A Practitioner's Guide to the RUP*. Addison Wesley.

Ledeczi, A., Maroti, M., Bakay, A., Karsai, G., Garrett, J., Thomason, C., et al. (2001). The generic modeling environment. In *Workshop on Intelligent Signal Processing*. Budapest, Hungary. Retrieved from http://www.isis.vanderbilt.edu/Projects/gme/GME2000 Overview.pdf.

Leymann, F., & Roller, D. (2000). *Production workflow: Concepts and techniques*. Prentice Hall.

List, B., & Korherr, B. (2005). A UML 2 profile for business process modelling. In *Perspectives in Conceptual Modeling, ER 2005 Workshops* (LNCS 3770, pp. 85-96).

MDAGuide. (2003). *MDA Guide Version 1.0.1*. Retrieved from http://www.omg.org/docs/omg/03-06-01.pdf.

Mernik, M., Heering, J., & Sloane, A. M. (2005). When and how to develop domain-specific languages. *ACM Computing Surveys, 37*(4), 316–344. doi:10.1145/1118890.1118892

Murata, T. (1989). Petri nets: Properties, analysis and applications. *Proceedings of the IEEE, 77*(4), 541–580. doi:10.1109/5.24143

oAW. *openArchitectureWare*. Retrieved from http://www.openarchitectureware.org.

Skogan, D., Grønmo, R., & Solheim, I. (2004). Web service composition in UML. In *Eighth IEEE International Enterprise Distributed Object Computing Conference (EDOC'04)* (pp. 47-57).

Stahl, T., Völter, M., Bettin, J., Haase, A., & Helsen, S. (2006). *Model-driven software development: technology, engineering, management*. Wiley.

Swithinbank, P., Chessell, M., Gardner, T., Griffin, C., Man, J., Wylie, H., & Yusuf, L. (2005). *Patterns: model-driven development using IBM rational software architect*. IBM Redbooks. Available at http://www.redbooks.ibm.com/abstracts/sg247105.html?Open.

Tolvanen, J.-P., & Rossi, M. (2003). MetaEdit+: Defining and using domain-specific modeling languages and code generators. In OOPSLA '03: Companion of the 18th annual ACM SIGPLAN conference on Object-oriented programming, systems, languages, and applications (pp. 92-93). New York: ACM.

van der Aalst, W. M. P., Hofstede, A. H. M., Kiepuszewski, B., & Barros, A. P. (2003). Workflow patterns. *Distributed and Parallel Databases, 14*(1), 5–51. doi:10.1023/A:1022883727209

White, S. (2006). *Business process modeling notation* (Version 1.0). Available at http://www.bpmn.org/Documents/OMG-02-01.pdf.

Windsor, J. (1986). Are automated tools changing systems analysis and design? *Journal of Systems Management, 37*(11), 28–33.

KEY TERMS AND DEFINITIONS

BPM Tools: A collection of modeling and implementation tools specialized for modeling a business process and implement it as a workflow in a workflow language.

Control Flow Behavior: A physical model of a business process. It specifies how the process should be implemented in BPEL.

Domain Specific Language: (DSL) A specialized programming or a modeling language that allows expressing solutions directly in concepts of a problem domain.

Eventmap: A model of all business events that may occur in a given business context.

Model Driven Development: A development paradigm that focuses on using models in software development. Models are used for analysis, simulation, verification and code generation

Model Transformation: A model transformation takes one or several source models and generates one or several target models, or textural documents. It is based on a transformation definition that specifies how to map elements in the source DSLs to elements in the target DSLs

Solution Process Flow: A logical or conceptual model of a business process. It specifies business logic for one business event.

Workflow Specification: A document that describes additional information required to implement a Solution Process Flow model in Danske Banks extended BPM system.

Chapter 3
Organizational Change, IT and Business Process Redesign

Claudio Petti
Scuola Superiore ISUFI, Università del Salento, Italy

Mark Klein
Massachusetts Institute of Technology, USA

ABSTRACT

Change in the business environment is pervasive and accelerating. New, agile, and often IT-based organizational forms are emerging. Recent management literature has paid a great deal of attention to observing and advocating this kind of organizational change. Relatively little attention has been given, however, to how to deal practically with these changes. How, for example, can companies foster the business process changes necessary to become agile? How can IT be leveraged for this purpose? In the attempt to provide some insights into these issues, this chapter will present a methodology for redesigning and inventing new business processes that relies on a handbook of process models, and is particularly suited to taking advantage of information technology to enable new organizational forms.

INTRODUCTION

Organizations nowadays are under increasing pressure to adapt their business processes to relentless technological, political, organizational, and other changes (Davenport and Perez-Guardado, 1999). As a consequence, being flexible and adaptable has become a matter of survival for companies. Under such conditions, being able to rapidly generate good new ideas about how to meet these challenges becomes a critical skill.

A body of process innovation techniques known collectively as Business Process Re-engineering (BPR) has emerged to address this challenge (Armistead and Rowland, 1996; Chen, 1999; Davenport and Short, 1990; Hammer, 1990; Grover et al., 1995; Hammer and Champy, 1993; Kettinger, Teng and Guha, 1997b; Kubeck, 1995, 1997; Nissen, 1998, 1999; Pandya and Nelis, 1998). Despite the widespread use

DOI: 10.4018/978-1-60566-669-3.ch003

of these tools, however, many process innovation initiatives fall short of delivering the hoped-for results. While they typically aim for revolutionary change, they often result in only incremental improvements (Stoddard and Jarvenpaa, 1995).

We can understand why this is so by considering the nature of current BPR techniques. While there are plenty of techniques (such as IDEF, Process Flowcharting, Statistical Process Control and so on) for modelling and analyzing *as-is* business processes, there are few structured techniques for designing *new* ones (Klein et al., 2003). The design of *to-be* processes is supported only by generic creativity techniques such as brainstorming and visioning, and the results of a redesign are typically highly dependent on the current process as well as the particular backgrounds of the participants.

The methodology proposed in this chapter is designed to address these limitations in existing techniques. The methodology, the fruit of a decade-long MIT research effort known as the *Process Handbook project*, is based on acquiring an abstract model of just the *core* activities and dependencies in the existing process, and then engaging in a structured and systematic exploration of process alternatives, utilizing for inspiration a large repository of best-practice business process models, i.e. a *Process Handbook*.

This chapter will present this methodology. We will begin with a brief description of how this methodology differs from traditional process redesign techniques, and review the key concepts on which it is based: Process Specializations and Inheritance, Dependencies and Coordination Mechanisms, Exception and Handlers. We will then use the case of a real-life risk management process to illustrate the steps of the methodology and demonstrate how some of its concepts (such as inheritance and exception handling) can be used to design more effective and robust IT-based processes by enabling easier and more structured gathering of software requirements, reducing the possibility of misunderstandings between IT experts and business people, and reducing software bugs. Finally lessons learned from the application of this methodology to IT-based process redesign will be drawn, and we will provide some perspectives on avenues for further research and improvement of the methodology.

BACKGROUND

Davenport and Stoddard observed, in 1994, that *"the popular management literature has created more myth than practical methodology regarding reengineering"* (Pg. 121). Despite the number of techniques that have been developed over the last decade, many reengineering initiatives still fall short in delivering the radical improvements expected, leading most of the times to incremental results, if not to the outright failure of many promising firm's organizational change efforts. To paraphrase Stoddard and Jarvenpaa (1995), BPR projects frequently attempt revolutionary – radical - change but because of political, organizational and resource constraints achieve only evolutionary – incremental – implementations.

Investigating the reasons for this inconsistency is an important step in understanding how to foster more effective organizational change. Many possible explanations have accumulated over the last fifteen years of research and practice. A reengineering project can, for example, be too radical, premature or initiated on the wrong business processes. It can be carried out in the wrong way or in the wrong place. Cultural issues, resistance to change and change management may come into play when the initial ambitions and radical innovations announced end up in the far more modest achievements of BPR projects. Looking more closely it can be easily seen that these explanations are mostly related to the way in which the BPR projects are implemented. These problems are still far from being solved so it is our contention that, to improve the situation, it might be wise to broaden the range of the inquiry from

Table 1. Synthesis of current techniques for process redesign activities (adapted from Kettinger, Teng and Guha, 1997bVan der Aalst et al., 2003; Rinderle, Weber, Reichert and Wild, 2005; Guenther et al., 2008)

Creativity Thinking Techniques Soft techniques based on intuition, spontaneous/group-based generation of ideas, experts advice, re-examining basic assumptions or imagination.	- Affinity Diagramming - Brainstorming - Visioning - Delphi Technique - Fast Cycle Full Participation Change Method - Nominal Group Tecnique - Out-of-the-Box Thinking
Process Analysis Techniques Process mapping and other *structured* techniques used in diagnose stage for documenting and analyzing existing processes.	- Cognitive Mapping - Computer-Aided Software Engineering - Dataflow Diagramming - Process Flowcharting - Hierarchical Colored Petri Nets - $IDEF_{0,3}$ - Role Activity Diagramming - Speech Interaction modeling - Process/Workflow Mining
Other techniques Techniques that cover partial aspects of redesign, simulation complex techniques or that entails detailed descriptions of the process.	- Activity-Based Costing - Assumption Surfacing - Costs/Benefits/Risks Analysis - Force Field Analysis - $IDEF_2$ - Workflow Design - Role playing - Simulation - Soft System Method - Adaptive Process Management

implementation issues to design issues, so that we also consider the design phase of the reengineering process, where new target processes are defined. Besides asking whether things are being done in the right way – that is always a good question - we should also ask if the right things are being done. So one more explanation, and the basic assumption of this work, is that the failure or the modest results of many process redesign efforts and related organizational changes, can be ascribed to the ways in which new processes are being conceived and designed, and in particular to the lack, among the different traditional process redesign techniques, of structured approaches to exploring, analyzing and defining new process designs (Klein et al., 2003).

A comprehensive survey of BPR techniques undertaken by Kettinger, Teng and Guha (1997b) covering BPR methodologies practiced by leading reengineering consulting firms, as well as more recent research on process mining/machine learning techniques for business process definition (such the ones of Van der Aalst et al., 2003; Rinderle, Weber, Reichert and Wild, 2005; Guenther et al., 2008), highlights those limitations (see Table 1).

At the redesign stage, where new process designs are developed, brainstorming, out-of-the-box thinking, visioning and other 'soft' creativity techniques are used to devise process design alternatives. Many techniques, aimed at other reengineering project stages and activities, were not developed originally for BPR purposes, but rather are simply the application, to BPR, of techniques developed in other problem-solving contexts. The more structured techniques normally used for process redesign - such as Integrated Definition (IDEF) or process flowcharting techniques - were mainly developed for documenting and analyzing as-is processes rather than exploring and defining 'to be' processes. There are, finally, many techniques that cover only partial aspects of process redesign, e.g. the assumption surfacing technique used in cost/benefits/risks analysis or adaptive process management, and others that are too complex to be broadly applied, e.g. simulations.

All this leads to a tendency to lavish effort on documenting and refining the existing business processes, what Hammer and Champy call "analysis paralysis" (Hammer and Champy 1993) rather than focusing on defining radical new alternatives (Klein et al 2003). And the design techniques that do exist do not support the systematic exploration of a full range of alternatives (Lee and Pentland, 2000; Pentland, 1995).

The re-designed business processes thus take too long to develop, tend to lag behind changes in the environment, and often represent minor variations of processes the designers are already familiar with and have spent so much time painstakingly documenting.

The BPR methodology described herein differs significantly from previous work:

- It encourages BPR participants to capture only the "essence" of the process they wish to re-design, focusing on core processes and key dependencies, to create an as-is process model that is simpler and therefore easier to understand. In this way designers are thus apt to consider a wider range of ideas than they would have generated on their own, and are more likely to take advantage of technological and managerial advances that have appeared in other contexts.
- While others have explored the use of reusable process knowledge libraries to enable BPR (Committee, 1992) (McNair and Leibfried, 1992) (Schank and Abelson, 1977) (Magazine, 1992) (Mi and Scacchi 1993), (Salancik and Leblebici, 1988) (Baligh, Burton et al., 1990) (Gasser, 1992), our approach is unique in that it draws together a repository of process best-practices (*the Process Handbook*), organized in innovative ways using coordination theory concepts, and exploited using recombination-based methodologies derived from experience with re-designing processes with Information Technologies.

This methodology is the result of a worldwide collaborative effort centered, for the last decade, around the MIT Center for Coordination Science, involving over 40 researchers, practitioners, companies and research institutions, including the e-Business Management Section at the Scuola Superiore ISUFI. Many of the results described in this paper came out of a three year collaboration between ISUFI and the Center for Coordination Science, with sponsorship by the MIT Center for Digital Business.

Currently the *Process Handbook* includes a database of over 5000 business processes in addition to software tools for viewing, searching, and editing the database contents (Malone et al., 1999; Malone T.W., Crowston K., and Herman, 2003). For more information about the contents of the Process Handbook, please refer to Malone et al. (2003) and to Herman and Malone (2003).

The basic concepts at the heart of the methodology are described herein.

Process Specializations

Practically all process representation techniques (including ours) use the notion of decomposition, i.e., that a process can be broken down (or "decomposed") into sub-activities. Our representation includes in addition to this the concept of *specialization*. While a sub-activity represents a *part* of a process, a specialization represents a type or *way of doing* the process (Taivalsaari, 1996; Van der Alst and Basten,

Figure 1. An example of inheritance in the specialization hierarchy. Adapted from (Malone et al. 1999)

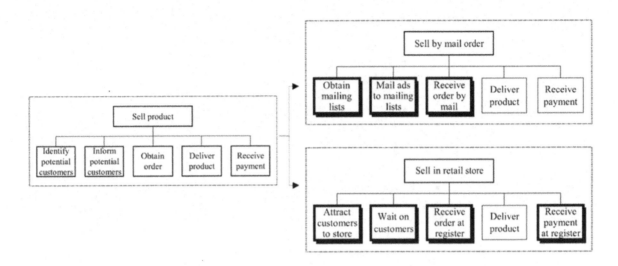

1999; Wyner & Lee, 2001). Using this concept, processes can be arranged hierarchically into a taxonomy, with very generic processes at one extreme and increasingly specialized processes at the other. As with other taxonomies, specialized entities automatically inherit properties from their more generic "parents", except where they explicitly add, delete or change a property.

Figure 1 illustrates this approach. Here, the generic process "Sell product" is decomposed into sub activities like "Identify potential customers" and "Inform potential customers". The generic process is also specialized into more focused process like "Sell by mail order" and "Sell in retail store". These specialized processes inherit, by default, the sub-activities and other characteristics of their "parent" process (AKA *generalization*):

Specialized processes can also add to or change the sub-activities they inherit. For instance, in "Sell by mail order", the sub-activities of "deliver a product" and "receive payment" are inherited without modification, but "Identify potential customers" is replaced by the more specialized activity "Obtain mailing lists."

In addition to processes like "sell by mail order" that can be viewed as general templates, the specialization hierarchy also includes "case studies" documenting creative solutions developed by organizations in response to particular process challenges. We have captured roughly 400 such case studies to date, ranging from "Hire human resources in advance of need {L-S Electro-Galvanizing}" to "Make using vendor assembly {VW Brazil}". Capturing such creative solutions in the repository enables their wider adoption by others.

We have found it useful to combine specializations into what we call "bundles". Each bundle represents a group of specializations that vary along some dimension. For instance, referring to the example in figure 1, a product can be sold either by mail order, or in a retail store. These specializations along with other possible ways in which the product can be sold (e.g. telemarketing, email or fax) can be grouped into a bundle that refers to "how" the sell activity is performed. In the Process Handbook bundles are expressed in form of questions. Generally speaking, the specializations under a bundle represent alterna-

Figure 2. An example of bundles in the specialization hierarchy

- P: Sell
  - ⊟[Sell how?]
    - ⊞P: Sell via face-to-face sales
    - ⊟P: Sell via direct marketing
      - P: Sell via direct mail
      - P: Sell via telemarketing
      - P: Sell via television direct response marketing
      - P: Sell via email / fax
    - ⊞P: Sell via store
  - ⊞[Sell via what channel?]
  - ⊟[Sell what?]
    - P: Sell product
    - ⊞P: Sell service
  - ⊞[Sell to whom?]
  - ⊞[Sell - views]
  - ⊞[Sell with what customization?]

tive answers to the question posed in the bundle. One can thus speak of "how" bundles (that gather different techniques for *how* the activity is performed), "who" bundles (that represent different alternatives for *who* performs an activity), "what" bundles (that represent different alternatives for *what* resource is manipulated by the activity), and so on. Figure 2 shows several examples of bundles in the specialization hierarchy for the "Sell" process, including "Sell how?" (which collects alternatives for how the sale is made), and "Sell What?" (which collects alternatives for what is sold):

Bundles can have associated tradeoff tables that capture the relative pros and cons of the different specializations in terms of their ratings on various criteria. Figure 3, for example, shows a tradeoff table for the specializations in the "Sell How?" bundle; specializations are the rows, criteria are the columns, and the cell contents are the values for each criterion and specialization:

The power of the specialization hierarchy comes from the fact that processes with similar functions are collocated, irregardless of the context (e.g. which industry) the process originally comes from. This

Figure 3. An example of tradeoff table

Alternative	Suggested products	Quality of service	Time to sell	Cost of selling
P: Sell via face-to-face sales	high margin, tailored	high	medium	high
P: Sell via direct marketing	specialty items	low	long	low
P: Sell via store	low margin commodities	medium	medium	medium

Figure 4. Three basic types of dependencies among activities Adapted from (Malone et al., 1999)

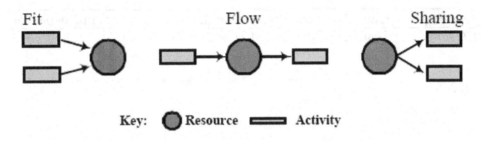

enables the cross-disciplinary fertilization of ideas and the leveraging of experiences across different industries.

Dependencies and Coordination Mechanisms

A second key concept is the notion that coordination can be viewed as the process of managing the resources (including documents, physical resources such as fuel, signals, and so on) that are shared, in some way, by the sub-activities in a process. We call these resource relationships *dependencies,* and distinguish dependencies into three basic types: flow, sharing and fit (Malone and Crowston, 1994) (Crowston, 1991) (Figure 4). *Flow* dependencies arise whenever one activity produces a resource that is consumed by another activity. Every flow dependency has three components: *timing* (ensuring the flow occurs at the right time), *accessibility* (ensuring the flow goes to the right place) and *usability* (making sure the right resource is transferred). *Sharing* dependencies occur whenever multiple activities all use the same scarce resource (e.g. when two people need to use the same machine). *Fit* dependencies arise when multiple activities collectively produce the components of a single resource (e.g. when several designers create subcomponents for a single system). Continuing with the process "Sell" example, Figure 5 shows an example of how dependencies are represented within the Process Handbook.

Figure 5. Dependencies in the process "Sell"

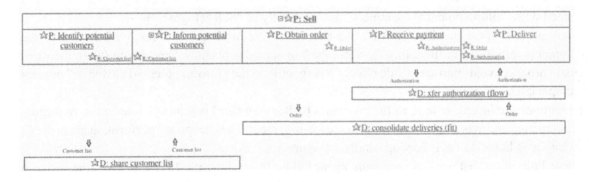

Figure 6. Examples of dependencies and associated coordination mechanisms

Dependency	Examples of coordination mechanisms for managing dependency
Flow: Timing	Transfer resource periodically Transfer resource on demand Transfer resource as it is generated
Flow:Access	Ship to consumer Make at point of use
Flow:Usability	Producer follows standards Consumer filters out sub-standard resources
Sharing	First come/first served Market-like bidding
Fit	Predefined subsystem interfaces Concurrent engineering design teams

One dependency concerns the "customer list" resource. Assuming multiple sales agents, we need to manage the sharing of customer lists amongst these agents. A second dependency concerns flow: the right delivery authorizations need to be transferred to the right delivery agents at the right time. Finally, there is a fit dependency between delivery authorizations: if there are multiple orders from one customer, it makes sense to try to consolidate these multiple orders for delivery purposes.

The resource relationships represented by such dependencies are managed by processes we call *coordination mechanisms*. As Figure 6 illustrates, each dependency type has its own set of mechanisms potentially relevant for managing it (Malone et al, 1999):

By consulting Figure 6 we can see, for example, that the sharing dependency in the "Sell" process can be managed by allocating customer names to sales agents on a first-come, first-served basis, or by sales agents bidding for customer names using some kind of market.

Exceptions and Handlers

The third key concept underlying the Handbook captures how processes deal with potential failures (Klein and Dellarocas, 2000). All processes in the Handbook repository are linked to the possible ways (*exceptions*) that the process may fail to achieve its goals. These exceptions, like all other process attributes, are inherited down the process specialization hierarchy. Consider, for example, the exceptions associated with "Inform potential customers", a sub-activity of "Sell" (Figure 7):

Every process in the Handbook inherits the exception "Performing agent dies" (which violates the goal "process terminates in finite time"), while the "unwanted solicitation" exception (which violates the goal "process avoids unwanted side effects") is specific to the "Inform potential customer" process and its specializations.

Exceptions are linked, in turn, to the processes (called *handlers*) potentially relevant to managing (i.e. anticipating and avoiding, or detecting and resolving) them. The exception "performing agent dies", for example, is linked to the following handlers (Figure 8):

These links show that one can *anticipate* agent failure by tracking the MTBF (mean time between

Figure 7. Exceptions for the process "Inform Potential Customers"

Goal	Exception
Unspecified	
G: process achieves optimal outcome	
G: process avoids negative side effects	E: unwanted solicitation
G: process uses minimal resources	
G: process terminates in finite time	E: Performing agent dies

failure) for that kind of agent, *avoid* failure by filtering out agents that are known to be unreliable, *resolve* the failure by replacing the failed agent, and so on.

THE HANDBOOK BASED PROCESS REDESIGN METHODOLOGY

The *Process Handbook* approach to BPR takes advantage of a process repository, organized using the concepts described above, to enable the systematic exploration of potential re-designs for a given process. The methodology described herein represents an integration and refinement of previously distinct techniques for designing the normative (Malone et al., 1999) (Klein et al, 2003) and exception-handling (Klein and Dellarocas, 2000) elements of a business process. To simplify understanding and provide insights into how to apply this methodology and its practical implications, a real-life example of a risk management process will be used to illustrate step-by-step the application of the methodology.

The approach begins by creating a "stripped-down" model of the as-is process, one that captures only the core activities and key dependencies. One then uses the Handbook repository as a source of ideas

Figure 8. Handlers for the exception "performing agent dies"

Handler
ANTICIPATED-BY *P: Track MTBF*
AVOIDED-BY *P: Filter out low-reliability resources*
DETECTED-BY *P: Monitor resource for failures*
RESOLVED-BY *P: Replace with other resource*
RESOLVED-BY P: Resurrect agent

concerning how the activities can be realized, the dependencies managed, and the possible exceptions handling according to the following steps:

1. Identification of the Process 'Deep Structure'
2. Specialization of core activities
3. Specification of coordination mechanisms
4. Specification exception handlers
5. Selection of alternatives

If, such in this case, an IT-based process is being envisaged, the definition of business requirements for the software is another step.

Step 1 – Identification of the Process 'Deep Structure'

The first step in re-designing a process is to identify a good initial abstraction of that process, what we can call the 'deep structure'. This involves identifying the core activities (i.e. those activities which are core to the functioning of the process) and key dependencies (i.e. the resource relationships that must appear between the core activities). So the goal is to capture the essence of the as-is risk management process, rather than become enmeshed in capturing details that we will probably want to radically re-design anyway. To do this access to relevant documentation and/or an interview with a domain expert is needed. The domain expert is a person knowledgeable about the business process being re-designed - the company's risk management process in this case – and is the person that will be able to identify especially promising re-design alternatives from among the ones generated using the methodology. In this phase its role is relevant in ensuring that the model captures all relevant activities, key dependencies, resources, and actors. So after having briefly explained the usage, the benefits and the expected outcomes of applying this methodology to the redesign of the business processes concerned – without going into the details of how it will be used – the interview goes on questions like 'what are the main activities of the risk management process?', 'what are basically the activities without such process could not exists?', 'which are the main resources consumed and produced?' and 'which are the main actors involved?'. The aim is to challenge the domain expert to further abstract its description to the core (a background knowledge on the process being analyzed and how it works inside the organization is necessary and for this having some preliminary documentation is useful). The result is a very simple representation that identifies two core activities: 'assess risks' and take action to manage it, that we have defined as 'reduce risks'. Both activities requires at least two resources: a person in charge, e.g. a *risk manager*, that assess risks and then act to mitigate the risks selected, signalled on a list, e.g. a *priorities' list* which identifies the risks to be managed. There is thus just one key flow dependency that manages the approval of the priorities' list, a supervising committee in the case analyzed. The deep structure might look like the following (Figure 9):

Common sense suggests that to assess something, you first must have a list of what needs to be assessed. So we decided to add another core activity, called 'identify risks', that creates that list. Here we may need someone who can identify which risks might occur in undertaking a set of activities, i.e. someone involved in the day-to-day operations of the organization, who is not necessarily the *risk manager* since that, especially in large organizations, is a specialized profile. We identified such activity as being done by *project managers*. Another key dependency has thus been recognized to ensure that the

Figure 9. Deep structure for the risk management process

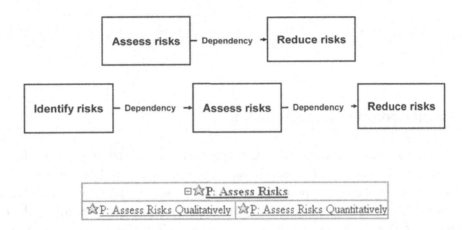

risks identified are transferred from the *project manager* to the *risk manager* to be assessed. This is a *flow dependency* (Figure 10).

This dependency might also, such in this case, include a *sharing* component (in the case the list is required by different risk managers that specialize in assessing different kinds of risks) and even a *fit* component (in the case the *risks' list* is assembled as a result of different meetings held by the *project manager* with projects' specialists).

A repository of business process models like the Process Handbook can prove valuable during the capture of the as-is deep structure, because it provides a collection of pre-defined process "building blocks". This can save time, because it is often quicker to hook together existing components rather than define them from scratch. This can also foster greater completeness, because the building blocks in the repository may include elements (e.g. sub-activities or exceptions) that we might otherwise forget to include. The Process Handbook repository's model for "assess risks", for example, is the following. (Figure 11)

We decided to use this process model as a "building block", so our risk management deep structure automatically includes (i.e. inherits) these sub-activities. When practical, the organization's domain expert can help validate whether the appropriate building blocks are being used. In our particular case, the availability of publicly available documentation rendered this interaction unnecessary.

Figure 10. Deep structure for the risk management process revised

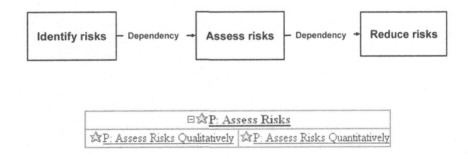

Figure 11. A decomposition for the assess risks activity

⊟☆P: Assess Risks	
☆P: Assess Risks Qualitatively	☆P: Assess Risks Quantitatively

Step 2 – Specialization of Core Activities

Once the deep structure has been captured in the repository, we can start exploring different ways of refining this abstract model into a fully-specified business process. Figure 12 below represents the deep structure of the process as being composed of three main parts, i.e. *"Identify Risks"*, *"Assess Risks"* and *"Reduce Risks"*, as well as two key flow dependencies that manage respectively the transfer and approval of the *"risks' list"* and *"priorities' list"* resources. Two actors are involved in this process: a *"Project Manager"* and a *"Risk Manager"* .

The first step is to replace the abstract core activities in the deep structure model with more specific ones. We wish for example better elicit and specify the 'reduce risks' part. A process knowledge repository such like the Process Handbook helps us to perform this exploration systematically, selecting the process alternatives from the process ideas already in the repository. There is already a specific process model called 'reduce risk' that heads the following branch in the Process Handbook's specialization hierarchy (Figure 13)

To specify how our process will reduce risks, we need only select one of the specializations from this branch. In such a case, where the "building block" was taken from the Process Handbook, this substitution can be made either by replacing the activity with one of its specializations, or by using the process recombinator to create a new process model with the specialized activity. Following this second approach, we can also use the trade-off tables to help us decide which specialization best suits our current needs. Figure 14 below shows the specialized process model with the specialized part 'reduce financial risk', which inherits such sub-processes as reduce liquidity, currency and capital risk. All the other parts have not been changed and are the same as indicated in Figure 12.

Figure 12. Risk Management deep structure in the Process Handbook

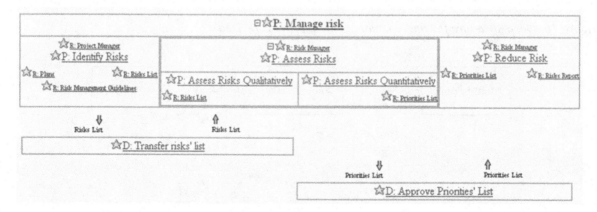

Figure 13. Reduce Risk branch in the Process Handbook specialization hierarchy

- ☐☆P: Reduce Risk
    - ☐☆[Reduce what risk?]
        - ⊞☆P: Reduce management risk
        - ☐☆P: Reduce financial risk
            - ☆P: Reduce liquidity risk
            - ☆P: Reduce currency risk
            - ☆P: Reduce capital risk
        - ☐☆P: Reduce technical risk
            - ☆P: Reduce risks related to the development of a product/system
            - ☆P: Reduce risks related to design of a product/system

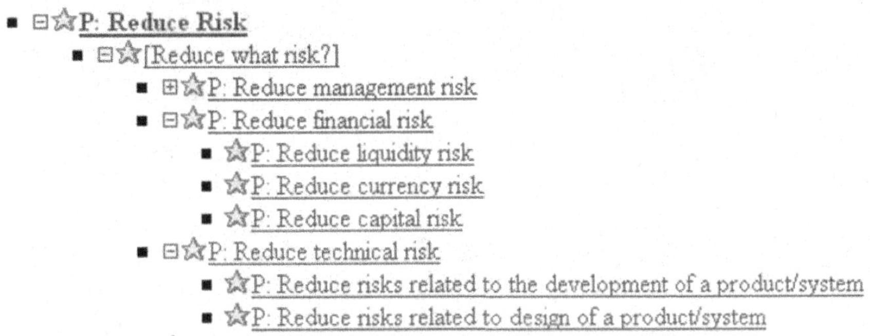

Step 3 – Specification of Coordination Mechanisms

In addition to specifying how the core activities in the 'risk management' process model can be realized, we also need to specify how the dependencies between these activities are managed. Each dependency type (flow vs fit vs sharing) has in the Process Handbook repository a corresponding branch of the specialization hierarchy that captures the processes - i.e. *coordination mechanisms* -that can manage that kind of dependency. These include the *manage fit*, *manage flow*, *manage sharing* branches of the process taxonomy. Let us consider, for example, the dependency between *identify risk* and *assess risk*. This dependency – where the risks identified by the *project manager* are transferred to the *risk manager* is in charge of assessing financial risks – is a *flow* dependency. We can thus specify how this dependency is managed by selecting a coordination mechanism from the manage flow branch of the repository.

Relying on the concept of bundle recombination we can generate composite transfer mechanisms choosing from the different bundles. We can, for example consider a transfer mechanism that relies on periodic updates of the list by the *project manager* (manage timing how? bundle) based on a common database that notify via e-mail updates (manage access how? bundle), according to a template that has been co-defined (manage usability how? bundle). (Figure 15)

Figure 14. Specialized Risk Management process model

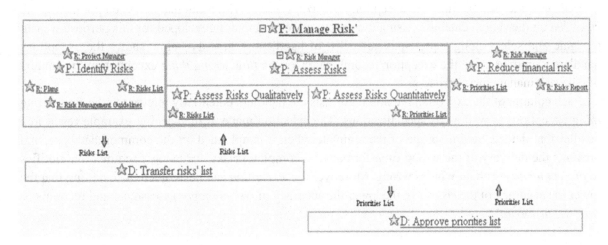

Figure 15. Coordination mechanism for the transfer risk list dependency

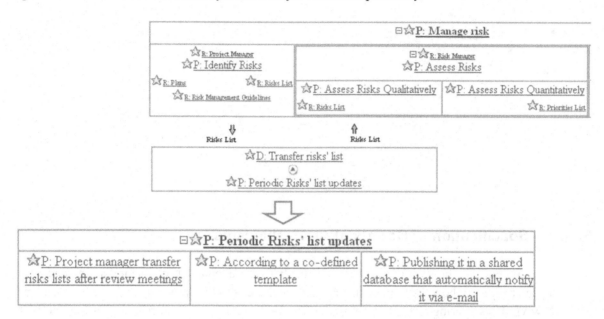

Step 4 – Specification of Exception Handlers

This stage involves specifying how the process might fail to achieve its goals, i.e. *exceptions*, and how these exceptions should be handled. We first need to identify, for every part in the 'risk management' process (core activities as well as coordination mechanisms), which exceptions are of concern. This can be done directly or starting from the identification of the goals each part/dependency needs to achieve. The work is facilitated since we have re-used Process Handbook entries, so we can on choose from a pre-enumerated list of exceptions – inherited from original process models - which ones are relevant to our particular context. Having done that we can then select, from a pre-enumerated list of handlers, which ones we might want to use to solve the selected exceptions. Figure 16 shows the 'risk management' process with the goals and exceptions inherited.

Let's consider for example the exception *flow wrong thing*, which can happen when publishing the *risks' list* on the shared database. Using the exception recombinator developed for this purpose we can navigate and select along a pre-enumerated list of handlers. Figure 17 below shows the exceptions handlers identified using the exception recombinator for the *flow wrong thing* exception in the context of our 'risk management' process.

Each column of the exception recombinator lists the handlers potentially relevant to the *flow wrong thing* exception, as well as its specializations. The selection made in the specific example result in a handler that detects the mis-usage of the template when it is uploaded on the common database, and prevents the delivery of the wrong (non-formatted/incomplete) *risks' list* using a sentinel that notifies to *project manager* about what is wrong. Moreover this *exception* can be avoided in signalling that the lower the accuracy of the *risks' list,* the lower the accuracy of *risk manager* assessment and recommendations (*tit-for-tat*)

Figure 16. Risk management process with goals and exceptions

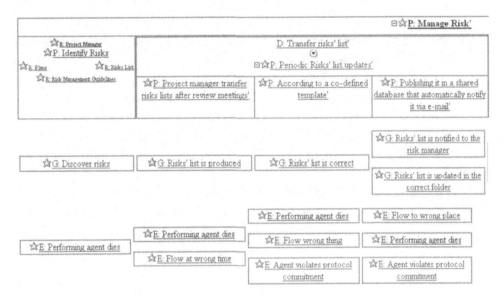

Figure 17. Using exception recombinator to specify handler for 'flow wrong thing'

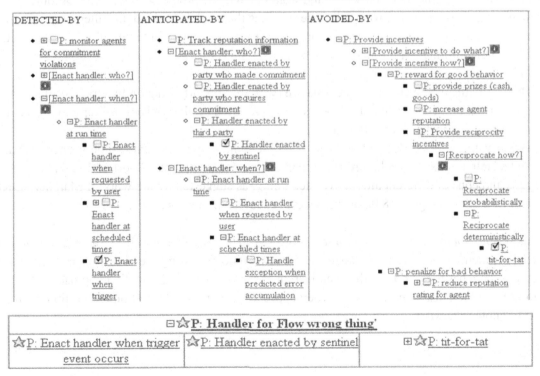

Figure 18. Using process metrics and trade-off tables to select alternative configurations

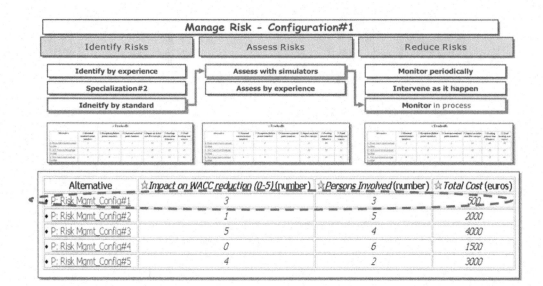

Step 5 - Selecting alternatives

As it can be seen, in this methodology, the bulk of the work is spent in exploring and generating new process alternatives, hopefully harvested from many sources and industries thanks to the usage of a Process Handbook-like knowledge repository. So those steps, repeated iteratively, allows us to generate a number of alternatives. Some might be innovative and well-suited to the process at hand, whereas others can be completely unsuited or even unworkable. There is thus the need to evaluate the alternatives generated and select the most suitable ones. This, according to the nature and complexity of the redesign activity as well as to the information made available by the organization, can be done in several ways:

- By having the organization's representative (with the support of qualitative trade-off tables) validate, critic, prune and refine the process ideas proposed on the basis of his/her experience, mandate or sense of what is an interesting solution
- By enriching process descriptions with a set pre-defined metrics, that can be further specialized and adapted to the particular process at hand using quantitative 'trade-off tables' that capture the pros and cons of different alternatives according, as suggested by the work of Margherita, Klein and Elia (2007). Figure 18 below provide an example of this approach:

This second approach, however, requires more significant involvement from the organization side, the need for metrics often leads to sensitive issues that hinders getting the necessary information, and sometimes there has been no formalized collection of such measures. So the first approach is the easier one to use and the most straightforward when appropriate metrics information and/or time is, for one reason or another, lacking.

Figure 19. Using the Process Handbook to identify software requirements

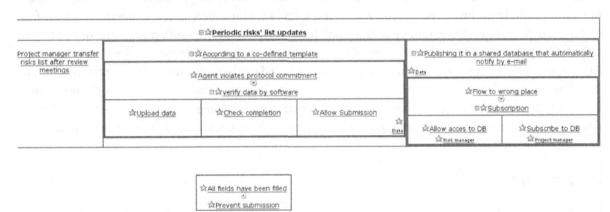

Definition of Business Requirements

Once the model of the redesigned process has been defined, we can then explore more specific process alternatives that describe the business requirements for the software applications that will be used to manage this process electronically. Starting from a business process design in this way means that its business guys can conceptualize and describe the process in their own way of thinking, while eventually creating a requirements model that a software developer or IT consultant can readily use to conceptualize, develop or describe the necessary enabling software applications.

Starting from the general model, the designer can refine each element of the process in order to clearly specify which is the expected behaviour of the associated software application and which are the different goals that should be reached through it. The ability to create bundles answering different key questions allows us, moreover, to define possible scenarios that explain how different actors interact with the application. This enables a more structured gathering of business requirements, starting from and directly involving business people. Through iterated refinements, IT experts can detail the functionalities of the software application, coming to the definition of real IT requirements. The output of this modelling activity could in fact represent the starting point for defining the specification of the software components through the traditional methodologies for software design.

Let's take for example the *transfer risk list* dependency. It could be interesting to design (or scout for) a software application that enable the shared, automatic and reliable management of the *risk list*. So starting from the process for *periodic risks' list updates* (Figure 15) we can think of a software application that allows the *project manager* to fill directly in the shared database (that is the *risks' list*) using a web-based form (that will act as a template) that prevents him from uploading risks if not all the elements asked for in the form are filled (so, in an automatic way, the *risk manager* is sure that the *risks' list* is looking at is always correct). Once the updates are uploaded, an e-mail notifies the *risk manager* that new risks have been added to the list. A subscription mechanism in which the risk manager 'invites' the project manager to fill in the database ensures appropriate delivery of the notification. Figure 19 shows how the *Process Handbook* was used to specify these business requirements

The figure shows that the Process Handbook represents a useful tool for bridging the 'language' gap between business and IT people when a software application is to be designed. In fact most of the existing software design approaches are usually oriented towards IT languages (such as UML) that are unfamiliar to and not close to the natural way of thinking of business people. This, together with the fact that these approaches often requires a well formulated description of what software should do to be used effectively, produces frequent misalignment between business expectations and real software features. This in turn results in time consuming and costly software adaptations and delays in its implementation. The *Process Handbook* on the other hand can be a 'complimentary tool' as it provides the possibility of starting from a general case defined by a domain expert and refining it iteratively with the software developer or IT consultant, obtaining in the end software applications able to manage specific cases.

CONCLUSION

The Handbook BPR methodology differs in important respects from previous work. Previous efforts have been predicated on capturing a detailed as-is model, but provide little guidance concerning what the to-be process should look like. The innovativeness and quality of the new process depends, as a result, on the experience and the creativity of the particular individuals involved. In addition, because creating the detailed as-is model is so resource-intensive, the new idea generation phase is typical time-limited, so often only a few new ideas are evaluated in any depth. The Handbook methodology turns this on its head.

BPR participants are encouraged to capture only the "essence" of the process they wish to re-design, focusing on core processes and key dependencies. This step is relatively quick, and creates an as-is process model that is simpler and therefore easier to understand. The BPR participants spend the bulk of their time systematically exploring ideas inspired by (recombinations of) 'best practices' harvested from many sources and industries. All elements of the deep structure, including those that 'have always been done that way', are subjected to scrutiny. Designers are thus apt to consider a wider range of ideas than they would have generated on their own, and are more likely to take advantage of technological and managerial advances that have appeared in other contexts.

While others have explored the use of reusable process knowledge libraries to enable BPR (Committee, 1992; McNair and Leibfried, 1992; Schank and Abelson, 1977; Magazine, 1992; Mi and Scacchi, 1993; Salancik and Leblebici, 1988; Baligh, Burton et al., 1990; Gasser 1992), our approach is unique in that it draws together a large repository of process best-practices, organized in innovative ways using coordination theory concepts, and exploited using recombination-based methodologies derived from experience with re-designing processes of realistic scope and complexity.

The discussion about the definition of software requirements shows such a kind of approach can support 'conversations' among people that come from different knowledge domains and specializations, thereby becoming a vehicle to accommodate and integrate the different perspectives needed to deal with the increasing complexity of business processes. This more clear, defined and systematic approach to the redesign of business processes has the potential of rendering process redesign more a science that an art, transforming it from a set of reactive actions into a controllable and predictable organizational change process that can help XXI century organizations respond, adapt and even generate change.

In this aim further research is needed, especially to address issues arising from the generative strength of the Process Handbook methodology. The ability to generate alternatives by recombination is in a sense, a two-edged sword, in that it is often easy to uncover an overwhelming number of process alternatives. For example, a deep structure model with 5 core activities and 5 alternative specializations per core activity produces 3125 (5^5) potential process alternatives, without considering alternatives for the key dependencies and important exceptions, if any. While many of these alternatives may be innovative and worthy of further exploration, many others will probably be unsuited to this particular domain, or even unworkable in general. The domain experts involved in the BPR engagement are thus called upon to be able to rapidly prune a large search space of possibilities so they can concentrate their effort on the most promising ones. While we do not expect to obviate the need for human judgment, we do plan to explore how the system can support human users by reducing the burden of traversing large design search spaces. One possibility involves the development of algorithms for automatically exploring the process design space for high-utility alternatives. Another promising direction involves enriching the metrics information captured in the process handboook through the development of a taxonomy of process attributes. Such a taxonomy can help identify which metrics should be captured in the Handbook's process descriptions and *tradeoff* tables, as well as help process designers with benchmarking and the generation of what-if scenarios.

Another promising direction for developing and strengthening the methodology is to use this kind of metrics-based approach for benchmarking purposes, in order to identify and prune process alternatives in a more systematic way. This might be either downstream (identifying the most suitable alternatives coming from top performers in one or more industries) or upstream (identifying which business processes can be used as a model according to target measures we are interested to, as suggested in the recent work of Margherita and Klein, 2007).

REFERENCES

Armistead, C., & Rowland, P. (1996). *Managing business processes: BPR and beyond.* New York: John Wiley and Sons.

Baligh, H. H., Burton, R. M., et al. (1990). Devising expert systems in organization theory: The organizational consultant. In M. Masuch (Ed.), *Organization, management, and expert systems* (pp. 35-57). Berlin, Germany: Walter de Gruyter.

Chen & Minder. (1999). BPR methodologies: methods and tools. In D. J. Elzinga, T. R. Gulledge, & C. Lee (Eds.), *Business process engineering: Advancing the state of the art.* (pp. 187-212). Norwell, MA: Kluwer Academic Publishers.

Committee, A. T. Q. S. (1992). *Benchmarking: focus on world-class practices.* Indianapolis, IN: AT&T Bell Laboratories.

Crowston, K. G. (1991). *Towards a coordination cookbook: Recipes for multi-agent action.* Ph. D. Thesis, MIT Sloan School of Management.

Davenport, T. H., & Perez-Guardado, M. A. (1999) Process ecology: A new metaphor for reengineering-oriented change. In D. J. Elzinga, T. R. Gulledge, & C. Lee (Eds.) *Business process engineering: Advancing the state of the art* (pp. 25-44). Norwell, MA: Kluwer Academic Publishers.

Davenport, T. H., & Short, J. E. (1990). The new industrial engineering: Information technology and business process redesign. *Sloan Management Review*, 11–27.

Davenport, T. H., & Stoddard, D. B. (1994). Reengineering, business change of mythic proportions? *MIS Quarterly*, *18*(2), 121–127. doi:10.2307/249760

Gasser, L. (1992). *HITOP-A: Coordination, infrastructure and enterprise integration*. Paper presented at the AAAI-92 Workshop on AI in Enterprise Integration.

Grover, V., & Kettinger, W. J. (Eds.). (1995). *Business process change: Concepts, methodologies and technologies*. Hershey, PA: Idea Group Publishing.

Gunther, C. W., Rinderle-Ma, S., Reichert, M., van der Aalst, W. M. P., & Recker, J. (2008). Using process mining to learn from process changes in evolutionary systems. *Int'l Journal of Business Process Integration and Management*, *3*(1), 61–78. doi:10.1504/IJBPIM.2008.019348

Hammer, M. (1990). Reengineering work: Don't automate, obliterate. *Harvard Business Review*, *68*(4), 104–112.

Hammer, M., & Champy, J. (1993). *Reengineering the corporation: A manifesto for business revolution*. New York: Harper Business.

Herman, G. A., & Malone, T. W. (2003) What is in the process handbook? In T.W. Malone, K. Crowston, & G.A. Herman, (Eds.), *Organizing business knowledge: The MIT process handbook*. Cambridge MA: MIT Press.

Kettinger, W. J., Teng, J. T. C., & Guha, S. (1997b). Business process change: A study of methodologies, techniques, and tools. *MIS Quarterly*, *21*(1), 55–80. doi:10.2307/249742

Klein, M., & Dellarocas, C. (2000). A Knowledge-based approach to handling exceptions in workflow systems. *Computer-Supported Collaborative Work. Special Issue on Adaptive Workflow Systems, 9*(3/4).

Klein, M., Herman, G. A., Lee, J., O'Donnell, E., & Malone, T. W. (2003) Inventing new business processes using a process repository. In T.W. Malone, K. Crowston, & G.A. Herman, (Eds.), *Organizing Business Knowledge: The MIT Process Handbook*. Cambridge MA: MIT Press.

Kubeck, L. C. (1995). *Techniques for business process redesign*. New York: John Wiley and Sons.

Kubeck, L. C. (1997). Techniques for business process redesign. *Interfaces*, *27*(4).

Lee, J., & Pentland, B. T. (2000). *Grammatical approach to organizational design*. Cambridge, MA: MIT Sloan School of Management. M+agazine, C. (1992). Back support for benchmarkers. *CIO Magazine June: 16*.

Malone, T. W., et al. (2003). Tools for inventing organizations: Towards a handbook of organizational processes. In T.W. Malone, K. Crowston, & G.A. Herman, (Eds.). *Organizing business knowledge: The MIT process handbook*. Cambridge MA: MIT Press.

Malone, T. W., & Crowston, K. (1994). The interdisciplinary study of coordination. *ACM Computing Surveys*, *26*(1), 87–119. doi:10.1145/174666.174668

Malone, T. W., Crowston, K., & Herman, G. A. (2003). *Organizing business knowledge: The MIT process handbook*. Cambridge MA: MIT Press.

Malone, T. W., Crowston, K., Lee, J., & Pentland, B. (1999). Tools for inventing organizations: Toward a handbook of organizational processes. *Management Science, 45*(3), 425–443. doi:10.1287/mnsc.45.3.425

Margherita, A., & Klein, M. (2007). An e-handbook for designing and implementing a benchmarking project. *International Journal of Process Management and Benchmarking, 2*(1), 10–28. doi:10.1504/IJPMB.2007.013315

Margherita, A., Klein, M., & Elia, G. (2007). Metrics-based process redesign with the MIT process handbook. *Knowledge and Process Management, 14*(1), 46–57. doi:10.1002/kpm.269

McNair, C. J., & Leibfried, K. H. J. (1992). *Benchmarking: A tool for continuous improvement.* New York: Harper Business.

Mi, P., & Scacchi, W. (1993). *Articulation: An integrated approach to the diagnosis, replanning and rescheduling of software process failures.* Paper Presented at the 8th International Conference on Knowledge-Based Software Engineering.

Mi, P., & Scacchi, W. (1996). A meta-model for formulating knowledge-based models of software development. *Decision Support Systems, 17*(4), 313–330. doi:10.1016/0167-9236(96)00007-3

Nissen, M. (1998). Redesigning reengineering through measurement-driven inferences. *MIS Quarterly, 22*(4). doi:10.2307/249553

Nissen, M. E. (1999). A configuration-contingent enterprise redesign model. In D. J. Elzinga, T. R. Gulledge, & C. Lee (Eds.) *Business process engineering: Advancing the state of the art.* (pp. 145-186). Norwell, MA: Kluwer Academic Publishers.

Pandya, Vinodrai, K., & Nelis, S. (1998). Requirements for process redesign tools. *International Journal Of Computer Applications in Technology, 11*(6), 409–418.

Pentland, B. T. (1995). Grammatical models of organizational processes. *Organization Science, 6*(5), 541–556. doi:10.1287/orsc.6.5.541

Rinderle, S., Weber, B., Reichert, M., & Wild, W. (2005). Integrating Process learning and process evolution – A Semantics based approach. In *Proceedings of the International Conference on Business Process Management - BPM'05* (pp. 252-267). Nancy, France.

Salancik, G. R., & Leblebici, H. (1988). Variety and form in organizing transactions: A generative grammar of organizations. In N. DiTomaso & S. B. Bacharach (Eds.), *Research in the Sociology of Organizations.* Greenwich, CT: JAI Press.

Schank, R. C., & Abelson, R. P. (1977). *Scripts, plans, goals and understanding.* Lawrence Erlbaum Associates.

Stoddard, D., & Jarvenpaa, S. (1995). Business process reengineering: Tactics for managing radical change. *Journal of Management Information Systems, 12*(1), 81–108.

Taivalsaari, A. (1996). On the notion of inheritance. *ACM Computing Surveys, 28*(3), 438–479. doi:10.1145/243439.243441

Van der Aalst, W. M. P., & Basten, T. (1999). *Inheritance of workflows: An approach to tackling problems related to change* (Tech. Rep.). Eindhoven: Eindhoven University of Technology.

Van der Aalst, W. M. P., Van Dongen, B. F., Herbst, J., Maruster, L., Schimm, G., & Weijters, A. (2003). Workflow mining: A survey of issues and approaches. *Data & Knowledge Engineering, 47*(2), 237–267. doi:10.1016/S0169-023X(03)00066-1

Wyner, G., & Lee, J. (2001). *Defining specialization for process models* (Tech. Rep. # 4159). Boston: MIT Sloan School of Management.

KEY TERMS AND DEFINITIONS

Bundle: A group of instances (processes, resources, others) put together according to a specific criteria of classification.

Coordination mechanism: A mechanism/process that manages a specific flow, fit or sharing dependency arising among parts of a process.

Deep Structure: The abstract structure of a process, expressed in terms of its core parts and the key dependencies arising among them.

Dependency: A relationship existing among two or more activities in terms of the use and production of specific resources as input/output.

Exception: A deviation from the normal execution of a process that causes a delay/failure in reaching the goals that the process is designed to achieve. It can be conceived as the violation of a commitment.

Goal: A desired state, i.e. an objective that the process or a part should achieve under normal conditions.

Handler: A mechanism/process that manages an exception by anticipating and avoiding, or detecting and resolving it.

Recombinator: A redesign-oriented tool that allows us specify an alternative structure for a process by creating different combinations of its specializations.

Specialization: A different alternative way of executing a process or a part of it. A specialization is usually defined in terms of why, where, who, when and how a process is executed.

Trade-Off Matrix: A redesign-oriented tool that allows us to compare alternative processes with respect to a given set of attributes. It allows us to evaluate the strengths and weaknesses of each alternative in terms of the attributes relevant to the redesign goals.

Chapter 4
Evaluating Adequacy of Business Process Modeling Approaches

Ilia Bider
IbisSoft AB, Sweden

Erik Perjons
Stockholm University/Royal Institute of Technology, Sweden

ABSTRACT

From the practical point of view, the most important parameter that describes the quality of a particular model is its adequacy to the task for which the model will be used. The selection of a "right for the task" modeling approach can substantially increase chances of creating a high quality model. To ensure the "right" choice of modeling approach the following three factors should be considered: (a) properties of the object to be modeled, (b) characteristics of the environment in which the model is being built, (c) intended use of the model. This chapter is devoted to the analysis of these factors for the domain of business process modeling. It presents a simplified classification of the approaches to business process modeling. It lists the most essential properties of business processes, it classifies modeling environments, and it discusses some practical tasks where a business process model can be used. Based on the analysis, practical recommendations on what modeling approach to choose are given dependent on the type of the process under consideration, the task at hand, and the environment in which the model is being built and verified.

INTRODUCTION

There are many different parameters that should be taken into consideration when measuring the quality of a particular model, like precision, level of details, formal correctness, etc. From the practical point of view, however, the most important factor is the adequacy of the model to a practical task that the model should help to solve. A formally incorrect model can be corrected, absent details can be added later, but an inadequate model may be of little practical use. It may be formally correct, precise, and very

DOI: 10.4018/978-1-60566-669-3.ch004

detailed, but the level of details may be too high in respect to the aspects that are of low interest for a given practical task, and too low for the aspects that are critical for this task.

The adequacy of a particular model depends, in a very high degree, on the type of the modeling approach (also called modeling method or technique) chosen for the given modeling task. Under modeling approach we understand modeling language, and related guidelines on how to use it in practice. In any particular application domain, there, usually, exist several, sometimes too many, competing modeling approaches. These approaches may be formally equivalent to each other; nevertheless, the choice of the "unsuitable" approach may seriously affect the chances for success. To make a right choice, a way of evaluation of the adequacy of a modeling approach to a practical task should be developed so that a "right" approach could be chosen for each particular modeling task.

In our opinion, the following factors are to be considered when making the choice:

1. Properties of the object to be modeled.
2. Characteristics of the environment in which the model is being built.
3. Intended use of the model.

Interpretation of these three factors depends on the application domain in which the modeling work is to be done. Thus, for each application domain, the following work needs to be completed in order to create a practical manual for selection a suitable modeling approach:

1. Classify the existing approaches to modeling according to the most important characteristics of the given application domain. This is extremely important when there exist too many approaches in a particular domain. In such a case, choosing an approach by comparing all of them can be both time consuming and confusing.
2. Select and describe the most essential properties of the modeling objects in the given application domain. Analyze which modeling approaches suit best for describing particular properties of the modeling objects.
3. Select and describe the most essential properties of the environment in which the modeling work is to be completed. Analyze which of the modeling approaches suit best for particular modeling environments.
4. List all thinkable tasks for which a model could be used in the given application domain. Analyze which modeling approaches are the most suitable for particular tasks.
5. Give the final recommendation on how to choose a suitable approach

This chapter presents an example of work completed according to the steps above. The work concerns the domain of business processes that we consider as quite representative for the task of testing the principles listed above. This is because:

- Based on our practice, there is no universal approach of business process modeling suitable for all possible projects in this field
- In this domain, there are far too many approaches and tools to consider all of them one by one to see which one suits best the needs of a particular project. Some classification of approaches is needed so that first a particular class can be chosen, and after that a approach that belong to the class.

The material presented in this chapter is written with the aim to give practical orientation on how to choose an appropriate approach for business process modeling. The chapter is written in a prescriptive manner having practitioners in mind. The number of references has intentionally been kept to the minimum to make the chapter easier to read for the intended audience. Despite the practical orientation of the chapter, some parts of it might be also of interest for researchers.

The chapter is based on the analysis of literature and on our own experience in the field of business process identification and modeling. Our own experience lies in the field of administrative processes, such as bureaucratic decision-making, lobbying (influence decision of others), processing customer feedback, inquiries, funeral arrangements, etc. For examples of such processes, see (Andersson et al., 2002, Perjons et al., 2007). This kind of processes has not received much attention in the literature, where the standard examples concern production, sales, insurance claims etc. The main characteristic feature of the administrative processes is their relatively loosely structure as far as the exact order of activities is concerned. Experience in modeling such processes complemented by literature on modeling more structured processes gave us a relatively broad basis for the work presented in this chapter.

The chapter is written according to the following plan. In Section "Business Processes – Main Notation", we introduce the general notions normally used when discussing business processes. In Section "Business Process Modeling – Informal Discussion", we discuss the idea of classification of business process modeling approaches informally through analogy with different kind of maps. In Section "Classification of Approaches", we introduce a classification of the approaches to business process modeling. In this classification, we have chosen to stress one particular aspect that we consider to be the most important for our practical task. This is the way of how the dynamics of business processes is represented. The classification is our own invention; it was worked out after a try to find an appropriate classification (for our task) in the literature.

In Section "Properties of Business Processes", we discuss the business process properties that are important to consider when choosing an approach to business process modeling. The properties on the list are more or less obvious for specialists in business process modeling. However, the list itself is our own invention; again, we could not find any readymade list in the literature. We attribute the absence of such lists and classifications of approaches due to that not enough attention is being paid to the practical perspective of choosing modeling approaches. In Section "Properties of the Modeling Environment", we consider the properties of environment in which the modeling work is being done. In Section "Intended use of Model", we consider some practical tasks for which a business process model could be used. While discussing properties of business processes, modeling environments, and project tasks, we refer to the classification of approaches from Section "Classification of Approaches", and give recommendations of what approaches suit best specific properties, or tasks.

In Section "What Approach to Choose?" we give some general recommendations based on combination of factors described in earlier sections. Finally, Section "Concluding Remarks" presents concluding remark to summarize the material. In Appendix 1, we place a short-overview of the state flow approach to business process modeling, as it is not well-known to general public.

BUSINESS PROCESSES: MAIN NOTIONS

We follow the most general definition of business processes, see, for example, (Hammer&Champy, 1994, Kueng&Kawalek, 1997), that defines a business process as a set of partially ordered activities aimed at reaching a well-defined goal. Some examples of goals are as follows:

- Reaching an agreement in business negotiations.
- Discharging a patient from the hospital in a (relatively) healthy state.
- Closing a sale.

This definition can be applied to main processes that produce some "value" to the customers, as well as to, so called, "support processes". Support processes are the processes that ensure that the main processes have enough resources to work problem free, e.g., hiring and firing personnel.

When discussing business processes, it is important to differentiate the process type from the process instance. The notion of *process type* is used to talk about the process in general, like:

- Sales process (in general),
- Processing insurance claims
- Decision-making

The notion of *process instance* is used to pinpoint a particular process, like:

- Processing a sales lead that concern a particular customer.
- Processing insurance claim #1345678.
- Passing an elderly care plan for 2002.

Two types of goals can be differentiated when discussing business processes: strategic and operational goals. Strategic goals, like customer satisfaction, growth, profit, etc. are associated with the process type. They explain why the process exists/should exist in the organization, and why it should be driven in a certain way. Analysis of the strategic goals results in the rules/procedures that dictate how the instances of the process should be run. All such rules for a given process type constitute a *process definition*.

Operational goals concern process instances, and they show when a process instance can be considered as finished. Examples of operational goals that correspond to the process types above are as follows:

- Understand a particular customer's needs and make an offer (sales process).
- Insure that all basic documents that concern a particular insurance claim are collected and that money is paid (processing insurance claims).
- Pass a decision on an elderly care plan based on the needs, available resources, and current legislation (decision-making)

Each process engages a number of participants, which can be roughly classified into artifacts, human beings (people) and organizations. The notion of *artifact* is used to represent any physical or abstract object like document, product, computer program, etc.

The notion of *human being* represents a person participating in the process. Very often, human beings participate in a business process on behalf of some company, political party, department, team, etc. Any of these unions can be represented by the concept of *organization*.

In relation to a particular process, the participants can be roughly divided into two categories: passive participants, and active participants. *Passive participants* are the participants that are subjected to transformation (or change) during the execution of activities, for example, a document being written, a car being assembled, a patient being treated in the hospital, an organization being reorganized.

Figure 1. Road map

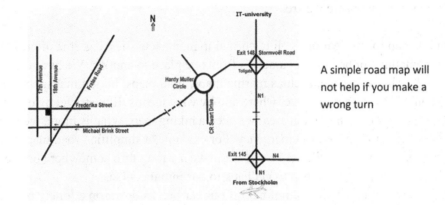

A simple road map will not help if you make a wrong turn

Active participants, or *agents*, are the participants that perform actions aimed at changing passive participants. The active participants can be considered on the level of individual people participating in the activity, or on the level of organizations that they represent. Artifacts can also play the role of active participants, e.g., industrial equipment, robots, computers, etc. Both human and non-human active participants are often called resources, as they should be distributed among various activities and process instances.

BUSINESS PROCESS MODELING: INFORMAL DISCUSSION

Business process model is a map that helps us to navigate through our business activities. In particular, it helps us to understand:

- Where we are right now,
- Where we need to go to,

Figure 2. Hiking map

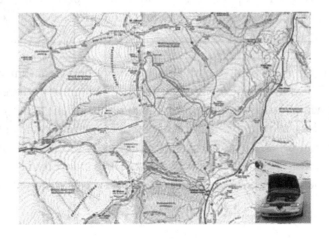

You may need a hiking map if your car breaks down on a lonely road in the mountains on a stormy day

- Where we came from, and
- How we got to where we are.

Using a map for navigation is quite normal in many activities, e.g. it is often a must when we need to move something or be moved ourselves from one place to another. We have different maps for navigating in the physical space, such as marine maps, road maps, hiking maps, etc. The choice of a map depends on what we want to move, where and by what means. If we travel by car we need a road map, if we travel on foot in a mountain area, we need a hiking map. What is more, we may need several different types of maps, in case of emergency. For example, a simplified road map that shows how to get from one point to another will not help if we make a wrong turn somewhere on the way, see Figure 1. We will need a detailed road map to get back to our initial course.

Even a detailed roadmap will not help if our car breaks down on a lonely road in a mountain area far from any human dwellings in a stormy weather. A hiking map can help us to find the shortest route to safety in this case, see Figure 2.

The most commonly used type of business process maps is a workflow map. The workflow shows in which orders activities (tasks) should be completed in order to reach a goal of the given business process. A workflow map is similar to a road map, more exactly, a simple road map. If you can follow it in the exact manner, you will reach the goal. However, if you need to make a turn because the road is temporally blocked, it might be difficult to get back.

A typical project in the area of Business Process Management (BPM) starts with describing business processes that exist in a given company or organization, so called as-is processes. It is very important to choose a right approach, i.e. right kind of maps, for creating these descriptions. For example, it does not make much sense to create a road map in the area where no roads exist (just small paths here and there). And it would not be enough just to draw a road map if you want to be able to find your way through even if you have been "blown off the road".

CLASSIFICATION OF APPROACHES

We consider that the most essential feature that differentiates various approaches to process modeling from each other is the way of presenting the development of a process instance in time, i.e. business process dynamics. There are many different approaches to representing process dynamics. However, in a simplified manner, we can classify all the approaches into four categories according to the main view they take over the business process dynamics:

1. *Input/output flow*. The focus is on passive participants that are being consumed, produced, or changed by the activities. This flow can be represented as a diagram (graph), where activities serve as nodes. The arrows connect the activities in accordance to results of one activity are being used in one or another way by the next activity. Such a diagram does not reflect the order of activities directly, it reflects the causal order, i.e. the results of one activity are used by another activity. However, the causality establishes a partial order between activities indirectly, i.e. the results should be produced before they could be used. The most common approach to represent this kind of flow is IDEF0 (FIPS, 1993).

2. *Workflow.* The focus is on the order of activities in time. This flow can be represented as a diagram (graph). Usually, nodes of the graph represent activities, while arrows represent the flow. Typical notations for representing workflows are IDEF3 process flow diagrams (Mayer et al., 1995), Activity Diagrams of UML (OMG, 2007), and Petri Nets (Aalst, 1999, Deiters&Gruhn, 1998). The Petri nets approach tries to combine the workflow with input-output flow, though the workflow is the dominating view.

3. *Agent-related view.* The focus is on the order in which agents get and perform their part of work. The typical notation to represent this kind of flow is Role-Activity Diagrams, RAD, (Huckvale&Ould, 1998), and Specification and Description Language, SDL (ITU-T, 2002).

4. *State flow.* Each activity produces changes in the part of the real world that embraces a given process instance. Some changes may concern the state of passive participants, e.g. their form, shape, or physical location. Other changes may concern the state of active participants, e.g. the state of the mind of a human agent trying to find a solution for a complex problem. However, the focus of the state flow view is on changes produced in the part of the world that embraces the given process instance. When the state flow is used as a complementary view, as in IDEF3 (Mayer et al., 1995), the flow is described in form of state-transitions diagrams. However, the state-transition diagrams exploit the state flow view only partially. For details of a full exploitation of the state flow view, see, for example, our papers (Khomyakov&Bider, 2000, Andersson et al., 2002). As this approach is not generally well-known, we place a short description of it in Appendix 1.

Let us illustrate our classification with the help of an example. We take one particular process and present fragments of it modeled, using different views. For this purpose, we use a decision-making process used by various committees in Swedish municipalities, see (Andersson et al, 2002). Informal description of this process is as follows:

- A committee decision-making process (instance) is brought into existence when a decision should be passed on a matter that concerns a given committee. The types of decisions range from simple decisions, e.g. deciding on certain information becoming publicly available to complex ones, e.g. approving the next year budget. However, the routines of preparing and making the decision are quite similar for all such cases.

- A decision-making process starts with some stimulus often fixed in a document. It can be an external document, e.g. a motion from a political party, information on a new regulation passed by a parliament, etc., or it can be an internal document, e.g. a protocol from the previous meeting, etc. Before the decision-making committee can pass a resolution, all basic information should be gathered, and somebody should review it and prepare a proposal.

- The basis for a decision usually consists of a number of documents, e.g. external or internal opinions (reviews) on the matter, laws and other regulations that should be taken into consideration, etc. At the moment of the process start, some of those ground documents may exist (e.g. laws and regulations); but others, e.g. internal or external reviews, should be prepared in the frame of the process.

A simplified workflow diagram of this process is presented in Figure 3. Here we used Activity diagram notation from UML 2.0. A fragment of this diagram is presented as an input-output flow in Figure 4. Here, we used IDEF0 notation. Another fragment of the workflow is presented as an agent-related

Figure 3. Possible simplified workflow of a decision-making process

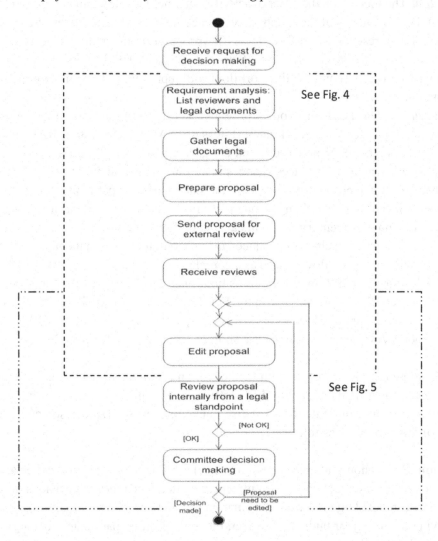

view in Figure 5. Here, we used RAD notation. Lastly, the state-structure for the state-flow model of this process is presented in Figure 6.

PROPERTIES OF BUSINESS PROCESSES

In this section, we will discuss different business process properties that are important to consider when choosing an approach to business process modeling.

Degree of Physicalness and Mobility of Passive Participants

In order to choose the right focus on the process dynamics, it is important to consider what kind of passive participants the process has. The passive participants can belong to one of the following two

Figure 4. A fragment of workflow in IDEF0

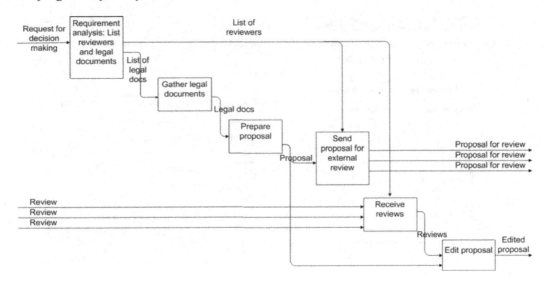

Figure 5. A fragment of workflow in RAD

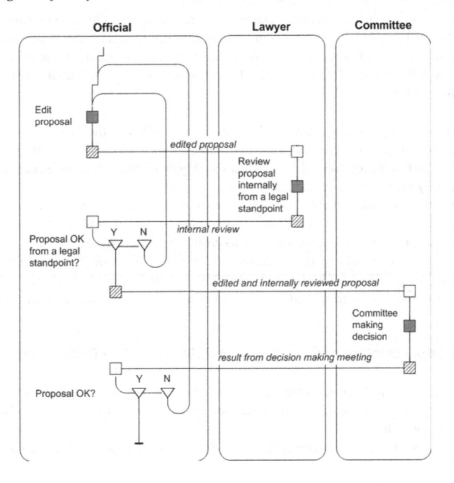

Figure 6. Possible state-structure for a decision-making process

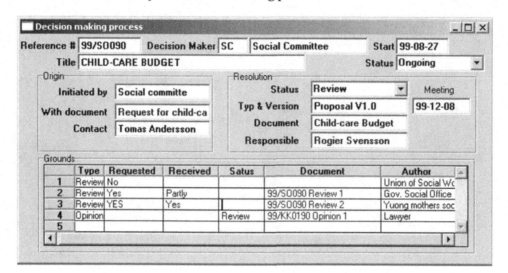

categories:

- Physical – parts of the car, a patient in the hospital, etc.
- Virtual – a decision being made, a company being reorganized (juridical, but not physical person), etc. Normally, a virtual object has some kind of physical representation. A decision being made is fixed in some document, first a proposal, then a law, regulation, order, etc. A company is represented by a number of documents that fixes its business, structure, etc. It may also have some physical office.

The degree of physicalness/virtualness determines the mobility of the passive participants. Heavy physical participants are not very mobile and need some efforts to be moved from one place to another. A virtual objects that are represented as documents are highly mobile, and with the current information technology they may be moved without any efforts.

If a process deals with immobile physical objects that should be passed around between different activities, then the input/output flow may be of great value as it can pinpoint all the logistical problems of the process. If the process deals mostly with the virtual objects, current technology may ensure that as soon as the object has been produced/changed it can be seen and used by whoever needs it. In this case, the input/output flow is of less interest. Workflow or state flow can be preferred.

In our *decision-making example,* all passive participants have virtual nature and as such are highly mobile.

Level of Specialization and Degree of Mobility of Active Participants

Active participants, called agents in the rest of the section, are people and equipment that are required for completing activities. They can be classified according to two dimensions: level of specialization, and degree of mobility.

As far as specialization is concerned, the level can be from a totally specialized agent to a totally universal agent. Totally specialized agent can be used only in one activity, e.g. a person who was trained to do only one thing, or some specialized equipment. Totally universal agent can be used in any activity. A typical example of a universal human agent is an owner of a one-man company. A computer represents a universal agent of non-human kind.

Note that specialization is not equal to agents' ability to do certain kind of job. Specialization may be imposed by laws and regulations that forbid one and the same person to complete two many activities in the frame of the same process instance (e.g., according to Sarbanes Oxley Act).

If a process in question has a lot of highly specialized agents, than the agent-related workflow, which shows the flow of activities through the agents, might be of interest. It may help in optimizing the usage of specialized agents. If most of the agents are universal, then the normal workflow might be better suited to describe the process.

The degree of mobility describes how easy, far and fast the agents can travel. Here, we can have totally immobile agents, like heavy equipment, and totally mobile agents like software that can be executed on site. The mobility/immobility factor of agents should be compared with mobility/immobility factor of passive participants. For example, if all passive participants are mobile, than the mobility of the agents is not important. Consider another example where some agents are highly specialized and immobile, and passive participant that the agents consume, produce, or change are physical but relatively mobile. Than both agent-related workflow view and input/output view are of interest when analyzing such a process.

In our *decision-making example,* some actions require specialized agents, for example, "review proposal from a legal standpoint" can be done only by a lawyer. This however, does not mean that this layer cannot serve as an officer who prepares a proposal in some other decision-making process instance. Specialization in the *decision-making process* is not rigid. It is more on restrictions in the frame of a process instance, than restrictions on the level of the process type.

Degree of Precision of Operational Goals

Operational goals have different level of precision. The operational goal may be very precise, like manufacture a new car, Volvo V-70, with such and such equipment, or less precise, like accept a plan for elderly care for year 2002. Less precise goals are specified in a "functional" manner, i.e. what is to be done and with what restrictions. Examples:

- Accept a plan for elderly care for year 2002 with a total budget of 1 000 000 euro, and main directions as described in law no 789 passed by the parliament on 5 January 2002.
- Create a software system that supports the decision-making process in the municipality of NN. The maximum budget is 100 000 euro, the deadline is 31 December 2002.

The functional specification does not precisely define the result that the process is supposed to produce. It only states constraints that should be observed when delivering the result. Even when an operational goal is defined functionally, there often exists a "projected" specification of what the result of the process should look like. This may take a form of proposals for the decision, or system specifications. The projected result may change in time, and sometimes the result may differ very much from the first projection. The degree of precision for functionally specified operational goals points to how much and how often the end-result can deviate from the initial projection.

When describing processes with functionally specified goals, a special consideration should be given to definition of operational goals in form of constraints, see Appendix 1. Very few approaches of process modeling give a clue of how to do it in a structural way. The state flow view presents a way of defining operational goals in form of constraints on the final states.

The degree of precision of operational goals has correlation with the nature of activities, and process flow. The more precise is the operational goal, the more exact the activities of reaching it could be defined. The same is true for the process flow.

In our *decision-making example,* degree of precision is low.

Autonomy and Characteristics of the Process' Environment

Each process interacts with its environment that is beyond the total control from the process participants. If the level of interaction is low, we speak of highly autonomous processes, for example, training personnel, pure manufacturing, etc. The flow of activities in this kind of processes normally follows the internal logic of the process, and it does not depend much on external events. The workflow approach to the description of the process dynamics will suit this kind of processes very well.

Processes that include interactions with external actors, like customers, supplies, etc., have lesser degree of autonomy. The order of activities for these processes depends not only on the internal logic of the process but also on the external, not always predictable events. For non-autonomous processes, it is important to understand if the environment in which they operate has a friendly collaborative nature, or a less friendly competitive nature.

In the collaborative environment, it is normal that external actors do their part of job as expected. For example, if during the purchasing process the vendor is asked to send a product description, we expect that he/she would do it with pleasure. A maximum disaster that can happen is that he/she forgets, and will need to send a reminder. A process that operates in a collaborative environment can behave like an autonomous process, i.e. the order of activities performed follows the internal logic of the process.

Typical examples of processes that operate in a competitive environment are sales in the presence of competitors, lobbying, negotiations, etc. The activities to be completed in this kind of processes may, at large extent, depend on how the environment is being changed by the actors whose actions are outside the control of the process. The processes of this type are sometimes called event-driven. The workflow view is not very helpful in this case. A state flow approach suits better the task of modeling the event-driven business processes.

In our *decision-making example*, the level of autonomy is usually high. However, all "big" decisions require external reviews from various interest groups, thus process instances related to such decisions have much less autonomy than those that concern simple decisions. When the decision is controversial, the environment can become hostile with interest groups sending negative reviews, and lobbying against the decision.

Nature of Activities

Some activities may be described in the exact manner, i.e. as an order of simple operations. For example, activity *attach a wheel to the car* can be presented in simple operations, like *screw a nut*. Most of the manufacturing activities are of this kind.

Other activities may be described only from the perspective of what results they should produce. For example, a description of activity *review a document* can state that the result should be in form of comments, but it is impossible to dictate exactly how and on what basis the comments should be produced. Many of intellectual activities have such a non-exact nature.

Activities that can be described in the exact manner have an advantage that the time and other resources consumed by an activity can be easily established. These parameters belong to the activity description. For activities that cannot be defined in the exact manner, such parameters may only be estimated on the case-to-case basis. The estimation belongs not to the activity definition, but to the process instance for which the estimation is being made.

For processes with exactly defined activities, it is possible to make simulations of the type "what happens if we cut the time consumed by a particular activity by 30%". For this kind of simulations, the workflow view on the process dynamics may be very useful.

For processes with many non-exactly defined activities, this kind of simulation is practically impossible. Thus, the advantages of time and resource related simulations are not of much importance for this kind of processes.

In our *decision-making example*, many activities have non-exact nature, e.g. prepare a proposal. However, it also includes some simple exact activities, e.g. send proposal to an external reviewer.

Orderliness of Process Flow

When choosing an appropriate view on the process dynamics, it is important to understand if the activities in the process flow follow each other in some exact predefined order, or only partial order can be established. The degree of orderliness correlates very much with other factors described in the previous sections, such as the precision of operational goals, degree of autonomy, friendliness of environment, nature of activities, etc.

For example, a highly autonomous process with a precise operational goal and exactly defined activities will have a high degree of orderliness. Such kind of processes can be properly represented by workflow diagrams. Suppose that in another example we have a non-autonomous process (like "sales") operating in a competitive environment with a functionally defined goal (like "sell something to X") and with non-exactly defined activities (like "analyze customer needs"). The degree of orderliness for such a process will be quite low, and it would be very difficult to present its dynamics with workflow diagrams. A state flow approach is more suitable for modeling such kind of processes.

In our *decision-making example*, orderliness is relatively high. However, with big controversial issues, a proposal can be "thrown back" for revision and new tours of external and internal reviews at any time. The workflow scheme on Figure 3 is much simplified, as it does not reflect such possibility.

PROPERTIES OF THE MODELING ENVIRONMENT

In this section, we will discuss the properties of environment in which the modeling work is being done

Level of Process Maturity in the Organization

The level of process maturity (McCormack&Johnson, 2001) characterizes the amount of knowledge an organization have about its own business processes. The following questions can help to determine the level of maturity:

- Are the processes identified?
- Have strategic and tactical goals been established for each process?
- Are personnel aware of in which processes they participate?

If the organization has a high level of process maturity, the process modeling can be done on the process-by-process basis. For each process, a group of experts who participate in the process can be assigned to investigate the details of workflow, state flow, etc.

If the level of process maturity is low, i.e. processes have not been identified yet, the first job is to find them in a functionally structured organization. One way to do this job might be by going through the organization on the department-by-department basis (and may be even on person-by-person basis). In this case, an input/output approach can be quite useful:

- First, identify what activities are performed in a particular department, wherefrom the input objects come, and where to the results are delivered.
- Sew together activities through their input/outputs.
- Select processes from the resulting cobweb.

For organizations that strictly define responsibilities for each position, the agent-related view may suit the task of identifying business processes. The identification process may start from listing activities for each position/role. Then points of cooperation/communication can be established, and one or several processes can be identified from the resulting net.

In our *decision-making example*, the project started with relatively low process maturity. However, the decision-making process has been identified relatively soon, after two sessions of discussions.

Professional Background of Human Participants

There are two ways to ensure that a process model corresponds to what is going on in the real world. One is to observe the part of the world related to the process in question in real-time. The other one is to discuss the process with the people engaged in it, read operational manuals, etc. The first method is quite expensive (in terms of time), and it is possible to use it only with the processes that produce physical results (e.g. manufacturing). For most of the processes that include intellectual tasks, like design, decision-making, etc., only the second method can be applied.

When the second method is applied, only the people engaged in the process can give a confirmation that a process model corresponds to what happens in reality. Therefore, the process description should be understood by the majority of people who are engaged in the process. Confirmation from the management only is not enough, as the management may not know all details of the process. As far as operational manuals are concerned, they may be out of date, and thus they cannot be considered as a reliable source of confirmation.

The way of presenting a process should be chosen in accordance to what kind of people are engaged in the process, their background and current assignments. If the process team consists mainly of the people with technical background, e.g. engineers, system developers, etc., it is possible to use highly formalized notations, complicated diagrams, etc. These kinds of people use formal definitions in their normal everyday work; thus, for them it will be easy to understand a formal description of business processes and find out what is incorrect.

If on the other hand, the people engaged in the process in question include specialists of non-technical professions, like office workers, doctors, nurses, lawyers, etc., the use of formal notations should be limited. Simple diagrams will help to understand the matter, but complicated many-pages diagrams are not suitable for this kind of professionals. They will not be able to detect errors.

The input/output flow, workflow, and agent-related view, all use diagrammatic notation for presenting the model. To the best of our knowledge, there are no non-diagrammatic approaches related to these views. When working with non-technicians on modeling a complex business process, the diagrammatic presentation can create additional hinder in communication between business analysts and experts in the business domain.

When using the state flow approach, the focus of discussions is placed on the state structure. The state structure can be expressed not only as a formal structure, but also as a two-dimensional picture. As far as our own practice is concerned, the state pictures are quite understandable for not-technical professionals. If a diagrammatic presentation may create an obstacle in communication with non-technicians, choosing the state flow view may help in eliminating this obstacle.

In our *decision-making example*, all human participants were non-technicians. The state flow view has been used to define and visualize the process, see (Andersson et al, 2002).

INTENDED USE OF MODEL

Below, we present a list of usual objectives (the list is not full):

1. To increase the level of process maturity, for example, to make the staff goal and process- conscious, to improve cooperation between colleagues, to educate new employers, etc.
2. Create a basis for process analysis and reengineering.
3. Create a basis for building computer support systems.

Each of these tasks is considered in more details in the subsections below.

In our *decision-making example*, the goal of the project was to write requirements for a computer support system.

Increasing Process Maturity

If increasing the process maturity is on the list of objectives, then we need to choose modeling approach that could help in communicating the process knowledge to all participants of the process. Here, it is particularly important to consider the background of the participants: technical/non-technical, and choose less formal approaches for non-technicians.

Table 1. How to choose a view on process dynamics.

System mission	Process view
Integrate existing systems	Input/output flow
Facilitate coordination / communication	Agent-related view
Introduce strict order in production-like processes	Workflow
Navigate each process to its goal	State flow

Analysis and Reengineering

If analysis and reengineering is on the list of objectives, then first, we need to understand what kind of analysis should/could be completed for a given process. Two types of analysis can be applied to a business process:

- Quantitative, or performance analysis
- Qualitative, or structural analysis

The quantitative analysis means evaluation of the process based on numerical values of important parameters, like rate of success, calendar time required for reaching the goal, costs in time and money, number of activities performed, customer satisfaction, etc. A typical example of this kind of analysis is ABC (Activity-Based Costing).

The quantitative analysis requires statistically reliable information on the process activities. Often, this information exists only for the processes with exactly defined activities. For such activities it is possible to establish how much time, material, manpower, etc. is needed for their execution. Based on this information, it is possible to calculate the costs of the process instance, or the needs for some specialized agents, human or not human. For the first task, a workflow view on the process may be useful. For the second task, an agent-related view may be of great use.

For the processes that have a great deal of non-exactly defined activities, it is difficult to make the quantitative analysis based only on the process model. The model itself would not provide the statistically reliable information, see deliberation on the topic in section "Nature of Activities". This kind of information is difficult to obtain without first introducing some kind of computer support for identified processes.

Qualitative or structural analysis means evaluation of the process based on matching the activities included in it against the goal of the process, i.e. whether they contribute to the goal and in what way. The qualitative analysis can be performed based on a model of the business process. This type of analysis requires detailed representation of the process goal. For relatively complicated goals, the state flow view on the process dynamics may be the only option.

Process reengineering means an approach aiming at improvements of processes, such as eliminate activities that do not contribute to the goal of the process. Results from both quantitative, and qualitative analysis can be used for reengineering. The results from the qualitative analysis can be used to detect the activities that do not lead to the goal (do not add value in other terminologies). Such activities can be eliminated. Another example is rearranging the order of activities execution in such a way that the activities directed at independent sub-goals are executed in parallel. This type of reengineering can be done based on the workflow view for the processes with high degree of orderliness, or based on the state flow view for the processes with low degree of orderliness.

Building Computer Support

If building computer support is on the list of objectives, the following should be understood:

1. If a new system is to be created, or the existing systems are to be integrated?
2. If the system will support only execution of activities, or it will help in running the process. The latter includes: help in keeping track of what has been done, planning new activities, reminding what has to be done, etc.
3. If a new system will impose a strict order in activities execution, division of responsibilities, etc., or it will allow choosing the course of action dependent on how the process is developing in time.

If an integration project is in view, then the input/output flow may help to understand how to connect various systems used in the organization. If the system should impose strict rules, the workflow view, or even agent-related view could be very helpful in building such a system. If the system should allow a high-level degree of flexibility, then the state flow approach can be the most appropriate. The result of deliberation above is summarized in the Table 1.

In our *decision-making example*, the goal corresponded to the last row of the table.

WHAT APPROACH TO CHOOSE?

Based on the discussions in the previous sections, we can conclude that there is no universal approach that would be equally suitable for all types of business processes, all types of objectives, and all levels of process maturity. An organization might need to choose several different approaches to apply at different stages of the process modeling work, and for different objectives.

As we have seen in the previous sections, many factors should be taken into consideration when choosing suitable approaches. Summarizing the discussion, we can give some general recommendations of what approach to choose.

• If an organization is functionally structured and processes are not identified, it is suitable to use input/output view (for example, IDEF0), or agent-related view (for example, RAD).

Input/output view suits organizations that have formal ways of internal communications via some objects, like documents, files, etc. Then the processes can be discovered by following the movement of these objects inside the organization. Agent-related view suits organizations that strictly define responsibilities for each position. The communication channels may be informal, like phone calls, informal meetings, etc. Then the identification process may start from listing activities for each role.

• When the processes are identified the workflow view, or state flow view, or both should be applied, as they are better suited for expressing details of each process. Workflow can be used only

Figure 7. Summary of approaches

Input/output flow	Agent-related flow
Focus on passive participants that are being consumed, produced, or changed by the activities. Important when there is a need to ensure that each passive participant has undergone a specified number of operations in a certain order. Who does the operations has less importance. 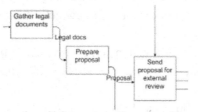 Process description according to this view represents a road map for "transporting" passive participants. Suitable for processes that deal with physical objects.	Focus on agent cooperation, i.e. order in which active participants get and perform their part of work. Important when there is a need to ensure each active participant doing his/her part of the job. How he/she does it is of lesser importance. 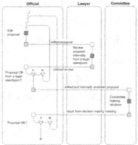 Process description according to this view represents a road along which the process passes through active participants. Suitable for processes with specialized agents, or with strict distribution of responsibilities, e.g. decision legalization.
Workflow	**State flow**
Focus on order of activities. Important when there is a need to ensure that all activities are completed in the right order. Who does the operations and what passive participants are changed during them has less importance. Process description according to this view represents a road map of activities. Suitable for processes with predefined order of activities (operations).	Focus on position reached in relation to the goal after execution of activities. Which activities are executed, and who executes them has less importance.  Process description according to this view is more like a hiking map that represents terrain and some paths across it. Suitable for loosely-structured administrative processes, the ones which do not have strict order of activities or distribution of responsibilities and which consume and produce information rather than physical objects. Also suitable for handling deviations from one of the three others road maps.

if there is some normal order in which activities are completed one after another. If this order is difficult to establish, the state flow view should be used.

In which way the end-result should be documented, depends on the tasks in which this result will be used, e.g. analysis and reengineering, building computer support, etc. Several views may be needed, each one for its own use.

- There is no need to work sequentially, i.e. first get a full input/output view, then identify the processes, than describe each process. As soon as (after initial analysis) some process has been suspected, a different approach can be applied to map this process. The work with input/output view can continue to identify other processes. We just span a new process-mapping project, and continue with identification.

The same is true when modeling a particular process. Suppose, for example, we want to represent results in a state-oriented way, but it is easier to start with workflow diagramming. We do not need to completely finish the workflow description before going over to the state flow description. As soon as we have enough information to make a sketch of the process state structure, we can continue processes mapping using the state flow approach.

Our recommendations are summarized in Figure 7.

CONCLUDING REMARKS

In the previous sections, we demonstrated a way of choosing business process modeling approach based on:

1. Classification of modeling approaches
2. Analysis of properties of modeling objects (business processes in this particular case), modeling environment, and the intended use of the model

We do not insist that our classification of approaches presented in this chapter is the only one, or it is the best one; we just found it useful for our practical task. The same statement concerns the list of business process properties, characteristics of modeling environment, and possible tasks for which a business process model could be used. The lists are not full and they should be complemented when new properties or tasks are discovered.

The material of this chapter has been used in several tutorials for researchers. It was also presented in printed and/or oral form to practitioners in the field, all of whom considered the material consistent with the common sense and their own experience. One particular group remarked that the material both "made the subject more complex and clearer". Under "more complex", they meant that there was a need to consider much more details than they anticipated, for example, the task for which a model was being built. Under "clearer", they meant that the material structured the reality in a way that shows how to complete their task.

The ideas presented in the chapter are also used in our own modeling practice, though not in every detail. Our main approach of modeling is the state-oriented one, thus the final model is expressed and documented in the terms of the state flow model. However, on initial stages of analysis, when the essences of the processes that exist in a particular organization have not been discovered yet, we use other approaches, e.g. simplified workflow diagrams.

The recommendations included in this chapter are not presented in a formal manner. Actually, the chapter does not give readymade answers on what approach to use in such-and-such situations. It gives only some directions on how to deliberate when considering modeling approaches. For the moment, we do not have any theory that can prove that our ideas are the right ones, and we do not know if such theory can be built. The only basis for our suggestions is common sense, and own experience complemented by analysis of the literature. However, the practitioners do need a methodology that can help to choose an appropriate modeling approach, and they need it now. We believe that our work can serve this aim until a more theoretically based methodology is worked out. We also hope that this chapter will stimulate researchers to pay more attention to the practitioners needs. The latter may result in appearing a more theoretically based methodology for choosing among numerous modeling approaches.

ACKNOWLEDGMENT

Many thanks to Paul Johannesson and Gil Regev whose comments helped to improve the text.

REFERENCES

Andersson, T., Andersson-Ceder, A., & Bider, I. (2002). State flow as a way of analyzing business processes – Case studies. *Logistics Information Management, 15*(1), 34–45. doi:10.1108/09576050210412657

Deiters, W., & Gruhn, V. (1998). Process management in practice. Applying the FUNSOFT net approach to large-scale processes. *Automated Software Engineering, 5*(1), 7–25. doi:10.1023/A:1008654224389

FIPS (1993, December). *Standard for integration definition for function modeling (IDEF0)*. National Institute of Standards and Technology (NIST). FIPS publication, 183.

Hammer, M., & Champy, J. (1994). *Reengineering the corporation – A manifesto for business revolution*. London: Nicholas Brealey Publishing.

Huckvale, T., & Ould, M. (1998). *Process modelling- Who, what and how: Role activity diagramming*. Hershey, PA: Idea Group Publishing.

ITU-T (2002). *Specification and Description Language (SDL), Z-100, 08/2002*. Telecommunication Standardization Sector of ITU.

Khomyakov, M., & Bider, I. (2000). Achieving workflow flexibility through taming the chaos. In *OOIS 2000 - 6th International Conference on Object Oriented Information Systems* (pp. 85-92).

Kueng, P., & Kawalek, P. (1997). Goal-based business process models: Creation and evaluation. *Business Process Management Journal, 3*(1), 17–38. doi:10.1108/14637159710161567

Mayer, R. J., Painter, M. K., & Menzel, C. P. Perakath, deWitte, B.P.S., & Blinn, T. (1995). *Information integration for concurrent engineering (IICE) IDEF3 process description capture method report*. Knowledge Based Systems, Inc. Retrieved from http://www.idef.com, 1995.

McCormack, K. P., & Johnson, W. C. (2001). *Business process orientation: Gaining the e-business: Competitive advantage.* St. Lucie Press.

OMG. (2007). *OMG Unified Modeling Language (UML), Superstructure, V2.1.2.* Object Management Group.

Perjons, E., Bider, I., & Andersson, B. (2007). Building and exploiting a business process model for lobbying: Experience report. [CIIMA]. *Communications of the IIMA, 7*(3), 1–14.

van der Aalst, W. M. P. (1999). *How to handle dynamic change and capture management information? An approach based on generic workflow models.* Retrieved from http://wwwis.win.tue.nl/~wsinwa/genwf.ps

KEY TERMS AND DEFINITIONS

Agent (or Active Participant): a process participant that perform actions aimed at changing the passive participants.

Agent-Related Flow: an approach to business process modeling in which focus is placed on agent communication.

Business Process: a set of partially ordered activities aimed at reaching a well-defined goal.

Input/Output Flow: an approach to business process modeling in which focus is placed on the flow of passive participants.

Modeling Approach: a modeling language and related guidelines on how to use it in practice.

Passive Participant: a process participant that is consumed, produced, or changed by the activities in a business process.

Process Participant: an artifact or human being engage in business process in one way or another.

State Flow: an approach to business process modeling in which focus is placed on changes produced in the real world.

Workflow: an approach to business process modeling in which focus is placed on the order of activities in time.

APPENDIX 1 – STATE FLOW VIEW ON BUSINESS PROCESSES

This appendix gives the main ideas of the state flow view on business processes and represents a modified and shortened version of discussion from (Khomyakov&Bider, 2000).

The main concept of the state flow view on business processes is the *process' state*. The process' state is aimed to show how much has been done to achieve the operational goal of a process instance, and how much is still to be done.

A *state* of a business process is defined by a construct that reflects the relevant part of the business world at a given moment of time. The internal structure of the state construct depends on the business process type to which the current instance belongs. An example, of such structure for a business process related to a customer order is represented in Figure 8, which is a screenshot from a state-oriented business process support system.

The state structure in Figure 8 includes: (a) attributes (variables), such as *To pay*, *Paid*, *Ordered*, etc., and (b) references to various human and non-human participants of the process, like *Customer*, *Products*, etc. The names of the attributes above correspond to the labels in the screenshot from Figure 8; the positions of some of these attributes are additionally pinpointed by arrows. Note that the state structure may include repeating groups, like *Products* in Figure 8, which means that some attributes, like *Ordered* and *Delivered* will have multiple values, one for each item of the group.

Figure 8. State representation of order processing from (Khomyakov&Bider, 2000)

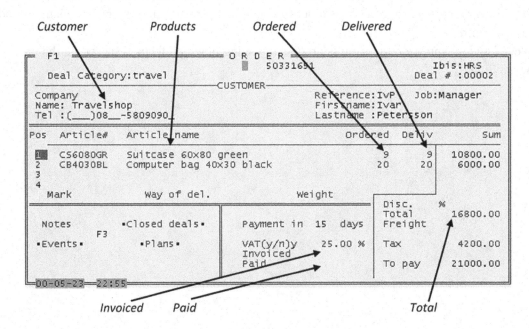

A *goal* of a business process can be defined as a set of conditions that must be fulfilled before a process instance can be considered as finished (end of the process instance trajectory in the state space). A state that satisfies these conditions is called a *final state* of the process. The set of final states for the process in Figure 8 can be defined as follows: (a) for each ordered product *Ordered = Delivered*; (b) *To pay = Total + Freight + Tax*; (c) *Invoiced = To pay*; (d) *Paid = Invoiced*. These conditions define a surface in the state space of this process type.

The process is driven forward through activities executed either automatically or with a human assistance. An activity can be viewed as an *action* aimed at changing the process state in a special way. Activities can be planned first and executed later. A *planned activity* records such information as type of action (goods shipment, compiling a program, sending a letter), planned date and time, deadline, name of a person responsible for an action, etc.

All activities currently planned for a process instance make up its *operational plan* or to-do list, see Figure 9 for an example. The plan lists activities the execution of which diminishes the *distance* between the current state of the process instance and the *projected* final state. The meaning of the term distance depends on the business process in question. Here, we use this term informally. For example, activities to plan for the process in Figure 8 can be defined in the following manner:

- If for some product *Ordered > Delivered*, *shipment* should be performed, or
- If *To pay > Invoiced*, an *invoice* should be sent, etc

The plan together with the "passive" state (attributes and references) constitutes a *generalized state* of the process, the plan being an "active" part (engine) of it. When an activity is executed, a process changes its generalized state. Changes may concern the passive and/or active parts of the state. At a minimum, the executed activity disappears from the plan. In addition, changes are introduced in attributes and references and/or new activities are planned to drive the process forward.

With regards to the generalized state, the notion of a *valid* state can be defined in addition to the notion of *final state*. To be valid, the generalized state should include all activities required for moving the process to the next state towards the goal. A business process type can be defined as a set of valid generalized states. A business process instance is considered as belonging to this type if for any given moment of time its generalized state belongs to this set. This definition can be converted into an operational proce-dure called *rules of planning*. The rules specify what activities could/should be added to/deleted from

Figure 9. Process's plan that complements the state from Figure 9.

	DeadLine	Activity	Resp	Counterpart
1	000526	Invoicing	HRS	Petersson
2				
3				
4				
5				

an invalid generalized state to make it valid. Using these rules, the process instance is driven forward in the following manner. First, an activity from the operative plan is executed and the state of the process is changed. Then, an operative plan is corrected to make the generalized state valid; as a result, some actions may be added to the plan and some be removed from it.

Section 2
Adaptive Technologies for Business Process Management

Chapter 5
Dynamic and Context–Aware Process Adaptation

Michael Adams
Queensland University of Technology, Australia

Arthur ter Hofstede
Queensland University of Technology, Australia

Nick Russell
Eindhoven University of Technology, The Netherlands

Wil van der Aalst
Eindhoven University of Technology, The Netherlands

ABSTRACT

This chapter re-examines the principles that underpin business process technologies to derive a novel approach that moves beyond the traditional assembly-line metaphor. Using a set of principles derived from activity theory, a system has been implemented, using a service oriented architecture, that provides support for dynamic and extensible flexibility, evolution and exception handling in business processes, based on accepted ideas of how people actually perform their work tasks. The resulting system, called the worklet service, makes available all of the benefits offered by process aware information systems to a wider range of organisational environments.

INTRODUCTION

Organisations are constantly seeking efficiency improvements for their business processes. To help achieve those goals, many are turning to Process-Aware Information Systems (PAIS) to configure and control those processes (Dumas et al., 2005; van der Aalst & van Hee, 2004) by supporting their modelling, analysis, enactment and management (zur Muehlen, 2004; Casati, 1998). The key benefits organisations seek by implementing PAIS solutions include: improved efficiency, better process control, improved customer service and business process improvement.

DOI: 10.4018/978-1-60566-669-3.ch005

The use of PAIS has grown by concentrating on modelling rigidly structured business processes that in turn derive well-defined workflow instances (Bider, 2005; Joeris, 1999; Reichert & Dadam, 1997). However, the proprietary process definition frameworks imposed make it difficult to support (i) dynamic evolution and adaptation (i.e. modifying process definitions during execution) following unexpected or developmental change in the business processes being modelled (Borgida & Murata, 1999); and (ii) deviations from the prescribed process model at runtime (Rinderle et al., 2004; Casati, 1998).

But change is unavoidable in the modern workplace. To remain effective and competitive, organisations must continually adapt their business processes to manage the rapid changes demanded by the dynamic nature of the marketplace or service environment. Also, a large proportion of workplaces undertake activities that do not easily conform to rigid or constricting representations of their work practices. And even in the most concrete processes deviations will occur within almost every instantiation.

If PAIS could be extended to meet the challenges of evolutionary and unexpected change in business processes, then their applicability would widen to include a far greater proportion of workplaces. Such support would not only benefit existing users of process-aware technologies, but would also introduce those businesses which employ more creative or ad-hoc processes to the range of benefits that PAIS offer.

This Chapter offers one solution designed to meet that challenge. The primary objectives of this Chapter are to provide:

- An overview of literature on approaches to exception handling and flexibility in Process-Aware Information Systems;
- A discussion of theoretical underpinnings of work practices;
- A discussion of a comprehensive framework for exception handling;
- The introduction of a concrete approach for exception handling based on this framework;
- The introduction of a concrete approach to processes that require on-the-fly change;
- A description of an (open source) implementation of these approaches within a state-of-the-art workflow system; and
- The presentation of an elaborated example.

BACKGROUND

A business process can be defined as a composite set of tasks that comprise coordinated computer-based and human activities (Leymann, 2006). A business process model or schema is a formal representation of work procedures that controls the sequence of performed tasks and the allocation of resources to them (Oberweis, 2005).

The development of a business process model typically begins with an analysis of current business procedures and processes. Subsequently, a model is developed based on those practices and business rules, then input into a PAIS and repetitively executed, supporting and giving formal structure and flow control to those processes. However, translating abstract concepts and descriptions of business practices and rules into tangible process models is a far from trivial exercise. There are sizeable development costs involved in mapping an abstract process to a structured schema, which must be weighed against the perceived cost benefits that the system will deliver. Therefore, current systems are most advantageous where they provide support for standardised, repetitive activities that do not vary between execution instances.

But even in highly structured environments, it is difficult (if not impossible) to successfully capture all work activities, and in particular all of the task sequences possible, in a static process model. It is also the case that, for any given human activity, the process for successfully completing the activity is constantly evolving. Change can also be introduced via many sources, including government regulation, new competitors, new markets, improvements in plant and equipment, workforce and resource availability and so on.

A recent Workflow Management Coalition survey found that 75 per cent of respondents reported they were currently performing work on improving existing processes (up to 92 per cent for the Finance sector) and 56 per cent were currently involved in a major business process redesign (Palmer, 2007). Such statistics underscore the frequency of organisational change and importance of providing a process management system which supports flexibility and the ability to adapt to change.

It is because of the discrepancies between real-world activities and formal representations of them that process instances typically experience *exceptions* during their execution. Rather than being considered an error, an exception in a business process is simply a deviation from the expected control flow or was unaccounted for in the original process model. Exceptions are a fundamental part of most organisational processes (Kammer et al., 2000); in fact, a substantial proportion of the everyday tasks carried out in a business can be categorised as exception handling work (Barthelmess & Wainer, 1995). Historically, exception handling within PAIS has fallen well short, particularly after execution has commenced (Kammer et al., 2000).

Thus a large group of business processes do not easily map to the rigid modelling structures provided, due to the lack of flexibility inherent in a framework that, by definition, imposes rigidity. This inflexibility extends to the management of exceptions, which places further limits on how accurately a process model can reflect the actual business process it is based on. Rather, process models are 'system-centric', meaning that work processes are *straight-jacketed* (van der Aalst et al., 2005) into the paradigm supplied, rather than the paradigm reflecting the way work is actually performed (Bider, 2005). As a result, users are forced to work outside of the system, and/or constantly revise the process model, in order to successfully complete their activities, thereby negating the perceived efficiency gains sought by implementing a process management solution in the first place.

Criteria for Process Adaptation

We propose six functionality criteria that a WfMS would need to meet to better support process adaptation, and thus a wider variety of work practices. Each criterion broadly represents a major topic area of workflow research and is outlined below.

Criterion 1: Flexibility and Re-use. The goal of any human activity may be realised in various ways through the use of different actions. Conversely, the same action can be a component of several different activities. While some workplaces have strict operating procedures because of the work they do (for example air traffic control) many workplaces successfully complete activities by developing a set of informal routines that can be flexibly and dynamically combined to solve a large range of problems. Thus, realising an activity in a contingent environment is aided considerably by having a set of actions to choose from (Bardram, 1997) for each task. This denotes a crucial factor for the representation of flexible workflows. At any point in time, there may be several possible sequences that can be followed utilising a sub-set of available actions to achieve the objective of the activity. Choices should be made dependent on the actual circumstances of the activity at that point in time. The availability of a catalog of actions would also encourage re-use. By using a modular approach, a resultant model may range from a simple skeleton to which actions can be added at runtime (supporting dynamic adaptation) or may be a fully developed model representing the *a priori* complete work practice, depending on user and organisational needs.

Criterion 2: Adaptation via Reflection. Workflow systems should support evolutionary adaptation of processes based on the experience gained during each execution of the process (Edmond & ter Hofstede, 2000). All human activity is guided by the anticipation of fulfilling the objective of that activity. An instantiation of a plan is fundamentally distinct from the plan itself. A plan is a work resource (Schael, 1998), detached from concrete activities, and is used to organise and divide the work amongst the participants involved. To achieve the expected result, the actions and operations contained in the plan (conceptual) have to be adjusted to the material conditions of each situation (contextual) (Symon et al., 1996). Depending on the context of the instantiation, some actions will mirror the plan, while other parts of the plan may be either discarded or augmented in some way. After completion, a comparison is made between the anticipated and actual outcomes, and any incongruities or deviations from the plan add to the experience of the participants, and so give rise to a learning situation. Typically, workflow systems ignore these deviations, resulting in systems that remain static in the face of change.

Criterion 3: Dynamic Evolution of Tasks. Workflow systems should support the evolution of tasks towards individual specialisations without risking the loss of motivation for the overall activity. Almost all work practices are collective activities that involve cooperation and mutual dependence between participants. Even so, practices generally evolve towards minimising mutual articulation among individuals, without jeopardising the overall objective of the collective activity. However, over-specialisation of an action may lead to deskilling, and therefore loss of motivation, of the workers involved (Kaasbøll & Smørdal, 1996). This phenomenon, referred to as context-tunnelling (Riss et al., 2005), becomes an issue when a participant is no longer motivated by the objective of the activity. Workflows structured as an assembly line are often the cause of such situations, because they force workers to become mere processors in a product delivery chain --- that is, the human contextual factors are ignored.

Criterion 4: Locality of Change. Modifications should be able to be fully applied by changing a minimal number of components, and should impact minimally on associated components. Related to support for flexibility is support for locality of change. Bass, Clement and Kazman (1998) suggest that increasing the adaptability of software is largely a function of how localised necessary modifications can be made. In terms of workflow process models, this idea suggests two desirable and related goals. Firstly, to ensure that a workflow process model is strongly adaptable, modifications should be able to be limited to as few components as possible. Secondly, any changes made within those components should impact on other components to the least extent possible.

Criterion 5: Comprehensibility of Process Models. Process models should be comprehensible to all stakeholders, and should support representation at different levels of granularity. A major limiting factor in the uptake of workflow systems is the complexity of the models developed for all but the most trivial activities. WfMSs that require the development of monolithic models fail to take into account the complexities in adapting and evolving those models. Also, there may be stakeholders that have difficulty in interpreting models that contain many possible paths on a single plane, and/or require different levels of abstraction to be presented.

Criterion 6: The Elevation of Exceptions to "First-Class Citizens". Workflow exceptions should not be regarded as errors but as events that provide an opportunity for a learning experience and therefore are a valuable part of any work practice. Generally, commercial WfMSs take the view that exceptions are to be considered errors. As such, they are seen to be annoyances which either should have been foreseen and therefore prevented from occurring in the first place, or perceived as impossible to predict and therefore best left handled off-system. However, exceptions (contradictions, diversions, tensions, deviations) are a normal and valuable part of every work activity, which can be used to refine or evolve the process towards improved efficiencies. As a result, exceptions should be implemented in a positive fashion to better reflect (within the workflow model) the actuality of the work practice it supports.

Survey of Literature and Related Systems

The following reviews the levels of support for flexibility and exception handling in several of the leading commercial process management products and a number of academic prototypes[1]. Unless explicitly stated otherwise, information regarding the products has been gleaned from product manuals, published literature and white papers. The version numbers specified for the commercial products are the versions that were reviewed.

Since the mid-nineties much research has been carried out on issues related to dynamic flexibility and exception handling in workflow management systems. Such research was initiated because, generally, commercial workflow management systems provide only basic support for handling exceptions (Russell et al., 2006; zur Muehlen, 2004) (besides modelling them directly in the main 'business logic'), and, where extant, each deals with them in a proprietary manner; they typically require the model to be fully defined before it can be instantiated; and changes must be incorporated by modifying the model statically. Further, there is minimal support for handling: workitem failures (and even when that support is offered, they must be manually terminated); external triggers; and only one system reviewed offers some constraint violation management (Russell et al., 2006).

Tibco iProcess Suite (version 10.5) (formerly *Staffware*) (TIBCO, 2006) provides constructs called *event nodes*, from which a separate pre-defined exception handling path or sequence can be activated when an exception occurs at that point. It may also suspend a process either indefinitely or wait until a deadline occurs. If a workitem cannot be processed it is forwarded to a 'default exception queue' where it may be manually purged or re-submitted. A compensation workitem may be initiated when a deadline occurs. Also, a workitem may be externally triggered, or 'wait' until an external trigger occurs. Certain tasks may be manually skipped at runtime.

An optional component of the iProcess Suite is the *Process Orchestrator* (Georgeff & Pyke, 2003), which provides for the dynamic allocation of sub-processes at runtime. It requires a construct called a "dynamic event" to be explicitly modelled that will execute a number of sub-processes listed in a pre-defined 'array' when execution reaches that event. Which sub-processes execute depend on predefined data conditionals matching the current case. There is no scope for dynamically refining conditionals, nor adding sub-processes at runtime.

COSA (version 5.4) (COSA, 2005) provides for the definition of external 'triggers' or events that may be used to start a sub-process. All events and sub-processes must be defined at design time, although models can be modified at runtime (but only for future instantiations). When a workitem fails the activity can be rolled back or restarted. A compensating activity can be triggered either externally or on deadline expiry. *COSA* also allows *manual* ad-hoc runtime adaptations such as reordering, skipping, repeating, postponing or terminating steps.

WebSphere MQ Workflow (version 6.0) (IBM, 2005) supports deadlines and, when they occur, will branch to a pre-defined exception path and/or send a notification message to a pre-defined user or administrator. Administrators can manually suspend, restart or terminate processes, or reallocate tasks. Only transaction-level exceptions are recognised, and they are simply recorded in the audit log.

SAP Workflow (version 6.20) (SAP, 2006) supports conditional branching, where a list of conditions (each linked to a process branch) is parsed and the first evaluating to true is taken; all branches are predefined. Exception events are provided for cancelling workflow instances, for checking workitem pre and post constraints, and for 'waiting' until an external trigger occurs. Exception handling processes may be assigned to a workflow based on the type of exception that has occurred, although the handlers for each are specified at design time, and only one may be assigned to each type – that is, filtering through a set of possible handlers based on the context of the case is not supported. When an exception occurs and a corresponding handler is found, all tasks in the block where the exception is caught are cancelled.

FLOWer (version 2.1) (Berens, 2005), is of the 'case-handling' paradigm); the process model (or 'plan') describes only the preferred way of doing things and a variety of mechanisms are offered to allow users to deviate in a controlled manner (van der Aalst et al., 2005). For example, a deadline expiry can automatically complete a workitem. Also, some support for constraint violation is offered: a plan may be automatically created or completed when a specified condition evaluates to true (Russell et al., 2006).

There have been a number of academic prototypes developed in the last decade (although activity was greater during the first half); very few have had any impact on the offerings of commercial systems (zur Muehlen, 2004). Several of the more widely acknowledged are discussed here.

ADEPT (Reichert et al., 2005) supports modification of a process during execution (i.e. add, delete and change the sequence of tasks) both at the model (dynamic evolution) and instance levels (ad-hoc changes). Such changes are made to a traditional monolithic model and must be achieved via manual intervention, abstracted to a high level interaction. The system also supports forward and backward 'jumps' through a process instance, but only by authorised staff who instigate the skips manually (Reichert et al., 2003).

The *AdaptFlow* prototype (Greiner et al', 2004) provides a hybrid approach to flexibility and exception handling. It supports ECA rules-based detection of exceptions and the dynamic adaptation of process instances, although an authorised user must confirm each adaptation manually before it is applied (alternate manual handling to override the dynamic adaptation offered is also supported). Also, the rule classifications and available exception handling actions are limited to medical treatment scenarios.

AgentWork (Muller et al., 2004) provides the ability to modify process instances by dropping and adding individual tasks based on events and ECA rules. However, changes are limited to individual tasks, rather than the task-process-specification hierarchy. Also, the possibility exists for conflicting rules to generate incompatible actions, which requires manual intervention and resolution.

A further approach using incompletely specified process definitions is found in the *SwinDeW (Swinburne Decentralised Workflow)* project (Yan et al., 2004). *SwinDew* is a peer-to-peer based decentralised model, where a process definition is split into a set of task partitions and distributed to peers, and on-the-fly process elaboration is performed at runtime. Thus, a multi-tiered process modelling and execution framework is provided.

CBRFlow (Weber et al., 2004) uses a case-based reasoning approach to support adaptation of predefined workflow models to changing circumstances by allowing (manual) annotation of business rules during run-time via incremental evaluation by the user. Thus users must be actively involved in the inference process during each case.

An approach, which integrates *CBRFlow* into the *ADEPT* framework, is described in (Rinderle et al., 2005). In doing so, semantic information about the reasons for change, and traceability data, are presented to the *ADEPT* user/administrator to support decision making processes. The information can also be used to facilitate reuse of ad-hoc changes from similar scenarios. When deviations from a process schema are required, the case-based reasoning component assists the user to find similar previous cases through a series of questions and answers, one of which may then be applied to the current instance. While the process is quite user-intensive, the approach does provide a good example of the combination of contextual information with exception handling techniques.

Pesic and van der Aalst (2006) point out that the majority of languages used to described and define business process models are of a procedural nature, which limits their effectiveness in very flexible environments, and introduce a declarative approach to process modelling, called *DecSerFlow*. A graphical language, it avoids many of the assumptions, constraints, conditions and rules that must be explicitly specified in procedural languages to perform flexible activities, the inclusion of which typically lead to an over-specification of the process.

In summary, approaches to flexibility and exception handling usually rely on a high-level of runtime user and/or administrator interactivity, which directly impedes on the basic aim of PAIS (to bring greater efficiencies to work practices) and distracts users from their primary work roles into process support activities. Another common limitation is the complex update, modification and migration issues required to evolve process models.

THEORETICAL FOUNDATION

Whenever a series of actions is undertaken with a view to achieving a pre-conceived result, some plan or set of principles is implemented that guide and shape those actions towards that goal. To be effective, a plan must be described using constructs and language that are relevant to both the actions being performed and the desired result, and be comprehensible by its participants and stakeholders. In business process terms, analysts seek to model some aspect of the real world by using a metaphor that bears some resemblance to the real world, but also represents an understanding of computational processes. Such metaphors are abstract constructs that form a common reference model that assist in representing the external world through computers.

The fundamental and widely understood *computational* metaphor (Stein, 1999) takes a set of inputs, performs a series of functional steps in a strict sequence, and, on completion, produces some output that represents the goal of the process. This metaphor describes a single, centralised thread of control, which very much reflects its mathematical ancestry but also reveals an underlying misconception in the common perception of technological 'progress'. Technological developments are, according to Holt (1997), "as much affected by fashion as clothing". Technologies do not evolve automatically (as Marx assumed) but rather reflect prevailing human culture (Mumford, 1963). That is, new technologies are derived from perceived needs and realised, not in isolation, but through the conventions and norms of their social *milieu*.

Thus the traditional computational metaphor reveals the influence of pioneers such as von Neumann and his team, and especially Turing, whose abstract machine proposed 'step-at-a-time' processing

(Turing, 1936), and which in turn reflects the influence on prevailing thought of the contemporaneous development of assembly-line manufacturing (Hendriks-Jansen, 1996).

As contemporary technological advances influenced the structure of early computers, so too has the computational metaphor become a significant model system for the conceptualisation and interpretation of complex phenomena, from cognition to economics to ecology (Stein, 1999). Of particular interest is the way the metaphor has been applied to the definition of organisational work processes. The computational metaphor remains applicable to well-defined problem domains where goal-directed, sequential, endpoint-driven planning is required (Stein, 1999). Such domains were the early beneficiaries of process management systems. Consequently, current commercial process management systems provide support for standardised, repetitive activities that do not vary between execution instances.

Adherence to the metaphor by PAIS has been an important factor in their acceptance by organisations with structured work practices. Descriptions can be found throughout the workflow literature to the 'processing', 'manufacturing' and 'assembly-line' modelling metaphors that are employed by commercial systems. However, while the Workflow Management Coalition claims that "even office procedures can be processed in an assembly line" (2002), there are many aspects where administrative and service processes differ from manufacturing processes (van der Aalst & Berens, 2001). It may be that the computational metaphor has been an inhibiting factor in the development of systems able to effectively support flexible work practices.

A process management system that better supports flexible work environments requires a sound theoretical foundation that avoids the computing metaphor, but rather describes how work is actually conceived, carried out and reflected upon. One such theoretical base can be found in *Activity Theory*.

Activity Theory is a powerful and clarifying descriptive tool, rather than a strongly predictive theory, and incorporates notions of intentionality, history, mediation, collaboration and development, focussing on understanding everyday practice in the real world (Nardi, 1996).

Activity Theory originated in the former Soviet Union during the 1920's and 30's as part of the cultural-historical school of psychology founded by Vygotsky, who began working on the theory at a time when the prevailing psychological theories were based on reflexology (which attempted to reduce all psychological phenomena to a series of stimulus-response chains).

In the form presented by Leontiev (1974), Activity Theory subsequently became one of the major Soviet psychology theories, and was used in areas such as the education of disabled children and the ergonomic design of equipment control panels.

In the 1980's and 90's, Activity Theory came to the attention of Scandinavian information technology researchers (for example: (Nardi, 1996), (Kuutti, 1996) and (Bødker & Greenbaum, 1993)). Their contribution was a revised formulation of Activity Theory, and also the application of Activity Theory to human-computer interface design.

Briefly, Activity Theory states that human activity has four basic characteristics (Bardram, 1997):

1. Every activity is directed towards a material or ideal object satisfying a need, which forms the overall motive of the activity.
2. Every activity is mediated by artefacts, either external (a tool) or internal (cognitive: using concepts, knowledge and experience).
3. Each individual activity is almost always part of collective activities, structured according to the work practice in which they take place. For example, a patient diagnosis can seldom be established

without reference to a diversity of medical information. Thus collective activities are organised according to a division of labour.

4. Finally, human activity can be described as a hierarchy with three levels: *activities* realised through chains of *actions*, and performed through *operations*:

   ◦ An *activity* consists of one or more actions, and describes the overall objective or goal.

   ◦ An *action* equates to a single task carried out to achieve some pre-conceived result. Each action is achieved through operations determined by the actual conditions in the context of the activity.

   ◦ *Operations* describe the actual performance of the action, and are dependant on the context, or conditions that exist for each action.

In Adams et al. (2003), ten fundamental principles, representing an interpretation of the central themes of Activity Theory applicable to an understanding of organisational work practices, were derived and are summarised below.

- **Principle 1: Activities are hierarchical.** An activity consists of one or more actions. Each action consists of one or more operations.
- **Principle 2: Activities are communal.** An activity almost always involves a community of participants working towards a common objective.
- **Principle 3: Activities are contextual.** Contextual conditions and circumstances deeply affect the way the objective is achieved in any activity.
- **Principle 4: Activities are dynamic.** Activities are never static but evolve asynchronously, and historical analysis is often needed to understand the current context of the activity.
- **Principle 5: Activities are mediated.** An activity is mediated by tools, rules and divisions of labour.
- **Principle 6: Actions are chosen contextually.** A repertoire of actions and operations is created, maintained and made available to any activity, which may be performed by making contextual choices from the repertoire.
- **Principle 7: Actions are understood contextually.** The immediate goal of an action may not be identical to the objective of the activity of which the action is a component. It is enough to have an understanding of the overall objective of the activity to motivate successful execution of an action.
- **Principle 8: Plans guide work.** A plan is not a blueprint or prescription of work to be performed, but merely a guide which is modified depending on context during the execution of the work.
- **Principle 9: Exceptions have value.** Exceptions are merely deviations from a pre-conceived plan. Deviations will occur with almost every execution of the plan, and give rise to a learning experience which can then be incorporated into future executions.
- **Principle 10: Granularity based on perspective.** A particular piece of work might be an activity or an action depending on the perspective of the viewer.

Table 1 shows a summary mapping of the ten principles to the set of criteria described in the *Background* section that a PAIS supporting the principles would meet.

Activity Theory offers a number of interesting insights into process management domains, particularly the related issues of adaptability, flexibility, evolution and exception handling. The principles derived

Table 1. Summary mapping of Activity Theory principles vs. workflow functionality criteria

	Flexibility & Re-use	Adaptation via Reflection	Dynamic Evolution	Locality of Change	Comprehensibility of Models	Exceptions as 'First Class Citizens'
Activities are Hierarchical	√			√	√	
Activities are Communal			√			
Activities are Contextual	√	√				
Activities are Dynamic		√	√	√		
Mediation of Activity	√	√	√			
Actions are Chosen Contextually	√					√
Actions are Understood Contextually			√	√		
Plans Guide Work		√			√	√
Exceptions have Value		√	√			√
Granularity Based on Perspective					√	

in this chapter have formed the theoretical foundations for the implementation and deployment of the system described in the following sections. Activity Theory was chosen as the theoretical framework because it provides, as demonstrated in this Section, a tight fit between actual work practices and the requirements of PAIS designed to support them. This Section does not claim Activity Theory to be the only applicable theoretical framework, but merely one from which sound principles of work practice for adaptive business processes could be derived.

CONCEPTUAL FRAMEWORK

In the previous section, a set of principles was derived from Activity Theory and applied to the issues of flexibility and exception handling for workflow systems. From that mapping of principles to issues, it was found that:

1.   Workflow management systems typically have trouble supporting all but the most rigid business processes precisely because their frameworks are based on computing metaphors rather than accepted ideas of actual work practices.
2.   A workflow management system that sought to overcome those issues must be built around a framework that better mirrors the way people perform work activities in organisational environments.

The consideration of these findings formed the conceptual foundations of a discrete service that transforms otherwise static workflow processes into fully flexible and dynamically extensible process instances that are also supported by dynamic exception handling capabilities. That service has been named the *Worklet Service*.

Worklets: A Conceptualisation

Fundamentally, a workflow management system that is based on the principles derived from Activity Theory would satisfy the following criteria:

- *A flexible modelling framework* — a process model is to be regarded as a guide to an activity's objective, rather than a prescription for it;
- *A repertoire of actions* — extensible at any time, the repertoire would be made available for each task during each process instance;
- *Dynamic, contextual choice* — from the repertoire at runtime by considering the specific context of the executing instance; and
- *Dynamic process evolution* — allow the repertoire to be dynamically extended, thus providing support for unexpected process deviations for all current and future instantiations of the process, leading to natural process evolution.

Thus, to accommodate flexibility, such a system would provide each task of a process instance with the ability to be linked to an extensible repertoire of actions, one of which to be contextually and dynamically chosen at runtime to carry out the task. To accommodate exception handling, such a system would provide an extensible repertoire of exception-handling processes to each process instance, members of which to be contextually and dynamically chosen to handle exceptions as they occur.

Using a service-oriented architecture, such a system, the Worklet Service, has been implemented. To support flexibility, the service presents the repertoire-member actions as *worklets*. In effect, a worklet is a small, self-contained, complete workflow process which handles one specific task (action) in a larger, composite process (activity)[2]. A top-level or parent process model is developed that describes the workflow at a macro level. From a manager process instance, worklets may be contextually selected and invoked from the repertoire of each enabled task, using an associated extensible set of selection rules. New worklets may be added to the repertoire of a task at any time (even during process execution) as different approaches to completing a task are developed, derived from the context of each process instance. Importantly, the new worklet becomes an implicit part of the process model for all current and future instantiations, avoiding issues of migration and version control (van der Aalst & Basten, 2002; van der Aalst, 2001; Kradolfer & Geppert, 1999; Joeris & Herzog, 1998). In this way, the process model undergoes implicit, dynamic, natural evolution.

In addition, for each anticipated exception, a separate repertoire of exception handling processes, known as *exlets* may be defined, to be dynamically incorporated into a running process instance on an as-needed basis. That is, for any exception that may occur at the task, case instance or specification level, a repertoire of exlets may be provided, the most appropriate one system-selected at runtime based on the context of the case and the type of exception that has occurred. Further, worklets that are invoked as compensation processes within an exlet are constructed *in exactly the same way* as those created to support flexibility, which in turn are constructed in the same way as ordinary, static process models.

In the occurrence of an unanticipated exception (i.e. an event for which a handling exlet has not yet been defined), then either an existing exlet can be manually selected (re-used) from the repertoire, one may be adapted on the fly to handle the immediate situation, or a new exlet constructed and immediately deployed, in each case allowing execution of the process instance that raised the exception to take the necessary action and either continue unhindered, or, if specified in the exception handler, to terminate, as required. Crucially, the method used to handle the new exception and a record of its context are captured by the system and immediately become an implicit part of the parent process model, and so a history of the event and the method used to handle it is recorded for future instantiations.

Context, Rules and Worklet Selection

For any situation, there are multiple situational and personal factors that combine to influence a choice of action. That set of factors that are deemed to be *relevant* to the current situation we call its *context*.

A taxonomy of contextual data that may be recorded and applied to a workflow instance may be categorised as follows (examples are drawn from a medical treatment process):

- **Generic (case independent):** data attributes that can be considered likely to occur within any process (of course, the data values change from case to case). Such data would include descriptors such as when created, created by, times invoked, last invoked, current status; and role or agent descriptors such as experience, skills, rank, history with this process and/or task and so on. Process execution states and process log data also belong to this category.
- **Case dependent with *a priori* knowledge:** that set of data that are known to be pertinent to a particular case when it is instantiated. Generally, this data set reflects the data variables of a particular process instance. Examples are: patient name and id, blood pressure readings, height, weight, symptoms and so on; deadlines both approaching and expired; and diagnoses, treatments and prescribed medications.
- **Case dependent with no *a priori* knowledge:** that set of data that only becomes known when the case is active and deviations from the known process occur. Examples in this category may include complications that arise in a patient's condition after triage, allergies to certain medications and so on.

Methods for capturing contextual propositions typically focus on collecting a complete set of knowledge from an 'expert' and representing it in a computationally suitable way (Kang et al., 1998). Such approaches depend heavily on the expert's ability to interpret their own expertise and express it in non-abstract forms (Manago & Kodraoff, 1987). Consequently, the lack of systematic dissemination of expertise has proved a major barrier to the development and use of improvements in exception handling methods in business processes (Klein & Dellarocas, 2000).

One bottom-up approach to the capture of contextual data that offers an alternative method to global knowledge construction is *Ripple Down Rules* (RDR), which comprise a hierarchical set of rules with associated exceptions, first devised by Compton and Jansen (1988).

The fundamental feature of RDR is that it avoids the difficulties inherent in attempting to pre-compile a systematic understanding, organisation and assembly of all knowledge in a particular domain. The RDR method is well established and fully formalised (Scheffer, 1996) and has been implemented as the basis for a variety of commercial applications, including systems for reporting DNA test results,

Figure 1. Example rule tree (ItemPreConstraint tree for DoShow task of OrganiseConcert)

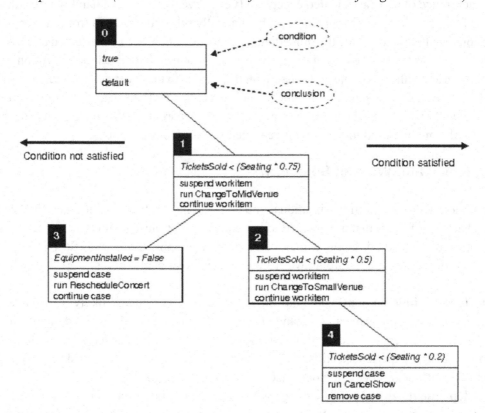

environmental testing, intelligent document retrieval, fraud detection based on patterns of behaviour, personal information management and data mining of large and complex data sets (Pacific Knowledge Systems, 2003).

An RDR Knowledge Base is a collection of rules of the form "if *condition* then *conclusion*" (together with other associated descriptors), conceptually arranged in a binary tree structure (cf. Figure 1). Each rule node may have a false ('or') branch and/or a true ('exception') branch to another rule node, except for the root node, which contains a default rule and can have a true branch only. If a rule is satisfied, the true branch is taken and the associated rule is evaluated; if it is not satisfied, the false branch is taken and its rule evaluated (Drake & Beydoun, 2000). When a terminal node is reached, if its rule is satisfied, then its conclusion is taken; if its rule is not satisfied, then the conclusion of the last rule satisfied on the path to that node is taken.

If the conclusion returned is found to be unsuitable for a particular instance — that is, while the conclusion was correct based on the current rule set, the context of the instance make the conclusion an inappropriate choice — a new rule is formulated that defines the contextual differences between the instance and the selected rule and is added as a new leaf node using the following algorithm:

- If the conclusion returned was that of a satisfied terminal rule, then the new rule is added as a local exception to the exception 'chain' via a new true branch from the terminal node.
- If the conclusion returned was that of a non-terminal, ancestor node (that is, the condition of the terminal rule was not satisfied), then the new rule is added via a new false branch from the unsatisfied terminal node.

In essence, each added exception rule is a refinement of its parent rule. This method of defining new rules allows the construction and maintenance of the rule set by "sub-domain" experts (i.e. those who understand and carry out the work they are responsible for) without regard to any engineering or programming assistance or skill (Kang et al., 1998).

Each rule node incorporates a set of case descriptors, called the 'cornerstone case', which describe the actual case context that was the catalyst for the creation of the rule. When a new rule is added to the rule set, its condition is determined by comparing the descriptors of the current case to those of the cornerstone case and identifying a sub-set of differences. Not all differences will be relevant — only the factor or factors that make it necessary to handle the current case in a different fashion to the cornerstone case are required to define a new rule. The identified differences are expressed as attribute-value pairs, using the normal conditional operators. The current case descriptors become the cornerstone case for the newly formulated rule; its condition is formed by the identified attribute-value pairs and represents the context of the case instance that caused the addition of the rule.

Rather than impose the need for a closed knowledge base that must be completely constructed *a priori*, this method allows for the identification of that part of the universe of discourse that differentiates a particular case *as the need arises*. Indeed, the only context of interest is that needed for differentiation, so that rule sets evolve dynamically, from general to specific, through experience gained as they are applied.

Ripple-Down Rules are well suited to the worklet and exlet selection processes, since they:

*   Provide a method for capturing relevant, localised contextual data;
*   Provide a hierarchical structuring of contextual rules;
*   Do not require the top-down construction of a global knowledge base of the particular domain prior to implementation;
*   Explicitly provide for the definition of exceptions at a local level;
*   Do not require expert knowledge engineers for its maintenance; and
*   Allow a rule set to evolve and grow, thus providing support for a dynamic learning system.

Each worklet is a representation of a particular situated action that relies on the relevant context of each instance, derived from case data and other (archival) sources, to determine whether it is invoked to fulfil a task in preference to another worklet within the repertoire. When a new rule is added, a worker describes the contextual conditions as a natural part of the work they perform[3]. This level of human involvement — at the 'coalface', as it occurs— greatly simplifies the capturing of contextual data. Thus RDR allows the construction of an evolving, highly tailored local knowledge base about a business process.

A Conceptual Framework For Exception Handling

The workflow exception patterns (Russell et al., 2006) were developed with the general aim of providing a conceptual framework for exception handling in workflow systems. They aim to describe the notion of a workflow exception in a general sense and the various ways in which they can be triggered and handled. An exception is anticipated to be a distinct, identifiable event which occurs at a specific point in time during the execution of a process instance. The manner in which the exception is handled will

Figure 2. Options for handling work items

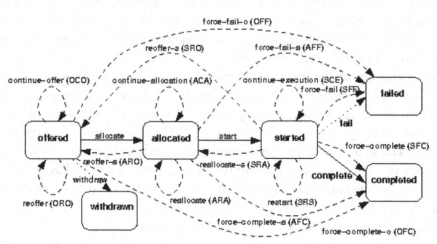

depend on the type of exception that has been detected. The types of events that give rise to exceptions can be classified into five distinct groups:

- **Work Item Failure** where during the course of its execution, a work item to unable progress any further. This may be a consequence of software or hardware failure or may be triggered by the user themselves as a means of signalling failure to the workflow engine;
- **Deadline Expiry** where a deadline that is associated with a work item (either for commencement or completion) is not met;
- **Resource Unavailability** where the resources that are required in order to commence or complete a work item are not available;
- **External Trigger** where signals are received from the operating environment that an event has occurred that impacts on the work item or process instance and requires some form of handling; and
- **Constraint Violation** where constraints have been specified in relation to elements in the control-flow, data or resource perspectives that need to be maintained to ensure the integrity and operational consistency of the workflow process is preserved.

The actual recovery response to any given class of exception can be specified as a pattern which succinctly describes the form of recovery that will be attempted. Specific exception patterns may apply in multiple situations in a given process model (i.e. for several distinct constructs), possibly for different types of exception. Exception patterns take the form of tuples comprising the following elements:

- How the work item (task) on which the exception is based should be handled;
- How the case and other related cases in the process model in which the exception is raised should be handled; and
- What recovery action (if any) is to be undertaken.

Exception Handling At Work Item Level. In general an exception will relate to a specific work item in a process instance and the way in which the exception is handled depends on the current state of execution of the work item. Figure 2 illustrates as solid arrows the states through which a work item progresses during normal execution. Figure 2 also shows fifteen strategies as dashed arcs from one work item state to another, which to distinct approaches for handling the current item in various states when a specific type of exception is detected.

Exception Handling At Case Level. Exceptions always occur in the context of one or more cases (process instances) that are in the process of being executed. In addition to dealing with the specific work item to which the exception relates, there is also the issue of how the case should be dealt with in an overall sense, particularly in regard to other work items that may currently be executing or will run at some future time. There are three alternatives for handling workflow cases:

1. **continue workflow case (CWC)** — the workflow case can be continued, with no intervention occurring in the execution of any other work items;
2. **remove current case (RCC)** — selected or all remaining work items in the case can be removed (including those currently executing); or
3. **remove all cases (RAC)** — selected or all remaining work items in both this and all other currently executing cases which correspond to the same process model can be removed.

In the latter two scenarios, a selection of work items to be removed can be specified using both static design time information relating to the corresponding task definition (e.g. original role allocation) as well as relevant runtime information (e.g. actual resource allocated to, start time).

Recovery Action. The final consideration in regard to exception handling is what action will be taken to remedy the effects of the situation that has been detected. There are three alternate courses of action:

1. **no action (NIL)** — do nothing;
2. **rollback (RBK)** — rollback the effects of the exception; or
3. **compensate (COM)** — compensate for the effects of the exception.

Rollback and compensation are analogous to their usual definitions. When specifying a rollback action, the point in the process (i.e. the task) to which the process should be undone can also be stated. By default this is just the current work item. Similarly with compensation actions, the corresponding compensation task(s) must also be identified.

IMPLEMENTATION

The *Worklet Service* has been implemented as a YAWL Custom Service (van der Aalst & ter Hofstede, 2005; van der Aalst, 2004). The YAWL environment was chosen as the implementation platform since it provides a very powerful and expressive workflow language based on the workflow patterns identified together with a formal semantics (van der Aalst et al., 2003). It also provides a workflow enactment engine, and an editor for process model creation, that support the control flow, data and resource perspectives. The YAWL environment is open-source and has a service-oriented architecture, allowing the worklet paradigm to be developed as a service independent to the core engine. Thus the deployment of the Worklet Service is in no way limited to the YAWL environment, but may be ported to other environments (for example, BPEL engines) by making the necessary links in the service interface.

Figure 3. External Architecture of the Worklet Service

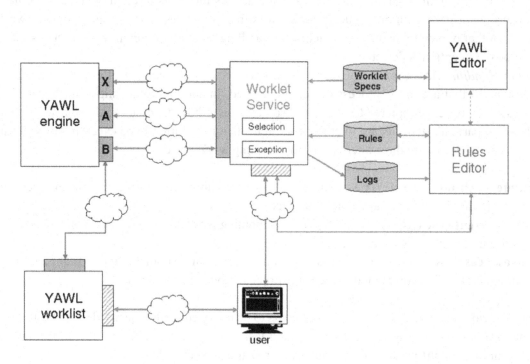

Custom YAWL services interact with the YAWL engine through XML/HTTP messages via certain interface endpoints. Specifically, custom services may elect to be notified by the engine when certain events occur in the life-cycle of nominated process instantiations (for example: when a workitem becomes enabled, when a workitem is cancelled, when a case completes), to signal the creation and completion of process instances and workitems, or to notify of certain events or changes in the status of existing workitems and cases.

The Worklet Service (including its rules editor), source code and accompanying documentation, can be freely downloaded from http://www.yawl-system.com.

Service Architecture

The service consists of a number of J2EE classes and servlet pages, organised in a series of packages.

The external architecture of the Worklet Service is shown in Figure 3. The entities 'Worklet Specs', 'Rules' and 'Logs' comprise the *worklet repository*. The service uses the repository to store rule sets, worklet specifications for uploading to the engine, and generated process and audit logs. Any YAWL specification may have an associated rule set. The rule set for each specification is stored as XML data in a disk file within the worklet repository. The YAWL Process Editor is used to create new worklet specifications, and may be invoked from the Worklet Rules Editor, which is used to create new or augment existing rule sets, making use of certain selection logs to do so, and may communicate with the Worklet Service via a JSP/Servlet interface to override worklet selections following rule set additions. The service also provides servlet pages that allow users to directly communicate with the service to raise external exceptions and to create and carry out administration tasks.

The Worklet Service comprises two discrete but complementary sub-services: a *Selection Service*, which enables dynamic flexibility for process instances, and an *Exception Service*, which provides facilities to handle both expected and unexpected process exceptions at runtime.

The Selection Service. The Selection Service enables dynamic flexibility by allowing a process designer to designate certain workitems to each be substituted at runtime with a dynamically selected *worklet*, which contextually handles one specific task in a larger, composite process activity. Each worklet is a complete extended workflow net (EWF-net) compliant with Definition 1 of the YAWL semantics (van der Aalst & ter Hofstede 2005). Each worklet may be designed and provided to the Selection Service at any time, *even while a parent process instance is executing*, as opposed to a static sub-process that must be defined at the same time as, and remains a static part of, the main process model.

An extensible repertoire of worklets is maintained by the service for each task in a specification. Each time the service is invoked for a workitem, a choice is made from the repertoire based on the contextual data values within the workitem and other sources, using a set of ripple-down rules to determine the most appropriate substitution.

The workitem is checked out of the workflow enactment engine, the corresponding data inputs of the original workitem are mapped to the inputs of the worklet, and the selected worklet is launched in the engine as a separate case. When the worklet has completed, its output data is mapped back to the original workitem, which is then checked back into the engine, allowing the original process to continue.

From an engine perspective, the worklet and its parent are two distinct, unrelated cases. The Worklet Service tracks the relationships, data mappings and synchronisations between cases, and creates a process log that may be combined with the engine's process logs via case identifiers to provide a complete operational history of each process instance and may be used as a data source for the evaluation of rule conditions.

Each task that is associated with a worklet repertoire is said to be 'worklet-enabled'. This means that a process may contain both worklet-enabled tasks and non-worklet-enabled (or ordinary) tasks. Any process instance that contains a worklet-enabled task will become the parent process instance for any worklets invoked from it.

Importantly, a worklet-enabled task remains a valid (ordinary) task definition, rather than being considered as a vacant 'placeholder' for some other activity (i.e. a worklet). The distinction is crucial because, if an appropriate worklet for a worklet-enabled task cannot be found at runtime (based on the context of the case and the rule set associated with the task), the task is allowed to run as an 'ordinary' task, as it normally would in a process instance. So, instead of the parent process being conceived as a template schema or as a container for a set of placeholders, it is to be considered as a complete process containing one or more worklet-enabled tasks, each of which *may* be contextually and dynamically substituted at runtime.

Worklets may be associated with either an atomic task, or a multiple-instance atomic task. Any number of worklets can form the repertoire of an individual task, and any number of tasks in a particular specification can be associated with the Worklet Service. A worklet may be a member of one or more repertoires — that is, it may be re-used for several distinct tasks within and across process specifications. In the case of multiple-instance tasks, a separate worklet is launched for each child workitem. Because each child workitem may contain different data, the worklets that substitute for them are individually selected, and so may all be instances of different worklet specifications.

The Exception Service. The Exception Service allows designers to define exception handling processes (called *exlets*) for parent workflow instances, to be invoked when certain events occur. It has been

Figure 4. Process – Exlet – Worklet Hierarchy

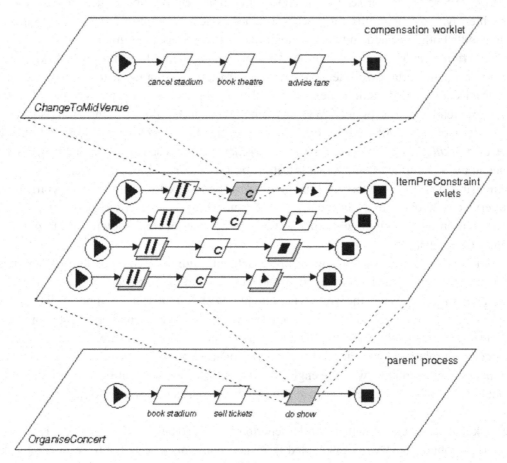

designed so that the enactment engine, besides providing notifications at certain points in the life cycle of a process instance, needs no knowledge of an exception occurring, or of any invocation of handling processes — all exception checking and handling is provided by the service.

The exception service uses the same repertoire and dynamic rules framework as the selection service. There are, however, two fundamental differences between the two sub-services. First, where the selection service selects a *worklet* as the result of satisfying a rule in a rule set, the result of an exception service rule being satisfied is an *exlet*. Second, while the selection service is invoked for certain nominated tasks in a process, the exception service, when enabled, is invoked for every case and task instance executed by the enactment engine, and will detect and handle up to ten different kinds of process exceptions.

As part of the exlet definition, a process designer may choose from various actions (such as cancelling, suspending, completing, failing and restarting) and apply them at a workitem, case and/or specification level. And, since the exlets can include compensatory worklets, the original parent process model only needs to reveal the actual business logic for the process, while the repertoire of exlets grows as new exceptions arise or different ways of handling exceptions are formulated.

An extensible repertoire of exlets is maintained by the service for each type of potential exception within each workflow specification. Each time the service is notified of an exception event, either actual or potential (i.e. a constraint check) the service first determines whether an exception has in fact

Figure 5. Example Handler Process in the Rules Editor

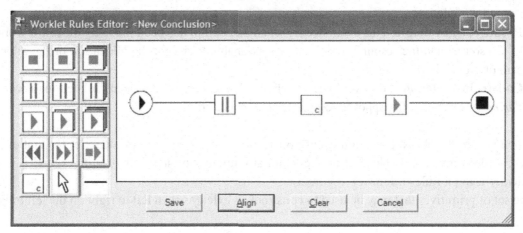

occurred, and if so, where a rule tree for that exception type has been defined, makes a choice from the repertoire based on the type of exception and the context of the workitem/case.

If an exlet executed by the exception service contains a compensation action (i.e. a worklet to be executed as a compensatory process) it is run as a separate case in the enactment engine, so that from an engine perspective, the worklet and its 'parent' (i.e. the process that invoked the exception) are two distinct, unrelated cases. Figure 4 shows the relationship between a 'parent' process, an exlet repertoire and a compensatory worklet, using an *Organise Concert* process as an example. Since a worklet is launched as a separate case, it is treated as such by the Worklet Service and so may have its own worklet/exlet repertoire.

The Service responds to the following exception types:

- **Constraint Types.** Constraints are rules that are applied to a workitem or case immediately before and after execution. Thus, there are four sub-types of constraint exception: *CasePreConstraint*, *ItemPreConstraint*, *ItemPostConstraint*, and *CasePostConstraint*. The service receives notification from the workflow engine when each of these constraint events occurs within each case instance, then checks the rule set associated with the specification to determine, firstly, if there are any rules of that exception type defined for the specification, and if so, if any of the rules evaluate to true using the contextual data of the case or workitem. If the rule set finds a rule that evaluates to true for the exception type and data, an associated exlet is selected and invoked.
- **TimeOut.** A timeout event occurs when a deadline set for a workitem is reached. In this case, the workflow engine notifies the service of the timeout event, passing to the service a reference to the workitem. If the workitem has an associated timeout rule set, the relevant exlet is invoked.
- **Externally Triggered Types**. Externally triggered exceptions occur, not through context internal to the process instance, but because of the occurrence of an event in the external environment, that may have an effect on the continuing execution of the process. Notification of these events is typically triggered by a user or administrator. Depending on the actual event and the context of the case or workitem, a particular exlet will be invoked if the associated rule exists. There are two types of externally triggered types, *CaseExternalTrigger* (for case-level events) and *ItemExternalTrigger* (for item-level events).

- **ItemAbort**. An ItemAbort event occurs when a workitem reports that it has been aborted before normal completion.
- **ResourceUnavailable**. This event occurs when an attempt has been made to allocate a workitem to a resource and the resource reports that it is unable to accept the allocation or the allocation cannot proceed.
- **ConstraintViolation**. This event occurs when a data constraint has been violated for a workitem *during* its execution (as opposed to pre- or post- execution).

When any of the above exception event notifications occur, an appropriate exlet for that event, if defined, will be invoked. Each exlet may contain any number of steps, or *primitives*, and is defined graphically using a Rules Editor (cf. Figure 5).

The set of primitives that may be used to construct an exlet (as seen left to right on the left of Figure 5) are:

- *Remove WorkItem*: removes (or cancels) the workitem; execution ends, and the workitem is marked with a status of cancelled. No further execution occurs on the process path that contains the workitem.
- *Remove Case*: removes the case. Case execution ends.
- *Remove All Cases*: removes all case instances for the specification in which the task of which the workitem is an instance is defined, or of which the case is an instance.
- *Suspend WorkItem*: suspends (or pauses) execution of a workitem, until it is continued, restarted, cancelled, failed or completed, or the case that contains the workitem is cancelled or completed.
- *Suspend Case:* suspends all 'live' workitems in the current case instance (a live workitem has a status of fired, enabled or executing), effectively suspending execution of the entire case.
- *Suspend All Cases:* suspends all 'live' workitems in all of the currently executing instances of the specification in which the task of which the workitem is an instance is defined, effectively suspending all running cases of the specification.
- *Continue WorkItem*: un-suspends (or continues) execution of the previously suspended workitem.
- *Continue Case*: un-suspends execution of all previously suspended workitems for the case, effectively continuing case execution.
- *Continue All Cases:* un-suspends execution of all workitems previously suspended for all cases of the specification in which the task of which the workitem is an instance is defined or of which the case is an instance, effectively continuing all previously suspended cases of the specification.
- *Restart WorkItem*: rewinds workitem execution back to its start. Resets the workitem's data values to those it had when it began execution.
- *Force Complete WorkItem*: completes a 'live' workitem. Execution of the work-item ends, and the workitem is marked with a status of *ForcedComplete*, which is regarded as a successful completion, rather than a cancellation or failure. Execution proceeds to the next workitem on the process path.
- *Force Fail WorkItem*: fails a 'live' workitem. Execution of the workitem ends, and the workitem is marked with a status of *Failed*, which is regarded as an unsuccessful completion, but not as a cancellation — execution proceeds to the next workitem on the process path.

- *Compensate*: run one or more compensatory processes (i.e. worklets). Depending on previous primitives, the worklets may execute simultaneously to the parent case, or execute while the parent is suspended.

Optionally, an *array* of worklets may be defined for a particular compensation primitive — when multiple worklets are defined for a particular compensation primitive via the Rules Editor, they are launched concurrently as a composite compensatory action when the exlet is executed.

The Selection and Exception sub-services can be used in combination within particular case instances to achieve dynamic flexibility *and* exception handling simultaneously.

EXEMPLARY STUDY

Film and television production is a multi-billion dollar industry. In Australia alone, there are over two thousand film and video production services actively employing almost twenty thousand people (Trewin, 2004). However, the industry is extremely competitive and has become progressively global in its scope. Even though the work processes of the industry are highly creative and goal-oriented, organisations are increasingly recognising the value of more conventional business management strategies, such as PAIS, to gain and maintain a competitive edge (Lee & Holt, 2006; Irving & Rea, 2006).

That is not to say that any workflow solution is able to be applied across the board to support all aspects of a film production process. But there are many aspects of the industry where meaningful benefits can be gained through the use of a workflow solution to assist in the management of a project, including:

- Back-office administrative and support processes;
- The allocation of resources to tasks;
- Routing of film stock, documentation and other materials amongst employees; and
- Facilitating inter-team communication and goal-setting.

This study will examine a process occurring in the post-production phase and discuss the applicability of implementing a worklet-service-based solution. The process originates from a cooperative project between the *Queensland University of Technology* (QUT) and the *Australian Film, Television, and Radio School* (AFTRS) within the context of QUT's *Centre of Excellence for Creative Industries and Innovation*.

Rather than coming at the end of production (as the name might imply), work within the post-production phase operates concurrently with several other phases of production. Tasks in this phase include the merging of video and audio components (voice, sound effects, music and so on) and editing to produce a coherent, final piece, and as such include tasks that are both acutely technical and highly creative. The process, referred to as the *Master* process, can be logically divided into three phases:

- **Pre-Edit**: The pre-edit phase begins with the delivery of the day's footage ('the rushes') to the post-production team. There are two possible entry points into the process, one for each type of media that may be used (film and videotape). It may be the case that both types of media are used for a particular set of rushes, so in terms of the model's entry points, inputs may arrive at both

Figure 6. Static Post Production Master Process (YAWL language)

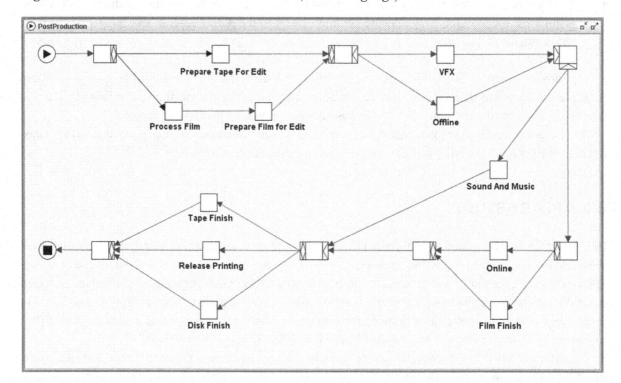

simultaneously. Videotape does not require the same degree of processing as film, but for both media types, a low resolution copy is digitised and stored on computer file to be used as a guide for the remaining process. Accompanying the film and/or tape is the 'rushes paperwork', a set of documentation which may include items such as an annotated script, and video and audio reports. This documentation is regarded as an important source of information about the footage, and is thus made available throughout the post production process.

- **Edit**: In the edit phase, the video and audio components are handled separately. Further, video editing is divided into low and high resolution edits. Low resolution editing is represented by the *Offline* task, which allows editing decisions to be made and documented before the high resolution editing begins. The result of the *Offline* task is the EDL (Edit Decision List). Video Effects Production takes place concurrently with the *Offline* task. When the *Offline* task completes, the high-resolution editing, along with the sound and music editing, can begin. For film, the high resolution editing takes place in the *Film Finishing* task, where the original negative is spliced into pieces, some of which are rejoined; for tape, it occurs in the *Online* task, where the video is rearranged using an editing suite and recorded to a tape master. Both take the EDL output from the low resolution edit and each performs the actions listed in the respective EDL on distribution quality media.

- **Post-Edit**: After the edit phase, an edited, high resolution, distribution quality film and/or tape, together with completed visual effects and sound and music, is completed, and now must be 'finished' for distribution. The finishing may be required for any or all of the film, tape and disk mediums, which are output in the form of a release print, master tape or release version respectively.

Figure 7. Post Production Master Process (Worklet-Enabled)

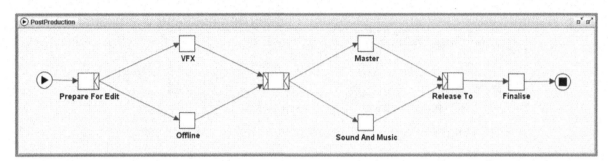

The process description reveals some of the complicating factors that come in to play when rendering this process to a particular modelling framework. For instance, it contains constraints which are designed to remove some tasks from the eventual process if certain preceding tasks were not included in a particular configuration of the process. For example, the removal of the *Prepare Film for Edit* and *Film Finish* tasks is required if the rushes were not received on film; similarly, the *Online* task will not be required if tape media was not received. In addition, because there are two entry points, there are three possible media combinations that may start a case instance (i.e. tape, film, or both tape and film), and so a nominal model will require a number of OR splits and joins to accommodate the various combinations and the tasks they entail.

A representation of the process in the YAWL language shows complications in the describing the process and its possible flow paths via a static model (Figure 6). There are several OR splits and joins; conditionals are required to be embedded into each OR split output arc to determine whether they 'fire' or not. All are dependent simply on which media formats have been supplied to the process. For example,

Figure 8. Selection Rule Tree for the PrepareForEdit task

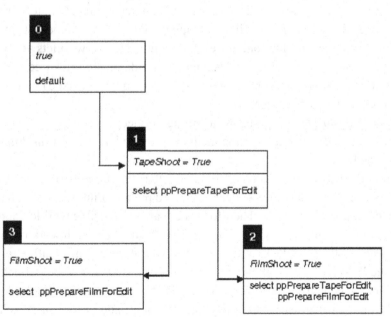

Figure 9. Worklets ppPrepareFileForEdit and ppPrepareTapeForEdit

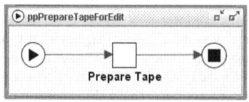

the first OR split task controls whether one or both arcs fire (one for tape, one for film); the OR split preceding the *Online* and *File Finish* tasks has a similar function, and so on. Thus in static representations such as this, the control flow logic is embedded into the business process logic. As a result, it is not obvious from the model which path may be taken during a particular instance.

With the flexibility mechanisms available through the WorkletService, the process can be modelled without much of the complexity, particularly by negating the need for the OR splits and joins. Figure 7 shows the worklet-enabled process. Immediately apparent is the fact that, in this case, all of the OR splits and joins have been removed from the process model.

The first task in the process, *PrepareForEdit*, is worklet-enabled. Associated with this task is the Selection rule tree shown in Figure 8. The rule tree shows that, if either tape or film has been supplied, the corresponding rule will be satisfied and the service will launch the appropriate worklet for that media. If the rushes have been delivered on both film and tape media, node 2 will be last satisfied, resulting in the launching of two discrete worklets, one for each medium (the two worklets are shown in Figure 9). Note that the conditional expressions for nodes 2 and 3 are identical in this tree, but their conclusions differ — node 3 will be tested if node 1 evaluates to false (i.e. there is no tape media), while node 2 will be tested only if node 1 evaluates to true.

The worklet-enabled *Master* task performs a similar service to *PrepareForEdit* — it will launch a worklet to carry out the *Online* process if tape media is provided, and/or for the *Film Finish* process if film media is provided.

The *Finalise* task models the processing of 'finishing' the output for distribution. There are three possible sub-processes to perform: tape finish, disk finish and release printing --- each has a corresponding worklet in the specification's repertoire. Therefore, there are six possible worklet launch combinations, as specified in the selection rule tree for the *Finalise* task (Figure 10). Each worklet consists of one task, corresponding to each of the three tasks at the post-edit end of the original static process model.

In summary, the Worklet Service allows a parent or master process to be defined without much of the explicit branching mechanisms necessary in the control flow of static models. As a result, the parent process models are cleaner, easier to verify and maintain, and easier for stakeholders to gain an

Figure 10. Selection Rule Tree for the Finalise Task

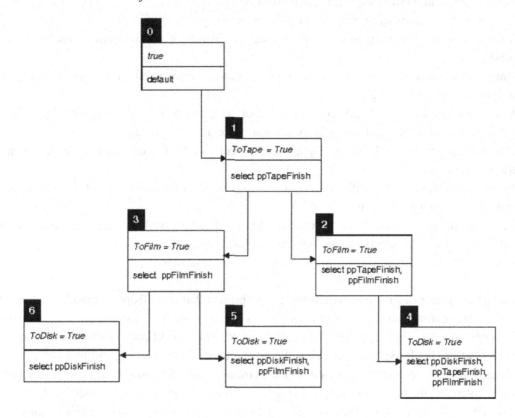

understanding of the process logic. Once the parent process is worklet-enabled, it is able to access all the features of the worklet paradigm, including support for exception handling. Some exceptions that may occur in a post production process include damaged film or tape stock, equipment malfunctions and breakdowns, and time and budget overruns, to name but a few. All of these exceptions may be handled by adding an appropriate exlet to the specification's repertoire. For a more complex example that uses a worklet solution in a gynaecological oncology domain, the interested reader is referred to the YAWL-4Health project: http://www.yawlfoundation.org/solutions/health.html.

CONCLUSION

This chapter began by identifying key problems that describe the fundamental limitations of current workflow technologies with respect to the rigidity enforced by the inflexible frameworks employed, and the consequent difficulties in placing more dynamic, information intensive processes within those frameworks. Then, a description of ten principles derived from Activity Theory that represent an interpretation of its central themes applicable to understanding organisational work practices was provided.

Based on the derived principles of Activity Theory, the Worklet Service was then conceptualised, implemented and validated. A primary feature of the service is that it has been designed and implemented as a discrete service, and so offers all of its benefits to a wide range of workflow management systems, allowing them to fully 'worklet-ise' their otherwise static processes. The Worklet Service:

- Keeps the parent model clean and relatively simple;
- Promotes the reuse of sub-processes in different models;
- Allows standard processes to be used as exception handling compensation processes, and vice versa;
- Maintains an extensible repertoire of actions that can be constructed during design and/or runtime and can be invoked as required;
- Allows a specification to implicitly build a history of executions, providing for a learning system that can take the appropriate actions for certain contexts automatically;
- Maintains a repertoire of fully encapsulated, discrete worklets that allow for easier verification and modification;
- Allows a model to evolve without the need to stop and modify the design of the whole specification when an exception occurs;
- By de-coupling the monolithic process model, models can be built that vary from loosely to tightly defined and so supports late binding of processes; and
- Allows a model to be considered from many levels of granularity.

There are a number of further research topic possibilities that arise from this work, such as: deeper empirical studies comparing the worklet approach to classic workflow approaches and measuring the relative benefits of each; porting the Worklet Service to other workflow systems (for example, IBM Websphere and/or Oracle BPEL); exploring the advantages of mixing different modelling styles and approaches, leading to recommendations of in what circumstances the various approaches are best used; and stronger support for process mining analysis using both the process logs generated by the service and the structure, content and evolution of the various ripple-down rule sets of specifications.

In summary, through a combination of the framework on which it is built and the mechanisms available through both its selection and exception handling sub-services, the Worklet Service offers a wide-ranging solution to the issues of flexibility and exception handling in process-aware information systems. In fact, the benefits offered through each sub-service can be combined to deliver a far-reaching set of capabilities that serve the needs of a wide variety of work environments and processes.

REFERENCES

van der Aalst, W. (2001). Exterminating the dynamic change bug: A concrete approach to support workflow change. *Information Systems Frontiers*, 3(3), 297–317. doi:10.1023/A:1011409408711

van der Aalst, W., Aldred, L., Dumas, M., & ter Hofstede, A. (2004). Design and implementation of the YAWL system. In A. Persson, & J. Stirna (Eds.), *Proceedings of The 16th International Conference on Advanced Information Systems Engineering (CAiSE 04)* (LNCS 3084, pp. 142-159). Riga, Latvia: Springer Verlag.

van der Aalst, W., & Basten, T. (2002). Inheritance of workflows: An approach to tackling problems related to change. *Theoretical Computer Science*, 270(1-2), 125–203. doi:10.1016/S0304-3975(00)00321-2 van der Aalst, W., & Berens, P. (2001). Beyond workflow management: Product-driven case handling. In S. Ellis, T. Rodden, & I. Zigurs (Eds.), *Proceedings of the International ACM SIGGROUP Conference on Supporting Group Work*, (pp. 42–51). New York: ACM Press.

van der Aalst, W., & ter Hofstede, A. (2005). YAWL: Yet another workflow language. *Information Systems, 30*(4), 245–275. doi:10.1016/j.is.2004.02.002

van der Aalst, W., ter Hofstede, A., Kiepuszewski, B., & Barros, A. (2003). Workflow patterns. *Distributed and Parallel Databases, 14*(3), 5–51. doi:10.1023/A:1022883727209

van der Aalst, W., & van Hee, K. (2004). *Workflow management: Models, methods and systems.* Cambridge, Massachusetts: The MIT Press.

van der Aalst, W., & Weske, M., & GrÄunbauer, D. (2005). Case handling: A new paradigm for business process support. *Data & Knowledge Engineering, 53*(2), 129–162. doi:10.1016/j.datak.2004.07.003

Adams, M. (2007). *Facilitating dynamic flexibility and exception handling for workflows.* PhD thesis, Queensland University of Technology.

Adams, M., Edmond, D., & ter Hofstede, A. H. (2003). The application of activity theory to dynamic workflow adaptation issues. In *Proceedings of the 2003 Pacific Asia Conference on Information Systems (PACIS 2003)* (pp. 1836–1852). Adelaide, Australia.

Bardram, J. E. (1997). I love the system - I just don't use it! In *Proceedings of the International ACM SIGGROUP Conference on Supporting Group Work (GROUP'97)*, (pp. 251-260). Phoenix, AZ: ACM.

Barthelmess, P., & Wainer, J. (1995). Workflow systems: A few definitions and a few suggestions. In *Proceedings of the ACM Conference on Organizational Computing Systems (COOCS'95)*, (pp. 138-147). Milpitas, CA: ACM.

Bass, L., Clement, P., & Kazman, R. (1998). *Software architecture in practice.* Reading: Addison-Wesley.

Berens, P. (2005). *The FLOWer case handling approach: Beyond workflow managment*, (pp. 363-395).

Bider, I. (2005). Masking flexibility behind rigidity: Notes on how much flexibility people are willing to cope with. In J. Castro & E. Teniente (Eds.), *Proceedings of the CAiSE'05 Workshops*, vol. 1, (pp. 7-18). Porto, Portugal: FEUP Edicoes.

Bødker, S., & Greenbaum, J. (1993). Design of information systems: Things versus people. In E. Green, J. Owen, & D. Pain (Eds.), *Gendered by design? Information technology and office systems* (pp. 53-63). London: Taylor and Francis.

Borgida, A., & Murata, T. (1999). Tolerating exceptions in workflows: A unified framework for data and processes. In *Proceedings of the International Joint Conference on Work Activities, Coordination and Collaboration (WACC'99)* (pp. 59-68). San Francisco, CA: ACM Press.

Casati, F. (1998). A discussion on approaches to handling exceptions in workflows. In *Proceedings of the CSCW Workshop on Adaptive Workflow Systems.* Seattle, WA.

Compton, P., & Jansen, B. (1988). Knowledge in context: A strategy for expert system maintenance. In J.Siekmann (Ed.), *Proceedings of the 2nd Australian Joint Artificial Intelligence Conference* (LNCS 406, pp. 292-306). Adelaide, Australia: Springer-Verlag.

COSA. (2005). COSA BPM product description. Retrieved March 13, 2008, from http://www.cosa-bpm. com/project/docs/COSA_BPM_5_Productdescription_eng.pdf

Drake, B., & Beydoun, G. (2000). Predicate logic-based incremental knowledge acquisition. In P. Compton, A. Hoffmann, H. Motoda, & T. Yamaguchi (Eds.), *Proceedings of the Sixth Pacific International Knowledge Acquisition Workshop* (pp. 71-88). Sydney, Australia.

Dumas, M., van der Aalst, W., & ter Hofstede, A. (Eds.). (2005). *Process-aware information systems: Bridging people and software through process technology*. New York: Wiley-Interscience.

Edmond, D., & ter Hofstede, A. H. (2000). A reflective infrastructure for workflow adaptability. *Data & Knowledge Engineering, 34*, 271–304. doi:10.1016/S0169-023X(00)00018-5

Georgeff, M., & Pyke, J. (2003). *Dynamic process orchestration* [White paper]. Staffware PLC.

Greiner, U., Ramsch, J., Heller, B., Löffler, M., Müller, R., & Rahm, E. (2004). Adaptive guideline-based treatment workflows with Adapt-Flow. In K. Kaiser, S. Miksch, & S. Tu (Eds.), *Proceedings of the Symposium on Computerized Guidelines and Protocols (CGP 2004)* (pp. 113-117). Prague: IOS Press.

Hendriks-Jansen, H. (1996). *Catching ourselves in the act: Situated activity, interactive emergence, evolution, and human thought*. Cambridge, MA: MIT Press.

Holt, A. W. (1997). *Organized activity and its support by computer*. Dordrecht: Kluwer Academic Publishers.

IBM. (2005). *IBM WebSphere MQ Workflow: Concepts and architecture*. Retrieved March 14, 2008, from http://publibfp.boulder.ibm.com/epubs/pdf/h1262857.pdf

Irving, D. K., & Rea, P. W. (2006). *Producing and directing the short film and video* (3rd ed.). Burlington, Oxford, UK: Focal Press.

Joeris, G. (1999). Defining flexible workflow execution behaviors. In P. Dadam, & M. Reichert (Eds.), *Enterprise-wide and cross-enterprise workflow management: concepts, systems, applications* (Vol. 24 of CEUR Workshop Proceedings) (pp. 49-55). Paderborn, Germany.

Joeris, G., & Herzog, O. (1998). Managing evolving workflow specifications. In *Proceedings of the 3rd IFCIS International Conference on Cooperative Information Systems (CoopIS '98)* (pp. 310-319). New York: IEEE Computer Society.

Kaasbøll, J. J., & Smørdal, O. (1996). Human work as context for development of object-oriented modelling techniques. In S. Brinkkemper (Ed.) *IFIP WG 8.1/8.2 Working Conference on Principles of Method Construction and Tool Support* (pp. 111–125). Atlanta, GA: Chapman and Hall.

Kammer, P., Bolcer, G., Taylor, R., Hitomi, A., & Bergman, M. (2000). Techniques for supporting dynamic and adaptive workflow. [CSCW]. *Computer Supported Cooperative Work, 9*(3), 269–292. doi:10.1023/A:1008747109146

Kang, B. H., Preston, P., & Compton, P. (1998). Simulated expert evaluation of multiple classification ripple down rules. In *Proceedings of the 11th Workshop on Knowledge Acquisition, Modeling and Management*. Banff, Alberta, Canada.

Klein, M., & Dellarocas, C. (2000). *A systematic repository of knowledge about handling exceptions* (ASES Working Paper ASES-WP-2000-03 ASES-WP-2000-03). Cambridge, MA: Massachusetts Institute of Technology.

Kradolfer, M., & Geppert, A. (1999). Dynamic workflow schema evolution based on workflow type versioning and workflow migration. In *Proceedings of the 1999 IFCIS International Conference on Cooperative Information Systems (CoopIS'99)* (pp. 104-114). Edinburgh, Scotland: IEEE Computer Society.

Kuutti, K. (1996). *Activity theory as a potential framework for human-computer interaction research* (pp. 17-44).

Lee, J. J., & Holt, R. (2006). *The producer's business handbook* (2nd ed.). Burlington, Oxford, UK: Focal Press.

Leontiev, A. (1974). The problem of activity in psychology. *Social Psychology*, *13*(2), 4–33.

Leymann, F. (2006). Workflow-based coordination and cooperation in a service world. In R. Meersman, & Z. Tari (Eds.) *Proceedings of the 14th International Conference on Cooperative Information Systems (CoopIS'06)* (LNCS 4275, pp. 2-16). Montpellier, France: Springer-Verlag.

Manago, M. V., & Kodratoff, Y. (1987). Noise and knowledge acquisition. In *Proceedings of the Tenth International Joint Conference on Artificial Intelligence* (Vol. 1, pp. 348-354). Milano, Italy: Morgan Kaufmann.

Muller, R., Greiner, U., & Rahm, E. (2004). AgentWork: A workflow system supporting rule-based workflow adaptation. *Data & Knowledge Engineering*, *51*(2), 223–256. doi:10.1016/j.datak.2004.03.010

Mumford, L. (1963). *Technics and Civilization*. Harcourt Brace Jovanovich, New York.

Nardi, B. A. (1996). *Activity theory and human-computer interaction* (pp. 7-16).

Nardi, B. A. (Ed.). (1996). *Context and consciousness: Activity theory and human-computer interaction*. Cambridge, MA: MIT Press.

Oberweis, A. (2005). *Person-to-application processes: Workflow management* (pp. 21-36).

Pacific Knowledge Systems. (2003). *Products: Rippledown*. Retrieved April 23, 2002, from http://www.pks.com.au/products/validator.htm

Palmer, N. (2007). A survey of business process initiatives. Retrieved April 4, 2008, from http://wfmc.org/researchreports/Survey_BPI.pdf

Pesic, M., & van der Aalst, W. (2006). A declarative approach for flexible business processes. In J. Eder, & S. Dustdar (Eds.), *Proceedings of the First International Workshop on Dynamic Process Management (DPM 2006)* (LNCS 4103, pp. 169-180).

Reichert, M., & Dadam, P. (1997). A framework for dynamic changes in workflow management systems. In *Proceedings of the 8th International Workshop on Database and Expert Systems Applications(DEXA 97)*, (pp. 42-48). Toulouse, France: IEEE Computer Society Press.

Reichert, M., Dadam, P., & Bauer, T. (2003). Dealing with forward and backward jumps in workflow management systems. *Software and Systems Modeling, 2*(1), 37–58. doi:10.1007/s10270-003-0018-x

Reichert, M., Rinderle, S., Kreher, U., & Dadam, P. (2005). Adaptive process management with ADEPT2. In *Proceedings of the 21st International Conference on Data Engineering (ICDE'05)*, (pp. 1113-1114). Tokyo, Japan: IEEE Computer Society Press.

Rinderle, S., Reichert, M., & Dadam, P. (2004). Correctness criteria for dynamic changes in workflow systems: a survey. *Data & Knowledge Engineering, 50*(1), 9–34. doi:10.1016/j.datak.2004.01.002

Rinderle, S., Weber, B., Reichert, M., & Wild, W. (2005). Integrating process learning and process evolution a semantics based approach. In W. van der Aalst, B. Benatallah, F. Casati, & F. Curbera (Eds.) *Proceedings of the 3rd International Conference on Business Process Management (BPM'05)* (LNCS 3649, pp. 252-267). Nancy, France: Springer Verlag.

Riss, U., Rickayzen, A., Maus, H., & van der Aalst, W. (2005). Challenges for business process and task management. *Journal of Universal Knowledge Management, 0*(2), 77-100. Retrieved January 27, 2007, from http://www/jukm.org/jukm_0_2/riss

Russell, N., van der Aalst, W., & ter Hofstede, A. (2006). Workflow exception patterns. In E. Dubois, & K. Pohl (Eds.) *Proceedings of the 18th International Conference on Advanced Information Systems Engineering (CAiSE 2006)* (pp. 288-302). Luxembourg: Springer.

SAP. (2006). *SAP advanced workflow techniques*. Retrieved March 17, 2008, from https://www.sdn.sap.com/irj/servlet/prt/portal/prtroot/docs/library/uuid/82d03e23-0a01-0010-b482-dccfe1c877c4

Schael, T. (1998). *Workflow management systems for process organizations* (LNCS 1096).

Scheffer, T. (1996). Algebraic foundation and improved methods of induction of ripple down rules. In *Proceedings of the 2nd Pacific Rim Workshop on Knowledge Acquisition*, (pp. 279-292). Sydney, Australia.

Stein, L. A. (1999). Challenging the computational metaphor: Implications for how we think. *Cybernetics and Systems, 30*(6). doi:10.1080/019697299125073

Symon, G., Long, K., & Ellis, J. (1996). The coordination of work activities: cooperation and conflict in a hospital context. *Computer Supported Cooperative Work, 5*(1), 1–31. doi:10.1007/BF00141934

TIBCO. (2006). *TIBCO iProcess Suite* [White paper]. Retrieved March 13, 2008, from http://www.staffware.com/resources/software/bpm/tibco_iprocess_suite_whitepaper.pdf

Trewin, D. (2004). *Television, film and video production in Australia* (publication 8679.0). Australian Bureau of Statistics. Retrieved April 13, 2008, from http://www.ausstats.abs.gov.au/ausstats/subscriber.nsf/0/14F1A528655E8486CA256EDE00782780/File/86790_2002-03.pdf

Turing, A. (1936). On computable numbers, with an application to the entscheidungsproblem. *Proceedings of the London Mathematical Society, 2*(42), 230–265.

Weber, B., Wild, W., & Breu, R. (2004). CBRFlow: Enabling adaptive workflow management through conversational case-based reasoning. In P. Funk, & P. A. Gonzalez Calero (Eds.), *Proceedings of the 7th European Conference for Advances in Case Based Reasoning (ECCBR'04)* (LNCS 3155, pp. 434-448). Madrid, Spain: Springer.

Workflow Management Coalition. (2002). *Introduction to workflow.* Retrieved November 14, 2004, from http://www.wfmc.org/introduction_to_workflow.pdf

Yan, J., Yang, Y., & Raikundalla, G. (2004). Towards incompletely specified process support in SwinDeW - A peer-to-peer based workflow system. In W. Shen, Z. Lin, J. Barthµes, & T. Li (Eds.), *Proceedings of the 8th International Conference on Computer Supported Cooperative Work in Design (CSCWD 2004)* (LNCS 3168, pp. 328-338). Xiamen, China: Springer.

zur Muehlen, M. (2004). *Workflow-based process controlling. Foundation, design, and implementation of workflow-driven process information systems.* Berlin: Logos.

KEY TERMS AND DEFINITIONS

Activity Theory: A meta-model or framework used to describe, theorise and research organised human activities, originating from Soviet cultural-historical psychology in the 1920's.

Exlet: An exception handling process, consisting of a number of exception handling primitives such as Suspend WorkItem, Remove Case, Compensate, and so on, which defines what action should be taken in the event of an exception of a certain type and context.

Process-Aware Information System (PAIS): A software system that manages and executes operational processes involving people, applications, and/or information sources on the basis of process models (Dumas et al., 2005, 7).

Ripple-Down Rules (RDR): A hierarchical, extensible set of rules of the form "if *condition* then *conclusion*", together with cornerstone case data, conceptually arranged in a binary tree structure.

Service-Oriented Architecture: A software architecture consisting of a number of discrete (usually web-based) services (software components that are accessed or communicate via standard network protocols), that link together as required in order to achieve some task.

Worklet: A (usually) small, self-contained, complete process definition which is designed to be invoked as a substitute for one specific task in a larger, composite process. Each worklet is a complete extended workflow net (EWF-net) compliant with Definition 1 of the YAWL semantics. A set of zero or more worklets may form the *repertoire* of a task.

ENDNOTES

[1]   Space considerations limit this discussion to the more popular and/or recent systems and prototypes; a more complete discussion can be found in Adams (2007)

2   In Activity Theory terms, a worklet may represent one action within an activity, or may represent an entire activity.

3   In practice, the worker's contextual description would be passed to an administrator, who would add the new rule.

Chapter 6
Flexibility for Distributed Workflows

Manfred Reichert
University of Ulm, Germany

Thomas Bauer
Daimler AG, Germany

Peter Dadam
University of Ulm, Germany

ABSTRACT

This chapter shows how flexibility can be realized for distributed workflows. The capability to dynamically adapt workflow instances during runtime (e.g., to add, delete or move activities) constitutes a fundamental challenge for any workflow management system (WfMS). While there has been significant research on ad-hoc workflow changes and on related correctness issues, there exists only little work on how to provide respective runtime flexibility in an enterprise-wide context as well. Here, scalability at the presence of high loads constitutes an essential requirement, often necessitating distributed (i.e., piecewise) control of a workflow instance by different workflow servers, which should be as independent from each other as possible. This chapter presents advanced concepts and techniques for enabling ad-hoc workflow changes in a distributed WfMS as well. Our focus is on minimizing the communication costs among workflow servers, while ensuring a correct execution behavior as well as correctness of ad-hoc workflow changes at any time.

INTRODUCTION

For a variety of reasons enterprises are developing a growing interest in aligning their information systems such that they become process-aware (Lenz, 2007; Müller, 2006; Mutschler 2006; Mutschler, 2008a). Such process-aware information systems (PAISs) offer the right *tasks* at the right *point in time* to the right *actors* along with the *information*, *resources* and *application services* needed to perform these tasks (Dadam, 2000). Business process management technology offers promising perspectives to

DOI: 10.4018/978-1-60566-669-3.ch006

achieve this goal (Weske, 2007). Examples include workflow management systems and case handling tools (Günther, 2008 a; Mutschler, 2008b).

A workflow management system (WfMS) enables computer-supported business processes (i.e., *workflows*) to be executed in a distributed system environment (Bauer, 1999; Muth, 1998; Shegalov, 2001). Usually, a WfMS provides powerful tools for implementing enterprise-wide, process-aware information systems (PAISs) (Dadam, 1999). As opposed to data- or function-centered information systems, a WfMS separates the specification of the process logic (i.e., the control and data flow between the process activities) from application coding (Dadam, 2000; Weber, 2007); i.e., process logic can be described explicitly in terms of a *workflow template* providing the schema for *workflow enactment* (workflow schema for short). The different *activities*, in turn, are implemented as loosely coupled *application services* that can expect that their input parameters are provided upon invocation by the WfMS and which only have to produce correct values for their output parameters. Usually, the core of the *workflow layer* is built by the WfMS which provides generic functions for modeling, configuring, executing, and monitoring workflows.

This separation of concerns increases maintainability and reduces cost of change (Mutschler, 2008a; Weber, 2008a); i.e., changes to one layer often can be performed without affecting other layers; e.g., changing the execution order of workflow (WF) activities or adding new activities to a *WF schema* can, to a large degree, be accomplished without touching any of the associated application services (Dadam et al., 2000). Furthermore, a *WF schema* can be checked for the absence of flaws already at buildtime; i.e., deadlocks, livelocks and faulty data flow specifications (van der Aalst, 2000; Reichert, 1998a) can be excluded in an early stage of the process lifecycle (Weber, 2009; Weber, 2006a). At run-time, new *WF instances* can be created and executed according to the underlying *WF schema*. When an activity becomes activated, a respective *work item* is assigned to the *worklists* of authorized users (which are determined based on the *actor assignment* associated with the corresponding activity). One example of such a WfMS constitutes the ADEPT system we have developed during the last years (Reichert, 2003c).

Problem Statement

A centralized WfMS shows deficits when being confronted with high loads or when supporting cross-departmental processes (Reichert, 1999; Dadam, 2000). In the ADEPT project, we have considered this by realizing a *distributed WfMS* made up of several WF servers (Bauer, 1997; Bauer, 1999; Bauer, 2003; Montagut, 2007). In this distributed variant of the ADEPT system, we allow WF designers to subdivide a WF schema into several partitions which are then controlled "piecewise" by different WF servers in order to obtain favorable communication behavior. Note that similar approaches have been discussed in literature (Alonso, 1995; Casati, 1996; Cichocki, 2000; Dogac, 1997; Gronemann, 1999; Guth, 1998; Kochut, 2003; Muth, 1998; Schuster, 1999; Sheth, 1997; Weske, 1999).

Comparable to centralized WfMS, also a distributed WfMS needs to be flexible to cover the broad spectrum of processes we can find in today's organizations (Bassil, 2004; Kochut, 2003; Lenz, 2007; Minor, 2007; Müller, 2006; Reichert, 1998 b). Thus, at the WF instance level it should be possible to flexibly deviate from the predefined WF schema during runtime. As reported in literature (van der Aalst, 2001a; Pesic, 2007, Reichert, 1998a; Mourào, 2007; Weber 2006a) such ad-hoc workflow changes become necessary to deal with exceptional and changing situations. Within the ADEPT project we developed an advanced technology for the support of such ad-hoc changes (Reichert, 1998a; Reichert, 2003a; Reichert,

2003b). In particular, ADEPT allows authorized users (or agents) to dynamically modify running WF instances, but without causing run-time errors or inconsistencies in the sequel (Rinderle, 2003).

In our previous work we considered distributed execution of a partitioned WF schema and ad-hoc WF changes as separate issues (e.g., Reichert, 1998; Bauer, 2003). In fact, we did not systematically examine how these two fundamental aspects of a large-scale WfMS interact with each other. Obviously, integrated support of respective features is by far not trivial as their goals are different. The support of ad-hoc WF changes and the correct processing of the WF instances afterwards prescribe a logically central control instance (i.e., a logically central WF server) to ensure correctness (Reichert, 1998a). This, however, contradicts to the accomplishments achieved by distributed WF execution (Bauer, 1997; Bauer, 2000). Note that one central WF server always decreases WfMS availability and increases communication costs between WF clients and WF server (Kamath, 1996). One reason for this lies in the fact that a central control engine must be informed of all changes concerning the state of a WF instance. In particular, information on instance states is needed to decide whether an intended ad-hoc change is applicable in a given context; i.e., whether the considered WF instance is compliant with the resulting WF schema (Reichert, 1998a; Rinderle, 2004a; Rinderle-Ma, 2008a).

Contribution

This chapter provides an extended version of the work we presented in (Reichert, 2007). It describes an approach which enables ad-hoc changes of single WF instances in a *distributed WfMS*; i.e., a WfMS with *WF schema partitioning* and *distributed WF control*. As a prerequisite, distributed WF control must not affect applicability of ad-hoc changes; i.e., each change, which is allowed for the central case, should be applicable in the context of distributed WF execution as well. The support of such ad-hoc changes, in turn, must not impact distributed WF control. In particular, distributed WF execution should not necessitate a great deal of additional communication effort due to the introduction of WF instance changes. Finally, ad-hoc changes should be correctly performed and as efficiently as possible.

To deal with these requirements it is crucial to identify the WF servers of the distributed WfMS to be involved in the synchronization of an ad-hoc change. Most likely we have to consider those WF servers currently executing the respective WF instance. These *active servers* need to know the schema and state of a changed WF instance in order to correctly control its execution afterwards. We need an efficient approach for determining the set of active servers controlling a particular WF instance. This must be possible without a substantial expense of communication efforts. In addition, we have to decide whether, when and how a changed WF instance schema has to be transmitted to other WF servers. As essential requirement the amount of communication should not exceed acceptable limits.

This chapter is structured as follows: We first give background information needed for the further understanding and we introduce basic issues related to distributed WF execution as accomplished in the ADEPT approach. Following this, we first describe how ad-hoc instance changes can be performed in the distributed variant of the ADEPT WfMS. Then we show how individually modified WF instances can be efficiently executed in such distributed WfMS. Finally, we describe our proof-of-concept prototype and discuss related work. The chapter concludes with a summary and outlook.

BACKGROUNDS

We first show how workflows can be modeled in the ADEPT WfMS. Following this we discuss fundamental issues related to ad-hoc changes of single WF instances.

Workflow Modeling and Execution in ADEPT

When implementing a workflow in a PAIS its control and data flow has to be explicitly defined based on the modeling constructs provided by the used *WF meta model*. More precisely, for each business process to be supported, a *WF type* represented by a *WF schema* is defined. For one particular WF type several WF schemes may exist representing the different *versions* and the *evolution* of this WF type over time. Figure 1 shows a simple example of a WF schema as modeled in ADEPT. The depicted schema comprises seven activities connected through *control edges*. Generally, control edges specify precedence relations between the activities. For example, activity *order medical examination* is followed by activity *make appointment*, whereas activities *prepare patient* and *inform patient* may be executed in parallel. Furthermore, the WF schema contains a loop structure, which allows for the repetitive execution of the depicted WF fragment.

The *ADEPT WF meta model* allows for the integrated modeling of different WF aspects including activities, control and data flow, actor assignments, semantical constraints, and resources. Here we focus on the first three perspectives.

Control flow modeling. As depicted in Figure 1, the control flow of a WF schema is represented as attributed graph with distinguishable node and edge types. This allows for efficient correctness checks and eases the handling of loop backs. Formally, a *control flow schema* corresponds to a tuple (N,E, ...) with node set N and edge set E. Each control edge e ∈ E has one of the edge types CONTROL_E, SYNC_E or LOOP_E: CONTROL_E expresses a normal precedence relation, whereas SYNC_E allows to express a wait-for relation between activities of parallel branches (Reichert, 2000). Finally, LOOP_E represents a loop backward edge. Similarly, each node n ∈ N has one of the node types STARTFLOW, ENDFLOW, ACTIVITY, STARTLOOP, ENDLOOP, AND-/XOR-Split, and AND-/XOR-Join. Based on these elements, we can model sequences, parallel branchings, conditional branchings, and loop backs. ADEPT adopts concepts from block-structured process description languages, but enriches them by additional control structures. More precisely, branchings as well as loops have exactly one entry and one exit node. Furthermore, control blocks may be nested, but must not overlap. As this limits expressive power, in addition, the aforementioned synchronization edges can be used for process modeling (Reichert, 2000).

Data flow modeling. Data exchange between activities is realized through writing and reading *WF variables* (denoted as *data elements* in the following). Data elements are connected with input and output parameters of WF activities. Each input parameter of a particular activity is mapped to exactly one data element by a *read data edge* and each activity output parameter is connected to a data element by a *write data edge*. An example is depicted in Figure 1. Activity *order medical examination* writes data element *patientID* which is then read by subsequent activity *perform examination*. The total collection of *data elements* and *data edges* constitutes the *data flow schema*. For its modeling, a number of restrictions has to be met. The most important one ensures that all data elements mandatorily read by an activity X must have been written before X is started. In particular, this must be ensured independent from the execution path leading to activation of X.

Figure 1. Example of a simple ADEPT WF schema

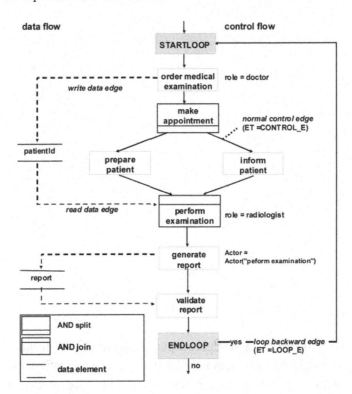

Based on a given *WF schema* new *WF instances* can be created and executed. ADEPT orchestrates them according to the defined control flow. Regarding a single activity, initially, its status is set to NOT_ACTIVATED. It changes to ACTIVATED when all preconditions for executing this activity are met. In this case corresponding work items are inserted into the worklists of authorized users. If one of them selects the respective item from his worklist, activity status changes to RUNNING and respective work items are removed from other worklists. Furthermore, the application service associated with the activity is started. At successful termination, activity status changes to COMPLETED. Generally, a large number of WF instances being in different states may run on a particular WF schema. To determine which activities are to be executed next, WF enactment in ADEPT is based on a well-defined operational semantics (Reichert, 1998a; Reichert, 2000). Furthermore, for each WF instance we maintain information about its current state by assigning respective markings to the nodes and edges of its WF schema. Figure 2 shows two WF instances running on the WF schema depicted in Figure 1.

Ad-hoc Workflow Changes in ADEPT

To allow users to flexibly react in exceptional situations and to dynamically evolve the structure of in-progress WF instances over time, ADEPT provides support for *ad-hoc changes*. Generally, WF flexibility can be achieved either through *structural adaptations* of WF schemes (Reichert 1998; Rinderle, 2004a; Rinderle, 2005) or by allowing for loosely specified WF schemes, which can be refined by users during runtime according to predefined criteria (Adams, 2006; Han, 1998; Sadiq 2001; Sadiq 2005; Weber,

Figure 2. Examples of two WF instances running on the WF schema from Figure 1

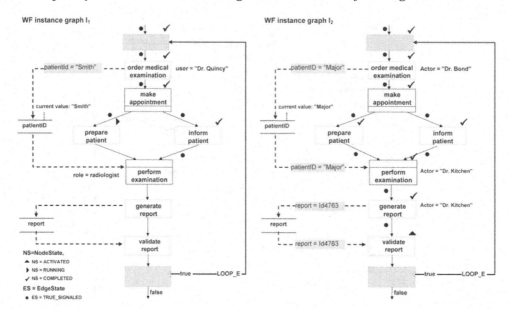

2007). This chapter focuses on structural schema adaptations of single WF instances; i.e., *ad-hoc changes* which can be applied to single WF instances in order to cope with exceptional situations.

Usually, the introduction of ad-hoc changes results in an instance-specific WF schema (Reichert, 1998a), which we also denote as the *execution schema* of the instance in the following; i.e., change effects are instance-specific and do not affect any other WF instance. In a medical treatment process, for example, current medication of a particular patient might have to be discontinued due to an allergic reaction of this particular patient.

ADEPT provides a set of high-level *change operations* and *change patterns*, respectively, for realizing structural schema adaptations. In particular, respective change operations abstract from the concrete schema transformations becoming necessary to realize a particular change. Examples of ADEPT change operations include the insertion of a schema fragment between two activity sets or the movement of a fragment from its current position within a WF schema to a new one. Generally, change operations can be applied to the whole WF schema, i.e., the region to which the respective change operation is applied can be chosen dynamically (as opposed to late modeling approaches where changes are restricted to a predefined region). Therefore, the ADEPT change operations are suited for dealing with exceptions. Furthermore, it becomes possible to associate pre- and post-conditions with them. This, in turn, enables us to guarantee soundness when applying the respective change operations (Reichert, 1998a). Preserving soundness will be of particular importance if ad-hoc changes are introduced by end users or – even more challenging – by software agents (Golani, 2006; Bassil, 2004).

We do not present all change patterns supported by ADEPT here, but only give three examples. For details on process change patterns as well as their formal semantics we refer to (Weber, 2007; Weber, 2008a; Rinderle-Ma, 2008b):

- *Insert fragment*: This operation can be used to add a schema fragment (i.e., a single activity or a complete block) to a WF schema. One parameterization describes the position at which the new

Figure 3. Insertion (a) and deletion (b+c) of process activities in ADEPT

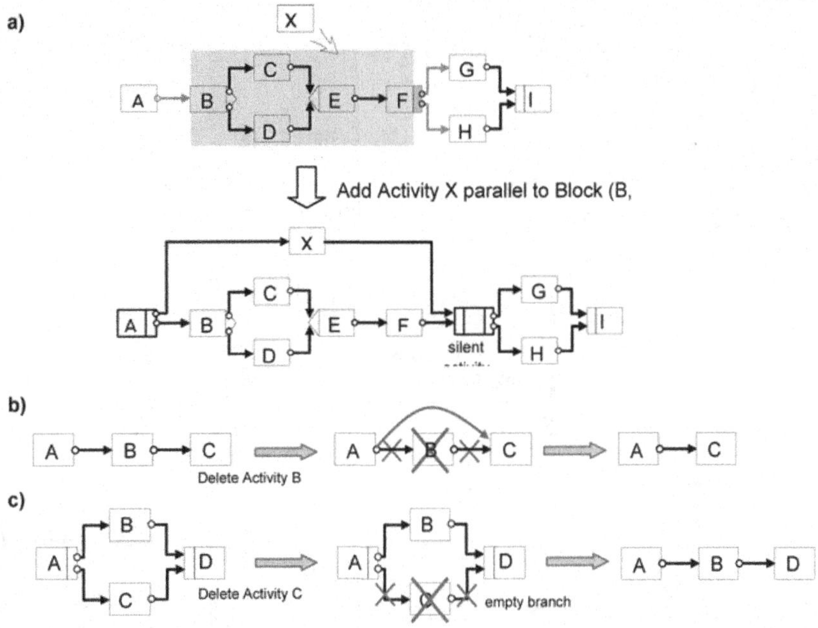

fragment is embedded in the respective WF schema. For example, ADEPT allows to serially insert a fragment between two directly succeeding activities as well as to insert new fragments between two sets of activities meeting certain constraints. Special cases of the latter variant include the insertion of a fragment in parallel to another one (*parallel insert;* see Figure 3a) or the additional association of the newly added fragment with an execution condition (*conditional insert*).

- *Delete fragment.* This operation can be used to remove single activities or blocks.
- *Move Fragment.* This operation allows users to move a fragment from its current position to a new one. Like for *Insert Process Fragment*, an important parameterization specifies the way the fragment is re-embedded in the WF schema. Although the move operation could be realized by the combined use of the insert and delete operation, ADEPT introduces it as separate operation, since it provides a higher level of abstraction to users.

By the combined use of these and other change operations, complex schema adaptations can be realized at a high level of abstraction.

So far, we have only considered structural issues. An example of an ad-hoc change applied at the WF instance level is shown in Figure 4. The depicted WF instance is modified by inserting new activity x in parallel to the existing activity b. Taking the user specification of the desired change ("insert activity x between a and c"), first of all, ADEPT checks whether this change can be applied; i.e., whether all correctness properties guaranteed by formal checks at buildtime are further met. If this is the case, ADEPT automatically calculates the *basic schema transformations* (i.e., change primitives like *insert node* or *delete edge*) to be applied to the execution schema of the given WF instance. In addition, it determines the new state of the WF instance in order to correctly proceed with the flow of control afterwards. In our example the state of the newly inserted activity x is automatically set to ACTIVATED; i.e., the cor-

Figure 4. (Simplified) example of an ad-hoc instance change in a centralized WfMS with a) WF execution schema, b) execution history, and c) change history

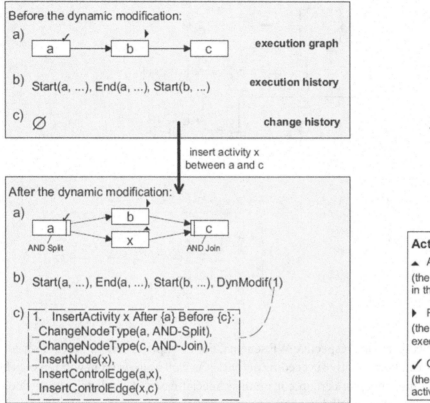

responding activity is immediately inserted into worklists of potential actors.

As illustrated in Figure 4 c, the required WF schema transformations (i.e., basic change primitives), together with the change specification, are recorded in the *change history* of the WF instance (Rinderle, 2006a). This history will be required, for example, if the WF instance has to be partially rolled back (Reichert, 2003a). Furthermore, ADEPT logs the occurrence of change events (and a reference to the corresponding change history entry) in the *execution history* of the WF instance as well. As example take the entry DynModif(1) in Figure 4 b which refers to the aforementioned ad-hoc change. Finally, the execution history contains other essential instance data, e.g., concerning the start and completion of activities.

Uncontrolled changes can lead to inconsistencies or errors. First of all, an ad-hoc change must result in a structurally correct WF instance schema. For example, deleting an activity can lead to missing input data for subsequent activities. This, in turn, can result in activity crashes or malfunctions when invoking the associated application service. Or, if a control edge is dynamically added without any checks, this can lead to deadlock-causing, cyclic dependencies. Besides structural soundness, we have to ensure that the respective WF instance is *compliant* with the modified WF schema (Casati 1998; Reichert, 1998; Rinderle, 2003; Rinderle, 2004a; Rinderle-Ma, 2008a); i.e., its execution log should be producible on the new WF schema as well. This will be not the case, if an activity is added to an already processed

Figure 5. (a) Migration of a WF instance (from s_1 to s_3); (b) resulting state of the instance

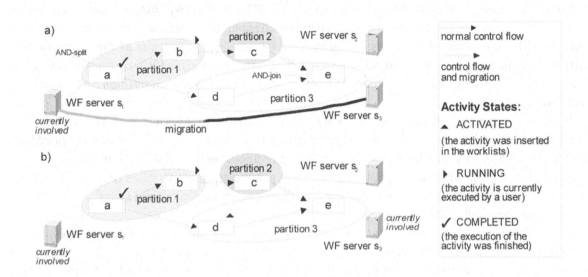

region of a WF schema. Generally, compliance is needed to avoid deadlocks or livelocks.

ADEPT precludes such errors and also ensures compliance. For this reason, formal pre- and post-conditions are defined for each change operation. They concern the state as well as the structure of the WF instance. Before introducing an ad-hoc change, ADEPT analyzes whether it is permissible on the basis of the current state and structure of the WF instance; i.e., whether the defined pre- and post-conditions of the applied change operations can be met. Only if this is the case the structure and state of the WF execution graph will be modified accordingly. Regarding our example from Figure 4, for instance, it would not be allowed to delete the already completed activity a or to add a new activity as predecessor of a.

DISTRIBUTED WORKFLOW EXECUTION IN ADEPT

We investigated the requirements of enterprise-wide and cross-organizational WF-based applications in detail (Reichert, 1999). In the following we provide a brief summary of fundamental concepts we developed for distributed WF control. Though illustrations are based on ADEPT, the general principles behind them can be applied to other WfMS as well.

Usually, WfMS with one central WF server will be not adequate if the WF participants (i.e., the actors working on the activities) are distributed across multiple enterprises or organizational units. In such a case, the use of one central WF server will restrict the autonomy of the involved partners and be disadvantageous with respect to response times. Particularly, if organizations are widespread, response times will significantly increase due to long distance communications between WF clients and central WF server. In addition, owing to the large number of users and co-active WF instances typical for enterprise-wide applications, the WfMS is generally subjected to an extremely heavy load (Kamath, 1996; Sheth, 1997).

For these reasons, in the distributed variant of the ADEPT WfMS, a WF instance may be controlled by multiple WF servers; i.e., its schema may be partitioned at buildtime, and the partitions be controlled piecewise by the different WF servers during runtime (Bauer, 1997).[1] As soon as the execution of a partition completes, control over the WF instance is handed over to the next WF server. We denote the hand-over of the instance control from one WF server to another as *instancemigration*.[2] An example is depicted in Figure 5.

When migrating a WF instance from one WF server to another, a description of its state has to be transferred to the target server before this server may take over control; i.e., before it may continue with instance execution. This includes, for example, information about the state of WF activities as well as WF relevant data; i.e., data elements connected with output parameters of activities. – To simplify matters, we assume that the WF templates (i.e., the WF type schemes) are replicated and stored on all relevant servers of the distributed WfMS.

To avoid unnecessary communication between WF servers, ADEPT allows to control parallel branches of an instance independent from each other – at least as long as no synchronization due to other reasons (e.g., ad-hoc changes) becomes necessary. In Figure 5 b, WF server s_3, which currently controls activity d, normally does not know how far execution has progressed in the upper branch (activities b and c). As advantage the WF servers controlling the activities of parallel branches do not need to be synchronized.

The partitioning of WF schemes and distributed WF control have been successfully utilized in other approaches as well (Casati, 1996; Muth, 1998). In ADEPT, we also target at the minimization of communication costs. Concrete experiences we gained in working with commercial WfMS have shown that there is a great deal of communication between the WF server and its WF clients (e.g., displaying worklists), oftentimes necessitating the exchange of large amounts of data. This may result in an overloaded communication system.

Hence, the WF servers responsible for controlling activities in ADEPT are defined in such a way that communication in the overall system is reduced: Typically, the WF server controlling a particular activity is selected in a way such that it is located in the subnet to which most of the potential actors of the respective activity belong. (Bauer, 1997) describes respective algorithms. This way of selecting the server contributes to avoid cross-subnet communication between the WF server and its WF clients. Further benefits are improved response times and increased availability. This is achieved since neither a gateway nor a WAN is interposed when executing activities. Finally, the efficiency of the described approach – with respect to WF server load and communication costs – has been proven by means of comprehensive simulations (Bauer, 1999).

Usually, WF servers are assigned to the activities of a WF schema already at buildtime. In some cases, however, this static approach is insufficient. Extensions will become necessary if *dependent actor assignments* exist; e.g., activity n may have to be performed by the same actor as preceding activity m. Consequently, the potential actors of activity n depend on the concrete actor who processes activity m. Since this set of prospective actors can only be determined at run-time, WF server assignment should be deferred to runtime as well. Then, a server in a suitable subnet can be selected; i.e., one that is most favorable for the actors defined. For this purpose, ADEPT supports *variable server assignments* (Bauer, 2000; Bauer, 1999); i.e., expressions like "server in subnet of the actor performing activity m" can be assigned to activities and then be evaluated at runtime. This allows for the dynamic selection of the WF server, which shall control the respective activity instance. Finally, (Bauer, 2004) deals with dynamic changes of server assignments in distributed WfMS.

REALIZING AD-HOC CHANGES IN A DISTRIBUTED WFMS

In a distributed WfMS it should be possible to perform ad-hoc changes of single WF instances just as in a central WfMS: The WfMS has to check whether the change may be applied taking the current structure and state of the respective WF instance into account. If the ad-hoc change is applicable (i.e., the instance has not progressed too far), the corresponding schema transformations will be determined and the WF schema belonging to the WF instance be modified accordingly (including adaptations of the WF instance state if required).

In order to check whether an intended ad-hoc change of a distributed WF instance is valid, first of all, the distributed WfMS needs to know the global state of the WF instance (or at least relevant parts of it). In case of parallel execution branches, for example, this state information may be distributed over several WF servers. It then has to be retrieved from these WF servers when the change shall be applied. How WF instance data can be efficiently transferred between the servers of a distributed WfMS has been described in (Bauer, 2001).

In the following we present a method for determining the WF servers on which the state information, relevant for checking the applicability of a particular ad-hoc change, is located. In contrast to a central WfMS, generally, in a distributed WfMS it is not sufficient to modify the execution schema of the WF instance solely on that WF server which controls the ad-hoc change. Otherwise, errors or inconsistencies might occur since the other WF servers might use outdated schema and state information when controlling the respective WF instance. In the following we show which WF servers have to be involved in the change procedure and how corresponding change protocols look like in ADEPT.

Synchronizing Workflow Servers in the Context of Ad-hoc Changes

An authorized user may invoke an ad-hoc change on any WF server which currently controls the WF instance in question. Yet as a rule, this WF server alone will not always be able to correctly perform the change. If other WF servers currently control parallel branches of the respective instance, state information from these WF servers might be needed as well. In addition, the WF server initiating the ad-hoc change must ensure that the change is also considered for the execution schemes of the respective WF instance, being managed by these other WF servers. This becomes necessary to enable these servers to correctly proceed with the flow in the sequel (see below). A naive solution would be to involve all WF servers of the WfMS by a broadcast. However, this approach is impractical in most cases as it is excessively expensive. In addition, all server machines of the WfMS must be available before an ad-hoc change can be performed. We come up with three alternative approaches:

Alternative 1 (Synchronize all Servers Concerned by the WF Instance). Alternative 1 considers all WF servers of the distributed WfMS which controlled the respective WF instance in the past, which are currently controlling respective WF activities, or which will be involved in the execution of future activities. Though the effort involved in communication is greatly reduced when compared to the naive solution mentioned above, it may still be unduly large. For example, communication with those WF servers which were involved in controlling the WF instance in the past, but which will not re-participate

Figure 6. Insertion of activity x between activities g and d by server s_4.

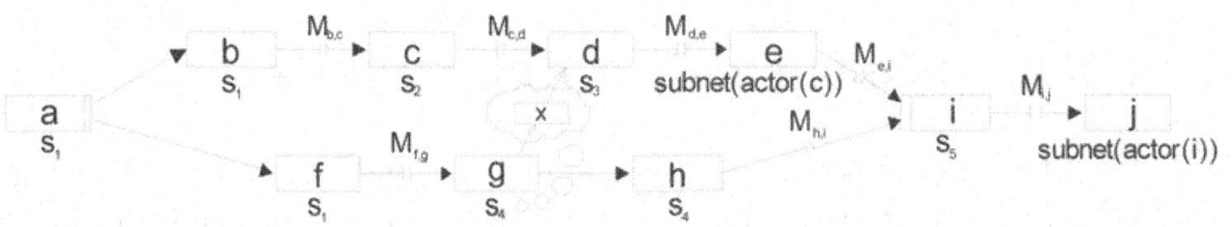

in future, is superfluous. They do not need to be synchronized any more and the state information managed by these WF servers has already been transferred in previous migrations.

Alternative 2 (Synchronize all Current and Future Servers of the WF Instance). To be able to control a WF instance, a WF server needs to know its current execution schema. This, in turn, requires knowledge of all ad-hoc changes performed so far. Therefore, a new ad-hoc change must be made public to those WF servers which are either currently active in controlling the WF instance or which will be involved in its control in future. Thus, it seems to make sense to synchronize exactly these WF servers. However, with this approach, problems arise in connection with conditional branches. For XOR-splits, which are evaluated in future, it cannot always be determined in advance which execution branch will be chosen. As different execution branches may be controlled by different WF servers, the set of relevant WF servers cannot be calculated immediately. Generally, it is only possible to determine those WF servers *potentially* be involved in the control of the WF instance in future.

The situation will become worse if variable server assignments are used. Then, for a given WF instance it is not possible to determine the WF servers that will be potentially involved in the execution of future activities. Note that runtime data of the WF instance, as required for evaluating WF server assignment expressions, may not even exist at this point in time; e.g., in Figure 6, during execution of activity g, the WF server of activity j cannot be determined since the actor responsible for activity i has not been fixed yet. Thus the system will not always be able to synchronize future servers of the WF instance when an ad-hoc change takes place. As these WF servers do not need to be informed about the change at this time (since they do not yet control the WF instance) we suggest another approach.

Alternative 3 (Synchronize all Current Servers of the WF Instance). The only workable solution is to synchronize exclusively those WF servers currently involved in the control of the WF instance, i.e., the *active* WF servers. Generally, it is not trivial at all to determine which WF servers these in fact are. The reason is that in case of distributed WF control, for an active WF server of a WF instance, the execution state of the activities being executed in parallel (by other WF servers) is not known. As depicted in Figure 6, for example, WF server s_4, which controls activity g, does not know whether migration $M_{c,d}$ has already taken place and, as a result, whether the parallel branch is being controlled by WF server s_2 or WF server s_3. In addition, it will be not possible to determine which WF server controls a parallel branch, without further effort, if variable server assignments are used. In Figure 6, for example, the WF server assignment of activity e refers to the actor of activity c, which is not known by WF server s_4. – In the following, we restrict our considerations to Alternative 3.

Determining the Set of Active Servers of a Workflow Instance

As explained above, generally, a WF server is not always able to determine from its local state information which other WF servers are currently executing activities of a specific WF instance. And it is no good idea to use a broadcast call to search for these WF servers, as this would result in exactly the same drawbacks as described above for the naive solution. We, therefore, require an approach for explicitly managing the active WF servers of a WF instance. The administration of these WF servers, however, should not be carried out by a fixed (and therefore central) WF server since this might lead to bottlenecks, thus negatively impacting the availability of the whole WfMS. For this reason, in ADEPT, the set of active WF servers (*ActiveServers*) is managed by a *ServerManager* specific to the WF instance. For this purpose, for example, the start server of the WF instance can be used as *ServerManager*. Normally, this WF server varies for each of the WF instances (even if they are of the same WF type), thus avoiding bottlenecks.[3]

The start WF server can be easily determined from the local execution history by any WF server involved in the control of the WF instance. In the following we show how the set of active servers of a specific WF instance is managed by the *ServerManager*, how it can be determined, and how ad-hoc changes can be synchronized.

Managing Active WF Servers of a WF Instance

As aforementioned, for the ad-hoc change of a WF instance we require the set *ActiveServers*, which comprises all WF servers currently involved in the control of the WF instance. This set, which may be changed due to migrations, is explicitly managed by the *ServerManager*. Thereby, the following two rules have to be considered:

1.   Multiple migrations of the same WF instance must not overlap arbitrarily, since this would lead to inconsistencies when changing the set of active WF servers.
2.   For a given WF instance the set *ActiveServers* must not change due to migrations during the execution of an ad-hoc change. Otherwise, wrong WF servers would be involved in the ad-hoc change or necessary WF servers would be left out.

As we will see in the following, we prevent these two cases by the use of several locks.[4] In the following, we describe the algorithms necessary to satisfy these requirements. *Algorithm 1* shows the way migrations are performed in ADEPT. It interacts with *Algorithm 2* by calling procedure *UpdateActiveServers* (remotely), which is defined by this algorithm. This procedure manages the set of active WF servers currently involved in the WF instance; i.e., it updates this set consistently in case of WF server changes.

Algorithm 1 illustrates how a migration is carried out in our approach: (Table 1).

Algorithm 1 is initiated and executed by a source WF server that hands over control to a target WF server. First, the *SourceServer* requests a non-exclusive lock from the *ServerManager*, which prevents that the migration is performed during an ad-hoc change.[6] Then an exclusive, short-term lock is requested. This lock ensures that the *ActiveServers* set of a given WF instance is not changed simultaneously by several migrations within parallel branches. (Both lock requests may be incorporated into a single call to save a communication cycle.) The *SourceServer* reports the change of the *ActiveServers* set to the

Table 1. Algorithm 1 (Performing a Migration)

```
input
        Inst: ID of the WF instance to be migrated
        SourceServer: source server of the migration (it performs Algorithm 1)
        TargetServer: target server of the migration
begin
        // determine the ServerManager for this WF instance from its execution history
        ServerManager = StartServer(Inst);
        // request a non-exclusive lock and an exclusive short-term lock from the ServerManager
        RequestSharedLock(Inst) → ServerManager;
        RequestShortTermLock(Inst) → ServerManager;
        // change the set of active servers (cf. Algorithm 2)
        ifLastBranch(Inst)then
                // the migration is performed for the last execution branch of the WF instance, that
                // is active at the SourceServer
                UpdateActiveServers(Inst, SourceServer, LogOff, TargetServer) → ServerManager;
        else // another execution path is active at SourceServer
                UpdateActiveServers(Inst, SourceServer, Stay, TargetServer) → ServerManager;

        // perform the actual migration and release the non-exclusive lock
        MigrateWorkflowInstance(Inst) → TargetServer;
        ReleaseSharedLock(Inst) → ServerManager;
end.
```

ServerManager, specifying whether it remains active for the concerned WF instance (*Stay*), or whether it is not involved any longer (*LogOff*). If, for example, in Figure 6 the migration $M_{b,c}$ is executed before $M_{f,g}$, the option *Stay* will be used for the migration $M_{b,c}$ since WF server s_1 remains active for this WF instance. Thus, the option *LogOff* will be used for the subsequent migration $M_{f,g}$ as it ends the last branch controlled by s_1. The (exclusive) short-term lock prevents that these two migrations may be executed simultaneously. This ensures that it is always clear whether or not a WF server remains active for a WF instance when a migration has completed. Next, the WF instance data (e.g., the current state of the WF instance) is transmitted to the target WF server of the migration. Since this is done after the exclusive short-term lock has been released (by *UpdateActiveServers*), several migrations of the same WF instance may be executed simultaneously. The algorithm ends with the release of the non-exclusive lock.

Algorithm 2 is used by the *ServerManager* to manage the WF servers currently involved in controlling a given WF instance. To fulfill this task, the *ServerManager* also has to manage the locks mentioned above. If the procedure *UpdateActiveServers* is called with the option *LogOff*, the source WF server of the migration is deleted from the set *ActiveServers(Inst)* (i.e., the set of active WF servers with respect to the given WF instance). The reason for this is that this WF server is no longer involved in controlling this WF instance. The target WF server for the migration, however, is always inserted into this set independently of whether it is already contained or not because this operation is idempotent.

The short-term lock requested by Algorithm 1 before the invocation of *UpdateActiveServers* prevents Algorithm 2 from being run in parallel more than once for a given WF instance. This helps to avoid an error due to overlapping changes of the set *ActiveServers(Inst)*. When this set has been adapted, the short-term lock is released. (Table 2)

Table 2. Algorithm 2 (UpdateActiveServers: Managing the active WF Servers)

```
input
        Inst: ID of the affected WF instance
        SourceServer: source server of the migration
        Option: indicates whether source server is further involved in the WF instance
                            (Stay) or not (LogOff)
        TargetServer: target server of the migration
begin
        // update the set of active WF servers of the WF instance Inst
        if Option = LogOff then
                ActiveServers(Inst) = ActiveServers(Inst) − {SourceServer};

        ActiveServers(Inst) = ActiveServers(Inst) ∪ {TargetServer};
        ReleaseShortTermLock(Inst); // release the short-term lock
end.
```

Performing Ad-Hoc Changes

While the previous subsection has described how the *ServerManager* handles the set of currently active WF servers for a particular WF instance, we now show how this set is utilized when ad-hoc changes are performed.

First of all, if no parallel branches are currently executed, trivially, the set of active WF servers contains exactly one element, namely the current WF server. This case may be easily detected by making use of the state and structure information (locally) available at the current WF server. The same applies to the special case that currently all parallel branches are controlled by the same WF server. In both cases, the method described in the following is not needed and therefore not applied. Instead, the WF server currently controlling the WF instance performs the ad-hoc change without consulting any other WF server. Consequently, this WF server need also not communicate with the *ServerManager*. For this special case, therefore, no additional synchronization effort occurs (when compared to the central case).

We now consider the case that parallel branches exist; i.e., an ad-hoc change of the WF instance may have to be synchronized between multiple WF servers. The WF server which coordinates the ad-hoc change then requests the set *ActiveServers* from the *ServerManager*. When performing the ad-hoc change, it is essential that this set is not changed due to concurrent migrations. Otherwise, wrong WF servers would be involved in the change procedure. In addition, it is vital that the WF execution schema of the WF instance is not restructured due to concurrent modifications, since this may result in an incorrect schema.

To prevent either of these errors we introduce **Algorithm 3**. It requests an exclusive lock from the *ServerManager* to avoid the aforementioned conflicts. This lock corresponds to a write lock (Gray, 1993) in a database system and is incompatible with read locks (*RequestSharedLock* in Algorithm 1) and other write locks of the same WF instance. Thus, it prevents that migrations are performed simultaneously to an ad-hoc change of the WF instance. (Table 3)

As soon as the lock has been granted in *Algorithm 3*, a query is sent to acquire the set of active WF servers of this WF instance.[7] Then a lock is requested at all WF servers belonging to the set *ActiveServers* in order to prevent local changes to the state of the WF instance. Any activities already started, however, may be finished normally since this does not affect the applicability of an ad-hoc change. Next the (locked) state information is retrieved from all active WF servers. Remember that the resulting global and

Table 3. Algorithm 3 (Performing an Ad-hoc Change)

```
input
        Inst: ID of the WF instance to be modified
        Modification: specification of the ad-hoc change
begin
        // calculate the ServerManager for this WF instance
        ServerManager = StartServer(Inst);
        // request an exclusive lock from the ServerManager and calculate the set of active WF servers
        RequestExclusiveLock(Inst) → ServerManager;
        ActiveServers = GetActiveServers(Inst) → ServerManager;
        // request a lock from all servers, calculate the current WF state, and perform
        // the change (if possible)
        for each Server s ∈ ActiveServers do
                RequestStateLock(Inst) → s;
        GlobalState = GetLocalState(Inst);
        for each Server s ∈ ActiveServers do
                LocalState = GetLocalState(Inst) → s;
                GlobalState = GlobalState ∪ LocalState;
        if DynamicModificationPossible(Inst, GlobalState, Modification) then
                for each Server s ∈ ActiveServers do
                        PerformDynamicModification(Inst, GlobalState, Modification) → s;
        // release all locks
        for each Server s ∈ ActiveServers do
                ReleaseStateLock(Inst) → s;
        ReleaseExclusiveLock(Inst) → ServerManager;
end.
```

current state of the WF instance is required to check whether the ad-hoc modification to be performed is permissible or not. In Figure 6, for example, WF server s_4, which is currently controlling activity g and which wants to insert activity x after activity g and before activity d, normally does not know the current state of activity d (from the parallel branch). Yet the ad-hoc change will be permissible only if activity d has not been started at the time the change is initiated (Reichert, 1998a). If this is the case, the ad-hoc change is performed at all active WF servers of the WF instance (*PerformDynamicModification*). Afterwards, the locks are released and any blocked migrations or modification procedures may then be carried out.

Illustrating Example

How migrations and ad-hoc changes work together is explained by means of an example. Figure 7a shows a WF instance currently controlled by exactly one WF server, i.e. WF server s_1. Figure 7b shows the same WF instance after it migrated to a second WF server s_2. In Figure 7c execution was continued. One can also see that each of the two WF servers must not always possess complete information about the global state of the WF instance.

Assume now that an ad-hoc change shall be performed, which is coordinated by WF server s_1. Afterwards, both WF servers shall possess the current schema of the WF instance to correctly proceed with the flow of control. With respect to the (complete) current state of the WF instance, it is sufficient that it is known by the coordinator s_1 (since only this WF server has to decide on the applicability of the desired change). The other WF server only carries out the change (as specified by WF server s_1).

Figure 7. Effects of migrations and ad-hoc changes on the (distributed) execution schema of a WF instance (local view of the WF servers)

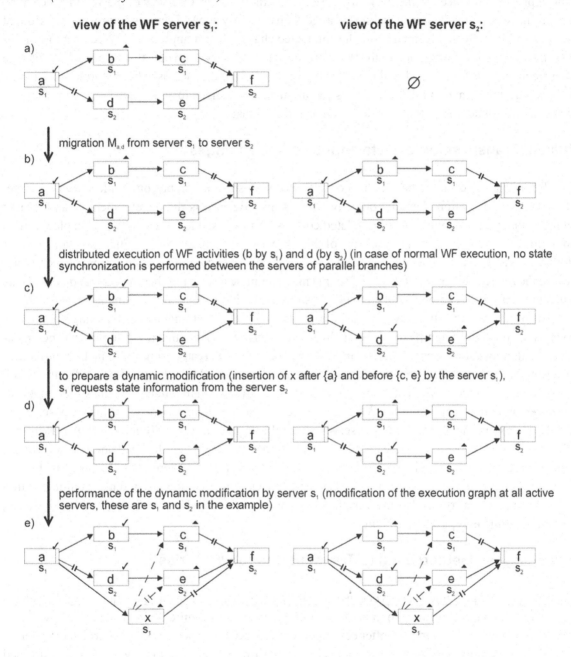

DISTRIBUTED EXECUTION OF A MODIFIED WORKFLOW INSTANCE

If a migration of a WF instance has to be performed its current state has to be transmitted to the target WF server. In ADEPT, this is done by transmitting the relevant parts of the execution history of the WF instance together with the values of WF relevant data (i.e., data elements) (Bauer, 2001). If an ad-hoc change was previously performed, the target WF server of a migration also needs to know the modified execution schema of the WF instance in order to be able to control the WF instance correctly afterwards. In the approach introduced in the previous section, only the active WF servers of the WF instance to be modified have been involved in the ad-hoc change. Consequently, the WF servers controlling subsequent activities still have to be informed about the conducted change. In our approach, the necessary information is transmitted upon migration of the WF instance to the WF servers in question. Since migrations are rather frequently performed in distributed WfMS, this communication needs to be performed efficiently. We first introduce a method that meets this requirement to a satisfactory degree. Then we present an enhancement that additionally precludes redundant data transfer.

Efficient Transmission of Data about Ad-hoc Changes

In the following, we examine how a changed WF execution schema can be communicated to the target WF server of a migration. The key objective of this investigation is the development of an efficient technique that reduces communication-related costs as best as possible. Obviously, the simplest way to communicate the current execution schema of the respective WF instance to the migration target server is to transmit this schema in whole. Yet this technique burdens the communication system unnecessarily because the related WF graph of this WF schema may comprise a large number of nodes and edges. This results in an enormous amount of data to be transferred – an inefficient and cost-intensive approach.

Apart from this, the entire execution schema does not need to be transmitted to the migration target server as the related WF template has been already located there. (Note that a WF template is being deployed to all relevant WF servers before any WF instance may be created from it.) In fact, in most cases the current WF schema of the WF instance is almost identical to the WF schema associated with the WF template. Thus it is more efficient to transfer solely the relatively small amount of data which specifies the change operations applied to the WF instance; i.e., to use the change history for this purpose. In the ADEPT approach, the migration target server needs this history anyway (Reichert, 1998a; Rinderle, 2006a), so that its transmission does not lead to additional efforts. When the base operations recorded in the change history are applied to the original WF schema of the WF template, the result is the current WF schema of the given WF instance. This simple technique significantly reduces communication efforts. In addition, as typically only very few changes are performed on any individual WF instance, computation time is kept to a minimum.

Enhancing the Method used to Transmit Change Histories

Generally, one and the same WF server can be involved more than once in the execution of a WF instance – especially in conjunction with loop backs. In our example from Figure 8, for instance, WF server s_1 hands over control to WF server s_2 after completion of activity b, but will receive control again later on in the flow to execute activity d. Since each WF server stores the change history until being informed that the given WF instance has been completed, such a WF server s already knows the history entries of the changes it has performed itself. In addition, s knows any changes that had been effected by other WF servers before s handed over the control of the WF instance to another WF server for the last time. Hence the data related to this part of the change history need not be transmitted to the WF server. This further reduces the amount of data required for the migration of the "current execution schema".

Figure 8. (a-d) WF instance and (e) execution history of WF server s_2 after completion of activity c. – In case of distributed WF control, with each entry the execution history records the server being responsible for the control of the corresponding activity.

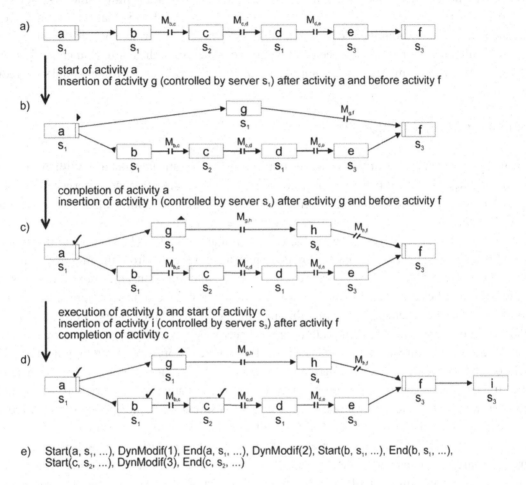

e)   Start(a, s_1, ...), DynModif(1), End(a, s_1, ...), DynModif(2), Start(b, s_1, ...), End(b, s_1, ...),
     Start(c, s_2, ...), DynModif(3), End(c, s_2, ...)

Transmitting Change History Entries

An obvious solution for avoiding redundant transfer of change history entries is as follows: The migration source server determines from the existing execution history exactly which changes the target WF server does already know. The related entries are then simply not transmitted when migrating the WF instance. In the example given in Figure 8, WF server s_2 can determine, upon ending activity c, that the migration target server s_1 does already know Changes 1 and 2. In the execution history (cf. Figure 8e), references to these changes (*DynModif(1)* and *DynModif(2)*) have been recorded before entry *End(b, s_1, ...)* (which was logged when completing activity b). As this activity was controlled by WF server s_1, this WF server does already know the Changes 1 and 2. Thus, for the migration $M_{c,d}$, only the change history entry corresponding to Change 3 needs to be transmitted. The transmitted part of the change history is concatenated with the part already being present at the target server before this WF server creates the new execution schema and proceeds with the flow of control.

In some cases, however, redundant transfer of change history data cannot be avoided with this approach. As example take migrations $M_{d,e}$ and $M_{h,f}$ to WF server s_3. For both migrations, using the above approach, all entries corresponding to Changes~1, 2, and 3 must be transmitted since WF server s_3 was not involved in the execution of the WF instance thus far. The problem is that migration source servers s_1 and s_4 are unable, from their locally available history data, to derive whether the other migration from the parallel branch has already been effected or not. Therefore, the entire change history has to be transmitted. Yet with the more advanced approach set out in the following, we can avoid such redundant data transfer.

Requesting Change History Entries

To avoid redundant data transmissions, we introduce a more sophisticated method. With this method, the necessary change history entries are explicitly requested by the migration target server. When a migration takes place, the target WF server informs the source WF server about the history entries it already knows. The source WF server then only transmits those change history entries of the WF instance yet missing on the side of the target server. In ADEPT, a similar method has been used for transmitting execution histories; i.e., necessary data is provided on basis of a request from the migration target server (Bauer, 2001). Here, no additional effort is expended for communication, since both the request for and the transmission of change history entries may be carried out within same communication cycle.

With the described method, requesting the missing part of a change history is efficient and easy to implement in our approach. If the migration target server was previously involved in the control of the WF instance, it would already possess all entries of the change history up to a certain point (i.e., it knows all ad-hoc changes that had been applied to the respective WF instance before this server handed over control the last time). But from this point on, it does not know any further entries. It is thus sufficient to transfer the ID of the last known entry to the migration source server to specify the required change history entries. The source WF server then transmits all change history entries made after this point.

The method described above is implemented by means of *Algorithm 4*, which is executed by the migration source server as part of the *MigrateWorkflowInstance* procedure (cf. Algorithm 1). This procedure also effects transmission of the execution history and of WF relevant data. *Algorithm 4* triggers the transmission of the change history by requesting the ID of the last known change history entry from the target WF server. If no change history for the given WF instance is known at the target WF server it will return NULL. In this case, the entire change history is relevant for the migration and is therefore transmitted to the target WF server. Otherwise, the target WF server requires only that part of the change history, which follows the specified entry. This part is copied into the history *RelevantChangeHistory* and transmitted to the target WF server. This data may be transmitted together with the mentioned WF execution data to save a communication cycle. (Table 4)

Algorithm 4 is illustrated by means of the example given in Figure 8: Concerning the migration $M_{c,d}$ the target WF server s_1 already knows the ad-hoc changes 1 and 2. Thus it responds to the request of the source server with *LastEntry = 2*. The migration source server then ignores the change history entries for changes 1 and 2, transmitting only the entry for change 3 to target WF server s_1. This result is identical to the one achieved in the approach for transmitting change history entries.

For the migrations $M_{h,f}$ and $M_{d,e}$, without loss of generality, it is assumed that $M_{h,f}$ is executed before $M_{d,e}$.[8] Since there has been no change history of this WF instance located on WF server s_3 yet, the target WF server of migration $M_{h,f}$ returns *LastEntry = NULL*. Therefore, the entire change history is transmitted

Table 4. Algorithm 4 (Transmission of Change History Data)

```
input
        Inst: ID of the WF instance to be changed
        TargetServer: server, which receives the change history
begin
        // start the transmission of the change history by asking for the ID of the last known entry
        LastEntry = GetLastEntry(Inst) → TargetServer;
        // calculate the relevant part of the change history
        if LastEntry = NULL then // change history totally unknown at the target WF server
                Relevant = True;
        else // all entries until LastEntry (incl.) are known by the target server
                Relevant = False;
        // initialize the position counters for the original and the new change history
        i = 1; j = 1;
        // read the whole change history of WF instance Inst
        whileChangeHistory(Inst)[i] ≠ EOF} do
                if Relevant = True then // put the entry in the result (if necessary)
                        RelevantChangeHistory[j] = ChangeHistory(Inst)[i];
                        j = j + 1;
                // check whether the end of that part of the change history, that is known by the
                // target WF server, is reached
                if EntryID(ChangeHistory(Inst)[i]) = LastEntry then
                        Relevant = True;
                i = i + 1;
        // perform the transmission of the change history
        TransmitChange(Inst, RelevantChangeHistory) → TargetServer;
end.
```

to s_3. In the subsequent migration $M_{d,e}$, the target WF server s_3 then already knows change history entries $1 - 3$, so that *LastEntry = 3* will be returned in response to the source server query. (When the *while* loop in Alg. 4 is run, variable *Relevant* is not set to *True* until history entries $1 - 3$ have been processed. Since there exist no further entries in the change history, *RelevantModificationHistory* remains empty with the result that no change history entries have to be transmitted.) Finally, the problem of redundant data transfer, as described at the beginning of this section, is thus avoided here.

To sum up, with the described approach not only ad-hoc modifications can be performed efficiently in a distributed WfMS, but transmission costs for migrating changed WF instances can be kept low as well.

PROOF-OF-CONCEPT PROTOTYPE

All methods presented in this chapter have been implemented in a powerful proof-of-concept prototype. It demonstrates feasibility of ad-hoc changes in a distributed WfMS and shows how the developed concepts work in conjunction with each other.

Buildtime Components

Our proof-of-concept prototype supports the WF designer by powerful tools. They support the definition of WF templates, the modeling of organizational entities and their relationships, the specification of access control constraints (e.g., authorizations concerning WF changes; Weber, 2005b), and the plug-

Figure 9. Workflow Editor

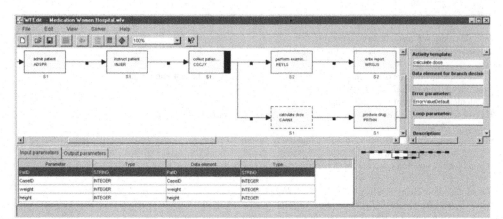

in of application services. All relevant information is stored in a repository. In addition, XML-based descriptions of the defined models can be created; e.g., to export them to other tools or to deploy them to the WF servers of the distributed WfMS.

For WF modeling we offer a syntax-driven, graphical WF editor. A sample screen is depicted in Figure 9. It shows a clinical workflow as modeled in ADEPT. The upper part of this screen shows the control flow of this workflow, whereas the lower part displays the input parameters of the currently selected activity *calculate dose* (as well as the mapping of these parameters to data elements). Additional information about the selected activity is shown on the right-hand side. Further down, a pacemaker box is displayed, which helps the WF designer to navigate through larger models. We explain the WF model from Figure 9 in more detail, since we refer to it in the following. This model describes the medication of a patient during a treatment cycle in a hospital. The workflow starts with the patient's admission to a ward (by a *ward nurse*). It then proceeds with activities *instruct patient* (by *ward physician*) and *collect patient data* (by *ward nurse*). Afterwards, the flow splits into two parallel branches which may be executed concurrently. The upper branch comprises the activities of a medical examination performed in another department (*perform examination* and *write report* both with user role *radiologist*), whereas the lower branch defines preparatory steps performed at the ward side (e.g., *calculate dose*, *produce drug*). These two branches contain some other activities (*read report*, *validate dose*) not displayed in Figure 9. When both branches are completed, they are joined and the produced drug is administered to the patient, some aftercare is provided, and the patient is discharged (also not displayed in Figure 9).

Our prototype supports the WF designer in calculating optimal WF server assignments for the respective WF activities; i.e., in partitioning the WF schema such that overall communication costs become minimal at runtime. For this purpose, we have implemented advanced algorithms which make use of the information from the organizational model (i.e., roles as well as locations of actors). Concerning our example from Figure 9, respective WF instances are controlled by WF servers s_1 and s_2. The calculated WF server assignments are displayed below the activity nodes. Accordingly, activities *perform examination* and *write report* are controlled by WF server s_2, whereas all other activities are carried out by WF server s_1.

Furthermore, the developed WF editor supports the designer in modeling error-free WF templates (e.g., by excluding deadlocks and by ensuring data flow correctness) – we denote this capability as *cor-*

Figure 10. Monitoring client (before applying an ad-hoc change to the depicted WF instance)

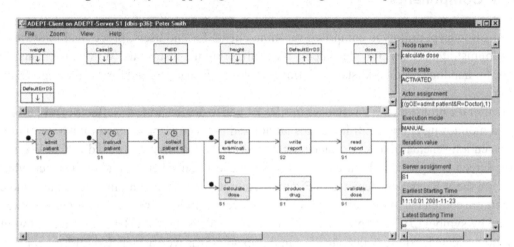

rectness by construction. To achieve it, both on-the-fly checks during editing and complete model checks initiated by the designer at any point in time are possible. In any case, a new WF template may only be released, if all correctness and consistency checks are successfully passed. Note that this is fundamental for the support of ad-hoc changes as well. An adaptive WfMS will only be able to guarantee consistency if a WF instance is consistent before a change as well. This, in turn, is crucial for the WfMS to guarantee a reliable and robust execution behavior of the distributed WF instances.

A new release of a WF template can be introduced to the distributed WfMS by deploying it to relevant WF servers. For this, an XML-based description is sent to the WF servers and imported into their run-time databases. – We omit descriptions of other build-time components since they are not relevant in the context of this paper (Reichert, 2003c).

Figure 11. Monitoring client (after applying the ad-hoc change to the depicted WF instance)

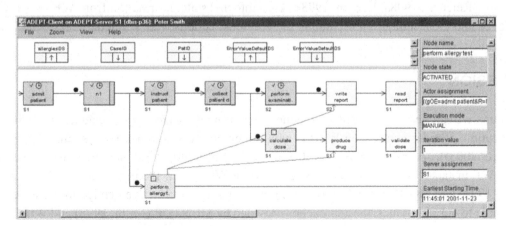

Runtime Components

Our proof-of-concept prototype comprises run-time clients for end users, process administrators, and system administrators. They provide support for configuring the distributed WfMS, for managing WF instances, for handling user worklists, for defining ad-hoc WF changes, and for monitoring WF instance execution.

To monitor the progress of WF instances in ADEPT and to demonstrate the effects of ad-hoc changes, we offer a monitoring component. It enables authorized users (e.g., process administrators) to visualize the execution schema of a WF instance together with the information related to that WF instance. A sample screen is depicted in Figure 10. It shows the execution schema of a WF instance which was created from the WF template depicted in Figure 9. Activities admit patient, instruct patient and collect patient data are completed (indicated by symbol ✓), whereas activity calculate dose is currently activated (expressed by symbol ☐). The upper part of Figure 10 displays the data elements read and written by the currently selected activity (calculate dose in this example) as well as detailed information about the activity (e.g., state, actor assignment, execution mode, server assignment, earliest / latest starting times, etc.). All relevant information is managed by WF server s_1 which controls activity calculate dose. We provides a powerful *application programming interface* for accessing respective information.

Actually, the depicted monitoring client only shows the execution schema from the viewpoint of WF server s_1 (to which this client is connected). However, WF server s_1 does not know how far execution has proceeded in the upper branch of the parallel branching (currently controlled by WF server s_2). For example, WF server s_1 does not know whether activity perform examination has been activated, started, or completed yet.

How can an ad-hoc change be realized in the given scenario? End users must be able to define such change at a high level of abstraction; i.e., without need to be familiar with the WF editor or to have knowledge about distributed execution of the WF instance. For this purpose we offer easy-to-use runtime clients to the actors.[9]

We now come back to our WF instance from Figure 10. Assume that an authorized user (connected to WF server s_1) wants to insert activity perform allergy test after activity instruct patient and before activities write report and produce drug; i.e., the user wants the allergy test to be started after instruction of the patient and to be completed before a report is written and the drug is produced. If this change is applied to the WF instance from Figure 10, the execution schema from Figure 11 will result. Here, node n1 represents an AND-split which resulted from the transformation of the change into respective schema adaptations (Reichert, 1998a; Dadam, 1998). Also note that state information from WF server s_2 had to be retrieved and the techniques presented in the previous sections were applied.

DISCUSSION

In literature, we can find a number of approaches addressing issues related to scalability and distributed WF execution. Besides centralized WfMS, which include most commercial systems (e.g. Staffware (Staffware, 2003)), several distributed WfMS consisting of multiple WF servers exist. Some of them assign a WF instance (as a whole) always to the same WF server. Examples include Exotica/Cluster (Alonso, 1994) and MOBILE (Jablonski, 1997); the latter approach was extended in (Schuster, 1999). Comparable to our techniques, the approaches provided by MENTOR (Muth, 1998) and WIDE (Casati,

1996) select the WF server for a WF activity next to its potential actors. CodAlf, BPAFrame (Schill, 1996), and METEOR$_2$ (Sheth, 1997), in turn, allocate the WF server for a WF activity on that node where its corresponding application service is located. Furthermore, completely distributed WfMS, like Exotica/FMQM (Alonso, 1995) and INCAs (Barbará, 1996}, use the machines of the actors as WF servers. Finally, there are approaches for distributed WF management, which do not have a special strategy for distributing the activities to the WF servers; e.g., EVE (Geppert, 1998), METUFlow (Dogac, 1997), MOKASSIN (Gronemann, 1999), WASA$_2$ (Weske, 1998; Weske, 1999), and the Petri-net based approach presented in (Guth, 1998).

Similarly, many groups deal with issues related to ad-hoc WF changes. They focus on different issues arising in this context. Like ADEPT (Reichert, 1998a), Chautauqua (Ellis, 1997), WASA$_2$ (Weske, 1998), and WF nets (van der Aalst, 2001a+b) deal with issues related to the correctness and consistency of modified WF instances. CBRFlow (Weber, 2004), ProCycle (Rinderle, 2005; Weber, 2005a; Weber, 2006b), and CAKE2 (Minor, 2007), for example, additionally apply knowledge-based techniques (e.g., case-based reasoning) to increase WfMS flexibility and to foster the reuse of ad-hoc changes. The approaches described in (van der Aalst, 2001b) uses generic WF models to deal with dynamic WF changes. In this context, a generic WF model describes a family of WF models (i.e., model variants) of the same WF type. Consequently, an (ad-hoc) change is handled by migrating a WF instance between different members of the same process family. This is supported by defining a minimal representative for each process family and by specifying rules for transferring a variant to the minimal representative (and vice versa). An approach based on inheritance, which uses generic inheritance-preserving transformation and transfer rules, is suggested by (van der Aalst, 2002). With this approach, certain errors in connection with changes can be avoided by choosing appropriate inheritance notions. Finally, there are several approaches aiming at the support of WF schema evolution and the propagation of the resulting schema changes to already running WF instances (if compliant to the new scheme). Corresponding work has been done in MOKASSIN (Joeris, 1998), WIDE (Casati, 1998), TRAM (Kradolfer, 1999), ADEPT2 (Rinderle, 2004a-c; Rinderle-Ma, 2008a), and WASA$_2$ (Weske, 1998).

There are only few projects which allow for ad-hoc changes as well as distributed WF control. In particular, how these two fundamental features of a large-scale WfMS impact each other has not yet been investigated in detail. The major objective of the aforementioned approaches was not to develop a scalable and flexible WfMS which is efficient with regard to communication costs. This has been systematically investigated in this chapter.

There are few approaches which address both WF changes and distributed WF execution. WIDE allows WF schema changes and their propagation to running WF instances (Casati, 1998). In addition, control of WF instances can be distributed (Casati, 1996). Thereby, the set of potential actors of an activity determines the WF server which has to control this activity. In MOKASSIN (Gronemann, 1999; Joeris, 1998} and WASA$_2$ (Weske, 1998+1999), distributed WF execution is realized through an underlying CORBA infrastructure. Both approaches do not discuss the criteria used to determine a concrete distribution of the WF activities; i.e., the question which WF server has to control a specific activity remains open. Here, changes may be applied at both the WF schema and the WF instance level.

INCAs (Barbará, 1996) uses rules for WF instance coordination. WF control is distributed with a given WF instance being controlled by that processing station that belongs to the actor of the current activity. The mentioned rules are used to calculate the processing station of the subsequent activity and, thereby, the actor of that activity. With this approach, it becomes possible to modify the rules, what results in an ad-hoc change of the WF instance behavior. As opposed to our approach, none of these works explicitly addresses how ad-hoc changes and distributed WF execution interact. The approach proposed in (Cichocki, 2000) enables some kind of flexibility in distributed WfMS as well, especially in the context of virtual enterprises. However, it does not allow to adapt the structure of in-progress WF instances. Instead, the activities of a WF template represent placeholders for which the concrete implementations are selected at run-time – a similar approach is provided by pockets of flexibility (Sadiq, 2001; Sadiq, 2005). Finally, DYCHOR allows for structural changes of process choreographies, but without taking state information into account (Rinderle, 2006b).

There are several approaches for distributed WF management where a WF instance is controlled by one and the same WF server over its entire lifetime; e.g., Exotica (Alonso, 1994) and MOBILE (Jablonski, 1997). The latter approach was extended in (Schuster, 1999) such way that a sub-process may be controlled by a different WF server to be determined at run-time. Though migrations are not performed, different WF instances may be controlled by different WF servers. Furthermore, since a central control component (i.e., WF engine) exists for each WF instance in these approaches, ad-hoc changes may be performed just as in a central WfMS. Yet there is a drawback with respect to communication costs (Bauer, 1999) since the distribution model does not allow to select the most favorable WF server for the individual activities. When developing our approach, we therefore did not follow such an approach since the additional costs incurred in standard WF execution are higher than the savings generated due to the (relatively seldom performed) ad-hoc changes.

SUMMARY AND OUTLOOK

Both distributed WF execution and ad-hoc WF changes are essential features of any WfMS in order to enable flexible process-aware information systems. However, each of these aspects is closely linked with a number of requirements and objectives that are, to some extent, opposing. Typically, the central control instance required for ad-hoc changes impacts the efficiency of (distributed) WF execution. For these reasons we cannot afford to consider these two fundamental aspects separately. In this book chapter, an investigation of exactly how these two features interact has been presented. Our results have shown that are, in fact, compatible. We have realized ad-hoc changes in a distributed WfMS efficiently. Our approach also allows for the efficient distributed control of changed WF instances. The described techniques make use of the fact that only a parts of the relatively small change history need to be transmitted when transferring a modified WF execution schema to another WF server. This is vital as migrations are frequently performed operations. As demonstrated with our proof-of-concept prototype, our approach succeeds in seamlessly integrating both distributed WF execution and ad-hoc changes into a single system.

There is room for further optimization regarding the selection of the WF servers that need to be synchronized in the context of an ad-hoc change. If such a change affects only a particular region of the WF schema, it could be performed by only those active WF servers controlling that region of the WF instance. This would reduce synchronization and communication efforts. In the extreme case, if only a single branch of a parallel branching has to be changed, only a single server must perform the change. However, activities belonging to parallel branches may be impacted by the change performed (e.g. due to dependencies in the data flow), thus necessitating synchronization of the respective WF servers in these cases. Our work has shown that the opportunity to deploy such an enhancement is fairly rare so that a significant improvement in the behavior of the system cannot be expected.

Generally, non-trivial interdependencies exist among the different features of a WfMS, which should be carefully analyzed and understood. One cannot implement such WfMS by adding one balcony to the other to deal with situation-specific problems. Instead a proper framework is needed which allows to argue about WF correctness and which covers all possible scenarios. The ADEPT1 project (Dadam, 1998) has reflected this way of thinking from the very beginning. In ADEPT2 (Reichert, 2005), we have extended respective research activities to other aspects as well, e.g., concerning the mining and evolution of access control constraints (Ly, 2005; Rinderle-Ma, 2007+2008c) or different techniques for learning from ad-hoc changes (Rinderle, 2005; Günther, 2006; Li, 2008). Recently, we have started our research on WF change patterns (Weber, 2007+ 2008a+2009; Rinderle-Ma, 2008b), WF refactoring techniques (Weber, 2008b), and data-driven WF coordination and adaptation (Müller, 2007+2008).

REFERENCES

Adams, M., ter Hofstede, A., Edmond, D., & van der Aalst, W. M. P. (2006). Worklets: A service-oriented implementation of dynamic flexibility in workflows. In *Proc. Coopis'06* (pp. 291-308).

Alonso, G., Kamath, M., Agrawal, D., El Abbadi, A., Günthör, R., & Mohan, C. (1994). Failure handling in large scale workflow management systems. *TR RJ9913, IBM Almaden Research Center.*

Alonso, G., Mohan, C., Günthör, R., Agrawal, D., El Abbadi, A., & Kamath, M. (1995). Exotica/ FMQM: Persistent message-based architecture for distributed workflow management. In *Proc. IFIP Working Conf. on Inf. Syst. for Decentralized Organisations*, Trondheim, Norway.

Barbará, D., Mehrotra, S., & Rusinkiewicz, M. (1996). *INCAs:* Managing dynamic workflows in distributed environments. *Journal of Database Management, 7*(1), 5–15.

Bassil, S., Keller, R., & Kropf, P. (2004). A workflow-oriented system architecture for the management of container transportation. In *Proc. BPM'04* (LNCS 3080, pp. 116-131).

Bauer, T., & Dadam, P. (1997). A distributed execution environment for large-scale workflow management systems with subnets and server migration. In *Proc. CoopIS'97* (pp. 99-108).

Bauer, T., & Dadam, P. (1999). Efficient distributed control of enterprise-wide and cross-enterprise workflows. In *Proc. GI-Workshop on Enterprise-wide and Cross-enterprise Workflow Management: Concepts, Systems, Applications* (pp. 25-32). Paderborn, Germany.

Bauer, T., & Dadam, P. (2000). Efficient distributed workflow management based on variable server assignments. In *Proceedings CAiSE'00* (pp. 94-109). Stockholm, Sweden.

Bauer, T., & Reichert, M. (2004). Dynamic change of server assignments in distributed workflow management systems. In *Proc. ICEIS'04* (pp. 91-98). Porto, Portugal.

Bauer, T., Reichert, M., & Dadam, P. (2001). Effiziente Übertragung von prozessinstanzdaten in verteilten workflow-management-systemen. *Informatik - Forschung und Entwicklung, 16*(2), 76-92.

Bauer, T., Reichert, M., & Dadam, P. (2003). Intra-subnet load balancing for distributed workflow management systems. *International Journal of Cooperative Information Systems, 12*(3), 295–323. doi:10.1142/S0218843003000760

Casati, F., Ceri, S., Pernici, B., & Pozzi, G. (1998). Workflow evolution. *Data & Knowledge Engineering, 24*(3), 211–238. doi:10.1016/S0169-023X(97)00033-5

Casati, F., Grefen, P., Pernici, B., & Pozzi, H. & Sánchez. G. (1996). *WIDE: Workflow model and architecture* (CTIT Technical Report 96-19). University of Twente, The Netherlands.

Cichocki, A., Georgakopoulos, D., & Rusinkiewicz, M. (2000). Workflow migration supporting virtual enterprises. In *Proceedings BIS'00* (pp. 20-35), Poznán, Poland.

Dadam, P., & Reichert, M. (1998). The ADEPT WfMS Project at the University of Ulm. In *Proc. 1st European Workshop on Workflow Management, Zurich, Switzerland.*

Dadam, P., & Reichert, M. (Eds.). (1999). Enterprise-wide and cross-enterprise workflow management: Concepts, systems, applications. In *CEUR Workshop Proceedings, Vol. 24.*

Dadam, P., Reichert, M., & Kuhn, K. (2000). Clinical workflows - The killer application for process-oriented information systems? In *Proc. 4th Int'l Conf. on Business Information Systems (BIS'00)* (pp. 36-59), Poznan, Poland.

Dogac, A., et al. (1997). Design and implementation of a distributed workflow management system: METUFlow. In *Proc. NATO Advanced Study Institute on Workflow Management Systems and Interoperability* (pp. 61-91), Istanbul, Turkey.

Ellis, C. A., & Maltzahn, C. (1997). The Chautauqua workflow system. In *Proc. 30th Hawaii Int. Conf. on System Sciences*, Maui, Hawaii.

Geppert, A., & Tombros, D. (1998). Event-based distributed workflow execution with EVE. In *Proc. IFIP Int. Conf. on Distributed Systems Platforms and Open Distributed Processing* (pp. 427-442).

Golani, M., & Gal, A. (2006). Optimizing exception handling in workflows using process restructuring, In *Proc. BPM'06* (LNCS 4102, pp. 407-413).

Gray, J., & Reuter, A. (1993). *Transaction processing: Concepts and techniques*. Morgan Kaufmann Publishers.

Gronemann, B., Joeris, G., Scheil, S., Steinfort, M., & Wache, H. (1999). Supporting cross organizational engineering processes by distributed collaborative workflow management - The MOKASSIN approach. In *Proc. 2nd Symposium on Concurrent Multidisciplinary Engineering*, Bremen, Germany.

Günther, C. W., Reichert, M., & van der Aalst, W. M. P. (2008a). Supporting flexible processes with adaptive workflow and case Handling. In *Proceedings WETICE'08, 3rd IEEE Workshop on Agile Cooperative Process-aware Information Systems*, Rome, Italy.

Günther, C. W., Rinderle, S., Reichert, M., & van der Aalst, W. M. P. (2006). Change mining in adaptive process management systems. In *Proc. 14th Int'l Conf. on Cooperative Information Systems (Coopls'06)* (LNCS 4275, pp. 309-326).

Günther, C. W., Rinderle-Ma, S., Reichert, M., van der Aalst, W. M. P., & Recker, J. (2008b). Using process mining to learn from process changes in evolutionary systems. *Int'l Journal of Business Process Integration and Management . Special Issue on Business Process Flexibility, 3*(1), 61–78.

Guth, V., Lenz, K., & Oberweis, A. (1998). Distributed workflow execution based on fragmentation of Petri nets. In *Proc. 15th IFIP World Computer Congress: Telecooperation - The Global Office, Teleworking and Communication Tool* (pp. 114-125).

Hallerbach, A., Bauer, T., & Reichert, M. (2008). Managing process variants in the process lifecycle. In *Proc. 10th Int'l Conf. on Enterprise Information Systems (ICEIS'08)* (pp. 154-161), Barcelona.

Han, Y., & Sheth, A. (1998). On adaptive workflow modeling. In *Proc. 4th Int. Conf. on Information Systems Analysis and Synthesis*, Orlando

Jablonski, S. (1997). Architecture of workflow management systems. *Informatik . Forschung und Entwicklung, 12*(2), 72–81. doi:10.1007/s004500050076

Joeris, G., & Herzog, O. (1998). Managing evolving workflow specifications. In *Proceedings CoopIS'98* (pp. 310–321), New York.

Kamath, M., Alonso, G., Günthör, R., & Mohan, C. (1996). Providing high availability in very large workflow management systems. In *Proc. EDBT'96* (pp. 427-442), Avignon, France.

Kochut, K., Arnold, J., Sheth, A., Miller, J., Kraemer, E., Arpinar, B., & Cardoso, J. (2003). IntelliGEN: A distributed workflow system for discovering protein-protein interactions. *Distributed and Parallel Databases, 13*(1), 43–72. doi:10.1023/A:1021565722755

Kradolfer, M., & Geppert, A. (1999). Dynamic workflow schema evolution based on workflow type versioning and workflow migration. In *Proc. CoopIS'99* (pp. 104-114), Edinburgh, Scotland.

Lenz, R., & Reichert, M. (2007). IT support for healthcare processes – Premises, challenges, perspectives. *Data & Knowledge Engineering, 61*, 82–111. doi:10.1016/j.datak.2006.04.007

Li, C., Reichert, M., & Wombacher, A. (2008). Discovering reference process models by mining process variants. In *Proc. 6th Int'l IEEE Conference on Web Services (ICWS'08)* (pp. 45-53), Beijing.

Ly, L. T., Rinderle, S., Dadam, P., & Reichert, M. (2005). Mining staff assignment rules from event-based data. In *Proc. Workshop on Business Process Intelligence (BPI)* (LNCS 3812, pp. 177-190).

Minor, M., Schmalen, D., Koldehoff, A., & Bergmann, R. (2007). Structural adaptation of workflows supported by a suspension mechanism and by case-based reasoning. In *Proc. WETICE'07* (pp. 370-375), Paris.

Montagut, F., & Molva, R. (2007). Enforcing integrity of execution in distributed workflow management systems. In *IEEE Conf. on Services Computing (SCC'07)* (pp. 1-8).

Mourào, H., & Antunes, P. (2007). Supporting effective unexpected exceptions handling in workflow management systems. In *Proc. SAC'07* (pp. 1242-1249).

Müller, D., Herbst, J., Hammori, M., & Reichert, M. (2006). IT support for release management processes in the automotive industry. In *Proc. 4th Int'l Conf. on Business Process Management (BPM'06)* (LNCS 4102, pp. 368-377).

Müller, D., Reichert, M., & Herbst, J. (2007). Data-driven modeling and coordination of large process structures. In: *Proc. 15th Int'l Conf. on Cooperative Information Systems (CoopIS'07)*, Vilamoura, Portugal, (LNCS 4803, pp. 131-149).

Müller, D., Reichert, M., & Herbst, J. (2008) A new paradigm for the enactment and dynamic adaptation of data-driven process structures. In *Proc. 20th Int'l Conf. on Advanced Information Systems Engineering (CAiSE'08)* (LNCS 5074, pp. 48-63).

Muth, P., Wodtke, D., Weißenfels, J., Kotz-Dittrich, A., & Weikum, G. (1998). From centralized workflow specification to distributed workflow execution. *Journal of Intelligent Information Systems, 10*(2), 159–184. doi:10.1023/A:1008608810770

Mutschler, B., Bumiller, J., & Reichert, M. (2006). Why process-orientation is scarce: An empirical study of process-oriented information systems in the automotive industry. In *Proc. 10th IEEE Int. Conf. on Enterprise Computing (EDOC '06)* (pp. 433-440), Hong Kong, China.

Mutschler, B., Reichert, M., & Bumiller, J. (2008a). Unleashing the effectiveness of process-oriented information systems: problem analysis, critical success factors and implications. [Part C]. *IEEE Transactions on Systems, Man, and Cybernetics, 38*(3), 280–291. doi:10.1109/TSMCC.2008.919197

Mutschler, B., Weber, B., & Reichert, M. (2008b). Workflow management versus case handling: results from a controlled software experiment. In *Proc. 23rd Annual ACM Symposium on Applied Computing (SAC'08)* (pp. 82-89), Fortaleza, Ceará, Brazil.

Pesic, M., Schonenberg, M., Sidorova, N., & van der Aalst, W. M. P. (2007). Constraint-based workflow models: change made easy. In *Proc. CoopIS'07* (LNCS 4803, pp. 77-94).

Reichert, M. (2000). *Dynamische Ablaufänderungen in Workflow-Management-Systemen*. PhD thesis, University of Ulm (in German).

Reichert, M., & Bauer, T. (2007). Supporting ad-hoc changes in distributed workflow management systems. In *Proc. CoopIS'07* (LNCS 4803, pp. 150-168).

Reichert, M., Bauer, T., & Dadam, P. (1999). Enterprise-wide and cross-enterprise workflow management: challenges and research issues for adaptive workflows. In *Proc. Workshop Informatik '99, CEUR Workshop Proceedings, Vol. 24* (pp. 56-64), Paderborn, Germany.

Reichert, M., & Dadam, P. (1998a). ADEPTflex – supporting dynamic changes of workflows without losing control. *Journal of Intelligent Information Systems, 10*(2), 93–129. doi:10.1023/A:1008604709862

Reichert, M., Dadam, P., & Bauer, T. (2003a). Dealing with forward and backward jumps in workflow management systems. *Int'l Journal Software and Systems Modeling, 2*(1), 37–58. doi:10.1007/s10270-003-0018-x

Reichert, M., Hensinger, C., & Dadam, P. (1998b). Supporting adaptive workflows in advanced application environments. In *Proc. EDBT Workshop on Workflow Management Systems* (pp. 100-109), Valencia, Spain.

Reichert, M., Rinderle, S., & Dadam, P. (2003b). On the common support of workflow type and instance changes under correctness constraints. In *Proc. 11th Int'l Conf. Cooperative Information Systems (CoopIS '03)* (LNCS 2888, pp. 407-425).

Reichert, M., Rinderle, S., & Dadam, P. (2003c) ADEPT workflow management system - Flexible support for enterprise-wide business processes. In *Proc. 1st Int'l Conf. on Business Process Management (BPM '03)* (LNCS 2678, pp. 371-379).

Reichert, M., Rinderle, S., Kreher, U., & Dadam, P. (2005) Adaptive process management with ADEPT2. In *Proc. Int'l Conf. on Data Engineering (ICDE'05)* (pp. 1113-1114), Tokyo.

Rinderle, S., Reichert, M., & Dadam, P. (2003) Evaluation of correctness criteria for dynamic workflow changes. In *Proc. 1st Int'l Conf. on Business Process Management (BPM '03)* (LNCS 2678, pp. 41-57).

Rinderle, S., Reichert, M., & Dadam, P. (2004a). Flexible support of team processes by adaptive workflow systems. *Distributed and Parallel Databases*, 16(1), 91–116. doi:10.1023/B:DAPD.0000026270.78463.77

Rinderle, S., Reichert, M., & Dadam, P. (2004b). Disjoint and overlapping process changes: challenges, solutions, applications. In *Proc. 11th Int'l Conf. on Cooperative Information Systems (CoopIS'04)* (LNCS 3290, pp. 101-121).

Rinderle, S., Reichert, M., & Dadam, P. (2004c). On dealing with structural conflicts between process type and instance changes. In *Proc. 2nd. Int'l Conf. Business Process Management (BPM'04)* (LNCS 3080, pp. 274-289).

Rinderle, S., Reichert, M., Jurisch, M., & Kreher, U. (2006a). On representing, purging, and utilizing change logs in process management systems. In *Proc. 4th Int'l Conf. on Business Process Management (BPM'06)* (LNCS 4102, pp. 241-256).

Rinderle, S., Weber, B., Reichert, M., & Wild, W. (2005). Integrating process learning and process evolution - A semantics based approach. In *Proc. 3rd Int'l Conf. on Business Process Management (BPM'05)* (LNCS 3649, pp. 252-267).

Rinderle, S., Wombacher, A., & Reichert, M. (2006b) Evolution of process choreographies in DYCHOR. In *Proc. 14th Int'l Conf. on Coop. Inf. Sys.* (LNCS 4275, pp. 273-290).

Rinderle-Ma, S., & Reichert, M. (2007). A formal framework for adaptive access control models. *Journal on Data Semantics IX* (LNCS 4601, pp. 82–112).

Rinderle-Ma, S., & Reichert, M. (2008 c). Managing the life cycle of access rules in CEOSIS. In *Proc. of the 12th IEEE Int'l Enterprise Computing Conference (EDOC'08)* (pp. 257-266), Munich, Germany.

Rinderle-Ma, S., Reichert, M., & Weber, B. (2008a). Relaxed compliance notions in adaptive process management systems. In *Proc. 27th Int'l Conf. on Conceptual Modeling (ER'08)* (LNCS 5231, pp. 232-247).

Rinderle-Ma, S., Reichert, M., & Weber, B. (2008b). On the formal semantics of change patterns in process-aware information systems. In *Proc. 27th Int'l Conference on Conceptual Modeling (ER'08)* (LNCS 5231, pp. 279-293).

Sadiq, S., Sadiq, W., & Orlowska, M. (2001). Pockets of flexibility in workflow specifications. In *Proc. ER'01* (pp. 513-526).

Sadiq, S., Sadiq, W., & Orlowska, M. (2005). A framework for constraint specification and validation inflexible workflows. *Information Systems, 30*(5), 349–378. doi:10.1016/j.is.2004.05.002

Schill, A., & Mittasch, C. (1996). Workflow management systems on top of OSF DCE and OMG Corba. *Distributed Systems Engineering, 3*(4), 206–233. doi:10.1088/0967-1846/3/4/005

Schuster, H., Neeb, J., & Schamburger, R. (1999). A configuration management approach for large workflow management systems. In *Proc. Int. Conf. on Work Activities Coordination and Collaboration*, San Francisco, 1999.

Shegalov, G., Gillmann, M., & Weikum, G. (2001). XML-enabled workflow management for e-services across heterogeneous platforms. *The VLDB Journal, 10*(1), 91–103.

Sheth, A., & Kochut, K. J. (1997). Workflow applications to research agenda: scalable and dynamic work coordination and collaboration systems. In *Proc. NATO Advanced Study Institute on Workflow Management Systems and Interoperability* (pp. 12-21), Istanbul, Turkey.

Staffware (2003). *Server Administration Guide*. Tool Documentation.

van der Aalst, W. M. P. (2001a). Exterminating the dynamic change bug: a concrete approach to support workflow change. *Information Systems Frontiers, 3*(3), 297–317. doi:10.1023/A:1011409408711

van der Aalst, W. M. P. (2001 b). How to handle dynamic change and capture management information: An approach based on generic workflow models. *Int. Journal of Computer Systems, Science, and Engineering, 16*(5), 295–318.

van der Aalst, W. M. P., & Basten, T. (2002). Inheritance of workflows: An approach to tackling problems related to change. *Theoretical Computer Science, 270*(1-2), 125–203. doi:10.1016/S0304-3975(00)00321-2

van der Aalst, W. M. P., & ter Hofstede, A. (2000). Verification of workflow task structures: A Petri-net-based approach. *Information Systems, 25*(1), 43–69. doi:10.1016/S0306-4379(00)00008-9

Weber, B., & Reichert, M. (2008b). Refactoring process models in large process repositories. In *Proc. CAiSE'08* (LNCS 5074, pp. 124-139).

Weber, B., Reichert, M., Rinderle, S., & Wild, W. (2006 a). Towards a framework for the agile mining of business processes. In *BPM'05 Workshop Proceedings* (LNCS 3812, pp. 191-202).

Weber, B., Reichert, M., & Rinderle-Ma, S. (2008). Change patterns and change support features - Enhancing flexibility in process-aware information systems. *Data & Knowledge Engineering, 66*(3), 438–466. doi:10.1016/j.datak.2008.05.001

Weber, B., Reichert, M., & Wild, W. (2006 b). Case-base maintenance for CCBR-based process evolution. In *Proc. 8th European Conf. on Case-Based Reasoning (ECCBR'06)* (LNCS 4106, pp. 106-120).

Weber, B., Reichert, M., Wild, W., & Rinderle, S. (2005 b) Balancing flexibility and security in adaptive process management systems. In *Proc. 13th Int'l Conf. on Cooperative Information Systems (CoopIS '05)* (LNCS 3760, pp. 59-76).

Weber, B., Reichert, M., Wild, W., & Rinderle-Ma, S. (2009). Providing integrated life cycle support in process-aware information systems. *Int'l Journal of Cooperative Information Systems (IJCIS), 18*(1), 115-165.

Weber, B., Rinderle, S., & Reichert, M. (2007). Change patterns and change support features in process-aware information systems. In *Proc. 19th Int'l Conf. on Advanced Information Systems Engineering (CAiSE'07)* (LNCS 4495, pp. 574-588).

Weber, B., Rinderle, S., Wild, W., & Reichert, M. (2005 a). CCBR-driven business process evolution. In *Proc. 6th Int'l Conf. on Case-Based Reasoning (ICCBR'05)* (LNCS 3620, pp. 610-624).

Weber, B., Wild, W., & Breu, R. (2004). CBRFlow - enabling adaptive workflow management through conversational case-based reasoning. In *Proc. ECCBR'04* (LNCS 3155, pp. 434-448).

Weske, M. (1998). Flexible modeling and execution of workflow activities. In *Proc. 31st Hawaii Int. Conf. on Sys Sciences* (pp. 713-722), Hawaii.

Weske, M. (1999). Workflow management through distributed and persistent CORBA workflow objects. In *Proc. CAiSE'99* (pp. 446-450), Heidelberg, Germany.

Weske, M. (2007). *Business process management: Concepts, methods, technology*. Springer.

KEY TERMS AND DEFINITIONS

Adaptive Workflow: refers to the ability of the workflow management system to dynamically adapt the schema (i.e., model) of in-progress workflow instances during runtime.

ADEPT: refers to an adaptive process management system developed at the University of Ulm. The ADEPT technology allows for dynamic workflow changes at different levels. It enables ad-hoc changes of single workflow instances as well as workflow type changes and their propagation to running workflow instances.

Ad-Hoc Workflow Change: refers to a change applied in an ad-hoc manner to a workflow instance (e.g., by dynamically adding, deleting or moving activities). Usually, ad-hoc changes of a workflow instance become necessary to deal with exceptions or unplanned situations not anticipated at workflow design time.

Compliance Criterion: refers to a well-established correctness criterion for adaptive workflows that can be applied to check whether a running workflow instance is compliant with a changed workflow schema; i.e., whether the change is valid for the workflow instance. For example, compliance will be always ensured if the execution log of the respective workflow instance can be produced on the new schema as well.

Distributed Workflow: refers to a workflow whose schema is subdivided into several partitions which are then controlled piecewise by different workflow servers. Accordingly, a distributed workflow management system (WfMS) is made up of several workflow servers that allow for such distributed workflow execution.

Migration: refers to the transfer of the control over a particular workflow instance from one workflow server to another.

Workflow Change History: refers to a log which captures all change events related to a particular workflow instance. Thus it complements the execution history of the instance which logs start and completion events of activities.

Workflow Change Pattern: allows for workflow schema adaptations at a high level of abstraction. Examples include high-level changes like the insertion, deletion and movement of process schema fragments. Workflow change patterns can be also used to assess the expressiveness of a change framework.

ENDNOTES

[1] To achieve better scalability, in ADEPT the same partition of different WF instances (with same type) can be controlled by multiple WF servers. Respective concepts, however, are outside the scope of this book chapter and are presented in (Bauer, 2003).

[2] In this context, migration should not be mixed up with the migration of a WF instance to a modified WF schema. Issues concerning the latter can be found in (Casati, 1998; Rinderle, 2004a-c).

[3] Using this policy there may be scenarios where the same WF server would be always used as all WF instances in the WfMS are created on the same WF server. (An excellent example is the server that manages the terminals used by the tellers in a bank.) In this case, the *ServerManager* should be selected arbitrarily when a WF instance is generated.

[4] A robust behavior of the distributed WfMS could also be achieved by performing each ad-hoc change and each migration (incl. the adaptation of the set *ActiveServers*) within a distributed transaction (with 2-phase-commit). But this approach would be very restrictive since during the execution of such an operation, "normal WF execution" would be prevented. That means, while performing a migration, the whole WF instance would be locked and, therefore, even the execution of activities actually not concerned would not be possible. Such a restrictive approach is not acceptable for any WfMS. However, it is not required in our approach and we realize a higher degree of parallel execution while achieving the same robustness.

[5] $p() \rightarrow s$ means that procedure p is called and then executed by server s.

[6] For details see Algorithm 3. The lock does not prevent several migrations of one and the same WF instance from being performed simultaneously.

[7] This query may be combined with the lock request into a single call to save one communication cycle.

[8] A lock at the target WF server prevents the migrations from being carried out concurrently in an uncoordinated manner. This ensures that migrations for one and the same WF instance are serialized; i.e., the lock is maintained from start of migration, while change history entries (and other

WF-related data (Bauer, 2001)) are acquired and transmitted, until the entries have finally been integrated into the change history at the target WF server. This lock prevents history entries from being requested redundantly due to the request being based on obsolete local information.

[9] To enable application developers to implement customized runtime components, we provide a powerful application programming interface (API) to them. Its functionality goes far beyond the APIs of existing WfMS. For example, our API provides powerful change operations, which hide as much of the complexity of an ad-hoc change as possible from users.

Chapter 7

Bayesian Agent Adaptation in Complex Dynamic Systems

Mair Allen-Williams
University of Southampton, UK

Nicholas R Jennings
University of Southampton, UK

ABSTRACT

Multi-agent systems draw together a number of significant trends in modern technology: ubiquity, decentralization, openness, dynamism and uncertainty. As work in these fields develops, such systems face increasing challenges. Two particular challenges are decision making in uncertain and partially-observable environments, and coordination with other agents in such environments. Although uncertainty and coordination have been tackled as separate problems, formal models for an integrated approach are typically restricted to simple classes of problem and are not scalable to problems with many agents and millions of states. We improve on these approaches by extending a principled Bayesian model into more challenging domains, using heuristics and exploiting domain knowledge in order to make approximate solutions tractable. We show the effectiveness of our approach applied to an ambulance coordination problem inspired by the Robocup Rescue system.

INTRODUCTION

As computing power and ubiquity increase, the use of multi-agent technology in complex distributed systems is becoming more widespread. Consequently, the scalability of such systems is becoming increasingly important. Furthermore, the inherent dynamism in many of these problems calls for timely online responses, rather than the offline computation of strategies. As an example, consider a street taxi business. Between fares, the taxis roam the streets looking for customers. If taxis are able to automatically share their locations using GPS and a dashboard display, they can attempt to spread out over different areas. Now, for multi-agent problems in which the complete state is not observed by any one agent, re-

DOI: 10.4018/978-1-60566-669-3.ch007

cent work has advanced the state of the art for finding offline solutions in networks of stationary agents, with solutions in systems containing at least fifteen agents (Marecki et al., 2008). Building on this, in this chapter we describe a related online approach which is suitable to complex dynamic processes with mobile agents, also scalable into tens of agents. In order to provide a focus, and as a motivation for this work, we will consider the disaster response domain. Disaster scenarios form rich grounds for multi-agent distributed problem solving, allowing us to explore several features of complex multi-agent problems. While there are many characteristics which may be present in disaster scenarios, we will find that there are two common themes: uncertainty, and coordination.

The first of these, uncertainty, may concern the environment ("What's going on?") and the agent's position in the environment ("Where am I?"); it may be about any other agents which might exist in the environment ("Who else is around? Where are they?") and their behavior ("What are they going to do?"). In these uncertain situations, each agent must do some form of discovery to determine the essential characteristics of the situation, including the agent's collaborators, before and alongside directly working to achieve its goals. This discovery phase in a multi-agent system is tightly linked with the presence of other agents in the system. As well as determining which other agents are present, agents may be able to cooperate to search over different regions, sharing information with each other as appropriate.

In addition to explicitly sharing information, observing the behavior of the other agents allows an autonomous agent to make inferences about the system. For example, in a scenario involving a burning building, a rational agent will not enter the building. Out of the disaster domain, consider perhaps a car manufacturing company, receiving orders from a regular customer base of car dealerships, able to make judgements about local economics based on the orders. Beyond discovery, there will continue to be interaction between the agents in a multi-agent system, whether explicit via communications and negotiations, or implicit through activity. Achieving some subgoals may involve a collaboration between several agents, as in a rescue operation where two ambulance members are required to carry a stretcher, or a car manufacturer where different parts are manufactured in different local factories.

Now, this general problem of taking others into account, coordination, is the second key issue we have identified for multi-agent systems. In uncertain, changing or open systems, fixed protocols for coordination must function against a background in which agents are not fully aware of the situation; their environment, the resources available to them, or the behavior of the other agents. For example, a particular car part manufacturer may be manufacturing parts in assorted colours without necessarily knowing what orders are coming in or whether a particular colour is newly in vogue in one of the key towns supplied by the factories. The negotiation of coordinated behavior in such systems is intertwined with the discovery phase, as agents interact with one another, perhaps cooperating to determine properties of the situation. Another example might be of a team of milkmen, needing to prepare for adjustments to their regular standing orders: they will expect that in the summer customers are more likely to go on holiday; they may be able to make inferences about school holidays within a particular catchment area, and the teams may be able to compare notes when they meet at the depot.

In order to achieve such a comprehensive model for planning and acting, we have built on existing techniques for coordinated decision making under uncertainty in dynamic systems. We have developed an algorithm which explicitly models other agents, demonstrating a principled approach to coordinated behavior in uncertain and partially-observable multi-agent systems. Over the next sections, we provide the background to this work and motivate a coordinated approach using finite state machines to model agent behavior. We then go on to describe this approach in detail. In order to validate our model we test it on a problem taken from the disaster response domain, describing the problem and comparing the performance of the our algorithm with previous approaches to partially observable uncertain systems. Finally, we conclude and describe directions for future work.

BACKGROUND

We ground our work in the disaster response domain. After a disaster such as an earthquake or a flood, the immediate situation and its environmental properties are typically unknown to the rescue teams, and may be changing quickly. Furthermore, the complete situation cannot be atomically observed by a single agent. Rescue teams may come from different regions but all must collaborate to search the area and rescue any disaster victims in a timely fashion. However, communication lines may be unavailable or restricted so that this collaboration is necessarily implicit or based on short one-way communications.

In more detail, we find that taking disaster response as our focus domain drives a particular interest in collaborative multi-agent domains which include the following properties:

Decentralisation: In these large and dynamic systems, providing a central controller is likely to be infeasible. Firstly, there are unlikely to be sufficient resources to allow communications between one central controller and every other node. Secondly, one central controller is almost certainly not going to be able to obtain a complete view of the system, and the potentially rapid changes as agents enter and leave the system would be difficult to track.

Dynamism: Realistic systems are rarely static. For example, in disaster recovery agents must adapt to changing weather conditions, any aftershocks, and unexpected events such as building collapse or fires. When taken together, this can lead to a turbulent dynamic environment.

Partial Observability: Along with decentralization, it is likely that no one agent is able to see the complete system all the time. Although communication between agents may extend a particular agent's view of the system, the agent must continually make judgements based on an incomplete view.

Bandwidth-limited: Limited communication is a characteristic common to disaster scenarios—for example, mobile phone networks often become jammed (National Research Council, 2005), or time constraints can limit opportunities for communication. Thus, agents may be able to exchange some information, but both time and bandwidth restrictions will limit these exchanges.

Openness: The rescue agents are likely to be entering or leaving the disaster scene throughout the rescue operation. Agents may be harmed at the scene and thenceforth be out of action, while new agents may arrive late. A collaborative model in a disaster response scenario must therefore be able to adapt to the continual arrival and loss of agents.

Similar properties may be present in many kinds of business process, such as the taxi dispatch firm with a variable (open) fleet of taxis to distribute, the gardener with a stable customer base but work depending dynamically on the weather and on the customers' personal activities, a busy hospital care team, the car manufacturing company mentioned previously, or a large bank trying to keep an appropriate cash float across its tills. Indeed, many parts of the disaster response problem can be considered as business processes, treating the disaster victims as customers, and negotiating resources such as ambulances, stretchers and fuel.

Keeping these driving forces in mind, we begin with a description of the most straightforward of this class of dynamic problems, the single agent observable Markov Decision Process (MDP). Building on the single agent MDP, we will generalize to partially observable and multi-agent environments, discussing means of coordination among agents. We will not discuss open systems in detail here.

In the most basic single MDP model, the agent perceives the state of the world through its sensory inputs, and decides on its immediate action based on this state. Following the agent's action, the world transitions into a new state, and the agent may receive some reward. This model forms the basis of Markov decision theory (Sutton & Barto, 1998). The fundamental feature of this theoretical model is the assumption that the immediate next state is dependent only on the previous state and choice of action—this is the Markov property.

Although the Markov property may not fully hold, it is often a sufficiently good approximation, and techniques which use this theory can get good results. This is demonstrated by many practical examples (Hoar, 1996) (Smith, 2002) (Abul et al., 2000). With the Markov assumption, if the models describing the transition and reward probabilities are completely known to the agent then the system can be solved, using a pair of recursive equations (Sutton & Barto, 1998) which determine the optimal action from each world state. These are the Bellman equations. For large systems, there are efficient ways of approximating these solutions—we do not go into these here as we will not be dealing with known MDPs, but refer the interested reader to (Sutton & Barto, 1998), chapter 9.

When there is uncertainty about the aforementioned models, the agent can learn the optimal actions through experimentation. To this end, reinforcement learning techniques, such as Qlearning, TD(λ) and SARSA (Sutton & Barto, 1998), provide techniques for the agent to do this. There are two types of learning: model-based or model-free. In the former, the agent aims to learn the system model, in this case the underlying MDP, and then solve that model (using the Bellman equations, as above) to decide an action. In the latter, the agent learns a direct mapping from the state to the optimal action. Model-free learning typically involves simple updates at each step; consequently, it is often more efficient for one-off problems. However, in comparison, model-based methods can be used to carry out many simulation steps alongside each real-time step, taking advantage of otherwise idle cpu cycles in relatively slow-progressing problems. Another advantage of model-based methods is the ability to bias the system towards a particular real model, using domain knowledge. Models or parts of models can also be re-used in different problems. Given this, we focus on model-based methods particularly because of these two properties: in scenarios such as disaster response, as in most business scenarios, we will have initial beliefs about the system based on the domain or similar disasters and would like to incorporate those beliefs into our solutions.

In particular, we focus on Bayesian model-based learning. By comparison to most model based learning methods, which maintain a point estimate of the models, a Bayesian learning method will maintain a probability distribution over all possible models, in the form of a belief state. This provides a principled solution to the exploration-exploitation problem: the decision an agent has to make between taking the action it currently believes to be optimal, and taking an exploratory action. In general, the more certain the agent is about its current model, the more likely it should be to take the currently optimal action. The Bayesian model pins this intuition down precisely.

Now, reinforcement learning, combined with the Bellman equations, will allow a single agent to solve any observable MDP which comes its way. However, although MDP models will form the basis of our environment, in large or complex scenarios it is common for an agent to make local observations which allow it to form inferences about the current state without observing the complete state directly (although in multi-agent systems, local observations may be augmented with communicated information). When the underlying process of moving from global state to global state is still (assumed to be) Markov, the scenario is described as a partially observable Markov decision process, or POMDP, and there are a host of POMDP-solution techniques.

For example, when the underlying environmental model is known, the POMDP can be converted to a continuous Markov decision process by defining a belief state as a probability distribution over states. The resulting continuous MDP, from belief state to belief state, can be solved using exact algorithms (Cassandra et al., 1997) or using approximations to make computation easier (Amato et al., 2006), (Kim et al., 2006). If the underlying model is not known, learning techniques must be used to refine a solution as the agent explores the system. Model-free approaches, such as (Aberdeen & Baxter, 2002), have had some success in using learning techniques to solve POMDPs. However, as discussed, we believe that model-based approaches may again have benefits—for example, (Shani et al., 2005) demonstrates a model-based algorithm which uses variable length suffix trees to address the fact that even if state transitions are Markov, the observable process may not be. However, existing approaches rely on a number of approximations and assumptions about the state space, hence are not entirely satisfactory. A principled approach may be to extend the Bayesian model described previously into partially observable domains (Ross et al., 2008).

Above, we have discussed agents reasoning about their environments. However, as well as reasoning about their environment, agents in a multi-agent system will be interacting with each other. This interaction can be modelled by defining a (hyper)sphere of influence for each agent within the environment. Overlapping spheres of influence indicate interactions between agents (Wooldridge, 2002). A model of how different spheres interact will form a part of the agent's model of the system, as will models of the behavior of the other agents. Making decisions in the context of these other agents is the fundamental principle of coordination (Durfee, 1999). Clearly, this is a central part of a reasoning agent in a multi-agent system. Thus, in the following sections we expand on how agents can reason about the behavior of others and incorporate that reasoning into their own behavior. (Table 1)

Perhaps the simplest example: agents functioning in uncertain worlds among other agents may include others' behavior in the Markov state transition model they develop. However, by doing this they may form inaccurate assumptions about the world, as agents adapt their behavior to one another (example 1). Consequently, maintaining models of the world and of other agents separately provides greater flexibility and may enable the agent to reuse a world model as agents come and go, or reuse models built for known agents in fresh scenarios. Below, we outline three common ways in which agents may develop and use models of the world to coordinate.

Three, potentially overlapping, coordination mechanisms are identified by Boutilier (1996): conventions, communication, and learning. Firstly, **conventions** are typically the simplest form of coordination. In a convention-based coordination system, there are a number of assumed "social rules" describing ways for agents to interact when they are aware of other agents. Coordination by convention is typically simple, scalable and requires no setup time (Fitoussi & Tennenholtz, 2000). However, it is inflexible,

Table 1. Example 1. The milkman making inferences about the world

A milkman loads up her float two or three times a day at the depot, based on her round and the availability of milk at the depot—milk is supplied to the depot several times a day, from different dairies. She must decide how to arrange her route so that when she returns to reload, she does not have to wait long for sufficient milk to be available; at the same time she must take into account her fuel requirements and time constrains.
She can ignore the presence of other milkmen in her world, estimating the milk availability purely on previous experience. However, if she takes into account the rounds of the other milkmen and the frequency with which they prefer to reload, she may be better able to adapt her model when, for example, particular milkmen are on holiday.

and relies on all participants knowing the conventions and complying with them. More complex models using conventions include role-based structures (Tambe et al., 1999) and self-organising structures (Wang, 2002). Secondly, **communication** is used for coordination in many kinds of system. Coordination through communication has a small setup time and some bandwidth costs. In most large systems there will be some form of communication in order to share information between agents; it will be impossible for any one agent to sense all the information it needs to function effectively in context (Dutta et al., 2004). However, we expect to make limited use of communication beyond information-sharing, as the bandwidth and timeliness constraints will typically preclude it. Finally, it is possible to extend single agent **learning** into the multi-agent domain. The uncertainties of our target domain make learning techniques a natural approach to problems within this domain. Learning techniques enable agents to evolve coordinated polices within uncertain state spaces, either with a group of learners exploring the space and converging towards an equilibrium (as in (Claus & Boutilier, 1998) and (Littman, 1994)), or by one agent explicitly learning about the behaviour of others in order to adapt its own appropriately (Chalkiadakis & Boutilier, 2003).

Distinct from the three approaches to coordination identified above, another research domain which investigates coordination from a theoretical angle is **game theory** (Leslie, 2004). In game-theoretic formulations, agents model the scenario as a game and try and derive, either through exact evaluation or through learning, a best response to the strategies of the other players in the game. If all the players iteratively keep playing best responses, and if strategies are mixed (stochastic) the play will converge to a (mixed) equilibrium, in which every player's strategy is a best response to every other player. One of the challenges of game theory is to direct the play so that convergence is not just to any equilibrium but to an optimal one (Claus & Boutilier, 1998). Game theory is an obvious model for scenarios with heterogeneous and competitive agents, but is also often a useful formulation for cooperative problems.

Within the domain of game theory, the form of multi-agent learning in which the agents maintain explicit models of the other agents is described as learning in stochastic games. One effective approach to extending single-agent reinforcement learning into this setting is the win-or-learn-fast (WoLF) approach: an agent's learning rate is adjusted according to its current performance, without explicitly modeling the other agents (Bowling & Veloso, 2001). However, WoLF techniques can be improved upon by using a Bayesian model in which agents maintain beliefs about the behavior of the other agents, as well as a probability distribution over world models (Chalkiadakis & Boutilier, 2003). The need for heuristically determined learning rates is then eliminated, while prior information about agents can be incorporated.

Considering these coordination techniques in the light of our domain requirements, we believe that "acting" and "coordinating" in uncertain systems should be completely integrated. That is, rather than use an explicit coordination layer, agents should include their beliefs about other agents' behavior in their action selection mechanism, and adjust their own action according to their beliefs about the other agents. By doing this, agents can smoothly make decisions about coordinated actions. Moreover, we believe that such an integrated approach should be based on sound theoretical principles, allowing us to reason about the behavior of agents. In uncertain and dynamic domains, this motivates the use of multi-agent learning models, since these provide a basis for such coordinated action selection and are designed for uncertain domains. Furthermore, although in large domains it may be impractical to learn a complete solution in real time, we have explained that learning methods can be used on top of other coordination mechanisms to provide adaptability on top of known conventions or communication languages, to select between coordination mechanisms, or to use learning for some subproblem. We therefore explore the application of multi-agent learning models to dynamic, partially-observable domains. Finally, we observe that within model based learning it is sensible for agents to maintain models of the other agents separately from the environment, as these models need not be treated as Markovian. Therefore, the game theoretic paradigm, computing "best responses" to agents within their environment, is appropriate and more flexible than treating other agents implicitly.

Given the aim of learning models of the environment, we have previously discussed reinforcement learning. However, learning models of other agents is typically a different kind of task from learning about the environment. In a fully observable domain with the Markov assumption, the optimal action will only ever depend on the current state. Therefore, agents can learn simple models of the strategies of the other agents, using multinomial distributions over actions (one for each state) and updating these distributions either using a simple frequency count or using Bayes' rule. This is known as fictitious play (Fudenberg & Levine, 1998). Conversely, in scenarios where the full state is unknown to the agent, simple fictitious play is not appropriate. Each agent may have knowledge of the environment and a model of the current world state—but this is not sufficient to respond optimally to the other agents. In a rescue scenario, some rescue tasks require several agents, and so the agents must come to the same conclusions about when these tasks are approached. If agents have differing views of the situation, they may not make the same decisions about urgency, resulting in an ineffective dispersal of agents.

In principle, each agent can maintain and update a POMDP in which the unknown POMDP "state" includes the world state, the other agents' world models, and behavioral models for the other agents. In practice, it is not tractable either to update such a model or to determine a best response within it without performing some approximations—for example, projecting just a small number of steps into the future, and using a domain-specific heuristic to estimate the values of those future states (Emery-Montemerlo et al., 2004). However, this approach relies on each agent being able to predict the computations of the other agents—each must be initialized with the same random seed. A different approach to approximation is to restrict the possible opponent strategies to those which can be described by regular automata, often called finite state machines or finite automata. An agent controlled by a finite state machine has a number of internal states, each associated with an action (or a probability distribution over actions)—this tells the agent how to act when it reaches this internal state. After taking an action, the agent's observations determine its movement to a new internal state. The finite state machine captures the notion that an agent's beliefs can be approximated, for the purposes of decision making, by a variable but finite sequence of past observations, and examples such as (Vu et al., 2006) (Carmel & Markovitch, 1996) demonstrate that it can be very effective. Furthermore, approximate best responses to finite state machines can be computed efficiently (Marecki et al., 2008).

However, to date previous work using finite state machines focuses on offline solutions to multi-agent problems, precomputing responses to every possible belief state. But it is impossible for every belief state to be reached: every belief state which is visited narrows the space of possible future beliefs (at least within a static environment). For offline solvers without tight time constraints, there may be no problem in generating redundant information. Other approaches use the intuition that the belief space need only be divided into sufficient chunks to determine the next action, for example using principal components analysis on a discretized state space (Roy & Gordon, 2002). The alternative to such techniques is to search for solutions online. This is the only way of approaching very dynamic systems, or systems where the problem parameters may not be known in time to perform a comprehensive offline search—as is likely to be the case in our target domain. Online solutions will, of necessity, be approximate, since any accurate solution projects infinitely far into the future and thus is effectively an offline solution.

In the next section we expand some of these ideas and describe in detail an algorithm for online co-operative action in partially observable multi-agent systems in which agent communication is limited to information-sharing. Our algorithm uses finite state machines to model the policies of the other agents and each agent computes online a best response to its beliefs about these finite state machines.

BAYESIAN LEARNING MODELS

As outlined in the previous section, we will use finite state machines to model individual agent policies in a multi-agent setting. In this section we flesh out the theoretical background behind this model. First, we outline an exact theory, then we show how the exact model can be approximated by a finite state machine model. Finally, we describe the finite state machine model in more detail.

Bayesian Learning

We begin by specifying our definitions. Throughout, we assume that there is some underlying world state, s, which changes in response to the joint actions of the agents. The progression of world states and joint actions forms an MDP. We assume that agents are not able to perceive s completely, but make some observations o from which they make inferences about the state. These observations may include communications from other agents—we do not treat those distinctly in this work. More formally, we will make use of the following definitions:

- $S = \left\{ S_0, \ldots, S_{n_s} \right\}$, a set of states. A state will generally be described by a set of state variables.

- $I = \left\{ I_0, \ldots, I_k \right\}$, a set of k agents

- $L \subset S = \left\{ L_0, \ldots, L_k \right\}$, a location variable for each agent. These determine the viewpoint from which agents make local observations.

- $A = \left\{ a_0, \ldots, a_{n_a} \right\}$, the set of individual actions. $A = A^k$ is the set of joint actions. Thus, we differentiate between a single action a and a joint action a by using bold for the latter, to emphasize that it is a vector. We may also use a_{-i} to refer to the vector a with the element corresponding to i removed, and $a \circ a'$ to refer to a with a' integrated.

- $O : \left\{ O_0, \ldots, O_{n_0} \right\}$, a set of observations

- $T_f : T_f(s_{t+1}, s, a_t) = P(s_{t+1} | s_t, a_t)$, the transition function from state to state, where $s_{t+1}, s_t \in S$ and $a \in A$.

- o_f: An n_0-dimensional function where $O_f(s_t, o_t)_i = P(o_t | i, s_t)$, the observation function for agent i, where $o_t \in O$ and $s_t \in S$.

- $R : \left\{ r_1, \ldots, r_{n_r} \right\}$, $n_r < n_s$, a set of possible rewards which an agent may receive

- $R_f : S \times A \times S \rightarrow R$, a reward function, specific to the agent. Typically, the reward will be associated with the immediate state, but for some problems it may be associated with the transition between states (for example, if actions have a cost).

When taken together, T_f, R_f and O_f describe the dynamics of the environment. We may use $\theta = (T_f, R_f, O_f)$ to refer to these dynamics as a whole. An individual agent, A, may also have:

- A (deterministic) policy $\pi : (p, h, o_t) \to a$ where p defines any prior or domain knowledge, h is all relevant historical information (observation sequences including communications from other agents), $o_t \in O$ is the current observation and $a \in A$ is a single agent action. Typically, (p,h) will be compressed to contain the sufficient statistics for a belief state (a probability distribution over states and unknown parameters).
- Beliefs over unknown parameters: for some variable X taking values $x_1, x_2, \ldots\ldots, b(x_i)$ is the probability that $X = x_i$, given the agent's prior information and subsequent observations.
- Models of the other agents' behavior: $P(\dot{A}|p,h)$ where π_i has the same form as π above and (p,h) refer to the prior and historical information of the agent A. To be clear, we assume that the other agents have deterministic policies, and our agent maintains beliefs over these deterministic policies.

Taking these definitions, we go on in the rest of this section to build up a formal model of learning in multi-agent systems. The following section explains an approximation which can be used to make implementing this model practical in a particular special case of interest to us. First, however, we introduce Markov Decision Processes.

MDPs and POMDPs

The transition function T_f has the Markov property: the probability of future states depends only on the current state and the action choices, and not on past state history. Consequently, {S, A, T, R} defines a Markov Decision Process (Figure 1):

In choosing an action at time $t = t_T$, the agent's aim is to optimize the expected discounted future rewards, defined by:

$$R_T^\gamma = \sum_t \gamma^t r_t \text{ (t ranges from T to } R_T^\gamma = \sum_t \gamma^t r_t \infty \text{ (t ranges from T to } \infty) \tag{1}$$

Figure 1. Markov Decision Process progression

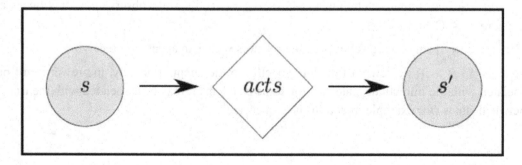

where $r_t \in R$ is the reward at time t. γ is a problem specific parameter which defines the agent's myopia; that is, to what extent it considers delayed future rewards to be important. It balances the importance we place on future states with our need to accumulate reward now. In practical terms it will be chosen to express the extent of lookahead appropriate to the problem (consider chess as an analogy: for the most part, say, 3 steps of lookahead are sufficient to play well). Typically, we will use a γ value of around 0.8, making lookahead negligible after around ten steps into the future—in a fragile disaster scenario we expect this to be sufficient for most planning purposes. It is most common for reinforcement learning algorithms to set γ between 0.7 and 1, although the choice will depend on the exact problem.

Now, in a fully observable world, $O = S$ and $P(o_t|s_t) = (1$ if $o_t=s_t$, 0 otherwise), i.e. the agent knows the complete state s_t at every timestep t. Given the Markov property, its optimal policy therefore need depend only on the current state. We can therefore define a policy in a fully observable MDP by $\pi(s) = a$, a function from states to actions. Then, if the strategies of the other agents are known, the agent can compute its own optimal policy via dynamic programming—effectively, this is the solution of the large simultaneous equation known as the Bellman Equations (2 and 3).

In more detail, $Q_\pi(s,a)$ is the (discounted expected) value of taking action a from state s, and then working to policy π. $Q^*(s,a)$ is the (discounted expected) value of taking action a from state s, and then working to the optimal strategy π^*. We will use "best response" to refer to the optimal single-agent action, a maximizing $Q(s,a)$ throughout this paper as we replace s with more complex models.

$$Q(s,a)=\sum_{s'} P(s'|s,a)\left[r(s')+^3 V(s')\right] \tag{2}$$

$$V(s) = \max_a Q(s,a) \tag{3}$$

$$\pi^*(s) = a \text{ such that } Q(s,a)=\max_a Q(s,a) \tag{4}$$

$$P(s'|s,a)=T_f(s',s,a \circ a_{-1}) \tag{5}$$

where a_{-1} is the joint actions of the other agents as defined by their strategies

There are various ways of efficiently approximating these solutions in large problems, and for solving in continuous systems. Briefly, the equations can be solved iteratively, and efficiency is achieved by (a) updating the states most likely to have changed first, and (b) updating "nearby" states when a state is updated (Sutton & Barto, 1998). We do not go into details of these solution techniques as realistically we are unlikely to know all the necessary parameters. In the next section we explain how this model is extended into systems with unknowns.

Partially Observable Systems.

It is often the case that the agent may not know (in the case of static parameters), or be able to observe (in the case of state-related values) all the details of the MDP. If the underlying state s cannot be observed, then the problem becomes a POMDP: a "partially observable" Markov decision process (Figure 2). At each step, the MDP proceeds behind the scenes, while the agent makes observations o derived from the underlying state s, where o is insufficient for the agent to reliably determine s. $Q_f(s,i)$ describes the probability density function $P(o|s)$ for agent i.

To solve this POMDP, we can derive from it a secondary MDP—a belief MDP. The multi-dimensional states of this secondary MDP have one continuous variable, b(s), for every possible value s of the underlying state. The value of b(s) indicates the probability that the underlying state is s, given the agent's prior knowledge and the history of observations and actions. The system proceeds from b to b' at each step using Bayes' rule (equation 6) to update the state probabilities (Figure 3):

$$P(\text{Model} \mid \text{observations}) \; \alpha \; P(\text{observations} \mid \text{Model})P(\text{Model}) \tag{6}$$

This belief MDP is, therefore, completely known, and although continuous and high-dimensional has an exact solution describing the optimal action in any belief state. This solution will inherently take into account the need for exploratory actions. In principle, any general techniques for continuous MDP solutions can be used to solve the belief MDP (Sutton & Barto, 1998). However, all belief-state MDPs fall into a particular class of continuous MDPs, since each belief state restricts the possible future belief states. More efficient solution techniques exploit the properties of these MDPs (Poupart et al., 2006) (Pineau et al., 2003).

Given this, we can extend the belief MDP idea further to consider cases where the environmental dynamics, θ, are not known or are partially known. In these cases, we can consider an underlying MDP which has the dynamics, θ, as one of its state variables. This MDP has a known transition function: $(s,\theta) \rightarrow (\theta(s),\theta)$. The observations for the POMDP associated with this MDP will include state transitions as well as the immediate observations. In principle, this POMDP can be solved exactly as described above. Finally, the same model extends into the multi-agent world by including the actions

Figure 2. Partially observable Markov Decision Process

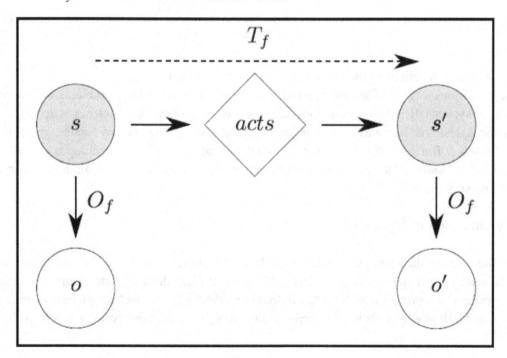

Figure 3. POMDP inducing a Bayesian belief state MDP

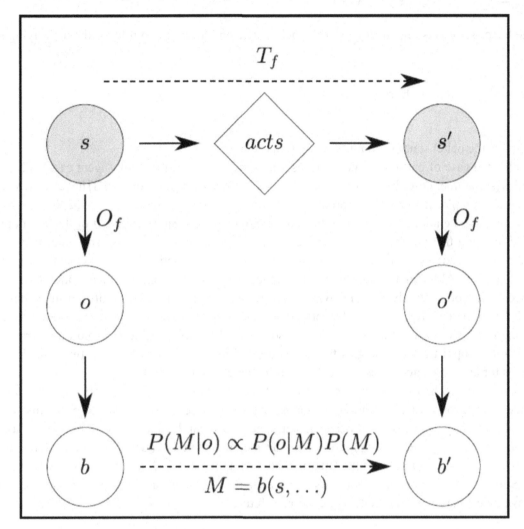

of other agents in the underlying state, and the behavior functions of other agents in θ. In a partially observable system, the behavior of another agent will depend on its beliefs about the state, and so we also add the beliefs over states of the other agents to our own MDP state:

$$S_{MDP} = \left\{ s, \forall j.(\sigma_j), \forall j.\left(b_j(s)\right), \theta \right\}$$

To date, existing work has studied some sub-cases of this general model: the fully-observable case where the dynamics are unknown, for single agent problems (Dearden et al., 1999) and multi-agent problems (Chalkiadakis & Boutilier, 2003); and the partially-observable case where the dynamics are unknown for multi-agent problems (Ross et al., 2008). All of these find online solutions using appropriate approximation techniques. In particular, in solving the Bellman equations, typically these techniques will only refer to a small number of belief states, beginning at the current one. Recall,

$$Q(s,a) = \sum_{s'} P(s'|s,a)\big[r(s') + \gamma V(s')\big]$$

The belief-state version, writing b for the belief state and leaving s to refer to the underlying state, is

$$Q(b,a) = \sum_{s'} P(s'|b,a)\big[E\big[r(s')|b\big] + \gamma V(b')\big]$$

where b' is the belief state resulting from the transition to state s' .

Finally, the case of particular interest to us, the partially-observable multi-agent case with known dynamics (sometimes described as a partially observable stochastic game, or POSG) has also been investigated. For example, in one online approximate algorithm (Emery-Montemerlo et al., 2004), each agent tries to compute the joint optimal action for that step, then executing its own part of this joint optimal action. Providing that all agents are initialized with the same information (in particular, they should share a random seed), every agent can compute the approximately optimal action so that the actions are truly cooperative. Although this algorithm is theoretically sound, it is computationally intensive and has only been tested on relatively small POSGs. More recent work has investigated offline algorithms for a special case of much larger POSGs, the networked POSG. In the case where the agents are networked according to a specific structure—such as a sensor network—it is possible to exploit this structure to develop more sophisticated strategies for agents located in critical parts of the network, and simpler strategies for agents located in less critical regions (Marecki et al., 2008).

An alternative technique for making approximate action choices is to gather together similar states, belief states or groups of observations, reducing the state space. In particular, in problems where a notion of proximity can be defined between states, an action can be decided for a new state based on experience of nearby states. Examples of the former include manual feature abstraction and hierarchies (Fischer et al., 2004). Examples of the latter include neural networks (Sutton & Barto, 1998), Kohonen maps (Smith, 2002) and belief compression via principal components analysis (Roy & Gordon, 2002). We leave investigation of such state aggregation to future work.

Finite State Machines

A finite state machine can be used to represent an agent's policy. We have discussed fully observable MDPs in which the agent's policy is decided on its immediate observations, and partially-observable MDPs in which the agent state is a continuous, high-dimensional belief-state derived from its entire history. A finite state machine policy falls between these two: the agent state is based on a variable length history. A fixed and finite number of agent states, more than the number of possible observations, are defined in the finite state machine and the agent moves from state to state of the machine based on its observation. In the next section we describe this model in more detail and explain how representing agent policies with finite state machines can be used to develop approximate online solutions in partially observable multi-agent problems.

BAYESIAN LEARNING APPROXIMATION USING FINITE STATE MACHINES

In this section we detail how to model agent policies using finite state machines. We then explain how these models fit with the multi-agent POMDP solution techniques described above, giving an algorithm for online learning and explaining how this model extends previous work in the area. First, however, we begin with the definition of a finite state machine.

Definitions

A deterministic finite state machine has:

- A set of n nodes $N = \{n_1, \ldots, n_n\}$
- A set of m edges $E = \{e_1, \ldots, e_m\}$
- For each node, an associated action a from the set of actions
- For each edge, an associated observation o from the set of observations

One of the nodes is designated as a start node, n_0. We write Act (n) to refer to the action associated with a node n.

An agent's policy is determined by such a state machine (algorithm 1): at each node (or agent state), the agent carries out the associated action. The resulting observations determine the agent's transition to a new node within the FSM. (Table 2)

Now, in order to use finite state machines as representations of agent policies in unknown multi-agent scenarios, we are proposing to do two things: (1) to learn the finite state machine models over time, from the sequence of observed actions and state observations, and (2) to derive an online policy as a best response to a set of (beliefs over) FSM policies. We describe each of these in turn, bringing them together at the end of this section.

Learning FSMs

In principle, learning a deterministic finite state machine from a set of observations can proceed as follows (Carmel & Markovitch, 1996):

- **Base case**: initialise the FSM with the single node n_0, setting the associated action to the first observed action
- **Recursion step**: given a FSM and an observation string, determine if the observation string is consistent with the FSM:

Table 2. **Algorithm 1** *A finite state machine policy*

1. The agent begins at the start node n_0. 2. The agent performs the action associated with the current node n. 3. When all agents have performed their action, the system moves to a new state s, supplying agents with observations o. 4. The agent moves along the edge associated with o, arriving at a new node n'. 5. Repeat from 2.

1.   Find a node whose action corresponds to the first action in the string: if there are no untested nodes remaining, FAIL

2.   Follow the FSM as prescribed by the observation sequence until (a) the action associated with a particular node does not match the action in the sequence: FAIL, return to 1 or (b) the end of the sequence is reached: CONSISTENT

If the observation string is consistent, then no further action need be taken. If the observation string is inconsistent, then we select a node from one of the failure points, and expand the FSM to include the new string.

Then, given a FSM and a particular (short-term) observation history (after applying the above algorithm to the history), we can construct a list of possible current nodes for the corresponding agent by considering each of the starting points consistent with the observation history and following the FSM through to a current node from each (abandoning any inconsistent nodes en route). The probability of each resulting current node will be the total probability of all start nodes which reached it, with that probability having been computed in a previous step.

However, there are two problems: one is that observation strings can be of indefinite length, i.e. we may find ourselves storing the entire observation history in order to accurately build the FSM. The second is that although the FSM is a deterministic model, the behavior it is modeling may be neither deterministic nor static. (A third issue is that we do not in fact know the observation strings, but rather have probabilities over them which are based on our own observations). We therefore wish to adjust our learning strategy to take these facts into account.

A point to note is that although we do not know the strategies of others or their optimal strategies, because we do know the MDP and the observation function, we can make some judgments about how much observation history is likely to be important in making decisions, providing us with a way of judging the optimal size of the FSMs.

We propose to sample possible observation strings from our belief state, and construct a candidate FSM for each sample, using the following tactics in learning these candidate FSMs:

*   Define a maximum number of nodes which can occur in the FSM
*   Break the observation history into overlapping observation strings of length 1
*   Assign each observation string a likelihood based on the frequency of occurrence and its sample probability, weighting more recent occurrences more highly. Discard completely observation strings older than n_t timesteps.
*   Rather than resolve inconsistencies by always creating new nodes, resolve inconsistencies by appealing to the likelihood of each of the inconsistent strings, and discarding the least likely

In the next sections we describe in more detail an algorithm for learning FSMs from observation strings.

A Polynomial FSM Learning Algorithm.

Now, finding the minimal FSM is NP-complete and cannot be approximated by any polynomial-time algorithm (Carmel & Markovitch, 1996). However, it is possible to learn compact FSMs in polynomial time, for many practical problems. The US-L* algorithm (Carmel & Markovitch, 1996) has polynomial running time and has been shown to be effective at finding compact models of agent behavior on small agent coordination problems—we propose to test it on larger problems.

This algorithm models the FSM using a table, with rows corresponding to observation string prefixes s, columns corresponding to string suffixes e, and the table entries corresponding to actions σ. The alphabet of possible observations is $\sum$. The table is then partitioned into equivalence classes:

$$C(s) = \left\{ \text{row}(s') | \text{row}(s') = \text{row}(s) \right\}$$

The table must be constructed in such a way that it describes a FSM: that is, it must be

- **consistent**: $s_1, s_2 \in S, \left[C(s_1) = C(s_2) \rightarrow \forall t \in \sum, C(s_1 t) = C(s_2 t) \right]$.
- **closed**: $\forall s \in S \sum, \exists s' \in S, s \in S, s \in C(s')$

From such a consistent and closed table a deterministic FSM can be described.

Specifically, US-L* marks entries in the table as either hole entries or permanent entries. The former are those which can be reassigned as the algorithm tries to re-adjust the table for consistency. Only when no hole entries can be reassigned is a new test added to the table. Permanent entries correspond to a fixed action.

The algorithm procedure is:

- Take a set of observation strings
- Initialise the table so that all the prefixes of the observation strings have an associated row in the table, and there is just one column with the empty string.
- Fill in the table entries using the observations, marking entries as hole entries if they are not supported by previous examples or permanent entries if they are are supported by previous examples. In order to bound the size of the automaton, we specify a maximum number of times a hole entry can be changed, basing the maximum on domain knowledge if it is available: the maximum should depend on the dynamism in the system (since an entry will change if the system is changing) and on the uncertainty in the system. In our work, we may adjust the maximum over time using learned domain knowledge.
- Adjust the table to make it consistent, adding new columns to the table where necessary (adding a new column enables the separation of one equivalence class into two—this adds at least one new state to the corresponding automaton).
- Adjust the table to close it, adding new rows where necessary.
- Take the next set of observation strings and loop as appropriate

This algorithm is designed to be used as an online algorithm for an adaptive agent to learn models of opponent behaviour, although Carmel and Markovitch only apply it to repeated two-player games. We will be investigating its application in our domain, specifying in advance a maximum size for the automata. Now, in order to make use of these finite state machine models of agent behaviour, our agent (maintaining these models) must be able to find an optimal response to what it believes to be the current situation. Referring back to our generic Bayesian model, this means evaluating Q(b, a) for a belief state b which includes beliefs over finite state machines. The next section explains how this is done.

Online Solutions: Best Response

Previous work (Vu et al., 2006), (Carmel & Markovitch, 1996) has considered fully observable, but non-Markov, repeated games. In such scenarios finding a best response is straight forward, since the state and consequently the reward can be computed for every step.

By contrast, in our work, the state is not known. This adds to the complexity of the situation (as previously discussed), since even if the policies of the other agents are known, we do not know what observations they may make and consequently cannot determine their actions. We consider first this idealised case where the policies of the other agents are known. Now, we can compute a best response to any belief-state b using the Bellman equations, as discussed in the previous section.

$$Q_i(b,a) = \sum_{s'} P\left(s' \mid b,a\right)\left[r(s')+^3 V(b')\right] \tag{7}$$

Where

$$P\left(b'\left(s'\right) \mid b,a\right) = \sum_{n_j,s',s} P\left(b'(s')|s,a \circ Act(n_j)\right)P(n_j,s|b) \tag{8}$$

and

$$P\left(b'\left(n_j'\right) \mid b,a\right) = \sum_{n_j,o',s} P\left(n_j'|o'\right)$$
$$P\left(o'|s,a \circ Act(n_j)\right)P(n_j,s|b) \tag{9}$$

Where

$$P\left(o'|s,a \circ Act(nj)\right) = \sum_{s'} P\left(s'|s,a \circ Act(nj)\right)P(o'|s') \tag{10}$$

$$\left(P\left(n_j'|o'\right) \text{ is 1 or 0}\right)$$

These equations are finite and can in principle be solved. In an online algorithm, $Q_i(b,a)$ can be computed from the current belief state by projecting k steps into the future. On the kth step, we replace $V(b')$ in equation 7 with some heuristic value. Possible heuristics include 0, a Q_{MDP}-based heuristic (Kaelbling et al., 1998) or some domain-specific heuristic (for example, the expected distance from any agent to a goal, or visible future rewards such as victims which can be saved, in a disaster problem). Algorithm 2 outlines this best response solution. Such finite horizon algorithms have been used in related belief-state problems in many cases: in observable problems with unknown parameters (the heuristic is to assume that the current parameters are correct, and solve the corresponding MDP (Chalkiadakis & Boutilier, 2003)), in finding offline solutions for networked POMDPs (Marecki et al., 2008), and in online partially observable stochastic games (Emery-Montemerlo et al., 2004). (Table 3)

In our partially observable setting, where the agent does not in fact have knowledge of the policies of the other agents, but rather has beliefs over these policies, we propose to estimate the best response to the belief state by sampling from the possible policies to obtain a selection of sets of FSMs, $F = \{F_1, \ldots, F_m\}$. For each sample FSM set F_s (containing a FSM for each other agent), the agent computes a best response action $BR_i(F_s, b)$. The action decision is then given by:

$$a = \max_{a_i} \sum_{i=1}^{m} P_i . \delta(BR_i(F_s, b) = a_i)$$

(where $\delta(A = B) = 1$ if $A = B$ and 0 otherwise).

An Online Learning Algorithm

We conclude this section with a complete description of our algorithm, which brings together several of the techniques described above. This is an algorithm implemented by a single agent who is aiming to adaptively find a best response to the behavior of the other agents in the system. Our intent is that when all agents are implementing this algorithm, adapting to each other, they should converge on a "good" solution for the problem. This algorithm, as described below, maintains models of the other agents in the form of finite state machines. These models are held in a belief state which is updated using Bayesian learning. At each step, the agent computes an approximate best response to the current models.

- An agent maintains a current belief state, $b(X)$, with beliefs over the variables $X = (s, \{o, F, n\})$ where s is the current state, and $\{o, F, n\}$ describes a set of triples: in each triple, o is an observation history and (F, n) are the induced FSM and current node in the FSM. The belief state contains one such triple for each other agent in the system. The agent also maintains historical information about $b(s)$ over a fixed number of steps.
- Several parameters are fixed initially: F_{max} the maximum number of nodes in any FSM, γ the myopia of the agent, n_t the horizon length to use in computing an approximate best response, o_1 the observation window length.

n_t may be determined based on γ: roughly, for a state n steps into the future, s_n contributes $\gamma^n . r(s_n)$ towards the discounted future reward. Thus with $\gamma = 0.8$ (a common myopia value), after 10 steps less

Table 3. Algorithm 2 Finite-horizon best response

• At timestep t, agent i has beliefs b over the state and the nodes n_j of the other agents j, and knows policies $n_j \rightarrow a_j$ for these agents.
• For some k, compute $Q_k(b, a)$ for each possible action a, using
• $Q_k(b, a) = \sum_{s'} P(s'\|b, a) \left[r(s') + {}^3 V_{k-1}(b') \right]$
• $V_k(b) = \max_a Q_k(b, a)$
• $V_0(b, a) = \sum_{s'} P(s'\|b, a) V_{heuristic}(s')$
• Execute the action a which maximizes $F_s(b, a)$

than 10% of the reward will be contributing towards the estimates of the future reward. This may be a small enough value to ignore. If γ is increased to 0.9, then it will take 21 steps before the fraction of the reward under consideration is reduced below 10%.

- initialize:

The belief state is initialized: b(s) is initialized either to uniform beliefs or biased based on domain knowledge. The observation strings o are all empty, and the F have a single node with uniform probabilities over all actions[1]

- at each step:
- The agent observes the actions of the others and makes observations about the state: these observations are used to update b(s) using Bayes' rule.
- The observation samples o are extended into the current time frame to obtain o', reweighting as appropriate. This is achieved by sampling from the expected observations of the other agents, given the current observation samples and b(s). When the length of an observation string exceeds o_1, the earliest observations are dropped. If a sample's likelihood falls below probability threshold p_s, the sample is discarded, and a new string sampled using b(s) and the storied history of b(s) over o_1 previous steps.
- For each observation sample o', update the FSMs F associated with the sample with the new information in o' using US-L*. The weighting given to the FSM F is the probability of the associated observation sample.
- For each sample FSM, compute an approximate best response, and thus decide the maximum likelihood best response action a from the FSM weightings as described above.
- Perform the action a
- Repeat

To reduce computational requirements, rather than doing all of this every step, we may prefer to collect behavioral samples over several steps and update our model less frequently. The best response is still computed every step.

Thus, in this section we have outlined a theoretical model for the online solution of partially observable multi-agent systems, based on the POMDP model, and then shown how we can approximate a particular (challenging) case of this model using finite state machines to model agent behavior. In order to demonstrate the effectiveness of this model, we have implemented it on a rescue problem. In the next section we outline the problem before going on to describe our results and how they compare with the state of the art.

MODEL INSTANTIATION

In order to test the algorithm on a challenging problem, we implemented a rescue scenario involving coordinating ambulances. We compared our algorithm with a current state of the art algorithm and a hand-written solution for this problem. In this section, we specify the problem as a multi-agent POMDP and explain how we simplify the observation space.

In more detail, in the rescue problem we have an n by m gridworld. k agents can move left, right, up or down (constrained, of course, at the edges of the grid). In the gridworld are buried victims, described by two parameters: D and R. D ('deadness') is a measure of the proximity of the victim to death. When it reaches a maximum level the victim is dead and subsequently ignored for the purposes of the rescue problem. R ('rescue needed') is a measure of the depth at which the victim is believed to be buried. Agents digging can reduce R. If R reaches 0 before the victim dies, then the victim is assumed to be safe. The urgency of the victim therefore increases with increased D and with increased R, unless R is sufficiently large compared with D that the victim can be considered a lost cause. Figure 4 shows one step on the grid for a 4x4 grid with three agents.

Specifically, taking the model we have described, the various parameters are instantiated in the following way:

States: A state of this world is described by using a pair of variables for each of the grid squares, characterizing the D and R values in the square (we make the simplifying assumption that there can be at most one victim in the square), and a variable for each agent, identifying its current square. We use l_d and l_r discrete levels to describe D and R, so for each square there are possible states, and for each agent there are $m*n$ possible states, making a total of $\left(\left(l_d * l_r\right)^{m*n}\right)$) possible states.

Agents: We assume that the number of agents, k, is fixed throughout each problem and known to each agent.

Locations: The location variable for each agent is its current square.

Figure 4. One step of the rescue problem on a 4x4 grid with three agents

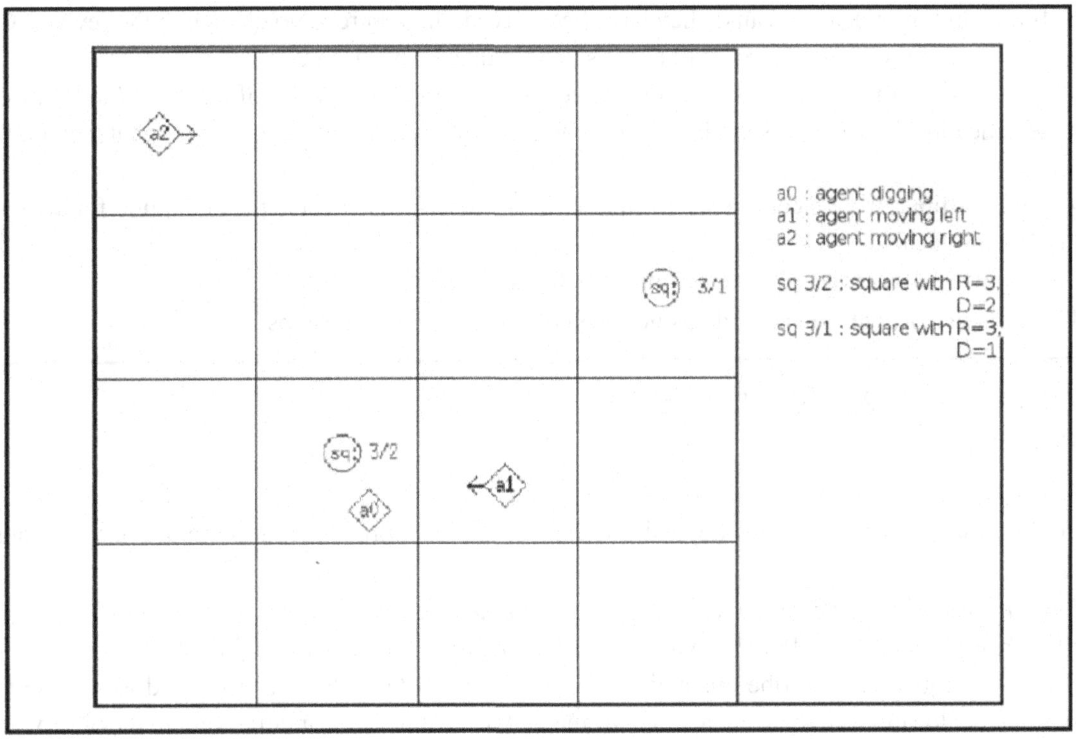

Actions: Agents may take Move actions (left, right, up or down), or Dig actions in their current square.

Observations: An agent observes some subset of the state variables, so there is one observation variable for each state variable. The values taken on by observation variables are those of the corresponding state variable, plus "null".

Transition function: Move actions move the agent one square in the requested direction, unless this is impossible in which case the action has no effect. Each square transitions (D, R) independently of other squares, so it is sufficient to define the transition function for one square. We use two global probabilities, p_d and p_r, to specify the probability of the D level changing (this is a constant probability independent of the action) and of the R level changing if there is a Dig action. If there is no dig action, R remains unchanged. We assume that if there are k digs in a square, they are concatenated. Finally, if a square is empty, we use a further parameter, p_a, to define the probability that a victim will appear in that square. If a victim does appear, the (D,R) levels it has are determined with uniform probability (greater than 0).

Observation function: Agents are able to see the squares (deadness, rescue-level, and any other agents in the square) to the left and right, and above and below them, as well as their own square. Additionally, we define a problem-specific parameter, v, for the visibility. For every other square, the agent will be able to see the agent-deadness D in that square with probability v and the rescue-level R in the square with independent probability v. Since all agent actions are fully observable, we assume that we can also observe all agent locations. This 'visibility' parameter could be justified as some level of communication with a centralised observer, say a helicopter viewing the scene. We assume no error in the observation: either a variable is completely and correctly observed or it is not observed at all.

Reward function: The reward function is a function of both the previous state and the current state. For each square, if a victim disappears because they have died, then the reward is decremented by one point. If a victim disappears because they have been saved, then there is no change to the reward. Consequently, for this problem rewards will always be less than or equal to 0.

The above definitions allow us to define beliefs over the values (D, R) of a square (and thus over the state, since locations are observable), and beliefs over the observations of other agents, given their locations:

Agent locations: We are certain for all squares how many rescue agents they contain / for all agents where they are located

The square is observed: We are certain of both its parameters

The square is not observed and has not been observed for t_i timesteps:

$$P(x_t{=}v_t|x_{t-1}{=}v_{t-1}){=}\sum_v P(x_t{=}v_t|x_{t-1}{=}v)$$
$$P(x_{t-1}{=}v|x_{t-1}{=}v_{t-1})$$

where the 1-timestep probabilities depend on p_d, p_r, p_a as appropriate, and the dig observations in that square.

The square has never been observed: This is just as above, but with $P(x_0{=}v_0)$ set to the problem-specific prior probabilities. Here, we assume that all squares are empty to begin with.

The above equations describe our beliefs about the world state: that is, the D and R values of the squares and the locations of the other agents. Similarly, we must define our beliefs about the observations of the other agents. Just as our beliefs about the state of each square are multinomial, the other agents' beliefs about the state of the square will be multinomial. Therefore, in the full POMDP model, our beliefs about other agents' beliefs over the state of the square would take on corresponding Dirichlet distributions. However, we are not trying to maintain beliefs about the other agents' belief states, only about their observations. Now, our own beliefs about the state of the square define exactly what we believe other agents will see if they see that square, as the observation function is deterministic and consistent for all agents. Because we know the location of the agent, we know of the (up to) four surrounding squares it definitely sees. Finally, we know that there is a v probability it will see any other square. Using this model, we investigate the behavior of our algorithm on the rescue problem.

EXPERIMENTAL EVALUATION

In order to test our strategy, we compare it against two other online algorithms: the state of the art for online partially observable stochastic games is the Bayesian game approximation using the finite-horizon approximation technique (Emery-Montemerlo et al., 2004), described previously ("POSG"). However, for large dynamic problems, this algorithm, which is exponential in the number of agents, proves to be very inefficient and we find that for all but the smallest variants of the rescue problem, POSG is too slow to be useful. Previous work on large dynamic rescue problems of a similar form (Paquet et al., 2005) compares with a handwritten strategy ("smart") tailored to the problem, and we do the same thing. Our handwritten strategy is the strategy that was used by the AladdinRescue team for ambulance distribution in the Robocup Rescue competition, which inspired this problem. The algorithm uses a greedy strategy to allocate ambulances to victims and is optimal in scenarios where (1) no new victims are arriving and (2) visibility is perfect (Ramamritham et al., 1989). It is therefore not an optimal strategy for the problem as we have stated it, but is a good approximation.

Comparing against these two algorithms, and using the null policy in which agents move randomly, but never dig and so never effect any rescues ("null") as a baseline, we investigate our algorithm, "best response" over different parameter settings on the rescue problem, and then focus on the scaling properties of the algorithm. Next, we identify the fixed parameters and then go on to our results.

Experimental Setup

Following experimentation, we fix the following parameters:

$$l_d = l_r = 4, \ p_d = 0.15, \ p_r = 0.4, \ l_d \ l_r \ p_d \ p_r \ p_a = l_r = 4, \ p_d = 0.15, \ p_r = 0.4, \ p_a = 0.05, \ v = 0.5.$$

In particular, we felt that the choice of four health and burial levels was sufficient to make the problem interesting without making the state space too huge. The other parameters were selected to generate scenarios requiring cooperation: victims were not arriving so fast that simply digging out the nearest was appropriate, victims might require more than one agent for rescue, and victims could survive long enough to be reached by agents some distance away.

We vary m, n and k as specified. We also experimented with increasing p_a towards problems where "dig nearby" becomes a viable strategy, and varying v. Finally, in the belief-state based algorithms, we must take samples from the belief state. We define the sampling rate as the number of samples taken for each variable, initializing it at a rate of 35 (for comparison, previous work on a single agent problem found that 20 samples was sufficient for good solutions (Dearden et al., 1999)).

In every experiment, we carried out several runs of the problem, varying the initial placement of civilians and randomizing their arrival and visibility. The same random seed was used to initialize each of the test algorithms in each run. The error bars included in the results show the 95% confidence intervals around each point. The rest of this section discusses our key results.

Examining the Learning Rate

To begin with, we compared the algorithms over the course of 1000 steps on a 7x7 grid, with three agents. We found that the POSG algorithm, which is exponential in the number of agents, did not complete in any reasonable time (we consider one minute per step to be "reasonable") on this size of problem, taking ten minutes for one agent to complete a single step. Figure 5 shows the performance of the smart policy with our algorithm over 1000 steps. Our aim was to examine the performance of the best response algorithm on a challenging problem, focusing on any changes in its behavior over time. To this end, we have used two different sampling rates for the best response policy, comparing how the agent learns when sampling very little information (samplerate = 10) or more information (samplerate = 50). We expect that the agent will both perform better, and learn faster at the higher sampling rate.

It is immediately clear from Figure 5 that the best response algorithm is outperforming the smart policy for these parameters. Now, if our algorithm (best response) is benefitting from learning, we expect to see that the advantage the best response algorithm has over the smart (handwritten) policy is increasing over time. From Figure 5(a) it is not clear that there is a large improvement in this advantage—that is, the lines are fairly straight. However, Figure 5(b) shows a closeup comparison of the two different sampling rates, showing the way in which the lower sampling rate is able to match the performance of the higher sampling rate after around 800 steps. We therefore see that with better information, the best response algorithm is able to perform well on this problem even without accurate models of the other agents, but when the sampling rate is very low, the best response algorithm is able to compensate for this by learning.

Consequently, it seems that the best response algorithm is performing well primarily on the basis of the sampled best response, rather than accurate estimates of the behavior of the others being critical. In order to investigate further, we compare the algorithms on some smaller problems which the POSG algorithm is able to run on, first looking at the effects of changing sample rates in more detail, and then varying two parameters relating to the character of the problem (visibility and victim distributions). This allows us to gain insights into the performance of our algorithm as the problem nature is changed. We also investigate parameters relating to the scale of the problem (number of agents, and size of grid). For each of these experiments we compare the total reward after 150 steps—from Figure 5 we can see that this is sufficient to show the differences between the algorithms or settings.

Varying the Sampling Rate

In order to examine how the best response algorithm will perform on challenging problems such as those we identified in our domain requirements, we will consider the effects of scale both on solution quality and on the computational requirements. Linked to the solution scales is the number of samples taken

Figure 5. Comparison of two algorithms over time on a 7x7 grid with 3 agents. Note that we use a log scale to show more clearly the differences between the algorithms, and the rewards are scaled up to > 0 for the logscale.

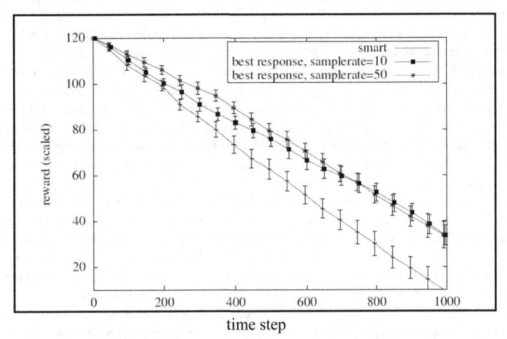

(a) **Algorithm performing over 1000 steps at two different rates**

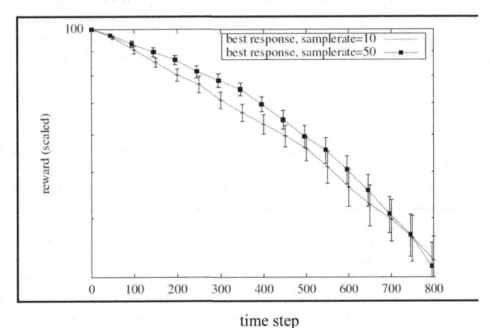

(b) **Closeup of the first 800 steps**

in estimating beliefs. The sensitivity of the solution to the number of samples is therefore relevant in considering the effectiveness of the algorithm.

For the POSG algorithm, on a 3x3 grid with two agents, table 7(a) shows the time/sample-rate ratios for 100 steps (to the nearest minute). Since our cut-off was one step per minute, we did not run any tests on the POSG algorithm beyond a sample rate of 75, the null policy and the smart policy do not do any sampling. For our own policy, which does not need to iterate over all joint policies, the scaling factor was much better: table 7(b) shows the equivalent rates. The POSG algorithm is exponential in the number of agents, since it iterates over all joint actions. It therefore scales badly as the number of agents is increased. By contrast, table 7(c) shows the times for the best response algorithm running on the larger problem of a 7x7 grid with three agents. Even on this larger grid the times are well within the "reasonable" range. We next investigate whether there is truly a need for higher sampling rates, since our earlier investigations indicated that the best response algorithm is able to perform quite well even at low sample rates.

To this end, Figure 6 shows the effect of changing the sample rate. As expected, neither the null policy nor the smart policy are susceptible to changing sample rates. However, the performance of the best response policy also does not vary much with the changing sample rates. It is also worth remarking that the error does not reduce noticeably as the number of samples is increased, suggesting that the same actions are selected with as few as ten samples. By contrast, the POSG algorithm performs noticeably better as the number of samples is increased, and the error around the points reduces.

These results indicate that similar actions are selected even with a small number of samples, perhaps because the best response can be estimated well, and the best response performs well with small sampling rates, making it possible for the algorithm to be very efficient. This compares favorably with the POSG algorithm which approaches optimality at high sampling rates but performs very badly at low sampling rates, at least for this type of problem. We do not investigate the POSG algorithm in the larger version of the problem (Figure 6(b)) but we see that as for the larger problems above, the best response algorithm slightly outperforms the smart policy, due to its better handling of imperfect visibility. The next section investigates the effects of visibility in more detail. (Figure 7)

Varying the Visibility

As the visibility increases and all agents have a better view of the scenario, we expect that the performance of all algorithms will improve. However, we expect the probabilistic algorithms (POSG and best response) to be at less of a disadvantage than the handwritten policy for the lower visibilities—this is because the handwritten policy always behaves as though the visibility is 100% thus does not do any exploration actions.

Figure 8 demonstrates the effects of varying visibility on a 3x3 grid and on a 7x7 grid, each with three agents. In Figure 8(a) we see the performance of the POSG algorithm is much worse than either the smart policy or the best response policy and fluctuating at lower visibilities, but noticeably improving as the visibility is increased. However, both the smart policy and the best response policy do reasonably well even at the lower visibilities, but there is no discernible difference between them. This is because three agents on a three-by-three grid can do fairly well using the very simple strategy of digging where they see victims and can probably directly observe most of the grid between them. By contrast, Figure 8(b) shows the performance on the larger grid. We do not show the slow POSG algorithm on this problem; the baseline of the null policy is at around -90. Here, we see that as expected the best response

Figure 6. Effects of changing the sampling rate with two and three agents

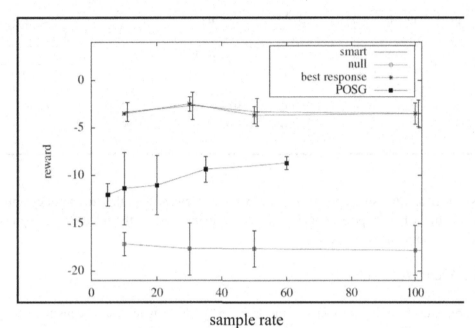

(a) 2 agents on 3x3 grid

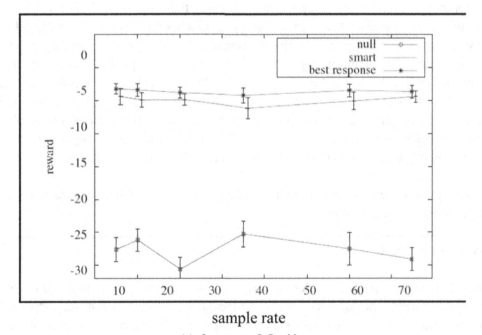

(a) 3agents on 5x5 grid

Figure 7. Time taken to complete one run of 150 steps

3x3 grid, 2 agents	
Sample rate	Time
10	12 minutes
20	19 minutes
35	38 minutes
60	67 minutes
75	113 minutes
(a) POSG algorithm	

3x3 grid, 2 agents	
Sample rate	Time
10	7 seconds
30	18 seconds
50	27 seconds
100	50 seconds
500	4 minutes
(b) best response algorithm	

7x7 grid, 3 agents	
Sample rate	Time
10	18 seconds
35	48 seconds
60	5 minutes
(c) best response algorithm	

policy does outperform the smart policy at lower visibility levels, with the smart policy approaching the performance of the best response policy as the visibility increases, although the best response policy continues to outperform the smart policy.

Varying the Victim Arrival Rate

As well as varying the visibility, we can vary the problem by adjusting the victim density. We expect that increasing the rate at which victims arrive, p_a, and thus the overall density of victims, will make the problem easier, as agents can do well with the simple strategy of digging out the victims around them. The reward for the null policy drops sharply—this is because there are more victims dying.

As the victim density increases, the optimal strategy approaches the very simple strategy of digging if there are any nearby victims. The point at which the simple strategy becomes optimal is indicated by the point where the smart policy stops making improvements over the null policy: between the 0.1 and 0.5 arrival rate on the small problem. The best response policy has matched the smart policy, and the POSG policy also catches up by the 0.5 data point. On the larger problem (Figure 9(b)), the smart policy and best response policy continue to improve across the graph, indicating that there is some sophistication needed in the strategies even at the high victim densities. As expected, on the larger problem, the best response policy slightly outperforms the handwritten strategy due to its better handling of the imperfect visibility.

For the next sections, we fix the visibility at 0.5 and the arrival rate at 0.05. We go on to investigate the scaling properties of the algorithms.

Varying Scaling Factors

The difficulty of the rescue problem scales exponentially with the size of the grid and the number of agents, which are related to the number of states and the number of joint actions respectively. Furthermore, in our implementation, all the agents were running on the same machine as one another and the environment; consequently, the memory requirements of the implementation scaled linearly with the number of agents. Nonetheless, we were able to test our algorithm on grids of up to 12x12 (2^{173} states), and with up to 7 agents (80,000 joint actions).

Now, although 7 agents is not a huge number for an algorithm which we would like to scale into dozens of agents, the primary limiting factor was the memory requirement for our implementation.

Figure 8. Effects of varying visibility

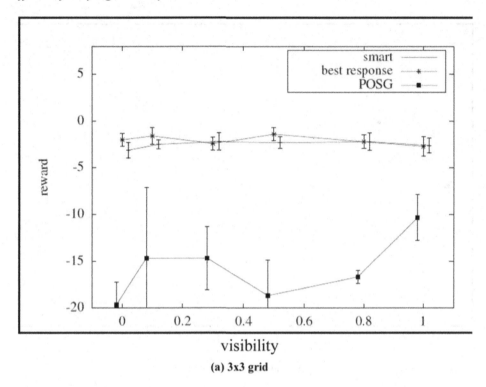

(a) 3x3 grid

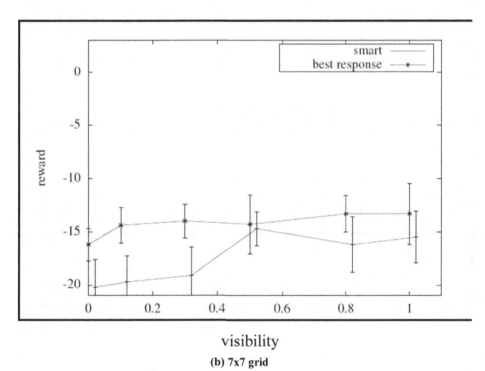

(b) 7x7 grid

Figure 9. Effects of varying victim arrival rate

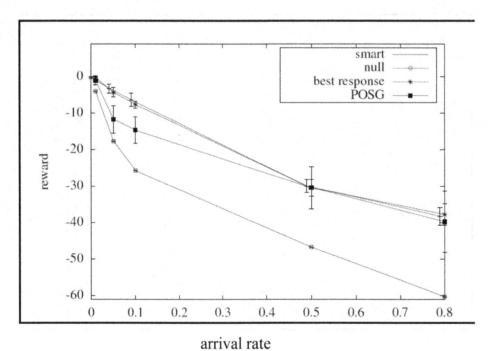

(a) 2 agents on 3x3 grid

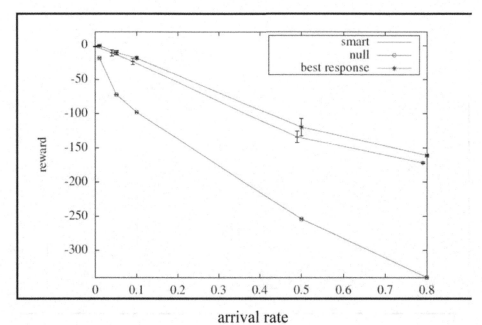

(b) 3 agents on 7x7 grid

Figure 10 shows the effect of increasing the number of agents on two larger grids, a 7x7 grid and a 9x9 grid. We observe that on the 7x7 grid as the number of agents is increased, the smart policy appears to saturate while the best response policy continues to improve. The results are similar for both the 7x7 and the 9x9 grid, although the smart policy does not saturate so much on the 9x9 grid—the larger problem space provides more room for improvement. Future work should involve a more efficient implementation, dividing the agents among several machines. We expect that the best response algorithm will then scale well as the number of agents is increased.

The best response algorithm also performs well on the large grids with many millions of states: with five agents nearly all the victims are rescued (the reward does not fall far below 0) even on the largest (12x12) grid. The smart policy falls away by comparison. This reflects the results we have seen earlier where the best response improves over the smart policy more as the grid size increases, a consequence of the way in which the best response policy incorporates uncertainty and the need for search on larger grids. The results are very similar for both three agents (Figure 11(a)) and five agents (Figure 11(b)) although, as expected, five agents are able to make more rescues than three agents (the lines are slightly flatter).

Thus, we have observed that the best response algorithm performs well by comparison with a handwritten strategy designed for the same problem, and requiring much less sampling than the POSG algorithm to achieve this performance. Furthermore, the best response algorithm scales well, solving problems with many states and increasing numbers of agents and improving on the handwritten strategy for these large problems.

CONCLUSION AND FUTURE WORK

In summary, we have considered the problem of taking other agents into account in uncertain and partially observable dynamic systems.

We developed an approach to this problem using a Bayesian learning mechanism, extending previous work on learning models of other agents, and demonstrated its effectiveness on a scenario from the disaster response domain. To emphasize, the novelties in this work lie in an extension of online model-based learning techniques into partially observable domains, using finite automata. As part of our theory, we outline a general Bayesian model of which our model forms a specific instantiation and show how other techniques, such as POMDPs and Bayesian learning, fit into this same model.

We have examined the performance of our algorithm on a cooperative rescue problem with respect to differing problem parameters, finding that its performance consistently outperforms a handwritten strategy for this problem, more noticeably so as the number of agents and the number of states involved in the problem increase. We also observe that reducing the sampling rate of our algorithm has only small effects on its performance, indicating that the best response calculation is the most important feature—this is encouraging as it enables us to use the best response algorithm with few samples, resulting in greater efficiency. However, we have commented that the limiting factor in running our algorithm, particularly as the number of agents increases, is the memory usage of our implementation, rather than the per-step time required. We therefore propose that future work should investigate more efficient implementations, and ways of distributing the problem across several machines—this is in any case a more accurate model of the problems of interest to us.

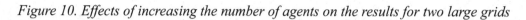

Figure 10. Effects of increasing the number of agents on the results for two large grids

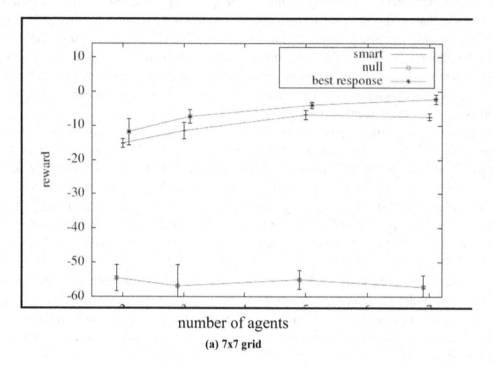

(a) 7x7 grid

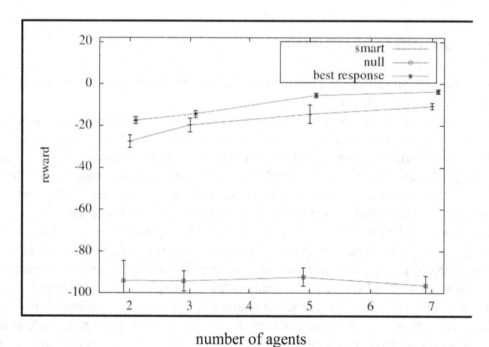

(b) 9x9 grid

Figure 11. Effects of changing the grid size on the results for 3 and for 5 agents

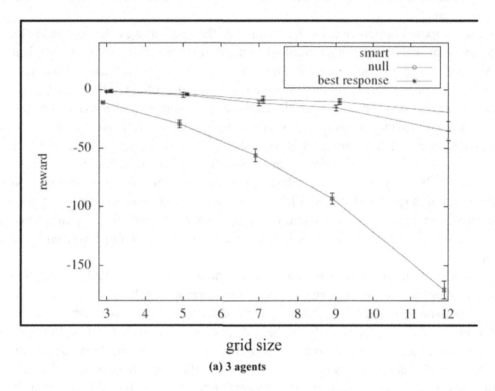

(a) 3 agents

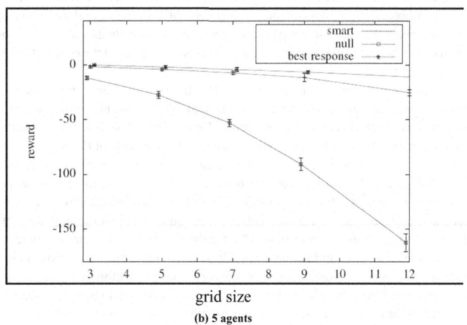

(b) 5 agents

Although the work described above is encouraging, there remain a number of areas in which improvement can be made. As well as scaling the model into higher numbers of agents and larger state spaces, using a more efficient implementation for the environment and agents, and running the agents on distributed machines, there are improvements which can be made to the model. We discuss each of these in turn below.

Firstly, we propose to improve upon the learning of the FSM, using automatic state clustering. In the rescue problem, and in many other problems, groups of states can be considered equivalent by the agents. As a simple demonstration, note that there are several symmetries in our example problem: at every step the grid can be rotated until our agent is towards, say, the bottom right, dividing state space into equivalence classes with four states in each class, one corresponding to each rotation (90°, 180°, 270°, 0°). More generally, we need only to divide up the states among the joint actions—that is, we need exactly as many abstract states as there are joint actions, associating every underlying state with its optimal joint action. In practice, particularly if we plan to re-use parts of our model, reducing it purely to joint actions is likely to be too abstract. Nonetheless, aggregating similar states may be useful. Now, an appropriate algorithm should be adaptable, allowing us to change our mind about which action should be associated with a particular state, should allow us to update clusters incrementally and should not tie us to any predefined set of clusters. We propose to use the statistical clustering described in (Hoar, 1996) for this purpose.

A second area of improvement is to better exploit the information available to agents. We are investigating a complex problem domain in which some domain knowledge can be assumed. We may also be able to assume some level of rationality in the other agents (akin to coordination conventions). As we develop our models of the agents, we have discussed how we can use these models to improve our beliefs about the agents' observations, applying Bayes' rule. However, it may be possible to make more sophisticated belief updates by considering the observations which we make and the observations which other agents will make to be correlated streams of information. Techniques such as the Kalman Filter (Welch & Bishop, 1995) are able to operate over correlated streams of information to make more accurate estimates about the value of any particular point and to estimate missing data (Osborne et al., 2008). These techniques could be applied (with caution) to our estimates of the observations of the other agents and of the current state.

Thirdly, we propose to move beyond the scope of the current work, considering cases in which the environmental dynamics are unknown or are changing, and in which agents are able to enter and leave the environment as the problem progresses. As discussed in the model description, the algorithm we have presented can in principle be used to learn fixed parameters such as parts of the environmental dynamics, by treating these parameters as a part of a "grand state" from which observations are made. Indeed, related work (Chalkiadakis & Boutilier, 2003) (Ross et al., 2008) has done this for some special cases.

In this context, given the uncertainties of our domain, it is clear that if the behavior of the other agents is completely unknown, and the current state is unknown, and the environmental parameters are completely unknown, an agent must stumble around "in the dark" for some considerable time before it can begin to get a handle on good or optimal behavior. However, in the typical scenarios motivated by our example domain of disaster response, an agent will have strong prior information about some or all of the unknown parameters. For example, the other agents may be assumed to be rational and cooperative, thus likely to behave in a near-optimal way. In our example problem, the form of the transition function may be known, but not the exact values of every parameter. By incorporating all the information available to the agent into its model, and particularly by correlating information, we anticipate that our model will be able to handle problems in which the environmental dynamics are not completely known using the theoretical form laid out previously.

Following on from this, our model can easily handle scenarios in which the number of agents changes (but is known to our agent) over time. This is particularly relevant to businesses where there is a mostly stable customer base, with new customers joining or old customers leaving at intervals—for example, the gardening firm, or a company providing lunchtime sandwiches to an office. Since the best response is computed at each step, there will be no difficulty in computing a best response over a subset of the other agents, or in adding a new agent model to the collection. Our agent will adapt continually during the problem run. Similarly, if the environmental dynamics change, the agent will adjust its model smoothly.

Future experiments will demonstrate this on more dynamic problems. Similarly, if the agent is learning the environmental dynamics, and those dynamics change, the agent can adapt concordantly.

With these improvements, we anticipate that the model we have described can be used as the basis of an algorithm capable of solving medium-sized distributed collaborative problems in the real world, such as traffic management, controlling search robots in a building after a fire, or distributing resources as disparate as sandwiches and taxis. Similar algorithms could also be included in software which could be loaded onto handheld devices to aid human decision-making during critical situations such as war or a large-scale disaster.

ACKNOWLEDGMENT

Thanks to Georgios Chalkiadakis and Zinovi Rabovich for discussions on the early versions of this work.

REFERENCES

Aberdeen, D., & Baxter, J. (2002). Scaling internal-state policy-gradient methods for POMDPs. In *Proceedings of the 19th international conference on machine learning* (Vol. 2, pp. 3-10). Sydney, Australia: Morgan Kaufmann.

Abul, O., Polat, F., & Alhajj, R. (2000). Multiagent reinforcement learning using function approximation. In *IEEE transactions on systems, man, and cybernetics, part c* (Vol. 30, p. 485-497).

Amato, C., Bernstein, D. S., & Zilberstein, S. (2006). Solving POMDPs using quadratically constrained linear programs. In *Proceedings of the fifth international joint conference on autonomous agents and multiagent systems* (pp. 341-343). New York: ACM Press.

Boutilier, C. (1996). Planning, learning and coordination in multiagent decision processes. In *Proceedings of the 6th conference on theoretical aspects of rationality and knowledge* (pp. 195-210). San Francisco: Morgan Kaufmann Publishers Inc.

Bowling, M., & Veloso, M. (2001). Rational and convergent learning in stochastic games. In *International Joint Conferences on Artificial Intelligence* (p. 1021-1026).

Carmel, D., & Markovitch, S. (1996). Learning models of intelligent agents. In *Proceedings of the thirteenth national conference on artificial intelligence* (Vol. 2, pp. 62-67). Portland, Oregon.

Cassandra, A., Littman, M., & Zhang, N. (1997). Incremental pruning: A simple, fast, exact method for partially observable Markov decision processes. In *Proceedings of the 13th annual conference on uncertainty in artificial intelligence* (p. 54-61). San Francisco: Morgan Kaufmann.

Chalkiadakis, G., & Boutilier, C. (2003). Coordination in multiagent reinforcement learning: a Bayesian approach. In *Proceedings of the second international joint conference on autonomous agents and multiagent systems* (pp. 709-716). New York: ACM Press.

Clark, A., & Thollard, F. (2004). PAC-learnability of probabilistic deterministic finite state automata. *Journal of Machine Learning Research, 5*, 473–497.

Claus, C., & Boutilier, C. (1998). The dynamics of reinforcement learning in cooperative multiagent systems. In *Proceedings of the fifteenth national/tenth conference on artificial intelligence/innovative applications of artificial intelligence* (pp. 746-752). Menlo Park:American Association for Artificial Intelligence.

Dearden, R., Friedman, N., & Andre, D. (1999). Model-based Bayesian exploration. In *Proceedings of the 15th annual conference on uncertainty in artificial intelligence* (pp. 150-15). San Francisco: Morgan Kaufmann.

Durfee, E. H. (1999). Practically coordinating. *AI Magazine, 20*(1), 99–116.

Dutta, P. S., Dasmahapatra, S., Gunn, S. R., Jennings, N., & Moreau, L. (2004). Cooperative information sharing to improve distributed learning. In *Proceedings of the aamas 2004 workshop on learning and evolution in agent-based systems* (pp. 18-23).

Emery-Montemerlo, R., Gordon, G., Schneider, J., & Thrun, S. (2004). Approximate solutions for partially observable stochastic games with common payoffs. In *Proceedings of the third international joint conference on autonomous agents and multiagent systems* (pp. 136-143). Washington, DC: IEEE Computer Society.

Fischer, F., Rovatsos, M., & Weiss, G. (2004). Hierarchical reinforcement learning in communication-mediated multiagent coordination. In *Proceedings of the third international joint conference on autonomous agents and multiagent systems* (pp. 1334-1335). Washington, DC: IEEE Computer Society.

Fitoussi, D., & Tennenholtz, M. (2000). Choosing social laws for multi-agent systems: Minimality and simplicity. *Artificial Intelligence, 119*(1-2), 61–101. doi:10.1016/S0004-3702(00)00006-0

Fudenberg, D., & Levine, D. K. (1998). *The theory of learning in games*. Cambridge, MA: MIT Press.

Hoar, J. (1996). *Reinforcement learning applied to a real robot task.* (DAI MSc Dissertion, University of Edinburgh)

Kaelbling, L. P., Littman, M. L., & Cassandra, A. R. (1998). Planning and acting in partially observable stochastic domains. *Artificial Intelligence, 101*(1-2), 99–134. doi:10.1016/S0004-3702(98)00023-X

Kim, Y., Nair, R., Varakantham, P., Tambe, M., & Yokoo, M. (2006). Exploiting locality of interaction in networked distributed pomdps. In *Proceedings of the AAAI spring symposium on "Distributed plan and schedule management"*.

Leslie, D. (2004). *Reinforcement learning in games.* Unpublished doctoral dissertation, University of Bristol.

Littman, M. L. (1994). Markov games as a framework for multi-agent reinforcement learning. In *Proceedings of the 11th international conference on machine learning* (pp. 157-163). New Brunswick, NJ: Morgan Kaufmann.

Marecki, J., Gupta, T., Varakantham, P., & Tambe, M. (2008). Not all agents are equal: Scaling up distributed POMDPs for agent networks. In *Proceedings of the Seventh International Joint Conference on Autonomous Agents and Multiagent System*s.

National Research Council. (2005). *Summary of a workshop on using information technology to enhance disaster management.* National Academies Press.

Osborne, M. A., Rogers, A., Ramchurn, S., Roberts, S. J., & Jennings, N. R. (2008, April). Towards real-time information processing of sensor network data using computationally efficient multi-output gaussian processes. In *International conference on information processing in sensor networks* (pp. 109–120).

Paquet, S., Tobin, L., & Chaib-draa, B. (2005). An online POMDP algorithm for complex multiagent environments. In *Proceedings of the Fourth International Joint Conference on Autonomous Agents and Multiagent Systems* (pp. 970-977). New York: ACM Press.

Pineau, J., Gordon, G., & Thrun, S. (2003, August). Point-based value iteration: An anytime algorithm for POMDPs. In *International Joint Conference on Artificial Intelligence* (pp. 1025 -1032).

Poupart, P., Vlassis, N., Hoey, J., & Regan, K. (2006). An analytic solution to discrete Bayesian reinforcement learning. In *Proceedings of the 23rd International Conference on Machine Learnin*g (pp. 697-704). New York: ACM.

Ramamritham, K., Stankovic, J. A., & Zhao, W. (1989). Distributed scheduling of tasks with deadlines and resource requirements. *IEEE Transactions on Computers, 38*(8), 1110–1123. doi:10.1109/12.30866

Ross, S., Chaib-draa, B., & Pineau, J. (in press). Bayes-adaptive POMDPs. In *Neural information processing systems.*

Roy, N., & Gordon, G. (2002, December). Exponential family PCA for belief compression in POMDPs. In S. Becker, S. Thrun, & K. Obermayer (Eds.), *Advances in neural information processing* (p. 1043-1049). Vancouver, Canada.

Shani, G., Brafman, R. I., & Shimony, S. E. (2005). Model-based online learning of POMDPs. In *European Conference on Machine Learning* (p. 353-364).

Smith, A. J. (2002). *Dynamic generalisation of continuous action spaces in reinforcement learning: A neurally inspired approach.* (Ph.D. thesis, Division of Informatics, Edinburgh University, UK.)

Sutton, R. S., & Barto, A. G. (1998). *Reinforcement learning: An introduction.* Cambridge, MA: MIT Press.

Tambe, M., Adibi, J., Alonaizon, Y., Erdem, A., Kaminka, G. A., & Marsella, S. (1999). Building agent teams using an explicit teamwork model and learning. *Artificial Intelligence, 110*(2), 215–239. doi:10.1016/S0004-3702(99)00022-3

Vu, T., Powers, R., & Shoham, Y. (2006). Learning against multiple opponents. In *Proceedings of the fifth international joint conference on autonomous agents and multiagent systems* (pp. 752–759). New York: ACM.

Wang, F. (2002). Self-organising communities formed by middle agents. In *Proceedings of the first international joint conference on autonomous agents and multiagent systems* (pp. 1333-1339). New York: ACM Press.

Welch, G., & Bishop, G. (1995). *An introduction to the Kalman filter* (Tech. Rep.). Chapel Hill, NC: University of North Carolina at Chapel Hill.

Wooldridge, M. (2002). *An introduction to multi-agent systems*. Wiley.

KEY TERMS AND DEFINITIONS

Agent: An agent receives input from the environment through its sensors and interacts with the environment to try and achieve some goal.

Bayesian probability: is an interpretation of probability which describes probability as a "personal belief", based on combining any prior with observed information.

Bayes' rule: Bayes' rule is the equation specifying how to update beliefs about the world, given new information: P(world = w | observations) ∞ P(observations | world = w)P(world = w).

Belief State: A belief state encapsulates the beliefs an agent has about its current state: that is, probability distributions for each variable within the state.

Coordination: When several agents are interacting with the same environment, their actions may affect one another, directly or indirectly—this is coordination.

Disaster Response: Large-scale disasters include earthquake, fire and terrorist attack, and require a timely coordinated multi-agency response.

Finite State Machine: A finite state machine has a set of internal states, and rules for movement between internal states. When describing the behavior of an intelligent agent, internal states prescribe actions, and movement between states is conditioned on observations from the environment.

Markov decision process: In a Markov Decision Process, changes in the environment in response to an agent's actions are determined only by the immediate state and actions, and not by any historical information.

Uncertainty: An agent in an uncertain environment does not know of all the parameters within that environment.

ENDNOTE

[1]   It would be possible to initialize with a more sophisticated set of F corresponding to shared conventions relating to the domain, for example encapsulating the knowledge that agents will run from a burning building. We leave that possibility to future work.

Chapter 8
Flow–Based Adaptive Information Integration

Dickson K.W. Chiu
Dickson Computer Systems, Hong Kong

Thomas Trojer
University of Innsbruck, Austria

Hua Hu
Zhejiang Gongshang University, China

Haiyang Hu
Zhejiang Gongshang University, China

Yi Zhuang
Zhejiang Gongshang University, China

Patrick C.K. Hung
University of Ontario Institute of Technology, Canada

ABSTRACT

Assembling a coherent view of distributed heterogeneous information and their processing is challenging but important for inter-organizational business collaboration and service provision. However, traditional integration approaches do not consider dynamic and adaptive issues such as human intervention and exception handling. Therefore, we propose a Workflow-based Information Integration (WII) approach, which is particularly suitable in a loosely coupled Web services environment. Our implementation framework comprises five layers: semantic, application, workflow, service, and message. We focus on the workflow layer for providing adaptiveness from the aspects of various types of flows such as control-flows, data-flows, security-flows, exception-flows and semantic-flows by using the Business Process Execution Language for Web Services (BPEL). We further extend this with our proposed data-integration, semantic-referencing, and exception-handling assertions in order to achieve dynamic and adaptive workflow-based information integration plans. We map information into SOAP messages and link the

DOI: 10.4018/978-1-60566-669-3.ch008

proposed exception-handling assertions in BPEL to SOAP-fault implementations. We also define semantic referencing in BPEL by using OWL Web Ontology Language. Lastly, we demonstrate the feasibility of our adaptive approach with an intelligence information integration case study at the application layer and examine some typical use cases of exception-handling with semantic support.

INTRODUCTION

There is a growing need for an integrated view of information from different sources with the blooming of information sources and services over the Web. Automation for the assembly of a coherent view of distributed heterogeneous information and information processing resources is a challenging and important process for inter-organizational collaboration and service provision. This process is defined as *information integration*, which deals with the problem of making heterogeneous, external data sources accessible via a common interface and an integrated schema. Users should perceive the collection of data as being managed by a single database system (Leymann & Roller, 2002). Information management involves dynamic and adaptive plan execution, involving steps such as access approval, continuous querying, query result accumulation, local persistent storage, and the linking of other actions to the results of queries (Barish et al., 2000). In this chapter, we advocate a workflow approach to address this problem. We further propose a formulation of information integration plans in a loosely coupled Web services environment in which each service provider acts as a data custodian or provides certain data analysis services.

Current trends in information and communication technology (ICT) accelerate the widespread use of Web services in information integration (Aversano et al., 2002). In this chapter, a Web service refers to an autonomous unit of application logic that provides some information processing resources to other applications through the Internet from a service provider (such as an enterprise). Here, an activity, i.e., a logical unit of work, is performed by a Web service. Web services are based on a set of XML standards such as Simple Object Access Protocol (SOAP), Universal Description, Discovery and Integration (UDDI), and Web Services Description Language (WSDL) (Weerawarana et al., 2005). In many cases, information integration plans may have to combine more than one information services to fulfill a need. Thus, information Web services must evolve to support interactions with access control in addition to simple procedures (Wiederhold, 1992). In addition, these Web services may require long duration enactment of multi-step activities, which can involve information processing tasks, interactions between information services providers, and human intervention (e.g., decision for approval). Thus, workflow technologies help providing dynamic and adaptive capabilities as further explained below.

A Workflow Management System (WFMS) (Georgakopoulos et al., 1995; Van der Aalst & Van Hee, 2002) is the application to support the specification, decomposition, execution, coordination, and monitoring of workflows (Jeston & Nelis, 2008). In general, a workflow includes many different entities, such as, activities, humans, events, and flows. An event is an atomic occurrence representing a specific state change of the system itself or an user application, which arise during the execution of an activity. We partition events into different types such as events related to control, data, semantic, exceptions, and security. A *flow* is a directed relationship that transmits events from a source activity to a sink activity. Hence, events partition activity relationships into corresponding types of flows, such as control-flows, data-flows, semantic-flows, exception-flows, and security-flows. In this way, a workflow specification is defined as a set of activities connected by these flows: every activity starts when one or more relevant events arrive; and when the activity finishes one or more events are generated inform other dependent activity/activities.

The Semantic Web helps providing explicit meaning to information available on the Web for automatic process and information integration based on the concept of ontology (Fensel, 2001). An ontology defines the terms used to present a domain of knowledge that is shared by people, databases, and applications. In particular, ontologies encode knowledge for providing adaptive capabilities, which possibly span different domains as well as describe the relationships among them. In this chapter, we define semantic references in Business Process Execution Language for Web Services (BPEL) by using the Web Ontology Language (OWL) (Lacy, 2005). OWL is a XML language proposed by the World Wide Web Consortium (W3C) for defining Web ontologies. An OWL ontology includes descriptions of classes, properties, and their instances, as well as formal semantics for deriving logical consequences in entailments.

An exception is a special event that deviates from normal behavior or prevent normal process execution. Upon unexpected exceptions, a comprehensive WFMS can support users to handle them manually. Frequent occurrences of similar exceptions have to be incorporated into workflow specifications as expected exceptions (Chiu et al., 1999; 2000; 2001). We link the proposed exception-handling assertions in BPEL to SOAP-fault implementations (Weerawarana et al., 2005) and examine some typical use cases of exceptions. To further increase the adaptiveness and alternatives in handling exceptions, we also discuss how to employ Semantic Web technologies in handling exceptions.

The combination of workflow technologies and Web services has become more and more popular in both the research community and the industry (Leymann et al., 2002). Based on our previous work for a healthcare environment (Hung & Chiu, 2003), we extend our proposed framework and generalize it in the context of Web services provisioning (Hung & Chiu, 2004) and in this chapter further explore the application of Semantic Web technologies in this context. The challenge addressed by this chapter is the development of a technical framework consisting of several logical layers that support the generation of information integration plans, targeting workflow systems in a loosely coupled Web services environment. Our proposed Workflow-based Information Integration (WII) framework comprise five layers, namely, semantic layer, application layer, workflow layer, service layer, and message layer. We express the control-flows, data-flows, semantic-flows, exception-flows, and security-flows of the conceptual workflow model using BPEL and OWL, extended with our proposed WII assertions in order to achieve dynamic and adaptive WII plans. This chapter demonstrates that the workflow concept is a suitable technology to support WII plans in an environment with autonomous and loosely coupled information services, especially when human intervention is required. In addition, Semantic Web technologies can effectively help exception handling for providing further adaptiveness in this context.

The remainder of this chapter is organized as follows. First, we review the relevant literature. Then we present the background information and overview for our proposed WII framework with a motivating example. Next we present the basic dynamic integration of control-flows, data-flows, and semantic-flows with BPEL and OWL. Then we detail our proposed security-flows and exception-flows extensions for WII for adaptive execution based on some typical use cases. We further illustrate how Semantic Web technologies can help exception handling to provide further adaptiveness. Finally we conclude this chapter with discussions and directions for future research.

BACKGROUND AND LITERATURE REVIEW

Prior research has proposed to abstract the information integration problem into querying an infrastructure mediation service (Wiederhold, 1992), which offers users and applications a location-independent virtual integrated schema in a common data model (Sheth & Larson, 1990). Although information integration issues are not new in database research communities, applying workflow technologies in different application domains has many unique properties that entail special integration design considerations, such as Sheng & Cheng (1990). Cheung et al. (2003) use a bottom-up data-driven methodology to extend information systems into Web services. However, this chapter presents a top-down approach and focus on a global view of the process.

Applying workflow technologies in health administrative data integration has been discussed in health informatics communities, such as the International Medical Informatics Association (http://www.imia.org), for a certain time. For example, Marsh (1997) introduces the concept of a virtual medical world that provides the potential to integrate existing medical information into future forms of medical data. Marsh (1998) also presents a multi-model medical information system for demonstrating the virtual medical world. Similarly, RIANE (Joubert et al., 1998) is a conceptual interface for providing end-users with easy-to-use heterogeneous databases and natural means to access and query them. On the other hand, Takeda et al. (2001) present a system architecture for supporting networked electronic patient records. Similarly, Liu et al. (2001) propose a web-based referral information system for sharing electronic patient records based on XML. Further, Grimson et al. (2001) propose a Synapses prototype system for supporting federated healthcare records that provides an integrated view of patient data from heterogeneous distributed information systems on the Internet. However, none of these works describe flows in their framework. In addition, none of these approaches provides a seamless integration that permits the use of workflow technologies to coordinate distributed information access from the aspects of data-flows generated from an information integration planning.

Web Services Description Language (WSDL) (Weerawarana et al., 2005) is an XML language proposed by the Web Wide Web Consortium (W3C) for describing Web services as a set of endpoints operating on messages that contain either document-oriented or procedure-oriented information. A WSDL document defines services as collections of network ports. A port is associated with a reusable binding by a network address, and a collection of ports defines a service. However, WSDL only describes the endpoint properties of Web services and does not consider the execution sequence of Web services activities (i.e., workflows). This is where workflow technologies are positioned to enhance the Web services applications such as information integration. For example, Thatte (2001) describes XLANG as a notation for the specification of message exchange behavior (i.e., interactions) among participating Web services in workflows on their BizTalk engine. XLANG is based on the WSDL service description with an extension element that describes the behavior of the services as a part of a business process. In XLANG, the behavior of each Web service is specified independently, and the interaction between Web services is only through message exchanges expressed as operations in WSDL. Similarly, Leymann (2001) describes the Web Services Flow Language (WSFL) on their MQSeries workflow engine that is also layered on the top of the WSDL. The WSFL is an XML language for the description of Web services compositions for supporting workflows. WSFL specifies the appropriate usage pattern of a collection of Web services in order to achieve a particular goal (e.g., information integration), and it also specifies the interaction pattern of a collection of Web services.

Next, the Web Service Choreography Interface (WSCI) (Nagappan, 2002) describes the flow of messages exchanged by a Web service participating in interactions with other Web services. In particular, WSCI describes the dynamic interface of the Web services participating in a given message exchange by means of reusing the operations defined for a static interface. Further, WS-Coordination (Foggon et al., 2003) defines an extensible framework for coordinating activities using a set of coordination protocols. Based on WS-Coordination, WS-Transaction (Foggon et al., 2003) presents an XML language to describe an atomic transaction for coordinating activities in a short period of time, and also a business activity for coordinating activities in a long period of time by applying business logic. However, none of these XML languages discuss data-flows, semantic-flows, exception-flows and security-flows in their models. Recently, the Business Process Execution Language for Web Services (BPEL) (Weerawarana et al., 2005), a formal specification of business processes and interaction protocols, has been proposed. BPEL defines an interoperable integration model that facilitates the expansion of automated process integration in both intra- and inter-corporate environment. In particular, the current version of BPEL claims that data flow will be allowed through links in addition to using links to express synchronization dependencies in the future version. Therefore, we demonstrate the proposed models with our proposed data-integration, semantic-referencing, and exception-handling assertions in the context of BPEL. In summary, all these XML languages facilitate defining Web services interacted activities in the format of a workflow. However, except SOAP-fault (Weerawarana et al., 2005) captures exceptions in the message level. Further, these languages do not provide any expression to capture exceptions comprehensively.

Exception issues have been widely investigated in the workflow research community. For example, Hwang et al. (1999) propose a model for handling workflow exceptions. The proposed model provides a rule base that consists of a set of rules for handling exceptions. If none of the rules match the current exception, a search on the previous experience in handling similar exceptions is conducted. They also describe several algorithms to identify the exception records by classifying the kind of information about exceptions, defining the degree of similarity between two exceptions, and searching similar exceptions. Similarly, Casati et al. (1999) present a methodology for modeling exceptions by means of activity graphs. They describe taxonomy of expected exceptions by categorizing and mapping them into activity graphs. They also show how to handle the exceptions in each class. Further, they also provide methodological guidelines in order to support exception analysis and design activities. Based on a taxonomy and meta-model, Chiu et al. (1999; 2000; 2001) developed a web-based WFMS, called ADOME-WFMS, to support automatic resolution for expected exceptions and human intervention for unexpected exceptions, through a unified framework of event-condition-action (ECA) rules. Advanced matchmaking was also supported with a role and capability model. Reichert & Dadam (1998) pointed out the possible occurrence of unexpected situations during workflow execution, if changes to a workflow are applied. Such changes can lead to violation of specific correctness properties which of a workflow system and must be handled accordingly. However, all of these works do not explicitly separate exception-flows from the control-flows and data-flows.

The Semantic Web is originally based on the research areas of knowledge representation and ontology in Artificial Intelligence (AI). DAML+OIL is a semantic markup language based on RDF and RDF Schema extended with richer modeling primitives (Lacy, 2005). DAML+OIL provides a language for expressing far more sophisticated classifications and properties of resources than RDFS. Recently, the OWL Web Ontology Language has been developed by the W3C Web Ontology Working Group as a revision of the DAML+OIL web ontology language. OWL has been proposed to provide three increasingly expressive sub-languages for specific communities of implementers and users, namely, OWL Lite,

OWL Description Logics (OWL DL), and OWL full. OWL Lite supports the basic need for a classification hierarchy and simple constraints. For example, while it supports cardinality constraints, it only permits cardinality values of 0 or 1. Thus, OWL Lite provides an easier implementation and a quicker migration path for thesauri and other taxonomies. OWL DL supports maximum expressiveness while retaining computational completeness (all conclusions are guaranteed to be computed) and decidability (all computations will finish in finite time). OWL DL includes all OWL language constructs, but they can be used only under certain restrictions (for example, while a class may be a subclass of many classes, a class cannot be an instance of another class). OWL DL is so named due to its correspondence with *description logics*, a field of research that has studied the logics that form the formal foundation of OWL. OWL Full supports maximum expressiveness and the syntactic freedom of RDF, but with no computational guarantees. For example, in OWL Full a class can be treated simultaneously as a collection of individuals and as an individual in its own right. OWL Full allows an ontology to augment the meaning of the pre-defined (RDF or OWL) vocabulary. Thus, ontology developers adopting OWL should consider which sub-language best suits their needs. In this chapter, ontology is described in OWL, in particular in OWL DL, because OWL provides a standard set of elements and attributes with defined semantics, for defining terms and relationships in ontology. In addition, OWL contains a set of logic-based primitives that are specifically useful in intelligence informatics. Furthermore, we decided to deploy OWL instead of DAML+OIL because OWL has been designed as a standard in W3C (Chen et al., 2003).

In summary, the development of solutions for workflow-based information integration is promising and challenging. Even current research on WII is still in an emerging stage. To our knowledge, none of the prior research studies the use of workflow technologies to materialize information integration from the control-flows, data-flows, security-flows, and exception-flows in a unified approach for dynamic and adaptive WII. Such application in security and intelligence informatics is novel.

FRAMEWORK OVERVIEW AND MOTIVATING EXAMPLE

Figure 1 depicts an overview of our adaptive WII approach, which also involves security and human intervention. In response to user requests from the input phase, the WII service in the planning phase generates a plan consisting of: source-specific requests to materialize data; control relationships among information services specifying coordination plans; activities to transport data among information services; exception relationships identifying expected exceptions; access control requirements, semantic referencing and source specific requests to invoke some operations (such as filter, transform, merge, or join) on data. In general, the WII service has a knowledge base that contains a set of information integration templates for generating different execution patterns for providing adaptiveness. Given an integration plan, the execution service in the execution phase coordinates the execution of requests at information services to generate integrated results for the output phase. Request execution at information services may occur synchronously or in parallel, depending on control-flow relationships nominated in the plan. Data-flow relationships in the integration plan specify how data transmission should occur among Web services. Semantic-flow relationships in the integration plan provide a domain of knowledge for supporting other flows to execute the workflow. Exception-flow relationships describe what to do with expected exceptions. Security-flow relationships specify how to satisfy the security requirements in the integration plan. Figure 1 also depicts the underlying technologies to support the adaptive planning and execution phases, which are WFMS and Web services respectively in this framework.

Figure 1. A schematic input, planning, execution and output phases

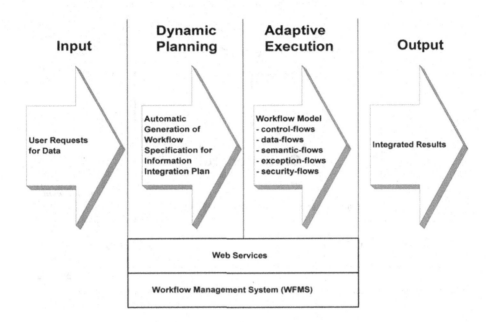

To illustrate our framework, we present a motivating example of intelligence information integration. Our example shows the investigation of a suspect through the provision of an integrated view of heterogeneous information and information processing resources that are distributed across autonomous organizations in a loosely coupled environment. In particular, after the tragedy of September 11, 2001, change of emphasis from enforcement to prevention requires much more of such investigations. To improve intelligence informatics, a dynamic and adaptive approach is a key to success. Detectives must be able to flexibly access comprehensive, accurate, and timely integrated intelligence information. For example, a detective investigates a suspect by inspecting an integrated view of records (e.g., criminal records, border control, and bank transactions) sourced from different government and commercial organizations depending on different situations. In particular, bank transactions within one month before and after a trip and above a certain threshold amount are retrieved. To illustrate, Figure 2 shows a sample WII schema with the following relations and attributes (in parentheses):

- *IDrecord (id-no, tax-file-no, name, sex, date-of-birth, area-code, phone-no, address, postal-code)*
- *CrimeRecord (id-no, crime-description, sentence, day-of-event)*
- *BorderRecord (id-no, entry-or-exit, place, vehicle, day-of-event)*
- *BankRecord (tax-file-no, bank-no, account-no, transaction, amount, balance, day-of-event)*

Figure 3 shows our architecture of WII with semantic support that consists of a set of intelligence Web services (e.g., databases and data analysis services) located at M different locations (M is a cardinal number), a WFMS, ontologies, and system interfaces. Typically, to provide dynamic and adaptive WII, the WFMS (i) accepts user requests with login information from the system interfaces, (ii) generates an

Figure 2. A sample intelligence information integration data schema

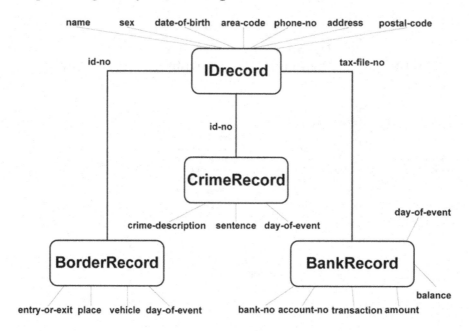

authenticated security-token (e.g., SAML) (Weerawarana et al., 2005) for this user, and (iii) connects the Web services from different intelligence providers with the user's security-token. Afterwards data-sets from chosen Web services (with the data custodian or intelligence provider's read-access approval) get collected and (iv) integrated to a view, and then (v) presented to the user. We focus on read-only interactions between the WFMS and Web services, because queries occur more often while updates usually involve only one intelligence provider. During this process, different parties such as users, data custodians, and service providers may have to reference a set of ontologies for executing the workflow. Thus, the WFMS integrates the datasets from various autonomous databases through Web services into integrated views, with the help of Semantic Web technologies.

Figure 4 summarizes our multi-layer framework that describes the conceptual and technical model for WII. A multi-layer framework describes a model with layers, which contains meta-models with a set of operations. This approach is analogous to prior research that recommends separating the description of the semantic, application, workflow, service, and message layers in a conceptual model (Casati et al., 1999; Hung et al., 2007). In addition, Figure 4 shows the mapping of each layer's conceptual and technical model, introducing the technologies which underlie each conceptual layer .

Figure 5 presents the workflow layer of our multi-layer framework with flow technologies to manage and monitor the control-flow, data-flows, security-flow, exception-flow and semantic-flow. This flow technology is becoming an integral part of modern programming models (Leymann & Roller, 2002), each flow is therefore separated and depicted in the context of a multi-layer framework, leading to what is called *flow independency*. The separation of flows results in increased adaptiveness of the information Web services in executing workflows. Thus, the workflow modelers can easily change or update the information integration plans for different situations (Leymann & Roller, 2002), as illustrated in further examples in this chapter.

Figure 3. System architecture of WII with semantic support

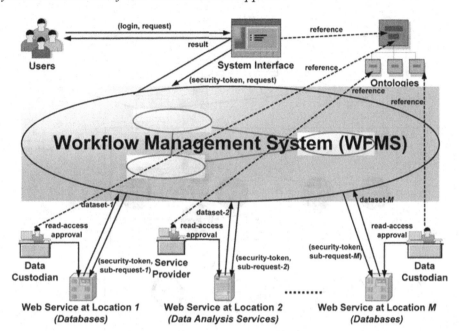

BASIC DYNAMIC EXECUTION WITH SEMANTIC, CONTROL, AND DATA FLOWS

In this section, we focus on the workflow layer for basic dynamic execution from the aspects of control-flows, data-flows, and semantic-flows by using the BPEL in the technical model, extended with our proposed WII assertions. Each service provider provides Web services at the service layer and BPEL orchestrates them together in order to achieve dynamic WII plans.

Figure 4. Mapping between the conceptual and technical model of WII

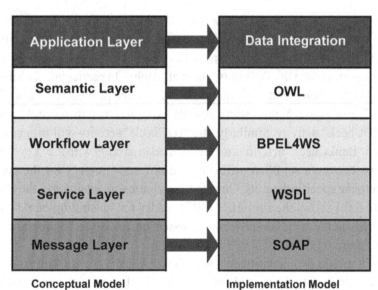

Figure 5. An example of control-flow, data-flows, security-flow, exception-flow, and semantic-flow for WII

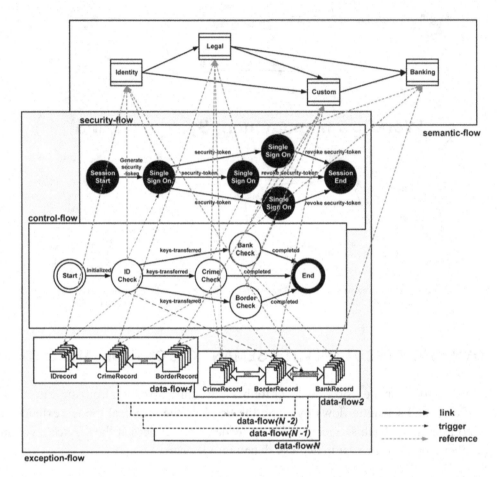

Based on the above example, Figure 5 describes a workflow that all the activities (in circles) are performed for retrieving the datasets from various databases (labeled by the activity's name), and are coordinated by a set of events (in single arrow lines). Each activity is assigned to a Web service for execution by a matchmaking process in the WFMS (Chiu et al., 1999). In particular, each activity has to obtain a read-access approval from each data custodian and data service provider as shown in Figure 3. Referring to the *control-flow* in Figure 5, the "Start" activity generates a control event "initialized" to trigger the execution of "IDCheck" activity. Similarly, the "IDCheck" activity will trigger the "CrimeCheck," "BorderCheck," and "BankCheck" activities to be executed in parallel with the "keys-transferred" events. In this case, the *keys* contain a set of records (i.e., "id-no" and "ac-no") for the consequent activities (Web services) to retrieve specific datasets. Once these activities are *completed*, the *control-flow* is ended successfully. Figure 6 (b) shows the simplified BPEL codes for illustrating one data-flow of Figure 5. Additionally, we propose the semantic-referencing assertions in BPEL for supporting semantic-flows in WII plans, as in Figure 6 (a).

The interactions between two meta-models at different layers (i.e., the control-flow and data-flow) are triggered by external events (in dashed arrow lines). In this case, the external events contain the

Figure 6. A simplified BPEL code for illustrating (a) the semantic-flow and (b) one data-flow

```
<flow name="semantic-flow">                    <flow name="data-flows">
  <ontology activityName="IDCheck">             <integrate name="data-flow-1">
                                                  <dataset name="IDrecord">
<ontologyRef="http://www.example.org/identity.owl"/>   <attributes name="id-no" key="primary"/>
  </ontology>                                       <attributes name="sex"/>
  <ontology activityName="BankCheck">             <attributes name="age"/>
                                                    ...
<ontologyRef="http://www.example.org/banking.owl"/>  </dataset>
  </ontology>                                      <dataset name="CrimeRecord"
    ...                                             <attributes name="id-no" key="primary"/>
</flow>                                              <attributes name="crime-description"/>
                                                    <attributes name="sentence"/>
                                                    ...
                                                  </dataset>
                                                  ...
                                                </integrate>
                                                ...
                                              </flow>
```

datasets generated from the activities. Referring to Figure 5, there is a set of N data-flows (N is a cardinal number) that are performed corresponding to the *control-flow*. Each data-flow can be assigned to an information Web service chosen by a matchmaking process in the WFMS (e.g., searching for the bank at which the suspect owns an account). The *data-flow-1* is used to join (in double arrows) the datasets returned from the "IDCheck," "CrimeCheck," and "BorderCheck" activities into an integrated view for a particular user request. Similarly, the *data-flow-2* is used to join the datasets returned from the CrimeCheck," "BorderCheck," and "BankCheck" activities respectively. In the context of BPEL, we propose new data-integration assertions named <integrate>, <dataset>, and <dataLinkage> for generating the data-flows as shown in Figure 6 (b). Referring to Figure 5, both the control-flow and data-flows are referencing to the relevant ontology described in the semantic-flow.

Referring to Figure 6 (b), using the "id-no" as a join key, the *data-flow-1* joins the "IDrecord" dataset (with attributes "id-no," "sex," "age," etc.), the "CrimeRecord" dataset (with attributes "id-no," "Crime-description," "sentence," etc.), and the "BorderRecord" dataset (with attributes "id-no," "entry-or-exit," "place," etc.). Similarly, using the "id-no" as a join key, the *data-flow-2* joins the "CrimeRecord," "Border-Record" and "BankRecord" datasets, which can be seen in Figure 5. In particular, the data linkage (i.e., "id-no" and "tax-file-no") between "BorderRecord" and "BankRecord" are delivered by the "IDCheck" activity from the *control-flow*. In a general case, the workflow is ended once all the control-flow and data-flow(s) are completed successfully.

ADAPTIVE EXECUTION WITH SECURITY AND EXECUTION FLOW

In this section, we first focus on the workflow layer for adaptive execution from the aspects of security-flows and exception-flows, further extended with our proposed WII assertions. In the next section, we explore how Semantic Web technologies can help to form adaptive exception handling.

One of the most popular security technologies for this communication channel environment is WS-Security (Weerawarana et al., 2005). WS-Security describes and provides protection enhancements to SOAP messaging to provide quality of protection through message integrity, message confidentiality, and single message authentication. From another point of view, WS-Security is a messaging language that mainly focuses on secure communications. Based on the SOAP messaging, a major advantage of such a security token is that the security mechanisms for protection of such a token can rely on the existing mechanisms provided by WS-Security, such as XML Encryption and XML Signature. Referring to the technical architecture of WS-Security specifications, we propose to manage and store user's access control information as security tokens in the context of WS-Security.

Based on the security token defined in the SOAP header, we propose security flow assertions in BPEL as <sessionStart/>, <clearance/>, <securityToken/>, <tokenType/>, and <sessionEnd/>. The <sessionStart/> assertion is used to identify the time when the user's security token is generated by WII, and the <sessionEnd/> assertion is used to identify the time when the user's security token is revoked by WII. The security flow of WII is orchestrated with the control flow, by means of describing the security clearance of each activity specified in the control flow. In this scenario, we adapt the single-sign-on method for security clearance (Gross, 2003). The single-sign-on method allows a user to log into WII just once (session start), and then access is transparently granted to a variety of permitted Web services with no further login being required. A session gets ended, say, if the user logs out (session end). In particular, authentication in WII is not only based on the "Username" and "Password", but can also use other information such as the "SubjectName" and "SubjectLocation." Each of the activity can define whether the security clearance <clearance/> is required and the details such as the type of security token <securityToken/> and <tokenType/>. In this example, SAML (Weerawarana et al., 2005), an XML-based framework for exchanging security credentials in the form of assertions about subjects, is used to define authentication and authorization decisions in WII. Therefore, Web service providers submit SAML tokens to security servers for making specific security decisions.

Exceptional situations may be caused by system failures, or may be related to the semantics of the activity, such as when a deadline of an activity expires (Joubert, 1998; Chiu et al., 2001). In many cases, exceptions may cause denial of services. Denial of service is always referring to the loss of availability due to accidental or malicious user actions. In general, there are two types of exceptions in the proposed conceptual workflow model: expected and unexpected exceptions. Expected exceptions (Chiu et al., 2001) are predictable deviations of the normal behavior of the workflow. In our proposed workflow model, there are several common categories of expected exceptions, such as:

- Control exceptions, which are raised in correspondence to control-flows such as start or completion of activities.
- Data exceptions, which are raised in correspondence to data-flows such as data integration processes.
- Temporal exceptions, which are raised in correspondence to both, control-flows and data-flows such as reaching of a specific future timestamp or a the elapsing of a pre-defined interval.
- External exceptions, which are raised in correspondence to control-flows and data-flows explicitly notified by external services such as system failures.
- Security exceptions, which are raised in correspondence to access control or security violations.

External and temporal exceptions are in general asynchronous, but control, data, and security exceptions occur synchronously with activity executions. In our proposed workflow model, unexpected exceptions mainly correspond to mismatches between an activity specification and its execution. In many cases, human intervention is a mechanism for handling unexpected exceptions in order to provide adaptiveness. In this section, we discuss some common use cases of expected exceptions, with focus on control, data, and security exceptions.

Failed activities are defined as activities that raised a failure during execution or are unavailable and therefore not executable. In general, there are three common exception-handling procedures (Chiu et al., 2000):

Remedy: The workflow designer can debug or modify the activities to resume the execution, in which other activities are not affected. Common examples would be when dealing with damaged or invalid data, illegible operations such as a division by zero, or a dead loop occuring during the execution of an activity.

Forward Recovery: The workflow designer can assign an alternative execution path to replace the problematic activity. For example, an airline company could replace the role of an immigration office, in giving insight to a suspect's entry or exit record. The problematic activity may have to roll back to the original state before performing the alternate execution path. Some other approaches related to Forward Recovery are based on tolerating the inconsistencies and proceeding the workflow execution, if a proper explaination could be given (Borgida & Murata, 1999).

Backward Recovery: Completed operations are executed in the reverse order of their previous execution. The problematic activity may have to roll back to a former valid state before it can be re-executed. For read-only operations, Backward Recovery is usually not required.

Any system components which have an algorithmic flow also have the need of a pervasive exception-handling (Perry et al., 2000). Exception-flows (Chiu et al., 2000; 2001) are often asynchronous with respect to the control-flows, data-flows, and security-flows, both in their raising and in their handling. Figure 7 describes our proposed adaptive exception-handling approach in the context of different flows (i.e., control, data, and security) in the workflow layer and different protocols (i.e., BPEL and SOAP). In the workflow layer, the control-flows, data-flows, and security-flows are orchestrated by the BPEL codes discussed before. The execution of WII interacts with a set of SOAP messages. Once a control, data or security exception is raised, the correspondent Web service will generate a SOAP fault message as an exception event to trigger the exception-flows in the workflow layer. We propose some new assertions to describe the exception-handling procedures in BPEL. These assertions integrate with the exception-handling procedure specified by the conditions in BPEL, so that adaptive actions can be taken in the context of our specified control-flow, data-flows, and security-flow.

Referring to the scenario of security-flows, there are two circumstances in which a security exception can occur: *activity-specific* or *cross-activity*. An activity-specific exception only affects exactly one activity, but a cross-activity exception may affect more than one activity. For example, the Web service at the "BorderCheck" generates a SOAP fault message to the WFMS as shown in Figure 8. This SOAP fault message describes the exceptional situation in which the user is not authorized to access this service because of the unrecognized security token sent by the user.

In the context of BPEL, we propose new exception-handling assertion named <exceptionHandling>, <event>, <condition>, and <action> for generating the data-flows as shown in Figure 9. Moreover, the proposed conceptual workflow model requires a termination mechanism to prevent exceptions trigger each other indefinitely (Aiken et al., 1992). In the worst case, if the workflow designer cannot find any feasible exception-handling procedure, the problematic activity has to abort as well as the user request. This is known as failure determination and is an undesirable situation during a workflow execution. In this case, we propose a new exception-handling assertion named <exceptionHandlingDefault> for specifying the abort action if none of the rules can handle the exception as shown in Figure 10.

Figure 7. Proposed exception-handling approach

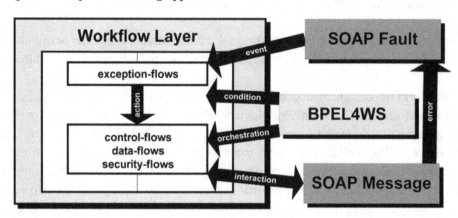

FURTHER ADAPTIVE EXECUTION HANDLING WITH SEMANTIC ASSISTANCE

In this section, we demonstrate the feasibility and advantages of employing Semantic Web technologies to assist in adaptive exception handling for remedy approach and forward recovery, respectively (cf. cases of Figure 9).

Consider when a security exception occurs at the "ID Check" activity in the security-flow. For illustration, the Web service of the "ID Check" activity generates a SOAP fault message to the WFMS as shown in Figure 11 (a). This fault message describes the exceptional situation of an authentication failure, in this case the Web service could not authenticate the user's location based on the "SubjectLocation" in the security token and the "postal-code" in the "IDrecord". Under this circumstance, the integration plan cannot be carried out properly, because the "ID Check" is the first critical activity in the workflow.

If there would be an "area-code" in the user record and the corresponding definition given in the ontology covers the postal codes of "SubjectLocation" and "postal-code," the "ID Check" activity can

Figure 8. The illustrative SOAP fault message

```
env:Envelope
xmlns:env="http://www.w3.org/2003/05/soap-envelope"
xmlns:e=http://www.WII.org/exceptionEvent
xmlns:xml="http://www.w3.org/XML/1998/namespace">
 <env:Body>
  <env:Fault>
   <env:Code>
     <env:Value>env:Receiver</env:Value>
     <env:Subcode>
      <env:Value>e:securityExceptionEvent</env:Value>
     </env:Subcode>
   </env:Code>
   <env:Reason>
     <env:Text xml:lang="en">
      Not authorize to access the BorderCheck service
     </env:Text>
   </env:Reason>
   <env:Detail>
   <e:securityToken>e:Unrecognized</e:securityToken>
   </env:Detail>
  </env:Fault>
 </env:Body>
</env:Envelope>
```

Figure 9. Proposed BPEL assertions for illustrating exception-flow

```
<flow name="exception-flow">
  <exceptionHandling name="rule-1">
    <event>anyActivitySpecificException</event>
    <condition>affectDataIntegration</condition>
    <action>remedyOrforwardRecoveryProcedure</action>
  </exceptionHandling>
  <exceptionHandling name="rule-2">
    <event>anyCrossActivityException</event>
    <condition>affectDataLinkage</condition>
    <action>backwardRecoveryProcedure</action>
  </exceptionHandling>
</flow>
```

authenticate the user. This case is referred to the remedy approach in the exceptional handling as shown in Figure 9.

The second example demonstrates the forward recovery approach as follows. Referring to Figure 5, there may be a security exception occurred at the "ID Check" activity if the Web service has to authenticate the "tax-file-no" besides the attributes specified by the security token. The corresponding SOAP fault message is shown in Figure 11 (b). In this case, the security token does not include the "tax-file-no," and so a failure of the authentication process occurs at the "ID Check" service. Based on the forward recovery approach, WII revises the control-flow to execute the "Bank Check" activity before the "ID Check" activity because of the missing "tax-file-no" attribute (see Figure 12).

SUMMARY AND OUTLOOK

This chapter proposes a WII framework from different aspects based on a flow concept, for adaptive information integration in an environment of autonomous organizations. In summary, the major advantages for using such a multi-layer framework are as follows.

Different aspects of information flows can be modeled in a single framework. As an indispensable part of any information system (Hung, 2001), information flows are the bridges between the information system and the users' activity model. The multi-layer framework has an advantage of visually depicting various types of flows in different layouts under different situations for dynamic and adaptive execution. In addition, separation of concern facilities requirements elicitation in the emerging field of security and intelligence informatics.

A multi-layer framework supports concurrent meta-models. Referring to Figure 5, the control-flow can trigger the execution of one or more data-flows ($1:N$) in parallel. This is a practical scenario for adaptive information integration because more than one user request may be supported by a single control-flow (an integration plan). Thus, scalability and reusability can be eased. Each meta-model can

Figure 10. BPEL Codes with Abort Assertion

```
<flow name="exception-flow">
  <exceptionHandlingDefault>
    <action>abortControlFlow</action>
  </exceptionHandlingDefault>
</flow>
```

Figure 11. Illustrative SOAP fault message, (a) showing an authentication failure, (b) pointing out a missing attribute

```
<env:Envelope
 xmlns:env="http://www.w3.org/2003/05/soap-envelope"
 xmlns:e=http://www.medicare.org/exceptionEvent
 xmlns:xml="http://www.w3.org/XML/1998/namespace">
 <env:Body>
  <env:Fault>
   <env:Code>
     <env:Value>env:Receiver</env:Value>
     <env:Subcode>
      <env:Value>e:securityExceptionEvent</env:Value>
     </env:Subcode>
   </env:Code>
   <env:Reason>
     <env:Text xml:lang="en">
      Cannot verify the user location at the Check ID service.
     </env:Text>
   </env:Reason>
   <env:Detail>
    <e:securityToken>e:authentication-failed</e:securityToken>
   </env:Detail>
  </env:Fault>
 </env:Body>
</env:Envelope>
```

```
<env:Envelope
 xmlns:env="http://www.w3.org/2003/05/soap-envelope"
 xmlns:e=http://www.WII.org/exceptionEvent
 xmlns:xml="http://www.w3.org/XML/1998/namespace">
 <env:Body>
  <env:Fault>
   <env:Code>
     <env:Value>env:Receiver</env:Value>
     <env:Subcode>
      <env:Value>e:securityExceptionEvent</env:Value>
     </env:Subcode>
   </env:Code>
   <env:Reason>
     <env:Text xml:lang="en">
      Not authorize to access the ID Check service
     </env:Text>
   </env:Reason>
   <env:Detail>
    <e:securityToken>e:missingAttribute(tax-file-no)</e:securityToken>
   </env:Detail>
  </env:Fault>
 </env:Body>
</env:Envelope>
```

be instantiated many times and reused for different integration plans to provide adaptiveness. From a technical point of view, each of these meta-models can be launched and executed in different systems on different platforms, especially facilitated through Web services over the Internet.

In addition, a multi-layer framework can enable the analysis, simulation, and validation of the model under study before proceeding to the actual implementation. The multi-layer framework also has an advantage of presenting all properties, relationships, and restrictions among meta-models, such as concurrency, synchronization, flow dependency, and temporal relationships. Once a system has been modeled as a net, a pre-execution analysis can be conducted. Thus, properties of the system can also be represented by similar means, and correctness proofs may be built using the methods of net theory (Michelis, 1999) and automata theory (Chiu et al., 2003).

Furthermore, we have outlined a technical framework based on contemporary Web services based on our conceptual model to facilitate the WII across autonomous organizational boundaries. We have

Figure 12. Revised control flow

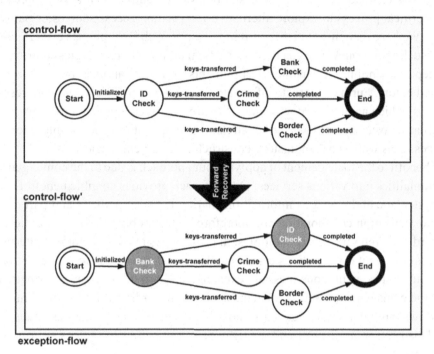

demonstrated the applicability and effectiveness of this technical framework through a practical example, so that intelligence information sources can handle enquiries with adequate security control and exception handling with semantic support. Further augmented with Web service technologies, organizations providing information initially do not have such an information system fully implemented. A minimal requirement is that they can be alerted with electronic messages or even through email (Kafeza et al., 2004) and respond required to the information requestor or reject the request. This is done through the Web-based application of the requestor, because Web service technologies facilitate any requestor to create and deploy such applications for intelligence partners to access. Further for legacy systems, wrappers may be built around them to enable compatibility with Web services. As such, existing intelligence processes can be gradually extended to the WII framework with adequate testing and streamlining of the switchover.

We have also formulated a pragmatic approach of specifying exceptions and their handlers for adaptive workflow-based information integration. A large variety of information sources may be required during different investigations, such as schools and universities for providing educational background, companies and labor departments for enabling access to job records, tax offices for information on incomes, hospitals for their stored medical records, etc. Each type of these organizations may have different access control requirements and access protocols. As such, *source-related* information access process templates can be formulated and stored in the repository. In contrast to healthcare information integration which is often related to the construction of the history of a single patient, there might be many targets for a particular investigation. Thus, the need for automation is impounding. In addition, investigation-related WII plans and templates stored in the repository can be extensively reused. They can further be modified in response to every changing regulation and policy.

Upon exceptions such as access denial, excessive delays, or requirement for extra approval or warrants, it is vital for a critical process to explore alternative information access sources or paths dynamically and adaptively. We have demonstrated that current Semantic Web technologies can effectively provides knowledge for such a solution. We further believe that Semantic Web technologies contribute unsurpassed power for exception handling in dynamic environments or critical applications in general, which has not been studied before. Further, alternate information access can provide means for cross-validation of vital information, which again adds power and reliability to critical applications. Thus, our framework employing Semantic Web technologies further streamlines applications such as intelligence information gathering processes as well as patient history construction under emergency.

The major benefit to the management of applying our approach is due to the convergence of disparate business functionalities into various services. Our approach provides tangible benefit for organizations by allowing systematic and managed information sharing between partners and participants. This facilitates cross-organization collaboration and therefore increases business opportunities. In particular, through standardized Web services technologies, the challenges in converging and interfacing different businesses across different organizations can be tackled in a proper approach. Our approach facilitates both synchronous and asynchronous message exchange and provides timely information to help (the right level of) the management to react and make decisions accordingly. Provision of monitoring facilities over the flows through the services is also possible for increasing the process transparency (Wong et al., 2008). This helps more flexible and timely exception handling as well as improves relationships with business partners.

In order to balance trust and security, the management of an organization would like to provide information on only the relevant part of its internal workflow to business partners. To achieve this, our approach organizes interactions with different business partners systematically into process views, so that customized interactions captured with flows. Overall, our approach helps capture and manage knowledge for business interactions across different types of business partners as well as to facilitate such related automation. These advantages in combination can also lead to cost savings as a major business advantage and can foster system stability.

If there appear unexpected exceptions that require human intervention, traditional databases themselves could not adequately represent knowledge without extensive pre-programming, especially if they are distributed across different organizations. Thus, using Semantic Web technologies to capture the ontology of relationships among available information, administrators can access a broader knowledge about the situation that has caused the exception. Further with the ability to carry out inferences, decisions could be made more effective and efficient in order to resolve or handle the exception. This direction is important for future research.

However, in order to further streamline interactions among organizations, there is a call for standardization of application layer semantics (such as content taxonomy and category definitions), protocols for interaction, and security policies, whereby Governments and regulatory bodies may get involved. A future goal therefore could be to form a service grid for seamless and large-scale use of such an adaptive WII, which is potentially useful for many public applications such as mobile and electronic tourism (Chiu et al., 2008b).

In addition, several other research directions can be explored, expanding the framework proposed in this chapter. In particular, security-flows and privacy-flows are conflicting but both are required according to laws and regulations, which lead to an important direction for future work (Cushmann, 1996; Ishikawa, 2000). As the proposed conceptual workflow model has to aggregate the datasets of previously isolated databases, the dynamic nature of this model raises a challenging domain for security and privacy issues as well. In particular, privacy-flow relationships describe which information Web service providers collect from individuals and under which purpose data will be processed (Hung et al., 2007). Further, process urgency requirement (Kafeza et al., 2004) during information integration (Chiu et al., 2008) is another issue to focus on for future exploring. The design of methodologies and the computer-assisted generation of the proposed WII workflows and the described exception handling mechanisms may also be important for several other application domains such as in financial content management (Chiu et al., 2005), e-Learning (Chiu et al., 2008), and e-Government applications (Wong et al., 2007).

ACKNOWLEDGMENT

This chapter is partially supported by the National Natural Science Foundation of China under Grant No.60873022, the Natural Science Foundation of Zhejiang Province of China under Grant No.Y1080148 and the Open Project of Zhejiang Provincial Key Laboratory of Information Network Technology of China.

REFERENCES

Aiken, A. Widom, J., & Hellerstein, J. M. (1992). Behavior of database production rules: Termination, confluence, and observable determinism. In *Proceedings of the ACM SIGMOD Conference on Management of Data* (pp. 59-68).

Aversano, L., De Canfora, G., Lucia, A., & Gallucci, P. (2002). Integrating document and workflow management tools using XML and Web technologies: A case study. In *Proceedings of Sixth European Conference on Software Maintenance and Reengineering* (pp. 24-33).

Barish, G., Di Pasquo, D., Knoblock, C. A., & Minton, S. (2002). A dataflow approach to agent-based information management. In *Proceedings of the 2000 International Conference on Artificial Intelligence (ICAI-2000)*, Las Vegas, Nevada, USA.

Borgida, A., & Murata, T. (1999) Tolerating exceptions in workflows: A unified framework for data and process. In D. Georgakopoulos, W. Prinz, & A.L. Wolf (Eds.), *Proceedings of the International Joint Conference on Work Activities Coordination and Collaboration (WACC'99)* (pp. 59-68), San Francisco, USA.

Casati, F., Ceri, S., Paraboschi, S., & Pozzi, G. (1999). Specification and implementation of exceptions in workflow management systems. *ACM Transactions on Database Systems*, *24*(3), 405–451. doi:10.1145/328939.328996

Chen, H., & Finin, T. & Joshi. A. (2003) *Using OWL in a pervasive computing broker*. Paper presented at the Workshop on Ontologies in Agents Systems.

Cheung, S. C., Chiu, D. K. W., & Till, S. (2003). A data-driven methodology to extending workflows across organizations over the Internet. In *Proceedings of 36th Hawaii International Conference on System Sciences (HICSS36)*. IEEE Computer Society Press.

Chiu, D. K. W., Cheung, S. C., Kafeza, E., & Leung, H.-F. (2003). A three-tier view methodology for adapting m-services. *IEEE Transactions on System, Man and Cybernetics . Part A, 33*(6), 725–741.

Chiu, D. K. W., Choi, S. P. M., Wang, M., & Kafeza, E. (2008). Towards ubiquitous communication support for distance education with alert management. *Educational Technology & Society, 11*(2), 92–106.

Chiu, D. K. W., & Hung, P. C. K. (2005). Privacy and access control in financial enterprise content management. In *Proceedings of the 38th Hawaiian International Conference on System Sciences (HICSS38)*, Big Island, Hawaii. IEEE Press.

Chiu, D. K. W., Li, Q., & Karlapalem, K. (1999). A meta modeling approach for workflow management system supporting exception handling. *Information Systems, 24*(2), 159–184. doi:10.1016/S0306-4379(99)00010-1

Chiu, D. K. W., Li, Q., & Karlapalem, K. (2000). Facilitating exception handling with recovery techniques in ADOME workflow management system. *Journal of Applied Systems Studies, 1*(3), 467–488.

Chiu, D. K. W., Li, Q., & Karlapalem, K. (2001). Web interface-driven cooperative exception handling in ADOME workflow management system. *Information Systems, 26*(2), 93–120. doi:10.1016/S0306-4379(01)00012-6

Chiu, D.K.W., Yueh, Y.T.F., Leung, H.-f., Hung, P.C.K. (2008b). Towards ubiquitous tourist service coordination and process integration: A collaborative travel agent system with semantic Web services. *Information Systems Frontier*. DOI: 10.1007/s10796-008-9087-2

Cushman, R. (1996). Information and medical ethics: Protecting patient privacy. *IEEE Technology and Society Magazine, 15*(3), 32–39. doi:10.1109/44.536299

Fensel, D., McGuiness, D. L., Schulten, E., Ng, W. K., Lim, E. P., & Yan, G. (2001). Ontologies and electronic commerce. *IEEE Intelligent Systems, 16*(1), 8–14. doi:10.1109/MIS.2001.1183337

Georgakopoulos, D., Hornick, M., & Sheth, A. (1995). An overview of workflow management: From process modelling to workflow automation infrastructure. *Journal of Distributed and Parallel Databases, 3*(2), 119–153. doi:10.1007/BF01277643

Grimson, J., Stephens, G., Jung, B., Grimson, W., Berry, D., & Pardon, S. (2001). Sharing health-care records over the Internet. *IEEE Internet Computing, 5*(3), 49–58. doi:10.1109/4236.935177

Gross, T. (2003). Security analysis of the SAML single sign-on browser/artifact profile. In *Proceedings of the 19th Annual Computer Security Applications Conference* (pp. 298- 307).

Horsch, A., & Balbach, T. (1999). Telemedical information systems. *IEEE Transactions on Information Technology in Biomedicine, 3*(3), 166–175. doi:10.1109/4233.788578

Hung, P. C. K. (2001). *Secure workflow model*. Ph.D.Thesis, Department of Computer Science, The Hong Kong University of Science and Technology, Hong Kong.

Hung, P. C. K., & Chiu, D. K. W. (2003). Workflow-based information integration in a Web services environment. In *Proceedings of the First International Conference on Web Services (ICWS'03)*, Monte Carlo Resort, Las Vegas, Nevada, USA.

Hung, P. C. K., & Chiu, D. K. W. (2004). Developing workflow-based information integration (WII) with exception support in a Web services environment. In *Proceedings of 36ᵗʰ Hawaii International Conference on System Sciences (HICSS36)*. IEEE Computer Society Press.

Hung, P. C. K., Chiu, D. K. W., Fung, W. W., Cheung, W. K., Wong, R., & Choi, S. P. (2007). End-to-end privacy control in service outsourcing of human intensive processes: A multi-layered Web service integration approach. *Information Systems Frontiers*, *9*(1), 85–101. doi:10.1007/s10796-006-9019-y

Hwang, S. Y., Ho, S. F., & Tang, J. (1999). Mining exception instances to facilitate workflow exception handling. In *Proceedings of the 6th International Conference on Database Systems for Advanced Applications* (pp. 45-52).

Ishikawa, K. (2000). Health data use and protection policy: based on differences by cultural and social environment. *International Journal of Medical Informatics*, *60*(2), 19–125. doi:10.1016/S1386-5056(00)00111-8

Jeston, J., & Nelis, J. (2008). *Business process management: Practical guidelines to successful implementations* (2ⁿᵈ ed.). Butterworth-Heinemann.

Joubert, M., Aymard, S., Fieschi, D., Volot, F., Staccini, P., Robert, J. J., & Fieschi, M. (1998). RIANE: Integration of information databases within a hospital intranet. *International Journal of Medical Informatics*, *49*(3), 297–309. doi:10.1016/S1386-5056(98)00084-7

Kafeza, E., Chiu, D. K. W., Cheung, S. C., & Kafeza, M. (2004). Alerts in mobile healthcare applications: requirements and pilot study. *IEEE Transactions on Information Technology in Biomedicine*, *8*(2), 173–181. doi:10.1109/TITB.2004.828888

Lacy, L. W. (2005). *Owl: Representing information using the web ontology language*. Trafford Publishing.

Leymann, F. (2001) *Web services flow language (WSFL 1.0)*. IBM Corporation.

Leymann, F., & Roller, D. (2002). Using flows in information integration. *IBM Systems Journal*, *41*(4), 732–742.

Leymann, F., Roller, D., & Schmidt, M.-T. (2002). Web services and business process management. *IBM Systems Journal*, *41*(2), 198–211.

Liu, C. T., Long, A. G., Li, Y. C., Tsai, K. C., & Kuo, H. S. (2001). Sharing patient care records over the World Wide Web. *International Journal of Medical Informatics*, *61*(2-3), 189–205. doi:10.1016/S1386-5056(01)00141-1

Louwerse, K. (1998). The electronic patient record; the management of access—Case study: Leiden University Hospital. *International Journal of Medical Informatics*, *49*(1), 39–44. doi:10.1016/S1386-5056(98)00008-2

Marsh, A. (1997). EUROMED - the creation of a telemedical information society. In *Proceedings of the IEEE Symposium on Computer-Based Medical Systems* (pp. 86-91).

Marsh, A. (1998). The creation of a global telemedical information society. *International Journal of Medical Informatics*, *49*(2), 173–193. doi:10.1016/S1386-5056(98)00039-2

Michelis, G. D. (1999). Net theory and workflow models. In *Proceedings of the 20th International Conference in Application and Theory of Petri Nets*, viii+423.

Nagappan, R., Skoczylas, R., & Sriganesh, R. P. (2002). *Developing Java Web Services: Architecting and developing secure Web services Using Java*. Wiley.

Perry, D. E., Romanovsky, A., & Tripathi, A. (2000). Current trends in exception handling. *IEEE Transactions on Software Engineering*, *26*(10), 921–922. doi:10.1109/TSE.2000.879816

Reichert, M., & Dadam, P. (1998). ADEPT$_{flex}$ – Supporting dynamic changes of workflows without losing control. *Journal of Intelligent Information Systems*, *10*(1), 93–129. doi:10.1023/A:1008604709862

Sheng, O. R. L., & Chen, G. H. M. (1990). Information management in hospitals: An integrating approach. In *Proceedings of Annual Phoenix Conference* (pp. 296-303).

Sheth, A., & Larson, J. (1990). Federated database systems. *ACM Computing Surveys*, *22*(3), 183–236. doi:10.1145/96602.96604

Takeda, H., Matsumura, Y., Kuwata, S., Nakano, H., Sakamoto, N., & Yamamoto, R. (2000). Architecture for networked electronic patient record systems. *International Journal of Medical Informatics*, *60*(2), 161–167. doi:10.1016/S1386-5056(00)00116-7

Tan, J. K. H. (2001). *Health management information systems: Methods and practical applications* (2nd ed.). Aspen Publication.

Thatte, S. (2001). *XLANG - Web services for business process design*. Microsoft Corporation.

Van der Aalst, W. M. P., & Van Hee, K. M. (2002). *Workflow management: Models, methods, and systems*. MIT Press.

Weerawarana, S., Curbera, F., Leymann, F., Storey, T., & Ferguson, D. F. (2005). *Web services platform architecture: SOAP, WSDL, WS-Policy, WS-Addressing, WS-BPEL, WS-reliable messaging, and more*. Prentice Hall.

Wiederhold, G. (1992). Mediators in the architecture of future information systems. *IEEE Computer*, *25*(3), 38–49.

Wong, J. Y. Y., Chiu, D. K. W., & Mark, K. P. (2007). Effective e-Government process monitoring and interoperation: A case study on the removal of unauthorized building works in Hong Kong. In *Proceedings of the 40th Hawaii International Conference on System Science (HICSS40)*. IEEE Press.

KEY TERMS AND DEFINITIONS

Activity: a logical unit of work in a workflow process.

Event: an atomic occurrence of something interesting to the system itself or user applications.

Exception: a special event that deviates from normal behavior or prevent normal process execution.

Flow: a directed relationship that transmits events from a source activity to a sink activity.

Information Integration (II): the field of study of techniques attempting to merge information from disparate sources despite differing conceptual, contextual, and typographical representations.

Semantic Web: an evolving extension of the World Wide Web in which the semantics of information and services on the web is defined, making it possible for the web to understand and satisfy the requests of people and machines to use the web content.

Web Service: an autonomous unit of application logic that provides some information processing resources to other applications through the Internet from a service provider (such as an enterprise).

Workflow: a depiction of a sequence of operations, declared as work of a person, work of a simple or complex mechanism, work of a group of persons, work of an organization of staff, or machines.

Workflow Management System (WFMS): the software to support the specification, decomposition, execution, coordination, and monitoring of workflows.

Chapter 9
Adaptive Exception Management in Uncertain Environments

Mati Golani
Ort Braude College, Israel

ABSTRACT

The ability to continuously revise business practices is limited when referring to traditional approaches in business process management systems. However, it is essential to organizations aiming at reducing their costs and increasing their revenues. In turbulent environments, the requirement for rapid and continuous changes to business processes, result in less control over the executed activities. As a consequence, process designers are limited in producing solid, well-validated workflow models. This chapter, reviews common approaches to exception handling, focusing especially on adaptive exception handling and introduces a mechanism that allows a flexible ad-hoc generated exception handling using backtracking and forward stepping at a process instance level. A dynamic approach in this domain is required, and can bolster the ability of a business process management system to deal with unexpected situations and to resolve, in runtime, scenarios in which such resolution both is called for and does not violate any business process constraints.

INTRODUCTION

Turbulent environments require organizations to continuously revise their business practices, seeking better business opportunities and continuously optimizing their processes. In the last decade, businesses have turned to technological solutions to assist them in this task. The use of electronic means to commerce, data mining, SLA's, and customer profiling are all recent technological developments that penetrate business activities. One of the most recent technological developments is the use of Web services, components with a well-defined interface that are embedded in cross-organizational business processes.

DOI: 10.4018/978-1-60566-669-3.ch009

Using Web services, the functional aspects of business applications are encapsulated (Aalst, 2003), with interfaces defined using standards such as BPEL4WS (BPEL4WS), and invocation controlled using approaches such as Service Oriented Architecture (SOA). Web services promise to deliver greater choice and flexibility to business processes.

Frequent and continuous changes to business processes carry with it risks, due to shorter (or even nonexistent) design time and less control over the executed activities. As a result, the ability of process designers to produce solid, well-validated workflow models is limited. Workflow management systems (WfMSs), serving as the main vehicle of business process execution, should recognize these risks and become more dynamic to allow the required business flexibility. To illustrate this point, two examples, involving Web services, will be used. First, an observation that the development of Web services is an ongoing task and new and improved services are continuously replacing existing ones. Currently, WfMSs provide little support to the re-execution of successfully processed tasks for running instances, even if the gains from such re-execution outweigh the costs. As another example, observe that Web services merely provide syntactic information regarding their input, output and processing logic, through standards such as WSDL. In most cases, such descriptions fail to convey all necessary constraints and restrictions. Modeling using Web services, therefore, is likely to make the validation of workflow models more difficult (Gaaloul, 2004), and more exceptions at run-time are to be expected. Efficient exception handling is a fundamental component of WfMSs and is critical to their successful implementation in real-world scenarios (Agostini, 2000).

The motivation for this work, lies in the need for flexible and dynamic WfMSs to support the growing number of exceptions that cannot be designed a priori, due to poor design or the lack of sufficient information regarding the internal logic of Web services. In particular, the introduction of a new and more beneficial Web service may trigger backtracking of a process for a re-execution to an activity in which the new Web service is performed, and then continue the regular execution while utilizing, to the extent possible, previously executed activities. In the case of an exception, the proposed algorithm identifies a feasible alternative that avoids the failing activity or communication channel. In this scenario, again, we backtrack to an activity from which it is considered safe to step forward. This is an elaboration of the work presented in (Golani 2005).

This chapter introduces the following:

- Model: An analysis of a workflow model, based on WSM nets, that generates a conceptual framework in which backtracking and forward stepping can be evaluated and implemented.
- Algorithms: algorithms for alternative route identification (at design time or run time) and forward stepping (at run time), to allow dynamic modifications to workflows.
- The meta-process concept, an efficient and a fully automatic mechanism (at the WfMS level) for activating the proposed algorithms. Four steps have to be completed when guiding the designer in the design of exception handlers:
  - Functional block detection, in which a workflow graph is analyzed and revised to fit certain properties that are needed for the next steps.
  - Alternative paths detection, in which a set of possible alternative execution is generated.
  - Parameter modification analysis, where the amount of change to earlier stages of the workflow is determined for each alternative path.
  - Exception handler construction, in which the designer is presented, in an iterative manner, with alternative paths from which it can choose.

We demonstrate related techniques with two somewhat different scenarios. First, we show how changes in Web services can be dynamically embedded into a workflow model, minimizing the costs related to re-execution of previously performed activities. Second, we propose an improved exception handler using forward stepping, backtracking, and alternative paths. Alternative paths, while not the only possible exception handling tool, can serve in a broad variety of cases, and can be easily produced automatically, either in design time (serving as a recommendation) or at run-time (serving as a crisis management tool, in the absence of immediate valid solutions).

BACKGROUND

Exception and modification handling -- *i.e.*, the way a workflow system responds once an exception or a modification notification occurs -- has been discussed in the literature for some time. The system may react in such cases either by terminating a process or handling an exception (Hagen 2000;Casati,1999). Another classification of the latter option as one of the available modification policies (which was called *Adapt*) to a given change in a running process (in Sadiq, 2000). This change is due to an unexpected exception, so the process should be handled differently than originally designed. Yet the authors do not define how to infer this modification.

Generally speaking, exception handling involves compensation flows (Du, 1997). Compensation flows provide rollback, a set of undo or compensating actions that leave the process in a consistent state. These flows are predefined. If compensation does not exist, the workflow operator may be willing to accept inconsistencies in which a completed activity is not voided. For example, assume an activity provides a customer with bonus points, on the assumption that a purchase will be made. Then another activity is chosen, which also awards bonus points. For a successful termination of the workflow (*e.g.*, a sale), an operator may be willing to grant double bonus points in this case.

Eder et al. describe several types of compensation in (Eder, 1996), and provide a three-step mechanism to handle exceptions (Eder, 1996; Eder, 1998). The first step entails rollback based on compensation type of activities in the workflow graph. In the next step, an agent determines whether to continue backward or to take an alternative path. The final step is a forward execution (which could lead to the same point of failure). In the event of rollback, existing work (Eder 1998) does not specify the stop point, implying that this point represent the decision on whether to continue. However, in many cases the parameter which drives this decision has been set before this point. Furthermore, these mechanisms are static (*e.g.*, during build time) (Du 1997; Kamath 1998; Eder, 1996). Our approach detects the actual/optimal stop point (via analysis), and can provide in run time an alternative execution that overtakes the failed activity.

A dynamic approach was presented by Hwang et al. (Hwang, 2003). Here, a failure recovery language supports multiple exceptions per activity, and applies rollback using ECP (end compensation point). This language uses the process parameters in order to determine its flow. The drawback of this approach is that it fails to make use of the user's insight (and output). It is impossible to accurately forecast all user intentions, and under different circumstances, individual users may make different choices based on the same input. Thus, the user's output is essential.

The rest of the chapter is organized as follows: Section 3 introduces a motivating example. In Section 4 we present the workflow graph-based model. In Sections 5,6,7 we present forward stepping, alternative path, and parametric analysis mechanisms, respectively – followed by a case study example

Figure 1.

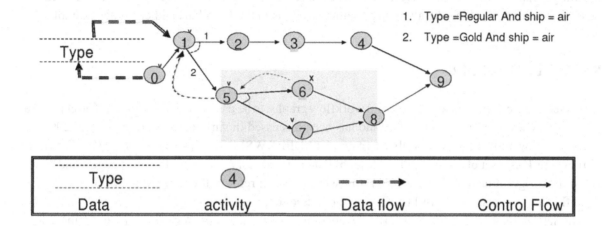

in Section 8. Finally, in Section 9, we introduce the architecture for implementation, and show the use of meta-processes.

ILLUSTRATIVE EXAMPLE

As an example, consider a process that handles registrations for package tours (see Figure 1). This process uses some local applications (member deals), as well as Web services (hotel registration: activity 0, flight reservation: activity 1) with some special offers available to gold members only (activities 5-8). We use two examples to illustrate the needs of a flexible business process. The first involves introduction of a new Web service that offers better hotels for cheaper prices, at a time when the process instance is already handling membership registration (activity 4), and hotel registration and flight ticket activities are already completed. The second event involves a failure of the special offer system for a gold customer (activity 6).

In the first example, nothing has gone wrong, but the world has changed (a new service has become available). Taking advantage of this new service may affect the customer's total cost, given penalties for canceling an existing order and the cost of creating a new one. Other activities or services may also need to be compensated or re-executed as a result of this update. For instance, activity 1 may require compensation if the original flight dates were modified based on the new hotel reservations. These costs must be quantified before the customer decides whether to continue with the original plan or to use the newly available service.

In the second event, the system will benefit by using a different path that allows successful completion of the business process while bypassing the special offers. Consider the example depicted in Figure 1. Activities 0, 1, 5, and 7 were performed in this instantiation, yet a failure at activity 6 blocks the process and prevents its completion. Alternative paths to the current path, to be formally defined in Section 3, are those paths in the graph that possibly lead to a successful termination of the business process, yet do not contain activity 6. Since activity 1 leads to activities 2 and 5 using a Xor condition, a rollback procedure to activity 1 would enable use of an alternative path to 9 through activities 2, 3, and 4.

This approach address only processes in which the alternative path has a real semantic alternative meaning. That means that an executed instance along one path can be logically executed (albeit, at a possibly higher cost) along the alternative path as well (as in the Regular/Gold customer example).

WORKFLOW MODEL

In this section we define basic constructs in workflow graphs, to be used later in the chapter. The classification of workflow constructs is not new and has been discussed in various works (*e.g.*, (Aalst, 2000)).

A workflow model can be described as a graph (ADEPT WSM net) $G(V,E)$ $[(V = V_a \cup V_d)$; $E = (E_c \cup E_d)]$, where V_a is a set of activities, V_d is a set of data parameters, E_c is a set of control edges, and E_d is a set of data edges. For simplicity, whenever possible, we will refer to the reduced graph $G' = G(V_d, E_c)$. Data flows (as appear in Figure 1) are discussed in Section 6.

An activity a in V_a has $in\_degree(G', a)$ incoming edges and $out\_degree(G', a)$ outgoing edges. Whenever it becomes clear from the context, we eliminate the graph reference and refer to $in\_degree(a)$ and $out\_degree(a)$. A *path* in G is a set of activities such that any two consecutive activities on the path are connected by an edge in E_c. We denote a path from a_i to a_j by $(a_i,...,a_j)$. The *length* of a *path* $(a_i,...,a_j)$ (denoted $length(a_i,...,a_j)$) is the number of edges in $(a_i,...,a_j)$. Finally, *Minlength* $(a_i,...,a_j)$ is the length of the shortest path in G that starts at a_i and ends at a_j .

We next define two graph constructs, namely splits and joins, based on the Workflow Management Coalition standard (WFMC). A Xor *split a* is a node (activity) with multiple outgoing edges ($out\_degree(a) > 1$), only one of which can be followed in the execution flow. The decision as to which edge to follow is based on the satisfaction of mutually exclusive conditions that are typically associated with the outgoing edges. Let $c_{a,a'}$ be a DNF (Disjunctive Normal Form) Boolean statement with a set of variables $Var(c_{a,a',})$ that must be satisfied in order to pass from activity a to activity a'. Activity 1 in Figure 1 is an example of a Xor split. Each Xor split a is associated with a Xor join (*e.g.*, activity 9 in Figure 1), an activity common to all paths that start from a. During runtime, when reaching a, the workflow engine evaluates the conditions on each of a's outgoing edges, and continues the execution along the edge whose associated condition is satisfied. The Xor join activity acts as a synchronization point in the execution.

An *And split* is a node with multiple outgoing edges whose execution flow follows all outgoing edges by parallel threading. Activity 5 in Figure 1 is an example of an And split. Threads of an And split a need to be synchronized at an *And join*, which is also a node in the graph that is common to all paths that start from a. Activity 8 is an example of an And join for activity 5.

Definition 1: *Xor split point* Let $G'=(V,E)$ be a workflow graph, and a be an activity in V. *A Xor split point of a* is a Xor split a_i with a Xor join a_j such that a_i is a predecessor of a.

Definition 2:*NXSP Nearest Xor split point* of a (NXSP(a)), is a Xor split point of a, a_i, which satisfies that any other Xor split point of a $(a_j)$is also a Xor split point of a_i .

And split point and *NASP* are similarly defined. Using the basic definitions given above, we now define blocks in a graph. Let $G'=(V,E)$ be a workflow graph and let a_i be a Xor split and a_j be the Xor join associated with a_i. A Xor *block* of a_i is a subgraph of G' induced by the nodes of all paths $(a_i,...,a_j)$ in G'. Similarly, given an And split a_i and the associated And join of a_i, a_j, an *And block* of a_i is a subgraph of G' induced by the nodes of all paths $(a_i,...,a_j)$ in G'. For example, the induced subgraph of activities

{5, 6, 7, 8} in Figure 1 (marked with grey rectangle) is an *And Block*. It models two threads that start after the execution of activity 5 and synchronize before the execution of activity 8.

Clearly, any activity *a* is within a Xor block defined by its Xor split point (can be null) and its associated Xor join. In particular, *a* is within a Xor block defined by *NXSP*(*a*) and its associated Xor join.

Definition 3: *Alternative paths* Let $G'=(V,E)$ be a workflow graph with a sink f, and let $P_1 = (a_i,...,a_j)$ and $P_2 = (a_i,...,a_k)$ be paths in G'. P_1 is an *alternative* to P_2 (and vice versa) if the following four conditions hold:

1. a_i is of type Xor Split.
2. *There is no activity a in $V\backslash\{a_i\}$ such that a is in P_1 and a is also in P_2.*
3. Any path $(a_j,...f)$ in G' does not include an activity in P_2.
4. *Any path $(a_k...f)$ in G' does not include an activity in P_1.*

It is worth noting that P_1 and P_2 share a common initial activity a_i. As an example, consider the alternative paths (1, 2, 3, 4) and (1, 5, 6, 7, 8) in Figure 1. Note that the paths (5, 6) and (5, 7) are **not** alternative paths, since activity 5 is not of type Xor Split (both activity 6 and activity 7 are part of the same And block).

The importance of *Xor blocks* in our analysis is related to the ability to provide an alternative paths analysis. In Figure 1, the *Xor Block* includes the entire graph save activity 0, and thus an alternative path for any activity (excluding activity 9) will start from activity 1. Therefore, once activity 6 fails, the *Xor Block* to which activity 6 belongs allows an alternative execution, using the paths that contains activities {1, 2, 3, 4}. We will present an algorithm for identifying alternative paths in Section 5.

We next discuss the normalization of Xor and And blocks. A normalized (Xor or And) block is a block in which neither the outgoing edges of the split activity, nor the incoming edges of the join activity, are connected to any activities outside the block. This property matches the WFMC definition (in interface 1) of *full-blocked workflows*. Formally,

Definition 4: *Normalized Block* Let G' *(V,E)* be a workflow graph with a source s and a sink f, and B a Block (either Xor or And) with split activity a_i and join activity a_j. B is *normalized* if a_j is on all paths $(a_i,..., f)$ in G' and a_i is on all paths $(s,..., a_j)$ in G'.

It is easy to show that if B is normalized, then *out_degree* $(G', a_i) = out\_degree(B,a_i) = in\_degree(G', a_j) = in\_degree(B, a_j)$. For brevity, we refrain from presenting the algorithm for block normalization in this chapter, however we manipulate a given process graph by modifying it (while using dummy activities) into a normalized structure as illustrated in Figures 2, and 3.

Given a workflow graph G'(*V,E*), *Inst*(*G'*) represents an instance of G'. *Inst*(*G'*) encapsulates instance-related data, such as activity state and input/output parameter values. *Inst*(*G'*) is a DAG and loop constructs in G'(*V,E*) are removed by duplicating loop blocks and re-labeling of activities.

An activity in *Inst*(*G'*) can be classified into one of the following states: uninitiated (yet, but on an execution path), void (on path that was not invoked), completed (finished on current path), compensated, or failed. (Figure 2 and Figure 3)

Figure 2. Pre normalization

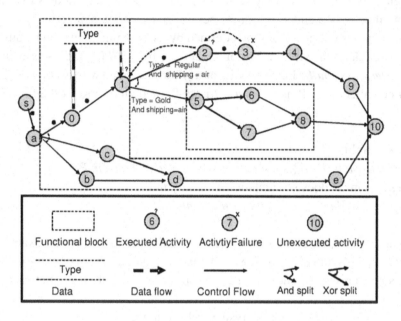

FORWARD STEPPING

In this section we present an efficient algorithm for forward stepping. Consider a path that begins from activity a_i, and assume that activity a_i needs to be re-executed due to exception or modification. Analyzing the state and dependencies of the activities (or Web services) that participate in a given process instance

Figure 3. Post normalization

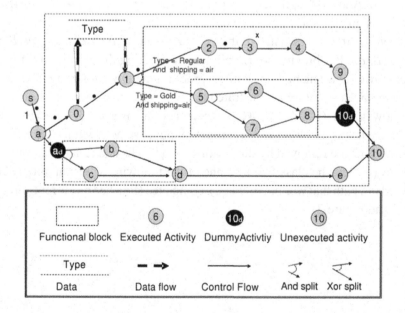

Table 1. Algorithm 1. Forward stepping

```
Input: G(V_a ∪ V_d, E_c ∪ E_d), a_i -first activity path, a_x - the stop activity (optional)
Output: potentialList - a list of potential activities to be re-executed, semanticList - a list of activities to be semantically executed
add a_i.successors into Q // Q is a Queue
put a_i into visitedList
put a_i.outputParameters into D
while Q not empty do
    put a_k = dequeue(Q) into visitedList
if ∃ a_k.inputParameter ∈ D then
        add a_k to potentialList
        add a_k.outputParameter to D
    else
        add a_k to semanticList
        endif
        if a_k ≠ a_x then
add a_k 's executed successor activities (as appear in Inst(G)) to Q . Add only activities that satisfy predecessor(a) ⊂ visited
        endif
    end while
    return potentialList, semanticList
```

can help determine which activities have not yet been executed, and which need to be re-executed. When we deal with exceptions, a stop (target) activity (a_x) is provided, so the forward stepping is executed until reaching this activity. In other scenarios, it is possible that no end point is given.

We assume *validity*, as follows. Activity a_i is *valid* if for a given input it has provided an output in the original instance, and this output is required for the forward stepping with the same input parameters values. Therefore, activities/services that have the same input as in the original process are *valid* and should not be re-executed, but rather semantically executed at the workflow level without invoking the underling application/service (*e.g.*, given that flight tickets have been ordered and been approved in the original instance, then if the forward stepping invokes this activity with the same destination and dates as input, it can use the confirmed reservation from the previous execution). In this case the WF system is notified by the client that the activity was executed, while no application/service was invoked. The required execution mode of activity a_i is evaluated (during run time) below, using the following notation. (Table 1)*Inst*(G') is the original instance*Inst'*(G') is the new/modified instance*input*($a,p,Inst(G')$) returns the value of p, which is an input parameter to activity a in *Inst*(G').

$$
\text{Exec}(a_i) = \begin{cases} \text{Reexecute} & \exists p \ input(a_i, p, Inst'(G')) \neq \\ & \quad\quad Input(a_i, p, Inst(G')) \\ \\ Semantic & Otherwise \end{cases}
$$

(1)

The forward stepping algorithm is given in Algorithm 1. Looking at the process structure, this - given it doesn't use instance data - can be invoked asynchronically with runtime instances (*e.g.*, in advance). *PotentialList* holds potential activities (derived from the process structure) for re-execution, of which only those satisfying the *Reexecute* condition in Equation 1 should be re-executed. During runtime, some of these activities may receive the same input values as in the original execution. Therefore, despite their dependency on other re-executed activities, we expect their previous output to be valid (due to the validity property). In such cases, semantic execution is sufficient, and there is no overhead cost for re-execution.

ALTERNATIVE PATHS DETECTION

In the case of an exception, undefined in advance, the workflow engine should rollback to an activity in the graph from which it can provide an alternative path to complete execution of the business process. We will refer to this activity as a *rollback point*. In an extended version of this work, we will elaborate on the heuristics of finding the best rollback point, and design time considerations in determining the suitability of alternative paths. This section details the necessary steps for rollback.

Definition 5: *Rollback point:* Let a_i be an activity in a normalized workflow graph $G' = (V,E)$ with a sink f. A *rollback point* of a_i in a given instance $Inst(G')$ is an activity a_j that satisfies the following conditions:

1. a_j was activated during $Inst(G')$ (*i.e.*, a_j's state in $Inst(G')$ is completed).
2. There is a path $P_1 = (a_j,...,a_i)$ in $Inst(G')$ of which all activities in $P_1 \backslash a_i$ are in state completed.
3. There is a path $P_2 = (a_j,...f)$ in G', such that P_2 is an alternative path to P_1.

A *nearest rollback point* of a_i in a given instance $(Inst(G')$ of $G')$ is a rollback activity a_k such that $minlength(a_k,a_i) \leq minlength(a_p,a_i)$ for any rollback point a_p of a_i.

Theorem 1:*Let a_i be an activity in a workflow graph $G' = (V,E)$. The nearest rollback point of a_i is $NXSP(a_i)$.*

Proof: Suppose that a_j is the nearest rollback point of a_i, and that $NXSP(a_i) = a_k \neq a_j$. From condition 3 of Definition 5 and Definition 3 a_j is of type Xor split, and furthermore there exists an alternative path to a_i that passes through a_j. In a similar manner, a_k also satisfies the requirements to be a rollback point of a_i. Given that a_j is the nearest rollback point, the condition requirement $minlength(a_j, a_i) \leq minlength(a_k, a_i)$ holds, and both being Xor split points of a_i it is clear that a_k is a predecessor of a_j, contradicting the requirement in Definition 2. Thus, $NXSP(a_i) = a_j$.

Rollback can be classified into three types, namely *single threaded, parallel threaded*, and *hybrid*. We will define each of these types and specify the rollback activities needed for each type, using Theorem 1 as a guideline.

Single-threaded rollback is a rollback in which the failing activity falls within a single thread. This means that upon failure, the rollback procedure should be applied only to this thread. The following rollback activity should be taken in a single-threaded type:$a_j = NXSP(a_i)$. Rollback until reaching a_j

Parallel-threaded rollback refers to a rollback in which the failing activity falls in one of multiple running threads. That means that there is an And split $(NASP(a_i))$ in the path $(NXSP(a_i), a_i)$. In this case, the rollback is performed for all parallel threads within the same And block, until the And split activity of the block containing the failing activity (marked as B_a) is reached. At this point it continues as single-threaded until reaching the nearest Xor split point. In the example given in Figure 1, there are two parallel threads running when activity 6 fails. The other thread, which executes activity 7, is forced to rollback until reaching activity 5, at which point the process continues as single-threaded. The following

Table 2. Algorithm 2. Rollback

Input: G, $Inst(G)$ -Instantiation, a_i -activity from which the rollback starts.
Output: $Inst'(G)$ - revised instantiation. Rollback of activities is performed to a_i 's nearest rollback point.
Process:
On the failure of activity a_i, $a_A = NASP(a_i)$ and $a_X = NXSP(a_i)$, if exist.
If $a_A = mull$ then
    Rollback as Hybrid threaded.
else if $length(a_x, a_i) < length(a_A, a_i)$ then
Rollback as Hybrid threaded.
else
    Rollback as parallel threaded.
end if

rollback activity should be taken in a parallel-threaded type:

Rollback all current executing and completed activities within B_a and proceed rollback as single-threaded.

Hybrid rollback is a rollback in which the failing activity a in $Inst(G')$ is part of a single thread, but some activities in $Inst(G')$ are part of an And block prior to the execution of a. For example, in Figure 1 assume that activity 8, which runs as single-threaded, fails. Since the process contains an And-block (activities 6 and 7 running in parallel), the rollback mechanism should apply to the entire And block and continue with the rollback until reaching $NXSP(8) = 1$. The following rollback activity should be taken in a hybrid-threaded type: $a_j = NXSP(a_i)$. Rollback until reaching a_j. For each

And-block, rollback all activities in the block and continue.

Algorithm 2 summarizes the mechanism for rollback discussed above. The correctness of Algorithm 2 stems immediately from Theorem 1. It is worth noting that single-threaded rollback is a special case of hybrid-threaded rollback, and therefore the algorithm refers only to the latter.

In case of a failure in one of the threads of an And block (*e.g.*, activity 6), one needs to rollback other threads as well (*e.g.*, activity 7 in Figure 1). However, there can be scenarios in which there is no need for rollback of the concurrent threads. In particular, if the failing activity occurs in a Xor block within an And block, an alternative path that does not require the rollback of all of the And block activities can be provided. This case is handled in Line 8 of the algorithm. (Table 2)

NASP and *NXSP* can be pre-assigned by analyzing the graph at design time. At each rollback step the compensation activity is assumed to execute in $O(1)$ (a more refined approach which addresses more complicated executions is deferred to an extended version of this work). There are $minlength(NXSP(a_i), a_i)$ steps to be taken, which is bounded by the cardinality of E. Therefore, the algorithm complexity is $O(E)$

.

PARAMETRIC MODIFICATION ANALYSIS

This section discusses scenarios, such as exception handling, that are handled with alternative paths. Once an alternative path has been discovered (see Alternative Path Detection section), it is necessary to evaluate the pre-conditions for performing this new path, and to request a change of values to satisfy these pre-conditions. We therefore turn our attention to the data flow of a business process. As an example, consider once more Figure 1, which introduces a data flow of a single data item, *Type*. This data item is updated during the execution of activity 0, and is retrieved by activity 1. Using common notation

(Rinderle, 2004), the data flow is marked using dashed double-line arrows. In what follows, we denote by *Update(var,a)* the nearest predecessor of *a* in which the variable *var* has been updated. This information can be generated offline and kept with each node, so that accessing it can be done in $O(1)$.

The parametric modification analysis is performed in two steps. The first entails identifying a set of variables whose modification would allow the use of an alternative path. The next is to identify the agents that have assigned the original values to these variables, and to request a change that would allow the use of the alternative path. We here detail each of these steps.

Satisfying Changes

Going back to Figure 1, recall that the original path to be taken was the path (0, 1, 5, 6, 7, 8, 9). Once activity 1 has been performed, the decision on whether to continue to activity 2 or to activity 5 is based on a mutually exclusive condition (regular or gold customer). Therefore, it becomes evident that the condition that enables us to proceed to activity 2 cannot be satisfied unless some of the variables are assigned different values.

For a given instance *Inst(G')*, each variable *var* in $Var(c_{a,a'})$ is assigned a value. Let $D(c_{a,a'}, Inst(G'))$ be **a set of sets** of assignments of the type *var = val* from *Inst(G')*, for which $c_{a,a'}$ **cannot be satisfied**. In the example given in Figure 1, $Var(c_{1,2}) = \{Type, Shipping\}$, and $D(c_{1,2}, Inst(G')) = \{Type="Regular"\}$, since under this instance, *Type* = "Gold".

Given an instance *Inst(G')* with an assignment *var = val*, where *var* is in $Var(c_{a,a'})$, one may consider a modified instance $Inst'(G') = Inst(G') \setminus \{var = val\} \cup \{var = val'\}$ in which *var = val* is replaced with *var = val'* . For example, a modified instance may include *Type* = Regular instead of *Type* = Gold.

Definition 6 *minimal satisfying change:* Let $c_{u,v}$ and Inst(G') be defined as before and let $D(c_{a,a'})$, Inst(G')) = \{set1\{var_{11} = val_{1l'} ..., var_{1n} = val_{1n}\}, set2\{var_{21} = val_{2l'} ..., var_{2m} = val_{2m}\}, ...\}$ Note that each set may be in different length, and some sets may share the same variables. A *satisfying change* to Inst(G') is a set of assignments $\{var_{i1} = val'_{i1'} ..., var_{in} = val'_{in}\}$ such that $c_{a,a'}$ can be satisfied under $Inst'(G') = Inst(G') \setminus \{var_{i1} = val_{i1'} ..., var_{in} = val_{in}\} \cup \{var_{i1} = val'_{i1'} ..., var_{in} = val'_{in}\}$

A *minimal satisfying change* is a satisfying change such that L (Equation 2) is the minimal of all possible satisfying changes. The *max* function is required since a *DNF* expression contains sets of predicates. Each set contain simple predicates with an *And* relation between them. All predicates in this set have to be satisfied in order to satisfy the set.

$$L = \max_{i=1}^{n} \left(\text{minlength} \left[Update \left(\underset{i}{var}, a \right) a \right] \right) \tag{2}$$

Definition 6 defines a minimal change to be the set of assignments in *Inst(G')* that can satisfy $c_{a,a'}$. Consider, for example, $c_{1,2}$ that includes the following statement:

(*Type* = "Regular" $\wedge$ *Shipping* = "air") $\vee$ (*Destination* = 972 $\wedge$ *City* = "TLV") and assume that all variables but *Type* are updated before activity 0. In this case, $Var(C_{1,2}) = \{Type, Shipping, Destination, City\}$. Assume an instance in which *Type* = Gold, *Shipping* = air, *Destination* = 33, and *City* = Hong Kong. Therefore, $D(c_{1,2}, Inst(G')) = \{\{Type = Regular\}, \{Destination = 972, City = TLV\}\}$. The *minimal satisfying change* would be $\{Type = Regular\}$.

It is worth noting that Definition 6 minimizes the maximal number of activities for which rollback is

Table 3. Algorithm 3: Parametric modification algorithm

```
Input: Graph G, Inst(G) -Instantiation, a_i -failed activity .
Output: Parameters - The parameters to be modified after Role approval
Process:
repeat:
//execute over the nested Xor blocks
A1 = NXSP(a_i)
for each e_{j,k} (an outgoing edge from A1) that does not lead to a_i do
        get c_{j,k}
        get Var(c_{j,k})
end for
L=getD(c, inst(G)) //list of satisfying changes.
Sort L by increasing length, using equation 2.
for i = 0 to size do
        parameters[val,val'] = L[i]
        for all set of assignments do
                var=val'
        end for
        if all assignments accepted then
                return (parameters)
        else
                continue // to the next satisfying change.
        end if
end for
A1 = NXSP(A1) // next Xor split point
until A1 = null
return null
```

needed. Such a definition seems reasonable when the rollback of any activity has the same cost, from the user's point of view. A more general approach would require the definition of a cost model to evaluate the impact of an activity rollback as well as a variable change, and to minimize this impact. We defer the introduction of this approach to the extended version of this work.

Variable Modification

Once the minimal satisfying change is computed, we can identify the variables that need to be modified. From the workflow model, using either a-priori information or mining procedures (Golani, 2003;Agrawal, 1998;WFMC-AD), one can identify the activity where those variables are modified. For example, in Figure 1 an exception occurs while executing activity 6. *NXSP* is detected as activity 1 and the minimal satisfying change is {*Type* = Regular}. This change can be set in activity 0. Let a_i be an activity in which a variable change is required. There are two possible sources for updated values, as follows:

A user-defined value: This is a value inserted by the agent that executed a_i. In this case, the user will be presented with a request for re-execution of the activity, with the specific condition needed to allow execution of the alternative path.

A derived value: This is an expression whose input includes both data flow and user input. If the user input affects the data value in such a way that the desired data value is feasible, the user's approval is requested for re-execution of a_i with a specific range of valid input to allow the alternative path execution.

Upon approval, the business process rollbacks to a_X (see Section 5), and forward stepping is performed from a_X to $NXSP(a_i)$. Once $NXSP(a_i)$ is completed, the expression is evaluated again, but this time the

Figure 4.

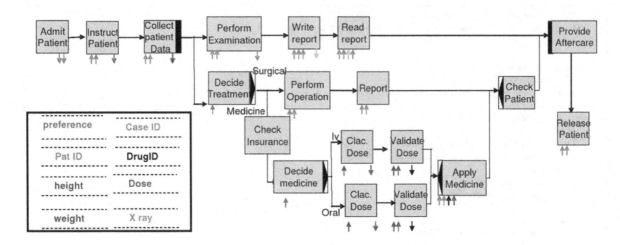

evaluation result redirects the execution to the alternative path.

In the case the modifying change request is rejected, the next minimal satisfying change is checked, and so on, until all changes have been exhausted. Then, the second nearest rollback point is computed, and the same procedure is applied to it. The *second nearest rollback point* (based on Definition 5), can be computed recursively as the nearest rollback point of $NXSP(a_i)$. Thus, the algorithm will recursively compute the same actions over the next nested Xor block (*i.e.*, $NXSP(NXSP(a_i))$). This process is summarized in Algorithm 3.

In the worst case the algorithm will iterate over all Xor split points, scanning all graph edges ($O(E)$). For each edge we generate (line 11) a list L of cardinality $|L|$, sorted (line 11) in $O(|L|log|L|)$. Therefore, the total complexity of Algorithm 3 is $O(|E||L|log|L|)$. It is worth noting that L may be exponential in $Var(C)$. However, under a reasonable assumption of rather simple conditions with a small $Var(c)$ with a constant upper limit, the algorithm complexity is $O(E)$. (Table 3)

Forward Stepping: Revisited

Given that a change to activity a_i was approved by the relevant agent, at least one of the output parameters (P_i) of an activity a_i must have been modified. The naïve approach assumes that the process can move forward in a semantic manner (see Section 4) until reaching the relevant Xor split point (a_x). However, along the path (a_i, a_x) there are activities which may be affected by the modified value of one of the output parameters of a_i. An activity which uses a modified parameter value as input should not be executed semantically, since the output parameters values may have been revised based on the modified input data. The mechanism for such an approach has been discussed in Algorithm 1 (combined with Eq 1). In this case, the algorithm is executed with a known stop activity a_x.

Figure 5. A meta-process structure

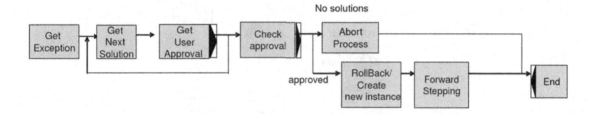

CASE STUDY

Consider Figure 4 that presents a scenario of a medical care within a hospital (based on a known scenario from the Adept-flex group at Ulm). The process begins with the patient's admission (assigned role nurse). It then proceeds with activities "instruct patient" (doctor) and "collect patient data" (nurse). Afterwards, there is a split into two execution branches which may run parallel to each other. The upper branch sets out the activities of a medical examination in another department ("perform examination" and "write report", both with user role "radiology doctor"), whereas the lower branch defines preparatory steps performed by the nurse (e.g., "calculate dose", "produce drug"), and a doctor ("validate dose").

The lower branch has further branching that is not taken in parallel. Mutual exclusive (Xor type nodes), that act as points for decision making (namely "Decide treatment", and "Decide medicine"). In first one, the doctor decides whether a surgery is required, or a medicine treatment is sufficient. The second activity refers to the type of medicine treatment (Oral vs. Iv). Then, the produced drug will be given to the patient, the patient with be evaluated, some aftercare will be provided, and the patient is discharged.

Consider a scenario in which the activity *"calc dosage (IV)"* is performed and the nurse finds out that there is no sufficient amount of the required medicine in the inventory. The raised exception creates a new process that analyzes and governors the situation (meta process -to be explained in the following section).

In this analysis, the first split point is (1)*"decide medicine"*, and the second one is (2)*"decide treatment"*. Both activities utilize the "preference" data as input parameter. This data is updated in activity (3)*"instruct patient"* which is assigned to a doctor. The doctor is then invoked with a new task requesting his approval for this satisfying change (Oral instead of IV). If the doctor agrees, the process is rolled-back/compensated until reaching the beginning of activity *"instruct patient"*. Both activities *"decide medicine"*, and *"decide treatment"* are added to the potential activities list (Algorithm 1). The activities on the first solution will modify the medical preference from *"IV"* to *"Oral"* affectively routing the process in an alternative path referring to oral medication. All activities are executed semantically except activities (1) and (2). Note that once the process arrives to activity *"decide treatment"*, this activity will be re-executed. It is in the *potential activity list* because its input parameters had been modified. Thus, the doctor role has the privilege of deciding of a surgical operation, although the original solution didn't "point" at this direction. If the doctor just approves the request for oral medical treatment, then the process will continue (forward stepping) until reaching the first detected Xor split point (1) and take the required alternative path.

Figure 6. Architecture

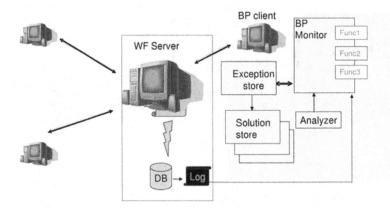

Suppose the doctor denies the modification request, then a request for the following satisfying change will be generated (operation instead of medicine) and the same mechanism (described above) is applied this time referring to the second Xor split point (2). The reader is required to consider the above scenario as a general example. Practically, further refinement that can be taken into consideration:

- If an operation begun or completed, in case of some exception (reduction in the patient stability), the path of the medicine treatment can be taken.
- After a medicine was taken, performing a surgery is forbidden. If a decision to take a medicine was taken, there is still an option of performing an operation on emergency cases unless the medicine was actually applied.
- Until the medicine is applied, one can switch - in case of short inventory- from oral to iv and vice versa.

The additional requirements can be modeled and handled, but are not in the scope of this chapter. The interested reader is referred to [Golani, 2008]

ARCHITECTURAL CONSIDERATIONS

We used the core functionality of a WfMS system to orchestrate our solution. A meta process is a process that manages other processes. Figure 5 presents a description of a *meta process* for exception handling. Slight modifications are needed to generalize it to the more general case. In our case, once a problem/ opportunity is monitored, the meta process is invoked and its activities are executed to provide the best solution. Each solution should be confirmed by the relevant agents prior to the semi-automated execution of the underlying process. Upon approval, those activities that are not affected by user input are semantically executed (assuming validity), while other activities are referred to their original responsible agent for execution. The result is a single meta process that can interact with all running processes using the system infrastructure and constructs, and that provides a transparent mechanism to handle such ad-hoc changes via backtracking and forward stepping.

Figure 7. Active monitor prototype

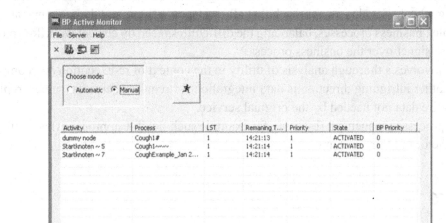

A meta process invokes a monitor that acts as a special workflow client (see Figure 6). The monitor receives modification notifications and exception-oriented messages (e.g., work items), and in response creates an instance of a process that requests a parameter change from the relevant agent. If the reply (again as work item) is negative, then the monitor seeks the next available solution and makes another request to an appropriate agent. This continues iteratively until there are no more solutions to suggest (as discussed in Algorithm 3). Once a positive answer arrives at the monitor, it rolls back to the required activity a_y (or creates a new instance that imitates and semantically executes the original instance activities until reaching a_y), and then starts the re-execution and semantic execution of the proceeding activities, until reaching an activity that was not on the original path.

A prototype was built over the ADEPT workflow system (see Figure 7). The BP monitor reads messages from the work items list. An exception is stored in the *exception Store*, while the analyzer analyzes the process graph and creates a list of solutions (for this exception) sorted from best to worst according to an estimation function (one of many within a repository). This list is stored in the *solution store*. At each iteration the *exception store* requests a new solution from the *solution store*.

CONCLUSION

This chapter proposes a mechanism for efficient management of flexible business processes - in particular, for forward stepping and backtracking. For illustration purposes, we demonstrate our techniques with two somewhat different scenarios. First, we show how changes in Web services can be dynamically embedded into a workflow model, minimizing the costs related to re-execution of previously performed activities. Second, we propose an improved exception handler using forward stepping, backtracking, and alternative paths. Alternative paths, while not the only possible exception handling tool, can serve in a broad variety of cases, and can be easily produced automatically, either in design time (serving as a recommendation) or at run-time (serving as a crisis management tool, in the absence of immediate valid solutions). Our goal is to develop an approach that allows (semi-) automatic dynamic management for arbitrarily complex business processes, balancing the difficulties faced by current workflow models and the control of a designer over the business process.

Future work involves a thorough analysis of utility in the context of re-execution and compensation of activities. Another intriguing direction is data integration for required services, since a replacement service may require data not needed by the original service.

Self healing process management (by using for example such flexible approaches) is likely to be the differentiating factor in future systems.

REFERENCES

Agostini, A., & De Michelis, G. (2000). Improving ‡flexibility of workflow management systems. In W. van der Aalst & J. Oberweis (Eds.), *BPM: Models, techniques, and empirical studies* (pp. 218-234). Springer Verlag.

Agrawal, R., Gunopulos, D., & Leymann, F. (1998). Mining process models from workflow logs. In O. Etzion & P. Scheuermann (Eds.), *Advances in Database Technology - EDBT'98, 6th international Conference on Extending Database Technology* (LNCS 1337, pp. 469-483).

BPEL4WS (n.d.). *Specification: Business process execution language for Web services* (Version 1.1). Retrieved from http://www-128.ibm.com/developerworks/library/ws-bpel/.

Casati, F., Ceri, S., Paraboschi, S., & Pozzi, G. (1999). Specification and implementation of exceptions in workflow management systems. *ACM Transactions on Database Systems, 24*(3), 405–451. doi:10.1145/328939.328996

Du, W., Davis, J., & Shan, M. C. (1997). Flexible specification of workflow compensation scopes. In *GROUP ACM*, 309-316.

Eder, J., & Liebhart, W. (1996). Workflow recovery. In *CoopIS* (pp. 124-134).

Eder, J., & Liebhart, W. (1998). Contributions to exception handling in workflow management. In O. Burkes, J. Eder, & S. Salza (Eds.), *Proceedings of the Sixth International Conference on Extending Database Technology* (pp. 3-10).

Gaaloul, W., Bhiri, S., & Godart, C. (2004 October). Discovering workflow transactional behavior from event-based log. In *On the Move to Meaningful Internet Systems 2004: CoopIS, DOA, and ODBASE* (pp. 3-18). Springer.

Golani, M. (2008). Workflow search space reduction – A model driven approach. [IJPAM]. *International Journal of Pure and Applied Mathematics, 44*(2), 265–280.

Golani, M., & Gal, A. (2005). Flexible business process management using forward stepping and alternative paths. In *Proceedings of the 3rd Business Process Management International Conference, BPM 2005* (LNCS 3649, pp. 48-63).

Golani, M., & Pinter, S. S. (2003). Generating a process model from a process audit log. In M. Weske, W. van der Aalst, & A. ter Hofstede (Eds.), *Proceedings of the Business Process Management International Conference, BPM 2003* (LNCS 2678, pp. 136-151).

Hagen, C., & Alonso, G. (2000). Exception handling in workflow management systems. *IEEE Transactions on Software Engineering, 26*(10), 943–958. doi:10.1109/32.879818

Hwang, G. H., Lee, Y. C., & Wu, B. Y. (2003). A new language to support flexible failure recovery for workflow management systems. In J. Favela & D. Decouchant (Eds.), *CRIWG* (LNCS 2806, pp. 135-150).

Kamath, M., & Ramamritham, K. (1998). Failure handling and coordinated execution of concurrent workflows. In *Proc. of the 14ᵗʰ Intl. Conf. on Data Engineering* (pp. 334-341).

Reichert, M., & Dadam, P. (1998). Adeptf lex-supporting dynamic changes of workflows without losing control. *Journal of Intelligent Information Systems, 10*(2), 93–129. doi:10.1023/A:1008604709862

Rinderle, S., Reichert, M., & Dadam, P. (2004). Correctness criteria for dynamic changes in workflow systems - A survey. *Data & Knowledge Engineering, 50*(1), 9–34. doi:10.1016/j.datak.2004.01.002

Sadiq, S., Marjanovic, O., & Orlowska, M. E. (2000). Managing change and time in dynamic workflow processes. *International Journal of Cooperative Information Systems, 9*(1-2), 93–116. doi:10.1142/S0218843000000077

van der Aalst, W. M. P., et al. (2000). Advance workflow patterns. In O. Etzion & P. Scheuermann (Eds.), *Cooperative Information Systems, 8th International Conference, CoopIS 2000* (LNCS 1901, pp. 18-29).

WFMC-AD. (1998). *Workflow management coalition 1998. Interface 5 - Audit data specification* (Tech. Rep. wfmc-tc-1015 issue 1.1). workflow management coalition.

WFMC-RM (1995). Workflow management coalition. *The workflow reference model* (wfmc-tc-1003).

Wohed, P., Aalst, W. M. P., Dumas, M., & Hostede, A. H. M ter (2003). Analysis of Web services composition languages: The case of bpel4ws. In Song et al. (Eds.), *Conceptual Modeling - ER 2003 - 22nd international Conference on Conceptual Modeling* (LNCS 2813, pp. 200-215).

World Wide Web Consortium. (n.d.). *WSDL Specification: Web services description language (WSDL) version 2.0.* Retrieved from http://www.w3.org/TR/wsdl.

KEY TERMS AND DEFINITIONS

Adaptivity: the ability to change the definition or routings of a running process.

Alternative Path: an execution plan of a business process that overtakes an activity on another path.

Back-Tracking: undoing/compensating already completed tasks in order to arrive to an earlier step in the business process.

Exception Handler: a mechanism that enables a business process to manage and heal from occurred and detected exception.

Flexibility: the ability to reconfigure a process given new demands and constraints. This is done by a designer/expert.

Forward Stepping: a section of the dynamic exception handler, in which the process advances forward (some of the underlying applications could actually not be invoked. See: semantic execution).

Full Blocked Workflow: For each JOIN (or respectively SPLIT) there is exactly one corresponding SPLIT (or respectively JOIN) of the same kind, and the Activity of the SPLIT and the corresponding JOIN are also the pairing BEGIN and END activities of an INLINE_BLOCK.

Meta Process: a process that models and manages other process models.

Process Model: a structure (one among petri net, BP graph, ADEPT WSM net) that describes the precedence of activities, roles, synchronization conditions etc.

Semantic Execution: execution on the workflow level only, meaning that the workflow engine is reported that task 'a' is completed while the underlying application for this task was not executed.

Chapter 10
Multiple-Step Backtracking of Exception Handling in Autonomous Business Process Management

Mingzhong Wang
University of Melbourne, Australia

Jinjun Chen
Swinburne University of Technology, Australia

Kotagiri Ramamohanarao
University of Melbourne, Australia

Amy Unruh
University of Melbourne, Australia

ABSTRACT

This chapter proposes a multiple-step backtracking mechanism to maintain a tradeoff between replanning and rigid backtracking for exception handling and recovery, thus enabling business process management (BPM) systems to operate robustly even in complex and dynamic environments. The concept of BDI (belief, desire and intention) agent is applied to model and construct the BPM system to inherit its advantages of adaptability and flexibility. Then, the flexible backtracking approach is introduced by utilizing the beneficial features of event-driven and means-end reasoning of BDI agents. Finally, we incorporate open nested transaction model to encapsulate plan execution and backtracking to gain the system level support of concurrency control and automatic recovery. With the ability of reasoning about task characteristics, our approach enables the system to find and commence a suitable plan prior to or in parallel with a compensation process when a failure occurs. This kind of computing allows us to achieve business goals efficiently in the presence of exceptions and failures.

DOI: 10.4018/978-1-60566-669-3.ch010

INTRODUCTION

A critical challenge in building practical business process management (BPM) systems is to allow users to maintain the system robustness and reliability with respect to the correct execution even in the presence of abnormalities. As the operating environment becomes increasingly complex, dynamic and error-prone, it is extremely challenging for designers and programmers to find out all possible combinations of exceptions as well as designing corresponding handling methods. Therefore, a flexible, systematic and autonomic approach for exception handling is essential for the success of applying complex BPM systems into wider fields of application.

Multi-agent systems have been extensively studied as a powerful high-level decomposition and abstraction tool in analyzing, designing, and implementing complex software systems (Jennings, 2001). Many researchers and practitioners have noticed the fundamental relationship between agents and workflow systems (Ehrler, Fleurke, Purvis, & Savarimuthu, 2006) and proposed various approaches to build dynamic and adaptive workflow systems with the concept of agents, and vice versa.

To manage the complexity arisen from the dynamic and complex running environment, we propose to apply the reactive BDI (Belief, Desire and Intention) (Rao & Georgeff, 1995) agent system to model and construct BPM systems, thus benefiting from its sound features of event-driven and means-end reasoning for the purpose of robustness, flexibility and adaptability.

Providing a higher level of abstraction, agents help to simplify modeling and construction of flexible BPM systems operating in open and distributed environments. To deal with exceptions, most multi-agent systems apply the mechanism of backtracking to recover and retry the failed execution. However, they back track in a rigid step-by-step manner until one alternative execution path is found. Moreover, they follow a defensive route of recovery-then-try pattern. Due to the dynamic and nondeterministic features of complex environments, rigid recovery on the reverse chronological order of execution history will in many instances become meaningless and inappropriate. Some attempt to consider starting a fresh plan after the exception. However, this approach is too computationally expensive and rarely practical to get deployed because it requires a complete knowledge about the running environment and needs to consider all previous actions. As a result, developers are forced to consider low-level details of disturbances, failure, or uncontrolled interactions between workflow actors for the requirement of robustness and reliability.

To address this issue, we propose to extend existing rigid backtracking strategy to support and enable execution backtracking in a multiple-step fashion (reverse chronological order with certain steps skipped). Instead of step-by-step backtracking through the execution tree, the system can "jump" back to an arbitrary history node and try another eligible execution path. Our approach maintains a tradeoff between replanning and traditional backtracking strategies.

To provide automatic and system-level support for concurrency control and exception handling, open nested transaction (Weikum & Schek, 1992) is integrated into our multiple-step backtracking model. Compared with other approaches which apply transaction models (Gray & Reuter, 1993) into workflow (Georgakopoulos, Hornick, & Manola, 1996) or multi-agent systems (Ramamohanarao, Bailey, & Busetta, 2001; Nagi, 2001), our method unites the beneficial features of event-driven and means-end reasoning from BDI agent systems and utilizes a flexible backtracking approach to allow the execution "jumping" back several levels at once to continue its execution towards the goal in case that backtracking to one level in the execution tree does not solve the problem.

Figure 1. PRS-style structure for BDI agent. (Adapted from (d'Inverno, Luck, Georgeff, Kinny, & Wooldridge, 2004))

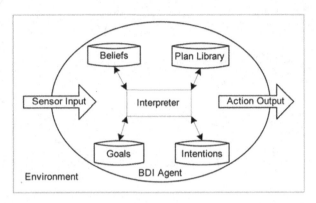

BACKGROUND

BDI Agents and Exception Handling

Software agents have the ability to provide autonomous and reactive behaviors, and to support decomposition and abstraction of functionality, making agent technology useful in analyzing, designing, and implementing complex software systems (Jennings, 2001). They are persistent entities that can perceive, reason and act in some environment. Often, agents are autonomous, reactive, and sociable (Woolridge, 2001).

In order to push agent technology into the mainstream of software development, various agent architectures (Woolridge, 2001) and agent programming languages have been proposed. Among them, BDI (Rao & Georgeff, 1995) is probably the most mature and accepted model. Most BDI platforms with PRS (Procedural Reasoning System) style share the following three features.

- An agent contains four key data structures as shown in Figure 1. *Beliefs* are the informational state representing what an agent knows about itself and the world which may be incomplete or even incorrect. *Goals* are the motivational state and correspond to what the agent wants to achieve. *Plans* represent the procedural knowledge about how to achieve a certain goal or react to a specific situation. *Intentions* are selected plans for execution and represent the deliberative state of an agent.
- The execution of an agent is event driven. Plans, which are usually represented in the form of *event* ← preconditions | *action_sequence*, are defined to react to a certain event which can be internal modifications to its goals and beliefs or external changes of environment. After *event* is triggered, the *preconditions* will be tested before *action_sequence* can be chosen for execution. Because events can occur non-deterministically, plans are executed reactively.
- The execution path to achieve a goal of an agent is generated by means-end reasoning. That is, the goal is treated as an initial event triggering a corresponding plan to run. *action_sequence* of the plan may contain primitive actions as well as subgoals. All sub-goals will be in turn treated as events to trigger sub-plans to run. This process continues recursively until all actions in sub-plans are primitive or atomic.

Figure 2. Event driven and means-end reasoning for BDI system execution

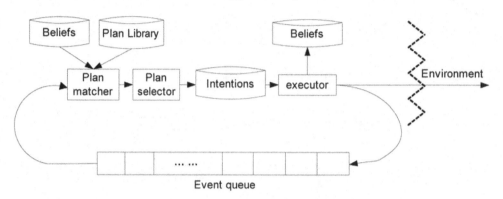

The execution process of a BDI agent can be abstractly depicted in Figure 2. This process is described by (Rao & Georgeff, 1995) and applied directly or indirectly by dMARS (d'Inverno et al., 2004) and 3APL (Dastani, Riemsdijk, Dignum, & Meyer, 2003).

The *plan matcher* will retrieve an event from the queue and search through the plan library to find the set of plans which can handle this event in that certain situation (determined by its beliefs). There might be more than one suitable plan found, and the *plan selector* will choose one of them and append it into the intention stack. Finally, the intention is executed, which results in internally updating the BDI state, including beliefs, desires and intentions, or externally operating to sense and change the environment.

Since agents usually work in open, dynamic and error-prone environment, they are more liable to conflicts and eventually failures. Without dealing with these problems appropriately, agent system can only remain as an experimental toy. Therefore, substantial effort is carried out with attentions to automate exception handling and execution resumption, thus making agent programming a serious platform to developers for developing complex applications.

On one extreme, replanning is proposed to have a fresh start by throwing away all the work that has been previously done in planning. However, it is too computationally expensive and rarely practical because it requires complete knowledge about the environment and business domain and involves a lot of programming efforts. On the other extreme, backtracking is applied to go back through all the work that previously been done in planning in a depth-first searching manner. Despite the feasibility of backtracking requires a rigid execution tree structure, it becomes the most widely applied for exception handling in multi-agent systems because it fits nicely to the hierarchical program architecture and enables systematic and platform-level recovery support.

To back track one step in the execution tree needs some compensation. Many existing agent programming languages provide some basic support for modeling exceptions and their compensations. They usually use a specified event to trigger a new plan to define compensating actions. For example, 3APL (Dastani et al., 2003) allows using plan revision rules to define compensating actions for a specified event. dMARS (d'Inverno et al., 2004) allows encoding of maintenance conditions, as well as success and failure actions, into a task definition. However, all of them lack a systematic way to organize and manage those exceptions and compensations, making complex system design and interaction management difficult and sometimes impossible.

Some researchers propose to apply transaction concepts to help build systematic and automatic platform for robust agent execution. TOMAS (Ramamohanarao, Bailey, & Busetta, 2001) applies a *nested transaction model* as the concurrency control and recovery mechanism to avoid performing conflict update operations on the agent. However, since a nested transaction model requires full control on the resources and no exposure of partial results, it is not feasible in most situated agent systems. Even if all agents perform database manipulation only, the model is still too rigid to be practical in a multi-agent system, because long-running activities can lead to locking resources for very long periods and can cause deadlocks. (Nagi, 2001) takes a more workflow-like approach by treating every action as an ACID (Atomicity, Consistency, Isolation and Durability) entity and putting them into *open nested transaction model* to create transaction trees. ECA (Event, Condition, and Action) rules are used to link two agents if one uses the partial results of another. But this approach does not allow changes of execution plans, which are quite common in agent applications. What is more, arbitrary and unstructured linkages among different agents breach the design principles of modularization and loose coupling.

As an extension to the compensation concept in advanced transaction models, (Unruh, Bailey, & Ramamohanarao, 2004) discusses the use of goal-based semantic compensation in the context of agents.

Compared with transaction-based solutions, Guardian (Tripathi & Miller, 2001) and Citizens (Klein, Rodriguez-Aguilar, & Dellarocas, 2003) separate the mechanisms and knowledge about exception handling from the agent system to a centralized exception manager. However, this separation only works well for some domain-independent exceptions. SaGE (Souchon, Dony, Urtado, & Vauttier, 2004) proposes to organize agents as well as their exception handlers in a hierarchical structure, but it lacks a precise model of what to do after the exception has been handled based on the exception-handling plan and the result of executing that plan.

Exception Handling in Workflow System

A primitive form of multi-agent system can be viewed as a workflow model in the sense that it has a predefined finite (static) execution flow. However, they share the same problem with regard to exception handling. It is therefore essential for the success of a workflow management system that it provides a powerful yet easy-to-use mechanism for maintaining system robustness and reliability, with respect to the correct execution of tasks even in the presence of abnormalities and exceptions.

(Georgakopoulos, Hornick, & Manola, 1996) argues that Customized Transaction Management (CTM) is one of the key infrastructure technologies for effective workflow management system. CTM can ensure the correctness and reliability of applications implementing business or information processes, while permitting the functionality each particular process requires (e.g., isolation, coordination, or collaboration between tasks).

The concept of transaction is a concise but powerful abstraction tool with the properties of concurrency control and failure atomicity. Traditional transactions have ACID properties (Gray & Reuter, 1993), which prevent inconsistency and integrity problems. *Atomicity* ensures that either all or none of operations of a transaction are performed. *Consistency* ensures that a transaction maintains its integrity constraints on the objects it manipulates. *Isolation* ensures that a transaction executes as if it were running alone in the system and intermediate transaction results are hidden from other concurrently executing transactions. *Durability* ensures the changes once made by successfully completed transactions are persistent even when systems crash.

In database applications, each transaction is enforced to have the ACID properties. Therefore, whenever there is an exception occurring, all work already done in the transaction is aborted and the system is restored to the starting state as if nothing has happened. However, ACID transactions require an activity to obtain full control of, and exclusive access to, its resources. In contrast to database applications where transactions can lock records to get exclusive access, and can restore any data from history, workflow tasks in nature usually work in an open environment and operate on physical objects where actions "always commit" and it is impractical or even impossible to satisfy either requirement. For example, a flight reservation task cannot lock the schedule to avoid flight changes or restore a bank account to the original amount by itself when cancelling a booking. Thus, traditional transaction mechanisms need to be extended for an open and shared environment before they can be applied to workflow systems.

The extended transaction models in workflow systems usually focus on the inter-dependency among the participating tasks. The overall workflow process is treated as a big transaction which organizes all participating tasks in a tree structure to ensure the criterion of correctness and reliability. Each task node is considered as sub-transaction which may not be required to hold all ACID properties. The relationships among these sub-transactions are depicted by task dependencies which can ensure the execution order and execution correctness.

Based on the dependencies among tasks, the workflow management system can generate plans to execute. Theoretically when exceptions occur, the system can retrieve all affected tasks and coordinate them to handle the exceptions together. Generally, the failure of a task at a given level may or may not affect its parent step. If it does, then the parent is to be rolled back and the procedure is repeated until a parent task is reached that is not affected. From this point on, a parent task may try an alternative child step to compensate or restart. Then the overall process is a two-phase remedy where the first phase, called the bottom-up phase, determines the highest ancestor task affected by the failure of the current task and a second phase, called the top-down phase, undoes the changes at each level starting from that ancestor (Kamathy & Ramamritham, 1996).

Another proposal is called sphere of joint compensation (Kamathy & Ramamritham, 1996). A collection of tasks in a workflow is grouped into a sphere S such that either all the tasks of S complete successfully or all of them are compensated. Thus a sphere is basically a failure-atomic unit. Spheres can overlap and be nested. Actually spheres are relaxed transactions with the property of atomicity and consistency. The problem is how to define the scope of the sphere.

Although these methods can guarantee the correctness of the system execution, they do not consider issues related to the context changes arising from dynamic and complex environment. For example, when a branch of the execution tree fails, other possible solutions need to wait until the recovery completes. If the running environment for recovery has become different from initial execution or design assumption, the overall system is taken down even though sometimes there are clear other approaches existing to continue the execution for achieving the business goals. As such, a more flexible recovery mechanism is required to organize transactional recovery and forward execution in complex interacting systems.

A Motivating Example

A travel management system with the goal of preparing a holiday for the customers is illustrated in Figure 3. All alternatives at the choice points are eligible for selection. Let us assume the system chooses *California* as the tour destination from all three possible places. Then it tries to book the flight and the hotel. After that, it chooses *Sailing* as the entertainment plan. Finally, it begins to rent a yacht. Unselected branches during the execution are cut off to simplify the presentation.

If yacht renting fails, traditional backtracking mechanism will go back to the choice point of *Entertainment* and try *Disneyland*. However, if tickets for the Disneyland are sold out, the system needs to

Figure 3. Travel management system

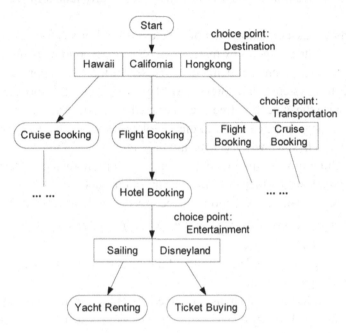

keep on backtracking by undoing hotel booking and flight booking to the choice point of *Destination* and try either Hawaii or Hongkong as the new destination.

However, this rigid step-by-step backtracking approach is sometimes not appropriate when the environment keeps on changing. First, its requirement of keeping the execution structure static for recovery purpose is hard to fulfill in a dynamic and non-deterministic environment, and recovery on the reverse order of the execution history will probably become meaningless in many situations. For example, the closure of the hotel after the booking has been made will invalidate any rollback or compensation attempts and result in the discontinuity of achieving the goal of holiday travel. Second, after exceptions occur, it requires complete compensation of failed plans before trying any further efforts to achieve the goal. Because applying other plans to approach the goal may not always conflict with the process of compensation, this requirement results in inefficiency with respect to goal achieving and sometimes brings unnecessary costs.

Addressing these drawbacks, we propose a multiple-step backtracking mechanism for recovering exceptions occurred in BPM systems running in dynamic and open environments. In our approach, when the system knows going back one level in the execution tree can not deal with the exception, it can jump back several levels at once instead to continue its execution towards the goal. We will also show how open nested transaction model is integrated into our flexible backtracking approach to provide systematic and automatic support for exception handling and concurrency control.

BDI-STYLE EXECUTION MODEL FOR BPM

In order to operate in complex and dynamic environment, the execution tree of a business process must be generated at run-time reactively to its surroundings. We propose to apply BDI framework to construct the dynamic composition of individual autonomous participants in the system to achieve a certain business goal.

The application domain has a predefined set of business rules. For a certain goal in a specified environment, it is broken down into sub-goals by matching it with corresponding plans. Each subgoal can be achieved by delegating to some agents, or being decomposed further with appropriate plans. Compared with conventional workflow systems, the proposed BPM execution model is more dynamic and adaptive to the environment because the execution tree is constructed at run time according to the real situation. For the purposes of the approach we describe in this chapter, we can assume without loss of generality a plan is a task to achieve. Thus, we will use *task* and *plan* interchangeably.

During the plan matching process for a goal, there may exist more than one feasible plan. Then, it is said the system has a *choice point* which is a key concept in our model.

Definition 1. A *choice point* of the execution tree records the applicable plans found by *plan matcher* to deal with a certain goal. It is denoted as $cp_{goal} = \{p_1, p_2, \ldots, p_n\}$ **where** p_i is an applicable plan. $S_{cp}(i)$ stands for the selection of plan p_i by *plan selector*.

Because the BPM system is modeled and built by following BDI agent systems, its execution shares the same features as multi-agent systems.

Principle 1. After a plan has made a change to the environment, if the whole system is still in a semantically consistent state satisfying system constraints, this state is acceptable even though the actions are later shown to be futile in working towards a goal.

This rule allows the execution of the BPM system to be treated in terms of independent small plan fragments. Each such fragment can be encapsulated in a transaction which can externalize its result after termination without causing long running transactions. For example, even if the travel management system cannot arrange any entertainment in California, the existence of flight and hotel booking does not prevent it from trying other options. Moreover, it is more important to achieve the goal of holiday arrangements for the system than to undo its payment of the booking deposit.

Principle 2. Cleaning up a side effect of a failed selection $S_{cp}(i)$ can have lower priority compared with trying its alternatives, or achieving the system's goal.

Compensation is usually used to release the consumed resources which are necessary for other attempts. However, it is the approach, not the purpose. All unrelated compensations can be processed in parallel with or even after the achievement of the goal to improve system throughput and efficiency. The applicability of this principle is based on the fact that system plans are dynamically composed when their events are triggered and their preconditions are satisfied. However, in resource-bounded situation compensation may have a higher priority.

Principle 3. If the system is consistent, any plan in its plan library can be selected for execution if the plan preconditions are met.

These rules allow us to continue system execution at any legal choice point after current execution encounters interruption. In other words, it is not necessary to conservatively roll back before trying other paths. The execution flow just needs to "jump" back to an appropriate choice point and continue. We will give a more detailed description of this concept in the next section.

FLEXIBLE EXCEPTION HANDLING MODEL

We first explain the multiple-step backtracking mechanism which maintains a tradeoff between replanning and rigid backtracking for exception handling and recovery. We then describe how we can incorporate the open nested transaction model to encapsulate plan execution and backtracking to gain the system level support for concurrency control and automatic recovery.

Multiple-Step Backtracking Recovery

Traditional Backtracking recovery tries to explore the solution domain in a depth-first search manner. The execution of the system is usually organized as a tree. When a task node fails, the system would go one step back to its parent by undoing or compensating the result done by the task. If there is still no solution in the parent node, the system would recursively back track to the upper level until reaching the root. Compared with this rigid search strategy, our approach can track back multiple levels at once by skipping intermediate steps according to the evaluation of the real time condition. Therefore, even in case step-by-step backtracking is invalid because of the environment changes, the system can still survive by recovering and continuing the execution flow from a higher level of control. This section at first introduces and defines the key concepts related to the flexible backtracking mechanism, and then shows the details about the backtracking algorithm for the recovery. Finally, the proposed approach is summarized and compared with the generally applied handling methods.

Key Concepts for Multiple-Step Backtracking

The system can use the knowledge of its set of choices at each choice point to decide which substitutable plan to choose if exceptions occur later.

Definition 2. **A choice point stack contains the choice points the system has met chronologically. It is denoted as** $cp\_stack = \{cp_n, cp_{n-1}, \ldots, cp_1\}$ where cp_i is the choice point occurred at time i.

When there is a failure of execution, it must happen at one branch of cp_n. The system can look through its stack for another applicable branch of a certain past choice point to continue achieving its goal. If possible, the new selected branch can be identical to the failed one as a retry. We call this process a "jump".

Definition 3. A jump is a continuation of the system execution flow at another selectable plan implied by elements of its choice point stack. To enable the jump to the jth choice of cp_i, **the preconditions of the plan** $S_{cp_i}(j)$ must be satisfied.

Preconditions of a plan usually specify the required resources and execution context. For example, after the failure of hotel booking, the travel management system may find there is not enough money left for Hong Kong or Hawaii because money has been paid for air ticket to California. The failed branch ($S_{cp_n}(f)$) and the new selected branch ($S_{cp_i}(s) \mid i \leq n$) may have three types of coordination with respect to their resource share or competition. Different type of coordination leads to different processing strategy.

- $S_{cp_n}(f)$ does not consume any resources which will be used by $S_{cp_i}(s)$. That is, $S_{cp_n}(f)$ has no access to the resources which must be guaranteed as preconditions of $S_{cp_i}(s)$. In this case, $S_{cp_i}(s)$

Figure 4. Different recovery strategy for different type of path coordination

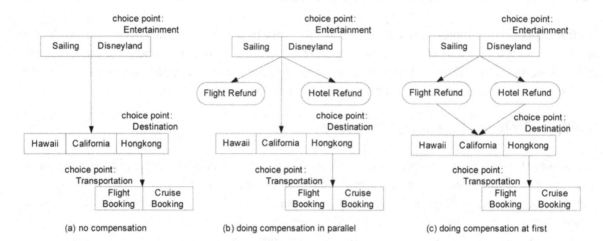

(a) no compensation   (b) doing compensation in parallel   (c) doing compensation at first

can be started directly prior to addressing the failure. However, there could be a background thread reclaiming the resources consumed by $S_{cp_n}(f)$.

- $S_{cp_i}(s)$ shares some resources with $S_{cp_n}(f)$. However, there are still enough resources left for $S_{cp_i}(s)$ after the consumption by $S_{cp_n}(f)$. The handling method of this case is the same as the first type. As shown in Figure 4 (a) and (b), the execution can jump directly to arrange travel at different destination because flight and hotel bookings have not spent anything, or only spent a small amount of money. The refund process can be ignored, or be carried out in parallel with the goal achieving or even after the goal of the agent has been achieved.

- $S_{cp_i}(s)$ shares some resources with $S_{cp_n}(f)$, of which too much has been used for $S_{cp_i}(s)$ to remain applicable. In this case, compensation must be applied first before execution can continue at $S_{cp_i}(s)$. As shown in Figure 4 (c), because the booking of flight and hotel has cost too much money, the agent must obtain the refund before continuing towards the goal.

Based on these different types of coordination, we have designed an innovative failure recovery algorithm to achieve non-stop execution towards the agent's goal. It is embedded in an open nested transaction structure tailored for BDI agents, thus enabling the build of robust and reliable BPM systems with architecture-level support of concurrency control and higher efficiency and throughput to deal with exceptions.

Recovery Mechanism and Algorithm

As shown in Algorithm 1, the overall execution flow of "jump" mainly consists of three parts operating on the data structure of choice point stack. (Table 1)

The choice points (including their sets of choices) encountered during the execution are stored into the stack as one static data structure of the BPM system. The stack is built and updated during the execution in accordance with the traversal along its execution tree structure. As the system traverses down the execution tree, it pushes the choice point it meets into the stack. When there is a failure preventing

Table 1. Algorithm 1. Execution flow of "jump"

Func buildStack() {   **if** *number of eligible plans > 1* **then**   **save plan choices into choice point stack;**   **}**

Func evalAndTry() {
 for *i = n; i > 0; i--* **do**
 	
 foreach *choice point* $S_{cp_i}(j)$ **do**
 if *isApplicable(* $S_{cp_i}(j)$ *)* **then**
 	
 continue at $S_{cp_i}(j)$;
 compensate previous work after cp_i ;
 remove $cp_n, cp_{n-1}, \ldots, cp_{i+1}$ **from stack;**
 break;
 end if
 end foreach
 end for
 }

Func backOneStep() {   **randomly select** $S_{cp_n}(r)$;   **add preconditions of** $S_{cp_n}(r)$ **as new subgoal;**   **}**

Func jump() {
 if *system execution fails* **then**
 if *evalAndTry() fails* **then**
 backOneStep();
 end if
 end if
 }

forward execution, the execution jumps back to a previous choice point. Meanwhile, all choice points coming after the selected one are removed from the stack altogether. Note that the selected choice point becomes the top element of the stack to indicate the current execution flow. These operations guarantee the correctness of the following theorem.

Theorem 1. If a choice point cp_i appears in the stack, all and only its ancestor choice points are present in the stack at the same time.

Proof. Let cp_a be the ancestor choice point of cp_i. Only two possibilities can result in that cp_a is not present in the stack: cp_a has not been visited at all or cp_a has been jumped by. In the first case, cp_i should also not be visited, and in the latter case cp_i should also be jumped by. However, this is conflict to the fact that cp_i is in the stack. Therefore, all ancestor choice points of cp_i are in the stack.

Let cp_j be a choice point in the stack which is not the ancestor of cp_i, then cp_j can only either be a descendant of cp_i, or have no relationship with cp_i at all. In the first case that cp_j is the descendant of cp_i, cp_i can not be the top element of the stack because cp_j should be visited later than cp_i. In the second case, cp_j is not on the path from the root to cp_i. In other words, cp_j can not be visited since it is not reachable in the execution towards cp_i, thus being unable to be in the stack. Therefore, only ancestor choice points of the top element are in the stack.

buildStack() is invoked by the plan selector in Figure 2 to build up the choice point stack for the "jump" process. *evalAndTry()* is the core method which searches through the stack to find a qualified plan to run in case of exception. This method utilizes event-driven feature of BDI agents. During this part, compensation to a failed branch may be carried out in parallel with or after the execution of a new selected branch. *backOneStep()* randomly selects a branch at the last choice point and creates new subgoals to achieve its preconditions if "jump" can not find an appropriate substitutable plan. This step relies on the means-end reasoning ability of BDI agents, and suspends the forward execution of the agent until compensation or other measures are taken. The compensation process generally comes from two methods. One is to compensate back step by step like sagas (Hector & Kenneth, 1987); another is to generate a compensation plan for all the backtracked steps altogether (Eiter, Erdem, & Faber, 2004). With the choice point stack, the method *jump()* can be added into the system deliberation cycle (Figure 2) as a general exception handling mechanism.

For the failed branch, its compensation may be carried out in parallel or after the execution of its alternatives. Thus, the result of the compensation may falsify the validity of the plan chosen in "jump" process.

However, if the compensation does not over-correct, but only partially or completely recover existing side effects, the order of execution will not affect the final result. Non-over-correction is denoted as $comp(r) \leq invl(r)$ where $invl(r)$ represents the amount of involved resource r in normal execution and $comp(r)$ is the reversal of r in the corresponding compensation. For example, if there is a refund for flight booking, the passenger will not pay more fines than the airfare, nor the air company refund more than the airfare.

Theorem 2. The result of compensation to the failed branch ($S_{cp}(f)$) will not affect the validity of the execution of the new selected branch ($S_{cp}(s)$) if the compensation has the feature of non-over-correction.

Proof. If the compensation occurs before any other progress is made, it can not invalidate the latter "jump" process.

For the compensation to occur after "jump", the initial resources r and the minimum requirement $r_{\min}$ for $S_{cp}(f)$ and $S_{cp}(s)$ satisfy $r \geq r_{\min}$. Otherwise, they cannot be saved as choice point options in the stack. If $S_{cp}(f)$ consumes resources $cons(r)$, the selection of $S_{cp}(s)$ means $r - cons(r) \geq r_{\min}$. Thus, the compensation is unable to invalidate the execution of $S_{cp}(s)$ after releasing some resources back. Conversely, if $S_{cp}(f)$ produces resources $prod(r)$, we get $r + prod(r) - comp(r) \geq r \geq r_{\min}$ under the feature of non-over-correction after the compensation. Then the precondition of $S_{cp}(s)$ is still guaranteed.

Relation to Existing Approaches

There are three primary possible strategies for recovery: replanning, which discards previous work; plan patching, which continues the current execution plan after repairing the cause of failure; and backtracking, which tries all alternatives in a depth-first searching manner.

Replanning should be the last resort because it is expensive to deploy. Plan patching is the most preferable approach; however, it is usually not available because of uncontrollability of the environment. Backtracking remains as the most feasible strategy which can be carried out systematically and protects existing work as much as possible. Moreover, it can be mapped to nested transaction structures and fulfilled by compensation.

Our model is essentially a variant of backtracking strategy to support and enable flexible recovery. However, we do not follow the standard backtracking journey of $compensate(nearestCP) - try()$ where $compensate(nearestCP)$ compensates the works done after the nearest choice point, and $try()$ will select a different branch to run. Here, "–" denotes sequential execution while "||" denotes parallel.

Instead, we argue that achieving the goal has higher priority than doing compensation. Thus, we introduce the operation *evalAndTry()*, which evaluates each choice point to find if there is a directly applicable plan. If one is found, it is selected for execution without waiting for the completion of compensation. So, the backtracking in our approach follows the journey of *evalAndTry()* || *compensate()*. If this procedure fails to find an applicable plan from any branch of the choice point stack, the execution pattern is converted to $compensate(nearestCP) \, || \, try()$. The compensation must complete before *try()* if and only if the previous execution has consumed too much resources to allow continuation. Our approach will have higher throughput because compensation and the substitutable plan can execute in parallel, and goal achievement becomes more efficient.

The approach implicitly makes the assumption that certain domain knowledge, such as goal preconditions and action effects, can be modeled with sufficient accuracy for such decisions. If this were not the case in some contexts, compensation can make subsequent actions more robust, since it helps avoid interactions that are not well modeled. Thus doing the compensation first can be adopted as the default handler to make the system more robust.

In fact, we can make some modifications to the last two functions of Algorithm 1 to simulate different backtracking strategies. For example, if *evalAndTry()* is constrained so that it will not return a directly executable plan, our approach becomes very similar to the standard one.

In case no eligible plans are found from the choice point stack, the system will make the replan from the existing situation to continue the execution, as described in the function *backOneStep()*. Compared with merely replanning, our approach uses the previous plan as a guide for further planning; therefore tries to keep finished work as much as possible to be valid.

Our method is more general than the conservative backtracking when plans in different tree branches become more and more independent. The introduction of a transaction manager also frees programmers from considering low-level error-prone details of concurrency control. (Eiter, Erdem, & Faber, 2004) describes a similar method which recovers from execution problems by backtracking to a past nondeterministic choice point, from which the system tries to "repair" the causes of failure and then continues. However, their aim is to generate a reverse plan to compensate back to a previous point and retry from there, which also follows the compensate-then-retry pattern. Their approach can be adopted to generate a compensation plan for the failed execution path.

Transactional Execution

The open nested transaction model will be integrated into the BPM execution platform to provide system level support of automatic recovery and concurrency control. The proposed platform brings the following benefits:

- It guarantees modularity and failure atomicity of plans. Thus, programmers only need to deal with two situations: the plan succeeds completely or fails without side effects. For example, if renting a yacht fails, the system will return back to the choice point of *Entertainment* with the details about the incomplete deal with the yacht company abstracted out.

- It enforces automation of exception handling and execution resumption. For example, after returning back to the choice point of *Entertainment* automatically, the system can retry renting again or choose to visit Disneyland instead.
- The nested structure of transactions also matches the tree structure of plan composition elegantly. It provides inter- and intra-task level support for distribution and concurrency control.

The flexible backtracking recovery strategy introduced in this chapter also helps to avoid the drawbacks of applying open nested transaction directly into BPM systems, such as the requirement of a rigid and static execution structure.

A plan may contain complex internal structure with respect to the goal decomposition, but it is its interfaces, not its implementation details, that are the concerns of the user. The internal execution of the plan is a black box for its caller.

Definition 4. **A plan is an atomic unit of work from the observer's point of view. Before the plan p is performed, it is in the start state** S_0, and after it finishes, it is in the end state S_n, denoted as $S_0 \xrightarrow{\quad p \quad} S_n$.

Figure 5 shows the interface of a plan. Plan p and its state changes are constrained by *enabling conditions (EC)*, *invariants (I)* and *termination conditions (TC)*. p can begin to execute if and only if its enabling conditions are satisfied, that is $S_0 \vDash EC \wedge I$ where $\vDash$ means satisfying. The change from S_0 to S_n is consistent if the invariants of the plan are satisfied. The termination conditions specify the desired outcome, or correctness criteria, of executing p. It is also possible that exogenous events, unanticipated interactions between agents, or non-deterministic action results may cause plan to be aborted when invariants are violated. The possible outcomes of p are:

- *Consistent* if S_n satisfies I, denoted as $I(S_n) \Rightarrow S_n \vDash I$.
- *Inconsistent* if S_n dissatisfies I, denoted as $\neg I(S_n) \Rightarrow S_n \nvDash I$.
- *Correct* if S_n is consistent and satisfies TC, denoted as $TC(S_n) \Rightarrow S_n \vDash TC \wedge I \subseteq TC$.
- *Consistent but not correct* if S_n is consistent but not satisfies TC, denoted as $\neg TC(S_n) \wedge I(S_n) \Rightarrow (S_n \nvDash TC) \wedge (S_n \vDash I) \wedge I \subset TC$.

Two kinds of plan models, an atomic plan and a composite plan, have been discussed above, they map to the same underlying model. Whether a plan is viewed as atomic, or composed of other plans, depends upon the abstraction level at which it is considered. If we need to access a plan's internal organization, we model it as compositional. If we just need to use its functionality as a building block, we model it as an atomic plan.

To avoid conflicts when accessing the shared resources such as bank account or available hotel rooms, traditional lock mechanisms are applied. However, it is a requirement that the lock is obtained only when the resource is visited and released as soon as possible after the visit. Otherwise, it is likely to cause the problem of long-running transactions which result in low efficiency and even deadlock. As long as the system is consistent, cascading rollback is avoided.

Figure 5. Interface of a plan

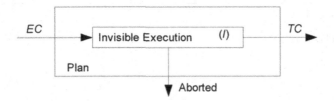

IMPLEMENTATION AND EXPERIMENTS

We have built a prototype of reactive workflow using 3APL-M (Koch, 2005) and JBoss Transaction Service (formerly Arjuna Transaction Service) (JBoss Inc., 2006) to simulate the travel arrangement example.

3APL-M is a lightweight version of 3APL (Dastani et al., 2003) and distributed under the GNU GPL. Its source code remains much simpler by leaving out supplementary components of 3APL, such as integrated development environment. It behaves as a programming library whose API allows a Java application to call 3APL logic and deliberation structures, and vice-versa. Because it is fully integrated with the Java platform and programming environments, 3APL-M is a good prototyping tool for cognitive agents. Further, programs written in 3APL-M can be easily migrated into 3APL because they share similar underlying language concepts and programming constructs.

JBoss Transaction Service is employed as the transactional execution manager, which guarantees the isolation of parallel plans. Its TxCore transaction engine supports both closed and open nested transaction and presents programmers with a toolkit of Java classes which can be invoked by 3APL-M agents directly to obtain desired properties, such as persistence and concurrency control.

As shown in Figure 3, a root goal of the system is decomposed into subgoals recursively, resulting in a tree structure. Each subgoal is achieved through a transaction-like function as shown in Algorithm 2. They are then organized in an open nested transaction structure. Whenever an exception occurs, the execution of that transaction is taken over by the function *jump*() shown in Algorithm 1. *jump*() will fork two threads: one is used to continue the execution at an earlier choice point, and the other is used to compensate the failed plan. (Table 2)

Because the rollback operation of traditional database transactions is usually not applicable in dynamic and open environments, it is not invoked in the prototype. Instead, if *jump*() succeeds, the failed task is allowed to commit, and its side-effects will be undone by its counterpart compensating transaction.

The "jump" algorithm is opportunistic, as it makes the assumption that the failure of one path of execution tree will not block others. In the worst case, where a failure state always holds resources required by other actions, the cost of maintaining and iterating the choice point stack increases. However, as different execution paths increase in independence from each other, the performance is improved.

FUTURE TRENDS

The shared theme of transactions, workflows, and multi-agents is to ensure the system correctness by executing concurrent tasks cooperatively towards their goals during normal execution, and to guarantee

Table 2. Algorithm 2. Pseudo-code for the travel agent

```
Func transactionFlightBooking() {
beginTrans();
sequence of actions for flight booking;
ifaction failsthen
system.jump();
commitTrans();
}
```

```
Func transactionHotelBooking() {
beginTrans();
sequence of actions for hotel booking;
ifaction failsthen
system.jump();
commitTrans();
}
```

```
......
```

```
Func TravelSystem.run() {
beginTrans();
switchsystem.select(Destination)do
caseCalifornia
transactionFlightBooking();
transactionHotelBooking();
break;
... ...
end switch
switchsystem.select(Entertainment)do
caseSailing
transactionYachtRenting();
break;
caseDisneyland
transactionTicketBuying();
break;
end switch
commitTrans();
}
```

the system reliability by repairing affected participating tasks coordinately to reach a semantically correct state when exceptions occur. As shown in Figure 6, a workflow system evolves into a multi-agent system when its operating environment becomes more and more complex and dynamic, and condenses into a database transaction when it obtains full control to the running environment.

As these three domains are closely related, more work is required to explore and identify the correlation among them. In fact, the boundary and criteria to classify real applications into one of the three types of systems are not clear.

To build a robust and reliable BPM system working in complex and dynamic environment, we have to assimilate the key concepts from transactions for structured concurrency and recovery management, and from multi-agents for adaptability and reactivity.

Due to the growing complexity and unpredictability, transactions as well as their extensions can not be straightforwardly adopted as a satisfactory solution for systems operating in dynamic and open environment. However, they still provide some invaluable concepts and features (e.g., failure atomicity, concurrency control, nested structure, compensation, and forward recovery) which can be used as components of the BPM system, especially for the problem of error handling and recovery. We can integrate these essential concepts into the sound features, such as autonomy and reactivity, brought by

Figure 6. Relations among transactions, workflows, and multi-agent systems

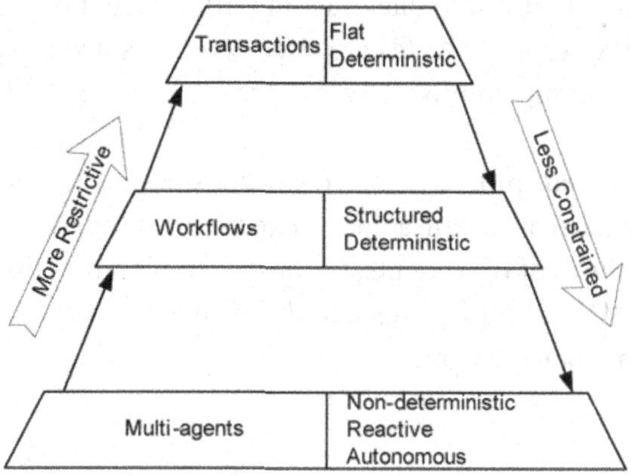

agent systems, thus designing a flexible and well-organized BPM recovery structure from a programming and software engineering perspective.

This chapter proposes an innovative backtracking mechanism utilizing the concept and features of BDI agent, and integrating open nested transactions to support its execution. A more general expression of our algorithm can be formalized to incorporate the full range of exception handling strategies between the two extreme ends of replanning and rigid step-by-step backtracking.

Our work does not go deep into the issue of distributed computation which is also essential for building BPM systems operating in complex and open environments. As agents are naturally distributed entities, multi-agent concepts can be further applied to benefit BPM systems to cope with a wide range of internal and external interactions and changes. As a result, our multiple-step backtracking mechanism needs to be further extended to embrace the distributed execution of BPM tasks. This is our future work.

CONCLUSION

This chapter has described a multiple-step backtracking mechanism to maintaining a tradeoff between replanning and rigid backtracking for exception handling and recovery, thus not suffering from the drawbacks of rigid backtracking. Our model encapsulated the business process execution in an open nested transaction to inherit the benefits of concurrency control and distribution management of participating plans.

Our approach mainly contained three parts. We first applied BDI agent model to design and construct BPM systems to operate in complex and dynamic environments with the advantages of adaptability and flexibility. Then we introduced the "jump" approach for exception handling and recovery which utilizes the beneficial features of event-driven and means-end reasoning of BDI agents. Finally, we used open nested transaction model to encapsulate plan execution and backtracking to gain the system level support of concurrency control and automatic recovery.

The nested tree structure was applied to depict the BPM system execution. During the construction of the tree structure along with the system execution, the choice points were stored and maintained in a stack. By iterating the stack, the system can find and execute a suitable plan from previously applicable ones to achieve its goal as soon as an exception occurs. This "jump" procedure struck a balance between complete replanning and rigid step-by-step backtracking after exceptions occur, by utilizing previous planning results in determining response to failure. Because the substitutable path is allowed to start prior to or in parallel with the compensation process, the system can achieve its goals more directly with higher efficiency.

Our approach also frees system programmers from considering low-level details of concurrency control and exception handling, because transactional execution automates these issues. Combining and utilizing several beneficial features of BDI agents, the open nested transaction model is tightly integrated into the BPM system. Both BDI data structures and the deliberation cycle are leveraged to maximize the functionality of transaction management.

REFERENCES

d'Inverno, M., Luck, M., Georgeff, M. P., Kinny, D., & Wooldridge, M. (2004). The dMARS architecture: A specification of the distributed multi-agent reasoning system. *Journal of Autonomous Agents and Multi-Agent Systems, 9*(1-2), 5–53. doi:10.1023/B:AGNT.0000019688.11109.19

Dastani, M., Riemsdijk, B. v., Dignum, F., & Meyer, J.-J. C. (2003). A programming language for cognitive agents goal directed 3APL. In *Programming Multi-Agent Systems* (pp. 111-130). Springer Verlag.

Ehrler, L., Fleurke, M. K., Purvis, M., & Savarimuthu, B. T. R. (2006). Agent-based workflow management systems (WfMSs). *Information Systems and E-Business Management, 4*(1), 5–23. doi:10.1007/s10257-005-0010-9

Eiter, T., Erdem, E., & Faber, W. (2004). Plan reversals for recovery in execution monitoring. In *10th International Workshop on Non-Monotonic Reasoning* (pp. 147-154).

Georgakopoulos, D., Hornick, M. F., & Manola, F. (1996). Customizing transaction models and mechanisms in a programmable environment supporting reliable workflow automation. *IEEE Transactions on Knowledge and Data Engineering, 8*(4), 630–649. doi:10.1109/69.536255

Gray, J., & Reuter, A. (1993). *Transaction processing: Concepts and techniques*. San Francisco: Morgan Kaufmann.

Hector, G.-M., & Kenneth, S. (1987). Sagas. *SIGMOD Record, 16*(3), 249–259. doi:10.1145/38714.38742

JBoss Inc. (2006). JBoss transactions 4.2.2 transaction core programmers guide. Retrieved May 7, 2008, from JBoss Inc.: http://labs.jboss.com/jbosstm/docs/4.2.2/manuals/pdf/core/ProgrammersGuide.pdf

Jennings, N. R. (2001). An agent-based approach for building complex software systems. *Communications of the ACM, 44*(4), 35–41. doi:10.1145/367211.367250

Kamathy, M., & Ramamritham, K. (1996). Correctness issues in workflow management. *Distributed Systems Engineering, 3*, 213–221. doi:10.1088/0967-1846/3/4/002

Klein, M., Rodriguez-Aguilar, J. A., & Dellarocas, C. (2003). Using domain-independent exception handling services to enable robust open multi-agent systems: The case of agent death. *Autonomous Agents and Multi-Agent Systems, 7*(1-2), 179–189. doi:10.1023/A:1024145408578

Koch, F. (2005). 3APL-M: Platform for lightweight deliberative agents. Retrieved 7 May, 2008, from http://www.cs.uu.nl/3apl-m/docs/3aplm-manual.pdf

Nagi, K. (2001). *Transactional agents: Towards a robust multi-agent system.* Berlin, Heidelberg: Springer-Verlag.

Ramamohanarao, K., Bailey, J., & Busetta, P. (2001). Transaction oriented computational models for multi-agent systems. In *Proceedings of 13th IEEE International Conference on Tools with Artificial Intelligence (ICTAI)* (pp. 11-17). IEEE Computer Society, Washington, DC, USA.

Rao, A. S., & Georgeff, M. P. (1995, June 12-14, 1995). BDI agents: From theory to practice. In *Proceedings of the First International Conference on Multiagent Systems* (pp. 312-319), San Francisco, California, USA.

Souchon, F., Dony, C., Urtado, C., & Vauttier, S. (2004). Improving exception handling in multi-agent systems. In *Software Engineering for Multi-Agent Systems II* (*Lecture Notes in Computer Science Vol. 2940*) (pp. 167-188). Springer Verlag.

Tripathi, A., & Miller, R. (2001). Exception handling in agent-oriented systems. In *Advances in exception handling techniques* (LNCS 2022, pp. 128-146).

Unruh, A., Bailey, J., & Ramamohanarao, K. (2004). Managing semantic compensation in a multi-agent system. In *International Conference on Cooperative Information Systems* (LNCS 3290).

Weikum, G., & Schek, H.-J. (1992). Concepts and applications of multilevel transactions and open nested transactions. In *Database transaction models for advanced applications* (pp. 515-553). San Francisco: Morgan Kaufmann Publishers, Inc.

Woolridge, M. (2001). *Introduction to multiagent systems.* John Wiley & Sons, Inc.

KEY TERMS AND DEFINITIONS

BDI agent: A software entity embedded in certain environment and behaves reactively to the changing situation in order to meet its design objectives. It has four key data structures: beliefs, desires, intentions and plans.

Choice Point: For a certain goal of the system, if plan matcher finds more than one eligible plan, the corresponding node in the execution tree is marked as a choice point.

Choice Point Stack: A choice point stack contains the choice points the system has met chronologically.

Consistent: The plan execution is consistent if it terminates at state S_n in which *invariants* are satisfied.

Correct: The plan execution is correct if it terminates at state S_n in which both *invariants* and *termination conditions* are satisfied.

Jump: A jump is a continuation of the system execution flow at another selectable plan implied by elements of its choice point stack.

Non-Over-Correction: The compensation process only partially or completely recovers the side effects made by the normal execution. Let $invl(r)$ represent the amount of involved resource r in normal execution and $comp(r)$ is the reversal of r in the corresponding compensation, then $comp(r) \leq invl(r)$.

Plan: A plan is an atomic unit of work from the observer's point of view. It is constrained by *enabling conditions* (*EC*), *invariants* (*I*) and *termination conditions* (*TC*).

Section 3
Collaborative Business Process Management

Chapter 11
Adaptive Development and Management of Business Collaborations

Bart Orriens
Tilburg University, The Netherlands

Jian Yang
Macquarie University, Australia

ABSTRACT

The IT infrastructure of organizations must be agile and dynamic in order to respond quickly to the new business models and requirements. This has led to an increasing demand from individual organizations for corporate business services that can easily adapt to changes through business collaboration. Popular solutions for business collaboration development and management do not properly cater for the specification of new collaborations nor do they facilitate the management of existing ones. In this book chapter we present a rule based approach for collaboration development and management. The proposed approach allows organizations to capture the requirements for their business collaborations in an explicit, manageable and uniform manner in the form of rules. These rules can then be used to drive and constrain the development and management of needed business collaboration models. Practical feasibility of the approach is demonstrated in the context of a complex insurance claim scenario using prototype tooling.

INTRODUCTION

Today's business climate demands a high rate of change with which Information Technology (IT)-minded organizations are required to cope. Organizations are facing rapidly changing market conditions, new competitive pressures, new regulatory fiats that demand compliance, and new competitive threats. All of these situations drive the need for the IT infrastructure of an organization to respond quickly in support of new business models and requirements. Organizations must therefore be agile and dynamic, for only in this way can they gear towards the world of fast occurring, hopefully automated, and complex

DOI: 10.4018/978-1-60566-669-3.ch011

electronic transactions. This has led to an increasing demand from individual organizations for corporate business services that can easily adapt to changes.

Unfortunately, current business collaboration solutions are too narrowly focused and are not capable of addressing the requirements of adaptive business collaboration development and management. Firstly, there is a lack of a coherent and cohesive vision on business collaboration development. Consequently there is no solution that is capable of designing collaborations where all different types of requirements (and dependencies between them) can be specified. Secondly, as a result these solutions for business collaboration design are unlikely to succeed as they can only offer limited support for adaptive development and management. As such, it is a costly and time-consuming effort to determine whether the developed business collaborations are compliant with the requirements as well as consistent with individual business processes. This is particularly the case when the impact of changes on the compliance and overall consistency of existing business collaborations need to be assessed.

In this book chapter we argue that the adaptive development and management of business collaborations can be achieved using a rule based approach. The idea behind the proposed approach is to make the business collaboration requirements of organizations explicit in the form of rules, and then use these rules to drive and constrain the development and management of business collaboration designs. As a result, design becomes a runtime activity where the business collaboration shapes itself to its specific circumstances by applying the appropriate rules. As such, business collaborations can be generated dynamically rather than statically pre-defined. This makes business collaboration adaptive in two ways: a) design of business collaborations is governed by explicitly defined and thus manageable rules, which can be further chained and used for making complex decisions and diagnoses; and b) business collaborations can be readily changed during design time and runtime by adding new rules and/or re-defining existing rules. Simultaneously, rules can also be applied to ensure that the generated business collaborations are and remain consistent.

Specifically, the chapter addresses the following questions: 1) what is the context in which business collaborations take place? 2) how can we represent the context of business collaborations in terms of formal models; 3) how do we make the development and management of business collaboration models adaptive; and 4) how can we ensure that business collaborations models are and remain conform to the requirements as well as consistent among themselves? In order to provide answers to these questions the chapter is structured as displayed in Figure 1.

As indicated in the road-map the chapter consists of eight sections. In the first part of the chapter the emphasis is on acquiring a clear picture with regard to the means that organisations currently lack for cohesive and agile business collaboration. This is twofold in nature: following the end of this introduction we start by investigating the exact requirements for business collaboration development and management. Subsequently, we survey the existing work in this area and contrast it with the identified requirements. On the one hand this will give us insight into what has already been done and how this positively contributes to facilitating business collaboration development and management. On the other hand it will allow us to identify the shortcomings of existing business collaboration solutions with regard to compliance, agility and consistency.

After these two sections the focus of the chapter shifts towards the rule based approach we developed to tackle the identified shortcomings. We start by discussing the Business Collaboration Context Framework (BCCF), which defines a comprehensive view on the context in which business collaboration takes place. On top of the BCCF we then introduce a model based approach with which organisations can capture their business collaboration context. A set of business collaborations models are generated

Figure 1. Chapter Road Map

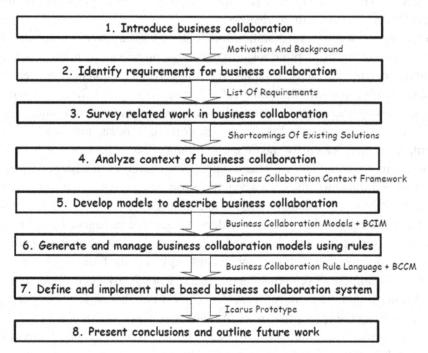

expressed in terms of a generic Business Collaboration Information Model (BCIM). Subsequently, we explain how organisations can express their requirements for business collaboration as rules using a Business Collaboration Rule Language (BCRL), and then use these rules to drive and constrain the development and management of the different business collaboration models by employing a Business Collaboration Conformance Mechanism (BCCM).

We illustrate with examples from a complex insurance claim handling case study described in (Grefen, Aberer, Hoffner, & Ludwig, 2000) that the design of models can be governed by explicitly defined and thus manageable rules. We also show that the models can be readily changed during design time and runtime by adding new rules and/or redefining existing rules. Moreover, we demonstrate that rules can be applied to ensure that generated models are and remain consistent. Lastly, we present a computer aided software engineering (CASE) tool set for modeling, analyzing, and managing rule based business collaborations with which we showcase the practical feasibility of the rule based approach. Finally, we draw conclusions and outline interesting future research directions.

REQUIREMENTS

In order to deliver the adaptive business services demanded by today's agile and dynamic business climate, organizations are increasingly focusing on utilizing existing services cross organizational boundaries. Such business collaboration is about cooperation between organizations by linking their business processes and exchanging messages between heterogeneous IT systems to achieve business related goal(s). Building and managing collaborations that cross independent organizational boundaries and their systems is challenging as it requires linking the elements of individual business together into a cohesive and consistent whole. Moreover, it must be carried out in compliance with organizational policies, relevant legislation, industry guidelines, technical capabilities and limitations.

Therefore organizations must be able to model their requirements for: 1) its internal business process (describing its private activities); 2) its public abstract process (describing how it can be interacted with); and 3) its partner's abstract process (describing what it expects from its partner). These requirements can be diverse in nature ranging from sequencing of activities, allocation of resources, defining security objectives, stipulating supported quality metrics, etc. Based on the resulting models the organizations must then have the means to establish possible collaboration strategies with others, and if necessary to negotiate a business collaboration agreement. This type of negotiation requires that the compliance to requirements and the consistency of private, public and agreed upon behavior is verifiable.

At the same time there is a strong interest from organizations in utilizing existing IT services in a configurable manner in order to deliver adaptive business services to their partners. Such configuration is about the proper usage of the services provided by the IT infrastructure in order to realize higher level-business services. Taking the example of a business service for ordering goods, it involves engaging IT services for checking pricing data, sending electronic order messages, automated billing, shipping, etc. This is challenging as well as necessary that the elements of business and IT can be intricately yet adaptively woven together in order to ensure that processes and their underlying message exchanges are properly aligned.

To this end, organizations must be able to specify different requirements applicable to their processes, abstract protocols and agreements: 1) the business requirements for delivering their business services; and 2) the technical capabilities of the available services provided by the IT infrastructure. On the basis of the resulting models organizations must then be able to quickly establish the possibility of engaging particular IT services for the realization of (part of) a business service followed by the development of business services and processes. Such development necessitates that the resulting business services are verifiable in terms of compliance to the business and IT requirements as well as the consistency of these different requirements.

Finally, the sketched development requires that organizations can foresee how future changes to their processes, protocols and agreements influence their ability to cooperate with others; and moreover how these can be managed in relation to existing collaborations. It also implies that organizations can assess how such changes impact the ability to deliver business services through the engagement of lower level IT services. In addition, enterprises need to be able to determine how changes may affect existing business and IT services, what need to be managed, i.e., properly defined, verified and versioned, and consistent results need to be delivered when executed. In summary, the challenge of managing agile collaborative business is to maintain both compliance and consistency for each partner in the collaboration as well as for the collaboration as a whole in the light of change.

RELATED WORK

Unfortunately, current business collaboration solutions are too narrowly focused and not capable of addressing the requirements of adaptive business collaboration development and management. As such, it is a costly and time-consuming affair to determine whether developed business collaborations are compliant with requirements as well as consistent. This is particularly the case when the impact of changes on the compliance and overall consistency of existing business collaborations must be assessed. When we look into the available technologies for business collaboration development, most works only facilitate partial specification of business collaboration requirements. Popular solutions like ebXML (ebXML Initiative, 2006, 2002), BPML and BPMN (Business Process Modeling Initiative, 2002) and workflow (Aalst, 1998; Aalst, Hofstede, & Weske, 2003; Georgakopoulos, Hornick, & Sheth, 1995; Workflow Management Coalition, 1995) focus on the definition of functional business requirements, whereas others such as BPEL4WS (Curbera et al., 2002), WSCI (Arkin et al., 2002), WSDL (Christensen, Curbera, Meredith, & Weerawarana, 2001) and WS-Choreography (Banerji et al., 2004) deal exclusively with technical requirements.

As such, these solutions are not capable of addressing both high level, business oriented demands and low level, technically related collaboration requirements. Moreover, they do not provide a way of linking these two types of requirement, which is crucial for organizations to ensure that business activities are supported by their IT-infrastructure. In addition, it is often unclear how extra-functional requirements are to be incorporated (or support thereof is very limited). High level notations such as UML based notations in (Booch, Rumbaugh, & Jacobson, 1998) are often used. However, this is typically done in an ad hoc manner and the resulting models lack formal semantics.

There are a number of research works that span both business and technical business collaboration requirements, for example the work in (Bresciani, Giorgini, Giunchiglia, Mylopoulos, & Perini, 2004). Others focus on relating business and IT such as done in (Casati, Shan, Dayal, & Shan, 2003) and (Zeng et al., 2003). The problem with these proposals lies in the fact that they do not take all requirements into consideration, and are unable to support high level, abstract requirement definition, and/or do not provide clear cut separation between business and technical requirements. Moreover, many approaches fail to provide uniform techniques for capturing private processes, public protocols and agreements, nor do they provide the means to capture dependencies among them. Exceptions are (Dijkman & Dumas, 2004) and (Traverso et al., 2004), however, these works concentrate on technical and business requirements respectively. No solution is provided for enforcing conformance and consistency verification.

More formally oriented proposals include languages based on simple finite-automata, Petri Nets (Aalst, 1998; Verbeek & Aalst, 2000), process algebras (Bergstra, Ponse, & Smolka, 2001) like (Hoare, 1985), (Bergstra & Klop, 1985) and (Milner, 1990). These proposals view both private processes and public collaborations as labelled transition systems, which are sets of states that is an abstraction of all the possible states of a concurrent system (Basten, 1998). Two other pursued avenues are logics such as found in (Rao, Kungas, & Matskin, 2006) and constraint satisfaction in (Aiello et al., 2002). Although we do not argue against the need for formal underpinnings of business collaboration design, such techniques also currently do not capture all the collaboration requirements. As such, it remains unclear whether and how their application might be achieved in context of business collaboration development.

When it comes to the management of service compositions and business collaborations in general, most work has focused on development without taking their management into too much consideration. Current solutions such as BPEL4WS (Curbera et al., 2002) and those specified by ebXML (ebXML Initiative, 2006, 2002) are pre-determined and pre-specified, have narrow applicability and are almost impossible to reuse and manage. The same applies to works from academia in the field of workflow in (Aalst et al., 2003; Bowers, Button, & Sharrock, 1995; Workflow Management Coalition, 1995), system development in (Bresciani et al., 2004; Traverso et al., 2004) and enterprise modelling in (Zachman, 1987). There have been numerous attempts though at making business collaboration development and management more adaptive.

Most approaches have turned to the use of rule based development and management in which the definition and modification of designs is guided by rules. In the area of workflow the works of for example (Deiters, Goesmann, & L˝offeler, 2000), (Reichert & Dadam, 1997) and (Reichert & Dadam, 1998), (Liu & Pu, 1997), (Joeris & Herzog, 1999), (Christophides, Hull, Kumar, & Simeon, 2000) and (Han, Sheth, & Bussler, 1998) proposed to built flexibility points into the workflow at which decisions can be made as to how to proceed. However, these approaches offer very limited adaptability by pre-definition of allowed changes at design time. Furthermore they only allow the flow of execution to be modified. (Casati, Ilnicki, Jin, Krishnamoorthy, & Shan, 2000) and (Zeng et al., 2003) are similar exponents of rule based design, though targeting for service-oriented computing based business collaboration development.

Further argument against the above approaches stems from the fact that they are not capable of capturing all business collaboration requirements. As such, they can only provide limited adaptability. (Zeng et al., 2003) for example doesn't clearly separate between business and technical requirements, and consequently no distinction is made between business and technical rules. Moreover, the issue of alignment of these two sets of requirements is not addressed. Another issue left to be addressed is how the semantics of rules differ depending on whether they are governing requirements for private or public behavior. (Bajaj et al., 2006) and (Andrieux, Czajkowski, & Dan, 2004) specify how to develop policies for web services, and agreements among services, but the focus is on technical requirements only. Furthermore, how consistency is maintained between policies and agreements is still unclear.

In conclusion we have found that current business collaboration solutions are simply not capable of facilitating dynamic business collaboration development and management. Firstly, there is a lack of a coherent and cohesive vision on business collaboration development. Consequently there is no solution that is capable of design of collaborations where all different types of requirements (and dependencies between them) can be specified. Secondly, due to this fact proposals for business collaboration design are unlikely to succeed as they can only offer limited support for compliant, consistent and adaptive collaboration development and management.

CONTEXT OF BUSINESS COLLABORATION

To remedy the lack of a clear and comprehensive view on business collaboration, we developed the *Business Collaboration Context Framework (BCCF)*. This framework captures the context of business collaborations in a structured manner by defining a modularized representation of the business collaboration context supporting the principal of separation of concern. As a result the complexity of business collaboration development and management is reduced by breaking up collaborations in more manageable chunks. To be concrete, the BCCF modularizes the business collaboration context by adopting a three dimensional view, being *aspect, level* and *part*. This modularization is shown in Figure 2.

Two organisations are displayed within a business collaboration context. As can be seen such context constitutes of three layers (depicted by the three colored rectangles), which going from top to down represent *strategic level, operational level* and *service level* respectively. At each layer three aspects are established, being *internal business process aspect, participant public behavior aspect* and *conversation aspect* (denoted by the rounded squared, octagon and hectagon shapes respectively). Each aspect consists of five parts: *material part, functional part, participation part, location part* and *temporal part,* which are represented as different shapes within each individual aspect. In order to visualize the dependencies

Figure 2. Business Collaboration Context Framework (BCCF)

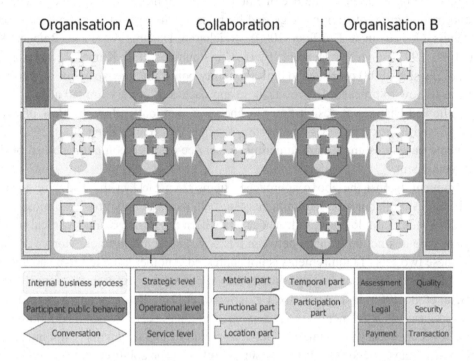

that exist between the different aspects, levels and parts their shapes are connected through vertical and horizontal block arrows. Finally, pervasive through these dimensions are requirements concerning (among others) *assessment* and *monitoring, legal issues, payment, quality, security* and *transactionality.*

In the following sections we will discuss the BCCF in more detail. For illustrative purposes we refer to the AGFIL case study. This case study describes a complex multi-party scenario, which outlines the way in which a car damage claim is handled by an insurance company (AGFIL). AGFIL cooperates with several contract parties to provide a service that enables efficient claim settlement. The parties involved are Europ Assist, Lee Consulting Services (Lee C.S), Garages and Assessors. Europ Assist offers a 24-hour emergency call answering service to policyholders. Lee C.S coordinates and manages the operation of the emergency service on a daily basis on behalf of AGFIL. Garages are responsible for car repair. Assessors conduct the physical inspections of damaged vehicles and agree repair upon figures with the garages.

Aspects of Business Collaborations

The first dimension, aspect, places emphasis on the different business collaboration behaviors that an organization exhibits in business collaboration. The aspect dimension encompasses three types of behavior captured in three corresponding aspects (inspired (Dijkman & Dumas, 2004), (Peltz, 2003) and (Traverso et al., 2004)): observable, exposed and internal behavior expressed in the conversation aspect, participant public behavior aspect and internal business process aspect respectively. The conversation aspect captures the externally visible behavior between organizations in a business collaboration. This observable behavior specifies from a global, organization independent point of view how the different parties in the AGFIL case study, such as Lee C.S, Garage Inc and AGFIL, are expected to behave to achieve efficient claim handling.

Rather than being global in nature, the participant public behavior aspect describes how an organization can publicly behave in a business collaboration and how it expects its partners to behave. As such, it is found at the edge of organizations forming the border with the outside (and therefore placed on the vertical dotted lines in Figure 2 to reflect this). For example, AGFIL is capable of interacting with Europ Assist to exchange claim information, and with Lee C.S to out-source part of the claim management to them. The internal business process aspect is also individual to each organization. However, it is only of interest to this particular party. Garage Inc for example internally will perform a series of private activities between receiving a car and reporting repair costs to Lee C.S.

Lastly, the conversation, participant public behavior and internal business process aspect are not independent from one another. Business processes support the different public behaviors an organization is exposing to other parties. For example, Garage Inc may have offer different conditions for handling a damaged car depending on customer status while in its private process the same activities are performed. A natural constraint in this regard is that the offered conditions should be internally supported by the corresponding business process. In turn, the conditions agreed upon by an organization should be supported by those described in its participant public behavior aspect. To illustrate, if Lee C.S expects Garage Inc to perform an activity supply repair information, based on the assumption that Garage Inc has the capacity to do so.

Levels of Business Collaborations

The second dimension, level, recognizes the fact that business collaboration involves linking both the processes and systems of organisations. As such, their different business collaboration behaviors comprise both a business and technical component. For this reason we adopt three layers of abstraction (inspired by work in (Object Modeling Group, 2003), (Bresciani et al., 2004) and (Zachman, 1987)). Firstly, the *strategic* level enables organisations to discuss and reason about the purpose and high level objectives of their business. Depending on the aspect that is considered, it is interested in capturing how they use and produce resources to further support their private strategies, the resources it wishes to acquire and/ or supply via cooperation with others, and the resource exchanges to which it has committed itself in actual collaborations. An example is AGFIL's commitment to share the resource claim management information with Lee C.S in order to help realize its objective of facilitate efficient claim handling.

Secondly, the *operational* level allows organisations to consider and examine how their day-to-day business activities help achieve the objectives set up at the strategic level. Internally the operational level concerns the routine in which private processes are conducted. The behavior exposed to others at this level captures an organization's potential to communicate with others, while the agreed upon communication between organizations is covered by the conversation aspect. For example, Lee C.S performs several concrete activities as it is managing a claim (like contacting the garage, selecting an assessor, and making a final report for AGFIL). Thirdly, the *service* level empowers organisations to capture and investigate how their IT infrastructure provides support for the operational activities in their private, exposed and agreed upon behavior. To illustrate, Lee C.S will offer a claim management service to AGFIL defining what electronic messages it can exchange and expect AGFIL to exchange.

Finally, dependencies exist among the business collaboration behaviors of organisations at different levels. Organisations accomplish their strategic goals through their business processes, which in turn are supported by the services provided by the underlying IT systems. For example, Lee C.S can operationalize its high level private activity of managing a claim by contacting an assessor to get an external damage estimate in case a garage's estimate is above a certain threshold. Alternatively, if the estimate is below a set level, then Lee C.S may immediately approve initiation of the repair. Similarly, an operational behavior can also be realized in different service behaviors. Garage Inc may e.g. use a function **send estimate** provided by its car repair service to realize its operational activity **report estimate** to notify Lee C.S of the repair estimate height.

Parts of Business Collaborations

The third dimension, part, reflects the fact that the different business collaboration behaviors conducted by organizations at the different levels cover many different considerations. Parts represent these different considerations by depicting the elements in a business collaboration behavior that have different contexts when observed from different levels. Five parts are distinguished (following work in (Curtis, Kellner, & Over, 1992), (Jonkers, Lankhorst, Buuren, Hoppenbrouwers, & Bonsangue, 2003), (Nguyen & Vernadat, 1994), (Scheer, 1992), (Vernadat, 1992) and (Zachman, 1987)): *material, functional, participation, location* and *temporal part*. These parts emphasise the structural, functional, participation, location and time-related characteristics of business collaboration behaviours respectively, where their exact semantics are dependent on the specific aspect and level that they describe.

To illustrate, the functional part in the observable behavior at strategic level captures the high level functionalities offered by parties like AGFIL and Lee C.S in business collaborations. Another example is the material part in the participant public behavior of Garage Inc at operational level, which captures the information that it can and wishes to exchange with other parties. Furthermore, the temporal part at service level in the internal behavior of Lee C.S comprises the technical occurrences that signal the progress of its business process in terms of the usage of the services of its IT infrastructure.

Like aspects and levels, individual parts interact with other parts where each part is related to every other part. The semantics of these interactions are specific to the individual level at which they take place. For example, at operational level the functional part is connected to the participation part expressing who is responsible for carrying out a task. For example, when a claim comes in at Lee C.S, and an assessor is required then the one most nearest to the garage of the customer will be contacted. This places restrictions on the relation between the how and who part. Another example is that the time frame to which Garage Inc is to adhere to concerning provision of the car repair cost estimate, can mean that some extra checks that the garage would normally perform are not carried out due to the limited time available.

Advanced Requirements

In addition to the dimensions identified thus far there exist several issues for business collaborations that are orthogonal to the BCCF levels, aspects and parts. Figure 2 portrays six potential issues encompassing assessment and monitoring, legislation, payment, quality, security and transactionality. Requirements related to these matters have different meaning depending on the specific level, aspect or part. For example, Garage Inc's security requirements at strategic level constitute security objectives that it has with regard to its business collaboration. In contrast, at operational level such requirements express which security mechanisms it employs to realize these objectives. Similarly, whereas quality requirements in the participant public behavior of Lee C.S constitute promises concerning quality, in the conversation aspect they represent agreed upon quality conditions.

Concretely, in relation to the BCCF we view these extra-functional, pervasive requirements as extending the different parts of business collaboration behaviors. To illustrate, a security requirement in material part at strategic level can convey that a resource must be sent in such a manner that it will not be disclosed to others. Similarly, a quality requirement in functional part at service level can express that a service operation must give a response to service requesters within a specific period of time. To further illustrate, a payment requirement in functional part at operational level can convey that an activity requires payment using electronic means. The advantage of this mechanism is that it ensures that the BCCF can easily be extended to include other pervasive business collaboration requirements besides the ones currently included.

Like aspects and levels, dependencies exist among pervasive requirements found in the different business collaboration behaviors at the different levels. For example, if Garage Inc decides to give up its objective of protecting car repair estimates against eavesdropping and unauthorized modification, then at operational level the conditions under which documents are communicated will change since there is no longer a need there to employ security mechanisms to encrypt these documents. Consequently Garage Inc may utilize its IT-infrastructure differently, as the used services are no longer required to possess the ability to use an encryption protocol like RSA or RC4 to ensure the confidentiality of exchanged electronic messages (carrying the documents as their payload).

MODELING BUSINESS COLLABORATIONS

The presented BCCF in the previous section provides us with a three dimensional view of the business collaboration context, modularizing collaboration development and management along the dimensions of aspects, levels and parts. It also gives us insight into the interdependencies that exist among these aspects, levels and parts. Moreover, the BCCF identifies several types of requirement pervasive throughout the dimensions, such as quality and security. In order to actually develop and manage business collaborations enterprises require a way to explicitly capture this context. We advocate a model based approach which is based on a generic *business collaboration information model* (BCIM), which is used to capture the parts at different levels and different aspects for each individual business collaboration based on the BCCF framwork. As a result, several *models* and *mappings* (expressing dependencies between models) can be generated based on the level and the aspect they represent. Figure 3 provides an overview of the different models and the relations between them.

As can be seen from the figure three sections were presented to represent the private, exposed and observable behaviors of organization A and B respectively (in line with the aspect dimension in the BCCF). The rounded rectangles represent the internal behaviors of party A and B at strategic, operational and service level respectively (following the level dimension in the BCCF), and are referred to as *processes*. The octagons capture the exposed behaviors of A and B referred to as *protocols*, whereas the hexagons express the observable behavior between both parties referred to as *agreements*. Vertically directed curved arrows represent v*ertical mappings* expressing dependencies between strategic, operational and service processes, protocols and agreements, whereas horizontally directed curved arrows define *horizontal mappings* to capture relations between private processes, protocols and agreements. Note that for reasons of clarity the modularization into parts of the different models has been omitted

Figure 3. Modeling The BCCF

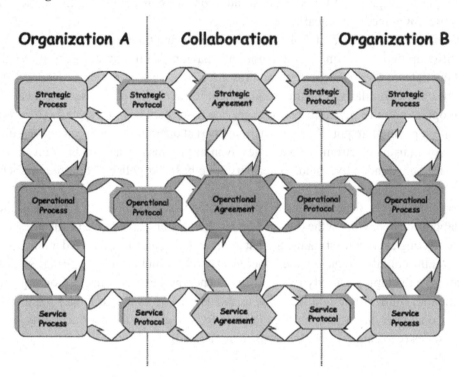

from the figure. In the remainder of this section we first introduce these collaboration models and mappings. After that we explain how they are defined using the generic BCIM.

Business Collaboration Models

Models provide design guidelines in terms of elements and their relationships to capture the different aspects at a particular level. Every model consists of five elements, where each element captures a particular part, i.e. for *material, functional, location, participation*, and *temporal* facet. Each element constitutes a set of logically related *properties*. Links connect the elements expressing dependencies among parts; whereas *attributions* capture relations among elements at different levels and aspects. In accordance with BCCF we have defined models for the strategic, operational and service level. Snippets of exemplary models for the AGFIL application describing an interaction between Garage Inc and Lee C.S are illustrated in Figure 4, showing the strategic, operational and service representation of this interaction respectively.

The models in Figure 4 are loosely based on UML conventions. That is, in order to distinguish between elements expressing different parts, we represent them in different shapes in their models: *material* part is shown as folded corners, *functional* part as rounded rectangles, *participation* part as octagons, *location* part as plaques, and *temporal* part as ellipses.

At strategic level, strategic models like the AGFIL-STM in Figure 4 capture purpose and high level requirements of business collaborations, akin to requirements analysis in e.g. (Bresciani et al., 2004; Traverso et al., 2004). Participant public behavior aspect (all elements at border of stakeholder like Lee C.S) specifies strategic capabilities of individual enterprises such as consume car, whereas internal

Figure 4. AGFIL Collaboration Models

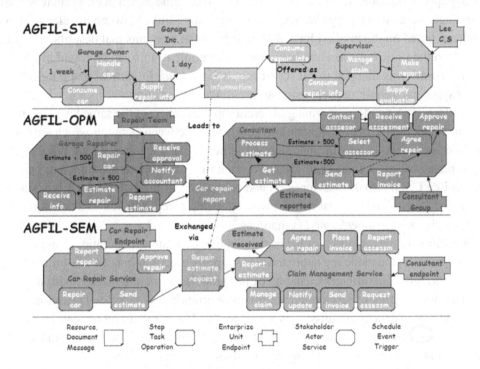

business process aspect (inside particular stakeholders) identifies the private enterprise processes (e.g. handle car) to realize these capabilities. When a strategic agreement is made, conversation aspect (all modeling elements external to or on boundary of stakeholders like garage owner) defines the exchange of resources like **car repair information** between enterprises.

At operational level, strategic models are concretized in operational models. In terms of aspects, in participant public behavior aspect (e.g. elements on border of garage repairer) the tasks an actor can perform are depicted e.g. **get estimate** (like ebXML CPP (ebXML Initiative, 2002)). Internal business process aspect (elements within actor) is similar to e.g. **BPML/BPMN (Business Process Modeling Initiative**, 2002) or workflow (Bowers et al., 1995), specifying how and when activities such as **estimate repair** are conducted. Conversation aspect (all elements on or outside actor borders e.g. consultant) captures operational agreements between enterprises by defining the flow of information between actors; like specified by RosettaNet (RosettaNet, 2006) or ebXML BPSS (ebXML Initiative, 2006).

At service level, operational models are translated into service models where specified activities are realized by services and their operations. Resembling interface behavior in (Dijkman & Dumas, 2004), the public participant behavior aspect is captured in models formed by elements placed on the border of individual services like **car repair service** depicting offered operations (akin to e.g. WSDL (Christensen et al., 2001)). Within a service the modeling elements depict internal business process aspect akin to orchestration; where a service internally engages other services to realize its functionality (not shown in Figure 4). Finally, conversation aspect (the elements on or outside the border of services) is akin to the notion of choreography (Banerji et al., 2004; Peltz, 2003) defining the agreed upon exchange of messages among services.

In order to express the dependencies that exist between the same aspect at different levels we employ vertical mappings. Vertical mappings are realized by providing links between the elements at different levels, which are based on the implicit links that exist between elements that describe the same facet at different levels in the same collaboration behavior. An example of this can be found in Figure 4 where **car repair information** is mapped to car repair report via a *leadsTo* vertical mapping; which itself is mapped to message **car repair request** using an *exchangedVia* relation.

In a similar fashion dependencies among different types of aspect at the same level are made explicit using horizontal mappings. Horizontal mappings define links between elements which are part of models describing different aspects, where the mappings are grounded on the implicit relations that exist among collaboration behaviors at an individual level. For example, the communication step consume repair information in Lee C.S internal behavior is related to the step of the same name in the corresponding exposed behavior via a *offeredAs* relationship; where the latter step is linked to a corresponding step in the observable behavior via a *performedAs* mapping.

Lastly, in addition to the definition of the basic structure of strategic, operational and service models (and their dependencies) the modeling approach also supports specification of extra-functional pervasive requirements. Currently the different elements of the models can be augmented with a wide range of assessment, payment, quality of service and security properties in order to specify assessment, payment, quality of service and security requirements respectively. These requirements can be defined for all different collaboration behaviors at all different levels, and dependencies among them have been made explicit. Due to space limitations we do not discuss these here any further.

Business Collaboration Information Model (BCIM)

In the previous section we introduced a wide variety of models and mappings to capture the business collaboration context provided by BCCF. Here we adopt the Business Collaboration Information Model to specify these different models in an uniform manner. BCIM constitutes a set of modeling description atoms to define individual models and mappings. An overview of the BCIM is provided in Figure 5.

Modeling description atoms constitute the basic building blocks with which we construct models to capture business collaboration behaviors. As the figure shows there are seven types of modeling description atom: *context, element, property, link, attribution, model* and *mapping*. These atoms serve the following purpose (where they are defined using a blend of a first order logic (FOL) and set theory like notation):

1. *Context*: identifies the position of a collaboration model within the business collaboration context. A context depicts a level and an aspect. Level must be equal to 'strategic', 'operational' or 'service', and aspect equal to 'internal business process', 'public participant behavior' or 'conversation'). A context **c** is formally defined as a tuple C(cl,ca,cm), where 'cl' is the level, 'ca' is the aspect, and 'cm' is the reference to the model to which the context belongs. An example is **C(strategic,conversation,AGFIL-STM)** representing the **AGFIL-STM** describing the strategic agreement between **Garage Inc** and **Lee C.S.**

2. *Element*: represents a part of a collaboration behavior, i.e. material, functional, participation, location, and temporal part. An element has a uniquely identifying name and a type. The element type reflects the kind of facet being represented. Each element has one or more properties. An element **e** is formally defined as E(en,et,em); where 'en' is the name of the model, 'et' is the type, and 'em'

Figure 5. Business Collaboration Information Model

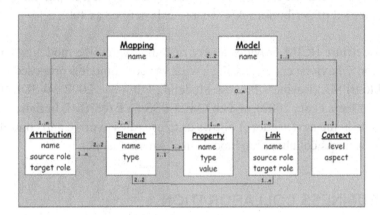

is the model reference. E(**supplyRepairInformation,step,AGFIL-STM**) expresses the **supply repair information** step performed by **Garage** Inc in **AGFIL-STM**.

3. *Property*: defines a characteristic of an element, enriching the description of a part (which can be both functional and non-functional in nature). A property **p** is formally defined as P(pn,pt,pv,pe,pm); where 'pn' is the name of the property, 'pt' the type, 'pv' the value, 'pe' the element reference, and 'pm' the model reference. To illustrate, in order to indicate that car repair information must be protected against modification the property **P(myProp,modification,true, carRepairInformation,AGFIL-STM)** can be specified.

4. *Link*: expresses connections between elements in the same model. A link **l** is formally defined as **L**(ln,ls,lso,lt,lta,lm); where 'ln' is the name of the link, 'ls' the source role, 'lso' the source element, 'lt' the target role, 'lta' the target element and 'lm' the model reference. For example, L(**myLink,responsibleFor,garageRepairer,allocatedTo,supplyRepairInformation, AGFIL-STM**) conveys that **garage repairer** is responsible for performing **supply repair information,** as stipulated in the agreement model **AGFIL-STM**.

5. *Attribution*: specify relations between elements from different models. An attribution can be 'vertical' in nature linking elements from models at different levels, or 'horizontal' connecting elements from models at different behaviors. An attribution a is formally defined as A(an,as,aso,at,ata) where 'an' is the name of the attribution, 'as' the source role, 'as' the source element, 'at' the target role and 'ata' the target element. Mapping A(**myMapping,leadsTo,carRepairInformation,resultOf,c arRepairReport**) defines such an attribution, stating that car repair information leads to car repair report.

6. *Model*: represents a collaboration model e.g. **AGFIL-STM**. It has a name, and constitutes one or more elements, properties and links. A collaboration model **CM** is formally defined as CM_{label}: c ∩ **ES** ∩ **PS** ∩ **LS**, i.e. the conjunction of a context c, a set of elements **ES**, a set of properties **PS** and a set of links **LS**. These sets are themselves defined as:

   ES: a set of elements defined as $\{e0...e_n\}$.

   PS: a set of properties defined as $\{p0...p_n\}$.

   LS: a set of links defined as $\{l0...l_n\}$.

7. *Mapping*: defines a mapping between two models such as the conversation models in AGFIL-STM and AGFIL-OPM. A mapping has a name, and consists of a collection of attributions. A mapping

MAP is formally defined as **MAP**: CM1 ∩ CM2 ∩ AS, i.e. the conjunction of two models CM1 and CM2, and the set of attributions AS; where AS is defined as $\{a0...a_n\}$.

Due to its generic nature BCIM provides a very rich and expressive modeling language to capture business collaboration behaviors; encompassing a wide variety of models proposed in literature including but not limited to BPML (Business Process Modeling Initiative, 2002), WSDL (Christensen et al., 2001), BPEL4WS (Curbera et al., 2002), and ebXML BPSS/CPP (ebXML Initiative, 2006). Moreover, as we will demonstrate in the next section it allows us to use rules to drive and control the development and management of business collaboration models in a generic manner.

RULE BASED BUSINESS COLLABORATION

The development of the described model based approach is an important step towards a more adaptive development and management of business collaborations. Compared to existing solutions the usage of multiple models allows organisations to describe collaborations in a much more comprehensive and accurate manner. Moreover, the adoption of mappings enables them to express dependencies among these models which are not often considered in other works. This gives them the means to trace how particular parts, levels and aspects are dependent on the other parts, levels and aspects. However, at the same time it leads to a much more extensive and complex business collaboration modelling effort, making it difficult to manually develop and modify collaboration models such that they are compliant and consistent.

Therefore, we propose a rule based approach for defining and managing business collaboration models that empowers organisations to do so in a compliant, consistent and agile manner. In a nutshell the idea is to allow them to make their business collaboration requirements explicit as rules. They can then use these rules to drive and constrain the development and management of the different collaboration models. This allows the design of models to be governed by the explicitly defined and thus manageable rules. It also allows models to be readily changed during design time and runtime by adding new rules and/or re-defining existing rules. Moreover, rules can be applied to ensure that generated models are and remain consistent.

Such rule based approach requires the ability to associate rules with models, an understanding of the types of necessary rule, and the capability to make these different rules explicit. Once we can define the rules that govern the development of business collaborations, the next step is to devise a way of 'finding' models and mappings that are in compliance with the resulting rules. To this end, we introduce the notion of conformance and explain how it caters for the adaptive, compliant and consistent generating and managing of business collaboration models.

Rules for Business Collaboration Modelling

As just observed, in a rule based approach for business collaboration the requirements of organisations are expressed in rules. Generally speaking a rule is an accepted principle or instruction that states the way things are or should be done, and tells you what you are allowed or are not allowed to do. In the context of business collaboration we refer to these rules as business collaboration rules. Such rules are statements that define or constrain some aspect of the business, which is intended to assert business structure or to control or influence the behavior of the business" (Ross, 2003). An example of an everyday business rule for Garage Inc is that "if the estimated repair cost is too high or the customer status is not 'gold', then report the cost to Lee C.S to obtain approval for repair".

Business collaboration rules are diverse in nature varying both in function and scope. Because we want to use rules to drive and constrain business collaboration, from a functional viewpoint we identify two types of rule: derivation rules and control rules. Derivation rules express in what manner models must be specified making their development adaptive. In relation to the literature on rule classification they comprise inferences, computations and action enablers in (Ross, 2003) and (Wagner, 2002)), and, deduction and projector rules in (Halle, 2002). In contrast, control rules place restrictions on the specification of models ensuring that they are consistent. They encompass both constraints and guidelines identified in (Ross, 2003), which express mandatory or optional control rules respectively. Both types of rule are found ranging over the different models and mappings that they govern.

Along level they fall into strategic goals, operational business rules, technical limitations, and rules governing the mappings between models at different levels. Along aspect they are divided into private regulations, promises to other parties, agreed upon commitments, and rules governing the mappings between models of different aspects. Along part derivation and control rules are sub-categorized into material rules, functional rules, participant rules, location rules, temporal rules, and rules governing the relations between different parts. These categories cover the typically mentioned types of rule in literature, such as data dependencies (material), control flow statements (functional), task allocation rules (functional-participation) and exception handlers (temporal-functional). Lastly, along pervasive requirements rules are grouped into (among others) basic, assessment, legal, payment, quality, security and transactionality rules.

This extensive classification illustrates that rules are found throughout the entire business collaboration context. The challenge for organisations is to specify all these different rules with a single language in a uniform and manageable way. Therefore we developed a generic and rich Business Collaboration Rule Language (BCRL) in which rule specification is grounded on the BCIM. An example policy is shown in Figure 6. A complete overview of the BCRL can be found in (Orriëns, 2007).

At the top of the figure we find the details for a policy containing the requirements for the service protocol of claim management service (offered by Lee C.S). The idea behind associating each business collaboration model with a policy is that it allows organisations to group all the rules that express requirements for the behavior described by this model. This allows organisations to group rules governing the same behavior in a logical structure, making it easier to maintain them. A policy has a name, last date of modification, as well as owner and manager information. In order to further facilitate rule structuring each policy constitutes one or more alternatives. Alternatives describe a certain course of action by defining a set of logically related rules such that they govern and constrain (some part of) the business collaboration in a coherent, consistent and meaningful manner.

The usage of alternatives enables organizations to cope with different business scenarios in an effective manner as new alternatives can be easily added to handle new situations while existing ones can be modified without affecting other alternatives. Figure 6 defines two alternatives catering for Garage Inc to deal with repair estimates of different height. In order to support organisations to express in which circumstances an alternative is applicable, guard conditions can be specified. For example, the guards of the first alternative in the figure state that the repair estimate must be greater than $500. In contrast, the second alternative is only applicable if the estimate is below $500. As such, the two alternatives are

Figure 6. Example of a Policy in the BCRL

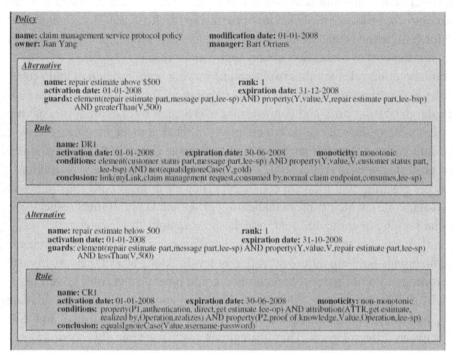

mutually exclusive, ensuring that it is always clear what course of action is to be followed in a given situation. Organisations can also stipulate the period in which an alternative is valid. Furthermore, they can define ranks to indicate an order of preference in case multiple alternatives are applicable under the same circumstances at the same time.

Each alternative constitutes a collection of rules expressing a set of related requirements. These rules comprise both derivation and control rules driving and controlling the behavior of the organisation in particular circumstances. In order to be able to uniformly specify different rules, they are expressed as constraints on the different modeling description atoms in the BCIM. For example, derivation rule DR1 in Figure 6 states the technical constraint that a car repair estimate must always be handled by normal claim endpoint if the customer status is not equal to 'gold'. Control rules are expressed in a similar way as derivation rules. The difference is that while derivation rules must always have a fact as conclusion (i.e. lead to deducing a new fact), control rules must always define an evaluation of an existing fact. An example is CR1 stating that if it is the case that task get estimate requires direct authentication and it is (partially) realized by an operation, then this operation must support a specific proof of knowledge mechanism (being a username/password combination).

Both derivation and control rules have an activation and expiration date to allow organisations to depict when rules are applicable (e.g. to handle older estimates differently than new ones). Also, rules have a monoticity which expresses whether a requirement must be met or is 'soft' in nature. Monotonic derivation rules must be enforced and can not be overridden. In contrast, non-monotonic derivation rules can be prioritized to indicate which requirement takes precedence over another in case of conflict (as detected by the control rules). 'Hard' control rules, i.e., monotonic control rules, express constraints that must not be violated. As such, in case such violation does occur, it must be resolved. On the other hand, 'soft' (i.e. non-monotonic) control rules function as guidelines and represent constraints that may be violated. An attempt to resolve such violations can be undertaken, but need not be successful. Prioritisation in this regard reflects the importance of violations with respect to each other, indicating which inconsistency is to be resolved first.

Finally, reuse is accommodated to further cater for the maintainability of rules through referencing and extension. Referencing is used to enable 'horizontal' reuse, that is, the reuse of policies, alternatives and rules through a 'pointer-like' inclusion. This means that a policy, alternative or rule is either defined in full or referenced in a pointer based on its name. Such referencing will reduce the effort required to define and maintain rules, for example by allowing organizations to define a rule in full once and then reference it whenever necessary. Thus, when the rule has to be changed, modification is only required at a single location. In contrast, extension is utilized to establish 'vertical' reuse expressing a generalization/specialization relation between policies, alternatives and rules. As a result, organizations can create hierarchies of policies, alternatives and rules, which makes their maintenance easier, e.g. alternatives can be added to a higher level policy which will be inherited by all policies extending it.

Generating and Managing Business Collaboration Models

The developed PRSL gives organisations the means to express their business collaboration requirements in a highly expressive and manageable manner. In such systems the interpretation of the meaning of a set of rules is given by the model that satisfies all the rules. A rule is satisfied if: 1) its conditions are met and so is its conclusion; or 2) its conditions are not met and neither is its conclusion. Based on this relation between a set of rules and its model we defined the notion of conformance. Informally speaking conformance expresses that a model must capture the semantics of its policy. This is the case when it satisfies the 'active' rules in the alternative applicable given the particular circumstances and time (see (Orriëns, 2007) for formal definitions). Based on this notion we then define the Business Collaboration Conformance Mechanism (BCCM), in which a model is compliant with requirements if it conforms to the derivation rules that are applicable to it.

Taking the protocol of claim management service as an example, suppose that the Garage sends a car repair estimate to Lee C.S whose value is $650. Upon arrival the policy of the protocol is evaluated. Since the value exceeds $500, the second alternative is applicable. This means that the protocol model must satisfy all rules in this alternative. Assuming that the customer status is not equal to 'gold', the conditions of DR1 are satisfied. Consequently, in order for the model to be conformed to this rule the modeling description atom link(myLink1,repair estimate request,consumed by,normal claim endpoint,consumes,lee-sp) must be added. Semantically this conveys that Lee C.S deduces that the estimate is to be handled by normal claim endpoint.

As a result, by defining different alternatives with different rules Lee C.S can generate protocols that handle different situations. Prioritization can play a role in this as well. For example, suppose that DR1 has no conditions and is non-monotonic. This rule will enforce the behavior of handling all repair estimates by normal claim endpoint. Lee C.S can override this 'default' behavior by defining another rule stating that if the repair estimate is above $500, but the claimant has a 'gold' status', the estimate should go to preferred claim endpoint, and then stipulating that DR2 has a higher rank than DR1. Here the result also will be a protocol that is tailored to the specific circumstances.

Compliance can also be utilized when managing changes. Let us assume for a moment that Lee C.S wishes to change the default endpoint to handle car repair estimates above $500 to new claim endpoint. One obvious advantage of the approach is that Lee C.S only needs to concern itself with re-defining rule DR1 to accomplish this new endpoint is used in new business collaborations. Moreover, Lee C.S can easily add new alternatives to accommodate more scenarios, e.g. to treat estimates from different garages differently. Also, refinement of existing alternatives can be done in a straightforward manner by simply adding new rules. Optionally it can also be the case that Lee C.S wishes to update its existing collaborations. This is done by evaluating the existing protocols to see if they satisfy the 'new' rules.

Let us assume that a protocol for claim management service already defines that normal claim endpoint handles car repair estimate. However, the underlying rule DR1 has been changed and thus this fact must be retracted. Lee C.S can define rules to state what should happen in such event, e.g. requiring that the old endpoint is notified that it must cease to work on estimates above $500. It will then apply the new DR1 to deduce that the estimate is now being handled by new claim endpoint (in order for the model to remain compliant with the rules). Interestingly, this can potentially cause conditions of earlier applied derivation rules to be no longer satisfied, and consequently prompt the removal of facts deduced using these rules based on this specific fact. This will continue until all no longer supported facts have been removed from the model.

During both model development and management Lee C.S also employs conformance rules to maintain consistency. A model is consistent if it conforms to all the control rules applicable to it, which in turn implies that the derivation rules to which it complies are consistent. In order to illustrate how it works, let us inspect the relationship between the exposed behavior of consultant and the claim management service. Suppose that the estimate in repair estimate request is $450. Also assume that there exists a derivation rule DR2 for consultant mandating direct authentication under these circumstances for task get estimate. Furthermore, assume that there is a rule DR_3 saying that get estimate is realized by operation report estimate. Finally, assume that DR_4 stipulates that operation report estimate does not demand an username and password from requesters.

Application of these rules will result in a violation of CR_1, as this rule states that such username/password must be asked for by report estimate. Resolution of this inconsistency is done by first identifying the derivation rules used to derive the facts satisfying the conditions of the violated control rule, then determining whether one of them has the lowest priority. If the prioritization information is inconclusive, then the inconsistency can not be resolved. If (like here) CR1 is non-monotonic, the inconsistency will be logged. In contrast, if CR1 is monotonic, then user intervention is required. If a lowest priority derivation rule can be found, then its concluding fact is removed. Supposing this is DR3, then the mapping between get estimate and report estimate is removed as well as any facts derived based on this mapping. Also, a new 'realising' operation must be found either by using another existing derivation rule or defining a new one.

PROTOTYPE

In order to demonstrate the practical feasibility of our approach we developed a prototype called **Icarus**. Icarus is a computer aided software engineering (CASE) tool set for modeling, analyzing, and managing rule based business collaborations. The Icarus platform uses Java technologies and is based on top of the open source OO jDREW reasoning engine for rule reasoning. Figure 7 shows the platform's architecture.

As can be seen in the figure the architecture consists of:

1. **Policy and model representation, storage and manipulation components** that provide support for creating, editing and storing policies for business collaboration models as well as generated models (for future reference and analysis), where storage is done in the form of easily exchangeable XML based representations.
2. **Analysis, simulation and management components** that offer functionality for analyzing policies with regard to missing, inconsistent and redundant rules, simulate models based on their policies conforming to particular circumstances, and effectuate changes to policies in existing models.
3. The **development environment** provides visual exploration for defining, modifying, and analyzing policies, and simulating and managing models satisfying these policies. It offers policy editors for the different business collaboration models in a project dialog environment and an automated visualizations of generated models, and access to the logic of the underlying individual model details.

In summary organisations utilize these different components as follows: first, they define their requirements in policies using the development environment. During this process organisations can employ the features provided by the **policy and rule analyzer** via the **analysis interface** to examine whether their defined policies miss any rules, have redundant rules or inconsistent rules. Once the problems have been resolved, organisations can then use the **model generator** component to simulate and verify that the policies lead to consistent and coherent models and mappings under different circumstances. Such simulation and verification is done via a sophisticated rule engine layered on top of the off-the-shelf **OO jDREW** rule engine to reason with non-monotonicity and prioritization, usage of alternatives, and status

Figure 7. Architecture for the Icarus Platform

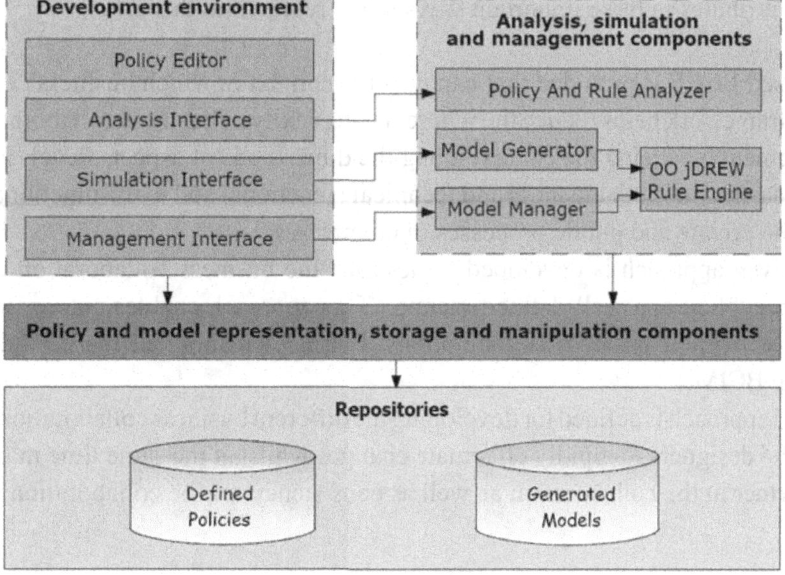

of rules and alternatives. The resulting models are next presented in a visually attractive manner in the **simulation interface**. Using this interface organisations can also analyze these models and investigate what rules were used to deduce and justify the different model details.

If satisfied, organisations can store the verified policies in the **policy repository**. Also, they may store generated models in the **model repository**. This allows them to retrieve these models later when managing existing models via the **management interface**. In this interface they can open a modified policy and assess its impact on an existing model (based on the original policy). The result is a visualization of the model according to the new policy as well as highlighting the parts no longer justified. We validated **Icarus**'s usefulness in several experiments. We applied its analysis component to detect and resolve issues with developed policies for the interaction between Garage Inc and Lee C.S, which reduces the time and effort to determine whether organisational requirements are complete. We simulated the design of models for this interaction in conformance with defined policies, which greatly enhances the capabilities of organisations to assess whether their requirements lead to coherent and desired behaviour. Lastly, we introduced changes to policies and automatically propagated their effects into existing models. This showed how the tool is effective for enabling organisations to determine the consequences of such changes on existing business collaborations.

CONCLUSION

Current web service development and management solutions are too narrowly focused and not capable of addressing the requirements of business collaboration. As a result, managing business collaboration in relation to changing requirements based on existing web service-based middleware technologies and standards is difficult. Many solutions have been proposed and most of them contribute in some way to solving the problem. What is missing is an approach that combines these different ideas in a holistic manner and provides enterprises with a set of methodologies and tools to support their activities in business collaboration development and management. In comparison, the work we presented in this chapter provides such a holistic and dynamic approach for business collaboration development and management. Specifically, it contributes in three important ways to the research in this area:

1. A modularised BCCF is provided that captures the context in which business collaboration takes place. This framework helps reduce the inherent complexity of business collaboration development and management by slicing the context along the dimensions of aspects, levels and facets, which covers a wide array of both business and technical (functional and extra-functional) requirements, as well as the private and public processes of enterprises.
2. A model-driven approach is developed to describe the business collaboration context given by BCCF in an explicit and well-defined manner. This approach enables enterprises to capture the entire context of their business collaborations. Formal semantics of these models are provided based on the BCIM.
3. A rule-based approach is defined for developing the different business collaboration models in which rules help the designers to rapidly effectuate changes whilst at the same time manage consistency for each partner in the collaboration as well as consistency for the collaboration as a whole.

In summary, we demonstrated that with the rule based approach organizations can gain the ability to adapt the manner in which they conduct their semi-automated, electronic transactions in response to new business models and requirements. We also reported an implementation of a development and management environment in the form of the Icarus prototype, which provides enterprises with the supporting environment needed to define, generate and manage cooperative processes. As a result, we have shown that with the presented approach business collaboration can be developed as independent from specific SOC implementation technologies as possible and can respond to any changes as effectively as possible. This is a vital ability if they wish to survive and prosper in a business climate in which change is the norm rather than the exception.

Work for future research will focus foremost on realising the automatic conversion of service models into web services based standards to make them executable. This will allow enterprises to dynamically define business requirements for their business collaborations, and map these to an executable web services based middleware solution. We believe that, once completed, our approach allows development and management of business collaboration to be as independent from specific SOC implementation technologies as possible and adaptive to changes as effectively as possible. Lastly, the workings of the approach will be explored in real life case studies in order to assess the extent to which it can be utilized to facilitate adaptive business collaboration development and management with regard to their complexity and manageability.

REFERENCES

Aiello, M., Papazoglou, M., Yang, J., Carman, M., Pistore, M., Serafini, L., et al. (2002, August). A request language for Web-services based on planning and constraint satisfaction. In *Proceedings of the VLDB Workshop on Technologies for E-Services*.

Andrieux, A., Czajkowski, K., & Dan, A. (2004, June). *Web services agreement specification* (WS Agreement).

Arkin, A., Askary, S., Fordin, S., Jekeli, W., Kawaguchi, K., Orchard, D., et al. (2002, August). *Web service choreography interface*.

Bajaj, S., Box, D., Chappell, D., Curbera, F., Daniels, G., Hallam-Baker, P., et al. (2006, March). *Web services policy framework (WS-Policy)*.

Banerji, A., Bartolini, C., Beringer, D., Chopella, V., Govindarajan, K., Karp, A., et al. (2004, March). *Web service conversation language (WSCL)*.

Basten, A. (1998). *In terms of nets, system design with petri nets and process algebra*. Unpublished doctoral dissertation, Department of Mathematics and Computing Science.

Bergstra, J., & Klop, J. (1985). Algebra of communicating processes with abstraction. *Theoretical Computer Science, 37*(1), 77–121. doi:10.1016/0304-3975(85)90088-X

Bergstra, J., Ponse, A., & Smolka, S. (2001). *Handbook of process algebra*. Elsevier.

Booch, G., Rumbaugh, J., & Jacobson, I. (1998). *The unified modeling language user guide*. Addison-Wesley.

Bowers, J., Button, G., & Sharrock, W. (1995, September). Workflow from within and without. In *Proceedings of the 4th European Conference on Computer-Supported Cooperative Work.*

Bresciani, P., Giorgini, P., Giunchiglia, F., Mylopoulos, J., & Perini, A. (2004, May). Tropos: An Agent-oriented software development methodology. *Autonomous Agents and Multi-Agent Systems, 8*(3), 203–236. doi:10.1023/B:AGNT.0000018806.20944.ef

Business Process Modeling Initiative. (2002, June). *Business process modeling language.*

Casati, F., Ilnicki, S., Jin, L., Krishnamoorthy, V., & Shan, M. (2000). *Adaptive and dynamic service composition in eFlow* (Tech. Rep. No. HPL-2000-39). HP Lab.

Casati, F., Shan, E., Dayal, U., & Shan, M. (2003). Business-oriented management of Web services. *Communications of the ACM, 46*(10), 55–60. doi:10.1145/944217.944238

Christensen, E., Curbera, F., Meredith, G., & Weerawarana, S. (2001, March). *Web service description language.*

Christophides, V., Hull, R., Kumar, A., & Simeon, J. (2000). Workflow mediation using VorteXML. *Bulletin of the IEEE Computer Society Technical Committee on Data Engineering, 24*(1), 40–45.

Curbera, F., Goland, Y., Klein, J., Leymann, F., Roller, D., Thatte, S., et al. (2002, July). *Business process execution language for Web services.*

Curtis, B., Kellner, M., & Over, J. (1992). Process Modeling. *Communications of the ACM, 35*(9), 75–90. doi:10.1145/130994.130998

Deiters, W., Goesmann, T., & L¨offeler, T. (2000). Flexibility in workflow management: Dimensions and solutions. *International Journal of Computer Systems Science and Engineering, 15*(5), 303–313.

Dijkman, R., & Dumas, M. (2004). Service-oriented design: A multi-viewpoint approach. *International Journal of Cooperative Information Systems, 13*(4), 337–368. doi:10.1142/S0218843004001012

ebXML Initiative.(2002, September). *Collaboration protocol profile and agreement specification.*

ebXML Initiative.(2006, April). *Business process specification schema.*

Georgakopoulos, D., Hornick, M., & Sheth, A. (1995). An overview of workflow management: From process modelling to workflow automation infrastructure. *Distributed and Parallel Databases, 3*(2), 119–152. doi:10.1007/BF01277643

Grefen, P., Aberer, K., Hoffner, Y., & Ludwig, H. (2000). Crossflow: Cross-organizational workflow management in dynamic virtual enterprises. *International Journal of Computer Systems Science & Engineering, 15*(5), 277–290.

Han, Y., Sheth, A., & Bussler, C. (1998, November). A taxonomy of adaptive workflow management. In *Proceedings of the CSCW Workshop Towards Adaptive Workflow Systems.*

Hoare, C. (1985). *Communicating sequential processes.* Prentice Hall.

Joeris, G., & Herzog, O. (1999, June). Towards flexible and high level modeling and enacting of processes. In *Proceedings of the 11th International Conference on Advanced Information Systems Engineering.*

Jonkers, H., Lankhorst, M., van Buuren, R., Hoppenbrouwers, S., & Bonsangue, M. (2003). Concepts for modelling enterprise architectures. In *Proceedings of the 7th IEEE International Enterprise Distributed Object Computing Conference.*

Liu, L., & Pu, C. (1997, November). ActivityFlow: Towards incremental specification and flexible co-ordination of workflow activities. In *Proceedings of the 16th International Conference on Conceptual Modeling.*

Milner, R. (1990). *Operational and algebraic semantics of concurrent processes.* Elsevier.

Nguyen, G., & Vernadat, F. (1994, May). Cooperative information systems in integrated manufacturing environments. In *Proceedings of the 2nd International Conference on Cooperative Information Systems.*

Object Modeling Group. (2003, June). *MDA Guide 1.1.*

Orriëns, B. (Ed.). (2007). *On the adaptive development and management of business collaborations* (No. 194). CentER.

Peltz, C. (2003, January). *Web services orchestration: A review of emerging technologies, tools, and standards.*

Rao, J., Kungas, P., & Matskin, M. (2006). Composition of semantic Web services using linear logic theorem proving. *International Journal of Information systems, 31*(4-5), 340-360.

Reichert, M., & Dadam, P. (1997, September). A framework for dynamic changes in workflow management systems. In *Proceedings of the 8th International Conference on Database and Expert Systems Applications.*

Reichert, M., & Dadam, P. (1998). ADEPTflex - Supporting dynamic changes of workflows without losing control. *Journal of Intelligent Information Systems, 10*(2), 93–129. doi:10.1023/A:1008604709862

RosettaNet. (2006). *RosettaNet Standards.*

Ross, R. (2003). *Principles of the business rule approach.* Addison-Wesley.

Scheer, A. (1992). *Architecture of Integrated Information Systems: Foundations of enterprise modelling.* Springer.

Traverso, P., Pistore, M., Roveri, M., Marconi, A., Kazhamiakin, R., Lucchese, P., et al. (2004, December). Supporting the negotiation between global and local business requirements in service oriented development. In *Proceedings of the 2nd International Conference on Service Oriented Computing.*

van der Aalst, W. (1998). The application of petri nets to workflow management. *Journal of Circuits . Systems and Computers, 8*(1), 21–66.

van der Aalst, W., ter Hofstede, A., & Weske, M. (2003, June). On the application of formal methods to process-aware information systems. In *Proceedings of the International Conference on Business Process Management.*

Verbeek, E., & Aalst, W. van der. (2000, June). Woflan 2.0 - A Petri-net-based workflow diagnosis tool. In *Proceedings of the 21st International Application and Theory of Petri Nets.*

Vernadat, F. (1992). CIMOSA - A European development for enterprise integration (Part 2): enterprise modeling. Pergamon Press Inc.

von Halle, B. (2002). *Business rules applied: Building better systems using the business rule approach.* John Wiley & Sons Ltd.

Wagner, G. (2002, June). How to design a general rule markup language? In *Proceedings of the Workshop XML Technologies for the Semantic Web.*

Workflow Management Coalition. (1995, January). *The workflow reference model.*

Zachman, J. (1987). A framework for information systems architecture. *IBM Systems Journal, 26*(3), 276–292.

Zeng, L., Benatallah, B., Lei, H., Ngu, A., Flaxer, D., & Chang, H. (2003). Flexible Composition of enterprise Web services. *Electronic Markets - The International Journal of Electronic Commerce and Business Medi*a, *13*(2), 141-152.

KEY TERMS AND DEFINITIONS

Abstract Business Processes: partially specified processes that are not intended to be executed. An Abstract Process may hide some of the required concrete operational details. Abstract Processes serve a descriptive role, with more than one possible use case, including observable behavior and process template.

Business Collaboration Model: the elements of the collaborative process and the relationships between these elements.

Business Process Management: a method of efficiently aligning an organization with the wants and needs of clients. It is a holistic management approach that promotes business effectiveness and efficiency while striving for innovation, flexibility and integration with technology.

Business Process Modeling: the activity of representing processes of an enterprise, so that the current process may be analyzed and improved. BPM is typically performed by business analysts and managers who are seeking to improve process efficiency and quality.

Business Rule: the operations, definitions and constraints that apply to an organization in achieving its goals.

Collaborative Business Process: an integrated business process which consists of relevant business processes across participating organizations.

Private Business Processes: those internal to a specific organization and are the type of processes that have been generally called workflow or BPM processes.

Chapter 12
Towards Dynamic Collaborations in Virtual Organisation Alliances

Xiaohui Zhao
Swinburne University of Technology, Australia

Chengfei Liu
Swinburne University of Technology, Australia

ABSTRACT

This chapter introduces a service oriented relative workflow model as a means of helping organisations promptly create flexible and privacy-safe virtual organisation alliances. It argues that virtual organisation alliances are highly advocated to adapt to dynamic B2B collaborations, driven by the fast changing service demand-and-supply requirements. However, the temporary partnership and low trustiness between collaborating organisations put challenges to effectively manage collaborative business processes, and correspondingly an organisation centred design method and a visibility mechanism are discussed in this chapter to provide a finer granularity of authority control at contacting and collaboration design phases. Furthermore, the authors hope that understanding the establishment of a virtual organisation alliance through the use of relative workflows will not only inform researchers a better business process design methodology, but also assist in the understanding of the dynamic behaviours inside a virtual organisation alliance and the supporting approaches.

INTRODUCTION

Recent years have witnessed the booming of global business collaboration which urgently drives organisations to dynamically form virtual organisation alliances. A virtual organisation alliance seamlessly integrates the business processes of different organisations to adapt to the continuously changing business conditions and to stay competitive in the global market (Osterle, Fleisch, & Alt, 2001; van der Aalst & van Hee, 2004).

DOI: 10.4018/978-1-60566-669-3.ch012

Different from virtual enterprises, which are typically large-scale organisations centred, a virtual organisation alliance is mainly constructed from small-to-medium sized organisations. These organisations join a virtual community to share each other's business services and capabilities. The collaborations in such a virtual organisation alliance are always motivated by prompt business service demand-and-supply requirements, such as service outsourcing or business service complementation. The collaborations are rather temporary and dynamic, which reluctantly conflict with the traditional pre-fixed inter-organisational workflow design mechanisms. In a virtual organisation alliance, each member organisation needs to publish and update its business services that can be provided or outsourced. In turn, other member organisations can choose partner organisations and create corresponding collaborations to best fit its requirements or profit benefits.

The dynamic structure and the collaboration openness mostly characterise the virtual organisation alliance. These two characteristics also put challenges to the management of collaborative business processes for virtual organisation alliances. Especially at contracting and collaboration design phases, the temporary and dynamic partnership requires high flexibility in describing and implementing collaboration processes between member organisations. Furthermore, the dynamics and temporality in turn result in the lack of trustiness between member organisations in loose-coupling business collaborations, and therefore complicates the authority control (Zhao, Liu, Sadiq, & Kowalkiewicz, 2008; Zhao, Liu, Yang, & Sadiq, 2007).

Aiming to solve these problems, this chapter extends our previously proposed relative workflow model into the service oriented computing environment to well support the collaboration behaviours of dynamic virtual organisation alliances. This model treats each participating organisation as an autonomous entity, and empowers the organisation to design inter-organisational workflow processes from its own perspective. With regard to the authority control, this organisation oriented mechanism enables the visibility differentiation for different partner organisations in the open collaborating environment of a virtual organisation alliance. In the proposed approach, contracts are not only used to define and regulate business service collaborations, but also to assist developing the visibility constraints for the business process integration. The research reported in this chapter is based on our previous work (Zhao, Liu, & Yang, 2006) with a lot of extension and improvements.

The rest of this chapter is organised as follows: Section 2 first presents the relation between business services and functional services, and then briefly reviews the proposed relative workflow model with an extension towards service oriented computing. Section 3 discusses how to support business collaborations in the environment of a virtual organisation alliance with the relative workflow model, especially at the phases of contracting and collaboration design. In Section 4, an application example is used to demonstrate how to practically apply the relative workflow approach to accommodate dynamic collaborations in a virtual organisation alliance. The implementation of a prototype is briefly introduced in Section 5 for the proof-of-concept purpose, and related work is given in Section 6, together with a discussion on our approach's advantages. Section 7 discusses the future trend of modelling collaborative business processes for virtual organisation alliances, and Section 8 concludes the whole chapter.

SERVICE ORIENTED RELATIVE WORKFLOW MODEL

Business Services and Functional Services

At high level, B2B collaborations are motivated by the synergy of service capabilities. At low level, such collaborations are implemented by fine-grained functional services. In regard to a virtual organisation alliance, it is established to quickly capture emerging market opportunities and enact business service collaborations, by the means of utilising and coordinating low-level functional services.

Technically, business services denote the business related procedures or work that can benefit others. In most cases, such business services are coarse-grained. For example, products manufacturing service, after-sales service etc. of a manufacturing company can be viewed as its business services. The notion of functional services comes from Service Oriented Computing (SOC), which is emerging as a new computing paradigm for distributed computing and business integration. A functional service denotes an Internet-accessible service (Leymann, Roller, & Schmidt, 2002). As building blocks of modern enterprise application architecture, functional services provide a good support on interoperability and flexibility. In this field, some leading companies and organisations, such as IBM, Microsoft and OASIS, have contributed a lot in defining specifications and developing architectures for service oriented computing. The notion of "functional service" has similar terms, such as Electronic Service or eService (Casati & Shan, 2001; Vissers, Lankhorst, & Slagter:, 2003), and nowadays Web service is considered as the most popular instance of practical functional services. Web services use Web Service Description Language - WSDL and Business Process Execution Language for Web Services - BPEL4WS to describe the service interfaces and interaction routines, respectively.

Figure 1 illustrates how business services and functional services come into architecting dynamic virtual organisation alliances at three layers. At the top layer, the collaborations between member organisations are represented in forms of business service interactions, business service outsourcing and business service composition; and the business services are supported by a single or multiple business processes, which streamline related handling procedures and regulate the usage of involved resources and staff at the intermediate layer, i.e. the process layer; at the bottom layer, i.e. the functional service layer, functional services provide a pool of basic functions for the workflow processes at the upper layer to invoke through service operations. The workflow processes streamline the related workflow tasks, and embed the orchestration and choreography of functional service invocations to fulfil a particular business goal. In the service oriented computing architecture shown in Figure 1, workflow processes and functional services together build up the fundamental infrastructure to support high-level business services.

Background of Relative Workflow Model

The motivation of relative workflows is to allow organisations to act as autonomous entities in B2B collaborations and provide a fine grained visibility control for preventing authority violation or privacy disclosure.

Traditional inter-organisational workflow design approaches follow the public view model, which means the collaboration choreography and orchestration of all participating organisations is normally determined by a leading organisation of participating organisations. As such, each organisation behaves as passively as a worker does in a pipeline workshop. We find that in most case, a participating organi-

Figure 1. Virtual organisation alliance architecture

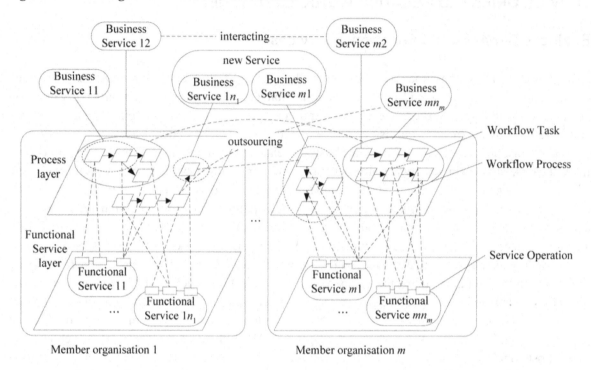

sation expects to choose its own partner organisations and define collaborative workflow processes by itself to adapt its own collaboration objectives and benefits rather than delegate to a third-party designer or a leading organisation. The public view approaches also fail to provide a fine granularity of visibility control. As the public inter-organisational workflow process is open to each involved organisation, either excessive information has to be disclosed or necessary collaboration information is not provided sufficiently.

We believe that business collaboration should be decided from the view of each individual organisation, i.e., an organisation defines its collaboration structure and behaviours by following the contracts signed with proper partner organisations, and may change them later by updating existing contracts or signing new contracts. In this way, each organisation acts as a highly autonomous collaboration participant, which is empowered with the authority to design its collaboration structure and behaviours in a proactive mode. In addition, this feature also highlights the flexible partnership between collaborating organisations. Privacy protection requires that the excessive information disclosure should be intentionally restricted, since high trustiness can hardly be granted between loosely-coupled organisations.

To support the above points, we proposed a novel approach, called relative workflow approach, which follows an organisation oriented perspective. Zhao, Liu and Yang (2005) have published a preliminary version of the relative workflow approach. In the context of relative workflows, each organisation can define the visible part of its own business processes to external organisations in the same collaboration. And each participating organisation only sees part of the collaboration picture. This part of the picture is changeable by the organisation. The ways the same organisation is seen by different organisations could be different.

Table 1. Visibility values

Visibility value	Explanation
Invisible	A task is said invisible to an external organisation, if it is hidden from that organisation.
Trackable	A task is said trackable to an external organisation, if that organisation is allowed to trace the execution status of the task.
Contactable	A task is said contactable to an external organisation, if the task is trackable to that organisation and the task is also allowed to send/receive messages to/from that organisation for the purpose of business interaction.

Extension of Relative Workflow Model

In this section, we extend the relative workflow model into the service oriented computing environment, by adding two definitions, *functional service* and *business service*. To hide private information during business collaborations, a participating *organisation* is allowed to wrap its *local workflow processes* into a series of *perceivable workflow processes* for different partner organisations, according to the *visibility constraints* defined in corresponding *perceptions*. And a *relative workflow process* is generated by linking an organisation's local workflow processes with perceivable workflow processes of its partner organisations. In this model, functional services work as building blocks to provide the basic supporting functions. And the orchestration and choreography of functional services is embedded in workflow processes.

Some key definitions are given below.

Definition 1 (Functional Service) A functional service is a discrete unit of application logic that exposes message-based interfaces suitable for being accessed across a network. A functional service s is defined as a set of operations $\{op_1, op_2, ..., op_n\}$. Each operation represents a message-based interface of a functional service. The message used by an operation op can be represented as a message description, $m \times \{in, out\}$, where m denotes the name of the message.

Definition 2 (Business Service) A business service bs of an organisation g represents a unit used for business collaborations. A business service is supported by a proper workflow process, which utilises necessary functional services to fulfil a particular business goal. This supporting workflow process may be a composite process, which consists of multiple collaborating local workflow processes.

Definition 3 (Local Workflow Process) A local workflow process lp is defined as a directed acyclic graph (T, R), where T is the set of nodes representing the set of tasks, and $R \subseteq T \times T$ is the set of arcs representing the execution sequence. Here, a task $t \in T$ may invoke one or more operations of functional services.

Definition 4 (Organisation) An organisation g owns a set of local workflow processes $\{lp^1, lp^2, ..., lp^n\}$ to support a set of business services. An individual local workflow process lp^i of g is denoted as $g.lp^i$. Here, $1 \leq i \leq n$, and n is the number of LWfPs.

During the collaboration, the organisation applies visibility control to protect the critical or private business information of some workflow tasks from entirely exposing to external organisations. Table 1 lists the three basic visibility values defined for business interaction and workflow tracking.

Due to the high diversity of business collaborations, these three values may hardly cover all possible visibility scenarios. In this chapter, we use these three values to provide a fundamental visibility mechanism, and this visibility value table is open for future extension.

Definition 5 (Visibility Constraint) A visibility constraint vc is defined as a tuple (t, v), where t denotes a workflow task and $v \in \{$ Invisible, Trackable, Contactable $\}$. A set of visibility constraints VC defined on a workflow process lp is represented as a set $\{vc:(t, v) \mid \forall t \ (t \in lp.T)\}$.

Definition 6 (Perception) A perception defines the information related to an inter-organisational interaction of a local workflow process. Once a business service oriented contract is assigned, the corresponding perception can be derived from the contract. The details about the derivation will be discussed later. A perception $p_{g_1}^{g_0 . lp}$ of an organisation g_0's local workflow process lp from another organisation g_1 is defined as (VC, MD, f), where

- VC is a set of visibility constraints defined on $g_0.lp$.
- $MD \subseteq M \times \{$ in, out $\}$, is a set of the message descriptions that contains the messages and the passing directions. M is the set of message names used to represent inter-organisational business activities.
- $f: MD \rightarrow g_0.lp_{g_1}.T$ is the mapping from MD to $g_0.lp_{g_1}.T$, and $g_0.lp_{g_1}$ is the *perceivable workflow process* of $g_0.lp$ from g_1.

Definition 7 (Relative Workflow Process) A relative workflow process $g.rp$ perceivable from an organisation g is defined as a directed acyclic graph (T, R), where (1) T is the set of the tasks perceivable from g, and T includes the following two parts.

- T_p, the set of tasks belonging to the local workflow processes in $g.rp$, defined on $\bigcup_k g.lp^k.T$, where, $1 \leq k \leq n$ and m is the number of g's involved local workflow processes.
- $T_{p'}$, the set of task belonging to the perceivable workflow processes in $g.rp$, defined on $\bigcup_i \bigcup_j g_i.lp_g^j.T$, where g_i is a neighbouring organisation of g. $1 \leq i \leq u$, $1 \leq j \leq v_i$, u is the number of g's neighbouring organisations and v_i is the number of g_i's related perceivable workflow processes for g. (2) R is the set of links perceivable from g, which is a union of the following three parts, where i, j and k are the same as in the definition of T.
- R_p, the set of the intra process links inside all local workflow processes in $g.rp$, defined on $g.lp^k$. $\bigcup_k g.lp^k.R$.
- $R_{p'}$, the set of intra process link inside all perceivable workflow processes in $g.rp$, defined on $\bigcup_i \bigcup_j g_i.lp_g^j.R$.
- L, the set of inter process links between local workflow processes and perceivable workflow processes, defined on $\bigcup_i \bigcup_j \bigcup_k \left(g.lp^k.T \times g_i.lp_g^j.T \cup g_i.lp_g^j.T \times g.lp^k.T \right)$.

The relative workflow model extended with business and functional services is shown in Figure 2, where rectangles, diamonds and rounded rectangles denote the workflow components, relationships and service components, respectively. With the discussed definitions, an organisation, say g_1, may first establish a business service by conjoining one or more local workflow processes to coordinate related functional services. Once this business service is involved in the collaboration with another organisation, say g_2, a perception can be generated to regulate the visibility control on each involved local workflow process. Afterwards, g_1 can wrap its local workflow process into an authority-safe perceivable workflow process for g_2, according to the visibility constraints defined in the perception. Finally, at the site of g_2,

Figure 2. Extended relative workflow model

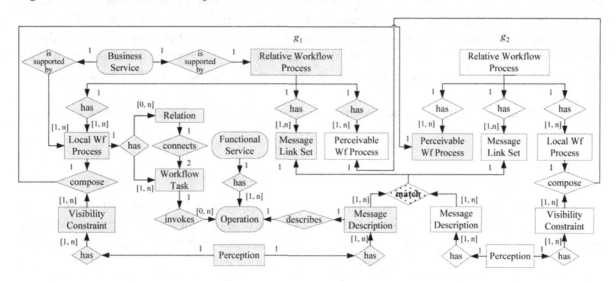

a relative workflow process will be assembled from related local workflow processes and perceivable workflow processes from g_1. Besides, a business service can also be supported by a pre-existing relative workflow process. Correspondingly, this business service may utilise the functional services of partner organisations to work for itself.

SUPPORTING VIRTUAL ORGANISATION ALLIANCES

Virtual organisation alliances are characterised by their dynamic nature and transient work arrangements. These characteristics in turn impose demanding requirements on workflow technologies that support for rapid business process assembling and changing partner relationships. In general, the business collaboration in a virtual organisation alliance can be represented as four phases, viz. contracting, collaboration design, collaboration execution and collaboration termination. This chapter focuses on the first two phases, i.e. how to organise business contracting and design inter-organisational business collaborations with the proposed service oriented relative workflow model in the virtual organisation alliance environment.

Why Relative Workflows Can Support Virtual Organisation Alliances

Support at Contracting Phase

Normally, B2B collaboration originates from contracting, where two or more parties come to an agreement to cooperate for a common objective, and this agreement is regulated by a legal document of contract.

Since a virtual organisation alliance enables the collaborations with a broad range of potential partners, each member organisation is empowered to quickly assemble the resources and expertise to capture emerging opportunities. To keep these options open, the partnerships between organisations are not static, but rather continuously evolve to stay competitive on the market. Correspondingly, this open partnership requires an open contracting mechanism, where an organisation posts the business services that it can offer and it may request to all potential co-operators in the virtual organisation alliance. Thereafter, some organisations with special interests may respond by referring to the business services. Finally, the involved organisations can come to negotiate the details of the contract for the collaboration. We call the organisation that issues the contract is a *host organisation*, and the responding organisations are *partner organisations*.

Different from the traditional closed contracting process, this open contracting process has following features.

- Low trustiness.

Since the contract may be established between parties with no prior partnerships, high trustiness can hardly be granted. The low trustiness requires authority control to prevent potential privacy disclosure during collaborations. As for this issue, the visibility constraint based visibility control mechanism of our relative workflow model is dedicated to guarantee the finer granularity of workflow visibility between cooperating organisations. With these visibility constraints, participating organisations can intentionally choose which tasks to be hidden or revealed to partner organisations according to the level of trustiness and the necessary interactions for collaborations.

- Uni-directional contracting.

Different from the normal contracting process which has defined concrete parties at the starting time, the open contracting process only involves a single party at the beginning, i.e. the host organisation. The uni-directional contracting process can be well supported by the process of posting business services in the context of the service oriented relative workflow model. Once a business service is prepared by deploying underlying supporting workflow processes, it will be published to all other member organisations to seek potential business collaborations. This service posting process also originates from one organisation, i.e. the host organisation, and propagates to all other organisations.

- Agile collaboration.

Because the involved organisations share a loosely-coupled relationship, the collaboration is dynamic with the low coordination, interdependence, short duration and few transactions. The agile collaboration requires the flexibility of collaboration structure and behaviours. Our relative workflow model supports a kind of "off-the-shelf" collaboration formation scheme, which empowers each organisation itself to choose partner organisations and define relative workflow processes from its own local workflow processes and the perceivable workflow process provided by other organisations. In this scheme, each participating organisation acts as an autonomous entity and it can change its partners or redefine its collaborations dynamically, to grasp the fast changing market opportunities.

Figure 3. Open relationship contracting

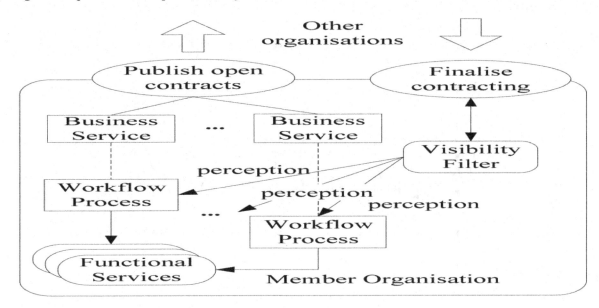

Support at Collaboration Design Phase

After all involved organisations sign the contract, they move to the collaboration design phase. In this phase, each participating organisation designs and coordinates the business collaborations amongst partner organisations by linking related business processes.

Practically, each member organisation may participate in multiple collaborations with different groups of partner organisations at the same time. Furthermore, each participating organisations may choose and combine several collaborations into a comprehensive one according to its own preference and management. Hence, complex partnerships may exist between organisations, and different participating organisations may own totally different forms of business collaborations at the whole picture level. For this reason, the collaboration should be treated from the individual perspective of each participating organisation rather than from a public perspective. Upon this point, our relative workflow model adapts to the various views from different organisations, as it designs and maintains inter-organisational workflow processes from a relative perspective.

How Relative Workflows Support Virtual Organisation Alliances

The discussion in previous section proves us that our relative workflow model well supports B2B collaborations at contracting and collaboration design phases for virtual organisation alliances. The relative perspective features our approach from conventional ones, and the visibility control mechanism and dynamic definition scheme also enhance the authority control and collaboration flexibility. Figure 3 illustrates how relative workflows support the collaborations of a member organisation in a virtual organisation alliance.

Figure 3 illustrates the open relationship contracting, where rectangles, ovals and rounded rectangles denote system components, interfaces with partner organisations, and internal services, respectively. In

Figure 4. Simplified contract model (modified from work (Griffel, Boger, Weinreich, Lamersdorf, & Merz, 1998))

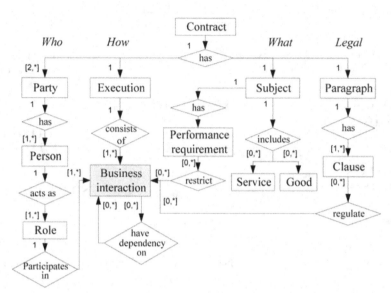

this figure, an organisation first creates its business services by composing related supporting workflows. Then, this organisation may post its demand-and-supply requirements in form of open contracts to the virtual organisation alliance that it joins. If another organisation responds its requirements, the two organisations may come to negotiate about the details of the intended collaboration, and confirm the collaboration by signing the open contract. Once this contract is finalised, the visibility filter will generate corresponding visibility constraints in the perceptions for the involved workflow processes. Afterwards, the two organisations come to the collaboration design phase, where a relative workflow process will be generated to conduct the business collaboration. This relative workflow process integrates the local workflow processes of the host organisation and the perceivable workflow processes of partner organisations. The generation of such a relative workflow process involves two operations, i.e. composing tasks and assembling relative workflow processes.

Business Service Level

Business services encapsulate the business logic and functions inside of an organisation into profitable items, such as making products, designing blueprints, etc. Such business services will be referred to establish contracts for business collaboration. From a technical point of view, these business services are implemented by aggregating the low-level functional services via workflow processes. Currently, the design of business services heavily relies on human assistance and influenced by business rules, policies and strategies.

Table 2. Algorithm 1. Generating perceptions

Input: c	a contract signed by organisation g_0 and g_1
g_0	the host organisation
g_1	the partner organisation
lp	an involved local workflow process of g_0
Output: p	the generated perception on g_0's lp from g_1
1.	// ----------- *Set all tasks invisible initially.* ------------
2.	$p.VC = \varnothing$; $p.MD = \varnothing$; $p.f = \varnothing$;
3.	**for** each task $t \in lp$
4.	$p.VC = p.VC \cup \{(t, \text{invisible})\}$;
5.	// ----------- *Set contactable tasks.* ------------
6.	$bsSet = participatedBS(lp)$;
7.	**for** each business interaction bi defined in contract c
8.	$interBS = interactedBS(bi)$;
9.	**if** $interBS \cap bsSet \neq \varnothing$ **then**
10.	**for** each business service $bs' \in interBS \cap bsSet$
11.	**for** each task $t \in lp.T$
12.	$invokedOP = invokedOPSet(t)$;
13.	**if** $invokedOP \cap bsOPSet(bs') \neq \varnothing$ **then**
14.	**if** $\exists (t, \text{invisible}) \in p.VC$ **then**
15.	$p.VC = p.VC \setminus \{(t, \text{invisible})\}$;
16.	$p.VC = p.VC \cup \{(t, \text{contactable})\}$;
17.	**end if**
18.	**for** each operation $op \in invokedOP \cap bsOPSet(bs')$
19.	**for** each message $md \in usedMD(op)$
20.	$p.MD = p.MD \cup \{ md \}$;
21.	$p.f = p.f \cup \{(md, t)\}$;
22.	**end for**
23.	**end if**
24.	**end for**
25.	**end if**
26.	**end for**
27.	// ------------- *Set trackable tasks.* ------------
28.	**for** each business interaction bi defined in contract c
29.	**for** each business service $bs \in interactedBS(bi)$;
30.	**for** each task $t \in lp.T$
31.	**if** $dependentTask(bs, t) = 1$ **then**
32.	**if** $\exists (t, \text{invisible}) \in p.VC$ **then**
33.	$p.VC = p.VC \setminus \{(t, \text{invisible})\}$;

Table 2. Continued

Input: c	a contract signed by organisation g_0 and g_1
34.	$p.VC = p.VC \cup \{(t, \text{trackable})\}$;
35.	end if
36.	end if

Perception Level

At the phase of contracting, organisations first publish their service demand-and-supply requirements. By means of auctions, bidding or free selections, a partner organisation may be determined by the host organisation. And once the contract is negotiated and signed by all the involved parties, the partnership is then confirmed. Corresponding perceptions will then be generated for involved workflow processes, due to the privacy concern. The setting of visibility constraints of a perception is subject to the business collaboration dependencies defined in the contract.

To analyse the obligations and dependencies implied in a contract, Griffel, Boger, Weinreich, Lamersdorf, and Merz (1998) have proposed a contract model in the Common Open Service Market for SMEs (COSMOS) project, which classifies a contract into four major parts of *Who, What, How* and *Legal Clauses*. As shown in Figure 4, the *How* part defines the execution details for the obligations defined in the *What* and *Legal* parts. The *execution* consists of *business interactions* that describe how the parties defined in *Who* part should interact with to fulfil the collaborations.

At business service level, each business interaction represents an invocation of business services.

Figure 5. Algorithm for composing tasks

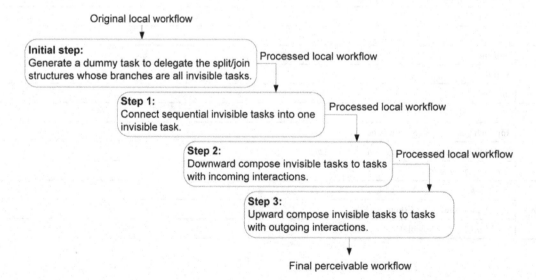

Figure 6. Toolmaking VOA

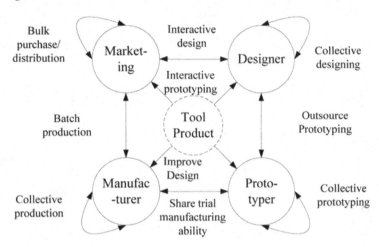

Due to the correlation in nature and the restrictions from *What* and *Legal* clauses, there may exist *dependencies* between business interactions, such as the logic relationship or tracking requirements etc. These dependencies may complicate the relationship between the tasks of supporting workflow tasks. In the contracting process, we call the organisation that issues a contract a *host organisation*, and the responding organisations *partner organisations*.

After the contract is finalised, the visibility filter starts setting up visibility constraints for these supporting workflow processes. These visibility constraints are determined according to these dependencies and the composition relation between participating business services and supporting workflow processes. On the one hand, this step enables the partner organisation's cognition of the host organisation's process details at a certain level. On the other hand, this step prevents the potential privacy disclosure to the partner organisation, and therefore guarantees the collaboration can be executed in an authority safe condition.

Algorithm 1 gives the detailed steps on generating a perception p for a local workflow process lp of the host organisation g_0 in the collaboration with the partner organisation g_1, according to the business interactions defined in contract c. In this algorithm, Function *bsOPSet(bs)* returns the set of functional service operations invoked by business service bs; Function *participatedBS(lp)* returns the set of business services that local workflow process lp participates in; Function *interactedBS(bi)* returns the set of business services that interact in business interaction bi; Function *invokedOPSet(t)* returns the set of functional service operations that task t may invoke; Function *usedMD(op)* returns the set of message descriptions used by operation op; Boolean function *dependentTask(bs, t)* returns "1" if business service bs has status dependency on task t, or returns "0" if not. (Table 2)

Because each business interaction involves the invocations of functional service operations for inter-organisational communication between business services of participating organisations, the "contactable" tasks are determined by matching the functional service operations used in business interactions and by business services. And the "trackable" tasks are determined according to the status dependence between workflow tasks and business services.

Figure 7. Business collaborations

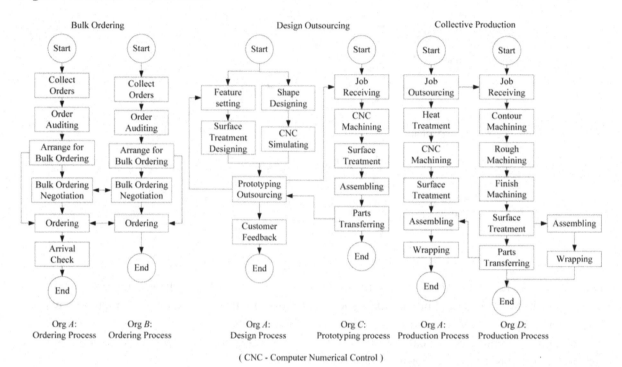

(CNC - Computer Numerical Control)

Process Level

Once the perceptions are set up, relative workflow processes can be generated with two more procedures, i.e., composing tasks and assembling relative workflow processes.

The purpose of composing tasks is to hide private tasks of local workflow processes. We choose to merge invisible tasks with contactable or trackable tasks into composed tasks, if not violating the structural validity; otherwise, those invisible tasks are combined into a dummy task. For example, according to the perception defined from the partner organisation, a local workflow process of the host organisation after this step becomes an authority safe perceivable workflow process. Figure 5 outlines the major steps of composing tasks of a local workflow process, and the detailed steps can be found in work (Zhao, Liu, & Yang, 2005).

In the operation of assembling relative workflow processes, an organisation may assemble its relative workflow processes from local workflow processes and the perceivable workflow processes of partner organisations, together with the messaging links. The messaging links are obtained by matching the message descriptions defined in perceptions of the host organisation and the partner organisation. Once this relative workflow process is generated, the inter-organisational service collaboration becomes formally prepared for collaboration execution phase. The detailed steps about this procedure are given in work (Zhao et al., 2005).

Figure 8. Relative workflow process for bulk ordering collaboration

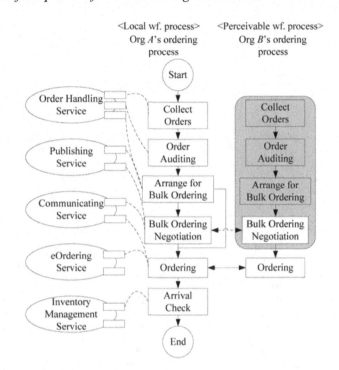

APPLICATION EXAMPLE

Overview

Australian toolmaking firms are relatively small and specialised, operating with minimal business infrastructures in an attempt to control overhead costs. This specialisation restricts access to additional customers or larger projects. In response to this increasing dilemma, toolmakers need to become effective in engaging and servicing a more geographically disperse clientele, and complementary toolmakers need to pool their resources. Technology-enabled collaboration can assist with dealing with this industry deficiency. In this section, we attempt to apply our relative workflow approach in supporting collaboration behaviours of a virtual organisation alliance for these toolmaking firms.

As Figure 6 shows, a virtual organisation alliance consisting of toolmaking firms may connect designers, manufacturers, prototypers and marketing companies together to collaboratively work for customer products. The possible business collaborations between these member organisations are labelled on the bi-directional arcs.

In Figure 6, we can see that various collaborations may occur between these member organisations. For example, manufacturers may batch the product orders from marketing companies for gains-to-scale. The marketing companies may report user requirements to designers and prototypers for product design and feed back the user comments to refine the product design. The prototypers may outsource its prototyping services to designers, and the manufacturers may share their manufacturing capabilities to prototypers. The manufacturers and designers may work together to improve product design for practical production. In addition, organisations of the same type may work collectively to improve the

Figure 9. Final relative workflow process

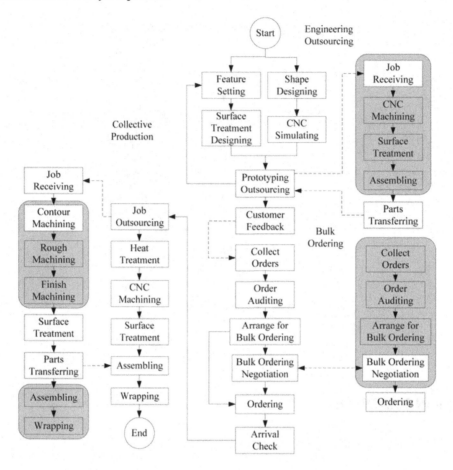

overall capabilities.

Figure 7 illustrates three possible business collaboration scenarios between four anonymous organisations. For simplicity, we only give key tasks of the involved workflow processes.

The collaboration of bulk ordering shown in Figure 7, indicates the economic of scale, as the organisations with orders for the same parts or parts from the same supplier batch their orders together for a better economical price. This collaboration lies between organisation *A*'s ordering process and organisation *B*'s ordering process.

In the collaboration of design outsourcing, organisation *A* outsources its prototyping task to organisation *C*, for the efficiency of time and cost, given organisation *C* has speciality in prototyping. This collaboration involves the interaction between organisation *A*'s design process and organisation *C*'s prototyping process.

In the collaboration of collective production shown in Figure 7, organisation *A*'s production process uses organisation *D*'s production service, which is supported by organisation *B*'s production process. Organisations *A* and *D* produce different kinds of parts, respectively, and finally assemble and package them into unitised tools at the site of organisation *A*. This collaboration is motivated by the production capability requirement, and reflects the synergy for small-to-medium sized organisations.

Figure 10. Relative workflow process from org D's view

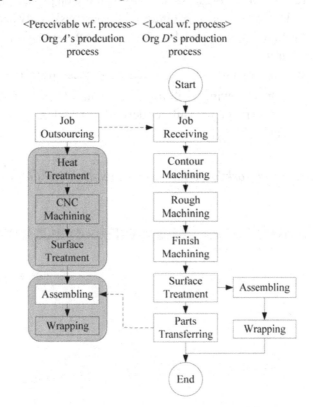

Workflow Setting

In the scenario of the bulk ordering collaboration, when organisation *A* collects orders from its production department(s), it will consider whether to seek a bulk ordering with potential co-buyers. If needed, it will publish a request for bulk ordering of listed parts or materials, to all other member organisations in this alliance. Suppose that organisation *B* has the same things to buy, and organisation *B* responds to organisation *A* to further negotiate the details about the amount for bulk ordering and the expected price, etc. Finally, a contract will be signed to regulate the agreement on bulk ordering, and the two organisations can conjoin their orders. This contract is motivated by seeking an economical price, and the collaboration is supported by the business services of parts ordering of the two organisations, with the underlying supporting workflow processes be organisation *A*'s ordering process and organisation *B*'s ordering process, respectively.

Since this collaboration concentrates on the bulk ordering negotiation, some tasks of ordering processes may be set invisible for the collaborating organisation, if these tasks do not directly participate in the bulk ordering negotiation. According to the algorithm mentioned in the previous section, the corresponding perception on organisation *A*'s ordering process from the view of organisation *B*, i.e. $p_B^{A.orderingprocess}$, may have the following visibility constraints. $VC_1 = \{$ ('Collect Orders', Invisible), ('Order Auditing', Invisible), ('Arrange for Bulk Ordering', Invisible), ('Bulk Ordering Negotiation', Contactable), ('Ordering' Contactable), ('Arrival Check', Invisible) $\}$.

These visibility constraints prohibit organisation B's cognition on private tasks, such as "Collect Orders", "Order Auditing" and "Arrange for Bulk Ordering". These tasks only handle internal procedures, and do not participate in the bulk ordering collaboration. Therefore, such prohibition does not affect the negotiation with organisation B.

Similarly, the perception on organisation B's ordering process from the view of organisation A, i.e. $p_A^{B.orderingprocess}$, may have the following visibility constraints. $VC_2 = \{$ ('Collect Orders', Invisible), ('Order Auditing', Invisible), ('Arrange for Bulk Ordering', Invisible), ('Bulk Ordering Negotiation', Contactable), ('Ordering' Contactable) $\}$.

Figure 11. User interface of local workflow editor and the relative workflow assembler. ©2009 Xiaohui Zhao. Used with permission.

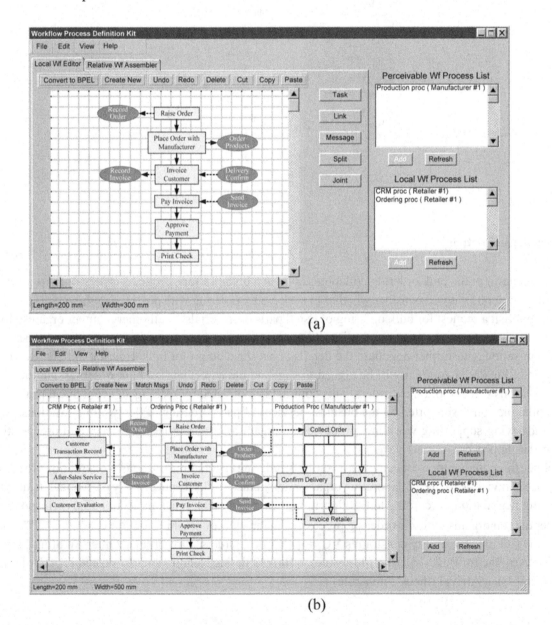

(a)

(b)

According to the visibility constraints defined in perception $p_A^{B.ordering\,Process}$, a relative workflow process can be generated from organisation A's perspective, as shown in Figure 8.

The invisible tasks to organisation A are marked with shadows. The ovals on the left denote the functional services invoked by organisation A's production process, and the small blank rectangles denote the operations of functional services. The two organisations collaborate at process level, while the functional services of organisation B may be hidden from organisation A. Therefore, only organisation A's related functional services are given in Figure 8.

Following this way, organisation A may also sign contracts with organisations C and D, for the design outsourcing and collective production. Therefore, organisation A is simultaneously participating in three collaborations with organisations B, C and D, respectively. These three collaborations together support organisation A's whole process of tools manufacturing. A relative workflow process integrating all these collaborations can be generated at the site of organisation A, to represent organisation A's comprehensive manufacturing business collaboration, as shown in Figure 9.

Figure 9 gives the relative workflow process from the perspective of organisation A. This relative workflow process combines organisation A's three local workflow processes, i.e. engineering process, ordering process and production process. In addition, this relative workflow process includes three other workflow processes of its partner organisations, i.e. organisation B's ordering process, organisation C's prototyping process and organisation D's production process, in their perceivable forms. For the simplicity, related functional services are not given in Figure 9.

However, another participating organisation, say organisation D, may own a different collaboration picture. As organisation D does not participate in the collaborations of bulk ordering or design outsourcing with organisation A, organisation D therefore has no authorities to perceive those two collaborations. This means that organisation D may even not know the existence of these two collaborations. The relative workflow process generated from the perspective of organisation D is given in Figure 10.

From the relative workflow processes shown in Figure 9 and Figure 10, we can see that different organisations hold different views towards collaborations. This reflects our relativity characteristics.

PROTOTYPE IMPLEMENTATION

To demonstrate the ideas discussed in this chapter, a prototype based on Sun Microsystems' Java Web Service Application Programming Interfaces (API) stack has been implemented. This newly re-architected API stack comprises Java API for XML Web Services (JAX-WS), Java Architecture for XML Binding (JAXB) 2.0 and SOAP with Attachments API for Java (SAAJ) 1.3. This API stack represents a logical re-architecture of Web services functionality in the open-source Java Enterprise Edition compliant application server, instead of the original XML Remote Procedure Call (XML-RPC) oriented APIs.

This business process management system implements our relative workflow methodology with the benefits from Web service's inherent advantages in distributed computing. For better integration and interoperability, Business Process Execution Language for Web Services (WS-BPEL) is deployed as the default business process definition language. Figure 11 (a) and (b) show the user interfaces of the local workflow editor and the relative workflow assembler in the workflow process definition kit, respectively. The two components enable users to model local workflow processes, set up visibility constraints, and assemble relative workflow processes to support collaborations. More details of the prototype implementation can be found in work (Zhao & Liu, 2006).

RELATED WORK AND DISCUSSION

During the last years, various efforts have been devoted to developing business to business applications. We briefly mention above some of such proposals, focussing on those which take into account supporting collaborative business processes in the environment of virtual organisation alliances.

ebXML consortium defined a comprehensive set of specifications for XML document exchange among trading partners, for the purpose of providing a framework in which EDI's substantial investments in business processes can be preserved. But a business process defined in ebXML mainly concentrates on exchange of business documents rather than control and data flows. The Partner Interface Process (PIP) blueprints by RosettaNet specify interactions using UML activity diagrams for the Business Operational View (BOV) and UML sequence diagrams for the Functional Service View (FSV) in addition to DTDs for data exchange. However, RosettaNet is primarily focusing on electronic markets with long-lasting pre-specified relationships between parties with one party (such as the market maker) imposing rigid business rules.

Many approaches attempt to precisely architect a virtual organisation alliance with diagrams at process level, resource level, function level, organisation level, and so forth. But these complex models fail in the flexibility and adaptability towards the characteristics of dynamics and openness (Berfield, Chrysanthis, Tsamardinos, Pollack, & Banerjee, 2002). Some approaches implicitly assume or explicitly model (Besembel, Hennet, & Chacon, 2002) business development functions in the virtual organisation alliances, which are often referred to as "broker", "business architect", "integrator", "project manager" (Katzy and Lon 2003) or similar names (Gazzotti, Palmirani, & Paganelli, 2001). These approaches always adopt an absolute view of collaborations, which presents the same picture of the structure and relationships to every member organisation in a virtual organisation alliance, and therefore neglect the aspects of authority control and privacy respect.

Recently, there have been a variety of platforms developed with business to business E-services and virtual enterprises in mind, such as E-speak (Casati, Sayal, & Shan, 2001) from HP, vorteXML (Christophides, Hull, Kumar, & Siméon, 2001) and CrossFlow project (Grefen, Aberer, Ludwig, & Hoffner, 2001). These systems provide supports for managing and monitoring virtual enterprises, along with some standards for communication. In the CrossFlow project, electronic contracts are used to specify the cooperation between E-Services. However, the contracts in this project did not include explicit visibility parameters. Compared with this work, our relative workflow approach provides a more systematic support in visibility control.

Chiu, Karlapalem, Li, and Kafeza (2002), and D. R. Liu and Shen (2003) borrowed the notion of 'view' from federated database systems, and employed a virtual workflow view (or virtual process view) for the inter-organisational collaboration instead of the real instance, to hide internal information. Schulz and Orlowska (2004) developed a cross-organisational workflow architecture, on the basis of communication between the entities of a view-based workflow model. Recently, Issam, Dustdar and Samir (2006) proposed another view-based approach to support inter-organisational workflow cooperation from the motivation of considering an inter-organisational workflow as a cooperation of several pre-established workflows of different organisations. In comparison, our relative workflow approach extracts explicit visibility constraints from commercial contracts to restrict the information disclosure. Different from the workflow view model, the relative workflow approach distributes the macro business collaboration into interactions between neighbouring organisations, and these interactions are performed by the relative workflows designed from the perspective of individual organisations.

With the proposed relative workflows, an organisation centric collaboration scheme can be realised. In this collaboration scheme, an individual organisation can actively choose partner organisations, and assemble proper 'off-the-shelf' perceivable workflow processes from partner organisations with its own workflow processes into a relative workflow process. This relative workflow process forms part of a collaborative workflow process for specific business collaboration. This collaboration scheme has the following appealing features:

- *High autonomy in collaborations*: As an autonomous entity, each organisation is in charge of choosing partners by issuing and signing proper contracts. In addition, each organisation is responsible for defining the collaboration structure and behaviours to fulfil its own business planning and management, without being forced to adapt the restrictions or irrationalities caused by the design of a leading organisation anymore. Therefore, each organisation owns the full control of its business collaboration, and participate collaborations in a proactive mode.
- *Fine granularity of visibility control*: The visibility control mechanism provided by our relative workflow approach prevents the business process privacy disclosure at the task level or at the process level. Such fine granularity of visibility control enables organisations to control the partner organisations' cognition on its business processes during collaborations according to the diverse partnerships. Regarding the low trustiness between the loosely coupled organisations in a virtual organisation alliance, this feature guarantees the authority control in collaborations.
- *Support of dynamic collaborations*: The proposed collaboration scheme can support business collaborations among loosely-coupled organisations in a dynamic or temporary manner. With the help of this scheme, a participating organisation is now able to easily redefine its collaboration structure and behaviours on the fly, e.g. to change partner organisations, to alter requirements for business collaboration with partner organisations, etc. In the environment of virtual organisation alliances, this feature enhances the dynamics of both the whole alliance and individual organisations, and therefore enables organisations to quickly grasp the fast changing market opportunities.

These features well satisfy the requirements of business collaborations in a virtual organisation alliance, especially at the contracting and collaboration design phases.

FUTURE TRENDS

The modelling of the collaborative business processes bridges the requirement engineering and business automation, and initiates the lifecycle of the business process management. Some business process languages, like WS-BPEL and Business Process Modelling Notation (BPMN), have been proposed to support the modelling of collaborative business processes, and are being adopted as industry standards. In this section, we are to discuss issues on contracting between organisations, object-oriented modelling perspective and human aspects in modelling, in the context of collaborative business processes in the virtual organisation alliances.

- *Contracting and process modelling*: Collaborative business processes are used to facilitate collaborations, while collaborations origin from contracting between organisations. Traditional BPM mainly attempts to automate business processes from a computer-oriented perspective, i.e., the approaches emphasis on the data, structural and other technical aspects of business processes. Actually, there is an outstanding difference between human-oriented contracts and computer-oriented business processes, and the interpretation of contracts affects the effectiveness of the modelled collaborative business processes. Previous work on contracting have ever discussed how to help human analysts interpret user requirements and convey them to business process modelling (Chiu, Karlapalem, Li, & Kafeza, 2002; Colombo, Francalanci, & Pernici, 2002). However, there are still a lot of open issues, such as the strategies of translating the descriptive words in contracts, the approaches for mapping the extracted information to data constraints, structural constraints, etc., the criteria on evaluating and validating the contract translation, and the reuse of previous knowledge or existing business processes when modelling new business processes, and so on.

- *Object-oriented view in modelling collaborative business processes*: Due to the heterogeneous nature of the application environment, the participating business processes of a collaborative business process exchange information and data in a loosely coupled mode, as most implementation approaches enable the communication in a collaborative business process with messaging mechanisms. In this communication mode, the object-oriented methodology is more appropriate to model the behaviours between the participating business processes. (Liu, Bhattacharya, & Wu, 2007) have investigated the deployment of object-oriented (or artifact-oriented) perspective in collaborative business process modelling, and the object-oriented perspective shows the advantages in representing the data flows inside or between business processes.

- *Human aspect concerns*: Human activities are considerably involved in most business processes, as business processes are originally developed to help people conduct businesses. However, recent efforts in BPM focus on enhancing the automation level of business processes, and therefore nowadays business process models become more computer-friendly, yet not that people-friendly. Integrating human activities to BPM will definitely better the controllability of business processes, and improve the practical performance of business processes. Some conceptual level and technical level initiatives towards this issue include process-aware information systems, BPEL4People, etc.

CONCLUSION

This chapter has presented a service oriented approach to support B2B collaborations in virtual organisation alliances. In this approach, services are widely used to characterise the collaboration motivation, guide workflow composition, and system infrastructure architecting. A visibility control mechanism is particularly applied to remove potential authority violation, and guarantee the safety on privacy between collaborating organisations. The proposed approach models inter-organisational business processes from a relative perspective, which provides more flexibility for each organisation to customise its collaboration, and therefore can accommodate the diverse partnerships between organisations. The proposed approach contributes to a full framework for supporting virtual organisation alliances with high autonomy, fine granularity control and dynamic collaborations.

ACKNOWLEDGMENT

The work reported in this chapter is supported by the Australian Research Council linkage project, "An Organisation Oriented Framework for Collaborative Business Processes" (LP0669660), with industry partner SAP Research, Australia.

REFERENCES

Berfield, A., Chrysanthis, P. K., Tsamardinos, I., Pollack, M. E., & Banerjee, S. *(2002).* A scheme for integrating e-services in establishing virtual enterprises. *Paper presented at the Research Issues in Data Engineering.*

Besembel, I., Hennet, J. C., & Chacon, E. *(2002).* Coordination by hierarchical negotiation within an enterprise network. *Paper presented at the 8th International Conference on Concurrent Enterprising, Rome, Italy.*

Casati, F., Sayal, M., & Shan, M. C. *(2001).* Developing e-services for composing e-services. *Paper presented at the International Conference on Advanced Information Systems Engineering.*

Casati, F., & Shan, M. C. *(2001).* Models and languages for describing and discovering e-services (Tutorial). *Paper presented at the International Conference on ACM SIG on Management of Data, Santa Barbara, USA.*

Chiu, D. K. W., Karlapalem, K., Li, Q., & Kafeza, E. (2002). Workflow view based e-contracts in a cross-organizational e-services environment. *Distributed and Parallel Databases, 12*(2-3), 193–216. doi:10.1023/A:1016503218569

Christophides, V., Hull, R., Kumar, A., & Siméon, J. (2001). Workflow mediation using VorteXML. *A Quarterly Bulletin of the Computer Society of the IEEE Technical Committee on Data Engineering, 24*(1), 40–45.

Colombo, E., Francalanci, C., & Pernici, B. *(2002).* Modeling coordination and control in cross-organizational workflows. *Paper presented at the DOA/CoopIS/ODBASE.*

Gazzotti, D., Palmirani, M., & Paganelli, P. *(2001).* WHALES: A project life-cycle management application for extended organisations. *Paper presented at the 7th International Conference on Concurrent Enterprising, Bermen, Germany.*

Grefen, P. W. P. J., Aberer, K., Ludwig, H., & Hoffner, Y. (2001). CrossFlow: Cross-organizational workflow management for service outsourcing in dynamic virtual enterprises. *A Quarterly Bulletin of the Computer Society of the IEEE Technical Committee on Data Engineering, 24*(1), 52–57.

Griffel, F., Boger, M., Weinreich, H., Lamersdorf, W., & Merz, M. *(1998).* Electronic contracting with COSMOS - How to establish, negotiate and execute electronic contracts on the Internet. *Paper presented at the 2nd Int. Enterprise Distributed Object Computing Workshop.*

Leymann, F., Roller, D., & Schmidt, M. T. (2002). Web services and business process management. *IBM Systems Journal, 41*(2), 198–211.

Liu, R., Bhattacharya, K., & Wu, F. Y. *(2007)*. Modeling business contexture and behavior using business artifacts. *Paper presented at the 19th International Conference on Advanced Information Systems Engineering, Trondheim, Norway.*

Osterle, H., Fleisch, E., & Alt, R. *(2001)*. Business networking - Shaping collaboration between enterprises. *Springer Verlag.*

van der Aalst, W. M. P., & van Hee, K. M. *(2004)*. Workflow management: Models, methods, and systems. *Cambridge, MA: MIT Press.*

Vissers, C. A., Lankhorst, M. M., & Slagter:, R. (2003). Reference models for advanced e-services. *Paper presented at the 3rd IFIP Conference on E-Commerce, E-Business, E-Government, São Paulo, Brazil.*

Zhao, X., & Liu, C. *(2006)*. Supporting relative workflows with Web services. *Paper presented at the the 8th Asia Pacific Web Conference, Harbin, China.*

Zhao, X., Liu, C., Sadiq, W., & Kowalkiewicz, M. *(2008)*. Process view derivation and composition in a dynamic collaboration environment. *Paper presented at the 16th International Conference on Cooperative Information Systems, Monterrey, Mexico.*

Zhao, X., Liu, C., & Yang, Y. *(2005)*. An organisational perspective of inter-organisational workflows. *Paper presented at the 3rd International Conference on Business Process Management.*

Zhao, X., Liu, C., & Yang, Y. *(2006)*. Supporting virtual organisation alliances with relative workflows. *Paper presented at the 3rd Asia-Pacific Conference on Conceptual Modelling Hobart, Australia.*

Zhao, X., Liu, C., Yang, Y., & Sadiq, W. *(2007)*. Handling instance correspondence in inter-organisational workflows. *Paper presented at the 19th International Conference on Advanced Information Systems Engineering, Trondheim, Norway.*

KEY TERMS AND DEFINITIONS

Business Process Management: a method of efficiently aligning an organisation with the wants and needs of clients. It is a holistic management approach that promotes business effectiveness and efficiency while striving for innovation, flexibility and integration with technology.

Business Process Modelling: the activity of representing both the current ("as is") and future ("to be") processes of an enterprise, so that the current process may be analysed and improved.

Collaborative Business Process: an integrated business process which consists of relevant business processes across participating organisations.

Contracting: the action of signing contracts to confirm a collaboration between different parties.

Process View: a partial representation of an actual business process, which may hide or omit some activities from the original business process.

Relative Workflow: a workflow model which describes inter-organisational workflows or collaborative business processes from the perspectives of individual participants, for the purpose of supporting privacy, openness and flexibility issues in the collaboration environment.

Virtual Organisation Alliance: a temporary alliance between a number of core competence based firms formed to take advantage of market opportunities.

Chapter 13
Inter–Workflow Patterns in Logistic Processes

Hyerim Bae
Pusan National University, South Korea

ABSTRACT

In logistic environments, a process, in that it manages the flow of materials among partners, inherently involves more than one organization. In this regard, a logistic process can be considered as a combined process consisting of multiple sub processes, each of which is managed by a single participant. In achieving systematic management of a logistic process, traditional Business Process Management (BPM) cannot be used for the entire flow, since it lacks the ability to manage interactions among partners. In this paper, then, we propose inter-workflow patterns that represent the relations among separate processes. We specify the inter-workflow patterns between processes, which patterns enable the generation of ECA (Event-Condition-Action) rules to control the execution of the logistic process. A rule engine can then take charge of managing the interactions among processes. A prototype system was developed for the purpose of demonstrating the effectiveness of our approach.

INTRODUCTION

In rapidly revolutionizing business environments, collaboration with partners is considered to be an essential element of success (Liu, 2007; Rhee, 2007b), because the competitiveness of a company is derived from the entire scope of business activity that delivers products to end users. Such collaboration is especially required in logistic environments (Jung, 2008), since a logistic process inherently involves multiple participants. Collaborative success is achieved by means of systematic interfaces among business partners, to the overall end of enhancing customer satisfaction (Gunasekaran, 2004; Liu, 2007; Rhee, 2007b).

DOI: 10.4018/978-1-60566-669-3.ch013

For the efficient management of supply chains, Supply Chain Management (SCM) has been introduced to plan, implement, and control collaboration among partners (Gunasekaran, 2004). SCM research has focused on a variety of areas such as strategic network optimization, strategic partnership, inventory decision (Seo, 2006), production scheduling (Mendez, 2006) and demand forecasting (Liang, 2006). However, execution issues such as the execution of inter-organizational processes have rarely been examined by SCM researchers. Inter-organizational process execution can be achieved by means of a systematic logistic process support.

Business Process Management (BPM) has been widely accepted as an effective and integrated way of managing and executing business processes (Basu, 2002; WfMC, 1995). The BPM system is considered to be a general methodology for increasing a company's productivity through the systematic design, management, integration and improvement of business processes (Basu, 2002; Rhee, 2007a; Rhee, 2007b). However, whereas logistic processes pursue inter-organizational optimization through the effective sharing of information, BPM, in its basic functionality, cannot be applied to the management of multi-organizational business processes.

In order to circumvent this obstacle, we employed a pattern-based approach to the management of interoperations among independent processes. Although the pattern-based approach has been actively researched for over a decade, existing workflow patterns are defined only within a single process, by specifying split and merging patterns such as 'AND', 'OR', 'LOOP', and others. Thus, those patterns cannot support logistic flow. For example, let us consider a delivery process. When goods flow from a manufacturer to customers, they are transported, by a truck, sometimes together in a box, and separately. This process will be repeated several times until the goods finally are delivered to respective customers. Such a process cannot be supported by any commercial BPM systems. In the present research, then, we defined inter-workflow patterns to support logistic processes involving multiple sub processes managed by multiple organizations. Accordingly, these patterns are converted into ECA (Event-Condition-Action) rules, which enable a logistic process to be executed by triggering the action of another process without requiring any separate process engine.

We admit that the pattern based approach to process modeling and execution has contributed to computerized process automation to some extent. At the same time, we claim that it is difficult, with a limited number of process patterns, to represent complex processes in real environments. However, inter-workflow patterns enable the predetermination of relations among independent processes, thereby providing a sound basis for systematic interoperations among participatory organizations. Furthermore, by utilizing ECA rules in implementing interactions among organizations, a third party rule engine can take charge of meditating processes. Thus, we can avoid the problem of where to locate a process server.

The main objective of this research is to develop a systematic method for managing inter-workflow logistic processes. We also established the following sub objectives, which are, at the same time, the three steps necessary for attaining the final goal.

- **Classifying inter-workflow patterns by modeling multi-organizational processes**: We develop a methodology to represent the logistics of business processes among companies and, based on that, establish a process model library.
- **Representing relations among processes using ECA rules**: We derive a process model and rule-based representation of relations among the processes in an environment, where materials and products flow among different partners.

- **XML-based rule representation and process execution using a rule engine**: We implement an XML-based representation of the ECA rules. We also develop an XML based rule controling mechanism by which logistic processes can be triggered and executed. For this purpose, we make BPM interoperable with a rule engine.

To achieve these goals, we first discover inter-workflow patterns that occur over logistic processes, and then derive rules to execute the patterns. We represent the rules in XML markup language enabling computer systems to interpret them. We expect that our relation patterns can contribute to the systematic management of the relations between two or among three or more independent processes.

BACKGROUND

Related Previous Work

The relevant previous research falls into one or another category: research on workflow patterns or on rule-based workflow execution. Certainly, a great amount of research has been conducted to model business processes using predefined patterns. WfMC (Workflow Management Coalition), an international standard organization on workflow, defines, for process split and merge, several types of workflow modeling semantics including 'AND', 'OR', and 'LOOP' (WfMC, 1995). Aalst et al. (2000) extend this specification defining 20 advanced workflow patterns. Workflow and BPM researchers, and most BPM systems, have adopted these standard patterns, and thus a basis for workflow interoperability has been established.

Several research efforts have been undertaken to apply rule-based approaches to the execution of business processes (Bae, 2004; Casati, 1996; Chen, 2006; Liu, 2005; Lucia, 2003). Bae et al. (2004) proposed automatic business process execution achieved by replacing a workflow engine with an active database enabling ECA rules. In order to generate ECA rules for process execution, they converted the predefined-pattern process structure into block structures and generated ACTA formalism, which is an advanced transaction model. Liu et al. (2005) introduced a method for modeling and automatic executing car allocation processes, in which method, rules governing the convenient designing of dynamic processes are utilized. Lucia et al. (2003) also applied rules to the execution of workflow, but their approach, unlike the previous ones, used object and activity diagrams. Chen et al. (2006) devised a set of ECA rules as well as a method for their execution required for service composition.

Although the previous research, in sum, provides a sound foundation for our research, our method clearly is unique. Whereas the previous studies developed process patterns and ECA rules for a single process, our research focused on the relationships and interfaces among multiple processes. Thereby, we provide ECA rule-based execution of multi-organizational processes in logistic environments, where the Business Process Management System (BPMS) is already installed. .

Basic Process Model

Prior to describing the relations among processes, we need to treat the concept of a basic process model. Our approach assumes that all partner companies participating in a logistic process have their own pro-

Table 1.

```
Rule (rule_name)
  ON (object).(event)
  IF conditionSet ={(condition_expression)}
  Do actionSet ={(object).(action)}
EndRule
```

cess management system. Based on that assumption, we provide a simple definition of a process model that represents the process of a participatory company (Bae, 2004).

Definition 1. *Process Model*

A process is defined as a directed graph $p = (T, L, A)$, such that

- $T = \{t_i \mid i = 1, ..., I\}$ is the set of tasks, where t_i is the i-th task, and I is the total number of tasks in P.
- $L = \{l_k = (t_i, t_j) \mid t_i, t_j \in T\ i \neq j \}$ is the set of links, where an element (t_i, t_j) indicates that t_i immediately precedes t_j.
- For a split task t_j, such that $|S| > 1$, where $S = \{t_k \downarrow (t_j, t_k) \in L\}$, and $f(t_j) = $ 'AND', if all t_ks should be executed; otherwise $f(t_j) = $ 'OR'.
- For a merge task t_j, such that $|P| > 1$, where $P = \{ t_i \mid (t_i, t_j) \in L \}$, and $f(t_j) = $ 'AND' if all t_i's should be executed; otherwise, $f(t_j) = $ 'OR'.
- $A_i = \{t_i.a_s \mid s = 1, ..., S_i\}$ is the set of attributes of a task t_i, where S_i is the total number of attributes in t_i and $A_k = \{l_k.a_s \mid s = 1, ..., S_k\}$ is the set of attributes of a link l_k, where S_k is the total number of attributes in l_k.

ECA (Event-Condition-Action) Rules

For the execution of a basic process, a process engine, which every BPM system provides, can be used. A global logistic process also requires an execution mechanism for seamless interoperation between participants. In the present study, ECA (Event-Condition-Action) rules were used. Even though previous research on the control of workflow processes using ECA has been actively conducted, it has not yet been applied to the relations between processes. In general, ECA rules observe the syntax below (Goh, 2001; Tan, 1999). (Table 1)

INTER-WORKFLOW PATTERNS

In this chapter, we introduce inter-workflow patterns that have been discovered through our several years of research on logistic process modeling.

Figure 1. Chained Service Model (CSM)

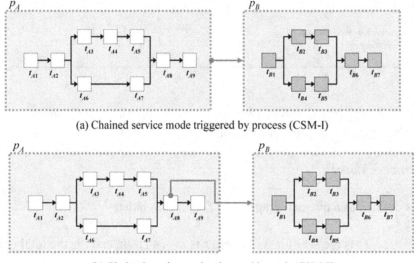

(a) Chained service mode triggered by process (CSM-I)

(b) Chained service mode triggered by task (CSM-II)

Pattern 1: Chained Service Model (CSM)

A Chained Service Model (CSM) is the simplest case, which was originally introduced by WfMC's standard specification (WfMC, 1995). In the CSM, once a process completes, another process is triggered and commences its execution. We classify the CSM into two sub-patterns according to its triggering object. If the succeeding process is triggered by the preceding process, we call it CSM-I. Otherwise, if

Figure 2. Nested Sub-process Model (NSpM)

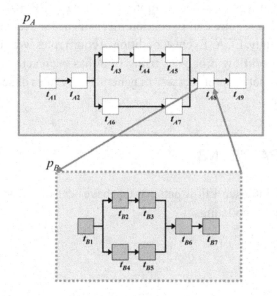

Figure 3. Parallel Synchronization Model (PSM)

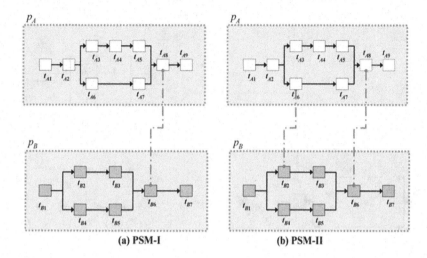

(a) PSM-I (b) PSM-II

the succeeding process is triggered by a task in the preceding process, we call it CSM-II. Figure 1 (a) shows that p_B is triggered by p_A and initiates after p_A completes. On the other hands, in Figure 1 (b), p_B is triggered by t_{A8}.

Pattern 2: Nested Sub-process Model (NSpM)

In the Nested Sub-Process Model (NSpM), a process becomes a unit task of another process, forming a parent-child relation, as shown in Figure 2. In view of p_A, the execution of p_B is treated exactly the same as the execution of t_{A8}.

Figure 4. Multiple Instance Model (MIM) and Instance Merge Model (IMM)

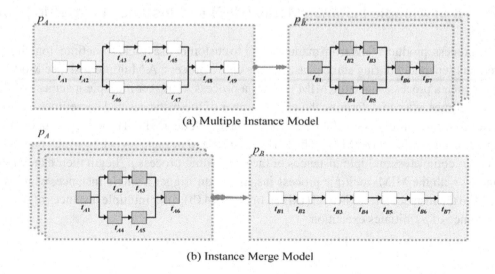

(a) Multiple Instance Model

(b) Instance Merge Model

Figure 5. Exception Handling Model

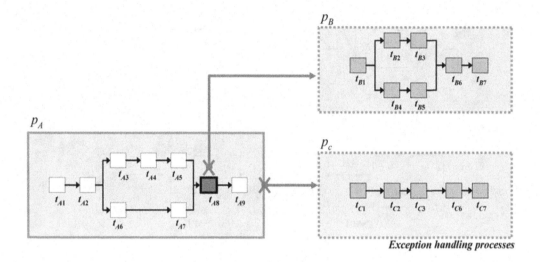

Pattern 3: Parallel Synchronization Model (PSM)

The Parallel Synchronization Model (PSM) comprises a relation pattern in which two different processes are executed in parallel and synchronized at a certain point. In other words, a process should wait at a certain stage until the other arrives at a predefined synchronizing point. The PSM can be classified into two models, the One-Point Synchronization Model (PSM-I) and the Multi-Point Synchronization Model (PSM-II), according to the numbers of synchronization points, and are represented in Figure 3 (a) and (b) respectively. In PSM-I (Figure 3 (a)), if a task t_{A8} in a process p_A completes without completing t_{B6} of p_B, p_A should hold execution until p_B reaches t_{B6}. The operation of PSM-II (Figure 3(b)) is similar to that of PSM-I, except for its multiple synchronization points.

Patterns 4 & 5: Multiple Instance Model (MIM) and Instance Merge Model (IMM)

In a logistic process, products flow from manufacturer to customer in a truck, sometimes together in a box and sometimes separately during some phases of the entire process. A Multiple Instance Model (MIM) is useful for such a process, since the MIM enables a process to trigger multiple instances of the other process. Sometimes, we can determine the exact number of the instances and sometimes we cannot. If we can determine the number, it is called the Static Instance Model (MIM-I) and if we cannot, it is called the Dynamic Instance Model (MIM-II). The MIM is illustrated in Figure 4 (a), in which model, as soon as a process p_A completes, multiple instances of the succeeding process p_B begin their execution.

In contrast with the MIM, multiple process instances can trigger a single instance, which situation corresponds to the Instance Merge Model (IMM). In Figure 4 (b), after multiple instances of p_A complete, a single instance of p_B initiates execution.

Figure 6. Cancellation Propagation Model

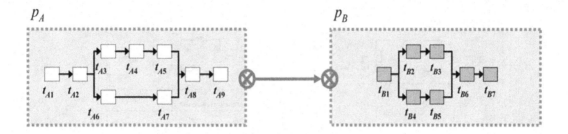

Pattern 6: Exception Handling Model (EHM)

The exception handling issue has already been dealt with by many researchers (Hagen, 2000; Klein, 2000; Kumar, 2005). Their approaches, however, provide only for task-level handling of workflow. But in logistic environments, exception handling might have to be provided by a separate process. In our Exception Handling Model (EHM), a process plays the role of exception handler for another process or task in which the exception takes place.

Figure 5 illustrates the EHM, where p_B is an exception handler for a specific task $p_A.t_{A8}$ and p_C is an exception handler for the whole process p_A. In p_A, if unexpected problems occur during execution of t_{A8}, then the control of the process is handed over to p_B. Otherwise, if problems occur in other tasks, the other handler p_C takes the control.

Figure 7. Complex Relationship Model

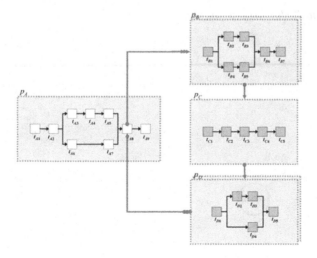

Figure 8. Sample logistic process

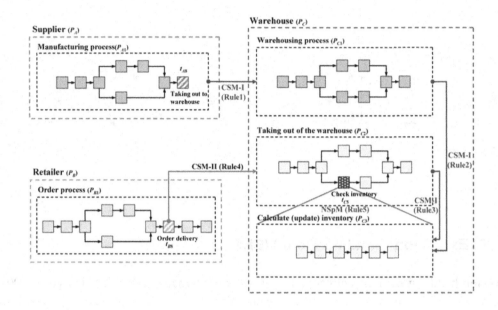

Pattern 7: Cancellation Propagation Model (CPM)

The Cancellation Propagation Model (CPM) is the relation pattern between two processes, by which process failure is propagated to the other process. As shown in Figure 6, if process p_A fails, then process p_B stops running.

Figure 9. State transition model for process objects

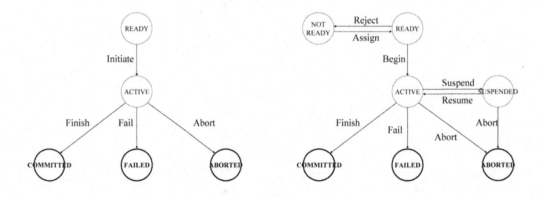

Table 2. Major events of business process

Object	Event		
	Event Name	**Corresponding Function**	**Description (When to be generated)**
Process (Instance)	*Create*	CreateInstance(int *n*)	When a process instance is created. *n*: number of instances generated
	Initiate	Initiate()	When a process begins.
	Finish	Finish()	When a process completes.
	Fail	Fail()	When a process fails.
	Abort	Abort()	When a process is aborted by a user.
Task (Instance)	*Assign*	Assign()	When a task is assigned to a user.
	Reject	Reject()	When a user rejects a task
	Begin	Begin()	When a task begins
	Suspend	Suspend()	When execution of a task is suspended.
	Resume	Resume()	When a suspended task resumes its execution.
	Finish	Finish()	When a task completes normally.
	Fail	Fail()	When a task fails.
	Abort	Abort()	When a task is aborted by a user.

Complex Relationship Model (CRM)

Sometimes, the relations among processes need to be represented by a combination of different models. In Figure 7, MIM, CSM, and IMM represent the relations among four different processes. After t_{A8} finishes, p_B starts. Successful completion of every instance of p_B is followed by an instance of p_C, which triggers the execution of p_D. If all of the instances of p_D finish, p_A finally precedes to t_{A9}.

Logistics Process Example

Using the inter-workflow patterns, we can establish relations between processes. Let us consider the supply chain illustrated in Figure 8. There are three organizations, each of which has its own process. In order to handle the manufacturers-to-customers logistics, all of the partners need to interoperate systematically. We use inter-workflow patterns to model the relations between processes and to automate their interoperation among them.

As shown in the figure, five processes (1 for a supplier, 3 for a warehouse, and 1 for a retailer) are interrelated by inter-workflow patterns. For example, the 'Manufacturing process (p_{A1})' of the supplier and the 'Warehousing process (p_{C1})' are inter-related by the CSM-I pattern. According to the definition of the CSM-I pattern, when p_{A1} completes, p_{C1} is triggered.

Table 3.

NULL..	(1)
$p_A.\ numberOfInstance() + p_B.\ numberOfInstance() < n$...........................	(2)
$p_A.isActivated() ==$ true	(3)
$p_A.numberOfCompletedInstance() > $ n	(4)

STATE TRANSITION AND EVENT-ACTION-CONDITION

State Transition Model of Process Objects

Process and task, the principal BPMS-managed objects, change their states while business processes are executed. Figure 9 (a) and (b) illustrate the state transitions of process and task respectively.

A process, after being designed and deployed, remains in the 'READY' state, and an authorized user can execute it generating the 'Initiate' event and transitioning the process into the 'DOING' state. If the process completes successfully, it enters the 'COMMITED' state. Or as a result of errors, it can be 'FAILED' or 'ABORTED' by users.

The state model of a task is more complex than that of a process. Let us consider a task in a process. When all of its preceding tasks complete, it is assigned to a user and a corresponding event, and 'Assign' is initiated. The state thereby changes from 'NOT READY' to 'READY'. If the user does not accept the task, the state will revert to the previous one, and if the user accepts the task, the 'ACTIVE' state is entered. The task can be suspended if the user so chooses. After the execution, the task state model enters one of 3 completed states, which are the same as those of the process.

Events, Conditions, and Actions of Business Process

Events in a business process take place according to the objects used in the BPMS, which are process, task, user, application, process variable and others. The present research uses events required only to interoperate among processes, which events are summarized in Table 2.

According to the ECA rules, the action is executed after the condition is evaluated by the system. Therefore, the condition has to be represented in a format that a computer system can interpret, and the system returns the Boolean value by evaluating operations on predefined objects.

In order to represent a condition, we use object, derived object, and operations. Objects evaluated for condition are those defined in the process meta model in Section 3. The following operations are used to express conditions and if a condition is satisfied, the Boolean value 'true' or 'false' is returned.

- Arithmetic: $+, -, *, /$
- Comparison: $<, >, ==, <>$
- Logic: NOT, AND, OR, XOR
- \NULL,
- Miscellaneous: BETWEEN, IN

A condition is expressed by combining objects, derived objects and operations. The followings are examples of conditions. (Table 3)

Table 4. Summary of major functions used in ECA rules

Function interface	Description
Time Process::delayed_time() *Time* Task::delayed_time()	This function returns the delayed time of a process/task
Process ProcessInstance::getProcessModel() *Process* Task::getProcessModel()	This function returns a process model of a process/task instance.
Task[] Task::getNextTasks()	This function returns the next task(s).
Boolean Process::isStopped() *Boolean* Task::isStopped()	This function determines if a process/task is currently stopped or not.
Boolean Process::isActivated() *Boolean* Task::isActivated()	This function determines if a process/task is currently in 'DOING' state or not.
Boolean Process::isTerminated() *Boolean* ProcessInstance::isTerminated ()	This function determines if a process (instance) has been terminated or not.
Boolean Process::isStarted() *Boolean* Task::isStarted()	This function determines if a process/task has already been started or not.
Int Process::numberOfCompletedInstance()	This function returns the number of process instances completed.
Int Process::numberOfTask()	This function returns the number of tasks in a process.
User Task::getUser() *User[]* Task::getUsers()	This function returns a user or users in charge of a task.
_____ _____*User:: 'COM-* *PLETE', 'ABORT'...})* _____ _____*User[]* ProcessInstance::getPresentUsers()	This function returns all users participating in a process instance.
Int Task::numberOfInstance () *Int* Process::numberOfInstance ()	This function returns the number of instances of a process/task.
Object ProcessVariable::value_of()	This function returns the value of a process variable.
Time Task::time_of(), Event_Name={'START', 'COMPLETE', 'ABORT'...}	This function returns the time stamp of a process/task event
long User::workload_of ()	This function returns the workload of a user.

Condition (1) indicates that an action can be invoked regardless of the condition. Condition (2) determines if the number of instances of a process p_A is smaller than n or not. Condition (3) determines if a process p_A is activated, and condition (4) determines if the number of process instances is larger than *n* or not.

After the condition is evaluated, an action is invoked based on the result. The actions are basic functions of business process execution, and include start, finish and suspend. These functions correspond to previously defined events, which are summarized in Table 2. All of the functions used in ECA rules and which pertain to BPM API are listed in Table 4.

Table 5. The ECA rules for inter-workflow patterns

Pattern	ECA (Event- Condition-Action) rules	
CSM	**RULE (R1-1:CSM-I)** **ON:**p_A.Finish **IF:** {$p_B.a_{pre\_condition}$} **DO:**$p_B.initiate()$ **ENDRULE**	**RULE (R1-2:CSM-II)** **ON:**$p_A.t_{A8}$.Finish **IF:** {$p_B.a_{pre\_condition}$} **DO:**$p_B.initiate()$ **ENDRULE**
NSpM	**RULE (R2-1: NSpM)** **ON:**$p_A.t_{A8}$.Begin **IF:** {$p_B.a_{pre\_condition}$} **DO:**$p_B.initiate()$ **ENDRULE**	**RULE (R2-2: NSpM)** **ON:**p_B.Finish **IF:** {$p_A.t_{A8}.a_{post\_condition}$} **DO:**$p_A.t_{A8}.commit()$ **ENDRULE**
PSM	**RULE (R3-1: PSM-I)** **ON:**$p_A.t_{A8}$.Finish **IF:** {$p_B.t_{B6}.a_{state} ==$ SUPENDED} **DO:** { $p_B.t_{B6}.resume(), p_B.t_{B6}.commit()$} **ELSE IF**$p_B.t_{B6}.a_{state} ==$ DOING **DO:** **ENDRULE**	**RULE (R3-2: PSM-II)** (*Do* **R3-1** *for multiple sync. points*) **ENDRULE**
MIM & IMM	**RULE (R4: MIM)** **ON:**p_A.Finish **IF:** {$p_B.a_{pre\_condition}$} **DO:**$p_B.createInstance(n)$ **ENDRULE**	**RULE (R5: IMM)** **ON:**p_A.Finish **IF:** {$p_A.a_{pre\_condition}$, ($p_A.numberOfCompleteInstance() == n$) } **DO:**$p_B.initiate()$ **ENDRULE**
EHM	**RULE (R6-1: EHM)** **ON:**$p_A.t_{A2}$.Fail **IF:** {$p_B.a_{pre\_condition}$ } **DO:** {$p_B.initiate(), p_A.t_{A2}.suspend()$} **ENDRULE**	**RULE (R6-2: EHM)** **ON:**p_B.COMPLETE **IF:** {$p_A.t_{A2}.a_{state} ==$ SUPENDED} **DO:**$p_A.resume()$ **ENDRULE**
CPM	**RULE (R7: CPM)** **ON:**p_A.FAILED **IF:** NULL **DO:**$p_B.stop()$ **ENDRULE**	

CONTROLLING INTER-WORKLOW PATTERNS

ECA Rules for Patterns

After the relations between processes are specified, they can be converted to ECA rules for run-time controlling. ECA rules, in our approach, use basic objects such as 'process', 'task', 'attribute', and 'user'. Almost every commercial BPM system predefines and provides events and functions for objects; we use them to specify the event, condition, and action elements in the ECA rules.

In this chapter, the ECA rules for each pattern are defined. The principal rules are summarized in Table 5.

XML Representation of ECA Rules

In order to deal with process execution patterns using ECA rules, the rules should be represented in a form that all logistic partners in different computing environments can recognize and use. This research

Figure 10. XRML representation for NSpM pattern, (a) An example of RIML

```
<RIML Version= "1.0w" >
    <Rule id= "BPR0001" type= "R2-1:NSpM">
      . <RuleTitle> order delivery </RuleTitle>
          <variable1 ObjType= "Process" >SP_ProcessID</variable1>
          <variable2 ObjType= "Task" >N_TaskID</variable2>
          <variable3 ObjType= "Process" >SB_ProcessID</variable3>
          <value1> 'p000238-001' </value1>
          <value2> 't000134-001' </value2>
          <value3> 'p000242-001' </value3>
      </Rule>
</RIML>
```
(a) An example of RIML

```
<RIML Version= "1.0w" >
    <Rule id= "BPR0001" type= "R2-1:NSpM">
      . <RuleTitle> order delivery </RuleTitle>
          <variable1 ObjType= "Process" >SP_ProcessID</variable1>
          <variable2 ObjType= "Task" >N_TaskID</variable2>
          <variable3 ObjType= "Process" >SB_ProcessID</variable3>
          <value1> 'p000238-001' </value1>
          <value2> 't000134-001' </value2>
          <value3> 'p000242-001' </value3>
      </Rule>
</RIML>
```

```
<RSML Version= "1.0w" >
   <RuleInvoke RuleID="BPR0001" InvokeNo= 1 >
      <IF >
          <Object> SB_ProcessID</Object>
          <Operation> CheckPreCondition</Operation>
          <Condition> ==</Condition>
          <Value> True </Value>
      </IF >
      <THEN>
          <Object> SB_ProcessID </Object>
          <Action>Initiate</Action>
      </THEN>
   </RuleInvoke>

   <RuleInvoke RuleID="BPR0001" InvokeNo= 2 >
      <IF >
          <Object> N_TaskID </Object>
          <Operation> CheckPostCondition</Operation>
          <Condition> ==</Condition>
          <Value> True </Value>
      </IF >
      <THEN>
          <Object> N_TaskID </Object>
          <Action>Commit</Action>
      </THEN>
   </RuleInvoke>

</RSML>
```
(b) An example of RSML

```
<RTML Version= "1.0w" >
   <WhenTrigger RuleID="BPR0001">
   <RuleTrigger TriggerNo = 1, InvokeNo=1 >
      <Object> N_TaskID </Object>
      <Event>Begin</Event>
   </RuleTrigger>
   <RuleTrigger TriggerNo = 2, InvokeNo=2 >
      <Object> SB_ProcessID </Object>
      <Event>Finish</Event>
   </RuleTrigger>
   </WhenTrigger>

   <Bring>
    <RuleTitle> order delivery </RuleTitle>
   </Bring>

   <Result>
    <RuleState> committed</RuleState >
   </Result>
</RTML>
```
(c) An example of RTML

introduces a modified version of eXtensible Rule Markup Language (XRML) developed by the Korea Advanced Institute of Science and Technology (KAIST) (Lee, 2003).

Figure 11. Rule-based controlling procedure

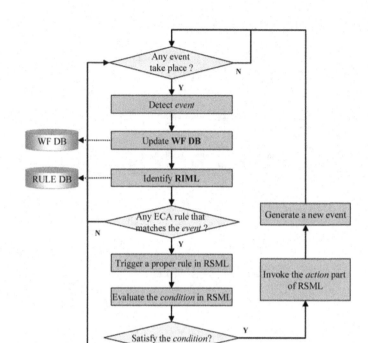

There exist three other XML-based rule markup languages, which are Business Rule Markup Language (BRML) (Grosof, 1999), Rule Markup Language (RuleML) (Boley, 2001), and Relational-Functional

Figure 12. Prototype System Architecture

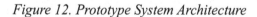

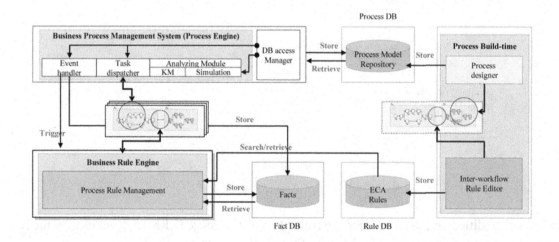

Figure 13. Modeled relationships between two processes using inter-workflow patterns at build time

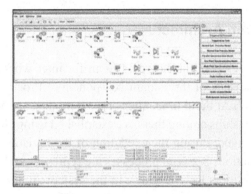

Markup Language (RFML) (Boley, 2000). However, because they cannot fully contain all three elements, Event, Condition and Action, we chose XRML as our rule presentation tool. However XRML, providing only a basic frame for representing ECA rules, did not exactly fit our purpose, so we applied a modified version of XRML to our system.

XRML consists of three different languages, which are Rule Identification Markup Language (RIML), Rule Structure Markup Language (RSML) and Rule Triggering Markup Language (RTML). The RIML defines rule identification information including rule title and variables, and it plays the role of meta data for rules. After the RIML is prepared, we define the RSML, which specifies the 'Condition' and 'Action' of a rule. Finally, we utilize the RTML to trigger rules and to specify results of rule execution. XRML representation of a rule in the NSpM pattern is illustrated in Figure 10.

Controlling Procedure of Inter-Workflow

Our system controls the execution of inter-workflow by using a rule engine that can interpret, manage, and infer rules from the ECA rules. The controlling procedure uses two repositories: the WF DB and the Rule DB. When an event takes place, our system first logs it into the WF DB and then tries to identify it in the Rule DB. If the corresponding RIML can be found, the system tries to match the event with the *event* of the ECA rules identified. Then, a proper RSML is retrieved by interpreting the RTML, and our system evaluates the *conditions* of the rule by evaluating them with reference to the facts, which are directly retrieved from or inferred from the existing facts in the WF DB. Then, if all of the *conditions* are proven to be true, the *action* is carried out. The performing of the *action* also generates events, and these are handled repetitively. The overall procedure is mapped in Figure 11.

PROTOTYPE IMPLEMENTATION

System Architecture

We developed a prototype system for inter-workflow management, illustrated in Figure 12. Our system consists of three main components: 'Process Build-time', 'Process Engine', and 'Business Rule Engine'. At build time, after process models are prepared using 'Process designer', the inter-workflow relationships among them are established using 'Inter-workflow Rule Editor'. Then, each basic process is managed, during the execution of the logistic process, by the process engine of its own BPMS. As the relations between processes are represented by ECA rules, the relations between them are managed by 'Business Rule Engine'. In the system architecture illustrated in the following Figure 12, all of the DBs are implemented using Oracle DBMS, and almost all of the modules are developed to work in J2EE environments.

Figure 13 shows the user interfaces used for editing inter-workflow between two processes. In the left Figure, a user opens two processes, which are already designed. Then, in the right Figure, he can establish the relationships by choosing inter-workflow pattern buttons, which are located on the right tool bar. Our system automatically generates ECA rules, and the user can adjust them simply by modifying some parameters. After the processes and relations among them are established, a process engine controls only the execution of processes, and a rule engine controls the interaction among the processes. This mechanism removes often delicate issue of where the controlling power should be placed, since the interaction between companies is managed by an independent rule engine.

CONCLUSION

In logistic environments, a material or a product is delivered from a provider to a consumer. The material or object, in such settings, undergoes several processes managed by different participants, who are the manufacturer, distributor, transporter, and retailer. In order to manage such flows, we provide inter-workflow patterns that represent the relations among the separate processes. When the inter-workflow patterns among the separate processes are specified at build-time, ECA rules are automatically generated for future controlling at run-time. We also provide XML-based rule representation, enabling partners with different computing environments to share and exchange rules.

While a global logistic process involving multiple organizations is executed, each unit process of a participatory company is managed by its own BPM system, and all of the interactions between the participants are controlled by a rule engine according to the codes of the ECA rules. Our contribution lies in integrating processes operated by multiple organizations and thereby enabling the connections between processes to be effectively and efficiently executed.

Inter-workflow patterns and rule-based management of interaction among processes provide several advantages in logistic environments. First, they enable the modeling and execution of inter-organizational logistic processes. Whereas traditional process patterns support only simple semantics within a single process and do not support logistic flow, inter-workflow patterns enable the representation of relations among partners participating in a logistic process. Second, triggering of a process from another process can be separated from process execution logics. After inter-workflow patterns and the pertinent rules are prepared, all of the process interoperations are executed and managed by a third-party rule engine, the rule engine being capable of automating the triggering of logistic flow. Third, since the rule DB is augmented by users, new types of relations among processes can be added. If the event, condition, and action of a new relation can be represented, they can be modeled and executed by our system.

There are several further research issues. First, we have focused only on the relation patterns that occur between two processes. We can extend them to patterns among three or more processes. Second, the introduced patterns pertain to one-way relationships. In other words, one process only sends signals, and the other process just takes action. However, either process can two-way interact with the other, in both giving and receiving instructions. Third, in order to execute the ECA rule codes, we need a more effective architecture to reconcile BPM and BRE. Finally, there are correctness issues in the inter-workflow patterns. Therefore, we need to develop an algorithm for avoiding a deadlock in the inter-workflow patterns, and also required is a method of correctly combining the patterns.

ACKNOWLEDGMENT

This work was supported by the Grant of the Korean Ministry of Education, Science and Technology (The Regional Core Research Program/Institute of Logistics Information Technology)

REFERENCES

Bae, H., Hur, W., Yoo, W., Kwak, B., Kim, Y., & Park, Y. (2004). Document configuration control processes captured in a workflow. *Computers in Industry, 53*(2), 117–131. doi:10.1016/j.compind.2003.07.001

Bae, J., Bae, H., Kang, S.-H., & Kim, Y. (2004). Automatic control of workflow processes using eca rules. *IEEE Transactions on Knowledge and Data Engineering, 16*(8), 1010–1023. doi:10.1109/TKDE.2004.20

Basu, A., & Kumar, A. (2002). Research Commentary: Workflow management systems in e-business. *Information Systems Research, 13*(1), 1–14. doi:10.1287/isre.13.1.1.94

Boley, H. (2000). Markup languages for functional-logic programming. In *Proceedings of 9th WFLP 2000*, Benicassim, Spain.

Boley, H., Tabet, S., & Wagner, G. (2001). Design rationale of RuleML: A markup language for Semantic Web rules. In *Proceedings of SWWS'01*, Stanford.

Casati, F., Ceri, S., Pernici, B., & Pozzi, G. (1996). Deriving active rules for workflow enactment. In *Proceedings of 17 Int'l Conference on Database and Expert Systems Applications* (pp. 94-110).

Chen, L., Li, M., & Cao, J. (2006). ECA Rule-based workflow modeling and implementation for service composition. *IEICE Transactions on Information and Systems . E (Norwalk, Conn.), 89-D*(2), 624–630.

Goh, A., Koh, Y.-K., & Domazet, D. S. (2001). ECA rule-based support for workflows . *Artificial Intelligence in Engineering, 15*(1), 37–46. doi:10.1016/S0954-1810(00)00028-5

Grosof, B. N., & Labrou, Y. (1999). An approach to using XML and a rule-based content language with an agent communication language. In *Proceedings of the IJCAI-99 Workshop on Agent Communication Languages (ACL-99)*. Stockholm, Sweden.

Gunasekaran, A., & Ngai, E. W. T. (2004). Information systems in supply chain integration and management. *European Journal of Operational Research, 159*(2), 269–295. doi:10.1016/j.ejor.2003.08.016

Hagen, C., & Alonso, G. (2000). Exception handling in workflow management systems. *IEEE Transactions on Software Engineering, 26*(10), 943–958. doi:10.1109/32.879818

Jung, H., Chen, F. F., & Jung, B. (2008). Decentralized supply chain planning framework for third party logistics partnership. *Computers & Industrial Engineering, 55*(2), 348–364. doi:10.1016/j.cie.2007.12.017

Klein, M., & Dellarocas, C. (2000). A knowledge-based approach to handling exceptions in workflow systems. *Computer Supported Cooperative Work, 9*(3), 399–412. doi:10.1023/A:1008759413689

Kumar, A., & Wainer, J. (2005). Meta workflows as a control and coordination mechanism for exception handling in workflow systems . *Decision Support Systems, 40*(1), 89–105. doi:10.1016/j.dss.2004.04.006

Lee, J. K., & Son, M. M. (2003). The eXtensible Rule Markup Language. *Communications of the ACM, 46*(5), 59–64. doi:10.1145/769800.769802

Liang, W.-Y., & Huang, C.-C. (2006). Agent-based demand forecast in multi-echelon supply chain. *Decision Support Systems, 42*(1), 390–407. doi:10.1016/j.dss.2005.01.009

Liu, R., & Kumar, A. (2005). An analysis and taxonomy of unstructured workflows. *Third International Conference on Business Process Management (BPM 2005)* Nancy, France (LNCS 3649, pp. 268-284).

Liu, R., Kumar, A., & Aalst, W. (2007). A formal modeling approach for supply chain event management. *Decision Support Systems, 43*(3), 761–778. doi:10.1016/j.dss.2006.12.009

Lucia, A. D., Francese, R., & Tortora, G. (2003). Deriving workflow enactment rules from UML activity diagrams: A case study. In *Proceedings of IEEE Symposium on Human Centric Computing Languages and Environments* (pp. 211-218).

Méndez, A., Bonfill, A., Espuña, A., & Puigjaner, L. (2006). Rigorous approach to coordinate production and transport scheduling in a multi-site system. *Computer Aided Chemical Engineering, 21*(2), 2171–2176. doi:10.1016/S1570-7946(06)80370-6

Rhee, S.-H., Bae, H., & Choi, Y. (2007). Enhancing the efficiency of supply chain processes through Web Services. *Information Systems Frontier: Special Issue on from Web Services to Services Computing, 9*(1), 103–118.

Rhee, S. -H., Cho, N., & Bae, H. (2007). A more comprehensive approach for enhancing business process efficiency (LNCS 4558, pp. 955-964).

Seo, Y. (2006). Controlling general multi-echelon distribution supply chains with improved reorder decision policy utilizing real-time shared stock information. *Computers & Industrial Engineering, 51*(2), 229–246. doi:10.1016/j.cie.2006.02.005

Tan, C. W., & Goh, A. (1999). Implementing ECA rules in an active database. *Knowledge-Based Systems, 12*(4), 137–144. doi:10.1016/S0950-7051(99)00028-3

van der Aalst W. M. P., ter Hofstede A. H. M., Kiepuszewski B., & Barros A. P. (2000). Advanced workflow patterns (LNCS 1901, 18-19).

WfMC-TC00-1003 (1995). *The workflow reference model*. Workflow Management Coalition, Lighthouse Point, FL.

KEY TERMS AND DEFINITIONS

Business Process Management: an integrated way of modeling, automating, managing and optimizing a business process to promote business effectiveness and efficiency. It strives for innovation, flexibility, and integration of enterprise information system.

ECA Rule: Event-Condition-Action (ECA) rule is referring to the mechanism of an active rule using IF-THEN-ELSE structure that attempts to execute an action based on certain conditions regarding to any incoming event.

Logistic Process: a process describing the flow of goods and information between the point of origin and the point of consumption to satisfy the customer demand.

Process Model: a logical and graphical description of a real business process. The purpose of process model is to analyze and improve processes.

Rule Markup Language: an XML-based markup language that is used to represent business rules.

Supply Chain Management: management of a network of interconnected businesses in order to fulfill the provision of product and service packages required by customers

Workflow Pattern: a set of predefined patterns of workflow which depicts a sequence of operations.

XML: a general purpose specification for creating custom markup languages, which is used both to encode documents and to serialize data.

Chapter 14
Engineering of Experience Based Trust for E-Commerce

Zhaohao Sun
Hebei Normal University, China & University Of Ballarat, Australia

Jun Han
Beihang University, China

Dong Dong
Hebei Normal University, China

Shuliang Zhao
Hebei Normal University, China

ABSTRACT

Trust is significant for sustainable development of e-commerce and has received increasing attention in e-commerce, multiagent systems (MAS), and artificial intelligence (AI). However, little attention has been given to the theoretical foundation and intelligent techniques for trust in e-commerce from a viewpoint of intelligent systems and engineering. This chapter will fill this gap by examining engineering of experience-based trust in e-commerce from the viewpoint of intelligent systems. It looks at knowledge-based trust, inference-based trust and their interrelationships with experience-based trust. It also examines scalable trust in e-commerce. It proposes a knowledge based model of trust in e-commerce and a system architecture for METSE: a multiagent system for experience-based trust in e-commerce. The proposed approach in this chapter will facilitate research and development of trust, multiagent systems, e-commerce and e-services.

INTRODUCTION

Generally, trust is a positive belief or expectation about the perceived reliability of, dependability of and confidence in a person, an intelligent agent, organization, company, object, process, or system (Schneiderman, 2000). Castelfranchi and Tan (2001) assert that e-commerce can be successful only if the general public trust is established in the virtual environment, because lack of trust in security is one

DOI: 10.4018/978-1-60566-669-3.ch014

of the main reasons for e-consumers and e-vendors not to engage in e-commerce. Therefore, trust has received an increasing attention in e-commerce and information technology (IT). For example, Finnie and Sun (2007) investigate trust in e-supply chains. Olsson (2002) examines trust in e-commerce. Pavlou (2003) integrates trust with the technology acceptance model to explore the customer acceptance of e-commerce. Salam et al. (2005) examine trust in e-commerce and notice that "many customers may still not trust vendors when shopping online". Wingreen and Baglione (2005) study the customer's trust in vendors from a business viewpoint. Xiu and Liu (2005) propose a formal definition of trust and discuss the properties of trust relation. Xiong and Liu (2002) propose a formal reputation-based trust model by combining amount of satisfaction, number of interaction and balance factor of trust in a peer-to-peer e-community. However, the majority of studies are on trust in online purchase settings, whereas there is relatively less research on trust in e-commerce from a viewpoint of logic and intelligent systems.

Multiagent systems (MAS) have been successfully applied in many fields such as e-commerce (Sun & Finnie, 2004) and e-supply chain management (SCM) (Finnie, Sun & Barker, 2004; Finnie & Sun, 2007). MAS has also been used as a development methodology in many studies (Henderson-Sellers & Giorgini, 2005). Further, trust has drawn some attention in MAS. For example, Chen et al. (2005) propose a fuzzy trust model for MAS taking into account direct trust, recommendation trust and self-recommendation trust. Xiu and Liu (2005) discuss trust in distributed systems. Tweedale and Cutler (2006) discuss trust in MAS by proposing a trust negotiation and communication model for MAS architecture. Schmidt et al. (2005) apply a fuzzy trust model to an e-commerce platform. However, they have not examined engineering of trust in multiagent e-commerce system (MECS), which is of practical significance for multiagent e-commerce and e-services. This chapter will be devoted to engineering of trust and experience-based trust in MECS.

Experience-based reasoning (EBR) is a reasoning paradigm using prior experiences to solve problems, and could be considered an advanced form of knowledge-based reasoning (Sun & Finnie, 2007). This chapter will apply EBR to trust among intelligent agents within the MECS. In particular, the use of experience in establishing trust in other agents will be explored. Any organization has some history of dealing with problems relating to orders and perturbations in the network and the solutions applied, as well as some formal processes for dealing with these. To respond automatically, software must be capable of reacting as one would expect a human agent to do. The information available to the agent may come from a variety of sources, including analysis of historical information/experience at the information/planning level (Finnie & Sun 2007).

The major contribution of this chapter is the establishment of a basis for understanding the new field of EBR and engineering of experience-based trust in e-commerce and the role it may play in the MECS environment. In addition, the issue of scalable trust and the role of experience in automating trust in e-commerce are appreciated. This chapter will resolve these issues by providing some methodologies, engineering and intelligent techniques for experience-based trust and scalable trust in e-commerce and MECS. These involve the use of EBR to enable agents in e-commerce to learn from prior experience in dealing with brokers and sellers and issues relating to trust and scalable trust in MECS.

There have been no studies that provide a unified treatment of trust and scalable trust in e-commerce, so far. This chapter will fill this gap by examining experience-based trust and case-based trust in e-commerce and their interrelationships from the viewpoint of intelligent systems. It will look at knowledge-based trust, inference-based trust and their interrelationships with experience-based trust and scalable trust in e-commerce respectively. The proposed approach in this chapter will facilitate research and development of trust, scalable trust, MAS, e-commerce and e-services.

The rest of this chapter is organized as follows: next two sections examine fundamentals of trust in e-commerce and provide the background for the research in this chapter. Then the following sections will propose a knowledge-based model for trust in e-commerce and look at experience-based trust in e-commerce. Furthermore, the chapter introduces a measure and evaluation for trust in e-commerce from a viewpoint of knowledge-based systems, proposes a case-based model for trust in e-commerce, and examines a fuzzy logic based model for scalable trust in e-commerce. Then the chapter will propose a system architecture for METSE: A multiagent experience-based trust system for e-commerce and discusses the future trends. Finally the chapter ends with some concluding remarks and future work.

BACKGROUND

Xiu and Liu (2005) propose a formal definition of trust and discuss the properties of trust relation. Their trust is based on the actions of an agent and its effects, whereas our trust, in particular, knowledge-based trust and inference-based trust in this chapter are based on knowledge-based systems.

Zhang, Lu and Yang (2004) propose a fuzzy set-based trust and reputation model in peer-to-peer (P2P) networks taking into account direct trust and reputation. The key idea behind it is that trusting other peers requires the review of one's experiences (direct trust) and the opinions of other peers (reputation). However, they have not detailed direct trust and reputation. Knowledge-based trust and inference-based trust in this chapter can be considered as a refined investigation into direct trust and reputation-based trust.

Wingreen and Baglione (2005) study e-commerce trust and knowledge-based trust. However, they emphasize the customer's trust in vendors (knowledge-based trust) and in technology (institution-based trust) from a business viewpoint, whereas this chapter examines knowledge-based trust from the viewpoint of intelligent systems.

Olsson (2002) examines trust in e-commerce and asserts that "if experience-based trust (EBT) can be evaluated automatically, then it would provide a foundation for decision support tool for e-commerce customers, because in e-commerce, a customer likes to conduct purchases online if she/he trusts the vendor based on the experience of herself/himself and other customers". This chapter can be considered as an attempt towards automation of EBT, because formalization, models and system modelling of EBT are a necessary premise of automation and engineering of EBT.

Xiong and Liu (2002) propose a formal reputation-based trust model by combining amount of satisfaction, number of interaction and balance factor of trust in a P2P e-community. Their work is at a higher level than what we have done in this chapter. Further, reputation is a complex phenomenon, which is certainly related to knowledge, experience, and problem solving methods in e-commerce and therefore reputation-based trust depends on knowledge-based trust and experience-based trust. In other words, knowledge-based trust and experience-based trust form a basis for reputation-based trust.

Schmidt (2003:25) proposes a framework to manage customer experience, which targets the business managers or consultants. This framework consists of the following five steps:

1. Analysing the experiential world of the customer
2. Building the experiential platform
3. Designing the brand experience
4. Structuring the customer interface

5.   Engaging in continuous innovation.

The customer interface is one of the key implementation strategies for managing customer experience in the MECS, because it affects retention through the exchanges and interactions which further determine whether the customers are satisfied with the MECS and whether they will buy the products or services again. Most customer relationship management (CRM) solutions merely record what can be easily tracked: the history and transactions of customer-company contracts (Schmidt, 2003:141). However, this is not enough for managing customer experience in MECS because the customer in MECS believes that the interface of the MECS is an agent of the MECS and s/he is communicating face-to-face with this agent. This is a new world, because the interaction between the customer and the agent of the MECS is different from traditional face-to-face interaction or communication in traditional business or service. However, in such an interaction, the customer will still try to obtain human-like interaction with the interface agent in the MECS (Finnie & Sun, 2007).

It should be noted that Schmidt's discussion on customer experience management (CEM) is essentially based on his business consultation experience, in particular, in the traditional business sectors, without regards to any intelligent techniques. Sun and Lau (2007) argue that intelligent techniques can improve management of customer experience in e-services, just as had been done in other fields such as in e-commerce. This chapter is an attempt towards engineering of experience-based trust in e-commerce using intelligent techniques such as fuzzy logic, multiagent systems and knowledge-based systems.

FUNDAMENTALS OF TRUST IN E-COMMERCE

This section first reviews the existing research on trust in e-commerce, then proposes an ontology for trust in e-commerce. It also looks at trust in e-commerce from a people-centered perspective and a system perspective. Finally, it examines scalable trust in e-commerce.

Introduction

Trust has been crucial to e-commerce, because it is an important factor in determining whether an e-customer chooses to or not to buy the goods or services via an e-store (Slyke, Belanger, & Comunale, 2006). Lack of trust usually leads e-consumers to hesitate to engage in the behaviors necessary for the widespread diffusion of e-commerce (McKnight, Choudhury, & Kacmar, 2002).

Trust has been of concern to researchers since the earliest research on MECS. In an open trading environment, trust can be established by external mechanisms such as using secret keys or digital signatures or by internal mechanisms such as learning and reasoning from experience (Finnie & Sun, 2007). As noted by Ramchurn et al. (2004), many current computer applications are following a distributed model with components available through a network e.g. semantic web, web services and grid computing. The open MAS with autonomous agents has been suggested as the logical computational model for such applications (Jennings, 2001). As a result, the implications of trust have broader relevance than that just in MECS.

Figure 1. Ontology of trust in e-commerce

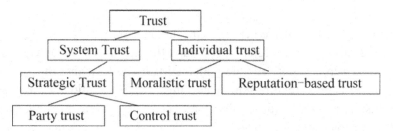

Ontology of Trust in E-Commerce

This subsection will review the definitions of trust in e-commerce and then introduce an ontology of trust in e-commerce, as shown in Figure 1.

There are many definitions of trust proposed in the literature. Slyke, Belanger and Comunale (2006) define trust in e-sellers (web merchants) as "truster's expectation about the motives and behaviors of a trustee", where a truster is an e-customer, and a trustee is an e-seller. Greenstein & Vasarhelyi (2002:120) defines trust in e-commerce as "the willingness of a trading partner to be vulnerable to the actions performed by the system of another trading partner based on the expectation that the other trading partner will perform a particular action or sequence of actions important to the truster, irrespective of the ability to monitor or control the other trading party". Therefore, trust is the expectation that arises within a community based on commonly sharing norms from one member to another of that community.

Ramchurn et al. (2004) provide an extensive review of research into trust in MAS and define trust as follows: "Trust is a belief of an agent that the other party will do what it says it will (being honest and reliable) or reciprocate (being reciprocative for the common good of both), given an opportunity to defect to get higher payoffs". They conceptualize trust as (a) individual-level trust (agent believes in honesty or reciprocation of interaction partners) and (b) system-level trust (the agents are forced to be trustworthy by the system). They further characterize individual-level trust models as learning (evolution) based, reputation-based or socio-cognitive based. Learning-based models are based on interactions with other agents. Reputation-based models work by asking other agents of their opinion of potential partners, often based on some form of social network (Sabater & Sierra, 2002). Rather than relying on interaction with other agents, socio-cognitive models operate on subjective perceptions of opponents. Wong and Sycara (1999) address two forms of trust i.e. trust that agents will not misbehave and trust that agents are really delegates of whom they claim to be. Vassileva et al. (2002) consider the formation of long term coalitions of customer and vendor agents using an agent trust model. Others have done research on agent learning in an untrustworthy environment, i.e. agents who will attempt to deceive each other in trading. For example, Wu et al. (2002) show that trust can be established if agents learn which other agents exhibit poor behavior and hence which agents not to trust.

Further, it is necessary to introduce (c) e-commerce-level trust. This level trust is a higher level one than the foregoing system-level trust, because e-commerce consists of many e-commerce systems such as MECS.

Uslaner (2004) classifies trust into two categories: strategic trust and moralistic trust. Strategic trust is the trust that reflects our experience or willingness with particular people doing particular things (e.g. specific exchanges) (Schneiderman, 2000). This kind of trust can be called business trust or transaction trust (Tan & Thoen, 2001), and then it is fragile and temporary (Schneiderman, 2000). Strategic trust can help us decide whether a specific website is safe and our information is secure there, etc. (Uslaner, 2004). Strategic trust can be improved by references from past and current customers (Schneiderman, 2000). One reason for Amazon's success (www.amazon.com) with online books selling is that it provides the peer (customers') reviews for almost every book available at amazon.com. The customer can read the peer reviews (as references) before buying the book. This is a process of building and improving strategic trust.

Moralistic trust is the durable optimistic view that strangers are well-intentioned (Schneiderman, 2000), which is a more general value that we learn early in life. This kind of trust will give us sufficient faith to take risks on the Web in the first place (Uslaner, 2004).

Tan and Thoen (2001) propose a generic model of trust for e-commerce consisting of two basic components: party trust and control trust based on the idea that the trust in a transaction with another party depends on the trust in the other party (party trust) and trust in the control mechanism (control trust) that ensure the successful performance of the e-transaction. This model can be used in designing trust related, value-added services in e-commerce.

Party trust and control trust constitute transaction trust (Tan & Thoen, 2001), because transaction trust is a kind of strategic trust. Therefore, party trust and control trust can be also considered as strategic trust, as shown in Figure 1. Moreover, party trust and control trust is supplementary to each other, because if there is not enough party trust between each other, then a control trust mechanism is prescribed. Based on the above discussion, Figure 1 shows an ontology model of trust in e-commerce.

It should be noted that trust ontology proposed here is a first attempt for understanding of trust in e-commerce. The proposed trust ontology will be gradually elaborated in the future. Further, every trust in the trust ontology (e.g. reputation trust) consists of knowledge-based trust, reasoning-based trust, experience-based trust and hybrid trust (see later in the chapter), all of these four kinds of trusts can be considered as computational trust (Teacy et al 2008). One of computational trusts is Bayesian trust (for details see Teacy et al (2008)), which can be also considered as a reasoning-based trust, because Bayesian inference is a well-known inference in AI (Nilsson 1998). Finally, individual trust can be generalized to group-based trust and institution-based trust, which is a part of scalable trust in e-commerce and will be discussed in later of this section.Control trust will be also discussed in the next subsection.

Two Perspectives on Trust in E-Commerce

This subsection will provide two models for trust in e-commerce from two different perspectives: A people-centred perspective and a system-oriented perspective.

There are three main parties involved in e-transactions in e-commerce: the buyer, seller and intermediary (Verhagen, Meets & Tan, 2006). In this chapter, buyers are either e-buyers or online customers or intelligent buyer agents (Sun & Finnie, 2004). Sellers are either e-vendors or Web merchants or Internet stores (Slyke, Belanger & Comunale, 2006) or intelligent seller agents (Sun & Finnie, 2004) or Web vendors (McKnight, Choudhury, & Kacmar, 2002), or online shops' websites related to e-transactions. Intermediaries are either e-agents or e-facilitators (Verhagen, Meets, & Tan, 2006) or e-brokers or intelligent (software) agents for any intermediary (Sun & Finnie, 2004). This consideration motivates the model of trust in e-commerce from a people-centered viewpoint, as shown in Figure 2.

The interrelationships between buyer trust, intermediary trust and seller trust have received substantial attention in e-commerce. For example, Verhagen, Meets & Tan (2006) explore intermediary trust and

Figure 2. A people-based model for trust in e-commerce (Sun & Lu, 2007), With kind permission of Springer Science and Business Media.

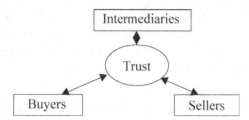

seller trust. Intermediary trust refers to "the trustworthiness of the intermediary operating the system. It reflects perceptions of security during transaction to the presence of guarantees, regulations, safety nets or other structures that are introduced by these institutions". Intermediary trust is related to seller trust and buyer trust.

Seller trust refers to the "perceptions of trust in the counterpart of transaction" (Verhagen, Meets & Tan, 2006). More specifically, seller trust refers to the subjective belief with which consumers assess that sellers will perform potential transactions according to their confident expectations, irrespective of their ability to fully monitor them. In e-commerce, the object of seller trust is the party selling the products. Buyer's trust in e-sellers is important in consumer-oriented e-commerce adoption decisions (Slyke, Belanger & Comunale, 2006).

In this model, buyers, sellers and intermediaries are working together in e-commerce in order to complete an e-transaction. However, all of them face trust issue in either e-commerce or MECS. Sometimes, they trust one another, sometimes they mistrust one another, and sometimes they distrust one another. If they trust each other, it is easy for them to complete an e-transaction satisfactorily. If they distrust each other, one of them might obtain the interest or benefit from the e-transaction.

From a system-oriented perspective, trust exists in the Web client, data transport, Web server, and Web operating system (OS) respectively (Sun & Lu, 2007). At the same time, trust constitutes a network, which can be called a trust network. The trust network links Web client trust, data transport trust, Web server trust, and Web OS trust, as shown in Figure 3.

Trust can be propagated along the trust network from Web client trust through data transport trust and Web server trust to Web OS trust (Sun & Lu, 2007). This trust propagation affects the trust of e-customers in the Web client, data transport, Web server, and Web OS sequentially in general, in e-commerce in particular. At the same time, this trust propagation also promotes the improvement of the Web browser, data transport, Web server, and Web OS. Therefore, the propagation of trust plays a vital role in e-commerce not only from the seller and buyer viewpoint, but also from a viewpoint of researchers of e-commerce. More generally, we should discuss scalable trust in e-commerce.

Figure 3. A trust network in e-commerce (Sun & Lu, 2007), With kind permission of Springer Science and Business Media.

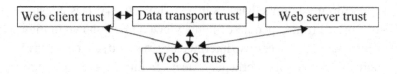

Scalable Trust in E-Commerce

There are many definitions about scalability in different fields (Zhao & Sun, 2008). For brevity, we consider the scalable system as the system can deal with the increase of users and resources under the condition of neither remarkably decreasing system performance nor notably increasing management complexity.

Based on the definition of scalable system, the scalability of MAS is a property that the system performance does not remarkably decrease when the system parameters change, such as agent number, heterogeneous agents, task scale and task heterogeneity. Then, the scalable trust of MAS can be defined as the trust that can fit for the change of system parameters changes; that is, these changes cannot lead to the input's remarkable increase or the output's remarkable decrease.

Scalable trust can be also considered as trust propagation. That is, the trust between one agent and another is extended to that between one agent and an agent network or group. The scalable trust between agents within a MAS is the trust that can fit for the remarkable expansion of the MAS system scale and the big increase of agent numbers, provided that the system still keeps appropriate efficiency and modest extra cost.

Scalable trust in the MECS can be treated through trust propagation from sociology and engineering perspectives respectively (Zhao & Sun, 2008). From the sociology perspective, the realization of scalable trust requests that trust in the MECS can be generalized to higher level social organizations. Social organizations from a low level to high level can be individual, network, group, organization and institution. Trust generalized from individual to network is called network based trust. Similarly, we can also call group-based trust, organization-based trust and institution-based trust. Trust generalization from individual interaction based trust to network-based trust, to group-based trust, to organization-based trust and to institution-based trust is an "up-scaling" process.

From the engineering perspective, with the drastic increasing of the agent number in the MECS, the non-scalability of the existed interaction-based trust models will lead to that the trust model has to maintain an enormous agent interaction database. The storage cost of the agent interaction experiences and the cost of selecting trusted agent also increase drastically, and finally these models cannot meet the requirement of the large scale application environment.

From the scalability viewpoint, the lowest level of trust is the individual-level trust (Zhao & Sun, 2008). This trust is just between individuals or agents themselves, one's trust to others cannot influence the trust building of another individual's trust in others. Network-based trust is at a higher level, and group-based trust is at a higher level than the network-based trust. The critical issue of the propagation from individual trust to network-based trust is that an individual's trust in others can efficiently contribute to the trust construction of another individual's trust in others in the network. The transformation from network-based trust to group-based trust requires at least one group head that represents the group to interact with others. How to propagate network-based trust to group-based trust, and how to successfully build group-based trust models are still open problems.

It should be noted that the above-mentioned network means relationship network with respect to one agent rather than computer network. How to generalize individual trust to network-based trust becomes significant for scalability of the system. The existing reputation-based trust models (Uslaner, 2004) provide the trust recommendation mechanism to make individual trust generalize to network-based trust. It is important for these models to have the ability of efficiently processing the dishonest recommendation information in the system in order to guarantee the scalability of trust successful.

Figure 4. A hierarchical model for scalable trust in e-commerce

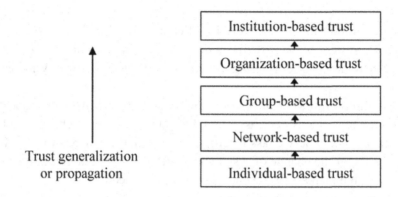

The still higher level trust is organization-based trust (Zhao & Sun, 2008). The differences of group and organization mainly are: (1) in organization, the relationship between members and the task representation are based on economic exchange such as wage and salary, and they are regulated by contracts. The loyalty to the controller is strengthened through the punishment to the contract violation. (2) Trust of the non-organizational member to the organizational members is free from organizational individuals. (3) Organizational members must act according to organizational rules. It still lacks sound contributions on how to propagate group-based trust to organization-based trust.

The top level scalable trust is institution-based trust. By using trustworthy ways, generalizing signals and symbols such as personal skill and ability make them not rely on group or organization that they belong to. For example, in our real life, education diplomas and driver's licenses conferred by one organization are these signals or symbols. The key of the realization of institution-based trust is to make the generalized signals and symbols trustworthy.

Based on the above discussion, scalable trust in e-commerce can be illustrated in a hierarchical structure, as shown in Figure 4.

It should be noted that individual-level trust, network-based trust and group-based trust have drawn significant attention in e-commerce and MECS, whereas organization-based trust and institution-based trust have not studied in depth in e-commerce.

A KNOWLEDGE BASED MODEL OF TRUST IN E-COMMERCE

This section will examine trust in e-commerce from the viewpoint of knowledge-based systems.

We assume that P is an agent and Q is another agent. P has a knowledge set K_P, which can be considered as the knowledge base in a knowledge-based agent, reasoning methods set R_P, which can be considered the problem-solving methods or strategies. Q has also knowledge base K_Q and reasoning set R_Q. Therefore, from the viewpoint of knowledge-based systems (Nilsson, 1998), the behavior of P and Q will be decided by (K_P, R_P) and (K_Q, R_Q) in the same environment.

It should be noted that K_P can also include one's experience, data, and information. R_P consists of traditional problem solving methods or reasoning methods and also non-traditional reasoning methods (Sun & Lu, 2007). In what follows, we consider trust between P and Q, which can be regarded as above-mentioned individual-level trust.

In the most general case, one of the essentially necessary conditions for "agent P trusts agent Q" is that agent Q has more knowledge and reasoning methods or problem solving methods than agent P, because this is the important premise of agent P placing confidence in agent Q. In other words, a necessary condition for "agent P trusts agent Q" is that at the time t, agent P and agent Q satisfy:

$$K_P \subseteq K_Q \text{ and } R_P \subseteq R_Q \tag{1}$$

Based on (1), we can see that trust as a binary relation satisfying (Sun & Lu, 2007):

1.   Reflexivity. Agent P trusts agent P itself.
2.   Anti-symmetry. If agent P trusts agent Q, then agent Q does not trust agent P. This is usually inconsistent with reality, because in e-commerce, agent P and agent Q can trust each other for an e-transaction in some cases; that is, trust is conditionally symmetric. This is the limitation of this model. However, if one agrees that trust is temporary, whereas distrust or mistrust is ubiquitous, then this model is still of practical significance.
3.   Transitivity. If agent P trusts agent Q, and agent Q trusts agent R, then agent P trusts agent R. For example, it is very common in e-commerce if customer A trusts his friend B, and B trusts eBay.com, then A trusts eBay.com. This is a kind of transitive trust or trust propagation in customer-to-business e-commerce. However, trust is not transitive in some cases. For instance, customer A trusts his friend B, and B trusts an e-commerce website, however, A does not trust this website.

Therefore, a trust relation is conditionally symmetric and transitive.

It should be noted that Xiu and Liu (2005) also discuss the common properties of trust as a binary relation, and they argue that a trust relation is reflexive and only symmetric, and transitive conditionally, which is consistent with the above discussion. Moreover, their formal definition of trust is based on the action of agent and its effect (action-effect), whereas our formal definition is based on the viewpoint of knowledge-based systems.

In reality, the condition (1) can be weakened to three different cases that lead to "agent P trusts agent Q."

1. $K_P \subseteq K_Q$
2. $R_P \subseteq R_Q$
3. $K_P \subseteq K_Q$ and $R_P \subseteq R_Q$

The first case is that "agent P trusts agent Q" because agent Q has more knowledge, data, information, and experience than agent P. For example, in a primary school, a student S with (K_S, R_S) trusts his teacher T with (K_T, R_T), because the latter has more knowledge and experience than himself; that is, $K_S \subseteq K_T$. The trust resulting from this case is called knowledge-based trust or agent P trusts agent Q with respect to knowledge. In other words, knowledge-based trust is based on one's knowledge and experience about competencies, motives, and goals of the agent (Branchund & Flinn, 2004).

The second case is that "agent P trusts agent Q" because agent Q has more reasoning methods or problem solving methods than agent P. For example, in a system development team, a fresh team member M with (K_M, R_M) trusts his team leader L with (K_L, R_L), because the latter has more problem solving methods than the former in systems analysis and design; that is, $R_M \subseteq R_L$. The trust resulting from the second case is called inference-based trust or agent P trusts agent Q with respect to inference. This implies that this trust is based on one's reasoning and problem solving abilities (Branchund & Flinn, 2004).

The third case is that "agent P trusts agent Q" because agent Q has more knowledge, experience and more reasoning methods or problem solving methods than agent P. For example, a patient P with (K_P, R_P) trusts an experienced doctor D working in a clinic with (K_D, R_D), because the doctor has more knowledge, experience and more methods in diagnosis and treatment than other doctors with (K_{DS}, R_{DS}); that is, $K_P \subseteq K_{DS} \subseteq K_D$ and $R_P \subseteq R_{DS} \subseteq R_D$. The trust resulting from the third case is called hybrid trust, or agent P trusts agent Q hybridly. In other words, hybrid trust is a combination of knowledge-based trust and inference-based trust.

Two agents P and Q in e-commerce or MECS may have trust relationships in one or more of the three cases. It is also common for agents P and Q in e-commerce or MECS to have a hybrid trust relationship, because the knowledge and reasoning methods of an agent are usually considered as his ability or reputation in particular in the case of trust as discussed in others' work such as Xiu and Liu (2005). Based on this idea, this investigation is more fundamental than reputation-based trust (Nielsen & Krukow, 2004) and ability-based trust (see later). In other words, reputation-based trust is a kind of hybrid trust. Furthermore, knowledge-based trust and inference-based trust can be considered as special cases of experience-based trust, because knowledge and reasoning are parts of human experience. Experience-based trust is also a more general form than hybrid trust, because experience-based reasoning contains more reasoning paradigms than that in knowledge-based systems (Nilsson, 1998; Sun & Finnie, 2005), which can be seen in the next section.

EXPERIENCE BASED TRUST IN E-COMMERCE

Experience-based reasoning (EBR) has been applied in e-commerce (Sun & Finnie, 2004). Experience-based trust has also been drawn attention in e-commerce (Sun & Lu, 2007). Experience-based trust is to use past experiences to help build the trust in the potential buyers or sellers in e-commerce. The feedback from other peers to the potential buyers or sellers also plays an important role in building of trust which is the basis for recommendation and judgement on the potential buyers or sellers (Xiong & Liu, 2002). This section extends inference-based trust and hybrid trust proposed in the previous section to experience-based trust in e-commerce.

From a logic viewpoint, there are eight basic inference rules for performing EBR (Sun & Finnie, 2007), which are summarized in Experience-based reasoning: Eight inference rules. They cover all possible EBRs, and form the fundamentals for all EBR paradigms. The eight inference rules are listed in the first row, and their corresponding general forms are shown in the second row respectively. The eight inference rules are *modus ponens* (MP), *modus tollens* (MT), abduction, *modus ponens with deception* (MPD), *modus tollens with deception* (MTD), *abduction with deception* (AD), inverse *modus ponens* (IMP), and inverse *modus ponens* with deception (IMPD). For simplicity, we denote them as

Table 1. Experience-based reasoning: Eight inference rules

MP	MT	abduction	MTD	AD	MPD	IMP	IMPD
P	$\neg Q$	Q	$\neg Q$	Q	P	$\neg P$	$\neg P$
$P \to Q$	$P \to Q$	$P \to Q$	$P \to Q$	$P \to Q$	$P \to Q$	$P \to Q$	$P \to Q$
$\therefore Q$	$\therefore \neg P$	$\therefore P$	$\therefore P$	$\therefore \neg P$	$\therefore \neg Q$	$\therefore \neg Q$	$\therefore Q$

$R = (R_1, R_2, R_3, R_4, R_5, R_6, R_7, R_8)$ respectively. The first four of them have been thoroughly used in computer science, mathematics, mathematical logic, philosophy and other sciences (Nilsson, 1998; Sun & Finnie, 2004). The rest were proposed in the past few years (Sun & Finnie, 2004, Sun & Finnie, 2007), to our knowledge. However, they are all the abstraction and summary of experience or EBR in real world problems. (Table 1)

We do not add an example for each of the inference rules here any more owing to space limitation. For such examples please see Sun and Finnie (2007) and Sun and Lu et al (2007).

It should be noted that the inference rules "with deception" such as MTD, AD, MPD and IMPD are non-traditional inference rules. However, they are real abstractions of some EBR, although few have tried to formalize and engineering them. The "with deception" is only an explanation for such models. One can give other semantic explanations for them such as "with trick" that is used previously (Sun & Finnie, 2005). One can also use exception oriented reasoning to explain them in the context of the stock market or medical/systems diagnosis (Sun & Finnie, 2004a).

In the rest of this section, we will discuss inference-based trust in the context of EBR.

As is well known, one reasoning or problem solving consists of a chain of inference rules (Sun & Lu, 2007). In other words, one agent P's reasoning method consists of a few fundamental inference rules. Therefore, we can use inference rules (how many times has an inference rule been used? how many inference rules an agent has used for a problem solving and in which way?) to measure the reasoning methods or problem solving methods. Based on this discussion, let $R = (R_1, R_2, R_3, R_4, R_5, R_6, R_7, R_8)$, $R_P \subseteq R$ and $R_Q \subseteq R$, then agent P trusts agent Q with respect to EBR *iff*

$$R_P \subseteq R_Q \tag{2}$$

This implies that "agent P trusts agent Q" because in the problem solving, agent Q has used more inference rules of EBR than agent P. For example, in a transaction of e-commerce, agent P trusts agent Q with respect to EBR, because agent Q uses *modus ponens* (MP), *modus tollens* (MT), abduction, abduction with deception (AD), inverse *modus ponens* (IMP) on some e-commerce occasions; that is, $R_Q = (R_1, R_2, R_3, R_4, R_7)$ and agent P only uses traditional inference rules, $R_P = (R_1, R_2, R_3)$. In particular, in negotiation of e-commerce, a seller agent always uses any possible inference rules of the EBR to make an e-customer agent trust him. Usually, an e-customer uses less inference rules of EBR than an e-seller in the negotiation of e-commerce (Sun & Finnie, 2007).

It should be noted Bayesian trust introduced by Teacy et al (2008) is a kind of experience-based trust based on Bayes networks (Nilsson, 1998:325) in essence. The difference between Bayesian trust and the foregoing experience-based trust lies in that the former are based on probability whereas the latter is based on logic.

MEASURE AND EVALUATION OF TRUST: A KNOWLEDGE BASED MODEL

Tweedale and Cutler (2006) examine trust in multiagent systems and note the measure of trust. However, they have not gone into it. In what follows, we will introduce a unified measure of trust based on the discussion of the previous section.

Generally, let the cardinality (size) of knowledge set K and reasoning methods set R be $|K|$ and $|R|$ respectively. Then the trust degree of agent P in agent Q can be denoted as taking into account (2):

$$T(P,Q) = \alpha(1 - \frac{|K_P|}{|K_Q|}) + (1-\alpha)(1 - \frac{|R_P|}{|R_Q|}) \qquad (3)$$

where, when $\alpha = 1$, T(P, Q) is the knowledge-based trust degree of agent P in agent Q. When $\alpha = 0$, $T(P, Q)$ is the inference-based trust degree of agent P in agent Q. When $0 < \alpha < 1$, $T(P, Q)$ is the hybrid trust degree of agent P in agent Q. For example, if $\frac{|K_P|}{|K_Q|} = 0.2$ and $\frac{|R_P|}{|R_Q|} = 0.6$, and $\alpha = 0.7$, then hybrid trust degree of agent P in agent Q is

$$T(P,Q) = 0.7 \times 0.8 + 0.3 \times 0.4 = 0.68$$

Further, $1 - \frac{|R_P|}{|R_Q|}$ implies that agent P's trust degree is greater whenever the size of knowledge set of the agent Q is greater than that of agent P taking into account (1). Similarly, $1 - \frac{|R_P|}{|R_Q|}$ implies that agent P's trust degree is greater whenever the size of reasoning methods of the agent Q is greater than that of agent P. The key idea behind it is that agent P easily trust agent Q if the latter has more knowledge and experience or problem solving ability than agent P taking into account (1). This case usually happens when a student trusts his teacher. With the age increasing the trust between any two persons will be decreasing. In other words, it is more difficult for one to trust others in the adult world. Therefore, $1 - \frac{|K_P|}{|K_Q|}$ or $1 - \frac{|R_P|}{|R_Q|}$ will be decreasing when the size of knowledge set of the agent P approaches to that of agent Q or the size of reasoning methods of the agent P approaches to that of agent Q. Therefore, the trust degree proposed in (3) is of practical significance. For simplicity, we use $T(P, Q)$ to denote either knowledge-based trust degree or inference-based trust degree or hybrid trust degree and do not differ one from another without specification.

It should be noted that Xiu and Liu (2005) assert that "trust evaluation result should be a Boolean value", which has been extended and revised by the above discussion.

Figure 5. CTMS: A case-based trust management system

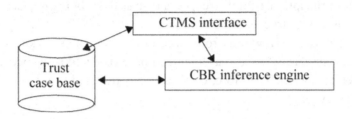

A CASE-BASED MODEL FOR ABILITY BASED TRUST

The intelligent model for trust introduced in the previous section is not valid for dealing with the ability-based trust. This section will focus on this kind of trust, which can be considered as a part of case-based trust in e-commerce.

Ability-based trust is related to the trustee's knowledge, skills or competency to perform as expected (Xiu & Liu, 2005). This kind of trust is related to one agent P and other agents or in particular agent team $Q = \{Q_1, Q_2, ...Q_n\}$ with respect to task t. Assume that for agent P, the satisfaction value that agent $Q_i, i \in \{1, 2, ..., n\}$ receives for completing task t is $s(P, Q_i, t)$, where $s(,,) \in [0,1]$, then the trust degree of agent P in agent Q_i, $T(P, Q_i, t)$, can be considered as $s(P, Q_i, t)$ (Xiong & Liu, 2002) (More generally, agent P should be replaced by a special standard for completing a task.); that is,

$$T(P, Q_i, t) = s(P, Q_i, t) \tag{4}$$

Therefore, the most trustworthy agent of agent P with respect to task t should be agent Q_J with a trust degree $T(P, Q_J, t)$ and $\exists J \in \{1, 2, ...n\}$ such that for any $i \in \{1, 2, ..., n\}$, $T(P, Q_J, t) \geq T(P, Q_i, t)$. We can briefly denote this as

$$T(P, Q, t)_{max} = T(P, Q_J, t) \tag{5}$$

Now there is a new task t_0 to be done by one of the agents in Q. t_0 is similar to task t. The question is who should be the most trustworthy agent for agent P to complete this task. To answer this question, we first review case-based reasoning (CBR).

Case-based reasoning (CBR) is a reasoning paradigm based on previous experiences or cases; that is, a case-based reasoner solves new problems by adapting solutions that were used to solve old problems (Sun & Finnie, 2004). Therefore, from a system viewpoint, we call CBR the form of experience-based reasoning, briefly,

CBR = Case base + Experience-based reasoning (6)

where case base (CB) is the set of cases, each of which consists of the previous encountered problem and its solution.

CBR is based on a principle about the nature of the world (Sun & Finnie, 2004): similar problems have similar solutions. Consequently, solutions to similar prior problems are a useful starting point for new problem solving. This principle also implies experience-based reasoning is based on the experience principle. For example, it is usually true in business activities that "Two MP4 digital players with similar quality features have similar prices." However, from a logical viewpoint, this is a kind of similarity-based reasoning. In other words, similarity-based reasoning can be considered as a special and operational form of experience-based reasoning. Therefore, CBR can be considered as a kind of similarity-based reasoning from a logical viewpoint.

CBR = CB + Similarity-based reasoning (7)

Similar to inference engine (IE) in expert systems (ES) (Nilsson, 1998; Sun & Finnie, 2004), one can also use CBR inference engine (CBRIE) to denote the inference engine in CBR system (CBRS); that is,

CBRS = CB + CBRIE (8)

where CBRIE performs similarity-based reasoning.

In the rest of the section, we propose a model for case-based trust management system (CTMS), as shown in Figure 5.

In this model, trust case base consists of all the trust cases with trust degree that agent i receives to complete task t, $T(P, Q_i, t)$, $i \in \{1, 2, ..., n\}$ and basic information of agent i such as its ID and speciality. The case-based inference engine processes the trust information of agents in Q based on similarity-based reasoning in order to answer the above mentioned question as follows:

Let t be similar to t_0, then $T(P, Q_i, t) \approx T(P, Q_i, t_0)$, $\approx$ is a similarity metric (Sun & Finnie, 2004), then the most trustworthy agent of agent P with respect to task t, agent Q_J with a trust degree $T(P, Q_J, t)$ that satisfies (5) will be recommended by the CTMS based on case-based reasoning to complete the new task t_0, which is a kind of experience-based recommendation; that is, it is based on the trust of agent P in the related agent team.

A FUZZY LOGIC MODEL FOR SCALABLE TRUST IN E-COMMERCE

As mentioned earlier, scalable trust has drawn some attention in e-commerce. However, how to measure scalable trust is still a big issue. This section will fill this gap based on the fuzzy operation (max-min) or approximate reasoning in artificial intelligence (Zimmermann, 1996).

We consider the scalable trust in the following scenario: agent P trust in agent $Q_1, Q_2, ..., Q_n$ which are all the agents within a MECS; that is, $Q = \{Q_1, Q_2, ..., Q_n\}$. The question is what trust degree of agent P is in Q.

For any $i \in \{1, 2, ..., n\}$, the trust degree of agent P in agent Q_i is $T(P, Q_i)$, and then the maximal trust degree of agent P in the agent team Q can be denoted as

$$T(P, Q)_{max} = Max\{T(P, Q_i), i \in \{1, 2, ..., n\}\}$$ (9)

The minimal trust degree of agent P in agent team Q can be denoted as

$$T(P,Q)_{\min} = Min\{T(P,Q_i), i \in \{1,2,...,n\}\} \tag{10}$$

The maximal trust degree of agent P in agent team Q implies that the agent P trusts the agent team Q with a trust degree $T(P,Q_K)$ and $\exists K \in \{1,2,...,n\}$ that satisfies

For any $i \in \{1,2,...,n\}$, $i \in \{1,2,...,n\}$ $T(P,Q_K) \geq T(P,Q_i)$, $T(P,Q_K) \geq T(P,Q_i)$ \hfill (11)

Therefore, this trust can be considered as "blind trust", because if the agent P trusts one agent of the agent team with a maximal trust degree, then s/he trusts the whole agent team in the MECS with the trust degree. An e-commerce owner or vendor hopes that his customers trust his company employees with maximal trust degree based on (9).

The minimal trust degree of agent P in the agent team Q implies that the agent P trusts the agent team Q with a trust value $T(P,Q_K)$ and $\exists K \in \{1,2,...,n\}$ that satisfies

For any $i \in \{1,2,...,n\}$, $i \in \{1,2,...,n\}$ $T(P,Q_K) \leq T(P,Q_i)$, $T(P,Q_K) \leq T(P,Q_i)$ \hfill (12)

This trust can be considered as "hostile trust", because he trusts the whole agent team in the MECS with the minimal trust degree that an agent within the MECS possesses. Currently, e-commerce owners or vendors try their best to avoid this trust degree that customers apply to their companies using customer relationship management and customer experience management (Sun & Finnie, 2004).

The above two different trust propagations or scalable trusts represent two extreme cases. In reality, the trust degree of agent P in the agent team in the MECS will be in the interval of $[T(P,Q)_{\max}, T(P,Q)_{\min}]$. This leads to the following model for scalable trust in e-commerce.

Let w_i be the weight of $T(P,Q_i)$, $i \in \{1,2,...,n\}$ with respect to agent P, then trust degree $T(P,Q)_w$ of agent P in the agent team Q, taking into account $W = \{w_1, w_2, ..., w_n\}$, is

$$T(P,Q)_w = \sum_{i=1}^{n} w_i T(P,Q_i) \tag{13}$$

Obviously, the above model for scalable trust in e-commerce satisfies:

$$T(P,Q)_{\min} \leq T(P,Q)_w \leq T(P,Q)_{\max} \tag{14}$$

These fuzzy logic based models can be used to propagate trust from individual-level through network-based and group-based as well as organization-based to institution-based or system-level in a hierarchical way.

In the rest of this section we illustrate these models with the following example.

Let agent P is an e-customer who is visiting an MECS to buy an MP4 digital player online. The MECS consists of a web client agent (a website) (Q_1), a product provider agent (Q_2), and e-transaction agent (Q_3), the trust degree of agent P in these three agents are $T(P,Q_1) = 0.7$, $T(P,Q_2) = 0.9$,

$T(P, Q_3) = 0.4$ respectively. Then

$$T(P, Q)_{\max} = \max\{0.7, 0.9, 0.4\} = 0.9 \tag{15}$$

and

$$T(P, Q)_{\min} = \min\{0.7, 0.9, 0.4\} = 0.4 \tag{16}$$

If this customer uses $T(P, Q)_{\max} = 0.9$ as his trust degree in the MECS, then he will buy the MP4 digital player because he has tried for some time to buy an MP4 digital player. However, if he uses $T(P, Q)_{\min} = 0.4$, then he is heavily concerned about the security of the e-transaction, and believes that the information from the product provider agent is incomplete or distorted, then he is reluctant to buy this product. If the agent P puts the weight to $T(P, Q_1)$, $T(P, Q_2)$, $T(P, Q_3)$ with 0.4, 0.4, and 0.2 respectively, then

$$T(P, Q)_w = 0.4 \times 0.7 + 0.4 \times 0.9 + 0.2 \times 0.4 = 0.72 \tag{17}$$

In this case, the agent P might buy the MP4 digital player taking into the above trust degree in the MECS.

METSE: A MAS ARCHITECTURE FOR EXPERIENCE-BASED TRUST IN E-COMMERCE

In the previous sections we have examined trust, scalable trust, and knowledge-based trust, experience-based trust based on software engineering, fuzzy logic, case-based reasoning and experience-based reasoning. All of these are the important approaches for automating or engineering experience-based trust in e-commerce. In what follows, we first provide a basic understanding of engineering and then propose a multiagent system architecture for experience-based trust in e-commerce.

From a viewpoint of computing, engineering of experience-based trust is the establishment and use of sound engineering principles in order to obtain economically experience-based trust for e-commerce (Pressman, 2001; Sun & Huo, 2006). More specifically, engineering of experience-based trust is the application of systematic, disciplined, quantifiable approaches to the modelling, processing, simulation, management and system development of experience-based trust in order to obtain economically trust for an individual or organisation, because engineering here is the analysis, design, construction, verification, modelling, management and system development of technical (or social) entities (Pressman, 2001).

From a viewpoint of systems development methodologies (Sun & Huo, 2006), engineering of experience-based trust is heavily affected by the research and development of its corresponding philosophies, methodologies, models and techniques, development tools and then applications and their interrelationships, which constitutes a unified hierarchical architecture as discussed in engineering of experience (Sun & Huo, 2006). We do not look at this architecture any more owing to the space limitation. In the rest of the section we examine engineering of experience-based trust in e-commerce through proposing a system architecture of METSE (Multiagent Experience-based Trust System for E-commerce).

Figure 6. METSE in a MECS

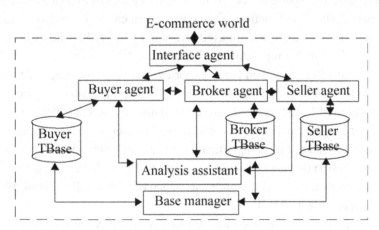

Multiagent systems (MAS) have been studied in the field of distributed AI (DAI) for more than 30 years (Weiss, 1999). Nowadays these systems are not simply a research topic, but are also an important subject of academic teaching and industrial and commercial applications. Recently, the term MAS is used for all types of systems composed of multiple agents showing the following characteristics (Sun & Finnie, 2004):

- Each agent has incomplete capabilities to solve a problem
- There is no global system control over agents
- Data are decentralized
- Computation is asynchronous.

Rationality is a compelling notion in MAS. An ideal rational agent is defined as follows: for each possible percept sequence, it acts to maximize its expected utility on the basis of its knowledge and the evidence from the percept sequence (Huhns & Singh, 1998:3-4).

Autonomy is also an important property of intelligent agents (Huhns & Singh, 1998:3-4), in particular for mobile agents, which can move from one location to another while preserving their internal state (Sun & Finnie, 2004). Autonomy is the ability of agents to handle human user-defined tasks independently of the user and often without the user's guidance or presence.

Based on the above discussion, we propose a multiagent system architecture for an experience-based trust in e-commerce, as shown in Figure 6. In this architecture, three rational agents (intelligent buyer agent, intelligent broker agent and intelligent seller agent) are autonomous. These three agents are mainly responsible for performing experience-based trust in one another respectively based on EBR or problem solving strategies towards an e-commerce transaction. In what follows, we discuss each of them in some detail.

1.   The buyer agent in the METSE is responsible for manipulating the buyer TBase (trust base) based on EBR to infer the experience-based trust in the seller agent and broker agent for an e-commerce transaction. This agent can be considered as an agentization of an experience-based expert system for trust which mainly consists of buyer TBase (similar to knowledge base in knowledge-based system

(Nilsson, 1998)) and an experience-based inference engine (EBIE) (that is not shown in Figure 6.) (Sun & Finnie, 2005). The function of the buyer agent can be extended to infer the experience-based trust based on fuzzy experience-based reasoning (Sun & Finnie, 2007). It should be noted that the function of the following mentioned agents can be also extended to infer the experience in the corresponding TBase based on fuzzy experience-based reasoning. The buyer TBase mainly consists of the history of buyer's trust in sellers and brokers in a form of rules or cases.

2. The seller agent in the METSE is responsible for manipulating the seller TBase based on EBR to infer the experience-based trust in the buyer agent and broker for the e-commerce transaction. This agent can be also considered as an agentization based on seller TBase and an experience-based inference engine (EBIE) that is not shown in Figure 6. The seller TBase consists of the history of seller's trust in buyers and brokers, which can be saved in the seller TBase like the cases in the CBR system (Sun & Finnie, 2004).

3. The broker agent in the METSE is an intelligent intermediary (Sun & Finnie, 2004), and is responsible for manipulating the broker TBase based on EBR to infer the experience-based trust in the buyer agent and seller agent for the e-commerce transaction. This agent can be also considered as an agentization based on broker TBase and an EBIE that is not shown in Figure 6. The broker TBase mainly consists of the history of broker's trust in buyers and sellers.

For the proposed METSE there are some other intelligent agents, shown in Figure 6. These are an interface agent, an analysis assistant and a trust base (TBase) manager. In what follows, we will look at them in some depth.

The *interface agent* is an advisor to help the buyer agent, broker agent and seller agent to know which rational agent s/he likes to ask for help. Otherwise, the interface agent will forward the problem of the e-commerce world to all agents in the METSE for further processing. The interface agent also, like an intelligent website, is responsible for displaying the intermediate or final results of experience-based trust for an e-transaction to buyer agent, broker agent and seller agent in the METSE.

The output of the experience-based trust provided by the METSE can be considered as a suboutput, which will be processed with the help of the *analysis agent*. Since different agents in the METSE use different experience-based trust strategies, and then produce different, conflicting results with knowledge inconsistency. How to resolve such knowledge inconsistency is a critical issue for the METSE. This issue will be resolved by the analysis assistant of the METSE. The analysis assistant will

*   Rank the degree of importance of the suboutputs from the METSE taking into account the knowledge inconsistency
*   Give an explanation for each of the outputs from the METSE and how the different results are conflicting
*   Possibly combine or vote to establish the best solutions
*   Forward those to the interface agent who will further forward the final result to the three main agents as a recommendation.

The *TBase manager* is responsible for administering the buyer TBase, seller TBase and broker TBase. Its main tasks are TBase creation and maintenance, trust retrieval, trust evaluation, trust reuse, trust revision, and trust retention. Therefore, the functions of the TBase manager are an extended form of the functions of a database manager (Sun & Finnie, 2005) or CBR system (Sun & Finnie, 2004) regardless of its case-based inference engine, because case base creation, case retrieval, reuse, revision and retention are the main tasks of the CBR system from a viewpoint of managing case base.

The rest of this section will show how the METSE works.

For an e-transaction in the e-commerce world, buyer agent asks the interface agent to solve the problem *p*, for example, to buy an MP4 digital player. The interface agent asks the buyer agent whether a special seller agent and broker agent should be needed. The buyer agent does not know. Thus, the interface agent forwards *p* (after formalizing it) to some seller agents in the METSE for further processing. However, the seller agent does not like to contact with the buyer agent directly in order to avoid the unnecessary trouble in the transaction, and then asks the interface agent to arrange broker agent for help. Therefore, the interface agent arranges some brokers to be involved in this transaction. From this time on, the trust conflict will arise: The buyer agent does not trust in some brokers, while the seller agent does not trust in some brokers either. At the same time, the broker also does not trust in either buyer agents or seller agents. How to resolve the trust conflict among them?

Each of the three agents uses either or all of trust evaluation (propagation) models (9), (10) and (13) to get an experience-based trust degree of the buyer in an appropriate seller and so on: the T1(buyer, seller), T2 (buyer, broker); T3(seller, buyer), T4(seller, broker); T5(broker, buyer), T6(broker, seller) taking into account non-symmetry of trust as a binary relation and then forwards these trust degrees to the analysis agent for analysis and recommendation. The analysis agent uses fuzzy logic techniques (Zimmermann, 1996) to analyze these trust degrees provided by buyer agent, seller agent and broker agent and then recommends each of them to revise one's trust degree in another in order to complete the e-transaction successfully. This is an iterative process or bargaining process for trust revision (Sun & Finnie, 2004).

After iterations or bargaining processes of trust, the buyer agent, broker agent and seller agent are all happy or satisfied with each other taking into account experience-based trust, and then complete the e-transaction successfully. Otherwise, they stop the e-transaction because of no-resolution of mistrust among them.

FUTURE TRENDS

We have examined engineering of experience-based trust in e-commerce based on software engineering, fuzzy logic, case-based reasoning, experience-based reasoning and intelligent systems. However, trust has been, is and will be a critical issue for the development of e-commerce, e-business and e-services from a people-centred perspective and a system-oriented perspective, just as trust has been a critical issue in traditional commerce, business and services for many centuries. Therefore, how to use techniques of information technology, artificial intelligence and artificial social intelligence to engineering trust and experience-based trust in e-commerce will be always a topic for future research. More specifically, we only list four topics for future research as future trends, owing to the space limitation.

The first topic for future research is to examine the trust, deception and negotiation in e-commerce and their interrelationships, because deception in e-commerce often affects the trust among agents negatively, while trust among agents can help to remove the deception among agents. The mistrust among agents in MECS can be improved through negotiation in e-commerce (Sun & Finnie, 2004). Therefore, this research can improve understanding of trust, deception and negotiation and facilitate the research and development of e-commerce.

The second topic for future research is to examine and develop protocols for trust among agents within a MECS. If the protocols for trust among the agents can be established, then the agents can perform e-transactions following the corresponding protocol for trust, and the trust among the agents will be certainly improved.

The third topic is to examine how logic/inference rules tie up to the idea of experience-based trust or learning from experience and provide detailed algorithms showing how an agent "evolves" its trust. To this end, it is significant to integrate Bayes network with foregoing experience-based trust.

The final topic for future research is to develop a real system for automating experience-based trust in e-commerce based on a real case study (or real examples) and techniques of multiagent systems in order to show how the approach proposed in this chapter to solve some real problems in e-commerce. In order to develop such a system, the related algorithms for trust propagation, trust evaluation, deception detection, negotiation-based trust should be analysed and designed. The system can improve our understanding of experience-based trust in e-commerce.

CONCLUSION

This chapter examined engineering of experience-based trust in e-commerce from the viewpoint of intelligent systems. More specifically, it examined fundamentals of trust and scalable trust in e-commerce and introduced ontology of trust in e-commerce. It proposed a knowledge-based model of trust in e-commerce and looked at experience-based trust in e-commerce. It examined knowledge-based trust, inference-based trust, case-based trust and fuzzy logic-based trust valuation in e-commerce and their interrelationships with experience-based trust from the viewpoint of intelligent systems. It proposed a system architecture for METSE: a multiagent system for experience-based trust in e-commerce. The proposed approach will facilitate research and development of trust, multiagent systems, e-commerce and e-services.

In future work, we will develop a system prototype for the proposed METSE and propose a spiral model for scalable trust in e-commerce and e-services. We will also explore scalable trust protocols and management in e-commerce.

ACKNOWLEDGMENT

This work is supported by the Education Ministry of Hebei Provice, China under a key research grant No. ZH200815.

REFERENCES

Branchaud, M., & Flinn, S. (2004). xTrust: A scalable trust management infrastructure. In *Proceedings of the 2nd Annual Conference on Privacy, Security and Trust.* (pp. 207-218). Fredericton, New Brunswick, Canada, 14-15 October.

Castelfranchi, C., & Tan, Y. H. (Eds.). (2001). *Trust and deception in virtual societies.* Norwell, MA: Kluwer Academic Publishers.

Chen, G., Li, Z., Cheng, Z., Zhao, Z., & Yan, H. (2005). A fuzzy trust model for multiagent systems (LNCS 3612, pp. 444-448.

Deloitte & Touche (2000). *E-commerce security: A global status report*. Rolling Meadows II: Information Systems Audit and Control Foundation.

Finnie, G., & Sun, Z. (2003). A logical foundation for the CBR Cycle. *International Journal of Intelligent Systems, 18*(4), 367–382. doi:10.1002/int.10093

Finnie, G., & Sun, Z. (2007). Negotiation, trust and experience management in e-supply chains. In Q. Zhang (Ed.), *E-Supply chain technologies and management* (pp. 172-193). Hershey, PA: Idea Group Inc.

Finnie, G., Sun, Z., & Barker, J. (2005). Trust and deception in multiagent trading systems: A logical viewpoint. In *Proceedings of the 11th Americas Information Systems* (AMCIS2005). The Association for Information Systems, Aug 11-14, 2005 (pp. 1020-1026) Omaha, NE, USA.

Ghosh, A. K. (1998). *E-commerce security: Weak links, best defenses*. New York: John Wiley & Sons, Inc.

Ghosh, A. K. (2001). *Security and privacy for e-business*. New York: John Wiley & Sons, Inc.

Greenstein, M., & Vasarhelyi, M. (2002). *Electronic commerce: Security, risk management, and control (2nd ed.)*. Boston: McGraw-Hill Irwin.

Hassler, V. (2001). *Security fundamentals for e-commerce*. Norwood, MA: Artech House.

Henderson-Sellers, B., & Giorgini, P. (2005). *Agent-oriented methodologies*. Hershey, PA: Idea Group Inc.

Huhns, M. N., & Singh, M. P. (Eds.). (1998). *Readings in agents*. San Francisco: Morgan Kaufmann Publishers.

Jennings, N. R. (2001). An agent-based approach for building complex software systems. *Communications of the ACM, 44*(4), 35–41. doi:10.1145/367211.367250

Jones, A. J. I., & Firozabadi, B. S. (2005). *On the characterization of a trusting agent, aspects of a formal approach*. Retrieved March 28, 2008, from http://www.sics.se/spot/document/TrustingAgent.ps

Koufaris, M., & Hampton-Sosa, W. (2002). *Customer trust online: Examining the role of the experience with the Web site* (CIS-2002-05). The CIS Working Paper Series, Baruch College.

McKnight, D. H., Choudhury, V., & Kacmar, C. (2002). The impact of initial customer trust on intentions to transact with a website: A trust building model. *The Journal of Strategic Information Systems, 11*, 297–323. doi:10.1016/S0963-8687(02)00020-3

Nielsen, M. & Krukow, K. (2004). On the formal modelling of trust in reputation-based systems (LNCS 3113, pp. 192-204).

Nilsson, N. J. (1998). *Artificial intelligence: A new synthesis*. San Francisco: Morgan Kaufmann Publishers.

Olsson, O. (2002). Trust in eCommerce: the ontological status of trust. In B. Wiszniewski (Ed.), *Proceedings of ECOM-02- Electronic Commerce - Theory and Applications* (pp. 89-96), Gdansk.

Pavlou, P. A. (2003). Customer acceptance of electronic commerce: Integrating trust and risk with the technology acceptance model. *International Journal of Electronic Commerce, 7*(3), 135–161.

Pressman, R. S. (2001). *Software engineering: A practitioner's approach* (5th Ed.). Boston: McGraw-Hill Higher Education.

Ramchurn, S. D., Huynh, D., & Jennings, N. R. (2004). Trust in multiagent systems. *The Knowledge Engineering Review, 19*(1), 1–25. doi:10.1017/S0269888904000116

Salam, A. F., Iyer, L., Palvia, P., & Singh, R. (2005). Trust in e-commerce. *Communications of the ACM, 48*(2), 73–77. doi:10.1145/1042091.1042093

Schillo, M., Funk, P., & Rovatsos, M. (1999). Who can you trust: Dealing with deception. In R. Falcone (Ed.), *Proceedings of Workshop on Deception, Fraud and Trust of the Autonomous Agents Conference*, Seattle, WA. Retrieved April 2, 2008, from http://www7.in.tum.de/~rovatsos/publications.shtml.

Schillo, M., Rovatsos, M., & Funk, P. (2000). Using trust for detecting deceitful agents in artificial societies. *Applied Artificial Intelligence Journal, 14*(8), 825–848. doi:10.1080/08839510050127579

Schmidt, S., Steele, R., Dillion, T. & Chang, E. (2005). Applying a fuzzy trust model to e-commerce systems (LNAI 3809, pp. 318-329).

Schneider, G. (2006). *Electronic commerce* (6th Ed.). Australia: Thomson Course Technology.

Schneiderman, B. (2000). Designing trust into online experiences. *Communications of the ACM, 43*(12), 57–59. doi:10.1145/355112.355124

Slyke, C. V., Belanger, F., & Comunale, C. L. (2004). Factors influencing the adoption of web-based shopping: The impact of trust. *The Data Base for Advances in Information Systems, 35*(2), 32–49.

Suh, B., & Han, I. (2002). Effect of trust on customer acceptance of Internet banking. *Electronic Commerce Research and Applications, 1*, 247–263. doi:10.1016/S1567-4223(02)00017-0

Suh, B., & Han, I. (2003). The impact of customer trust and perceptions of security control on the acceptance of electronic commerce. *International Journal of Electronic Commerce, 7*(3), 135–161.

Sun, Z., & Finnie, G. (2004). *Intelligent techniques in e-commerce: A case-based reasoning perspective.* Berlin, Heidelberg: Springer-Verlag.

Sun, Z., & Finnie, G. (2004a). Experience based reasoning for recognizing fraud and deception. In *Proceedings of International Conference on Hybrid Intelligent Systems* (HIS 2004). (pp. 80-85), December 6-8, Kitakyushu, Japan. IEEE Press.

Sun, Z., & Finnie G. (2005). MEBRS: A multiagent architecture for an experience based reasoning system (LNAI 3681, pp. 972-978).

Sun, Z., & Finnie, G. (2007). A fuzzy logic approach to experience based reasoning. *International Journal of Intelligent Systems, 22*(8), 867–889. doi:10.1002/int.20220

Sun, Z., & Huo, H. (2006). The engineering of experience. In *Proceedings of 6th Intelligent Systems Design and Applications*, vol. 2. (pp. 1114-1117), Jinan, China, 16-18 Oct. IEEE Press.

Sun, Z., Li, Y., & Zhao, S. (in press). Trust, deception and security in e-commerce. In B.K. Nescott (Ed.), *E-commerce coming into its own*. New York: Nova Science Publishers.

Sun, Z., Lu, S., Han, J., & Finnie, G. (2007). Experience-based trust in e-commerce. In W. Wang, Y. Li, Z. Duan, H. Li, & X. Yang (Eds.), *Integration and Innovation Orient to E-Society*. New York: Springer.

Tan, Y. H., & Thoen, W. (2001). Toward a generic model of trust for electronic commerce. *International Journal of Electronic Commerce*, 5(2), 61–74.

Teacy, W. T. L., Chalkiadakis, G., Rogers, A., & Jennings, N. R. (2005). Sequential decision making with untrustworthy service providers. In Padgham, Parkes, Müller & Parsons (Eds.), *Proc. of 7th Int. Conf. on Autonomous Agents and Multiagent Systems* (AAMAS 2008) (pp.755-762), May, 12-16., 2008, Estoril, Portugal.

Tweedale, J., & Cutler, P. (2006). Trust in multiagent systems (LNCS 4252, pp. 479-485), Berlin Heidelberg: Springer-Verlag.

Uslaner, E. M. (2004). Trust online, trust offline. *Communications of the ACM, 47*(4), 28–29. doi:10.1145/975817.975838

Verhagen, T., Meents, S., & Tan, Y. H. (2006). Perceived risk and trust associated with purchasing at electronic marketplaces. *European Journal of Information Systems, 15*, 542–555. doi:10.1057/palgrave. ejis.3000644

Wagealla, W., Carbone, M., English, C., Terzis, S., & Nixon, P. (2003). A formal model for trust lifecycle management. In *Proceedings of Workshop on Formal Aspects of Security and Trust (FAST2003) as part of the 12th Formal Methods Europe Symposium (FM2003)*. Retrieved April 23 2008, from http://www. cis.strath.ac.uk/research/publications/papers/strath_cis_publication_213.pdf.

Wang, Y., & Singh, M. P. (2007). *Formal trust model for multiagent systems*. Retrieved April 28 2008, from http://www.csc.ncsu.edu/faculty/mpsingh/papers/mas/ijcai-07-trust.pdf.

Weiss, G. (Ed.). (1999). *Multiagent systems: A modern approach to distributed artificial intelligence*. Cambridge, MA: MIT Press.

Wingreen, S. C., & Baglione, S. L. (2005). Untangling the antecedents and covariates of e-commerce trust: Institutional trust vs. knowledge-based trust. *Electronic Markets, 15*(3), 246–260. doi:10.1080/10196780500209010

Xiong, L., & Liu, L. (2002). Building trust in decentralized peer-to-peer electronic communities. In *Proceedings of International Conference on Electronic Commerce Research* (ICECR-5), Montreal, Canada, October.

Xiu, D., & Liu, Z. (2005). A formal definition for trust in distributed systems (LNCS 3650, pp. 482-489).

Zhang, S., Lu, D., & Yang, Y. (2004). A fuzzy set based trust and reputation model in P2P networks (LNCS 3177, pp. 211-217).

Zhao, S., Liu, H., & Sun, Z. (2008). Scalable trust in multi-agent e-commerce system. In *ISECS 2008*, August 3-5, Guangzhou, China, (pp.990-993). IEEE Computer Society.

Zhuang, H., Wongsoontorn, S., & Zhao, Y. (2003). A fuzzy-logic based trust model and its optimization for e-commerce. Retrieved May 2 2008, from http://www.eng.fau.edu/conf/fcrar2003/papers/FuzzyTrustModel21.pdf.

Zimmermann, H. J. (1996). *Fuzzy set theory and its applications*. New York: Kluwer Academic Publisher.

KEY TERMS AND DEFINITIONS

Case-Based Reasoning (CBR): a reasoning paradigm based on previous experiences or cases. As a system, a case-based reasoner solves new problems by adapting solutions that were used to solve old problems (Sun & Finnie, 2004). CBR is also a special form for experience-based reasoning (Sun & Finnie, 2007).

E-Commerce: already a discipline for research and development in commerce and information technology. The simple definition for e-commerce is doing business online. E-commerce can be also defined as the exchange of information, goods or services within business through the use of Internet technology (Sun & Finnie, 2004, p. 47). Usually, e-commerce and e-business is used interchangeably.

E-Services: a term for services on the Internet. E-services include e-commerce transaction services for handling online orders, application hosting by application service providers (ASPs) and any processing capability that is obtainable on the Web. There is a trend to integrate e-commerce and e-business with e-services.

Experience-Based Reasoning (EBR): a reasoning paradigm based on human experience. The human EBR consists of eight inference rules at fundamental level, as mentioned in this chapter. Therefore, it is a logical basis for natural reasoning in particular, for natural intelligence in general.

Expert System (ES): a special form of a knowledge-based system. Expert systems employ human knowledge to simulate expert performance, and they present a human-like facade to the users. Expert systems are one of the successful application fields in AI.

Fuzzy Logic: conceived by Lotfi Zadeh in 1965, is a mathematical technique for dealing with imprecise and fuzzy data/knowledge and problems that have many solutions rather than one. Although it is implemented in computers which ultimately make only yes-no decisions, fuzzy logic works with ranges of values, solving problems in a way that more resembles human logic. Fuzzy logic is used for solving problems with expert systems and other intelligent systems that must react to an imperfect environment of highly variable, volatile or unpredictable conditions (Zimmermann, 1996).

Knowledge-Based System: an AI application system mainly consisting of a knowledge base in a domain and inference engine. It is expected that everyday information systems will increasingly become knowledge-based and provide users with more assistance than they do today.

Multiagent Systems (MAS): have been studied in the field of distributed AI for more than 30 years (Weiss, 1999; Sun & Finnie, 2004). Recently, the term MAS is used for all types of systems composed of multiple agents showing the following characteristics (Sun & Finnie, 2004): Each agent has incomplete capabilities to solve a problem; There is no global system control over agents; Data are decentralized; Computation is asynchronous.

Scalable Trust: motivated from the scalable system. Scalable trust of MAS can be defined as the trust that can fit for the system parameter changes, which cannot lead to the input's remarkable increase and the output's remarkable decrease (Zhao & Sun, 2008). Scalable trust consists of individual-level trust, network-based trust, group-based trust, organization-based trust and institution-based trust. Trust propagation from individual-level trust to group-based trust is important for MECS at the moment.

Trust: firm reliance on the integrity, ability, or character of a person or thing. In e-commerce, trust is the expectation that arises within a community based on commonly sharing norms from one member to another of that community. More generally, trust indicates a positive belief or expectation about the perceived reliability of, dependability of and confidence in a person, an intelligent agent, organization, company, object, process, or system (Schneiderman, 2000).

Chapter 15
Addressing the Complexities of Global Process Harmonization

Jude Fernandez
Infosys Technologies Limited, India

Jyoti Bhat
Infosys Technologies Limited, India

ABSTRACT

Process harmonization is a complex initiative carried out by large companies seeking to standardize the process variants being executed by different business units across several countries or regions. Motivations for this exercise include cost pressures, mergers and acquisitions, customer satisfaction, need for agile and flexible processes, risk reduction in outsourcing processes etc. The complexity of this exercise is inherent as it involves multiple regions with special needs and characteristics, existing process and IT systems evolved over time, organizational dynamics around different business groups, etc. While a literature survey reveals quite a few cases of process harmonization, there are not many descriptions or research on the best approaches or methodologies to be used. In this chapter, we first define and examine the drivers of process harmonization. Subsequently, the challenges and constraints associated with such initiatives are identified, followed by some example cases. Further, we analyze a case study in detail to understand the practices followed. Based on these analyses, we propose a methodology to execute process harmonization initiatives.

INTRODUCTION

Large global corporations composed of different business groups across multiple countries and regions have grown over a period of time, either organically or inorganically. It is common to find that different business units have evolved their own business processes, policies and practices with IT systems supporting them. Such heterogeneous, complex, non-standard business processes make it difficult for the organization to meet the flexibility and agility required to remain competitive in the global economy.

DOI: 10.4018/978-1-60566-669-3.ch015

Multiple business challenges and constraints compel enterprises to harmonize their process across different regions and business groups. The drivers for process harmonization are varied and include scenarios like mergers and acquisitions, providing uniform customer experience, developing agile and flexible processes, reducing risks in outsourcing of processes, organization restructuring, optimizing cost of IT operations etc.

While an increasing need for process harmonization is felt by enterprises, the focus on developing relevant approaches and methods is at a nascent stage. It is still in the domain of management consultants with the individual consultant approaching the problem based on previous experience and expertise. The term 'Process Harmonization' itself, is not clearly defined or understood by all. Terms like process improvement and process standardization are so closely related to process harmonization that there is a need to clarify these terminologies to ensure a uniform understanding.

Process Harmonization Defined

Harmonization as an initiative is being undertaken across the world across industries, products, standards, etc. For defining process harmonization we have considered some of the definitions and meanings associated with the word *harmonization* by different groups taken from varied contexts. Below are some of the definitions for harmonization which we found:

"The act or state of agreeing or conforming" (Roget's II, 1995)

"The process and/or results of adjusting differences or inconsistencies to bring significant features into agreement" (US Department of Defense, 2005)

Almost all the definitions of harmonization define it as the ***process*** towards ***achieving agreement*** *on the standards*. Studying the charters and mission statements of the harmonization programs in different contexts we find certain commonalities:

- All of them consider harmonization as the process or effort to achieve uniformity
- Taking into account everyone's concerns appears to be the core of the program
- It is accepted and acknowledged that harmonization can result in more than one standard being accepted for use
- It is assumed that the common aspects across the different groups will be greater than the differences
- The harmonization effort is towards identifying the differences and reaching consensus.

In our literature review, we found very few formal definitions of process harmonization. Interestingly, we found some ambiguity in the use of the terms process harmonization and process standardization. Richen & Steinhorst (2005) viewed Process Standardization as creating uniform (and strictly standard) business processes across various divisions or locations, while they considered Process Harmonization as ensuring that there are a finite and manageable set of process standards (for a particular process) in the organization across different regions. However, we found the terms process harmonization (Hibbert, 2004) and process standardization (Manrod & Vitasek, 2004) being used interchangeably to mean Process

Harmonization as defined by Richen & Steinhorst (2005). Accordingly, we define *Process Harmonization as the process of designing and implementing business process standardization across different regions / units so as to facilitate achievement of the targeted business benefits arising out of standardization whilst ensuring a harmonious acceptance of the new processes by the different stakeholders.* From another angle, the process of arriving at standardized processes by ensuring an optimal number of standards for a process is Process Harmonization.

Organizations may undertake standardization by following a one-size-fits-all approach by enforcing a single standard process across different geographies and units. An alternate approach seen more commonly for process standardization is to have two or three standard processes to ensure the different requirements of the business are met (for instance different standard processes for each sales channel or product line). As in the case of process design and improvement, useful reference aids are available in the form of process standards and industry reference models. These include SCOR for supply chain processes (Supply-Chain Council, 2008), eTOM for Telecom processes (TM Forum, 1998), ISO 9000, CMMi for Software process management, etc.

In the software industry, process standards like CMMi are used to aid harmonization (Maidantchik, Rocha, & Xex´eo, 1999). An organization at CMMi Level 3 (SEI, 2006) has standard processes defined at the organization level with tailoring guidelines which allows for customization/localization of the process to the specific project. The challenge faced by the organization is to define standard processes which can cater to all kinds of projects considering variations in project size, technology, location, etc. Software organizations take the route of forming working groups and steering committees and piloting the processes while defining the standard processes. But which is the base process on which the variants can be built? How do you decide how many different standard processes are required for a process? The CMMi model does not provide answers to these questions on which organizations need help. Using industry process standards like SCOR and eTOM would also raise similar challenges.

Examining what Process Improvement means, it is found that Business Process Improvement aims to improve the performance of the current business process on various process measures. Process improvement involves identifying, analyzing and improving existing processes within an organization to meet new goals and objectives. There are different process improvement methodologies like TQM, Juran, Six Sigma, Lean, BPR etc, which are used by organizations based on their needs.

While some or all of the techniques and methods of process improvement may need to be deployed in a Process Harmonization program, the methodologies and best practices need a different treatment as the challenges of harmonization have some finer nuances and differences. The variables to be dealt with in process harmonization include the presence of multiple process owners across lines of business, geographies and units, different geographical and regulatory requirements, different IT systems supporting the variants of the business process, multiple definitions of some of the business entities (e.g., customer, item codes) amongst others.

Drivers for Process Harmonization

Organizations take up process harmonization due to various business challenges. In this section, we provide a short analysis of the most common business drivers observed for process harmonization.

Process Harmonization provides opportunities for companies seeking to reduce operational costs by centralizing appropriate sections of their processes into a single operations group (for e.g., a single back-office group to process loan applications for all worldwide business groups of a bank). This also has a significant impact in reducing the risks associated with business process outsourcing as found by Wullenweber & Weitzel (2007) in their exploratory analysis of data from 218 business processes in 126 banks.

In a majority of the process harmonization cases studied, cost reduction is the driver with the focus on the opportunity of reducing IT costs. Companies are realizing that it is not very smart to continue to maintain multiple IT systems supporting similar processes for business groups across the world. Consequently, several firms have embarked on initiatives to design and build single IT systems to replace the multiple duplicate systems that have existed for the different regions. Process harmonization supported by uniform IT systems provides economies of scale and common practices like savings through group buying, data sharing across units, etc.

Harmonizing the operations across global companies helps in establishing an optimal set of operational standards and reduces the inherent complexity of running a global organization. Other drivers for harmonization include ensuring a uniform customer experience from the process across all regions and lines of business of the organization. This is in the case of those customers of the company who interface with the same process across regions / countries and encounter different experiences leading to dissatisfaction. Standardized processes and systems have the benefit of more efficient integration with customers, partners and suppliers.

Another driver is organizational agility and flexibility through standardized processes across geographies and lines of businesses which makes introduction of process changes and new products quicker and more efficient across the organization.

In some cases, process harmonization is done with the objective of providing control and visibility to senior management by means of having standard processes and process metrics in all regions.

Mergers and acquisitions are another trigger for harmonizing processes between the two merging organizations to ensure greater synergy in the processes and supporting IT systems. Organization restructuring like integration of subsidiaries, geographical units or lines of business is a driver for process harmonization in some organizations.

Most organizations look at harmonizing their processes based on one or more of the above triggers. The case studies and literature study found that predominantly, it is the IT function that proposes the need for process harmonization as it faces the challenges in maintaining different systems to support different process variants.

EXAMPLES OF PROCESS HARMONIZATION

Many organizations have taken up process harmonization with varying objectives and results. While several success stories are evident there are also a few cases where the initiative ran into complexities. In this section, a few snapshots of process harmonization cases are provided which highlight the drivers, complexities, challenges and lessons.

Tesco

Tesco, the global retail giant, is on a large-scale process harmonization program to standardize its business processes and IT systems to support plans for global expansion. The company aims to achieve a single way of working across more than 3000 stores in 14 countries. Tesco believes that standardized processes and better quality data will allow it to understand markets, cut costs and simplify its IT systems and build localizations and customizations of the process in a better and faster manner. Tesco's business leaders are involved in developing standard business processes and selecting systems while the CIO is responsible for developing the systems (Hadfield, 2007).

Exxon Mobil

This oil company's focus was on business process standardization for achieving economies of scale. Standardization of business processes at Exxon has enabled standardization of its IT systems which in turn provided for greater agility in response to business dynamics. It also helped significantly during Exxon's merger with Mobil. Exxon faced the issue of over-standardization impeding its adoption of leading edge technology and business practices and adopted a balanced approach of standardization along with business flexibility (Mitchell, 2006).

Unilever

In the late 1990's, Unilever's Home and Personal Care Business Group in Europe embarked on a vision to simplify its business by standardizing processes, at the same time adhering to local regulations, so as to leverage the organization's scale for greater growth. The company created a single set of processes from the existing local systems and changed the business to comply with it. Crucial success factors for the initiative included getting the buy-in and support of the line managers in each country, ensuring IT and business groups work together in a co-operative mode and finally having a strong program management structure including all key stakeholders (Hibbert, 2004).

Nestle

In the late 1990s, Nestle USA, (subsidiary of Nestle SA), embarked on a multi-million dollar SAP investment with the aim to establish common processes, systems and organization structures across nine autonomous divisions. However, years of autonomous operation proved a major stumbling block and also the implementation team overlooked the key aspect of business process change before implementing the systems. Subsequently, structured harmonization of all relevant business processes was carried out and the new systems were accepted by the users leading to substantial savings for the organization (Worthen, 2002).

Modus

At the time of the case study in 1996, Modus, a large high technology company was operating in 12 countries. It began a global process standardization drive to ensure its global customers get the same level of quality irrespective of location. In addition to a very systematic method for process identification and benchmarking of performance, and process standardization, the company also carried extensive communication and change management programs to ensure the success of the program (Manrod & Vitasek, 2004).

Hammer & Stanton (1999) provide a few more examples of process harmonization (IBM, Johnson & Johnson, Hewlett-Packard, Owens Corning) elaborating how these initiatives have helped the firms realize significant value and at the same highlighting change management aspects that were involved in these cases.

In all of the above cases, the key challenge, to begin, with centred on designing a uniform and universal process that could replace the existing process variants across different regions. Only when this was done was it possible to design the "single" IT system or the "single" operations center. The uniform process also had to cater to the different and distinct needs of the various regions and its success was measured by the extent it was able to satisfy the needs of the regional business groups. Process Harmonization has the dual complexity of process and technology; the first is related to the challenges and decisions of creating harmonized processes from the various existing process variants and the other is the challenge of identifying and harvesting the best from the current IT investments to orchestrate and execute the new business process.

CHALLENGES AND CONSTRAINTS FOR PROCESS HARMONIZATION

Process harmonization requires the application of process engineering concepts coupled with organizational change management and industry best practices. The challenges for process harmonization are in some ways similar to those encountered during process improvement, however there are distinct differences due to the inherent nature and complications of multiple processes and systems in different regions, business units etc.

Balancing Needs of Stakeholders and Change Management

One of the biggest challenges for process harmonization is to design the new process in a way that is most acceptable to the different groups of stakeholders. These groups include corporate groups, regional process owners, IT groups, and external customers from different regions. Even the best managed initiatives will ultimately have to be sold to the different stakeholder groups, more so to those groups which have to make significant changes in their way of operations. A robust change management approach needs to be built early into the entire program to ensure wider acceptability of the new process in the shortest time (Worthen, 2002). Whether the process harmonization is initiated by the IT department, or by business groups, in most of the cases the implementation of the new process is through a new or modified IT system. Sometimes, these initiatives are labelled as "Single implementation of XYZ system across the globe". While, on one hand, it is imperative that IT should understand that such an initiative involves significant process change, it is also crucial that business should not view it as *only an IT initiative*. Getting buy-in from business is critical in such cases and hence establishing clear business drivers for the initiative and ensuring the required commitment from the business groups needs to be addressed at the beginning (Worthen, 2002).

Cost and Complexity of the Harmonization Initiative

As harmonization involves multiple stakeholder groups from different regions (typically from across the world), the initiative can easily go overboard in terms of the cost and complexity of ensuring its success. Costs include travel to cover different regions / countries, cost of system changes, consultant and vendor fees, etc, while complexity arises from the multitude of the process variants being followed, eliciting and understanding the local process needs and challenges (Hibbert, 2004). One of the questions encountered is, *"Do we have to capture all variants of the process followed across all regions?"* This is a very relevant question as each additional process modelled can add to the time and cost of the initiative. Additionally, this complex exercise can involve substantial amount of risk and some firms have lost control while attempting to harmonize long-standing processes (Worthen, 2002). Ensuring availability of stakeholder representatives to help in designing the process, reviewing and finalizing it adds another dimension to the complexity challenge. Ideally, they should be involved from the beginning and at all key stages; however, cost and other commitments may prevent this from happening (Hibbert, 2004; Manrod & Vitasek, 2004).

Regional Constraints

Some regions may have constraints such as non-availability or shortage of certain skills, raw materials (at the appropriate cost) which will impact decisions on carrying out the relevant business functions from there (Manrod & Vitasek, 2004). There will be differences in the markets across regions; for example in the consumer goods market, in some regions customer orders are cash transactions, while in advanced markets the orders are processed electronically. Other needs to be fulfilled include local government and statutory regulations. In several cases, some of these requirements might be in variation and conflict with each other. Cultural differences across regions may impact the processes and ways of conducting business in those markets.

Decision Making on Re-Use of Existing Processes and IT Infrastructure and Assets

As the organization undertaking process harmonization will have multiple variants of the process supported by an equal number of varied IT systems and applications, tough decisions need to be taken as to whether and what to reuse, which existing process or system is better and so on. Decisions to reuse all or part of the existing IT infrastructure will put certain restrictions on the new process so as to comply with the processes defined in it. On the other hand, prior decisions on implementation of a new package-based solution, e.g., ERP / CRM etc, will require the new process to comply with the processes defined in the package which are not amenable to change (Mitchell, 2006). Daneva (2000) offers pointers on how process harmonization can influence the amount and the benefits of the reuse of ERP requirements.

BRIEF DESCRIPTION OF THE CASE STUDY AND METHODOLOGY

Description of the Company

The company, referred to as OilCo, is one of the world's leading players in providing solutions that help oil exploration and production companies maximize value from their hydrocarbon-bearing assets. Operating in multiple countries, the company caters to several large oil giants having operations in multiple countries. OilCo's large global clients interface with its different units and services across different regions and geographies.

Outline of the Methodology Followed

Scoping, Business Case and Initiative Planning

One of the major dissatisfaction points of the clients of OilCo was that their experience of OilCo's processes across different geographies varied widely and this unpredictability caused problems for the clients while integrating their systems with those of OilCo's. Added to this, customers had issues related to the visibility into process performance. Hence, OilCo selected its customer-facing processes of the company (involving requirements, quotations, invoicing etc.) as candidates for process harmonization.

The business case defined focused on establishing a standard process and systems for appropriate product lines and regions with a view to improve data accuracy and metrics capture for better visibility of the process and its performance (including for external customers), increased efficiency of the process through automation and process improvement.

OilCo decided to launch a large initiative to harmonize its processes in chosen areas to address these issues and then build a single instance of an IT system which would then be deployed across different regions. The initiative was sponsored by the Operations Vice President (VP), while the program execution was under the control of IT with the Executive Director-IT playing the driving role. The process signoffs (As-Is and To-Be) were to be done by the Product Champion (Quality and Operations representatives) and the four regional VPs.

OilCo brought in an IT services and consulting firm to carry out this exercise in partnership with its internal IT and business groups. Senior executives from OilCo were involved in defining the high-level roadmap, objectives and timelines for the initiative before bringing the consulting firm to carry out the assignment.

Discovery of the As-Is Process Variants

Elicitation of the Process variants and Process Capture: The consulting firm was given charge of the initiative at this stage and it brought in teams with an appropriate mix of senior and middle level consultants well-versed in the domain, organizational dynamics, change management, program management, process modeling etc. Different regions of OilCo with its own process variants were identified and teams were allotted to each region. Key stakeholders from OilCo in each region were identified and interviewed to elicit the relevant portions of the process. One of the complications was that within each region there were different product line variants. So the team categorized the variants into product families. Where the differences were high, the variants were captured as separate processes. The process details were initially captured in a written form and later converted into structured process models. The specific needs of customers, local regulations and other unique situations for each region were documented in the As-Is process documents.

Process Modeling: The processes in each region were modeled using a standard process modeling tool supported by guidelines and methodologies for process hierarchy and granularity. A total of 15 different process maps were captured and the modeling was done till the workflow level.

Capture of As-Is Metrics, Pain-points: The existing processes did not have any metrics defined or captured. During the As-Is process capture, feedback was taken on the ideal set of Key Performance Indicators (KPIs) / metrics for each process (Days Sales Outstanding, cycle time etc). Key customer requirements were captured as customer KPIs. The team also captured the pain points and issues experienced by the process stakeholders.

Analysis of As-Is Process Variants and Design of the To-Be Process

The challenge faced at this stage was to consolidate all of the process variants into a coherent and logical process before considering the improvement of the processes. To facilitate this, a workshop was planned involving all the key consultants (of the consulting firm) involved in the As-Is process capture and modeling, with two days allotted for each business process. The consultant-anchor for each region presented on the merits and demerits of their respective process variants.

After initial discussions it was agreed to review in detail the process variant of *Region A* considering its strengths and weaknesses and pain-points/issues faced currently. The reasons for choosing this region was that it was well documented (though a manual process), well-structured with check points, review points and handovers defined clearly. After detailed discussions, the group finally agreed that the *Region A* process was superior to the others and could be used as the base process for consolidation. Other variants could be added on top of this.

During the process of selecting the most appropriate segments for each process and sub-process, the anchors from different regions were asked to take positions – "put yourself in the shoes of your region's Process Owner". The team experience was quite high, in terms of overall business maturity, domain understanding and experience as well as process expertise and this was a critical factor in the decision-making on which process segments from which region was the most appropriate.

As the process variants were discussed and finalized it was captured online using the modeling tool. The discussion around the issues and pain-points in the process also led to identifying improvement opportunities. Solutions for pain-points were identified along with best practices and the To-Be process was created so as to address the issues and pain points. The processes were standardized till the sub-process level and below this, process variants were identified as applicable to particular regions or product lines.

To-Be Review and Buy-in for Finalization

Product champions and regional VPs had committed their time for reviews and sign-offs, but, in reality, getting the required time from the operations representatives for the review of the process was a challenge. Hence the team planned a 2-day workshop inviting all key stakeholder reps and facilitated the process walk-throughs during these sessions. Also the user interface (UI) mockups which were designed for the "to-be" process elicited a more positive participation and response from all the reviewers. This proved to be very effective as the interviewee put it, "...*in approximate terms we had about 60 to 70 changes suggested during the process reviews and over 500 during the UI mock ups reviews of the same process. The impact (effectiveness of review) when they can visualize is more...*"

To-Be Rollout and Buy-in

In OilCo, after the signoff by the operations representatives at the overall level, the process was taken for rollout across the regions. This was planned and carried out as a series of road shows involving the regional teams using a combination of process walkthroughs and UI mock ups. The workshops were more helpful than offline or individual interviews in creating the shared understanding required for process reviews and refining the process. They were also effective as a means for obtaining the buy-in for the new process.

OilCo is currently deploying the new process on an enterprise resource planning system along with a business process management (BPM) system and other workflow products.

ANALYSIS OF THE METHODOLOGY IN THE CASE STUDY

For the analysis of the methodology we will refer to the earlier section on Challenges and Constraints and ascertain the extent to which these have been addressed. Wherever possible, we have brought in references to other process harmonization examples to elaborate each point.

Balancing Needs of Stakeholders and Change Management

Active involvement of senior executives at different stages of the initiative helps in managing change. In OilCo, the key regional stakeholders were brought in as part of the steering committee of the program. In addition, the process reviews and sign-offs were done by representatives from each region. This helped ensure that the individual needs of the regions were considered during the design and finalization of the To-Be process.

In the Unilever example, the regional Process Owners took the ownership of sign-off on the process which ensured buy-in of the process at the regional levels. Additionally, there was a strong coalition of senior line managers to steer this program over its duration. The sponsor and champion for the initiative was a senior executive responsible for all the regions where the harmonization is being carried out, so as to emphasize the ownership.

The harmonization approach at Modus (Manrod & Vitasek, 2004), had as its first step, the development of a robust process that took care of the needs of all stakeholders across the regions. For this the requirements from all regions (including client and other requirements) were rationalized and streamlined and built into the standard process. This was followed by the rollout of the process to secondary facilities where the process was further expanded to take into account any additional regional or client specific uniqueness. The approach here was to modify the process to accommodate the needs of all regions but to keep it standardized.

In several of the cases seen, the program managers brought in suitable mechanisms to ensure good teamwork between IT and business to avoid potential functional barriers. The companies involved in the initiative also felt the need for getting the buy-in from the business line managers on the need for the common processes and brought them in early on (Hibbert, 2004; Hadfield, 2007; Worthen, 2002).

Cost and Complexity of the Harmonization Initiative

In OilCo, each region had process variants for different product lines, and hence the team concluded that the process can be standardized by product families, especially when the differences were significant. So each product family had at least one process standard.

During the review of the To-Be processes, to address the challenge of getting the required time from the operations representatives from each region, the team organized a workshop review involving all

Figure 1. Proposed Methodology for Process Harmonization

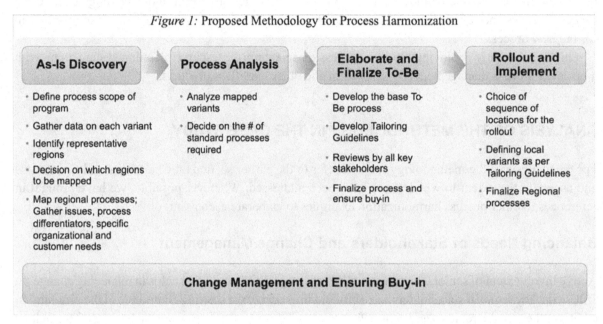

the representatives. This helped in speeding up the process of the review and also enabled more effective reviews.

Unilever addressed the complexity of standardization by approaching the end goal in stages with the initial brief being to harmonize the processes. Upgrading to best-in-class processes was viewed as the second step needing more time. This meant that, for the first phase, processes of some group companies became more sophisticated; while others took a step backwards. Additionally, the scope of the process harmonization was defined tightly at the start and throughout the program no change was made to the authorized scope without a clear view of the consequences. This helped to manage within the costs and timelines. To minimize the risk of impact on the supply chain, most of the rollouts were carried out on public holidays. During rollout of the processes, it was decided to pilot with the larger companies first so as to prove its applicability. However, as was seen in other examples, it is also important to verify (in parallel) that the process is suitable for the smaller regions as well.

Regional Constraints

The harmonization program will need to consider constraints peculiar to a region such as availability of skills, raw materials, local regulations, culture, specific customer requirements etc.

One of the examples seen of addressing conflicting needs and constraints across regions was at Modus where a two step process of rollout was used (Manrod & Vitasek, 2004).

Decision Making on Re-Use of Existing Processes and IT Infrastructure and Assets

The company in the OilCo case did not consider re-using the existing IT systems as they had decided to go in for a new system.

In the case of the process standardization program at Tesco, the process chosen took precedence and once this was finalized, the IT systems that were aligned to the new process were taken forward for the new architecture. Non-standard systems that had been installed by individual regions were dropped (Hadfield, 2007).

How many standardized processes are to be there? A question that will come up during standardization is should there be one process applicable to all situations across regions, and business units or can there be more than one? In the OilCo case, the company decided to have standard processes for distinct product lines.

In other cases, cited in Hammer & Stanton (1999), Hewlett-Packard had decided on a single, standard process for some areas, such as procurement, while they have allowed process variants for product development, reflecting the wide variation in its products and in the customers who buy them. On the other hand, Johnson & Johnson has largely standardized its R&D processes in its pharmaceutical business units to encourage them to share people and ideas and to enable all R&D projects to be managed as a single coherent portfolio. At the same time, different units have been given the liberty to design their own sales and manufacturing processes based on their unique needs. Hammer & Stanton (1999) propose that companies should standardize their processes as much as possible (as the rewards are greater) without interfering with their ability to meet diverse customers' needs.

PROPOSED METHODOLOGY

Process harmonization is a non-trivial exercise and the need for a structured approach is important to ensure that the initiative succeeds in delivering the planned benefits on time and within budget.

Based on the learnings from the case study as well as the practices seen in the other examples, we propose the foundation for a structured methodology for a process harmonization initiative. Figure 1 shows the high-level view of the proposed Process Harmonization methodology. Some parts of it have been tried out successfully in different companies, while other practices are proposed to be tested and vetted out. Some areas need more research to validate the methods suggested and elaborate on it so that it can be brought into practice.

As-Is Discovery

An important first step is a clear definition of the scope of the harmonization program clearly defining the set of processes being harmonized and the process architecture / hierarchy for the chosen set of processes. The processes selected and its scope should be aligned to the business drivers for the harmonization initiative.

The data to be gathered on each regional process variant will include process aspects such as customer needs, customer types, products / services handled, volume of transactions, process performance data (KPIs, customer feedback etc). In the absence of process performance data, the team can use guesstimates

Figure 2. Alternate approaches for developing the To-Be

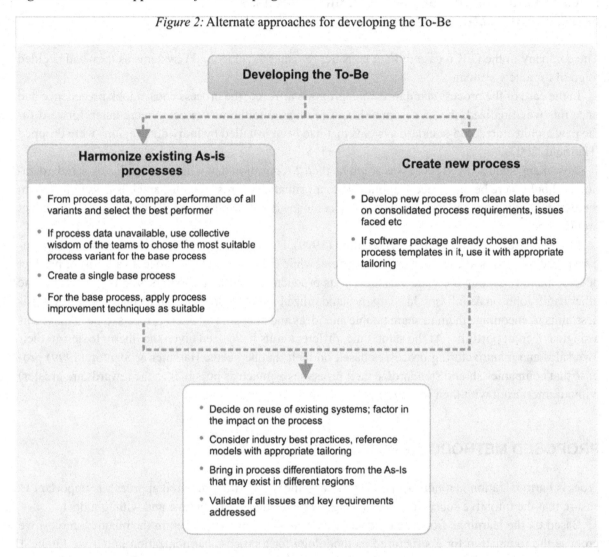

Figure 2: Alternate approaches for developing the To-Be

by process users and experts (which have worked well in some cases that we have observed).

At the outset, the team should finalize on governance practices for the capture of the processes. These cover the use of a standard process modeling tool, suitable process modeling methodology including process templates for capturing data. All members of the team should be trained on these aspects to ensure its consistent use throughout the program. This will help ease the subsequent stages of process analysis and To-Be creation.

The question on whether we need to elicit and map all regional variants or only some representative regions has been addressed in previous sections. While the safest way would be to cover all regions and map the processes of each individually, this will increase the complexity and cost of the program. Hence we propose an alternate approach which involves identification of representative regions. These are regions having an inclusive set of process parameters and characteristics which can best represent the other regions. The criterion for identifying these regions is, "Can processes developed for these representative regions, be taken forward for others with minimal customization, tailoring etc.?" Once the representative processes are mapped, they can be used as the base to build the maps for the regional variants. In case there is not much difference, this will reduce the process elicitation and modeling effort considerably. This approach will contribute to the overall efficiency of the methodology, however we are yet to see this in practice and so this approach needs to be researched further.

During mapping of the regional processes, additional data need to be gathered such as issues / pain-points faced in that region, process differentiators that may be part of that process (which are differentiators vis-à-vis competition) and specific organizational, market and customer requirements. Detailed process performance data are gathered at this stage. The team can also get feedback on the appropriate set of process indicators for that region.

Process Analysis

Process Analysis will cover the analysis of different characteristics of the process variants such as issues and pain-points, process performance data, customer feedback, process differentiators etc. In addition, requirements of the process need to be consolidated and rationalized considering the requirements (organizational, market and customer related) of all regions.

At this stage, a decision can be taken whether to have a single standardized process or to have two or more standard processes. This should be based on the different aspects affecting the process like different product lines (e.g., order-to-cash process for trucks versus cars), different channels (electronic channel versus a walk-in store), etc. The team will need to identify, define and explore all such organizational parameters that might warrant a separate process. In addition, different entities in the process will also need to be standardized in terms of its definition, for instance, customer (identifying the customers of the process), item names / numbers for raw materials and products.

Elaborate and Finalize To-Be

Develop the Base To-Be Process

The creation of the To-Be involves a choice of two paths: consider the existing As-Is processes and create a harmonized process out of these; alternatively, ignore the As-Is and define a new process.. Figure 2 depicts these approaches.

Harmonize Existing As-Is Processes

The first approach is to decide upon a base process on the basis of which the To-Be will be built. The options are either to choose one of the regional variants or to create a new base process by a combination of one or two regional variants. Selection of the base variants needs to be done based on available data. Process performance data, if available, is a good yardstick to compare the processes. However, relying only on process performance data can be misleading. A regional process with lesser complexity and challenges may show better performance as compared to another region with higher complexity and challenges (e.g., more demanding customers, complex regulations, greater competition etc). For e.g., in the OilCo case it was found that the US process was more complex than the Europe variants as the market, regulations and other aspects in the US were more varied and demanding as compared to that of Europe. A straightforward comparison of the process performance of the US with that of Europe would have been misleading. Hence, care is to be exercised so that only processes with similar business contexts in their regions are compared.

To select the base process, it is useful to focus on those regions with greater complexity and variation in the business context. The assumption here is that if such a process is chosen as the base standard To-Be process, it will be easier to scale it down or tailor it for the lesser complex regions.

In the absence of process data, the team will have to rely on its collective wisdom to glean out the most appropriate process configuration to form the base standard To-Be process as was seen in the OilCo case.

Process improvement techniques can then be applied to the base To-Be process to address the improvement objectives, pain-points etc.

Create New Process

In the second approach, the decision is made to ignore the existing process and adopt / build a new one. This decision may be due to any of several factors: for e.g., a new software package has been adopted which has its process templates to comply with; the existing As-Is processes are of poor quality; competitive pressures are forcing a drastic change of the process; existing processes have little or no competitive differentiators, etc. The options for developing the To-be process will include, adopting the process templates from the software package chosen (with the required tailoring) or developing the To-Be from a clean slate based on the consolidated requirements of all regions.

In either of the above paths of defining the To-Be, process differentiators from different regions gathered during the As-Is stage are then added on top of the base To-Be process. The impact of the decisions made on reuse of existing IT systems also needs to be analyzed and factored into the To-Be process.

References to appropriate industry best-in-class process reference models and standards can aid in adopting best practices.

Before the finalization of the base To-Be process, the process has to be validated for inclusion of all key requirements (organizational, market and customer) have been taken care of. Decisions need to be taken as to which requirement is part of the base To-Be process and which can be added as tailorable features.

Refine and Finalize To-Be

Once the base To-Be has been created, tailoring guidelines and policies will need to be created specifying which aspects of the process can be modified, in what manner and under what conditions. The capture of this information can leverage the capabilities of process modeling tools, e.g, in the form of business rules, role definitions in swim lanes etc.

Reviews by stakeholder representatives are a vital part of the process. A good practice used by the team in the OilCo case is to conduct the review in a workshop mode involving all the stakeholders. An additional good practice was the use of UI mock-ups to give the process reps a good feel of what they will experience in the process.

The feedback from the review workshops will lead to refinements of the process before the finalization of the To-Be standard process.

Rollout and Implement

Rolling out to the different regions will involve more of change management and less of process engineering. There are two possible approaches that can be adopted.

The first involves defining the To-Be process for each of the regions with customizations as per the tailoring policies decided. Once all the regional processes are finalized, the single, integrated system for all regions can be planned, developed and rolled out in a phased manner.

The second approach involves a phased roll-out of the process along with the system. In this case, the process for each region is finalized after required tailoring and then the system is built and rolled out. A decision required here is to decide on the sequence of the rollouts: which regions to be first and which to follow. At Unilever, the new process along with the systems was first implemented in two regions with varied and complex requirements. A good guideline to be followed is to pilot the process among regions with lesser resistance to change. Additionally, the representative regions (chosen during the As-Is stage) may also be suitable as pilots since the tailoring required will be lesser for the additional regions.

In all the above approaches, it is important to have suitable change management practices built in, including proper communication on the business need for the new processes and systems and adequate championing by the regional sponsors and other change agents.

CONCLUSION AND FUTURE RESEARCH

Process harmonization can be viewed as a variant of process improvement with the added dimensions of framing out a To-Be process from a multitude of existing As-Is processes. It has similar challenges related to methodology, approach and change management as any Business Process Management (BPM) initiative. While we have proposed a methodology to approach harmonization in a structured manner based on the analysis of the case study and other examples seen, many questions need to be studied in detail to support this methodology with methods and techniques. Further, this methodology will need to be refined and strengthened based on actual field implementation experiences. Some of the questions include, should all the As-Is processes be modeled before the To-Be; alternatively should the As-Is be discarded and the To-Be built from zero or is there a pragmatic via-media approach? How do we choose which processes from which regions are most suited to be taken forward? Should the IT systems underlying the process be reused or should we consider custom-built new systems or bringing in package-based systems? Currently most of these questions are answered based on the collective opinions of the stakeholders involved and not using any well researched conclusions and recommendations. Another aspect not well studied is the technology support required for process harmonization initiatives. A possible area for further exploration is the capabilities, templates and features provided by the BPM tools such as process modelers, process simulation tools etc.

As in any other organization initiative, the success of process harmonization depends to a great extent on change management. Since harmonization usually results in implementing a single new system across the organization the questions on who should own the initiative, how should senior management and stakeholders be involved are bound to arise. These questions are similar to the ones being asked about any other BPM initiative.

REFERENCES

Daneva, M. (2000). Reuse measurement in the ERP requirements engineering process. In *Proceedings of the 6th International Conference on Software Reuse: Advances in Software Reusability* (LNCS 1844).

Forum, T. M. (1998). *NGOSS Business Process Framework – eTOM*. Retrieved May 29, 2008, from http://www.tmforum.org/BestPracticesStandards/NGOSSBusinessProcess/1648/Home.html

Hadfield, W. (2007), Tesco standardizes IT for global expansion. Retreived May 20, 2008, from http://www.computerweekly.com/Articles/2007/04/24/223408/tesco-standardises-it-for-global-expansion.htm

Hammer, M., & Stanton, S. (1999). How process enterprises really work. *Harvard Business Review*, 77(6), 108.

Hibbert, G. (2004, February). Unileverage. *Financial Management*, 30-31.

Maidantchik, C., Rocha, A. R. C., & Xex'eo, G. (1999). Software process standardization for distributed working groups. In *Proceedings of the 4th IEEE International Symposium and Forum on Software Engineering Standards.*

Manrod, K. B., & Vitasek, K. (2004). Global process standardization: A case study. *Journal of Business Logistics*, 25(1).

Mitchell, R. L. (2006). *Exxon gets power from IT standardization.* Retrieved May 20, 2008, from http://www.computerworlduk.com/management/it-business/it-organisation/case-study/index.cfm?articleid=377

Richen, A., & Steinhorst, A. (2005). *Standardization or harmonization? You need both.* Retrieved September 26, 2008, from http://www.bptrends.com/publicationfiles/11-05-ART-StandardizationorHarmonizationv-RickenSteinhorst.pdf

Roget's (1995). *Roget's II: The new thesaurus* (3rd ed.). Houghton Mifflin Company. (Accessed September 26, 2008)

SEI. (2006). CMMI® for Development, Version 1.2 (CMU/SEI-2006-TR-008). Retrieved May 27, 2008, from http://www.sei.cmu.edu

Supply-Chain Council. (2008). *Supply-chain operations reference-model.* Retrieved May 29, 2008, from http://www.supply-chain.org/galleries/public-gallery/SCOR%209.0%20Overview%20Booklet.pdf

US Department of Defense Dictionary of Military and Associated Terms. (2005). Retrieved September 26, 2008, from http://handle.dtic.mil/100.2/ADA439918

Worthen, B. (2002). Nestle's enterprise resource planning (ERP) odyssey. Retreived May 20, 2008, from http://www.cio.com/article/31066

Wullenweber, K., & Weitzel, T. (2007). An empirical exploration of how process standardization reduces outsourcing risks. In *Proceedings of the 40th Hawaii International Conference on System Sciences – 2007.*

KEY TERMS AND DEFINITIONS

Process Harmonization: Process of designing and implementing business process standardization across different regions / units so as to facilitate achievement of the targeted business benefits arising out of standardization whilst ensuring a harmonious acceptance of the new processes by the different stakeholders.

Process Standardization: Used interchangeably with the term Process Harmonization.

As-Is Process: A definition (model) of the process (including the sub-processes, workflows and activities) as it happens currently in the organization.

To-Be Process: The definition (model) of the future state process which has been designed to achieve the targeted process performance and requirements (current and future) of the organization, thereby also addressing the issues faced with the current process.

Process Analysis: The systematic examination of the As-Is process focused on identifying and developing ideas for improvement of the process.

Business Process Management: A continuous approach to design, improve and deploy processes that are aligned to organizational objectives using appropriate IT systems that can quickly adapt to process changes.

Process Variants: Different shades of the same process that are being executed in an organization by different business units / regions.

Chapter 16
Tending and Trekking towards Composite Oriented Architecture (COA)

Pethuru Raj Chelliah
Wipro Technologies, India

ABSTRACT

*With the noteworthy spurt of service orientation (SO) principles, the spur and surge for composition paradigm have taken a fabulous and fruitful dimension and perspective. Composites are emerging and establishing as the promising, proven and potential building-blocks in the pulsating ICT space. Enterprises are very optimistic and sensitive about the shining days of composites in their day-to-day dealings and obligations to their restive partners, government agencies, venerable customers, demanding end-users, and loyal employees. In short, composites are bound to increasingly and illuminatingly participate and contribute towards fulfilling the goals of realizing integrated, optimized, smart and lean business processes that in turn can lead to extended, connected, **adaptive**, and **on-demand** businesses. As next-generation ICT is presumed to thrive on spontaneous and seamless **collaboration** among systems, services, servers, sensors, etc. by sending messages as well as smartly sharing a wider variety of connected and empowered resources, there arises a distinct identity and value for progressive, penetrative and pervasive composites. Already we started to read, hear and experience composite applications, services, and views. As composition is to flower and flourish in a positive fashion, the future IT is definitely on right track. In this chapter, you can find discussions about how rapidly and smoothly services enable business-aligned composites realization. There are sections dealing with prominent composition paradigms, patterns, platforms, processes, practices, products, perspectives, problems and potentials.*

DOI: 10.4018/978-1-60566-669-3.ch016

INTRODUCTION

Service orientation gracefully and gleefully supports the long-cherished and unfinished goal of reusability. SO equips and enables designers and developers to compose sophisticated business solutions as a collection of simple yet sophisticated services. This enforces the view of creating and keeping up some common services that can be utilized and reutilized by many types of clients across domains more frequently and readily to construct a variety of business systems for a variety of purposes. IT departments in glowing enterprises, product vendors, system integrators (SIs) and independent software vendors (ISVs) are more keenly leaning towards producing and maintaining a growing community of enterprise assets (primarily reusable, reliable, sustainable, smart, secure, scalable, and supple services for preparing the unfolding service era) to revitalize their crumbling and struggling enterprise systems and also to realize new-generation, resilient, and versatile enterprise solutions at the business speed. Precisely speaking, the next-generation IT will revolve around services and their distinct yet unexplored territories and capabilities.

As a way for enhancing the reusability of not only modernized systems but also existing and expensive artifacts, composition idea has been picking up fast. Another trend is to close-in the widening gap between the business movements and IT realities. That is why **process-centricity** has become a huge and hot topic that ultimately empowers business executives and analysts to play around with enterprise IT systems. That is, there is an urgent need for a tighter coupling, closer **collaboration**, and deeper alignment between business dynamics and IT innovations. Service-based composites have solidified and sharpened as the silver bullet for all the ills and limitations of current enterprise IT. Therefore the popularity of composites is soaring and its acceptance and adoption rates are unbelievably high with overwhelming support across industries.

Process-Centrism – Service oriented architecture (SOA) (Koskimies, 2006) heavily impacts all the layers in any enterprise system architecture. Particularly we all know that processes guarantee the extreme success, flexibility, openness, dynamism and real-time responsiveness of applications and therefore, there are all-out efforts and endeavors in bringing out a gamut of right optimizations through innovations in arriving at lean, integrated, and nimble business processes. As **process-centricity** acquires a vital proportion in this service era (there is a close interlinking between processes and services with the unveiling of SOA, the first and foremost business-driven architectural pattern, style, and approach), there is a continued evolution of process compactness, consolidation, composition, etc. By leveraging standards-compliant BPM tool sets and suites, organizations have embarked on streamlining and automating their everyday tasks effortlessly. Besides concepts, algorithms and tools are extensively leveraged to reduce turnaround time and time-to-market significantly in order to ensure regulatory compliance and organizational obligations very strictly.

However for BPM suites to realize their true potential, they must evolve consistently beyond simply enabling structured processes. Structured processes account for hardly 10+% of the total work being performed within organizations each day. The other 90% of work is done in a completely dynamic, adhoc, and unstructured manner. In order to help organizations become more anticipative and competitive in this exceedingly connected world especially at this recessionary period, BPM suites need to become sophisticated and smart enough to visualize the unforeseen and accordingly equip themselves to satisfactorily and seamlessly fuse into dynamic business systems that define tasks on the fly. BPM suites need to allow business managers to assign, delegate and track mission-critical tasks in real time. BPM suites must also become value-added tools for knowledge workers, edifying them to quickly and easily leverage the collective knowledge and information assets of entire organization as they go ahead with their daily chores.

The advantage of static and structured BPM is that processes have been modeled based upon the best practices gained and gleaned. They include links to information bases, subject matter experts (SMEs), and other critical resources that enable the knowledge worker perform the assigned tasks optimally based upon the understanding of what has worked well in the past. However this would fail in a truly dynamic world. That is, there is no standard way to know in advance what a task will entail and therefore no way to draw on the best practices and key metrics from a historical model. So efforts are actively underway to bring the salient and sustainable benefits of the conventional capability, visibility, and productivity of existing BPM systems into this ever-changing world. In short, empowered processes are imperative and supremely fit for seamlessly incorporating all kinds of extra features in futuristic ICT systems. This enforces the view for unearthing a set of robust and versatile technologies, toolsets, and standards for realizing empowered (analytics-attached, communication-enabled, **event-driven**, etc.), **adaptive**, and composite processes.

Next-Generation Business Process Management (BPM 2.0) – According to Scott Byrnes (http://www.ebizq.net), BPM 2.0 must address the two important concerns of today's forward-thinking organizations: 1) managers' lack of visibility and control over daily business processes, and 2) knowledge workers' lack of expert guidance and value-added resources to accomplish their work. Considering the vagaries and variations encountered in modern business systems, process complexity is constantly on the rise. This lays the foundation for understanding the significant value-additions that can be brought to the table by new-generation BPM principles and products.

a.   **Dynamic BPM** – Dynamism is an important buzzword today. Systems are slated to be dynamic in their interactions, interfaces, and interpretations. In that line, the forthcoming BPM suites need to be extremely dynamic. The dynamic BPM helps overcome the above-mentioned challenges by dynamically modeling the day-to-day activities within an organization and by providing deeper visibility, vitality, complete control and accountability for mission-critical activities. Dynamic BPM also empowers executives to quickly create ad-hoc yet high-priority tasks that can be subdivided and forwarded to leverage the most knowledgeable human minds and systems assets quickly. Leadership team can have a complete visibility of all the short-term and long-running processes (structured and unstructured). This trend would enhance the much-needed accountability and allow for accommodating on-the-fly changes. Managers gain actionable insights into performance standards such as how long it takes an employee to finish a task successfully, how many activities an employees can undertake and how often an employee delegates tasks. Dynamic BPM also helps professionals to focus on the bottom line by providing immediate access to individual, team and corporate performance besides alerting executives to negative trends or bottlenecks before they become monstrous problems. Additionally, heads can gain deeper visibility and controllability into goals tracking, business trends, juggling market sentiments, varying users' expectations, and overall company performance, collectively providing a succinct and clear picture of their organization's status. In a nutshell, dynamic BPM is a strategic artifact.

b.   **Context-sensitive BPM** – Context-awareness is very important for next-generation ICT solutions to be contributive, constructive and competitive. This nice yet challenging feature ultimately leads to dynamism. BPM 2.0 has to understand and provide the business context for every task assigned. By understanding exactly what a worker is being asked to do, a futuristic BPM solution can intelligently identify and offer value-added resources and information assets at the nick of time that will help the worker to accomplish the task successfully and efficiently. For example, by understanding that an employee has been asked to estimate 2007 budget numbers by his manager for recruiting expenses and considering the coming year's employee growth projections, a BPM solution can proactively search the company's knowledge as well as content management systems for effective decision-making. In addition to that, a BPM solution might serve up the 2006 financials that have a line item for recruiting costs and also a PowerPoint presentation delivered by the COO that discusses employee growth projections for 2007. Extracting and delivering this kind of context-sensitive insights will be a stepping stone for improved employee productivity.

c. **Collaborative BPM** - Collaborative BPM significantly expands the scope and the effectiveness of traditional BPM. It provides a pliable environment to coordinate the dynamic activities of human-driven and collaborative processes. Optimization of the collaborative works of employees, through a more structured sequence of steps, helps an organization to transcend the limits of status quo to realize a new phase and pace of enterprise productivity. Collaborative BPM is unique as it focuses on empowering specific activities to work collaboratively to reach the desired business goals. For example, it can plan a meeting automatically, call a client, open and record a chat session etc. to finish the initiated process successfully. **Collaboration,** without an iota of doubt is a key driver for BPM 2.0

d. **Event-driven BPM** – Events are the new work-units doing extremely well in enterprise computing. The basic driver is that business events happen in hordes and there is a stringent necessity for capturing event messages instantaneously, analyze at faster pace, and leverage the generated insights effortlessly to make enterprise systems more dynamic, predictive, sensitive, and proactive. Already we are very familiar with event-driven programming in desktop and web computing and as the enterprises are ticking towards globalized, events directly or indirectly associated with businesses do have impacts and implications on the business execution and service delivery models. With extreme distribution, liberalization, and globalization, system architecture ranges from centralized, federated, to combined models. Event-driven computing, event heap and cloud are a few of the sparkling buzzwords in IT circles. Event driven architecture (EDA) is the architectural approach for efficient event production, routing, mediating, processing, and consumption. Business software vendors have come out with event servers, event stream processing (ESP) and complex event processing (CEP) infrastructures to capture and consolidate simple as well as complex events.

Our working environments wear an altogether different look these days with email emerging as the widely used business facilitation tool. In addition, instant messaging, web conferencing, unified communication etc are becoming popular and pervasive. In this progressive scenario, it is not possible to predetermine the next thing to happen. Therefore the traditional BPM is all set to be obliterated and soon **event-driven** BPM will be shining upon us soon. That is, there will be a smooth convergence between CEP and BPM to arrive at next-generation BPM tools. Real-time BPM is the ultimate result out of a series of advancements in aspects such as event generation / triggering, streaming, gleaning, consumption, processing, mining, aggregation, dissemination etc.

CEP software handles many low-level events to recognize actionable insights in the form of trends, patterns, associations, etc., that in turn trigger a business activity at right time. CEP usually refers to event processing that assumes an event cloud as input, and thereby can make no assumptions about the arrival order of events. The combination of CEP & BPM gives the best of both worlds. This enables modeling our businesses as best we can in advance along with the inherent flexibility to change that model in real-time to take advantages of incoming opportunities or catch problems before they happen. CEP engines are capable of correlating and corroborating complex and continuous events creating realizable, recognizable and recordable knowledge. Based on this extracted wisdom, CEP engine in sync with the relevant business rules subsequently alerts and modifies the BPM processes appropriately to take correct actions based on the identified pattern. CEP engines thus have stabilized as the mainstream EDA infrastructure. We can let the CEP system automate as much as we want or simply do the alerting piece to our administrators with recommendations on what to change in our business processes. **Event-driven** BPM can transform streams of scattered emails and business conversations into intuitive and informative charts, illustrating the origins and objectives of each task with a step-by-step snapshot of the task from inception to completion.

e.   **Agent and AI Technologies empower CEP** – According to "http://tibcoblogs.com/cep/", CEP happens to be an inspiring solution for semi-structured processes. Agent and AI technologies have emerged as the potent ones for processing unstructured processes. Agent technology successfully tackles extreme scalability issues by traversing from database processing (single instruction, multiple data records) to "via message" processing (instruction decomposition via separate multiple agents and their intercommunication). Agents are generally characterized by being self-organizing, self-configuring, self-healing, self-optimizing, goal and policy-aware etc. As indicated above, CEP engines can be autonomous and interactive to the extent that they simply respond to multiple (complex and continuous) events but adaptivity can be via machine-learning or more commonly via statistical functions. The main trait of CEP engines is to keep the event histories in memory and this presumably is an added advantage in intelligent distributed agents too. One issue coming in the way is the latency issues in communications between agents, especially for time-constrained problems. Agent techniques may be ideal for things like continuous scheduling where they might be controlled by a CEP engine that determines when to reschedule. A tighter synchronization between CEP and other critical technologies say agents will result in cross-fertilization and this mixing and mashing will lead to trendsetting techniques.

As processes are being continuously pampered and powered by powerful technologies, achieving adaptive businesses will become easier and quicker. The structural and the behavioral aspects of processes are undergoing numerous advancements. The utility and usability of standards-compliant BPM tools are bound to go up sharply due to the rising complexity of new-generation ICT systems. Increased focus on process modeling, integration, composition, and innovation along with a growing repository of diverse assets (system building-blocks, tools, containers, engines, design patterns, frameworks, methodologies, best practices, utilities, platform-independent models (PIMs), infrastructure-neutral software modules, etc.) will do a lot of good in constructing and sustaining agile and on-demand corporations.

DEMYSTIFYING SERVICE COMPOSITION

We have gone through the importance of creative processes and BPM platforms as manipulation at process level is easier not only for developers, assemblers but also for business analysts. Process excellence is the heart and soul of enterprise applications. Flexible processes result in elastic systems. Besides that

Figure 1. The Evolution of Software Building-Blocks

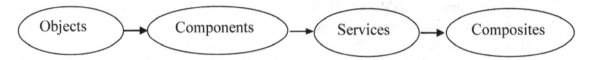

suppleness, we need adaptivity too. As we all know that dynamic and knowledge-based composition of system components guarantees **adaptive** systems, the discipline of service composition gains much traction and talk these days especially with the growing popularity of SOA.

Besides **process-centricity**, service ubiquity, transparency, interoperability, self-description, openness, reusability, and autonomy are the principal drivers for services to be elegantly composed. There are methodologies, containers, engines, grids, fabrics, architectures, identification and discovery schemes etc. popping up for simplifying and streamlining the target and task of service aggregation. There are articles and articulations by prominent people on how composites perfectly participate and facilitate in implementing full-fledged business systems at very rapid pace. Researchers are keenly associating themselves in order to set in industry-strength standards for service **collaboration** and governance. Composites are highly reusable, business-aware, evolvable, and manageable. In other words, composition has gained some leeway and clearly passed the initial litmus test after service science (SS) started to sparkle in the recent past. In short, composition immensely participates in dynamically evolving system construction. As we know, composites are playing a very telling role in shaping up service-oriented business applications (SOBAs), dynamic business applications (DBAs), multi-enterprise business applications (MEBAs) rich enterprise applications (REAs), and cloud applications (CAs).

The method of composing discrete, atomic, and fine-grained (local as well as global) services to create **coarse-grained** and composite applications that are more closely aligned to business goals and strategies has become very popular among the IT services and solutions providers to achieve significant cut in the developmental complexity, cost and time. The figure 1 pictorially depicts about the evolution of prominent software building-blocks. As services are becoming more acceptable and adoptable for software community, composites are all set to play a compelling, and mind-blowing role in shaping up the future requirements being imposed on software professionals by clients as well as end-users.

There are some design considerations and constraints for services to be composed efficiently. Firstly, services need to be platform-neutral and ready for integration. Other qualities of services include reusability, accessibility, interoperability, composability, and extensibility. Service vitality, viscosity, viability, and visibility are also other worthy characteristics of services. When some preexisting / legacy services are combined to work together in order to achieve a specified business goal, the correctness of this composition also needs to be validated. A composite needs to guarantee connectivity, scalability, availability and other non-functional QoS requirements such as security, dependability, performance, timeliness etc.

Service Composition Approaches – There are a number of composition languages, methodologies, frameworks, architectures, patterns, platforms and application domains brewing at steady pace.

- Process-based Composition (BPEL (EAI), CDL (B2B) & SOA)
- Activity-based Composition (Activity-oriented Computing & SOA)
- Component-based Composition (SCA & SOA)

- Event-Driven Composition (EDA & SOA)
- Model-Driven Composition (MDA & SOA)
- Agents-sponsored Composition (Multi-agent system(MAS) & and SOA)
- Semantic Composition (Semantic SOA)
- Artificial Intelligence (AI) planning, machine learning (ML), case-based Reasoning (CBR), Business Rules (BR) and Knowledgebase-based composition

Composition Types and Techniques (Dustdar, 2005) - Service orientation has been showing exemplary forward movement in this era of globalization, decentralization, distribution, and digitalization. As new services are being built from the scratch or existing assets get wrapped, enabled and modernized to be exposed and accessed via XML-based open standards, the discipline of interoperability has acquired a new dimension and meaning too. Composition is an essential ingredient of dispersed services to find one another in order to interact instantly and instinctively. Several organizations are collaboratively working towards service composition standards, toolkits, verification & validation approaches, key guidelines, ROI metrics, TCO insights, and best practices. Experts see that service composition can happen in three major ways: manual, semi-automatic and automatic composition.

Services are generally classified into two types based on their abstraction levels. On the one hand, basic, primitive, or simple services are elementary functionalities and on the other hand, we have integrated, and composite services that aggregate a set of discrete functionalities (atomic services) distributed and deployed in different localities into new-generation, high-end and personalized applications that are closer to the users' actual needs.

a. **Manual Composition** – This is a relatively easier one yet labor-intensive in which relevant services are determined at design time itself for subsequent composition. Currently there are two main mechanisms. The first approach (service orchestration) combines available services by utilizing a central coordinator (the orchestrator) that is responsible for invoking and combining them. The second approach (service choreography) does not assume the exploitation of a central coordinator but each service participating in the process is made aware of its role, when to interact and with which partners. Following this approach, the overall goal is achieved as the composition of peer-to-peer interactions among the collaborating services. XML-based orchestration languages include business process execution language (BPEL) and choreography description language (WS-CDL) for static composition.

BPEL is an XML-based language supporting process-oriented service composition. BPEL composition interacts with a set of services to achieve a given task. The composition result is called a process, participating services are partners, and message exchanges are called activities. A process interacts with external partner services through a WSDL interface. BPELJ, a combination of BPEL and Java allows developers to include Java code inside their BPEL code. Developers can use BPEL with two more specifications: WS-Coordination coordinates the actions of services when a consistent agreement must be reached on the service activities' outcome and WS-Transaction defines the transactional behavior of services. In short, BPEL enables representation of composition where information flow and the binding between services are known a priori.

Service choreography concerns the interactions of services with their clients/users. It is a model of the sequences of operations, states, and conditions, which control how the interactions occur. Successfully following the pattern of interaction prescribed by a choreography has to result in the completion of some useful function, for example, making inquiry of vehicle registration number, finding out the detail of the registered owner, and his or her accident records, or putting the system into a well-defined error state. Service choreography permits the description of how services can be composed, how roles and associations can be established, and how the state, if any, of composed services is to be managed. **Proactive composition**, a kind of static or manual composition, means offline or pre-compiled composition. Services that compose in a proactive manner are usually stable and highly reusable.

The **component approach** is termed as a packaging mechanism for developing distributed applications in terms of combining existing services. This facilitates developing value-added services by combining existing elementary or complex services offered by different enterprises. For instance, a travel plan service can be developed by composing elementary services such as hotel reservation, ticket booking, car rental and sightseeing trip services. The main idea here is that a service can be described as a class that represents a public interface in terms of performed functionality and the composite logic is encapsulated inside the class definition. A public interface of such component can be published and used for discovery and use. Thus the process of service composition deals with reusing, specializing and extending the available components.

b. **Automated Composition** – Realistically this runtime / dynamic / late composition is more tricky and risky compared to manual / early / static / design-time composition. The need for this intrigue composition arises due to a few valid reasons. Some special requirements could not be met by existing standalone and independent services. However an adroit combination of them could accomplish the identified need. There are practical difficulties in intelligent anticipation, automatic discovery, adept matchmaking and decision-taking, and finally runtime utilization. In this unpredictably changing world, it is not at all possible to visualize and freeze all the business and technical needs in advance. Services are being created by dispersed and diverse developers and deposited in geographically distributed and decentralized servers. That is, very frequently there will be new or upgraded services being posted on the Web. It is therefore not feasible to keep an eye on all the services or the functionality of each service being readied and registered on the consistently expanding web infrastructure.

Changing scopes and strategies make businesses jittery and panicky and hence enterprises are investing heavily in business agility, resiliency, continuity and competitiveness solutions, services and strategies. Though SOA is one enabling business tool, robust and versatile service aggregation practices, platforms and patterns have to be in place so that organizations as well as end-users can fully benefit out of the thriving service orientation paradigm. Service aggregation has to be comprehensively supported by concepts and containers that facilitate automated discovery, assessment and access of diverse services. This enablement will ultimately result in workflow execution (runtime) providing elegant composites. To that end, several methods such as artificial Intelligence (AI), process algebras, agent and semantic web technologies are overwhelmingly promising.

Price comparison service is one motivating example. In the absence of automated composition of services, the user has to waste considerable amount of time and resources in determining and visiting numerous B2C web sites, entering or polishing his / her preferences repeatedly, integrating or aligning the different types of results oozing out from different sites. It is preferred that the user enters information once and receives the expected results from the most appropriate services with minimal additional assistance. http://www.addall.com/ is an automated search and comparison web application. There are several promising frameworks and techniques formulated and published for service composition. Readers can find a survey of dynamic service composition techniques in (Alamri, 2006).

i. **A Service Composition Framework** – The paper entitled as "A Survey of Automated Web Service Composition Methods" has proposed a general framework for automatic services composition. This framework is in high-level abstraction, without considering any particular language, platform or algorithm used in composition process. The composition system has two kinds of participants: service provider and service requester. The system also contains the following components: translator, process generator, evaluator, execution engine, and service repository. The translator translates between the external languages used by the participants and the internal languages used by the process generator. For each request, the process generator tries to generate a plan that composes the available services in the service repository to fulfill the request. If more than one plan is found, the evaluator evaluates all plans and proposes the best one for execution. The execution engine executes the plan and returns the result to the service provider.

ii. **Semantic Composition** – Services are a relatively new formulation for building distributed systems. Service description, discovery and interaction are being facilitated by familiar standards such as WSDL, UDDI, and SOAP. These do not implicitly permit to embed relevant semantics in service description, registration, message etc. This limitation means that two identical XML descriptions could mean totally different things, depending on the context in which they are used or vice versa (i.e., two distinct descriptions could mean one thing). That is, descriptions are syntactically correct whereas semantically wrong. This in several ways complicates match-making as well as decision-making tasks and hence there is a renewed call for attaching descriptive and contributive semantics in service messages, schemas and contracts. This puts systems in forefront instead of humans to plan viable alternatives, work out counter measures, wriggle out of dilemmas and dead ends, to decide the best route and services to perform the goals scripted, etc. The effort to integrate semantics into services started with the now standardized RDF and evolved with the creation of DAML+OIL and in particular with DAML-S and OWL-S (where S stands for Services). These languages happened to be the initial step in the creation of the new Web Ontology Language called OWL. Thus dynamic discovery and utilization will see the light through a host of semantic web technologies such as XML, RDF, RDF schema, ontology, etc. OWL-S is a service ontology that enables automatic service discovery, invocation, composition, interoperation and execution monitoring.

Semantics enables Seamless Composition – Composition has to be seamless and spontaneous. Composition happens in an integrated environment, which boasts of highly interoperable software modules. Services are highly interactive, integrative, and independent of any technology / platform details and are the best bet for generating policy, goal, business, network and identity-aware composites and for business modernization and integration. Sadly the current SOA fulfills syntactic integration that fails on many accounts and hence researchers have creatively laid down the foundation for embedding semantics. This incorporation goes a long way in realizing semantic services that intrinsically supports dynamic finding, comparing service capabilities, and utilization. This empowerment paves the way for purposeful, uninhibited and **on-demand** service **collaboration**.

Strict adherence to standards insures and ensures the goal of loose coupling. Attaching semantics with messages being transmitted empowers unambiguous understanding of the distinct capability of each service participant. How services mandated to converse, coordinate, collaborate, etc could be correctly identified by attached semantics. In order for data to flow unimpeded in any SOA implementation, there needs to be an uncompromising detachment between service providers and consumers on each other's data formats. Services should be more concerned with the semantic meaning of the data, not the structure of the data. Thus for having meaningful and seamless composition, technologies fulfilling semantic technologies are the need of the hour.

Semantic Markup of Services for Automated Composition – The paper "Automatic Web Services Composition Using SHOP2" has very interesting details about the semantic markup of services will enable the automation of various kinds of tasks, including discovery, composition, and execution of services. Sufficiently rich, machine readable descriptions of services would allow the creation of compound services with little or no direct human intervention. One part of DAML-S, namely its process ontology, provides a standard language for describing the composition of services.

SHOP2 is a domain-independent hierarchical task network (HTN) planning system exploiting promising AI techniques for planning for automatic service composition. More specifically, they have built an agent that can plan a collection of service requests to achieve user's goals. Among all planning techniques, HTN planning seems very promising because the concept of task decomposition in HTN planning is very similar to the concept of composite process decomposition in DAML-S process ontology. HTN planning is an AI planning methodology that creates plan by task decomposition. This is a process in which the planning system decomposes tasks into smaller subtasks till primitive tasks are found that can be performed directly. Planning for tasks in the order that those tasks will be performed makes it possible to know the current state of the world at each step in the planning process, which makes it possible for SHOP2's precondition-evaluation mechanism to incorporate significant inferring and reasoning power, including the ability to call external programs. This makes SHOP2 ideal as a basis for integrating planning with external information sources as in the web environment. In order to do planning in a given planning domain, SHOP2 needs to be given the knowledgebase about that domain. SHOP2's knowledge base contains operators and methods. Each operator is a description of what needs to be done to accomplish some primitive task and each method tells how to decompose some compound task into partially ordered subtasks.

iii. **Agent-based Service Composition** - The drawbacks of passive composition lead many to ponder and propose new approaches for dynamic service selection and composition. Agents, especially multiagent systems (MAS), seem to be very assuring and articulate in establishing dynamism in service selection and utilization. First of all, service composition could be performed dynamically through agent **collaboration** without predefining abstract plans. Moreover, agent technology offers well-developed approaches to formally express and utilize richer semantic information, such as non-functional characteristics of services or qualitative constraints on the results proposed by a service. Finally, local and reactive processing in MAS can avoid centralized systems' bottlenecks and improve scalability.

The publication titled as "Dynamic Service Composition and Selection through an Agent Interaction Protocol" has prescribed an agent-based approach for intelligent composition. The authors' overall composition approach is broadly decomposed into three steps.

1.   Formalise and decompose the user's requirements into one or several interdependent requests, which are sent to a mediator agent responsible for the discovery of candidate services
2.   Discover and retrieve the candidate services from a centralised registry using keywords extracted from the user's requests
3.   Select and compose the services' functionalities through the interactions of the mediator agent and the agents providing the candidate services, until the user's requirements are completely satisfied.

Through building robust agents and interaction protocols, the authors have showcased their agent-based solution for ensuring dynamic composition.

iv.   **Service Composition with Case-based Reasoning (CBR)** – The research paper "Web Service Composition with Case-Based Reasoning", has unveiled a reactive composition mechanism via CBR. Reactive composition means creating a compound service on the fly. It requires a component manager to take the total responsibility of collaborating with the different sub-services to provide the desired composite service to the client. The interaction cannot be predefined and varied according to the situation. It is better to exploit the present state of services and provide certain runtime optimisations based on real-time parameters like bandwidth, and cost of execution of the different sub-services.

CBR has been a leading problem solving approach leveraging the AI machine learning techniques and the basic idea behind CBR is to solve new problems by comparing them to old problems, which have already been solved in the past. The existing problems and their solutions are stored in a database of cases, called a case-base. When a new problem is presented, the CBR system tries to retrieve the most similar existing problems from the case-base. The idea is that, if two problems look similar, then the solutions to these problems are also possibly similar. The concept of case-similarity measure plays a critical role in performing these processes.

CBR is applied in the service discovery process and this composition model integrates the two behaviours of proactive and reactive service compositions. The proactive composition phase provides the pre-assembly of the composition service, which includes the sub-services, parameters and relationships among sub-services, while the reactive composition phase deal with the processes of service discovery and integration of the existing sub-services. There are three main components in this model: request analyst, outsource agent, and services composers.

v.   In the **algebraic service composition** approaches, services are modeled as mobile processes. Pi-calculus, the leading process-modeling theory, provides a conceptual framework and mathematical tools for expressing mobile systems and reasoning about their behaviors. The example of a mobile system is cellular phone that can change the connection to a network of base station as the phone is carried around. The advantage of using Pi-calculus for a service composition is that it is capable of modeling mobile systems and reasoning about their behaviors. Since the service environment is intrinsically dynamic where everything changes without prior warning, it can be considered as a perfect mobile system. Pi-calculus also ensures safety and liveness properties of created service composition.
vi.   In the **conversation specification** approach, individual services communicate through asynchronous messages. Each individual service has a queue for incoming messages and there is a global

"watcher" to keep track on messages. The conversation is a sequence of messages and this conversation among the peers models the global behavior of the service composition. Services are modeled as Mealy machines, a kind of finite state machines (FSM) with input and output. In this approach, the correctness of a service composition can be verified by checking correctness inside a workflow specification.

Secure Composition – As the Internet is an open channel and steadily establishes as the acclaimed global-scale business platform, security aspects have gained traction as service messages are being transmitted on the Internet. Multi-channel delivery is another requirement. Rock-like security is being guaranteed through upgraded measures on various security principles such as authentication, authorization, confidentiality, integrity and non-repudiation. Trust is an emerging security-enforcing mechanism for service interaction and intermediation. As distributed enterprise services are increasingly found and bound over the web, message integrity and confidentiality are very serious issues not to be easily sidestepped. Also services are meant to be repeatedly leveraged by different clients operating in diverse domains to formulate a variety of large-scale distributed applications. As services are autonomous, standalone, and capable of finding other services in their vicinity or in their networks for earnestly working together to be highly usable for accomplishing stated business goals, there arises a gamut of challenges in the form of threats, risks, vulnerabilities, hacking, adware, malware, etc. Due to the message-passing nature of services, many subtle, sleepy, and shattering errors might silently creep in when several services are put together (The most probable letdowns include messages that are never received, deadlocks, incompatible behaviors, etc.).

Formal methods come in handy in these situations. The major advantages accrued out of using formal languages and models with a clear and formal semantics is that this enables the use of automatic tools to verify whether a system matches its finalized and formalized requirements and works properly. It is also found that formal methods and tools can be used to guarantee secure service compositions.

Quality of Service (QoS) Composition is to leverage, aggregate and bundle each individual service's QoS properties to ensure the desired QoS of the resulting composite service. The leading QoS properties are scalability, security, dependability, flexibility, availability, performance, etc.). SOA infrastructures such as enterprise service bus (ESB), complex event processing (CEP) and orchestration engines, service grids and fabrics are expected to work together in guaranteeing the QoS requirements for composites.

FORMAL METHODS AND TOOLS FOR COMPOSITION

The discipline of formal methods (Ter Beek, 2007) has a long history and a slew of unambiguous and uncompromising models and methods for elegantly describing (both structural as well as behavioral aspects) a spectrum of ICT systems has arrived and being adopted by the concerned. As the futuristic business IT systems are primarily service-centric, model and **event-driven**, proactive and **on-demand**, scientists and researchers are firm and fast in leveraging the most promising formal methods and tools. Formal methods are strong and solid in description, validation and verification of sophisticated and flexible business processes. With SOA is heavily process-centric, service representation and composition domains are at advantageous position with the availability and advancements of formal methods.

a.   **Automata** (labeled transition systems) are a well-known model for formal specifications of systems. An (finite) automaton consists of a set of (finite) states, a set of actions, a set of labeled transitions between states, and a set of initial states. Labels represent actions and a transition's label indicates the action causing the state transition. The intuitive way in which an automaton can model a system's behavior has lead to a variety of automata-based specification models such as Input/Output (I/O) automata and their many derivatives, timed automata, team automata etc.

I/O automata were originally introduced to model distributed computations in asynchronous networks and as a means of constructing correctness proofs of distributed algorithms. An I/O automaton is an automaton whose set of actions is partitioned into input, output and internal actions. Primarily I/O automata and their variants are utilized to describe reactive and distributed systems.

   Team automata are an extension of I/O automata and are used to model components of groupware systems and their interconnections. They were further developed as a formal model to provide a general theoretical framework for the study of synchronization mechanisms in automata models. By dropping a number of restrictions of I/O automata, team automata allow the flexible modeling of various kinds of **collaboration** in groupware systems. Team automata impose hardly any restrictions on the role of the actions in the various components and their composition is not based on a priori fixed way of synchronizing their actions. This allows the definition of a wide variety of protocols for the interaction between a system and its environment.

   Timed Automata were introduced to model the behavior of real-time systems in a formal way. They extend automata with timing constraints by using a finite number of real-valued clocks, which can be reset and whose values increase uniformly with time. At any moment in time, the value of a clock equals the time elapsed since the last time it was reset. These clocks can be used to guard the transition from one state to another. A transition is enabled if and only if the timing constraint associated with it is satisfied by the current values of the clocks. Automata-based models are very appropriate to formally describe, compose, and verify service compositions.

b.   **Petri Net** is a directed, connected and bipartite graph which consists of place nodes, transition nodes and arcs connecting places with transitions. Places may contain tokens. Petri nets are apt for modeling concurrent systems efficiently and effortlessly. Several aspects of concurrent systems can be easily identified mathematically and conceptually via Petri nets.

Petri nets are very popular in business process modeling and related fields due to the variety of process control flows that they can capture. Especially the dead-path-elimination technique used in business process execution language (BPEL), an XML-derived language, to bypass activities, whose preconditions are not met, can be readily modeled using Petri nets. There are ways to map all BPEL control-flow constructs to labeled Petri nets. This output can subsequently be used to verify BPEL processes by means of the open-source tools. There are a number of papers linking service composition with Petri nets. For example, there is a Petri net-based algebra to compose services based on control flows.

   Each service in a pool has a Petri net where transitions are assigned to methods and places to states. A Petri net describes service behavior and has one point for input and one port for output. When a Petri net definition for each service is finished, a composition operator performs the composition. As a result of composition process, new services can be created. Petri nets are good at proving the absence of deadlocks and correct termination. Some of the non-functional properties can be modeled by using colored Petri nets (CPN) that extend classical Petri nets with time and resource management

c.   **Process Algebras** (Rao, 2004) are a popular means to describe and reason about process behaviors. Their underlying semantic foundation is based on labeled transition systems. There are many variants and the most well-known process algebras are Milner's Calculus of Communicating Systems (CCS), Hoare's Calculus of Sequential Processes (CSP), the Algebra of Communicating Processes (ACP) and the Language of Temporal Ordered Systems (LOTOS). Like Petri nets, process algebras are precise formalisms that allow the automatic verification of certain properties of their behaviors. The pi-calculus is a process algebra that has inspired modern composition languages such as BPEL. The pi-calculus is a formal model to describe processes and this significantly simplifies the automatic verification of properties of the behavior of models expressed in such a model. As far as composition is concerned, the pi-calculus offers stimulating constructs to compose activities in terms of sequential, parallel and conditional execution.

Formalization helps a lot in process-intensive system engineering. Today we do process modeling using business process modeling language (BPML), process execution via BPEL, system implementation, system checking followed by deployment, management and maintenance. This ordering is not acceptable as if deviations, misunderstandings, and misinterpretations need to be identified at the beginning stage itself in order to significantly reduce development cycle. With formal methods such as Petri net and Pi-calculus, standardized processing modeling, direct mapping to BPEL, and model verification and validation are done at the earliest resulting in huge savings of developmental time and cost. It is no exaggeration that formal methods and languages are growing in their stature in order to capture and captivate IT professionals in this recessionary and down time.

ARCHITECTURAL APPROACHES FOR SERVICES COMPOSABILITY

Novel application architectures are emerging to disrupt and displace the existing static and stagnant schemes for application implementation. We used to hear, read and sometimes experience the significant turnarounds being brought in through these architectural styles such as service component architecture (SCA), model-driven architecture (MDA), **event-driven** architecture (EDA), web-oriented architecture (WOA), etc. Basically these have flowered and flourished due to the emergence of potential building-blocks (services, events, models, aspects, agents, portlets, etc.) for new-generation systems. Composite applications can be achieved from these abstraction artifacts through a smart combination. In the sections to follow, we are to discuss how SCA and EDA facilitate composite creation / generation and sustenance. There are PhD theses that insist on model-driven and policy-based service composition too.

a.   **SCA** is a set of specifications which describe a standardized programming and an assembling model for rapidly building and connecting service systems in a radically differentiating manner. SCA extends and complements prior and proven approaches to implement services and SCA simplifies and streamlines a growing portfolio of services built on flexible and open components that implement business logic, which offer their capabilities through service-oriented interfaces. These service components could consume functions offered by other components (local as well as remote) via service-oriented interfaces, called service references. SOA is primarily a design approach whereas SCA lessens the complexity of developing or assembling and deploying SOA solutions through its simple development, wrapping, and reusing model. Ultimately SCA encourages seamless composing of old, new and even refurbished service components out of existing application code.

SCA architecture - SCA divides the steps of building of a SOA application into two major parts:

- The implementation of components which provide services and which consume other services
- The assembly of the implemented components to build business systems through appropriate wiring of service references to services

SCA offers a viable mechanism to package and deploy sets of closely related components, which are developed and deployed together as a well-knit unit. It decouples service implementation as well as assembly from the details of infrastructure capabilities and from the mechanisms for invoking external participants. This enables extreme portability of services between different infrastructures, protocols, and languages.

How SCA Works? - The SCA provides an open and technology-neutral (XML-based) scheme for implementing value-added business services that are defined in terms of a business function. Moreover SCA cleanly abstracts all the low-level and laborious tasks and makes middleware functions more accessible to application developers. SCA provides a well-defined model for the smooth assembly of adroit business-solutions from a growing collection of geographically dispersed services. SCA provides a model for the assembly of tightly coupled services and also for the assembly of loosely coupled service-oriented systems. SCA divides up the steps in the building of a SOA system into two major parts. The first step involves the implementation of contributive components which provide services and which consume other services (local as well as remote). Second the existing or implemented components are leveraged to build the desired business system through the compact wiring of service references to services.

In addition to that, SCA provides the inherent capability to build **coarse-grained** service components as assemblies of several fine-grained components. The SCA approach aims to reduce or eliminate the incidental complexity to which application developers are currently exposed when they deal directly with debilitating middleware APIs. While it allows developers to focus on writing business logic, SCA also complies with existing standards under the covers to preserve existing investment in standards, middleware and tools. SCA also supports a variety of component implementation and interface types as first class citizens. For example, the implementation of an SCA component may be a BPEL process, and its interface may be defined in WSDL, or the component may be a Java class with an interface defined as a Java interface. This gives businesses the required flexibility to incorporate a wide-range of existing and future assets into value-added and insights-driven service-oriented systems with little or no bridging or gluing code required.

Service Implementations and Clients - Service implementations are concretization of business logic, which provide services and/or consume services. Services can be implemented in any programming languages such as Java, BPEL or C++. An implementation can provide a service, which is a set of methods / operations implemented and exposed via a public interface that could be automatically identified, matched, and handled by other components. Implementations can also use other services via service references, which indicate the implementation's dependency on services provided elsewhere.

An implementation may also have one or more configurable properties. A property is a data value that can be externally configured and this affects the business function of the implementation. SCA services typically use document-style business data for parameters and return values, and preferably these parameters are represented using "Service Data Objects "(SDOs).

Services, references and properties are the configurable aspects of an implementation. Configuring a reference is done by binding the reference to a target service, which will then be used by the implementation when it invokes the reference. Configuration of a property involves setting a specific data value for the property. In a SCA framework, one implementation can be used to build multiple components. Each component could have a different configuration of the references and properties. Components and their services are used by other local as well as remote components. SCA has been an enabling architectural framework for service systems. Precisely speaking, the goal of simplifying the process of composing legacy as well as modern services over networks is being accomplished by SCA. That means, existing investments are preserved and incrementally value-added. Service-enabling the staggering number of performing modules is the gist of SCA so that composite applications could be easily readied in an affable and affordable fashion through tools-based leveraging of them.

b. **Event-Driven Architecture (EDA)** - Events are turning out to be very crucial in implementing customer-delight systems. Business events are many, pervasive and penetrative. Enterprise systems therefore need to be sharpened to consume internal as well as incoming events. Not only that, they need to be processed according to the rules laid down, users' preferences, and as per the changing business context. Further on, a kind of mining and match-making software infrastructure has to be in place in order to extract and spit out actionable insights out of a heap of streaming data. In a nutshell, business events and their skilful utilization and manipulation are anticipated to play a telling role in shaping up and sharpening the future enterprise elegance, exuberance and agility.

Enterprise IT has to take care of business events in a systematic and synchronized manner. That is, businesses need to act and react to impulses (events within as well as from the environment). Events monitoring, meshing, analysis, processing, and management are extremely essential for nimble and lean businesses. Events are expected to do a stellar job in dynamically linking service components to create composite applications (Van Hoof, 2007). Events are generally asynchronous and are expected to simplify asynchronous service interaction, which in turn leads to the realization of concurrent or parallel systems. Precisely speaking, when something happens somewhere, this incident / activity / event (alternatively referred to as state change) would be passed as a message to the centralized or decentralized middleware / broker / engine that in turn pass on the informational and intended message to all the subscribers to intelligently ponder about the next possible move. This is a recursive operation.

For a fitting example, if we order a book on SOA in Amazon.com, there are a number of business intelligence (BI) services (asynchronous events) waiting to capture this ordering (initiating event). These events on the server side collaborate together and leverage contextual details to arrive at a smart decision, which ultimately leads to new revenue generation for amazon.com. Thus not only capturing events, but also extracting the essence, strategically valued association, progressive trends, hidden intelligence, cues and patterns behind those events are very much essential for businesses to thrive in this competitive and knowledge-based market environment. A composite service resulting out of event generation and consumption can be implemented as pictorially illustrated in figure 2.

Figure 2. Implementing Composite Service using Events

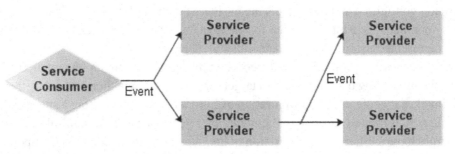

The service consumer (initiator / user agent / client) sends the initiating event that is delivered (through a pub/sub engine) to a set of event services (service providers) that have subscribed to this originating event. One or more of these service providers on receiving the message, can, in turn, formulate counter measures, which will be again routed via compact messages through the broker to another set of services. This sequencing of events effectively creates a composite service. The realization of composite services through pub/sub infrastructure has the following characteristics.

- It is significantly more flexible, compared to programmatic implementation. By changing a set of services, subscribed to a particular topic, it is possible to completely change implementation of composite services. Alternatively the same can be achieved by changing the topic to which consumer sends the original event.
- Events-based implementation does not provide a well defined place for the composite service context. This makes an implementation of composite services more complex. One of the solutions is to attach the context data to the events content, which usually makes messages voluminous, which leads to increased network usage and performance degradation.
- Events-based implementation does not provide the notion of the composite service instance, which makes it very difficult to coordinate events, implementing a composite services instance.
- This also makes it very difficult to implement any form of transactional support to ensure correct behavior in the case of failures of participating services.

Further improvements of composite service implementation can be achieved through usage of an orchestration engine for implementation of service mediator (fig. 3). This implementation improves the programmatic implementation by using orchestration language instead of general programming language for composite implementation. This allows programming and maintaining composition logic using visual editors, tailored specifically to simplify this kind of programming. It also allows utilizing the power of orchestration engines providing built-in capabilities for asynchronous invocations, state management, exception handling, compensation support, etc. The enhancements accumulated by employing orchestration engine in event-based service composition eliminate most of the difficulties and limitations of the previous mechanism. The orchestration engine can be further refined and retrofitted towards constructing compact and QoS-compliant service composites. A specific event message routed through a set of logically related services results in composite service. The runtime identification of services and dynamic manipulation of event consumers, brokers and producers all contribute for pro-

Figure 3. Implementing Composite Service using Orchestration Engine

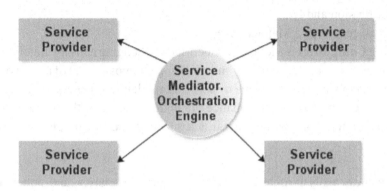

ducing smarter composites.

In summary, there are various options being considered for smooth implementation of service composition. These days there are overwhelming supports for model-driven architecture (MDA) and model-driven system development (MDSD). As models establish their unique capabilities and strengths to emerge as the most flexible, virtualized and abstracted building-blocks for next-generation system production and sustenance, the discipline of model-driven composition is all set to capture the heart of many in order to reach out greater heights in the days to come. Researchers are sincerely unearthing a variety of ways and means of simplified (through tools, patterns, frameworks, widgets, wizards, etc.) implementation of model-driven composition. In the world of Web 2.0, data and service **mashup**s (Bloomberg, 2006) are very prominent and dominant. Distributed data sources from heterogeneous systems are being collected, cleaned up, polished, synchronized and presented in order to create a kind of unified view for users. Similarly services too are being meshed, mixed and mashed up for creating novel applications. Pioneering and path-breaking processes and practices are being worked out for services getting smartly mated to arrive at robust and resilient services. Composition has become a mainstream task being carried out in all the domineering layers in the enterprise system stack ranging from presentation, process, application, service, information to infrastructure layers.

COMPOSITE DEVELOPMENT LIFE CYCLE (CDLC)

Composites highlight their uniqueness and distinction on fully implementing business processes. It is argued that composition via service interconnection and intermediation leads to more sophisticated services and applications. Composites are more aligned with business realities and provide a single point of access to desired business goals. It is all about the automated discovery, matching, ranking, selecting and adroit combination of participating services into differentiated and virtualized services. As existing services from different vendors are assembled over networks, on one hand, we achieve service reusability and on the other hand, we reap value-added, authenticated, and business-aligned services. Composites thus are an indispensable cog in conceptualizing, constructing and commanding affordable and affable software solutions. As every tangible thing or developmental activity has a well-defined life cycle, composites development too has to go through a standard life cycle.

a. Composite Modeling
b. Composite Evaluation and Execution
c. Composite Management and Maintenance
   a. **Modeling Composites** is a long-cherished and challenging activity. Lately modeling incorporates both analysis and design portions. Creating composites out of a heap of discrete services is a no mean job and hence a tinge of hardcore modeling is necessary in order to mitigate the threatening complexity and to enhance the understanding of the nuances of composites and their functioning. A model in general is a succinct and unambiguous representation of the system.

Models help business analyst, architects, and developers to analyze and understand the business problem at hand and to design best-in-class solution by drastically diminishing the complexity of them by mapping complex and murkier details into simple and standardized notations. They establish a conceptual abstraction of the key business entities, their relationships and the interactions between them. Models communicate the desired structure and behavior of the system to distributed project teams. Models also help to visualize and control the system architecture. Models enable to better understand the final system we are building, often opening a spectrum of opportunities for simplification and reuse. Finally, models power us to mitigate and manage any kind of risks. Models could be persisted, uniformed represented and stored. They in a way lead to consistent and commendable innovations in the field of software development.

i.   **Composite Analysis** - Analysis has been a very important and incredible task in arriving at composites that satisfy the decided and decoded requirements (operation as well as service-level). A clear and unambiguous understanding of the business context, problem, and goals besides the details on implementation technologies, frameworks, containers, and existing IT assets goes a long way in precisely and concisely documenting requirements (both functional as well as non-functional) of the proposed system. Empowered with relevant knowledge of both the composites and the problem domain, architects and programmers could think ahead in visualizing any kind of risks, deviations, constraints, problem areas, etc and these could come handy in effective and unified change, version, variance, configuration, vulnerability, and threat management. In other words, analysis helps to decide the "what part" of the total project implementation. What each composite needs to have and do (individual capability of each service component and the collective contribution of the composite through expert coordination) is being decided in this activity.

ii. **Composite Design** – There are two design models (logical as well as physical). The logical design gives the overall structure for resulting composites but the details about the specific services would not be indicated in the logical design. In the physical design, the participating service components need to be specified apart from the actors and the high-level interaction among system modules. In order to detail about each contributive service, service identification through automated matching of functions and features of each service with the overall requirements of the planned composite is mandatory.

iii. **Composite Diagramming** - As far as composite design is concerned, a composite service is expressed using service chart diagrams that leverage state charts. Encoding the flow of method invocations as state charts is especially attractive for several reasons. First, state charts possess a formal semantic, which is essential for reasoning about composite service specifications. Next, state charts are becoming a standard process-modeling mechanism as they have been incorporated into the latest UML standard. Finally, state charts offer a good number of control-flow constructs such as branching, concurrent threads, structured loops etc. for easier and quicker design of resilient composites. UML, being the standard modeling language, will go through recommendations, revisions and releases in due course of time in order to capture and accommodate all the specialized characteristics of composites in a more matured and synchronized fashion.

iv. **Service Discovery and Identification** – Deciding all the participating services has to be performed for creating physical composite design. Composite design is concerned about designing creative business solutions based on available services. The design transparently specifies what component services are utilized and how they interact with one another. Before involving and invoking them, the correct services need to be searched, studied (matched, ranked, validated, and verified) of their capabilities, compatibilities, and characteristics, and selected. There are proven matchmaking algorithms popping up for automated service selection.

For developing business-scale composites, there ought to be an easier and enabling mechanism to lookup and wade through a set of fulfilling services from the service repository. An easily searchable and navigable registry repository product has to be in place for service discovery. Besides keyword-based searching for syntactic discovery, there is a need for automatic discovery too. This automation becomes possible when we have semantic services and semantic ESB backbone in place. Semantics-attached services expose more to requesting agents and this helps to arrive at a concise and precise understanding of service capabilities and context. Service filtering mechanism comes in handy in lessening the workload.

Policy-based service selection is gaining much ground. Conventional means of selecting a service are predominantly based on the results returned from service discovery. Typically most approaches employ a kind of matchmaker, which works in tandem with a service registry and user preferences based on the functionality of services. Non-functional attributes are not taken into considering while selecting and deciding the right and relevant services that fruitfully participate in service chaining. Therefore an extended architecture has been materialized and this facilitates consumers to easily notify their non-functional inclinations (performance, timeliness and QoS) before filtering and freezing the right services.

v. **Service Matchmaking** is the ideal and indisputable way of selecting the desired services. The user or program has to look for right services by using textual descriptions provided by service providers in order to understand their unique functional capabilities and non-functional properties. The order of linking is also very important. By matching output parameters with input parameters, if it is found that their data structures are different, then it calls for necessary transformation.

Composition Patterns – Patterns are too evolving consistently. Any complex entity has to have a set of unique patterns embossed inside in a hidden nature and extracting them goes a long way in realizing software-intensive business systems. Architectural patterns such as business, application, and runtime patterns are making waves. Similarly integration, modernization and composition patterns are being adopted in big ways. If decomposition demystifies complicated ICT systems, then composition guarantees adaptivity of them. Composition has penetrated into the deep of the IT landscape and experts are focusing on brining out robust and resilient composition patterns that in turn streamlines and simplifies composite development.

Figure 4. Hierarchical Service Composition Pattern

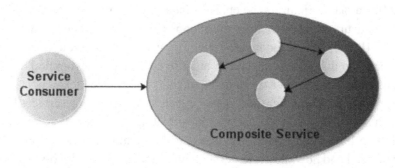

Hierarchical composition pattern entails invoking the composite service in its entirety each time to use this service. This approach is a common way of designing workflows where the process comprises a series of activities, each of which may correspond to a sub-process or a task performed by a person or a program. Here the composition as a whole consumes an input and, if appropriate, produces an output. The relationship between the composite service and the component services is that of containment. The composition itself is transparent to the consumer (block box). A consumer invokes this type of composite service, waits until its execution completes and uses the results (either directly or in a form of side effects) of its execution (fig. 4).

This composition approach is good for implementing full-fledged systems that internally supports the hierarchical decomposition. Every level of hierarchy is implemented as an independent composite service, coordinating execution of lower level (composite) services. It is also a common way of modeling high level solutions in workflow systems by composing a series of activities, each of which may correspond to a lower level business process, or a task to be performed by a person or a program. While any composite service may be monitored or interrupted by the outside system using it, it does not support any other functional interactions with the service consumer except for an original invocation.

Although this black box composition approach is a very powerful way of dealing with complexities, there are situations when a consumer needs to control execution of the composite service based on the intermediate execution results of service execution. The other type "Conversational Composition" supports this need. In this case the implementation of the composite service is also completely opaque to the service consumer, but selected intermediate execution results are exposed (grey box).

Conversational composition pattern supports a conversation between a service and its consumer. The conversation has state and thus this type of service represents one of the exceptions from stateless services. In fact, the appearance of stateful invocations in SOA is an indicator for usage of a conversational composite service. In conversational composition, the interaction between a consumer and a composite service is not limited to a single exchange as it is the case with hierarchical composition. It is perfectly conceivable to have a conversation that spans multiple and separate exchanges.

This is achieved by supporting an explicit conversation state by composite service and exposing multiple interfaces to a service consumer – one for the initial service invocation and others to get intermediate results and control execution based on them (fig. 5). In this type of composition, the interacting consumer and provider are viewed as peers, exchanging data and control signals. Since both models are viable ways of designing compositions, the question is how to pick between them. On the one hand,

Figure 5. Conversational Service Composition Pattern

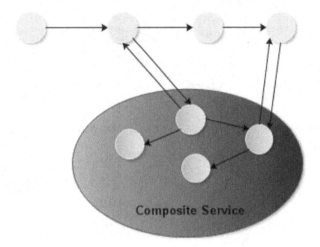

using a strict hierarchy is a useful way of modeling complex business processes, as demonstrated by the success of workflow technology.

On the other hand, conversations have an expressiveness that makes it easy to capture common business interactions (the acts of negotiation, monitoring of results and so on) through explicitly modeling the messaging interactions between a consumer and a composite service.

vi.   **Service Linking and Chaining** – Once the right and the rightful services are identified, then the linking task has to happen based on the agreed ordering or sequencing of the services to be ultimately useful. This ensures correct interaction among the component services according to the finalized design. Composite service crafted out of a set of interactive services then will be subjected to necessary configuration and then will be deployed in the composite container. There are predominantly two methodologies for service linking to realize composites.

Mediator-based topology assumes a single service playing the role of a mediator that controls the interactions of the component services.

1.   For mediator-based **hierarchical services**, mediator's design revolves around the definition of the coordination of component services in order to achieve a specified goal within specified constraints. There are various techniques for implementing the coordination, including orchestration, OWL-S compositions, Petri Nets etc.
2.   For mediator-based **conversational services**, the mediator's design revolves around specifying states and state transitions based on the system events. Typical implementation techniques use transition system or finite state machine (FSM).

Mediator-based methodology (fig. 6) assumes a single service, called the mediator, which has the specialized role of interacting with the service consumer and controlling the execution of the other services (component services) participating in composition.

Figure 6. Mediator-based Composition Methodology

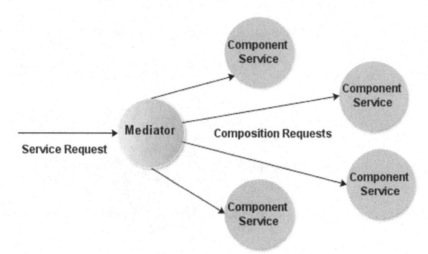

In the case of mediator-based hierarchical services, the mediator implements an orchestration schema that defines invocation sequence of component services in order to achieve a specified goal within specified constraints. In the case of mediator-based conversational services, the mediator implements service states and states transitions, based on the consumer inputs. In the case of peer-to-peer methodology, there is no notion of a mediator service. Every participating service (component service) can execute (partial) composite service (fig. 7).

A composition, in this case, is defined as a messaging template and component services can be plugged into it. The target behavior is specified as a family of permitted message exchange sequences, which should be realized by the system. Typically this methodology is used only for the implementation of the hierarchical services due to the lack of mechanisms required for support of the conversational state. Composites thus developed can be accordingly configured, deployed into composite container, optimized through consolidation based on performance monitoring, resource utilization, and virtualization. Further on composites need to be governed as services are empowered for automatic interactions.

b. **Composite Evaluation and Execution -** Once a composite is realized, it has to be subjected for thorough investigation of its functional as well as business capabilities. There are several mechanisms and tools available in order to quicken the process of automated testing and debugging. In addition to that, we also can employ a string of simulators and emulators that help in locating any pain points, loopholes, and junctions where a suite of innovations can be seamlessly introduced. Thus evaluation of the composite developed through examination could lead to competent and compact composite. Subsequently all the necessary configuration and preferred performance details can be specified so that composites are ready for deployment, fine-tuning and execution.

c. **Composite Management and Maintenance -** SOA has conquered the unquenchable minds of both developers and executives alike. SOA has been sparkling and spreading its wings far and wide. Technocrats are tending towards SOA for its unprecedented technical capabilities and entrepreneurs are embracing for its business automation advantages. A variety of horizontal and vertical services are being implemented and several of them are modernized version of existing IT assets. These are

Figure 7. Peer-to-peer Composition Methodology

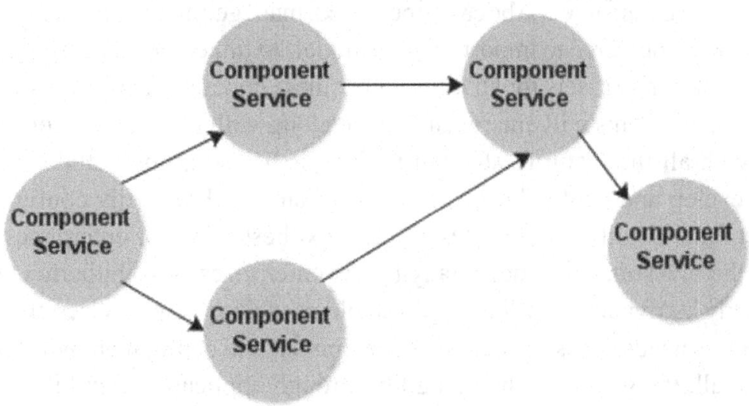

being combined for generating value-added services in the form of composites. Services are being registered in public registries to be made use of by other clients for other tasks and thus a kind of service landscape is unfolding. Enterprises are betting and banking on service ecosystem for their day-to-day operations and offerings to be accomplished in an agile and lean fashion. Services are being emboldened with various supporting techniques and high-end infrastructures to guarantee their quality of service (QoS).

Besides, firms are devising a growing array of enforceable policies, best practices, proven strategies, evaluation metrics, and key guidelines in ensuring usability, availability, sharability, composability, elasticity, fidelity and reusability, the prime qualities of any typical SOA system. Now with the arrival of **event-driven** SOA, the complexity and chaotic nature of services will shoot up. Governability is the emerging criterion for establishing a consistent and complete platform on which a group of related services could exhibit their capabilities and deliver on their promises. Both design and run-time governance solutions are being produced and they will go a long way in empowering individual services, assigning and fixing responsibilities, enforcing business rules, controlling any kind of deviations, overseeing and guaranteeing the contractual obligations, sequencing runtime service behaviors towards the business goals. In short, service autonomy would include self-governing attribute too. The impact will be actionable and controllable IT.

COMPOSITE ORIENTED ARCHITECTURE (COA)

Composition is gaining significant momentum and traction. Having convinced about the special capabilities of composites for software development community in the long run, professionals and pundits are keenly collaborating together to come out with promising composition languages, patterns, standards, middleware, and proven approaches. This section briefs about the need for COA and its supporting infrastructures. As indicated before, one or more composites are generally employed to fully automate a business process. With the publication of OMG's MDA standard specifications, platform-independent models (PIMs) have taken the center stage. Software components are being readied in PIM form. Process models and PIMs will jointly contribute for halving developmental complexity, cost and time. Models being supple, affable, and extensible can be easily persisted, managed and maintained. The next-generation BPM suites are getting empowered to import process models to tinker them accordingly. In short, process models are reusable enterprise assets for all kinds of business domains. This means composite modeling techniques, tools, and platforms will emerge and shine along with next-generation process models.

Another trend with all the maturity attained in SOA is to increasingly and consistently make use of composites to develop and deploy business systems that could be easily configurable to supply an altogether different functionality. Composites are the next best thing for enterprises as they can create business value for the investments made already by the enterprises. Also hitherto unheard applications can be created quickly by dynamically locating both old as well as new services and linking the chosen ones as per the business needs. Thus application development and deployment will become faster, easier and cheaper. Above all, the goal of business agility through application flexibility can be fulfilled. In order to transform COA a mainstream architectural strategy and style, the need for versatile and resilient products such as a standard composition modeling language, integrated development and deployment environments, composites registry repository, composites fabrics for safely and smartly routing, mediating, transcoding, and transmitting messages, and other middleware functionalities is on the rise.

1. **Composites Modeling Language** – A modeling language allow the specification which services participate as component services, the order of their invocation, and the determination of possible parameters. The resulting specification is called composition schema. The language is specifically designed for the composition of services and the composition schema is then a program written in this language.

2. **Integrated Development Environment (IDE)** enables designers to specify a composition schema. Typically, this is achieved by providing a graphical user interface to the designers. They compose a new service by modeling component services and control flow graphs on a canvas. The result is then a composition schema which can also be translated into a textual representation.

3. **Composites Container** takes care of the execution of the composition schema. This includes the invocation of the component services and the verification of the correct order of messages as defined in the composition schema. Such an environment is often called composition or orchestration engine.

COA in a way is the amalgamation of several enterprise architectures such as SOA, SCA, EDA, MDA, etc. Hence it is imperative to integrate SCA runtime with SOA enterprise system bus (ESB) backbone so that heterogeneous components running on disparate platforms can be found and connected to implement competent SOA-based composites. Standards-compliant MDA toolkits in order to create services from the platform-independent models (PIMs) directly are mandated. Composites will be high-performing, mission-critical and enterprise-scale components. Besides designing, developing, testing, and deploying composites, governance is very critical for the effective functioning and for fulfilling the operational agreements made out between composites providers and consumers.

COMPOSITE APPLICATION FRAMEWORK (CAF)

Any typical composite application framework has to have a string of modular and standards-based process, presentation, information and integration infrastructures.

1. **Business Process Management (BPM) 2.0 Suite** empowers business process analysts and managers with the ability to visually model, create, simulate, integrate, validate and optimize sophisticated business processes. Due to the emergence of value-added processes such as communication-enabled business processes (CEBPs), analytics-attached business processes (AABPs), etc., BPM 2.0 is becoming hot. Composites hence need an army of matured technologies including business intelligence (BI) 2.0 to be effective and contributive for the forthcoming service era.

2. **Composites Server** enables the easier deployment, administration, configuration, execution, performance monitoring, refinement, and lean management of composites. Also problems identification and resolution capabilities need to be incorporated. **SCA runtime** also ought to become a part of this system. **Visual composer** is another interesting wizard for generating composites visually

3. **Composite Testing Tools** are to automate the testing of functionalities, and features of composites developed

4. **Composites Governance Solution** is to enforce composites to strictly adhere or comply to various business rules / policies, best practices, key guidelines, user preferences, goals, etc

5. **Business Activity Monitoring (BAM)** facilitates deeper and broader levels of business intelligence (BI) for process execution and performance across the enterprise

6. **Business Process Optimization (BPO) Engine** – This will help to identify the lacunae and holes in business processes and to optimize them accordingly. Business processes need to be nurtured and optimized

7. **Business Rules (BR) Engine** is to simplify embedding business rules in composites on demand and to guarantee policy-based management

8. **Orchestration Engine** is for orchestration of various services towards the composed one that automates a full business process.

9. **Security Services** that provide the security, confidentiality, and integrity mechanisms such as authentication, authorization, access control, encryption / decryption, non-repudiation, etc

10. **Web Workbench is** for developing rich Internet and enterprise applications using fast emerging web 2.0 technologies such as AJAX, mash-ups etc. for empowering composites with rich and intuitive interfaces

11. **An Integrated Composite Development Environment (CDE)** is an integrated environment in which SOA-based composite applications are quickly modeled, designed, developed and debugged.

12. **MDA Toolkit** – As machine-readable models are to play a key role in realizing composites, there is a need for MDA-compliant tools to create service components automatically from the business requirements-specific models

13. **XML Engine** is for parsing, processing, mining, transforming, displaying, and transcoding XML files as service messages carry XML-based data.

14. **Agent Runtime** is the execution platform for scores of intelligent software agents that are very critical in accomplishing several tasks connected to the art and act of composite realization

15. **Master data management (MDM)** framework for coordinating and synchronizing critical business data across different applications and databases efficiently.

16. **Composites Repository** – We have service registry repository for runtime finding and binding of services. Naming and directory services are also being strengthened to store, filter, and matchmaking, categorize, and select services. Taxonomy-sponsored composite registry repository needs to be established

17. **Composites Integration Bus (CIS)** – This is an advanced version of ESB with the following capabilities.
    1. **Distributed Messaging** – The message oriented middleware (MoM) provides a reliable and distributed transport facility using store-and-forward mechanism that guarantees message delivery even in the case of network failures
    2. **Location Transparency** – A composite client invoking a composite provider only needs to be aware that the composite exists. The client does not need to know where the composite is running. The CIS locates the composite when it gets invoked.
    3. **Transport Transparency** – Many communication protocols such as HTTP, SOAP, JMS etc. will be supported and any one can be leveraged for message transmission
    4. **Quality of Service (QoS)** – Composites will satisfy several non-functional characteristics such as scalability, throughput, amenability, security, accessibility, high availability, dependability, trustworthiness, etc
    5. **Content-based Routing** introduces a set of rules or business logic that is applied to the content of the message at the routing stage and enables the CIS to route messages to specific service providers based on the content
    6. **Open Standards** – Standardization facilitates interoperability among the containers, engines, modules and services.

CIS has to provide a slew of transport, transformation, routing, brokering, analysis, and mediation services to facilitate the integration of diverse and geographically distributed composites. Composite integration will become a neat reality through CIS. Composites can be described using composite WSDL and registered in a UDDI-kind registry. Composites can use SOAP and REST for composites interaction. Messages and documents will be the prime means for composites to interact and collaborate dynamically. CIS will act as a contributing intermediary to enable intelligent communication between different composites. A CIS guarantees that the message, whatever it may be, gets delivered from consumer to composite or vice versa. Composites are **event-driven** and hence CIS has to handle events. A CIS can be an integrated, generic yet adept communication backbone and integration infrastructure. This empowers businesses to sense and act proactively on any kind of business events and situations including incoming opportunities and insidious threats. Apart from a MoM for events processing and a well-defined policy engine ought to be attached as composites are linked and leveraged based on the business rules.

Composites, being **coarse-grained** and complex services, can be realized at design time as well as at runtime. Composites can be visualized, developed and deposited in composites repository. There are critical yet demarcated roles for software agents, service components, and machine-readable models in realizing the era of composites. Composites will become the dominant application realization mechanism for optimal and connected enterprises. Composites, being process-centric, can be integrated to form complex applications instantly. Composites can be leveraged for business consolidation as multiple enterprises can configure accordingly and reuse them. Composites achieve business agility as they support rapid construction of business-specific applications that adapt to business changes intrinsically.

Composites will be semantic and hence semantic discovery, matchmaking, selection and integration among composites will become commonplace.

CONCLUSION

Composites are significantly positioned for growing businesses. Business challenges such as efficiency, resiliency, continuity, dexterity, leanness, sensitivity, and smartness are being increasingly addressed at the process level. Composites are tightly aligned with the incredible processes. It is hence clear that advancements being made out in composite paradigm are distinctively beneficial for system engineering. However engineering composites, utilizing, manipulating, persisting, and governing them to be proud participants in the hot enterprise ecosystem and finally forming composite processes, services, applications, data, views, etc are not an easy task. In this chapter, we have laid down the solid groundwork for composite engineering and discussed about the significant business and technical impacts. We also have described about composite development methodologies, frameworks, platforms, etc. Hopefully this will act as a stimulating document in taking forward the grand vision set for the field of service composition to scintillating heights in the years ahead. Efforts are underway in conceiving and consolidating composite patterns. People are at work in unearthing relevant assets, appliances, artifacts and tools empowering composite realization. Besides setting up composites repository, the special traits of composites are being studied and leveraged by professionals. In short, composites and clouds will lead to the era of real-time, adaptive, and on-demand, enterprises.

REFERENCES

Alamri, A., Eid, M., & El Saddik, A. (2006). Classification of the state-of-the-art dynamic web services composition techniques. *International Journal of Web and Grid Services*, *2*(2), 148–166. doi:10.1504/IJWGS.2006.010805

Bloomberg, J. (2006). Composing services into enterprise mashups – Empowering business users with enterprise Web 2.0. Retrieved from http://www.zapthink.com

Dustdar, S., & Schreiner, W. (2005). A survey on web services composition. Int. *J. Web and Grid Services*, *1*(1), 1–30. doi:10.1504/IJWGS.2005.007545

Koskimies, M, (2006). *Composing services in SOA: Workflow design, usage and patterns*.

Rao, J., & Su, X. (2004). A survey of automated web service composition methods. In *Proceedings of the First International Workshop on Semantic Web Services and Web Process Composition (SWSWPC 2004)*, California. Springer-Verlag.

Resources, S. O. A. (n.d.). Retrieved from http://www.peterindia.net/SOA.html

Ter Beek, M., Bucchiarone, A., & Gnesi, S. (2007). Web service composition approaches: From industrial standards to formal methods. In *Proceedings of the Second International Conference on Internet and Web Applications and Services*. IEEE.

Van Hoof, J. (2007). SOA and EDA: Using events to bridge decoupled service boundaries. *The SOA Magazine*. Retrieved from http://www.soamag.com/I4/0207-2.asp

KEY TERMS AND DEFINITIONS

Composite Services: are collections of business and IT services. Composites work together to provide on-demand business solutions. Composites are aggregates generated via orchestration or choreography methods and are supposed to automate business processes. There is a direct mapping between composites and processes and hence composites, being highly business-aligned and **coarse-grained**, could be easily handled and manipulated by business analysts and executives.

Enterprise Service Bus (ESB): is a flexible, open and standards-compliant messaging, routing, brokering, and connectivity infrastructure for finding, binding, and linking distributed applications and services in order to create an integrated IT ecosystem. ESBs are continuously maturing and evolving to become the unified and resilient platform comprising a wider variety of adaptors for smartly connecting disparate systems to enable spontaneous and seamless **collaboration**. In short, ESB is a kind of core integration backbone and reflective middleware.

Services: are loosely coupled, highly cohesive, self-describing, autonomous, publicly discoverable, network addressable, accessible and actionable, technology-agnostic, interoperable, reusable, composable and evolvable software modules. Services are a repeatable and recoverable unit of capability. Services are the apt abstraction entities and the base building-blocks for mitigating system complexity and for enabling application integration, modernization and composition.

Service Oriented Architecture (SOA): brings in a suite of paradigm shifts in software development, modernization, and integration principles and practices. SOA clarifies the structural as well as behavioral aspects of interactive software modules (services) in realizing a range of open enterprise systems. SOA guarantees business transformation and optimization. SOA enables process innovation that in turn accomplishes creative and cognition-enabled software solutions.

Web 2.0: represents the next-version of the current web. Due to the unprecedented articulation and adoption of social computing and networking technologies, Web 2.0 is alternatively referred to as the social web that enables intimate user-participation and cyber-**collaboration**, real-time experience of web applications, knowledge sharing for enhanced productivity, and synchronized and smart presentation of facts on the web interface through seamless aggregation of right and rightful information from distributed sources over the Internet.

Section 4
Practical Issues in BPM Technology Development

Chapter 17
Semantic Business Process Mining of SAP Transactions

Jon Espen Ingvaldsen
The Norwegian University of Science and Technology, Norway

Jon Atle Gulla
The Norwegian University of Science and Technology, Norway

ABSTRACT

This chapter introduces semantic business process mining of SAP transaction logs. SAP systems are promising domains for semantic process mining as they contain transaction logs that are linked to large amounts of structured data. A challenge with process mining these transaction logs is that the core of SAP systems was not originally designed from the business process management perspective. The business process layer was added later without full rearrangement of the system. As a result, system logs produced by SAP are not process-based, but transaction-based. This means that the system does not produce traces of process instances that are needed for process mining. In this chapter, we show how data available in SAP systems can enrich process instance logs with ontologically structured concepts, and evaluate techniques for mapping executed transaction sequences with predefined process hierarchies.

INTRODUCTION

To describe the current situation in dynamic business process environments we need tools that can assist rapid modeling. Process mining tools meet this requirement by extracting descriptive models from event logs in the underlying IT-systems to construct the business process descriptions from actual data.

SAP systems are promising domains for process mining. SAP is the most widely used Enterprise Resource Planning (ERP) system with a total market share of 27 percent worldwide in 2006 (Pang, 2007). Even though there may be blue print models defined for how the systems should support organizational business processes, there are often gaps between how the systems are planned to be used and how the employees actually carry out the operations. The magnitude of data sources in a running ERP

DOI: 10.4018/978-1-60566-669-3.ch017

system is large, and within SAP there are several event and transaction logs that can be analyzed with process mining.

In this process mining work, we use transaction data that describe document dependencies between executed transactions. A transaction in a SAP system can be viewed a small application. An example of a transaction is "*ME51 – Create Purchase Requisition*". As the name indicates, this transaction enables a user to create a purchase requisition. "*ME51*" is the unique identifier for this transaction, called the transaction code. Such a transaction would produce a purchase requisition, which further can be referred to by a purchase order created in another transaction, like "*ME21 – Create Purchase Order*". By tracing such document dependencies, we are able to extract transaction sequences that can be explored and analyzed with use of process mining.

Data in the underlying databases of SAP systems contain

- Transactional data – Daily operations, such as sales orders and invoices.
- Master data – Business entities such as customers, vendors and users.
- Ontological data – Metadata for interpretation and structuring of instances.

The transactional data are the basis building blocks for process mining analysis and describe events that are carried out. In the transactional data we typically find execution timestamps and relations to involved master data sources. The ontological data in SAP databases can be used to extract descriptions of the transactions and related entities. For instance, in the SAP database there are table structures that contain full text descriptions of transactions and business processes and their internal relationships.

Construction and maintenance of ontologies is work-intensive and has so far been a bottleneck to realization of many semantical technologies. Ontologies tend to grow huge and complex, and both domain expertise and ontology modeling expertise are needed in ontology engineering (Gulla, 2006). In the underlying databases of SAP systems there are lots of structured data that can be extracted to form and populate ontologies. In semantic business process mining of SAP transactions, we can exploit available data structures to limit the extent of ontology engineering work.

One particular challenge with process mining of SAP transactions is the many-to-many relationship between transactions and defined business processes. Figure 1 shows an example from the business process hierarchy in SAP. In SAP systems, business processes are defined at four levels, "Enterprise Area", "Scenario", "Group" and "Business Process". At the second lowest level, Figure 1 shows two business processes, "*Subsequent debit for empties and returnable packaging*" and "*Sales activity processing (standard)*". As shown in the hierarchy, both of these business processes can involve the transaction "*V+01: Create Sales Call*". The transaction logs in SAP systems contain no information about business process context. If we do process mining on transaction logs where "*V+01: Create Sales Call*" occurs, there is no available data that explicitly states whether this transaction was carried out in the context of "*Subsequent debit for empties and returnable packaging*", "*Sales activity processing (standard)*" or another business process.

Transaction sequences themselves can be used as input to process mining algorithm to extract flow models and performance indicators. However, if we could map the executed transactions precisely to concepts in the defined business process hierarchies, we would be able to extract business process models with aggregated levels, and relate performance indicators to higher level process definitions.

Figure 1. Example of business process hierarchies

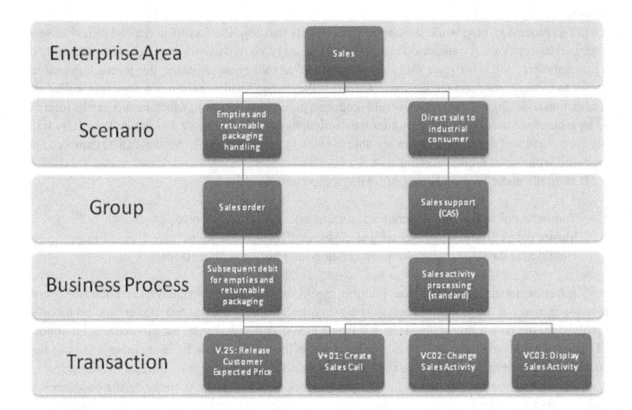

In this chapter we will show how transaction sequences extracted from SAP systems can be enriched with relations to ontological concepts and we will evaluate three techniques for mapping executed transactions with the standard business process hierarchies in SAP.

BACKGROUND

In the past year, Semantic Web technology has gained a substantial interest from Business Process Management (BPM) research. Traditional process mining has successfully been shown to extract flow models that describe how activities and organizational units depend on each other in dynamic business process environment. Semantic business process mining (SBPM) takes advantages of the rich knowledge expressed in ontologies and associated process instance data and extracts semantic models that enable reasoning in a wider context than traditional process mining. SBPM has been proposed as an extension of BPM with semantic web and semantic web service technologies in order to increase and enhance the level of automation that can be achieved within the BPM life-cycle (Alves de Medeiros, 2007; Ma 2007).

Contemporary information systems (e.g., WFM, ERP, CRM, SCM, and B2B systems) record business events in so-called event logs. Process mining takes these logs to discover process, control, data, organizational, and social structures (van der Aalst, 2007). Within the BPM life-cycle, process mining can be applied to gather knowledge about the past and find potentials for change and optimization.

Approaches for semantic process mining have been proposed by incorporating ontologies, references from elements in event logs to ontological concepts and ontological reasoners. Ontologies define the set of shared concepts necessary for the analysis, and formalize their relationships and properties. The references associate meanings to syntactical labels in event by pointing to defined ontology concepts. The reasoner supports reasoning over the ontologies in order to derive new knowledge, e.g., subsumption, equivalence, etc. (Alves de Medeiros, 2008).

Alves de Medeiros (2007) point out two important potentials for leveraging process mining with a conceptual layer:

1. To make use of the ontological annotations in logs and models to develop more robust process mining techniques that analyze on conceptual levels.
2. Use process mining techniques to discover or enhance ontologies based on the data in the event logs.

Pedrinaci (2008) argue that business process analysis activities require semantic information that spans business, process and IT levels and is easily retrieved from event logs. They have developed the Events Ontology and the Process Mining Ontology that aim to support the analysis of enacted processes at different levels of abstraction spanning from fine grain technical details to coarse grain aspects at the business level.

ProM is an open source process mining framework that is built up of plug-ins that targets different process mining analysis (van der Aalst, 2007). Already, there are developed plug-ins and input format for ProM that targets ontological reasoning. The Semantically Annotated Mining eXtensible Markup Language (SA-MXML) format is a semantic annotated version of the MXML input format used by the ProM framework. In short, the SA-MXML format opens for linking elements in logs to concepts in ontologies. The Semantic LTL Checker is a ProM plug-in that allows for semantic verification of properties in SA-MXML logs (Alves de Medeiros, 2008).

EXTRACTION OF SEMANTICALLY ENRICHED TRANSACTION SEQUENCES

SAP systems contain data structures (typically hierarchical) that can be exported to form and populate ontologies. Such data structures include:

*   Organizational structures: Employees, roles, departments, controlling areas, etc.
*   Geographical structures
*   Material and product groupings
*   Business process compositions

In some cases these structures can be utilized directly as complete domain ontologies, while in other cases they require manual processing before they can be used as complete domain ontologies or as input to populate general or incomplete ontologies.

Extraction of long transaction sequences from SAP systems is a task that involves large amounts of data and multiple database tables. EVS ModelBuilder is a tool that is designed to support extract entries

Figure 2. Three SAP tables that are used to describe events related to the creation of purchase orders.

USR03, User address data	
Attribute	Description
BNAME	Username
NAME1	Full name
ABTLG	Department

EKKO, Purchase Order Header	
Attribute	Description
EBELN	Purchase order id
AEDAT	Creation date
LIFNR	Vendor
ERNAM	User

LFA1, Vendor Master	
Attribute	Description
LIFNR	Vendor number
LAND01	Country
ORT01	City
ORT02	District

from SAP systems that are suitable for process mining. The tool is created in cooperation between Businesscape AS and the Information Systems group at the Norwegian University of Science and Technology. In EVS ModelBuilder, the user can describe on a type-level how business object and events are related. Based on these descriptions, the program carry out necessary database queries, merge data sources and exports transaction logs that can be processed and explored by analysis tools like ProM. More details about how this tool can support the preprocessing phase of process mining projects are described in (Ingvaldsen, 2007).

POPULATING ONTOLOGIES FROM AVAILABLE DATA STRUCTURES

We will use a simple example to show the magnitude of structured context information available in the transaction logs in SAP systems. Figure 2 shows three SAP tables that can be involved in a semantic process mining project. The EKKO table contains data describing purchase order headers. Entries in this table contain references to a vendor and the user that created the purchase order. Both the user and the vendor are described more in detail in separate database tables. USR03 is one of the tables that describe SAP users in detail. It contains the full name of the user and describes which department the user belongs to. LFA1 include vendor details such as their location, specified by country, district and city.

Based on data found in the EKKO table, we are able to extract events for creations of purchase orders. Data in the two other tables can be used to populate two distinct ontologies; one describing the breakdown of the company into departments and employees, and one describing how countries, districts, cities and vendors relate to each other. Figure 3 shows how our example data can describe events in detail and relate them to structured ontological data. In both of the ontologies, human knowledge is used to structure and place different concepts into hierarchical levels, but the population of ontological concepts are done by use of data available in the SAP tables.

In real systems, the three tables in figure 2 involve many more attributes that describe the entity properties. To limit the extent of this example, we have only involved a subset of available attributes. By including other attributes and related tables into this simple process mining example, we can enrich the event further with context details and link the event to other events like creation of purchase requisition and receipt of order confirmations and goods.

In SA-MXML, the event information and ontologies are is stored in separate files. The event log files describe the process instances that are carried out, the work items they consist of, relations to aggregated process definitions, involved users, and execution timestamps. These elements can further point to ontological concepts by use of Uniform Resource Identifiers (URIs) .

Figure 3. An example of a "Create purchase order" event that is related to two ontological concepts

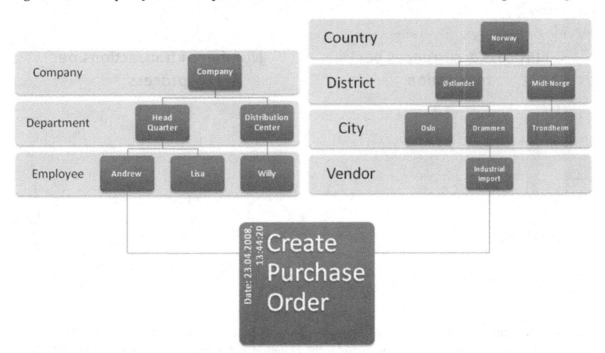

MAPPING EXECUTED TRANSACTIONS TO DEFINED BUSINESS PROCESSES

Much process mining work assumes that event logs extracted from the IT systems contain relations between the executed events and higher level business process definitions. Such information is very helpful if we want to do delta analysis. That is, comparing the actual processes with predefined process models. By comparing the predefined process models with models discovered by use of process mining, discrepancies between them can be detected and used to improve the processes (van der Aalst, 2005).

By linking entries in SAP transaction logs to aggregated business process definitions we can lift the models and performance indicators that we discover from process mining from a somewhat system technical level to higher business levels.

Predefined business process hierarchies are available and serialized in database tables in SAP systems. As shown in figure 1, this hierarchical structure consists of four levels. An enterprise area depicts a business structure, which represent a homogeneous unit in the sense of process-oriented structuring. Examples of enterprise process areas are enterprise planning, production and sales. Business scenarios are assigned to a particular enterprise process area, and describe on an abstract level the logical business flow across different application areas involving the processes. Process groups contain individual processes that are bundled such that they can be visualized more easily. Processes describe the smallest self-contained business sequences and represent the possibilities within its transactions, where detailed functions are carried out. Examples of business scenarios, process groups and processes for the sales enterprise area are shown in figure 1.

In this paper we will focus on the sales enterprise area for evaluating techniques for mapping entries in transaction logs to defined business processes. The sales enterprise area deals with the tasks of performance utilization and thus organizes the business relationships in the market. The task of this enter-

Figure 4. a) Distribution of process occurrences per transaction within sales. b) Number of transaction per process

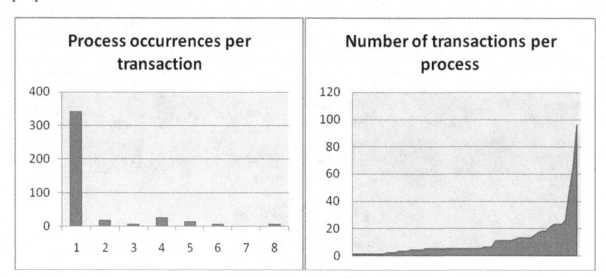

prise area is to provide customers with the goods produced in the enterprise, or with financial or other services offered by the enterprise. This includes the planning and control of distribution channels, from advertisement, inquiry and quotation processing, sales order processing, delivery processing, invoicing, and down to checking of incoming payments (Keller, 1998).

A process can be carried out by completing one or more transactions. Figure 4a shows how many processes transactions are involved in within the enterprise area "sales". Most transactions are only involved in one single process, and in average a transaction is involved in 1.55 processes. This means that for very many of the transactions in a transaction log we can identify the correct process easily.

On the other hand, there are a significant number of transactions that occur in many processes. For the enterprise area "sales" some transactions occur in up to eight processes. These transactions can be seen as the most common transactions, and these are the transactions we find most frequently in the transaction logs. For such transactions, it is much more challenging to identify the correct process for a given execution context.

Figure 4b shows that the number of transactions a process can involve vary significantly. In total the sales enterprise area consists of 59 standard processes, and in average a process involves 10.92 transactions. Most processes contain only a handful of transactions, but there are processes that can involve close to a hundred transactions.

Mapping Approaches

A transaction sequence is a list of executed and related transactions that are ordered by their execution timestamp. They are related in the sense that they produce and consume the same set of resources. I.e., an execution of the transaction "ME51, Create Purchase Requisition" produces a purchase requisition that can be consumed (referred to) by the transaction "ME21, Create Purchase Order".

Figure 5 shows a transaction sequence with seven entries and a hierarchy with defined business processes. From the transaction logs in SAP systems, we can extract transaction sequences as shown at the

Figure 5. A transaction sequence where each entry is mapped to a defined business process.

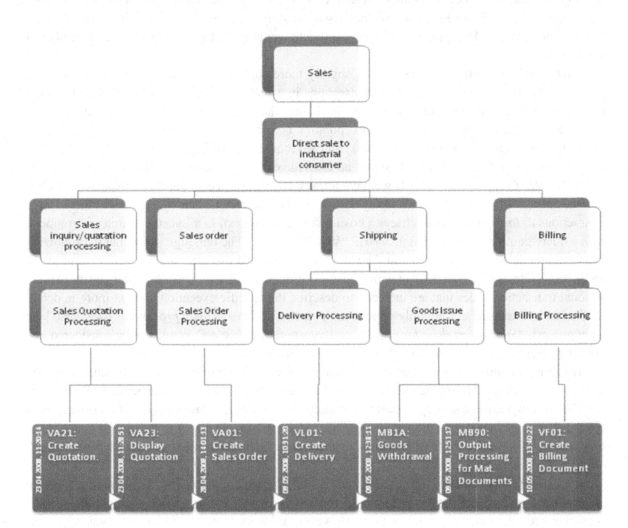

bottom of the figure, but the mapping to business process definition is not explicitly stated in the data.

Transaction sequences typically span multiple process boundaries, and therefore each transaction in the sequence must be mapped to the correct business process context.

Although the relations between transaction executions and defined business processes are not explicitly stated in the transaction logs there are approaches for identifying likely mappings. We will propose and evaluate three such approaches: Simple lookup, search and indexing of processes, and graph operations.

Simple lookup is the naïve approach of searching for processes that contains the transaction execution we want to enrich with business process context. In cases where several processes contain the given transaction the one with the least number of transactions is selected as the correct business process context. If we use simple lookup to identify the business process context for the transaction "*VL01: Create Delivery*", we would search for all processes where this transaction occurs. Such a query would result in the following process candidates from the sales enterprise are: "*Batch search strategy processing (standard)*", "*Delivery for returnable packaging subsequent debit*"," *Delivery for returns*", and " *Delivery processing*". Here, the first process candidate would be as this contains the least number of transactions.

Search and indexing of processes is a slightly more sophisticated approach where the defined processes are indexed by their involved transactions in a search index. Then, instead of just using a single transaction to form a search query, we also include the other entries of the transaction sequence. The idea behind this approach is that by incorporating neighbor transactions of a transaction we have more information about the execution context and are more likely of identifying a unique and correct business process definition. Figure 1, shows an example of two processes that both include the transaction "*V+01: Create Sales Call*". If we have a transaction sequence where this transaction, "*VC02: Change Sales Activity*" and "VC03: Display Sales Activity" occurs together, we can include all the three transactions to form a query and retrieve a business process context. In a Lucene[1] search environment, such a query could be expressed as +"V+01" "VC02" "VC03". The plus sign states that the following transaction code is required to exist in the result set entries, and this plus sign is used in front of the transaction code that we want to map with a business process definition. The other query terms express optional transaction codes that are included to describe the specific execution context more in detail. As the last two transactions are only present in the process "*Sales activity processing (standard)*" the other process, "*Subsequent debit for empties and returnable packaging*", would not be considered as a candidate process for this execution of "*V+01: Create Sales Call*".

Graph operations are an alternative approach that views the set of candidate solutions as a graph with nodes and edges. The problem that motivated this approach is that several standard SAP processes contains exactly the same set of potential transactions. For instance, "*Master transfer for contact documents*", "*Message transfer for billing documents*", "*Message transfer for sales documents*", and "*Message transfer for supplies*" are all processes that involve exactly the same set of transactions: "*VL14: Mail control decentralized shipping*", "*VL20: Display Communication Document*", "*VL70: Output From Picking Lists*", "*VPAK: Packing list*", and "*VT70: Output for Shipments*". Neither simple lookup or search and indexing of processes would be able to distinguish and select one such process as they contain exactly the same set of transactions. However, in longer transaction sequence typically spans several processes, and a process, like "Master transfer for contact documents", is often just one of several processes. This process is more likely to be the correct process if the other transactions in the same transaction sequence are within the same process group, process scenario or at least enterprise area. For each entry in a transaction sequence, this approach uses simple lookup to retrieve sets of solution candidates. Then, Dijkstras shortest path algorithm is used find the shortest distance through the business process hierarchy between the set of process candidates and the transactions in the actual transaction sequence. For a given transaction, the business process with the lowest average distance to all entries in the actual transaction sequence is selected as the right candidate.

Evaluation

To evaluate the three approaches we constructed ten transaction sequences spanning alternative routes through the following sales processes: Sales Quotation Processing, Sales Order Processing, Delivery Processing, Goods Issue Processing, and Billing Processing. The sequence between these processes and the transactions they can involve are shown in figure 6. This set of possible transactions is used together

Figure 6. Typical sales processes and their transactions. The process sequences are read from left to right.

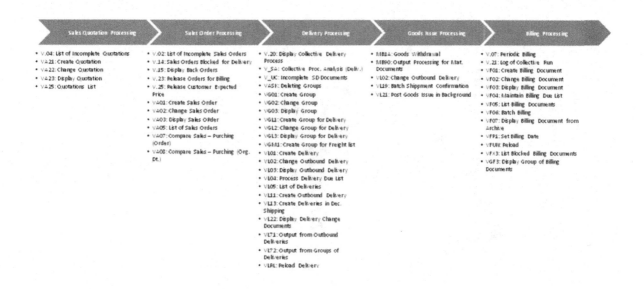

Figure 7. Test set of ten transaction sequences where each entry is labeled with a correct business process.

TEST 1	Sales Quotation Processing			Sales Order Processing		Delivery Process	Goods Issue Processing		Billing Processing	
	VA21	VA23	VA22	VA01	VA03	VL01	MB1A	MB90	VF01	VF02
TEST 2	Sales Order Proce	Delivery Process	Goods Issue Processing		Billing Processing					
	VA01	VL01	MB1A	MB90	VF01					
TEST 3	Sales Order Processing			Delivery Processing			Goods Issue Processing		Billing Processing		
	VA01	VA03	VA02	VL01	VL03	VL02	MB1A	MB90	VF01	VF02	VF03
TEST 4	Sales Quotation Processing		Sales Order Processing							
	VA21	VA22	VA01							
TEST 5	Sales Quotation Processing			Sales Order Processing				Delivery Processing		Goods Issue Processing			Billing Processing		
	VA21	VA23	VA22	VA01	VA03	VA02	VA02	VL01	VL03	MB1A	MB90	VL02	VF01	VF03	VF02
TEST 6	Delivery Processing		Goods Issue Processing		Billing Processing						
	VL03	VL02	MB1A	MB90	VF01	VF02					
TEST 7	Sales Order Proce	Delivery Processing		Goods Issue Processing							
	VA01	VL01	VL03	MB1A							
TEST 8	Sales Quotation I	Sales Order Processing			Delivery Processing		Goods Issue Processing		Billing Processing		
	VA22	VA01	VA02	VA02	VL01	VL02	MB1A	MB90	VL02	VF01	VF03	VFP1
TEST 9	Sales Order Processing			Delivery Processing		Goods Issue Processing			Billing Processing		
	VA01	VA02	VA02	VL01	VL02	MB1A	MB90	VL02	VL19	VF01	VF03	VFP1
TEST 10	Sales Quotation Processing			Sales Order Processing				Delivery Processing		Goods Issue Processing			Billing Processing		
	VA21	VA23	VA22	VA05	VA01	VA05	VA02	VL22	VGL1	MB1A	MB90	VL02	VF01	VF03
TEST 11	Sales Quotation Processing			Sales Order Proce	Delivery Processing		Goods Issue Processing		Billing Processing		
	VA21	VA23	VA22	VA01	VL22	VL01	MB1A	MB90	VL02	VF01	
TEST 12	Sales Quotation I	Sales Order Processing		Delivery Processing		Goods Issue Processing		Billing Processing		
	VA21	VA01	VA03	VL22	VGL1	MB1A	MB90	V.07		

Figure 8. Percentage scores for how many correct business process mappings the three approaches are able to identify. The scores are shown as bars for each of the 12 tests.

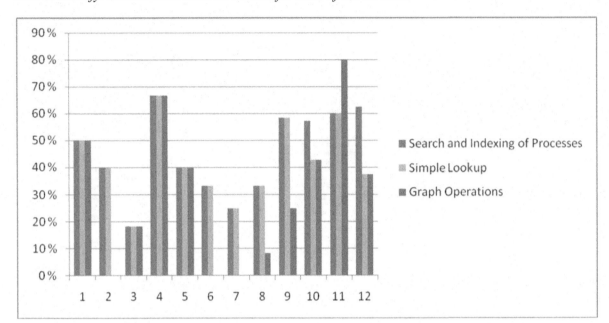

with process definitions in (Keller, 1998) to construct transaction sequences for testing that are realistic and annotated with correct business process context.

In total 12 test transaction sequences was constructed. To make them realistic with respect to typical process mining logs, the constructed transaction sequences have a lot of variation in length, and some are incomplete with respect to describe end-to-end processes. In process mining, extracted transaction logs typically contain transactions carried out within a certain time frame. Entries that are close to the start or end of are frequently incomplete as only parts of their history overlaps with the selected time frame. Cancelled processes lead also to incomplete transaction sequences. The test transaction sequences and their business process annotations are shown in Figure 7.

Figure 8 shows how to which extent each approach is able to identify the correct mapping for the twelve test sequences. In average *search and indexing of processes* identify the correct mapping in 45% of the test cases. For simple lookup and graph operations the average scores are 42% and 31% respectively. In four of the test cases they have the same score.

The graph operations approach has the highest deviation in its overall performance. In several of the test sequences this approach identifies none of the mappings correctly. A reason for this might be that this approach can fall into local areas of the business process hierarchy where the shortest path criterion is optimized, but the identified mappings are distant from the correct solution.

Search and process indexing outperforms the *simple lookup* approach in two of the test cases. In both of these the *search and process indexing* finds the correct mapping because the query contains context information that enable the system to limit the solution space and eliminate false candidates.

All of the three approaches could be modified and tuned to improve the performance. In the evaluations all approaches describe the context by including a varying number of transaction codes. These descriptions could also be extended with information like involved documents, users, vendors, products, geographical locations, etc. As we get a better and more complete picture of context around the execution of a transaction we can limit our solution space further and increase the probability of identifying correct mappings. However, such systems would also require manual labeling of training sets or search indices where such context information is related to the defined business process hierarchies.

Another alternative for improving the mapping between transaction executions in the transaction logs with defined business processes is to combine the method. *Search and process indexing* or *simple lookup* could be chosen to the main strategy for suggesting the right business process, and in those cases where the business process candidates contain the same set of transactions the graph operations approach could be applied to make a suggestion.

FUTURE TRENDS

In the last years there has been a consolidation between ERP and Business Intelligence (BI) systems. The largest ERP vendors, SAP and Oracle, have acquired the two BI vendors Business Objects and Hyperion and integrate their solutions into their customer offerings. Now, ERP does not only provide a shared data source for various organizational units, but also a valuable data source that companies can utilize to extract knowledge and competitive advantages.

Software vendors that focus on supporting the Business Process Management (BPM) lifecycle, like IDS Scheer, have already shipped products that borrow elements from process mining. The ARIS Process Performance Manager enables companies to relate performance indicators to real business flows. As ERP solutions also are moving into directions of Service Oriented Architectures (SOA) and (BPM), we believe that future business applications in the ERP and BI area will focus more on analysis of business flows. This will create need for information systems that create event logs that contains a lot of structured context information and relations to higher level process definitions.

In this paper we have focused on showing how elements in the event logs can be linked to ontological concepts. In addition, event logs can also be enriched with numerical and date attributes. For a purchase process, events can be enriched with order amounts, values, expected delivery dates, and so on. With such information available in the event logs we can not only describe how dynamic business processes are executed, how the loads are distributed and where most of the time is consumed, but also to which extent the actual processes are meeting expectations.

As shown throughout this paper the amount of information that can be related to event logs is enormous, and there are large potentials for merging elements from process mining, data mining and ontological reasoning. Process mining is used to find out how people and systems work. Ontological reasoning provides answers to test hypotheses, and data mining can extract descriptive and predictive models that support the whole picture.

If the core of ERP systems was originally designed for business process management and monitoring of process instances we would not need techniques to identify mappings between historical transaction executions and defined business processes. Traces of process instance information in transaction logs would create valuable opportunities for using process mining to describe the real business flow and measuring the deviations against business process definitions and procedures. However, as large software vendors needs to be backwards compatible with older systems and customers, it is difficult to do major modification of the kernel design. Until traces of process instance information are provided in the event log structures, a process miner needs tools that can assist the mapping of transaction executions and defined business processes.

CONCLUSION

Transaction logs in SAP systems contains substantial amount of context information that can be utilized to create references from the execution instances to ontological concepts. Also, SAP databases contain ontological data that describe relations between concepts involved in transaction executions. This availability of context information and ontologically structured concepts reduce manual ontology engineering work and make SAP systems a promising arena for semantic process mining.

General ontologies, like the Process Mining Ontology, are important for semantic interpretation of common process mining terms. However, customized domain ontologies are also important for being able to reason over enterprise specific concepts. As the reusability of such enterprise specific ontologies are low, tools that utilize available data to assist or automate parts of the ontology engineering process is of great value.

In this paper we have shown how available data structures in SAP systems can be utilized to populate ontologies and construct transaction logs for semantic business process mining. We have in particular focused on the challenge of making use of the business process hierarchy definitions available in SAP systems. Three approaches for mapping entries in transaction sequences with predefined business process hierarchies are evaluated, and the results from these evaluations shows that it is difficult to completely automate the process of identify such mappings. By including a more complete information picture around the execution of transactions, we can limit the solution spaces and increase the probability of identifying correct business process mappings.

Correct mappings between transaction log entries and defined business processes, enable process mining techniques to construct models that are lifted from a somewhat system technical transaction flow focus up to aggregated levels that describe higher level business terms. This makes process mining models valuable both for IT and business people.

REFERENCES

Alves de Medeiros, A. K., Pedrinaci, C., van der Aalst, W. M. P., Domingue, J., Song, M., Rozinat, A., et al. (2007). An outlook on semantic business process mining and monitoring. In *OTM 2007 Workshops* (pp. 1244-1255). New York: Springer.

Alves de Medeiros, A. K., van der Aalst, W. M. P., & Pedrinaci, C. (2008). *Semantic process mining tools: Core building blocks*. Paper presented at the 16th European Conference on Information Systems, Galway, Ireland.

Gulla, J. A., Borch, H. O., & Ingvaldsen, J. E. (2006). Unsupervised keyphrase extraction for search ontologies. In *Natural Language Processing and Information Systems* (pp. 25-36). New York: Springer.

Ingvaldsen, J. E., & Gulla, J. A. (2007). Preprocessing support for large scale process mining of SAP transactions. In *Business process management workshops* (pp. 30-41). New York: Springer.

Keller, G., & Teufel, T. (1998). *SAP R/3 process oriented implementation*. Reading, MA: Addison-Wesley.

Ma, Z., Wetzstein, B., Heymans, S., & Anicic, D. (2007). Semantic business process repository. In *Proceedings of the International Workshop on Semantic Business Process Management (SBPM 2007)*, CEUR Proceedings.

Pang, C., Eschinger, C., Dharmasthira, Y., & Motoyoshi, K. (2007). *Market share: ERP software, worldwide, 2006.* Gartner report.

Pedrinaci, C., & Domingue, J. (2007). Towards an ontology for process monitoring and mining. In *Proceedings of the Workshop on Semantic Business Process and Product Lifecycle Management (SBPM-2007), CEUR-WS*

van der Aalst, W. M. P., Reijers, H. A., Weijters, A. J. M. M., van Dongen, B. F., Alves de Medeiros, A. K., Song, M., & Verbeek, H. M. W. (2007). Business process mining: An industrial application. *Information Systems, 32*(1), 713–732. doi:10.1016/j.is.2006.05.003

van der Aalst, W. M. P., van Dongen, B. F., Günther, C. W., Mans, R. S., Alves de Medeiros, A. K., Rozinat, A., et al. Verbeek· H. M. W., & Weijters, A. J. M. M. (2007). ProM 4.0: Comprehensive support for real process analysis. In *Petri Nets and Other Models of Concurrency – ICATPN 2007* (pp. 484-494). New York: Springer.

van der Aalst, W. M. P., & Weijters, A. J. M. M. (2005). Process mining. In M. Dumas, W.M.P. van der Aalst & A.H.M ter Hofstede (Ed.), *Process aware information systems* (pp. 235-255). Wiley Interscience

KEY TERMS AND DEFINITIONS

Process Mining: Research area that aims at creating tools for discovering process, control, data, organizational and social structures from event logs.

SAP Systems: ERP solutions delivered by SAP for large organizations.

Semantic Business Process Management (SBPM): An extension of BPM with semantic web and semantic web service technologies in order to increase and enhance the level of automation that can be achieved within the BPM life-cycle

Transaction: A small application within SAP systems that have a unique transaction code.

Transaction Log: Data source in a transaction based information system that describes historical events.

Transaction Sequence: An ordered chain of events that describe transaction carried out, how they depend on each, when they were executed, and relations to involved entities like users, vendors, products, etc.

ENDNOTE

[1]   Lucene is an open source information retrieval library, supported by the Apache Software Foundation. See: http://lucene.apache.org/

Chapter 18
A Domain Specific Strategy for Complex Dynamic Processes

Semih Cetin
Cybersoft Information Technologies, Turkey

N. Ilker Altintas
Cybersoft Information Technologies, Turkey

Ozgur Tufekci
Cybersoft Information Technologies, Turkey

ABSTRACT

This chapter identifies the issues that might create orthogonal complexities for process dynamism, and decouples the components implementing them in a "domain specific" way. Authors believe that traditional process management techniques for modeling and executing the processes still fall short to improve the dynamism of an enterprise. Some of the reasons are: using too "generic" techniques and tools for process management that are not scalable enough for typical business cases, having lack of architectural coverage to manage the tradeoffs between dynamism and other business quality issues, insufficient support for integrating legacy business processes, and unbalanced guidance between "primary" and "supportive" processes. In order to improve the business agility particularly with dynamic processes, effective abstraction and composition techniques are needed for the systematic design of primary and supportive processes in an organization. Authors bring in the "Domain Specific Kit" abstraction as a way to improve the dynamism of complex processes.

INTRODUCTION

For many decades, enterprises have been looking for efficient, reliable, flexible and adaptable processes. The increasing agility in business world enforces organizations to be more dynamic in every possible way. But, traditional process management techniques for modeling and automating the core business processes fall short to enhance the dynamism in an enterprise. In traditional business process management, IT mainly abstracts the complexities of business processes with automated methods and tools that

DOI: 10.4018/978-1-60566-669-3.ch018

unsurprisingly introduce the categorization of processes as "primary" and "supporting" ones.

In order to improve the dynamism of complex business processes, IT departments should no longer be the roots of this process categorization, but rather they should provide the right toolset to business departments for flexible process modeling and execution. However, this is not that much easy to achieve. Proposals abound to segregate the business and IT perspectives for dynamic processes, but these efforts have fallen short so far for many practical cases.

Some of the issues behind this incapability can be detailed as follows: first, existing approaches are too "generic" to be used for every sort of complex [business] process. On the other hand, organizations run the business in different domains and expectedly, they have to comply with different process requirements. One example is integrating different processes of two organizations, one from banking domain and the other from automotive domain, for the processing of consumer loan for automobile sale transaction. The composition of their processes could not be simply orchestrated at run time without having a process choreography model at design time. The generic "process orchestration" models or strategies cannot easily solve service-oriented quality issues such as cross-domain security protocols (Tufekci et al., 2006; Aktas and Cetin, 2006).

The second issue is the lack of architectural coverage. The "dynamism" of a complex process is primarily a "non-functional requirement", which cannot be achieved by using pure "functional" approaches. Rather, architectural modeling plays an important role here to ensure the process quality. Hence, modeling the business processes with declarative approaches and implementing them using only Web Services will not be enough for process dynamism. This minimalist "functional" thinking cannot help design the architectural aspects (i.e. security, performance, flexibility, modifiability, extensibility and adaptability) of dynamic complex processes. Instead, a reference architecture model (in a meta-level) is needed to conceptually design the domain specific components of process management. That is why Service Level Agreements (SLA) is still a debate in the Service-Oriented Architecture (SOA) community to compose services of different processes (Keller and Ludwig, 2002).

The third drawback is the lack of support for integrating the legacy processes. We know that enterprises still have to run the business with legacy processes worth of billions of dollars, which cannot be simply reshaped in a night. Thus, any strategy to improve the dynamism of complex processes should consider the existing process assets accordingly. The domain specific abstractions could help in that sense to abstract the complexities of existing services and processes so that they can be migrated in a reasonable period of time (Sneed, 2000; SEI, 2005; Ziemann et al., 2006; Cetin et al. at ICPS, 2007; Cetin et al. at ICSEA, 2007).

Additionally, existing approaches focus on the dynamism of "primary processes" but, on the other hand, they mostly neglect the dynamism of "supporting processes" and "organizational processes" (Havey, 2005; Tufekci et al., 2006). This degrades the overall process dynamism since supporting and organizational processes used by IT departments may easily put a barrier against the agile processes of business departments. This is almost the case when IT departments should comply with software process improvement standards (Yeh, 1991; Cetin et al. at EuroSPI², 2006).

The last difficulty occurs in the setup procedures of service and process execution infrastructures for business agility. The classical way of setting up information systems to model and execute the complex processes follows agile or heavyweight methodologies, but with one common characteristic in mind that "business people asks and IT people provides". This approach usually ends up with "highly tailored" models that cannot be flexible or extensible for future expectations. On the other hand, many concerns such as business rules, workflows, services, content generation and batch processing can be segregated from the actual application to facilitate the dynamism of process modeling and process execution. This way of isolated process development requires selective development lifecycles where related functional and non-functional requirements need to be identified, encapsulated, modeled, designed and implemented in a "domain specific" way (Fowler, 2002; Cetin and Altintas, 2008; Altintas, 2007).

The chapter will define a strategy in an extensive manner and explain the details how this strategy can overcome the introduced challenges for dynamic complex processes. The strategy given here is not a mere conceptual or academic study. Rather, it has been already put into action for the implementation of MEROPS (Central Operations Management) of a mid-scale bank in Turkey. MEROPS is a specialized unit in the bank responsible for management of documents and associated workflows in a very dynamic business environment coping with ever-changing business requirements of more than 2500 bankers every day. In order to meet the business needs in a timely manner, a complete infrastructure has been designed and implemented due to the strategy given here where business workflows, business rules, business services and associated content can be created and modified dynamically by means of Domain Specific Kits and Choreography Modeling. This work has been partly supported by TUBITAK[1].

BACKGROUND

Business processes are highly complex, involve many different participants and spawn multiple information systems. Running business processes is no longer possible without support from modern information technology. Moreover, optimizing business processes is crucial for business success of companies. Therefore, the processes have to be continuously improved and have to be flexible enough to deal with dynamic environment in times of global competition (Burmeister et al., 2006).

However, the existing picture of enterprise process management is rather different. Processes are almost statically modeled, lack of standard and flexible process execution infrastructures, and far from being managed declaratively. In traditional business process management, IT mainly abstracts the complexities of business processes by means of hard-coded methods and primitive tools that unsurprisingly introduce the categorization of processes in an enterprise. Inspired by software process modeling, which derives the well-known standards like ISO 12207, ISO/IEC 15504 SW-CMM and CMMI, Figure 1 proposes a categorization template to deal with the major vertical and horizontal relations and feedback mechanisms inherited in process categories (Tufekci et al., 2006).

In Figure 1, "primary processes" represent the processes constituting the core business of an organization. They can be figured out by itemizing those services the organization is established for. In order to exemplify, acquisition and development processes are primary processes for the software industry, and manufacturing processes are primary processes for the automotive industry.

Primary processes are accompanied by "supporting processes", which do not typically result in final products of the organization, but rather indirectly contributes to the value added. They are performed to control and maintain integrity of the product or service developed by primary processes. Additionally, they ensure that products and processes comply with predefined provisions and plans. Documentation, configuration management, verification, training and audit process are supporting processes. Surely the categorization is relative to the business domain. As an example, audit process is the primary process of an audit organization whereas it is a supporting process for an ISO 9001 certified manufacturing company.

Figure 1. Major process categories

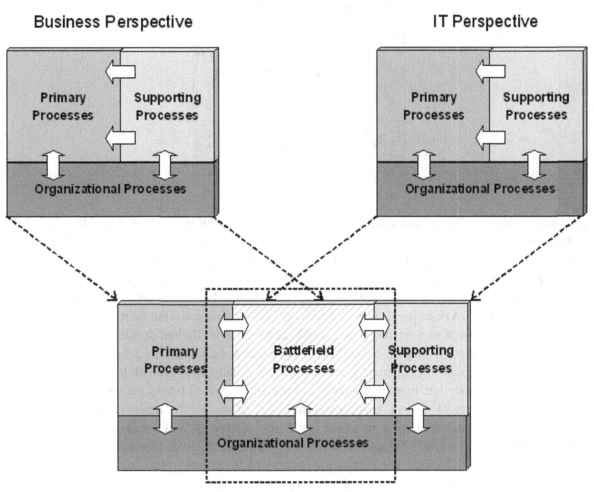

Finally, "organizational processes" include the processes establishing business goals of an organization. They are formed as generic activities that apply to all processes either primary or supporting. Managerial processes, resource and infrastructure processes, and improvement processes are all in organizational process category. The interference of organizational processes with other processes is bi-directional; they provide the goals, plans and resources to other processes and accumulate the operational data for measurement analysis and improvement.

The traditional view of business process modeling originates from two distinct perspectives of business and IT experts, and their respective primary and supporting processes. For instance, consider a bank. Undoubtedly the banking processes are the primary processes. On the other hand, software development is considered as a supporting process for a bank, whereas it is a primary process for an IT vendor or IT department. The identical processes are perceived as primary or supporting from different angles. The business and IT perspectives are two distinct viewpoints to the same software development process. Business people primarily concentrate on the functional requirements, business rules, and need to employ the new system as well as alter the system as needed in a very short time. In contrast, IT people will be focusing on the architectural issues, quality factors such as reliability, robustness, etc. These two different

Figure 2. Discrepancy between perspectives

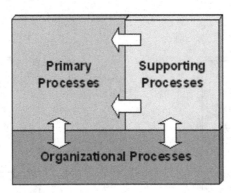

perspectives define different "domains" both for business and IT departments. A "**domain**" is defined here at its simplest form as "the bounded area of interest and dedication for problem solving". The problem usually occurs when these two distinct domains have to be harmonized somehow, where IT and business experts are expected to understand each other's domain terminology entirely. As an example, banking experts are expected to know what Web 2.0 stands for, whereas IT experts are expected to know, for example, what EBITDA (Earning Before Income Tax, Depreciation and Amortization) actually means. The discrepancy between two perspectives is mostly apparent in inefficient development cycles, over-budget and over-time software projects, architectural problems, performance issues, etc.

The traditional process management given in Figure 1 usually ends up with lengthy development time, loss of communication, more dependency to business-unaware IT professionals, vicious change management cycles, etc. One way to manage the challenges of process dynamism is separating the perspectives of primary and supporting processes in different viewpoints and composing them through a common strategy (see Figure 2). Figure 2 shows the segregated perspectives of business and IT where the supporting processes of business perspective are joined with the primary processes of IT perspective.

A "**battlefield process**" in Figure 1 is the one that cannot be clearly identified as either IT process or business process. Rapid prototyping of user interface (screens and reports) is a typical battlefield process. In most of the information system development efforts, battlefield processes are well known as the "risky loss of communication" as almost every software development life cycle suggests iterative / incremental approaches to reduce the risk accordingly. Optimizing the battlefield processes will affect the primary business processes, the supporting IT processes and, above all, the organizational processes positively. Thus, the effective management of battlefield processes is crucial to the success of both IT and business perspectives.

Figure 2 summarizes the following vision: IT departments should no longer be the roots of process categorization; rather they should provide the right toolset to business departments for flexible process modeling and execution. By doing so, both business experts and IT experts can be focused on their own domains and the interaction between the two perspectives can be limited to the battlefield processes. Declarative approaches might help a lot to synthesize the languages (Domain Specific Languages [DSLs] such as Business Process Execution Language) specific to these completely different domains for the better management of battlefield processes. The similar strategy has been put by previous research such as (Pesic and van der Aalst, 2006; Küster et al., 2006). However, existing research has not concentrated enough on **domain specificity** (Domain Specific Modeling, use of Domain Specific Languages or Domain Specific Toolset) for complex dynamic processes management.

Some proposals abound to achieve the separation between business and IT perspectives for more flexible, adaptable and dynamic processes, too. For example, workflow management models, methods and systems have been categorized and presented by (van der Aalst and van Hee, 2002). Workflow patterns have been classified and presented extensively by (Russell et al., 2006; van der Aalst et al., 2003). Likewise, process patterns have been catalogued by (Ambler, 1998). Workflow flexibility and process patterns contributed a lot to process dynamism, but existing research on how legacy implementations can take part in workflow or process patterns have not been detailed so much. Especially, the non-functional issues of process integration with legacy systems are still major research questions.

From the industrial standards perspective, modeling and execution languages for business processes have been put forward to manage them in dynamic environments. Abstract modeling languages like Business Process Modeling Language (BPML, 2002) and execution languages such as (BPEL, 2004) for business processes have been defined, and even a Business Process Modeling Notation (BPMN, 2004) has been put forward to design business processes in a more abstract way. Later, WS BPEL 2.0 has been the convergence path for different languages from different vendors in order to specify business processes based on Web Services, which has completely changed the former BPEL approach (WS-BPEL 2.0, 2007). Supportively, associated frameworks and tools have been developed to manage complex business processes in a dynamic environment. WS-BPEL 2.0 is the widely accepted standard for today's industrial applications, however the non-functional issues of service selection and composition urge system vendors such as IBM, Oracle, SAP and Microsoft to focus on more aspect-oriented service bus implementations, which are still researched at laboratories. The research results might change the WS-BPEL structure in the near future to synthesize the different Enterprise Service Bus implementations.

Process modeling plays an important role for process dynamism. The previous research has shown that Model-Driven Development (MDD) can help transform the business process models into actively running dynamic processes. For example, (Scacchi, 1998) has researched the challenges of process modeling especially for visualizing and enacting in complex organizations, and proposed an approach for modeling the processes accordingly that helps for dynamic management. (Kumaran et al., 2007) has introduced a modeling framework, which adapts and extends workflow technologies to address the unique requirements of the IT service management domain. These extensions are primarily in three areas: life-cycle management, dynamic process execution, and federated workflow. (Shi et al, 2005) provided a service-oriented and business process model driven platform for developing on-demand (dynamic) business systems, where the platform uses two separate views (business and IT views) to relieve them from unfamiliar domains. The platform contains a reasoning engine to support the key rules that are presented for automatic process transformation from business view to IT view. The research for the use of MDD in complex dynamic process management has mainly concentrated on the Model Driven Architecture (MDA) of Object Management Group (OMG). However, the challenges of complex dynamic process management urge us to further research the potential value of Domain Specific Modeling especially from aspect-oriented and architecture-based perspectives.

Aspect orientation is another technique to help achieve process dynamism. By using the key principles of Aspect-Oriented Software Development (AOSD), the crosscutting concerns such as business rules and workflows can be designed separately and weaved into the final picture dynamically. For instance, the previous research has shown that business rules can be segregated from the business processes to improve process dynamism (Cetin et al. at DPM, 2006; Cibran and D'Hondt, 2006; Date, 2000). Similarly, workflows can be totally separated from the applications using aspect-oriented techniques. (Tombros, 1999) has proposed an aspect-oriented workflow model to separate the static and dynamic aspects of a workflow system. This approach empowers business modelers to control and monitor the dynamic parts of a business model for improving the process dynamism.

Domain specific approaches and their use for modeling dynamic processes are not new at all. More than two decades ago, (Winograd and Flores, 1986) suggested a different way to look at computers and the way they are being used. Their vision had its roots in philosophy, biology and architecture. Extrapolating from cognition as a biological phenomenon, they conclude that the most successful designs are not those that try to fully model the **domain** in which they operate, but those that are "in alignment" with the fundamental structure of that domain, and that allow for modification and evolution to generate new structural coupling. Then, (Dragos and Johnson, 1998) improved this philosophy to present an infrastructure for process and product models where structural coupling plays a central role. They have described the components of a common infrastructure as a "domain model engine" that stands on the shoulders of first version of the "Adaptive Object Model (AOM)". Two years after the introduction of "domain model engines", (Yoder and Razavi, 2000) rephrased the AOM and introduced the "micro-workflow" where a domain specific model engine has been designed for adaptive workflow systems that tackles the workflow problem at the object-level.

By addressing the use of domain specific approaches for dynamic processes, (Dou et al., 2005) have already mentioned the "data perspective" of **domain specificity** for achieving dynamic business processes, where the extracted workflow constituents can be represented by domain specific applications. Accordingly, a hybrid workflow system could be treated as a collection of domain-specific applications integrated across application frameworks. Similarly, (Wild et al., 2006) have presented the dynamic engines, which allow for the flexible IT support of business processes in highly dynamic environments like the logistics industry, by extracting process logic and business rules from application programs, and applying the cases on domain specific calculation functions.

THE PROPOSED STRATEGY

The process modeling today tends to demarcate the perspectives of business and IT experts, and their respective primary and supporting processes. In addition to separating the perspectives of business and IT domains, dynamism in complex [business] process management can be achieved by paying attention to concerns such as flexibility, extensibility, modifiability and adaptability that are all known as "architectural aspects". Architectural modeling of enterprise applications that can execute complex business processes is probably more complicated than any other part of the software design process. For that reason, the architecture of enterprise applications should be modeled by taking multiple concerns and their tradeoffs into account. These concerns and tradeoffs usually exist orthogonal to the software processes (Harrison, 2002; Cetin et al. at ICSEA, 2006). Moreover, it is worth to mention that such crosscutting aspects that are orthogonal to actual business processes will be the main cause of "battlefield processes" given in Figure 2.

In order to manage the tradeoffs among flexibility, modifiability and adaptability across different processes, proper abstraction and composition techniques need to be used for the architectural design of process execution. To this end, the proposed strategy here first identifies the architectural components that might create orthogonal complexities for process dynamism and implements them in a domain specific manner. Then, it introduces a choreography platform (a choreography language and an engine) to compose the previously isolated domain specific parts. The proposed strategy is based on the following issues:

− Separation of business and IT perspectives (**domain**s): the clear separation of business and IT domains facilitates both parties to focus on their own domains (field of interest), which will lessen the burden of learning each other's domain terminology.
− Abstraction of business and IT perspectives with domain specific approaches: both parties (business and IT) have different process viewpoints where each one has its own complexities to be dealt with. Besides that, providing dynamism for each one has certain different characteristics. For instance, the process dynamism that can be introduced by workflow flexibility might pay off at maximum level for the business perspective, but not exactly for the IT perspective.
− Composition of both perspectives throughout **battlefield process**es: the distinct processes of each perspective should be aligned at certain points which are named as "battlefield processes" in Figure 1. The strategy adopts a choreography-based strategy to align these processes. In doing so, a descriptive choreography language is used to bind the business and technical contexts of both perspectives.
− Abstracting legacy integration in a domain specific way: actually, integration with legacy processes means two different things for business and IT. Hence, generic approaches to address both perspectives usually fall short for any one of them or sometimes for both at the same time. The domain specific approaches adopted for separating both perspectives will also help at this point to integrate the legacy processes. The use of **Domain Specific Language**s and **Domain Specific Engine**s to execute them will have dedicated keywords for the integration of legacy processes.
− Achieving quality by means of process choreography reference architectures: apart from achieving process dynamism, other quality factors should be concerned especially against potential tradeoffs. For instance, process dynamism with declarative workflow flexibility might introduce security leaks in process management unless designed carefully. The strategy has a choreography setup based on reference architectures for certain business domains. As an example, different architectural templates at meta-level are expected to be designed for different business domains such as banking, insurance, or automotive.
− Simplifying the setup process: the setup process should not further complicate the business and IT perspectives. Domain specific languages shorten the learning curves, and improve the feedback between parties with simplified prototyping and pilot runs. Moreover, configurations can be abstracted in every possible way by means of domain specific engines instead of generic workflow engines or enterprise service busses.

The proposed strategy has been mainly driven by the Software Factory Automation (SFA) vision (Altintas et al., 2007; Altintas, 2007). The SFA vision is highly motivated by the fact that constructing versatile software products or setting up complex business processes can no longer be managed by means of generic approaches such as "Extreme Programming is the right software process model for every kind of business agility" or ".NET framework and Java application servers are sufficient for all sort of transactional applications". Instead, SFA envisages that ever-growing complexity of primary and supporting processes should be identified individually and managed independently.

This motivation, however, requires having a broad palette of expertise within an organization that can be continually used for every new case, which is almost impossible. This is the actual picture in automotive industry for example, where automobile manufacturers cannot have the expertise for every detail like airbags or parking sensors. The way to tackle this challenge is setting up a factory process with moving assembly lines for integrating the in-house manufactured parts with the ones acquired from third parties. Then, the following questions come to mind: who will set up the factory and which sort of expertise is needed to form the assembly processes?

The answers have already been found for "industrial factories": there are different organizations around just to set up factories for the manufacturing of typical products. These organizations are known as "[industrial] factory automation vendors", which have well defined, tested and proven processes to set up factories. After setting up such a factory, the factory management is then putting its own processes or customizing the factory automation vendor's processes to manage the product-manufacturing life cycle. In short, industrial factory owners are far beyond to setup their own factories by themselves since this requires completely different expertise and associated processes. Instead, they ask for the help of industrial factory automation vendors to set up the factories for themselves. But, once the factory has been established, the factory owners can use the facilities (infrastructures, processes, etc.) provided by factory automation vendors to create and dynamically manage the actual processes.

What is the existing picture for delivering the software products? It is totally different since many organizations feel confident enough to set up its own IT processes even without getting help from the experts. Open source madness and dominance of agile software processes nowadays encourage enterprises to walk alone. But, the final outcome does not usually differ so much: they end up with monolithic, non-maintainable, static, and incapable primary (business) processes. To top it off, supporting and organizational processes are mostly ad-hoc and unmanageable, too. On one hand, manufacturing processes have been improved for "zero defect" products even in avionics industry, but on the other hand, software industry is still discussing the value of "unit tests" and "refactoring" for dynamic complex processes. The dilemma between these two pictures has been mentioned as "essential difficulties" and "accidental difficulties" in the famous article of (Brooks, 1987). He points out that essential difficulties for an enterprise should be the ones having direct effects on core business such as the difficulties in setting up a sales process to minimize the sales force costs for a mobile vendor. However, accidental difficulties are the ones helping achieve the core business functionality but not having direct effects on that such as the difficulties of using Java instead of C++ for implementing the sales business processes. Both primary and supporting processes in software industry need to be deal with essential difficulties rather than accidental ones. The rise of Python, PHP and Ruby against C++, Java and C# for Web-based process implementations is just one simple evidence.

Software Factory Automation is inspired by the way other industries have been realizing industrial factory automation for decades. Industrial factory automation utilizes the concept of "Programmable Logic Controllers (PLCs)" to facilitate the production of domain specific artifacts in isolated units. PLCs may also take place in moving assembly lines to unify the production process. Factory automation in milk factories, for example, bridges diverse units of pasteurization, bottling, bottle tapping, and packaging through moving assembly lines, all designed by the use of PLCs. Bottle and bottle tap in this example are both domain specific artifacts that can be reused in the production of various milk products such as regular, skimmed or semi-skimmed, or even in bottling of straight or sparkling water, not just milk.

PLCs improve the reusability of domain specific artifacts with a consistent design in mind: PLC has a Programmable Processor (PP) to be programmed with a Computer Language (CL) through a

Figure 3. Software Factory Automation analogy with Industrial Factory Automation

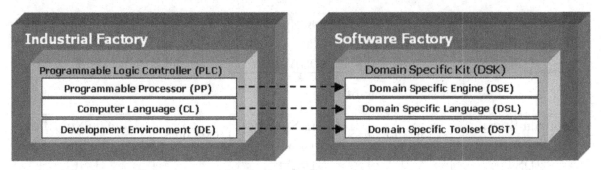

Development Environment (DE). So does the **Domain Specific Kit** (DSK) abstraction of SFA model. Figure 3 shows that a Domain Specific Kit has a **Domain Specific Engine** corresponding to Programmable Processor, a **Domain Specific Language** corresponding to Computer Language, and a **Domain Specific Toolset** corresponding to Development Environment of PLC concept. As the way PLCs are used for abstracting a wide range of functionalities like basic relay control or motion control, Domain Specific Kits in Software Factory Automation approach can be designed specifically to abstract certain things such as screen/report rendering or business rule execution in software factories. Such a vision in product development naturally abstracts the associated processes from each other and clearly draws the boundaries of business and supportive processes.

SEPARATING THE CONCERNS WITH DOMAIN SPECIFIC KITS

Domain Specific Kits have been devised to isolate discrete concerns in the solution domain and specify reusable Domain Specific Artifacts to abstract them. They let the modeling and development of software artifacts in isolation and enable their composition via a choreography model (Cetin et al. at MoRSe, 2006). DSK introduces a set of domain specific terms (constituents) and Figure 4 depicts the interrelation among these constituents:

- **Domain Specific Language** (DSL) is a language dedicated to a particular domain or problem with appropriate built-in abstractions and notations. An example to a DSL is the Structured Query Language (SQL) of relational database management systems, which can command the backend database engine both for data description (Data Description Language - DDL) and data manipulation (Data Manipulation Language – DML).
- **Domain Specific Engine** (DSE) is an engine particularly designed and tailored to execute a dedicated Domain Specific Language. An example to a DSE is the "Database Engine" of relational database management systems, which can be commanded by SQL and execute the database queries as specified so.
- **Domain Specific Toolset** (DST) is an environment to design, develop, and manage software artifacts of a dedicated Domain Specific Language. An example to a DST is the "Interactive SQL (iSQL) Tool" that can be used by database designers and user to retrieve database schema graphically, construct the queries visually, and execute the SQL commands directly.

Figure 4. Conceptual model of Domain Specific Kits

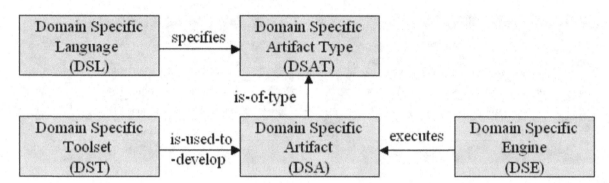

- **Domain Specific Kit** (DSK) is the composite of Domain Specific Language, Domain Specific Engine and Domain Specific Toolset. An example to a DSK is the "Relational Database Management System" that includes SQL as the DSL, Database Engine as the DSE, and iSQL Tools as the DST.
- **Domain Specific Artifact Type** (DSAT) is a software artifact type that a certain Domain Specific Kit can express, execute and facilitate the development. An example to a DSAT is "Stored Procedure" or "Trigger" that can be used to command the database engine for bulk or event-based operations.
- **Domain Specific Artifact** (DSA) is an artifact that is expressed by a Domain Specific Language, developed by a Domain Specific Toolset, and executed by a Domain Specific Engine. An example to a DSA is the "Stored Procedure for Personnel Database Export" that can be expressed in SQL and executed directly by the Database Engine.

(Griss and Wentzel, 1998) used the term "**Domain Specific Kit**s" first within the context of "flexible software factories". However, the Domain Specific Kit concept in Software Factory Automation model diverges from the Griss's definition and attributes a new content to the old term. DSKs in SFA are lightweight and loosely coupled with each other; so their artifacts (DSAs) can be designed as composable with others. The artifacts are defined and composed by declarative approaches. Furthermore, artifacts can be developed and contained within reusable software assets. In order to achieve that, DSK design aims to maximize the reuse of Domain Specific Artifacts like screen and report layouts or certain business rules (Altintas et al., 2008). Finally, DSKs are not particular to a product family, and even they can be reused across different product lines (Altintas and Cetin, 2008).

In order to exemplify the Domain Specific Kit abstraction, a Business Rules Management System (BRMS) has been discussed here briefly. A BRMS enables the segregation of business rules from the application where they crosscut almost every tier from content to service (Cetin et al. at DPM, 2006). In our designs, we abstract the business rules management from the rest of the picture with a practical Aspect-Oriented Framework so called RUMBA ([RU]le-based [M]odel for [B]asic [A]spects), which provides a declarative environment with a GUI console for rule-based business process modeling. It basically enables the design of any business entity (e.g. person) through the dynamic composition of feature-driven "basic aspects" (e.g. identity as a permanent feature and instructorship as a varying feature used when person is expected to be an instructor). Moreover, every basic aspect such as instructorship

Figure 5. *Software Factory Automation for service-oriented computing*

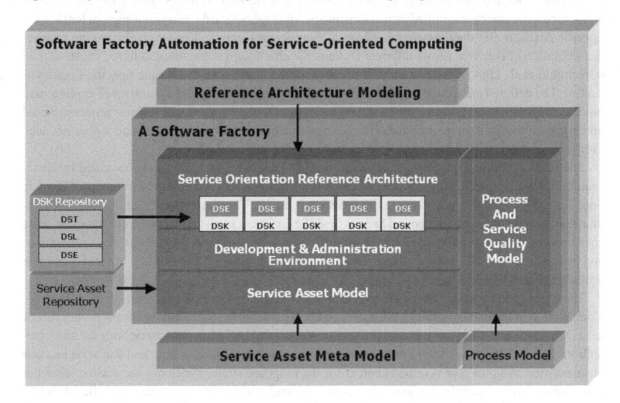

may contain other basic aspects, recursively. RUMBA allows the dynamic definition of facts, rules, and rule-sets, too.

RUMBA can be referenced as a Domain Specific Kit, which isolates the business rules management from the rest of the picture as follows: it has a very lightweight rule inference engine as the Domain Specific Engine, a visual rule editor as the **Domain Specific Toolset** that can dynamically manage the business rule changes, it uses the RuleML (RuleML, 2004) as the Domain Specific Language: Moreover, rule and composite-rule are the Domain Specific Artifact Types. RUMBA can take part in business choreography with API-based, service-based, or other type of interfaces.

COMPOSING THE CONCERNS WITH CHOREOGRAPHY

Domain Specific Kit abstraction enables the separation of concerns in different domains. Each concern has been expressed and executed by a different Domain Specific Language and the associated Domain Specific Engine like PLCs are controlling certain concerns in industrial automation. Naturally, every separation should end up with a composition as well. For the composition of domain specific artifacts expressed in a Domain Specific Language, Software Factory Automation employs a choreography model (a language and an engine) that relies on SOA as a paradigm for managing resources, describing process steps, and capturing interactions between a service and its environment (see Figure 5).

Software Factory Automation anticipates the use of a choreography language for describing the interaction of artifacts according to choreography's goal. Composing Domain Specific Artifacts declaratively with a choreography language enables the independent development of Domain Specific Artifacts and also ensures interoperability of them. Domain Specific Engines are the execution engines for Domain Specific Artifacts and they are composed via a choreography engine. Choreography engine requires the separation of concerns across different Domain Specific Engines and, thus, deferred encapsulation (Greenfield et al., 2004) can be achieved through plugging in and out any Domain Specific Engines as needed. The deferred encapsulation enables the flexibility, modifiability and dynamism of implemented processes. This provides an execution model for collaborative and transactional business processes based on a transactional finite-state machine. This is a non-monolithic execution model, and it does not need every sort of detail to be specified at once in the beginning of process design.

The features mapped into specific Domain Specific Languages are going to be executed by corresponding Domain Specific Engines. Therefore, dynamic pluggability and context-awareness of Domain Specific Engines are crucial for the runtime execution model. The choreography engine enables communication and coordination among Domain Specific Engines. It ensures context management, state coordination, communication, produce/consume messaging, nested processes, distributed transactions, and process-oriented exception handling. The flexibility resulting from composition of loosely coupled artifacts is crucial for process dynamism.

The choreography model of the strategy has been designed in compliance with the Web Services Composite Application Framework (WS-CAF, 2003). It provides the coordination among parties (in our case Domain Specific Engines), manages the common context and manages transactions for interoperability across existing transaction managers, for long running compensations, and for asynchronous business process flows. The common context for the proposed strategy includes the session identifier and session context, security attributes, transaction identifier and context, protocol specific attributes, client identifier, business domain specific identifiers, such as "branch code" or "customer id" for banking context.

Domain Specific Kits bring out the concept of reusable, configurable, specialized work units in terms of services within the context of business processes. The proposed strategy abstracts the details of business services with Business Service Description DSLs and makes them available for the integration with other business services and software artifacts through the choreography model. This aids business service and business process designers to model the core business rather independent from the other process quality issues such as security and availability. Such aspects should have been dealt with during the design of the reference architecture specific to that business domain.

SETTING UP A SERVICE-ORIENTED SOFTWARE FACTORY WITH SFA APPROACH

The Software Factory Automation approach with Domain Specific Kits enables the specification of coarse-grained reusable asset models as collections of Domain Specific Artifacts and their composition rules. This strategy encapsulates the correlated features (hence artifacts) within more cohesive software asset models and manages them with higher-level abstractions. As an example from the financial product family systems, "Alert and Notification Manager" and "Blacklist Manager" are two examples of software assets, which are highly abstract with respect to objects, components and even services used by traditional business process management approaches (Altintas et al., 2008).

Table 1. List of Domain Specific Kits used in banking system

DSK Name	Description	Artifact Types
Rich Client Kit	*Business domain independent XML-based technology used for power screen design in Internet applications*	*Page, Region, Popup*
Reporting Kit	*Business domain independent XML-based technology used for report content generation, rendering and presentation in Internet applications based on an open source project JasperReports that can be retrieved from http://jasperforge.org/sf/projects/jasperreports*	*Report*
Business Services Kit	*A lightweight kit for development, publishing, administration of business services with a registry, repository, meta-model and policy management services*	*Service*
Business Rules Kit	*Business domain independent kit for business rules segregation where all aspects, facts, rules and rule-sets can be defined and managed dynamically by means of a GUI console. It has been based on RUMBA Framework (Cetin et al. at DPM, 2006)*	*Rule and Composite-Rule*
Business Processes Kit	*A jBPM-based kit for business process management providing design, development and execution of business processes. jBPM is the open source project implemented by JBoss, and can be retrieved from http://www.jboss.com/products/jbpm*	*Process*
Data Persistence Kit Also known as Persistent Object Model [POM] Kit	*An XML-based Object-to-Relational (O2R) mapping kit for defining, deploying and executing SQL queries by mapping to Plain Old Java Objects (POJOs)*	*POM*
Batch Processes Kit	*A special purpose kit for defining, scheduling and execution of batch jobs with enterprise-class features, based on open source project Quartz that can be retrieved from http://www.opensymphony.com/quartz/*	*Job*

Figure 5 shows that SFA instantiates a dedicated **software factory** for a product or a sufficiently complex information system where business components can be integrated into the Service-Oriented Architecture. Here, two different process types exist: one for setting up the relevant software factory and the other for constructing the product or information system from that software factory. The processes for setting up the software factory are rather straightforward and defined within the context of SFA vision (Altintas et al., 2007).

The software factory setup first instantiates a concrete architecture from the SOA-based product line reference architecture, organizes the development environment, describes the service asset model, and aligns the primary and supporting processes from standard process models. For example, the software factory can be set up with supportive processes selected from the software process library of Lighthouse (Cetin et al. at EuroSPI², 2006), such as ISO 9001 compliant or CMMI compliant. Similarly, primary processes can be selected as declarative implementations with Business Processes Kit (see Table 1) based on jBPM (JBoss Java Business Process Management) or service-based hard-coded implementations.

The selection of primary and supporting processes from the software factory template will form the concrete "Process and Service Quality Model" in the instantiated software factory (see Figure 5). The final activity will be selecting or implementing the proper Domain Specific Kits and integrating them.

In our software factories, we use Aurora (Altintas and Cetin, 2005) as the SOA-based reference architecture for product line design and software artifact compositions. However, SFA approach enables other reference models such as Spring Framework (Spring, 2003) to be used in software factories. Aurora is a platform independent product line infrastructure based on rich client and enterprise integration models for Web applications with drag_&_drop design and development environments / tools. Aurora adopts rich-client strategy where a dedicated rendering engine is placed automatically on Web clients, which renders the screen layouts and executes the GUI events specified in an XML structure known as EBML (Enhanced Bean Markup Language). EBML is capable of declaratively expressing the reusable screen regions, defining sanity checks and arithmetic expression rules, executing local and remote method calls, versioning and caching structural parts separately, dealing with static reference data, managing the client context and multi-lingual support (Altintas and Cetin, 2005). EBML descriptions are automatically recognized by the rendering engine (ERE – EBML Rendering Engine) on Web clients. ERE completely takes away the need for static GUI codes and empowers the business service and business process designers to manage the cases dynamically at run time.

ERE can also instantiate business processes and invokes business services implemented at the backend. Backend services are quite lightweight in Aurora reference architecture. The backend Aurora servers (simple Java servlet extensions) interpret the business service and business process requests expressed in XML and automatically convert them to POJO (Plain Old Java Object) calls. In this transformation, service names are matched with the previously registered Java service interfaces and service parameters are transformed into composite and indexed Java data structures known as CSBag. Then, the service can be invoked dynamically as a high performance Java call. After service execution, service results are transformed back from composite Java data structure (CSBag) back to XML constituents specified at EBML remote call section.

This SOA vision provides a very scalable, secure, high performance and dynamic service infrastructure, and even Java based business processes expressed in jBPM can be incorporated. Moreover, data persistency can be managed in a transactional manner with Aurora Persistent Object Model (POM) Kit (see Table 1). Aurora SOA baseline surpasses the bottlenecks of using Web Services in enterprise applications but providing almost the similar benefits. In the case of actual Web Service interoperability, Aurora provides automatic transformations from Aurora services to Web Services forth and back. This way, any Aurora business service or business process can take place in the orchestration of Web Services for intra process management.

DYNAMIC PROCESS MANAGEMENT WITH DOMAIN SPECIFIC KITS

Dynamic process management strategy with Domain Specific Kits identifies primary and supporting processes pertaining to a domain, isolate them from each other for every domain, model them in a domain specific way relying on a service-oriented reference architecture, compose the individualized processes in a process composition model based on process choreography, and provide the automation support for supporting and organization processes. The underlying conceptual model of dynamic process management strategy based on Domain Specific Kits has been given in Figure 6.

In this strategy, Domain Specific Kits play a key role for the separation of concerns for dynamic process management. The "reference architecture" underlies the composition of Domain Specific Kits (Engines) as well as constrains the design of "Process Composition Model". Process Composition Model is based on choreography and executed by a common choreography engine. "Modeling Environment" utilizes the constraints of "Reference Architecture" in providing toolsets for the specification of Domain Specific Artifacts expressed in a Domain Specific Language as well as the specification of process composition in a choreography language. "Software Process Automation" manages them all, where

Figure 6. Conceptual model of dynamic process management strategy

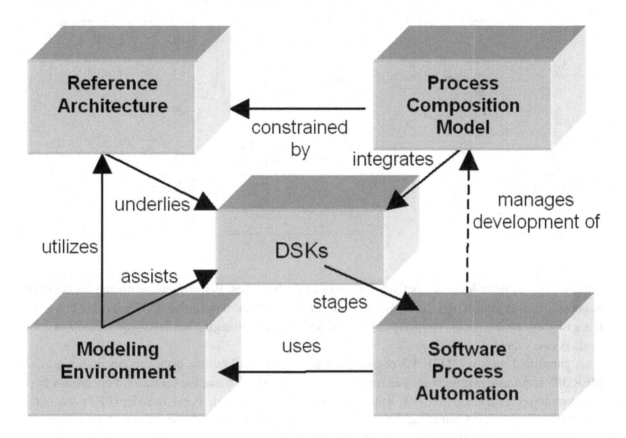

repositories keep the different versions of such specifications. Software Process Automation plays again a key role here to manage the "**battlefield process**es" and complying with different software process management standards such as CMMI and SPICE (Cetin et al. at EuroSPI[2], 2006).

The DSK approach enables the process designers to link processes to each other and to other relevant artifacts in a very loosely coupled manner. Both process definitions and the choreography can be specified declaratively and process execution is left to proper Domain Specific Engines and Choreography Engine. Moreover, it also facilitates the production planners to manage the configuration (as well as commonality and variability) issues according to the reference architecture of the **Software Factory**. The design of Domain Specific Engines and Choreography Engine has different variability management techniques ranging from parameterization to bytecode injection at low level, which facilitate the process designers to easily deal with process customization and integration at higher levels.

CASE STUDY: CENTRAL OPERATIONS MANAGEMENT IN A BANK

The strategy presented here has been already put into action for the implementation of MEROPS (Central Operations Management) of a mid-scale bank in Turkey with 250 branches and 1.5 million customers. MEROPS is a specialized unit in the bank responsible for the execution of banking operations, which

Figure 7. MEROPS high-level process flow

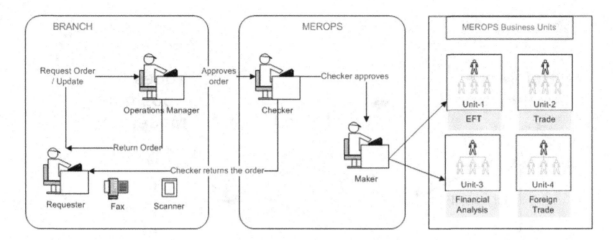

usually require higher-level competence on behalf of the branches. Performing the operations centrally requires the management of documents and associated workflows between MEROPS and 250 branches. It is a very dynamic business environment to cope with the ever-changing business requirements of 2500 bankers every day.

A simplified view of MEROPS organization and business flow has been presented in Figure 7. MEROPS requires dynamic processes from several perspectives. First, the centralized operations have different completion characteristics: some of them such as Electronic Fund Transfer (EFT) orders are executed and completed immediately; on the other hand, the requested operation may be a financial analysis report that usually takes two weeks to complete.

Another major issue is the diversity of documents accompanied to different processes and sub-processes. Following the same example, EFT operation requires a simple customer order form whereas financial analysis report requires a set of documents including company balance sheets, tax declarations and sector-specific information. A sample process is given in Figure 8.

The third difficulty occurs at the organization of central units. Considering the same example again, EFT order processing unit is a simple one consisting of 4 makers and 1 checker. However, financial report preparation unit has many experts preparing different parts of the report, and they may be specialized in different domains. Management of the report pools and approvals requires the execution of several sub-processes within the central unit.

The last but the most complicated dynamism needs stem from the centralization strategy of banking operations. It is naturally not a one-shot transformation process, which raises managerial issues for the coexistence of legacy and brand new business processes. Since reengineering of the banking processes has been going on, a single process for a limited set of branches can be decided for centralization at a time. Hence, while the selected branches have been diverted to MEROPS, all other branches should be executing their existing operations locally. In short, both central and non-central business processes might be running across different branches at the same time.

In order to respond to the business needs in a timely manner, a new infrastructure has been designed and implemented due to the strategy given here where business workflows, business rules and business services can be created and modified dynamically. We have devised several Domain Specific Kits to

Figure 8. MEROPS main process flow

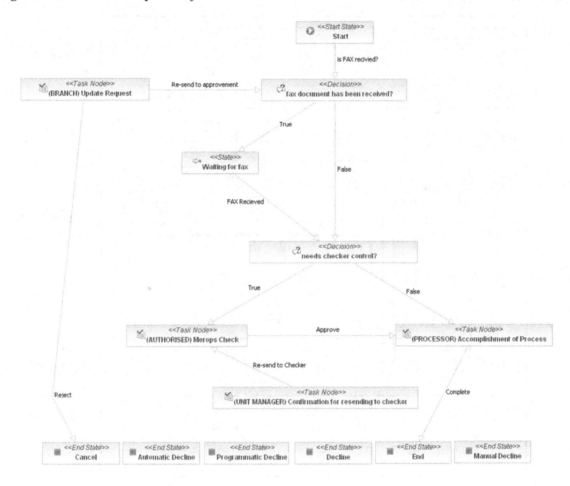

isolate the technical concerns. The corresponding Domain Specific Engines have been employed in the reference architecture (see Figure 9) of the banking infrastructure. The Domain Specific Kits have been listed in Table 1.

A simplified view of the reference architecture is depicted in Figure 10. The reference architecture for banking system employs a choreography model that has been designed in compliance with the Web Services Composite Application Framework (WS-CAF, 2003). The choreography model handles the global context management, coordination, and transaction management of all parties (Domain Specific Engines). The common context includes the session identifier, session context, security attributes, transaction context, protocol specific attributes, and business domain specific identifiers for banking. The interaction model of composition relies on SOA as a paradigm for managing resources, describing process steps, and capturing interactions between an artifact and its environment.

The composition model of Domain Specific Artifacts has been driven by extending the Process Description Language (jPDL) of the Business Processes Kit (see Table 1) due to the requirements of the bank. jPDL is an XML-based language that can express business processes and service interactions declaratively. Business Processes Kit has extended the jPDL to include Aurora service calls and trans-

Figure 9. Reference architecture for banking system

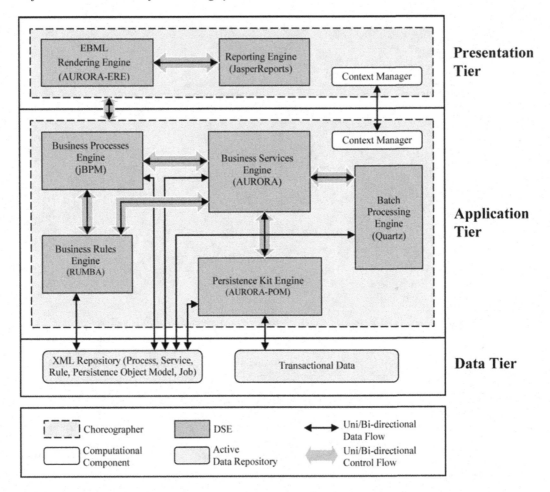

actional support. Such an extension includes the nodes for time and amount controls, task nodes with built-in approval mechanism, integrating process model with banking organization model, conditional service execution nodes where multiple services can be chained by linking their inputs and outputs. Those extensions enable the modeling of dynamic MEROPS processes.

After the bank has started using the implementation, the primary processes of both parties have been totally separated. What IT expects from the business turned out to be the upper level process specifications modeled by using Domain Specific Toolsets (business processes, business rules, business services, and the user interfaces all given in declarative form) and specified in proper Domain Specific Languages. In fact, since the toolsets are automatically generating the artifacts in the so-called Domain Specific Languages; IT department has not expected anymore that business people should be DSL-savvy. The specifications are put into a common repository with versions, IT experts check in to that repository, and collect the related ones. Repository management tools also monitor this process so that non-repudiation issues between IT and business departments have been resolved automatically. The face-to-face communication between IT and business departments has been limited. The only communication required at battlefield area left to business analysts who are the members of the IT department. The business analysts are also expected to resolve the misunderstandings and conflicts through prototyping and pilot sessions by using the same toolset. They also act as "client advocates" to meet the specific process requirements of the business departments. This approach has reduced the process development cycles, limited the conflicts, dramatically lowered the ratio of bugs, and improved IT service and product quality.

FUTURE TRENDS

Information systems and complex product structures are changing the world that we live in. Ubiquitous computing requires the context awareness and Service Level Agreements at every detail, which degrades the dynamism of primary and supporting processes. Form the other hand; high performance computing needs necessitate the use of backend service grids and even in a virtualized way. The virtualization in service-oriented computing draws new requirements for "dynamic SOA governance" and "autonomous services". The Web content is growing dramatically every day. The way to provide attractive content is not possible without mashing up the brand new content with existing ones. Web 2.0 trends challenge every organization to change the way to construct software products and information systems. Maybe, the biggest challenge will be the integration of legacy content with the new one.

In order to overcome the existing and future challenges of service-oriented computing, people are searching for ways ranging from Model-Driven Development to Aspect-Oriented Software Development. Another research area is providing "formal modeling techniques" for business processes to enable the "complete coverage" and "formal verifications" as well.

The last but not least trend is the widespread use of mobiles and rich clients for business processes. Emerging business fields such as customer relationship management and sales force automation come with their own challenges in dynamic process management. Such challenges are exemplified as dynamic routing in line with location-based services and integrated process management in business merges and acquisitions.

CONCLUSION

This chapter has provided the challenges of dynamic process management from an industrial perspective and introduced a strategy to meet these challenges. Inspired by the Software Factory Automation vision, this strategy uses Domain Specific Kit abstraction to separate the concerns of primary and supporting actors in Domain Specific Kits and then compose them through a Choreography Model including the choreography engine and choreography language.

In the real-life case study, we have used seven basic Domain Specific Kits given in Table 1. This is our observation that even with this restricted set of Domain Specific Kits, we can quite effectively segregate the complex processes from each other and manage them individually. After setting up this strategy, we could manage to deploy new business processes very efficiently such that the business people (bankers in our case) could manage to create, enact, and execute business processes without demanding to IT personnel as long as there is no technical barriers such as extending the capabilities of Domain Specific Kits or composing the Domain Specific Artifacts much more conveniently.

The proposed strategy helped us to overcome the challenges given in the introduction as follows: we refrain from using generic approaches and techniques for process modeling by partitioning the big picture into domain specific parts. We have dedicated a Domain Specific Kit for each partition and aligned the primary and supporting processes accordingly. This strategy enabled us to integrate external processes and services quite effectively. For example, Financial Gateways Family System has been designed with such a vision, which integrated more than 30 external business processes and services to a banking system.

The second challenge was the lack of architectural coverage of existing approaches. The proposed strategy here treats the architectural coverage as a first class entity. First, it uses the service-oriented reference architecture (Aurora) to instantiate the software factories. Second, every Domain Specific Kit should have a dedicated Domain Specific Engine that has to be designed and implemented by taking the functional as well as non-functional requirements of that domain. This can resolve the orthogonal complexities of architectural aspects crosscutting the process management.

The third drawback was the lack of support for integration of the legacy processes and coexistence of new processes with the legacy ones. The proposed strategy has introduced an integration model using service mashups with Domain Specific Kits, where front-ends of legacy applications can be integrated with screen scrapper Domain Specific Kits and back-ends with B2B wrapper Domain Specific Kits.

Another difficulty was having dynamism not only in primary processes, but also in supporting and organizational processes as well. The proposed strategy isolates every process (not only primary processes) of a particular domain from the rest of the picture. This facilitates the software process managers to define and manage the activities of software artifacts implementation. Moreover, the feedback from primary processes helps to improve the Domain Specific Engines and Domain Specific Language constructs for more dynamic process definitions, hence enriches the common business vocabulary.

The last challenge was the way to follow heavyweight setup procedures of service and process execution environments. Since the proposed strategy uses a **software factory** approach, it has been already armed with charted roadmap for instantiating the reference architecture. The reference architecture model provided by Aurora as well as the dedicated Domain Specific Kits such as Business Processes Kit and Business Rules Kit help establish the execution infrastructures for business services and processes effectively and to achieve reliability by employing the existing kits.

REFERENCES

Aktas, Z., & Cetin, S. (2006). We envisage the next big thing. *IDPT-2006 Integrated Design and Process Technology Conference* (pp. 404-411). San Diego, California.

Altintas, N. I. (2007). *Feature-based software asset modeling with domain specific kits*. Doctoral dissertation, Middle East Technical University, Department of Computer Engineering. Ankara, Turkey. Retrieved from http://etd.lib.metu.edu.tr/upload/12608682/index.pdf

Altintas, N. I., & Cetin, S. (2005). Integrating a software product line with rule-based business process modeling. *TEAA-2005 Trends in Enterprise Application Architecture Workshop, VLDB-2005 Conference* (LNCS 3888, pp. 15-28).

Altintas, N. I., & Cetin, S. (2008). Managing large scale reuse across multiple software product lines. *ICSR-2008 10th International Conference on Software Reuse* (LNCS 5030, pp. 166-177). Beijing, China.

Altintas, N. I., Cetin, S., & Dogru, A. (2007). Industrializing software development: The "factory automation" way. *TEAA-2006 2nd Trends in Enterprise Application Architecture Conference* (LNCS 4473, pp. 54-68).

Altintas, N. I., Cetin, S., & Surav, M. (2008). OCTOPODA: Building financial gateways family system using domain specific kits. *ICONS-2008 Third International Conference on Systems* (pp. 85-92). Cancun, Mexico. DOI 10.1109/ICONS.2008.57

Ambler, S. W. (1998). *Process patterns*. Cambridge University Press/SIGS Books.

BPEL. (2004). *BPEL: Business process execution language*. Retrieved March 30, 2008, from http://bpel.xml.org/.

BPML. (2002). *BPML: Business Process Modeling Language*. Retrieved April 12, 2008, from http://www.ebpml.org/bpml.htm.

BPMN. (2004). *BPMN: Business Process Modeling Notation*. Retrieved March 12, 2008, from http://www.bpmn.org/.

Brooks, F. P. (1987). No silver bullet: Essence and accidents of software engineering. *Computer*, *20*(4), 10–19. doi:10.1109/MC.1987.1663532

Burmeister, B., Steiert, H. P., Bauer, T., & Baumgärtel, H. (2006). Agile processes through goal- and context-oriented business process modeling. *DPM-2006 Dynamic Process Management Workshop at Business Process Management 2006 Conference* (LNCS 4103, pp. 217-228).

Cetin, S., & Altintas, N. I. (2008). An integration model for domain specific kits. *IDPT-2008 Integrated Design and Process Technology Conference*.

Cetin, S., Altintas, N. I., Oguztuzun, H., Dogru, A., Tufekci, O., & Suloglu, S. (2007). A mashup-based strategy for migration to service-oriented computing. *ICPS'07 IEEE International Conference on Pervasive Services* (pp. 169-172). Istanbul, Turkey.

Cetin, S., Altintas, N. I., Oguztuzun, H., Dogru, A., Tufekci, O., & Suloglu, S. (2007). Legacy migration to service-oriented computing with mashups. *ICSEA'07 International Conference on Software Engineering Advances* (pp. 21-30), Cap Esterel, France. DOI 10.1109/ICSEA.2007.49

Cetin, S., Altintas, N. I., & Sener, C. (2006). An architectural modeling approach with symmetric alignment of multiple concern spaces. *ICSEA'06 International Conference on Software Engineering Advances* (pp. 48-57), Tahiti, French Polynesia. DOI 10.1109/ICSEA.2006.261304

Cetin, S., Altintas, N. I., & Solmaz, R. (2006). Business rules segregation for dynamic process management with an aspect-oriented framework. *DPM-2006 Dynamic Process Management Workshop at Business Process Management 2006 Conference* (LNCS 4103, pp. 191-202).

Cetin, S., Altintas, N. I., & Tufekci, O. (2006). Improving model reuse with domain specific kits. *MoRSe'06 Model Reuse Strategies Workshop* (pp. 13-16). Warsaw, Poland.

Cetin, S., Tufekci, O., Buyukkagnici, B., & Karakoc, E. (2006). Lighthouse: An experimental hyperframe for multi-model software process improvement. *EuroSPI²-2006 European software process improvement and innovation conference.* Joensuu, Finland.

Cibran, M. A., & D'Hondt, M. (2006). High-level specification of business rules and their crosscutting connections. *Aspect-Oriented Workshop at AOSD-2006*, Bonn, Germany.

Date, C. J. (2000). *What not how: The business rules approach to application development.* Addison Wesley Longman Inc.

Dou, W., Chueng, S. C., Chen, G., Wang, J., & Cai, S. J. (2005). A hybrid workflow paradigm for integrating self-managing domain-specific applications. *GCC-2005 4th International Conference on Grid and Cooperative Computing* (LNCS 3795, pp. 1084-1095). Beijing, China.

Dragos, A. M., & Johnson, R. E. (1998). A proposal for a common infrastructure for process and product models. In *Proc. OOPSLA Mid-year Workshop on Applied Object Technology for Implementing Lifecycle Process and Product Models* (pp. 81-82). Denver, Colorado.

Fowler, M. (2002). *Patterns of enterprise application architecture.* Addison-Wesley.

Greenfield, J., Short, K., Cook, S., & Kent, S. (2204). *Software factories: Assembling applications with patterns, models, frameworks, and tools.* Wiley.

Griss, M. L., & Wentzel, K. (1994). Hybrid domain specific kits for a flexible software factory. In *Proceedings of the Annual ACM Symposium, Applied Computing* (pp. 47-52). Phoenix, Arizona.

Harrison, W. H., Ossher, H. L. & Tarr, P. L. (2002). *Asymmetrically vs. symmetrically organized paradigms for software composition.* IBM Research Division, Thomas J. Watson Research Center, RC22685 (W0212-147).

Havey, M. (2005). *Essential business process modeling.* O'Reilly.

Keller, A., & Ludwig, H. (2002). Defining and monitoring service level agreements for dynamic e-business. In *Proceedings of LISA '02: Sixteenth Systems Administration Conference* (pp. 189-204). Philadelphia, PA, USA.

Kumaran, S., Bishop, P., Chao, T., Dhoolia, P., Jain, P., & Jaluka, R. (2007). Using a model-driven transformational approach and service-oriented architecture for service delivery management. *IBM Systems Journal, 46*(3), 513–529.

Küster, J. M., Koehler, J., & Ryndina, K. (2006). Improving business process models with reference models in business-driven development. *BPD-2006 Business Process Design Workshop at Business Process Management 2006 Conference* (LNCS 4103, pp. 35-44), Vienna, Austria.

Pesic, M., & van der Aalst, W. M. P. (2006). A declarative approach for flexible business processes management. *DPM-2006 Dynamic Process Management Workshop at Business Process Management 2006 Conference* (LNCS 4103, pp. 169-180), Vienna, Austria.

Rule, M. L. (2004). *RuleML: Rule markup language.* Retrieved April 15, 2008, from http://www.ruleml.org

Russell, N., ter Hofstede, A. H. M., van der Aalst, W. M. P., & Mulyar, N. (2006). *Workflow control-flow patterns: A revised view*. BPM Center Report BPM-06-22. Retrieved from http://www.BPMcenter.org

Scacchi, W. (1998). Modeling, integrating, and enacting complex organizational processes. In K. Carley, L. Gasser, & M. Prietula (Eds.), *Simulating organizations: Computational models of institutions and groups* (pp. 153-168). MIT Press.

SEI (2005). *SMART: The service-oriented migration and reuse technique* (CMU/SEI-2005-TN-029).

Shi, X., Han, W., Huang, Y., & Li, Y. (2005). Service-oriented business solution development driven by process model. *CIT-2005 Fifth International Conference on Computer and Information Technology* (pp. 1086-1092). Shanghai, China.

Sneed, H. M. (2000). Encapsulation of legacy software: A Technique for reusing legacy software components. *Annals of Software Engineering, 9*, 293–313. doi:10.1023/A:1018989111417

Spring. (2003). *The Spring Framework*. Retrieved April 19, 2008, from http://www.springframework.org/.

Tombros, D. (1999). *An event- and repository-based component framework for workflow system architecture*. Doctoral dissertation, University of Zurich. Retrieved February 22, 2008, from http://www.ifi.uzh.ch/archive/diss/Jahr_1999/thesis_tombros.pdf.

Tufekci, O., Cetin, S., & Altintas, N. I. (2006). How to process [business] processes. *IDPT-2006 Integrated Design & Process Technology Conference* (pp. 624-631). San Diego, California.

van der Aalst, W. M. P., ter Hofstede, A. H. M., Kiepuszewski, B., & Barros, A. P. (2003). Workflow Patterns. *Distributed and Parallel Databases, 14*(3), 5–51. doi:10.1023/A:1022883727209

van der Aalst, W. M. P., & van Hee, K. M. (2002). *Workflow management: Models, methods, and systems*. Cambridge, MA: MIT Press.

Wild, W., Wirthenson, R., & Weber, B. (2006). Dynamic engines - A flexible approach to the extension of legacy code and process-oriented application development. *WETICE-2006 Proceedings of the 15th IEEE International Workshops on Enabling Technologies: Infrastructure for Collaborative Enterprises* (pp. 279-284). Manchester, UK

Winograd, T., & Flores, F. (1986). *Understanding computers and cognition: A new foundation for design*. Addison-Wesley, Norwood, NJ.

WS-BPEL 2.0. (2007). *WS-BPEL 2.0: Web services for business process execution language*. Retrieved April 25, 2008, from http://docs.oasis-open.org/wsbpel/2.0/OS/wsbpel-v2.0-OS.html.

WS-CAF. (2003). *Web services composite application framework (WS-CAF)*. Retrieved July 28, 2007, from http://www.oasis-open.org/committees/tc_home.php?wg_abbrev=ws-caf

Yeh, R. T. (1991). System development as a wicked problem. *International Journal of Software Engineering and Knowledge Engineering, 1*(2), 117–130. doi:10.1142/S0218194091000123

Yoder, W., & Razavi, R. (2000). Adaptive object-models, *Conference on Object-Oriented Programming Systems Languages and Applications* (pp. 81-82). Minneapolis, Minnesota.

Ziemann, J., Leyking, K., Kahl, T., & Dirk, W. (2006). Enterprise model driven migration from legacy to SOA. *Software Reengineering and Services Workshop.*

KEY TERMS AND DEFINITIONS

Domain Specific Kit: is the composite of a "Domain Specific Language" to specify software artifacts pertaining to that domain; a "Domain Specific Engine" to interpret and execute a Domain Specific Language; and a "Domain Specific Toolset" to design, develop, and manage software artifacts of a dedicated Domain Specific Language. An example to a Domain Specific Kit is the "Relational Database Management System" that includes SQL as the Domain Specific Language, Database Engine as the Domain Specific Engine, and iSQL Tools as the Domain Specific Toolset.

Domain Specific Process: is the set of activities dedicated to construct the software artifacts in a particular domain. Domain Specific Processes are mainly discrete and isolated from each other in software construction. The best way to integrate them is through well-defined and unified process choreographies. In relational database management domain; database management system installation process, database schema creation and maintenance processes, and database backup-restore processes are all known as Domain Specific Processes.

Primary Process: represents the activities constituting the major purpose of existence of an enterprise, which figure out services the organization is established for. They are also known as "business domain processes", which carries the utmost value for an organization. Credit Card Management, Loan Management, Account Management are all "primary processes" in the banking domain.

Supporting Process: is performed to maintain integrity of the product or service developed by "primary processes" as well as it ensures that products and processes comply with predefined provisions and plans. Supporting processes accompany the "primary processes", which do not typically result in final products of the organization, but rather indirectly contributes to the value added. Documentation, configuration management, verification, training and audit process are all supporting processes.

Organizational Process: includes activities that establish the business goals of the organization and develop process, product and resource assets which, when used will help to achieve business goals. Managerial processes, resource and infrastructure processes are all in organizational process category.

Software Factory Automation: is the vision to set up software factories as the way other industries have been establishing the industrial factories for manufacturing. It requires different know-how, expertise, infrastructures and processes to put forward the integrated software construction environments. Software Factory Automation analyzes the functional and non-functional requirements of a product domain, establishes the product line, provides core assets, and preliminary processes. It leverages the actual software construction in many ways including dynamic process management and time-to-market issues.

Software Product Line Engineering: is the combination of life cycle management as well as architectural setup of a software product line. A Software Product Line is a set of software-intensive systems that share a common, managed set of features satisfying the specific needs of a particular market segment or mission and that are developed from a common set of core assets in a prescribed way. Software Product Line Engineering can enable rapid market entry and flexible response, and provide a capability for mass customization of a software product.

ENDNOTE

[1] The concepts given here have been researched mainly within the context of OCTOPODA Project that is partially supported by Technology and Innovation Funding Programs Directorate (TEYDEB) of The Scientific and Technological Research Council of Turkey (TUBITAK) (ProjectNo/Date: 3060543 and 01.09.2006).

Chapter 19
Lightweight Workflow

Hajo A. Reijers
Eindhoven University of Technology, The Netherlands

ABSTRACT

This chapter describes lightweight workflow as a possible approach to counter many of the issues related to the introduction and sustained use of operational workflow management systems. Aside from a description of the essential features of lightweight workflow, this chapter also provides a reflection on the application of lightweight workflow in practice. Lightweight workflow is a very relevant direction to be aware of for practitioners who consider the use of workflow technology. Researchers may find inspiration from this chapter to further the adoption of workflow management technology.

INTRODUCTION

Workflow management systems (WfMSs) are among the core technologies associated with process management. At the introduction of this technology, some two decades ago, many expected that the technology would be widely adopted by industry (White & Fischer, 1995; Koulopoulos, 1995). But despite its supposed effectiveness to support operational business processes in their execution (van der Aalst & Hee, 2002), it is fair to say that the technology has not lived up to this expectation yet.

It can be argued that the reason for this is that the application of a WfMS makes business process execution too rigid, obstructing users to react freely to the breakdowns occurring during their evolution (Bowers et al., 1995). Some blame the rigidity on the use of formal workflow models; others on the strict coupling between modeling and execution (Dourish et al., 1996). Especially the lack of flexibility to deal with unforeseen situations is a very widely felt shortcoming of many commercially available

DOI: 10.4018/978-1-60566-669-3.ch019

WfMSs. It has resulted in research as well as industrial approaches to alleviate the problem, for example see (Reichert & Dadam, 1998; Kammer et al., 2000; van der Aalst et al., 2005; Kaan et al., 2006).

Over the years, commercial workflow technology has become an increasingly sophisticated type of software system. A commercial system may include extensive functionalities to deal with both regular and exceptional cases, to support process modeling and simulation, to allow for run-time monitoring as well as for the generation of periodic management information, and many, many other features. Although this development addresses some of the shortcomings of the technology that were just touched upon, a new type of problem emerges: The technology becomes too expensive, too extensive and too complex to use. Many small- and medium sized organizations seem reluctant to look into workflow technology for this reason (Smith & Fingar, 2003). And even if an organization can afford the technology, it may seem a disproportionate investment if the processes that need to be supported are highly structured and relatively simple.

This chapter elaborates on an approach that is opposite to the direction of most developments in the workflow field: It focuses on workflow systems that can do less, not more. We will refer to such systems as lightweight workflow. The purpose of this chapter is not to position lightweight workflow as a replacement of full-fledged workflow technology, but rather as a niche alternative. In this way, the core principles of this idea can be expanded to address the needs of more organizations than currently seem to take advantage of this technology.

The structure of this chapter is as follows. We will first provide some background on workflow in general and lightweight workflow in particular. We will provide a comprehensive overview of the issues that lightweight workflow aims to address and provide a definition and the characteristics of this technology. Next, we will reflect on the actual effectiveness of this technology in two case studies we performed. Finally, we will reflect on related trends in the workflow landscape after which we will come to a conclusion.

BACKGROUND

A workflow management system (WfMS) is a software system that supports the specification, execution, and control of business processes (Jablonski & Bussler, 1996; van der Aalst & Hee, 2002). Conceptually, it can be said to do so by separating the logistics of the business process – as managed by the WfMS – from the content of the process – which is managed with other applications and carried out by various types of performers. The logistic side of a business process is taken care of by a WfMS on the basis of a predefined workflow plan, which can be used to hand out work items to the right performers in the right order, at the right time. The advantages of using a WfMS in this way are fourfold (Reijers et al., 2003):

1. Less coordination effort: The WfMS liberates human actors from the routine work they need for coordination – it's the WfMS that will take care of this.
2. Higher quality: The WfMS will offer to actors at least the work which is required to deliver the preferred quality of service – the plan describes what should be done at a minimum.
3. Higher efficiency: The WfMS will offer to actors at most the work which is required to produce an acceptable result – if the plan did not cover a step under certain conditions, it is in principle not required for the case under consideration.

4.   Higher maintainability: Ejecting the business control-flow from traditional applications and moving it towards a WfMS simplifies the adjustment of both the logistics and the content of work separately from each other.

From this expose, it can be seen that the workflow plan is a fundamental concept in the working of a WfMS. But many variations exist with respect to how such a plan exactly determines or influences process execution. For example:

−   The plan in a production-workflow management system like TIBCO completely determines the execution;
−   The plan in a case handling system like FLOWer only indicates what would be the usual execution order and allows for deviations, for example skipping a step;
−   The plan in an adaptive workflow system like ADEPT can be flexibly changed and augmented during its execution.

Note that a comprehensive treatment of all the variations in workflow technology is out of the scope of this chapter, but the interested reader is referred to (Reijers et al., 2003; Weber et al., 2007) for more pointers.

Currently, no clear definition is available for a specific subcategory of WfMSs that we would like to refer to as lightweight workflow. Unmistakenly, various researchers have alluded to a simpler, less complex type of workflow in proposing their approaches. Probably the first development in this area was the Mentor-Lite system, see (Weissenfels et al., 1998; Muth et al., 1999). Another notable development is the Milano system (Agostini & de Michelis, 2000a; Agostini & de Michelis, 2000b). Somewhat related also, are the so-called proclets (van der Aalst et al., 2000), which are proposed as autonomous, lightweight workflow processes. It should be noted, however, that these are all research initiatives that have not found wide acceptance in industry. Moreover, all these solutions are proposed in an isolated manner, without an attempt to consciously reflect on the overall category of lightweight workflow.

At this point, we will shift our attention to the common problems associated with traditional WfMSs to establish a better understanding of lightweight workflow and the issues they are intended to solve.

PROBLEMS WITH TRADITIONAL WORKFLOW

Lightweight WfMSs are developed to overcome particular problems which exist with are related to traditional WfMSs. Traditional WFMSs are 'heavy weighted' and support numerous functionalities. At this stage it will be clear to the reader that lightweight WFMSs can be seen as stripped versions of regular WFMSs, with limited functionalities. We will refer to three classes of problems associated with the current use of workflow-technology to come to a sharper description of lightweight workflow. Two problem classes are associated with:

1.   The *implementation* of current WfMSs,
2.   The *footprint* of current WfMSs, and

The different problems are described in the following subsections, as well as the way that lightweight workflow deals with them.

Implementation Problems of Traditional Workflow

The implementation of a WfMS can be roughly divided into 2 phases; (1) the initial implementation of the WFMS and (2) the incremental adaptions. When a company has decided to use a WFMS, this system is usually bought from a workflow vendor. The WFMS cannot be used immediately; a complicated installation is needed to configure the WFMS to the business processes. Usually, a third party consultancy firm is needed for the initial implementation. Thus, the initial implementation is often complex and requires significant effort.

After a WfMS has been in use for some time, incremental adaptions are inevitable. There are three reasons for incremental implementations. (1) Errors in the development of the software which causes the WFMS to malfunction. These design-related mistakes are generally made in the development phase of the WFMS. Design related mistakes should be prevented because it is much more expensive to change the software when the system is already in use then during the design phase. Another type of change is related to the (2) administration/management of the WFMS. An example of this are the security patches that are necessary, which should keep the WFMS safe from intruders. The third type of change is related to changes in the (3) organization, like a re-distribution of responsibilities over departments and participants.

Incremental implementations can be divided into run-time and build-time implementations. Run-time implementations are changes made while the system is running. An example is a change in the routing of cases. Ideally, these changes should be made on-the-fly without stopping the system. Making changes is complex in current WfMSs and therefore experts are often needed to make these changes. This causes changes in the process model to be expensive and time consuming. Build-time changes require the WFMS to be stopped and therefore should be avoided when possible. An example of build-time changes are adjustments to the process models. It is clearly better to be able to change things at run-time than be forced to do this at build-time (Weber et al., 2004).

Obviously, for the initial implementation of a WfMS considerable technical expertise is required. When numerous features need to be installed initially, the installation is obviously more demanding. All features need to be fine-tuned with the organization and furthermore it may be necessary to couple some features to other software packages used in the company. Integrating the WfMS with other (legacy) systems is arguably the most complex task in the initial implementation. The solution that lightweight workflow provides in this respect is that it has fewer features than regular WfMSs and therefore allows for a simpler and shorter initial implementation phase.

With respect to the incremental adaptions, lightweight workflow attempts to limit the occasions that shutdowns are required of the system for a build-time change, in favor of using run-time changes. Various of existing lightweight approaches that explicitly try to circumvent shutdowns of this kind are described in (Muth et al., 1999; Agostini & de Michelis, 2000a). Often, the end-users themselves are targeted to take care of such adoptions, which limits an organization's dependency on technical experts. In this way, lightweight workflow allows for a less intrusive use of workflow technology in the light of the inevitable changes that will occur.

Table 1. Characteristics of lightweight WfMSs

Number	Characteristic
1	Provide less functionality than traditional WfMSs
2	Allow for faster, non-intrusive implementation than traditional WfMSs
3	Cause a smaller footprint than traditional WfMSs
4	More heavily involve end-users than with traditional WfMSs

Footprint Problems of Traditional Workflow

Conventional WfMSs can be said to leave a big "footprint" in an organization (Muth et al., 1999), which denotes the negative impact on and introduction of relation with all kinds of organizational aspects. There are basically three different types of footprints that can be distinguished; the financial footprint, the human footprint and the technical footprint.

The financial footprint of a WfMS is related to the purchasing and licencing cost of a workflow system. The organization has to pay for the whole WfMS, usually independent of the features that will be used. The second aspect of the footprint of a WfMS is the influence it has on the work procedures. Even when work basically stays the same as it ever was, employees need to get accustomed to new software (e.g. the workflow in-basket interface) and may not be able to use procedures and/or software that they did before (e.g. the creation of letters is something that is now out of their control). The third aspect in footprint of a WfMS is the technical footprint. Some WfMSs e.g. require installing a fat client, a Database Management System (DBMS), or an application server. Also, current WfMSs rely heavily on the network infrastructure and this network often becomes a bottleneck (Fakas & Karakostas, 2004). In this way, the introduction of a WfMS introduces new technologies and increased dependencies between the systems.

Lightweight workflow is an approach to diminish the traditional workflow footprint in various ways. The financial footprint is addressed because lightweight is mostly a simpler system, which is more affordable. Human footprint issues are addressed by putting much more emphasis on the involvement of end-users in the configuration and maintenance of the WfMS, in contrast to the top-down approach that is often used in workflow implementations. This approach, which positively affects user influence, is clearly only possible because lightweight workflow is in a technical sense not too complex. Finally, lightweight workflow often not aims at a full integration with all important systems already in place, in this way limiting the new dependencies that are introduced along with the workflow system.

LIGHTWEIGHT WORKFLOW

In the light of the problems identified in the previous section, the characteristics of lightweight workflow can be summarized as shown in Table 1.

Using these characteristics, we propose the following definition of a lightweight WfMS.

Figure 1. Features of a lightweight WfMS

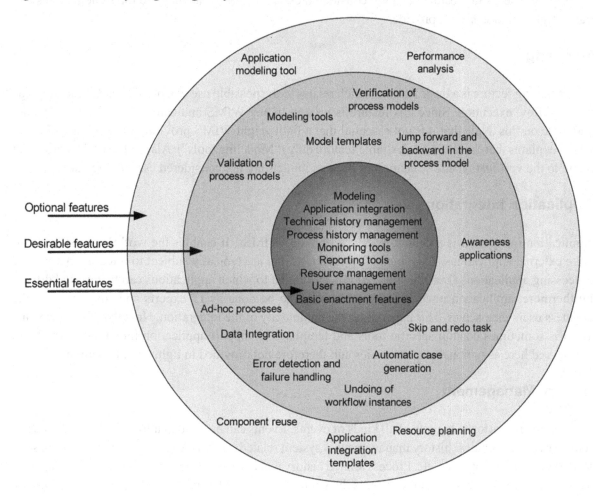

Definition "Lightweight Workflow Management System":

Lightweight workflow management systems are workflow management systems that only provide the most basic functionalities and are characterized by a relatively small and non-intrusive effort to implement and adopt them, in particular by depending on the involvement of business users.

The main question that now can be raised is what the set of basic functionalities should be. Clearly, different researchers and vendors can put different emphases in this discussion. Shown in Figure 1 is a set of concentric circles that show the various layers of features that can be observed in many WfMSs, where the most central circle provides the essential list of features that a WfMS cannot do without. These are the features that any lightweight WfMS will need to provide. Moving towards the outer circles, desirable features can be distinguished for any WfMS. The more these kinds of features are included in a lightweight WfMS, the 'heavier' it will get. The outer circle contains features that are optional for WfMSs in general, but typically not encountered in a lightweight solution.

We will discuss the features that are considered essential shortly, as they are the basic features any lightweight solution should provide.

Modeling

The modeling feature is a basic feature, which relates to the possible use of a pre-defined model to guide the workflow execution. Since this feature is present in any WfMS and cannot be left out we do not elaborate on this. Note that it is not essential that a lightweight WfMS provides a modeling tool *itself*, which explains that the latter is a desirable feature only ("Modeling tools"). Also, advanced features that relate to the verification and validation of process models are not considered essential features.

Application Integration

Application integration is a common feature of many WfMSs: It enables the workflow system to invoke external applications. Examples of applications that are typically subject to integration are word processing applications (Zur Muehlen, 2004). The extent to which applications can be invoked differs. Furthermore, application integration sometimes has to be done by IT experts and sometimes by the business users themselves. This depends on the complexity of the integration. Note that "heavyweight" WfMSs sometimes contain specific tools and templates to support application integration, which are considered here as optional characteristics and therefore not provided in lightweight solutions.

History Management

This feature refers to the logging of all kinds of events. Events can be divided into technical and process-related events. Technical history management is system related, such as user log-on and log-off, system shutdowns, version updates, etc. Process related history management keeps track of process related data. This is a so called audit trail and represents the whole route a case has taken. Examples of these logs are activity start time, activity duration and activity completion.

Monitoring Tools

Monitoring tools report about the operational processes and often do this real-time. TIBCO's product I-process inside is an example of a monitoring tool. It can monitor e.g. the number of cases in a process in real-time. Monitoring tools make it possible to analyze the workflow process from different dimensions. They can show several aspects of the workflow process such as the current activities, the current deadline violations or the priority in activities. More advanced, "awareness" tools, can actively warn stakeholders of process deviations but they are typically not encountered in lightweight solutions.

Reporting Tools

Reporting tools are somewhat different from monitoring tools. They provide information on a higher level and they do not do this real-time. TIBCO's product I-process analytics is an example of a reporting tool. It provides information for management, e.g. the number of cases which have been started in a specific month.

Resource Management

A WfMS routes work packages to the right performers. To do so, the WfMS needs to be aware of the available resources and corresponding roles. The resource management feature enables the WfMS to integrate resources during process execution. More advanced, related features – but typically not encountered in lightweight solutions – are resource planning based on predictions and work balancing using actual utilization levels.

User Management

With the user management feature all users of the WMS can be managed. So, different roles and different authorizations can be defined for specific performers that are active within the scope of a WfMS. A manager of a department has for example more rights in the system then a regular employee. User management is a common feature which is present in all WfMSs.

Basic Enactment Features

Any WfMS should provide some basic features to let the system operate. Examples are the process management facility (creates workflow instances), the control flow manager (handles state changes) and the work list handler (creates work items). More advanced features, such as the automatic case generation in case of external events, are not lightweight features. In particular, various features that support advanced exception handling are not considered basic features.

Now we have identified what a lightweight workflow solution typically looks like, it is worthwhile to reflect on some real-life experiences to determine whether light-weight workflow is effective to deal with the problems we associated with more traditional kinds of WfMSs. This will be done in the next section.

CASE STUDIES

To gather insights into the effectiveness of lightweight workflow solutions, we worked together with Pallas Athena[1], a multinational company offering various workflow solutions. Among their offerings is a software package that is called *Protos Activate*. The software package supports all essential features as we related on in the previous section, as well as many desirable features like, for example, its own process modeling tool. It does not, however, support from the desirable features any functionality to deal with exceptions or to raise awareness of the process state. In this sense, the tool is very different from many (research) workflow systems that are currently under development. In addition, none of the optional features from Figure 1 are part of Protos Activate. This means, in particular, that the facilities to integrate this system with other systems are limited. Typically, a Protos Activate implementation aims at integrating with an application like Word and/or Excel only. The whole philosophy behind the software is that the role of experts is limited and that end users can model their own process and "activate" it. Also, the purchasing price is very limited to what is common for commercial systems. For more information on this software package, the interested reader is referred to the public information available at the vendor's website.

Table 2. Evaluation cases

Problems addressed by lightweight WfMS		
Initial implementation		
	Technical installation	4.00
	Configuration of the system	2.00
	Acceptation by user groups	4.50
	Involvement user groups	4.50
	Effort	5.00
	Duration initial implementation	5.00
	Average score	**4.17**
Adoptions		
	(Re)Configuration of the system	4.00
	Acceptation by user groups	4.50
	Involvement user groups	4.50
	Effort	5.00
	Duration incremental implementation	5.00
	Average score	**4.60**
Footprint		
	Human footprint	3.00
	Technical footprint	2.00
	Effectiveness	2.00
	Average score	**2.33**
Functionality		
	Specific features:	
	Modeling tool	5.00
	Data integration	1.00
	Error detection and failure handling	3.00
	Average score	**3.00**
	Total average score	**3.53**

Protos Activate has been implemented at various worldwide locations and we selected two implementation sites to consider in more detail.

Case 1: Computer Manufacturer

This case concerns the implementation of Protos Activate at a large computer manufacturer, based in the Netherlands. The implementation concerns a process in the software sales department, where the package was used to . The case characteristics are that is concerns an environment with high process complexity – the process was difficult to model –, a low volume of cases being handled by the workflow process (typically causing only a 20% utilization of the involved resources) and a medium need for data integration (only with Word and Excel).

Case 2: Mortgager

The second case study concerns a mortgager that is also based in the Netherlands. The mortgager operates in a business to business environment and does not have direct contact with end users. The volume of cases is typically much higher than for the first case study, but the process is much simpler. The amount of data integration is similar.

For both cases, we have held ex-post interviews with the involved consultants of Pallas-Athena, being two individuals for each implementation. These people played a supportive role only in these projects, as much of the modeling was done by the end-users themselves. Because these consultants had extensive knowledge of more traditional workflow packages, in particular the FLOWer system also offered by their company, it was possible to had them reflect on issues that were actually encountered by using Protos Activate and *comparing* them to a situation where a more traditional solution would have been used. The aggregated outcomes of this evaluation are summarized in Table 2.

As can be seen in this table, the three main categories of problems were addressed as introduced in this chapter. Furthermore, three specific features were singled out for evaluation. The subjects were asked to give scores on a scale of 1 to 5. For the problems, a low score implied that the they considered the lightweight solution to be a poorer solution to handle these than a traditional WfMS would have. For example, the score of '2' for the configuration of the system indicated that, on average, the consultants thought that this particular aspect would have been dealt with slightly easier and more effectively with a traditional WfMS.

Similarly, for the functionalities, a low score implied that the four consultants on average considered the lightweight workflow system to provide a less satisfactory support than they would expect from a traditional solution. For example, the score of a '1.0' for the data integration functionality indicated that this would have been dealt with much more satisfactorily with a traditional WfMS.

The overall average (which aggregates over all the averages of the sub-categories) of 3.5 hints at a slight preference for the lightweight workflow system in comparison to having used a more traditional WfMS for the considered cases. This is not a very strong preference and should certainly not be interpreted as a statistical significant result.

What is more interesting are the relative differences in the scores. As more or less expected, the lightweight solution performs very strongly with respect to the initial implementation and subsequent adoptions (average scores of 4.17 and 4.60 respectively). The involved consultants mentioned as main benefits that the lightweight system could be implemented in a faster and easier way and that acceptation by the end-users was much better than they were used to in conventional cases. The results were relatively better for the mortgager, where end-user involvement was higher. In this sense, lightweight workflow seems very effective to deal with the troublesome implementation issues we identified.

However, and more surprisingly, the footprint was not so well addressed by the lightweight solution (average score of 2.33) issues. Recall that one of the basic premises of lightweight solutions is that fewer features would lead to a smaller technical and financial footprint. In our interviews with the consultants, they indicated that the technical footprint would have been more favorable when a regular WfMS had been used because the data integration feature was supported in a very limited way (see also the score of 1.00 for the specific feature). In the computer manufacturers' case, a lot of information was stored in proprietary databases, such as software prices, offers and customer information. To use this information, scripting was necessary. As similar problem occurred in the case of the mortgager, since correspondence to clients had to be done in a particular industry format.

Therefore, this evaluation suggests that lightweight workflow is a two-edged sword. By reducing the features of a WfMS the implementation becomes easier, cheaper, and faster, particularly so because end-users can take care of many of the implementation and adoptions tasks. However, as soon as a more difficult technical challenges occur, the absence of rich technical (data integration) features are felt.

FUTURE TRENDS

In this chapter we have briefly mentioned some approaches to bring more flexibility to WfMSs and paid considerable attention to a direction that we referred to as lightweight workflow. Another development that takes place in the workflow landscape that are worthwhile to mention.

In this chapter, we have solely considered stand-alone workflow applications – Gartner refers to them as *pure play* workflow – where there is clear trend to include this type of functionality in other types of systems, such as Product Data Management or Enterprise Resource Planning (ERP) systems. It cannot be ruled out that workflow technology will become *absorbed technology* in the long run. Various organizations that we have worked with exchanged their workflow system for an ERP system in the past years, see e.g. (Reijers & van der Aalst, 2005).

Another trend is that workflow functionality is not absorbed in other types of applications, but in operating systems. A good example is the Windows Workflow Foundation[2], a form of a lightweight workflow, which is included in Windows Vista. Even though this functionality is not as advanced as regular WfMSs, it is very easy to install and configured by non IT-experts. This trend perhaps best shows that lightweight workflow has much potential.

CONCLUSION

Lightweight workflow is a solution to offer *less* features in a workflow system. The underlying idea is that in many situations, especially when flexibility and application integration are not big issues, a "lighter" workflow system provides a better proposition to arrive at a successful and satisfactory workflow implementation.

Lightweight workflow is by no means the final word in the workflow landscape. It is certainly not the right answer for many of the industrial situations where case variation and data integration are big issues. Yet, it is an interesting counter-proposition to the dominant direction of various efforts to extend the functionalities of WfMSs with the aim of making them even more flexible, even more suitable to integrate with other applications, even more capable of providing management information, etc. The inevitable side-effect of increasingly more complex workflow systems is that they will become increasingly difficult to implement, with negative repercussions on user adoption. It is questionable whether, in the long run, the workflow paradigm would profit from continuing in such a direction only. It seems more fruitful to work on a broad range of workflow solutions so that the right trade-off can be selected for each particular case.

Clearly, what is in actual demand are more thorough evaluations of lighweight workflow as being applied in practice. In particular, it should be determined in what situations the lesser support lightweight systems require will outweigh the increased efforts to integrate such a system with its environment (e.g. enterprise systems, databases, etc). The involvement of end-users and system integrators will be essential for such an evaluation.

ACKNOWLEDGMENT

The author wishes to acknowledge the help of Chris Sonnenveld in defining and evaluating leightweight workflow.

REFERENCES

Agostini, A., & de Michelis, G. (2000a). A light workflow management system using simple process models. *Computer Supported Cooperative Work*, *9*(3-4), 335–363. doi:10.1023/A:1008703327801

Agostini, A. & de Michelis, G. (2000b). Improving flexibility of workflow management systems (LNCS 1806, pp. 218-234).

Bowers, J., Button, G., & Sharrock, W. (1995). Workflow from within and without: Technology and cooperative work on the print industry shopfloor. In *Proceedings of the Fourth Conference on European Conference on Computer-Supported Cooperative Work* (pp. 51-66).

Dourish, P., Holmes, J., MacLean, A., Marqvardsen, P., & Zbyslaw, A. (1996). Freeflow: Mediating between representation and action in workflow systems. In *Proceedings of the 1996 ACM Conference on Computer Supported Cooperative Work* (pp. 190-198).

Fakas, G. J., & Karakostas, B. (2004). A peer to peer (P2P) architecture for dynamic workflow management. *Information and Software Technology*, *46*(6), 423–431. doi:10.1016/j.infsof.2003.09.015

Jablonski, S., & Bussler, C. (1996). *Workflow management: Modeling concepts, architecture and implementation*. London: International Thomson Computer Press.

Kaan, K., Reijers, H. A., & van der Molen, P. (2006). Introducing case management: Opening workflow management's black box. In *Proceedings of the 4th International Conference on Business Process Management (BPM 2006)*.

Kammer, P. J., Bolcer, G. A., Taylor, R. N., Hitomi, A. S., & Bergman, M. (2000). Techniques for supporting dynamic and adaptive workflow. *Computer Supported Cooperative Work*, *9*(3-4), 269–292. doi:10.1023/A:1008747109146

Koulopoulos, T. M. (1995). *The workflow imperative: Building real world business solutions*. New York: John Wiley & Sons, Inc.

Muth, P., Weissenfels, J., Gillmann, M., & Weikum, G. (1999). Integrating light-weight workflow management systems withinexisting business environments. In *Proceedings of 15th International Conference on Data Engineering* (pp. 286-293).

Reichert, M., & Dadam, P. (1998). Adeptflex: Supporting dynamic changes of workflows without losing control. *Journal of Intelligent Information Systems, 10*(2), 93–129. doi:10.1023/A:1008604709862

Reijers, H. A., Rigter, J., & van der Aalst, W. M. P. (2003). The case handling case. *International Journal of Cooperative Information Systems, 12*(3), 365–391. doi:10.1142/S0218843003000784

Reijers, H. A., & van der Aalst, W. M. P. (2005). The effectiveness of workflow management systems: Predictions and lessons learned. *International Journal of Information Management, 25*(5), 458–472. doi:10.1016/j.ijinfomgt.2005.06.008

Smith, H., & Fingar, P. (2003). *Business process management: The third wave*. Meghan-Kiffer Press.

van der Aalst, W. M. P., Barthelmess, P., Ellis, C. A., & Wainer, J. (2000). Workflow modeling using Proclets (LNCS 1901, pp. 198-209).

van der Aalst, W. M. P., & Hee, K. M. (2002). *Workflow Management: Models, methods, and systems*. Cambridge: MIT Press.

van der Aalst, W. M. P., Weske, M., & Grunbauer, D. (2005). Case handling: A new paradigm for business process support. *Data & Knowledge Engineering, 53*(2), 129–162. doi:10.1016/j.datak.2004.07.003

Weber, B., Rinderle, S., & Reichert, M. (2007). Change patterns and change support features in process-aware information systems (LNCS 4495, pp. 574-588).

Weber, B., Wild, W., & Breu, R. (2004). CBRFlow: Enabling adaptive workflow management through conversational case-based reasoning (LNCS 3155, pp. 434-448).

Weissenfels, J., Muth, P., & Weikum, G. (1998). Flexible worklist management in a light-weight workflow management system. In *Proceedings of EDBT Workshop on Workflow Management Systems, Valencia*.

White, T. E., & Fischer, L. (1995). *New tools for new times: The workflow paradigm*. Future Strategies Inc.

Zur Muehlen, M. (2004). *Workflow-based process controlling: Foundation, design and application of workflow-driven process information systems*. Logos, Berlin.

KEY TERMS AND DEFINITIONS

Lightweight Workflow Management System: Lightweight workflow management systems are workflow management systems that only provide the most basic functionalities and are characterized by a relatively small and non-intrusive effort to implement and adopt them, in particular by depending on the involvement of business users.

Workflow: the computerized facilitation or automation of a business process, in whole or part.

Workflow Management System: A system that completely defines, manages and executes workflows through the execution of software whose order of execution is driven by a computer representation of the workflow logic.

ENDNOTE

[1]   See http://www.pallas-athena.com, last accessed September 28th, 2008.

[2]   See http://msdn2.microsoft.com/en-us/library/ms735967.aspx, last accessed September 28th, 2008.

Chapter 20
Testing Complex and Dynamic Business Processes

Krishnendu Kunti
Infosys Technologies Limited, India

Bijoy Majumdar
Infosys Technologies Limited, India

Terance Bernard Dias
Infosys Technologies Limited, India

ABSTRACT

In this chapter we deal with testing of business processes implemented using computer systems. We have discussed challenges associated with business process testing, identified aspects of business processes that need to be tested and capabilities that the testing tool(s) or environment should have in order to perform such testing. The chapter also discusses a commonly used software testing methodology in light business process testing for provisioning of structured mechanism for business process testing. One of the aspects of managing complex and dynamic business processes is making sure that the process delivers what is required of it at all times. Dynamics of the business may require frequent changes in the business process and whenever such changes takes place there is a need to test the process thoroughly to ascertain that the process is still working according to the requirements laid down for it. This becomes even more important if the business process is implemented using computer systems since over a period of time the computer software becomes more prone to error as it is updated frequently to accommodate the business changes hence the requirement for testing complex business processes.

INTRODUCTION

Traditionally, business processes (BPs) and roles were defined within organizations. These processes became mature and robust over a period of time. As business grew, computer systems were developed in order to cater to business needs. But since, in erstwhile times the advantages of modular and distributed systems were not very well known, most of the systems developed were monolithic in nature.

DOI: 10.4018/978-1-60566-669-3.ch020

These monolithic applications worked in silos; performed high level activities required by individual business units and used custom data formats. This did not matter much since these systems required very little communication with other systems and whenever they did communicate, they used point to point, tightly coupled batch mode file transfers. As a result of the monolithic and closed nature of these systems, business functions could not be reused across systems. Such a scenario led to replication of business function across multiple systems. The resulting system architecture offered predictability but at the same time took away flexibility and hence any scope of easy evolution of the process concerned. Over the years as organizations grew in size, mergers and acquisitions took place. Also, more and more activities of the organization started getting outsourced. This led to steep increase in the number interactions and interacting partners. The competition also increased over time and there was a need to modify BPs quickly to stay ahead of the competition. This led to the need of agile or dynamic business processes by which new processes and products can be delivered to the customer quicker and with minimal effort. Supporting dynamic BPs required loosely coupled architecture which could not possibly be achieved using traditional tight coupling between processes where a whole range of activities were bundled into a single system. The solution lay in functional decomposition of monolithic systems into smaller modules, which could be exposed as services and arranged in the most desired format according to need of the BP. Such architecture enabled wider access of business functions (often defined using standard based interfaces) which in turn facilitated re-usability, increased flexibility and eased communication.

Modern BP principles along with enabling architecture paradigms like Service Oriented Architectures (SOA (Service Oriented Architecture, 2008) and technologies like Process modeling/enactment engine, Rules engine, composite applications, etc. allow creation of dynamic BP. While dynamic BPs are great for business they are difficult to manage on the technical front. One of the many challenges associated with managing complex and dynamic BP implementations is its testing. This chapter will discuss the challenges in testing of BP implementations as well as an approach for BP development and testing using the V-Model for software development. It also discusses the aspects of BP implementation that needs to be tested, scope of BP testing and capabilities that a BP implementation testing system should possess. Finally, it talks about the future trend in this area and the conclusion.

Since this chapter deals with testing of BP implementation using computer systems rather than testing the BP itself, from here onwards we will refer to BP implementations simply as BPs for better readability.

BACKGROUND

BPs differs from traditional application in that they may span across multiple stakeholders, enterprise IT layers, standards, security zones, may be partially automated, may partially require human intervention or may comprise of both legacy and new applications. Also, they may involve some complex rules and business policies. The process should also be flexible enough architecturally so that it can be modified quickly to meet the constantly changing business needs. Although this has become possible today with adoption of SOA, the challenges involved in testing such BPs have multiplied manifolds. Existing approaches of development and testing can be used for BPs, however testing requirements in BPs differ a lot from other applications. This is an important area and there is very little literature available on it. In this chapter we hope to discuss the various aspects of BP testing to some level of detail so that it may be useful to any team trying to develop and test dynamic BPs.

CHALLENGES IN TESTING BUSINESS PROCESSES

As we have mentioned earlier modern BPs are very different from conventional applications. Some of the challenges faced in testing such BPs because of these differences are mentioned below:

- A BP comprises of many smaller business functions. These business functions may be located in different physical locations. They may use different message formats and different transport protocols to communicate. Because of this varied nature of functions it becomes extremely difficult to comprehensively test such BPs. This requires capability to support transport protocols, message formats, security standards, interface definition formats, etc. to name a few . It is often difficult to support these testing requirements using traditional testing tools geared towards testing individual applications that did not involve aforementioned complexities.

- Each of these functions that participate in BP can either be a frontend, a backend, or a middleware application in traditional sense. However, on whole it is often difficult to clearly classify a BP as either a frontend, backend or middleware application. Traditional tools cater to testing either of these tiers but not all the tiers. Hence, conventional means of testing a single application and associated tools and solutions might not meet all requirements for testing a BP.

- As a BP may be spread across different systems, the number of failure points are larger than that in a normal system. Testing on an function is done with the intention of finding bugs and defects and fixing them. But in BPs with increased number of failure points it is very difficult to pinpoint the cause of defect or bug.

- Adoption of architectural paradigms like SOA and composite application have facilitated creation of loosely coupled and flexible business processes. Such BPs are flexible and can be easily modified. The dynamic nature of business causes the BP to change very often and every time any change occurs, it needs to go through few rounds of thorough regression testing. Therefore, testing BP is difficult because of its constantly evolving nature.

- Many BPs caters to the needs of an organization's external clients and partners i.e. the BPs are exposed to outside world. This makes the organizations systems vulnerable to malicious attacks. A BP exposed to the external world needs to be secure and this means the security needs to be tested extensively. Also since a large number of users may be using it, the performance of the process needs to be tested thoroughly as well.

- The functions that participate in a BP, in most cases are developed by different teams. It is often difficult to co-ordinate between different teams and to ensure that proper processes are being followed in all the teams. Also, chances of miscommunication increase if processes are not followed properly and chances are that requirements may not be met exactly. Therefore at many times the different functions may differ and it may be difficult to integrate and test them.

- In a BP involving human participants, delegation model is another challenge. Apart from the normal business process execution, the various allocation mechanism or hierarchy model needs to be valid throughout the process execution. This criteria mandates user hierarchy knowledge and their corresponding calendar details for efficient business process testing.

IDENTIFYING ASPECTS OF BUSINESS PROCESSES FOR TESTING

Testing a computer system includes activities like definition of test plan/strategy and test cases, setup of testing environment, test case execution, bugs reporting and finally bug fixing. While the actual execution of test cases, bug reporting and bug fixing can happen only when the system to test is built, but it is important that the use cases and requirements for each phase of the BP project life cycle are not lost and that the system is testing for every requirement laid down.

To fit this requirement, the V-Model is a suitable development methodology to enforce testing discipline throughout the BP project life cycle. The V-Model approach for software development and testing was first described by Perry. W. E. (1995) in his book "*Effective Methods for Software Testing*". This model is now widely used for ensuring system quality in projects that employ the traditional software development life cycle.

The V-Model approach states that testing an application becomes much easier if it is taken up in phases like the development process. It states that each artifact in the development phase maps to a corresponding artifact in the testing phase. Starting the testing process right at the beginning of the BP project life cycle ensures that the use case and requirement for each stage can be easily converted into test cases for testing the output of that phase. This ensures the thorough testing of BP at all levels of software architecture. Therefore, the V-Model helps the project team to continually determine how they would successfully test the project deliverables.

The V-Model is a suitable test methodology to deliver BPs due to the following reasons:

- It supports top-down approach in identifying the relevant entry and exit criteria at each level with respect to defining the BP requirements, functional/technical design, program specification, etc.
- It provides a bottom-up test approach by supporting message validations and testing of - functions within an application, individual application, interoperability between applications, set of integrated applications and the complete system.
- It helps to effectively test all the project deliverables throughout the Software Development Life Cycle by providing the mapping between the deliverables and the type of testing as applicable.

This mapping between the phases of development and testing lifecycle is shown in Figure 1 below:

In this section we will discuss the different aspects of BP that need to be tested using the V-Model.

In the business discovery phase the business analysts come up with a business use case for new BP or a change in the existing one. This is the phase in which the need for the BP is identified. Also, the benefits-to-cost ratio is calculated to justify it. The corresponding activity in the testing phase is the release testing. The release testing plan which is based on the information collected during the business use case phase tries to verify if the final BP that is implemented is still valid in the current business scenario. Many times the development and testing of the BP does not finish in time, i.e. it takes longer than the initially estimated period to finish. During this period, there is a possibility that the BP has become obsolete or needs some modifications to still be applicable in the current business scenario. Release testing is the testing phase at which the validity of the BP is verified. Release testing is the last test that happens on BP before it goes into production.

In the requirements specifications phase, the business requirements for the BP are gathered by the development team from the business analysts who have designed the BP. This phase includes gathering

Figure 1. V-Model for software testing. Adapted from Wikipedia 2008 (http://en.wikipedia.org/wiki/V-Model_(software_development)).

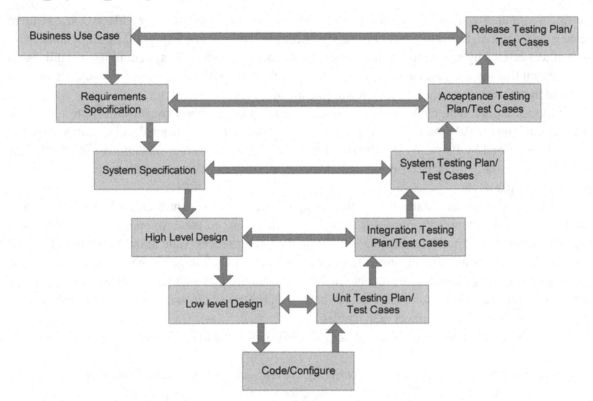

functional as well as non-functional requirements about the process. The counterpart in the testing phase is the Acceptance Testing. The Acceptance Test Cases are developed from the information gathered during this phase. The acceptance testing is done to ensure that the delivered BP meets all the business requirements specified. This test is usually done by testers who have enough understanding about the business and the requirements for the BP.

The following table shows the information that needs to be collected at the requirements specification phase and how it maps to test requirements that can be used during the acceptability testing phase: (Table 1)

In the system specification phase the overall view of the environment is described, i.e. what the overall system will look like once the BP is integrated with it. It indicates where and how he newly developed BP will fit into the existing environment. This phase also defines the functional as well as non-functional requirements for the different systems that interact with the BP. The System Testing Phase tests that the system specifications are being met. It tests the system view of the BP, i.e. how the overall system behave if the BP is integrated with it. This testing phase mainly determines the affect that the new BP has on the rest of environment. This testing is probably the most difficult testing to conduct since all aspects of the complete environment need to be tested. The number of things to test and the number of test cases are very large. Nevertheless this testing needs to be conducted to ensure that BP fits into the overall environment without causing any problems to the existing systems. The information collected at the system specification stage and the corresponding tests required are shown in the table below: (Table 2)

Table 1. Requirement specification mapping to acceptance testing

Process Requirements Specification Phase	Process Acceptability Testing Phase
Identify business processes and sub-processes that need to be created/developed and what each process and sub-process is suppose to do.	Come up with test cases to test each of the process/sub-process if it meets the requirement specified.
Identify associated roles for each business process, domains to which each role belong and role specific information if any.	Come up with Test Cases to test that the business process is only accessible to the roles for which it should be accessible.
Identify rules, policies applicable for the process and how these policies are applicable for roles involved, applicable geographic locations, line of business, etc.	Design test cases for testing that rules and policies are implemented properly for the BP
Identify non-functional requirements of security and performance related Service Level Agreements for processes and roles.	Design test cases for testing the non-functional requirements in the BP.

During high level design stage the functional view of business process gets created. Each of the business functions that make up the process is identified and designed. It the business function already exists then it need not be created. They just need to be tested to see if they meet all the requirements for the BP. But the business functions that are not already available have to be designed, developed and tested. The business function design could include:

- Business data format (e.g. Flat file, XML (eXtensible Markup Language, 2001), data definitions (Flat file structure and delimiter, XML schema (XML Schema, 2001),
- Business data constraints (e.g. user Id field can be only 12 characters long with alpha numeric characters) and associated information (e.g. if the XML is a domain specific syntax or based on common enterprise entity definition) for individual business functions identified in the prior stage.
- Data transport protocol (e.g. which transport is used for moving data to and from an interface).
- Roles and Domains applicable to each function are identified and their participation in overall process is determined. Also, decisions like identity management and access management system to be used are taken.
- If there are any rules and policies that are applicable for the individual function, then decisions like rule engine to use needs to be taken.

Table 2. System specification mapping to system testing

Process System Specification Phase	Process System Testing Phase
Identify how the process/sub-process implementation will interact with the rest of the environment.	Identify test cases to ensure that the BP is integrated with the rest of the environment properly and also that the remaining functionality in the other systems is intact.
Identify how the newly defined roles relates to other roles that already exist and are used in other processes.	Identify test cases to test the newly introduced roles and domains affect the other processes.
Identify what rules and policies will be applicable to already existing system. Also if there is any common data that the rules and policies are applied to.	Identify test cases to test the impact of the rules and policies to the other processes.
Identify if the security or performance specification for the overall environment after the BP is integrated with the other systems. This is especially important if this process is meant to be a sub-process of a larger process.	Identify test cases to test the overall security and performance of the environment.

- The non-functional requirements for each function are also identified. The usage of security servers and gateways for security and load balancing and clustering for performance needs to be considered.

At the process level, the following design aspects need to be considered:

- Translations and enrichments i.e. enriching and mapping output data from one function to data input for another function. This is usually required if existing functions are used and they do not fit the requirement of the current BP exactly. In such cases some data manipulation and customization is required before it can be used by the function.
- The integration may include control mechanism for transfer of control between functions. Some of the most commonly used control mechanisms are process orchestration or choreography language such as Business Process Execution Language (BPEL (Business Process Execution Language, 2006)) or Business Process Modeling Language (BPML (Business Process Modeling Language, 2002)), etc. But since all these standards are based on WSDL (Web Services Description Language, 2007) specification, they do not support all kinds of transports and message structures. Therefore, some organizations come up with their own process representation to accommodate their different systems.

At this stage the testing scope identified during the business discovery stage further gets refined. The following testing requirements are identified at this stage: (Table 3)

During the low level design phase, the implementation and code level details are defined. For example, if you are using an object oriented language for implementation, it will includes information like the number of classes and objects, the content of each class i.e member variables and methods and the relationship between objects, etc. During the coding phase, the components are coded and corresponding unit test cases are developed to test for all possible paths, boundary values, etc. of the class and it is made sure that the classes are working as intended. The roles, domains, etc. are created and conFigured in the identity and access management systems and tested thoroughly. Similarly, the rules and policies are conFigured on rules engine and tested. The performance of each class is tested using profilers for various parameters like memory utilization, leaks, execution time, etc. so that performance is built into the BP from the code level itself.

Finally, when the testing phases start, test units or stubs are created for each newly created function. These test units test a business interface as well as functional unit using required message structure over required transport protocol. Individual test units are used not only for functional testing but also for regression testing, performance testing and security testing as described in the tables above. For a business process that involves more than one function deployed across platforms, a BP testing system should take care of data translation requirements, control flow requirements, tracking/reporting requirements. Other requirements of a BP testing system are described in details in next section.

Identification of testing requirements starting at business discovery stage and continuing it through subsequent stages ensures that implementation of the business process is indeed happening in accordance with requirements. This practice enables modular design of business functions in deployment, incorporation of rules and policies in a manner such that it becomes easy to change, incorporation of Service Level Agreement (SLA) and security requirements for individual function and process; and development of a robust test suite for comprehensive test coverage of business process.

Table 3. High level design mapping to integration testing

Process High Level Design Phase	Process Integration Testing Phase
Identify how the business processes/sub-processes will be implemented i.e. what are the functions that will make up the complete business process. Design each business function that is not available.	Identify how to test newly developed business functions and existing ones as standalone entities and as part of the overall business process. Identify test cases for testing if the functions send and receive proper message formats over their respective protocols.
Design how functions identified in the prior stage interact with one another with respect to data flow and control flow. Data flows represent flow of business data across process and control flow represent the sequence in which functions coordinate with one another.	Identify Test Cases to test the interaction between the functions that need to interact with each other.
Identify if there are any roles and business domain demarcation at the function level and how they impact the overall business process. Identify how roles and domains for a function will be implemented.	Identify test cases for testing roles and business domains for individual business functions and existing ones as standalone entities and as part of the overall business process. Identify roles and their corresponding domains that need to be tested. Also, the proper access rights for each role are assigned. This testing will depend on how the roles and their access are implemented. i.e. If any identity management servers, etc. are used, the testing will be specific to those servers.
Identify if there are any rules and policies required at the function level and how they affect the rules and policies of the entire business process. Identify how rules, policies applicable for functions will be implemented.	Identify test cases for testing rules and policies of individual business function and aggregate rules and policies when the functions are integrated. Identify rules that need to be tested. This testing will depend on how the rules are implemented, i.e. if a rule engine is used, the testing will be specific to that particular rule engine.
Identify security and performance requirements for each business function. Identify how non-functional requirements for security and performance related Service Level Agreements will be implemented.	Identify test cases for testing security and performance requirements for each business function and the performance of the system when the different functions are put together. Identify test cases for testing the security and performance requirements based on how they are implemented. i.e. if security server is used, the testing will be specific to that server.

REQUIREMENTS FOR BUSINESS PROCESS TESTING

The whole testing process can be very difficult and time consuming if it involves writing some custom code for every test case. It almost becomes impossible to test a computer system comprehensively if you are not using any automation. Therefore, a lot of tools are available in the market today that can greatly improve the whole testing process. The greater the automation in testing, the better and faster is the testing process. An efficient testing process needs to be assisted by an efficient BP testing product. Testing a BP requires some basic set of capabilities to be present in testing tools. Some of these capabilities are mentioned below:

Ability to Manage and Test Varied Functions

A BP might comprise of a number of business functions. In order to test such a process, individual functions which need to be tested as a part of process are physically represented as a testing unit. Testing units are configurable functions which have an associated message structure and transport and physical system specific information if required (e.g. database URL, HTTP endpoint, etc). A BP testing solution should allow testing of individual function by allowing creation of testing unit. A set of testing units are combined to create a test scenario that depicts the real life BP. Since in a BP the same function may be used in different BPs, the testing unit once created should be re-usable. The ability of a BP testing solution to test decomposed process units (business functions) and re-use these testing units across business scenarios is a key testing requirement towards testing individual systems as a part of single process.

Also, in order to test a BP, a testing system should support a number of protocols and message formats. This is important because the business functions may be made up of a number of sub-functions which are defined in terms of system specific information.

For e.g., consider a funds transfer function. The function involves the following system steps:

- User submits a fund transfer request to fund transfer web service and the web service saves the data to a database.
- A batch script extracts the fund transfer data from database and sends it to fund transfer process hosted on a remote application server and exposed via Messaging queue (MQ).
- The server sends funds transfer response to destination MQ, from where the response is received and sent to a FTP location from where it is picked and reconciled by mainframe.

In order to perform end-to-end testing of the above function, a functional decomposition is performed and individual sub-functions are identified which need to be tested. The stated function can be decomposed into the following sub-functions:

1. Fund transfer web service
2. DB extraction for fund transfer data
3. Fund transfer process deployed on the application server and
4. Reconciliations process hosted in mainframe.

Since a function may consists of many sub-functions, a testing unit should be able to generate required message structure for the sub-function and deliver it to the endpoint using required transport protocol. These message formats may be custom to enterprise like delimited values in a flat file or standards based (e.g. SOAP (Simple Object Access Protocol, 2007) based on WSDL (Web Services Description Language, 2007). The format may also be based on domain specific syntax (e.g. SWIFT (Society for Worldwide Interbank Financial Telecommunication, 2008) for banking domain). Also the protocol over which the message needs to be sent may be standard based like FTP or HTTP or it may be custom to a particular platform. A BP based testing system should offer extensible mechanism to incorporate message syntax and underlying transport, and associate these with testing units to test diverse application and services.

Ability to Perform Functional, Regression and Performance Testing

Functions in a BP are required to be tested for functional correctness, consistency after code change (e.g. a new build) and for performance SLAs. The performance testing part is especially important since a BP is formed out of many different smaller functional units and one lower performing functional unit can slow down the entire business process. Therefore, it is important to make sure that the performance of each functional unit is meets the performance requirement and is not causing a bottleneck in the business process. Since the functional unit may be used in other business processes it is important to also factor the number of processes in which a particular functional unit will be participating while coming up with the performance requirement for it. Therefore, a BP testing system should allow functional,

Figure 2. BP test tool simulating the upstream and downstream systems

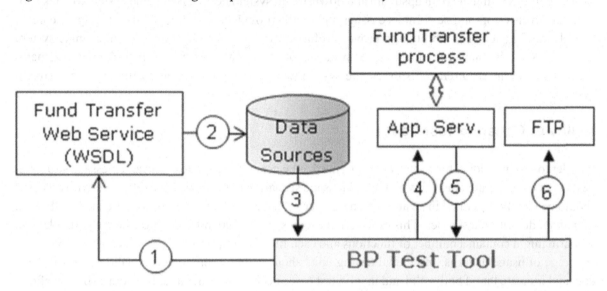

regression and performance testing and generate test unit level metrics and cumulative metrics for all three above mentioned requirements.

Ability to Simulate Upstream and Downstream Function

In order to perform end-to-end testing of a process, functions need to be tested in certain sequence. And to properly test this sequence, the input and output of each of the functions needs to be monitored. One way of doing this is by configuring functions don't communicate directly with one another as in case of real life interaction, but via a testing system that simulates both upstream (client) and downstream (server) system for a particular function. Testing units defined in the testing system behave as upstream and downstream systems for functions.

In the scenario depicted in Figure 2, BP Test Tool performs the following functions through test units created for corresponding functions:

- It simulates a web service client (upstream system) that generates SOAP message structure and submits it over HTTP to web service.
- It acts as a batch extraction script that extracts data from database, generates test cases and translates it to XML format required by fund transfer function hosted on application server.
- It simulates an MQ sender (upstream system) and sends the XML created in the prior step to fund transfer function hosted in application server.
- It simulates an MQ receiver (downstream system) to receive response from fund transfer process hosted in application server.
- It simulates FTP sender (upstream system) that uses received file from the prior step and sends file to folder using FTP.

The ability to simulate both upstream and downstream system helps a BP testing system to track sub-function levels errors and performance issues and finally provide testing for exhaustive usage scenarios at each sub-function. This ability also proves useful in scenarios that require testing of a single system in isolation and its impact on downstream systems. For e.g., if a patch has been applied to intermediate system and the requirement is to test the system without using the actual upstream or downstream system.

Ability to Generate Test Cases

In order to test individual functions, test cases need to be generated from test data and message structure. Test cases are generated in such a manner that usage scenarios are comprehensively covered. Test cases should be ideally generated in an automated manner so that individual tester is not burdened by the task of manual definition test cases. This especially becomes applicable in BP testing where a particular test scenario might contain a number of functions and each function requires a set of test case to provide full coverage of usage patterns. Individual testing units should allow users to define valid and invalid test data and indicate that if both valid and invalid test cases need to be generated. It would also be useful to be able to specify some rules which allows the tester to specify inclusion and omission criteria for data within a test case. For e.g., the tester should be able to specify if there is some test data or combination of test data that should be included in all the test cases or excluded from all the test case. This will help eliminate invalid test cases.

Business scenarios involve testing of more than one function and hence participation of more than one testing unit. Test data received from upstream testing units are used to generate test cases for downstream testing units. BP testing system should allow dependency mapping of data from upstream system to data for downstream system. These mapped data is used for test case generation for the next testing unit in a test scenario. While testing a set of business scenarios there might be common traversal paths across scenarios, in BP testing it should be possible to optimize traversal paths across business scenarios which would lead to considerable saving of testing effort. For instance if there are two business scenarios A-> B -> C and B-> C-> D, where A, B, C, D are functions, if the first scenario has already been tested then traversal path of B-> C can be omitted for the second scenario if the same test data is to be used. But at the same time a BP testing platform should allow test case optimization in such a way that possible combinations of values occurs in at least one test case.

Ability to Track Request, Response and Exceptions and Reporting Capability

Messages - both input and output - need to be captured for every testing unit or a set of testing units as a part of test scenario. The testing system should allow configuration to optionally capture exceptions. Information capture while test case execution is used for a variety of purposes which includes: input and output messages capture, generation performance statistics, capturing of errors, capturing control flow and data flow. In BP testing system monitoring of test execution should be possible both at run times and in form of consolidated report at the end of test execution. These reports may include:

- Run time reporting: These reports capture information pertaining to progress of test execution, execution request-response logging and error/exception capture, etc.

- Functional testing reports: These reports capture the information of functional testing of the functions as well as the complete business process. In automated testing the request is fired and the response is examined for error/exception. Finally a report is generated on which test cases passed and which ones failed and what was the error/exception received for the ones that failed.
- Regression testing reports: These reports capture information pertaining to how request- response differed in execution of test case or test scenario as compared to a baseline request response set. These reports indicate success or failure at individual test case as well as at a cumulative level of test scenarios, i.e. for a function as well as the whole process. This helps determine if the changes made have affected the other aspects of the application.
- Performance testing reports: These reports capture information about the performance of each function as well as whole process. These reports may include metrics on response times, maximum numbers of users possible, maximum number of requests from each user processed in a given time, the system resource utilization, etc.

Ability to Test Other Non-Functional Requirements Like Security, Rules, Etc.

Functions in a BP based process might have other non-functional requirements like security, policies, data rules, etc. associated with them. Usually testing of non functional requirements would require associating certain additional data while generating test data. This data forms an integral part of message to be processed by application/service. A BP testing tool should provide following generic capability for testing non-functional requirements:

- Application of data rules to generated test data e.g. a data rule might necessitate that two data values should always occur simultaneously or a particular field will always change and hence need not be considered for regression testing.
- Application of standards based tokens to message constructs, these tokens might be required for a number of purposes including security, confidentiality, non-repudiation, etc.
- Application of syntactical rules in generated test data e.g., a data rule might necessitate that fields confirm to certain syntactical rule.

Please note the requirements described above are by no means exhaustive, there might be requirement for testing of other non-functional requirements.

Requirements To Support Standards Based Testing

A large amount of work in the BP implementation technology space is driven by standards like BPMN (Business Process Modeling Notation, 2006), BPEL (Business Process Execution Language, 2006), Web services (Web Services, 2004), etc. If the BP is based on any of the standards then the BP should also be tested for standard compliance. But as we stated earlier all organizations might not go for these standards because of its limitations to support different message structures and protocols that the enterprise systems are using. Some organizations however, have realized the advantages of standards and are enabling web services on their systems to support these standards. Standards are applicable not only for interface definition but also for definition of process, security, role based access, etc. BP testing tool should have the following capabilities to check for standards compliance:

Figure 3. BP test scope for different phase

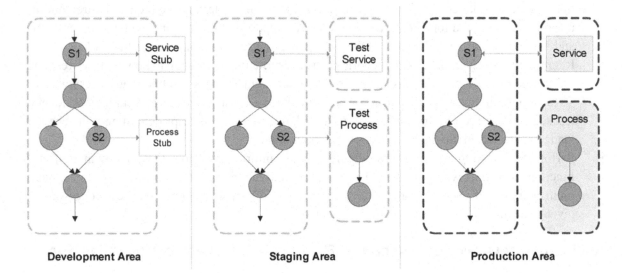

- Capability to understand a standard and check for syntactic compliance
- Capability to generate message structure based on standards based interface definition and to create test cases either provisioning of valid values or directly from interface definition.
- Capability to support domain specific standards like ACORD (ACORD Insurance Domain standard, 2002), FIX (Financial Information eXchange, 2005), etc.
- Capability to check for syntactical correctness of defined flow, ensure logical termination and test possible traversal paths

BUSINESS PROCESS TEST SCOPE

One of the major advantages for BPs is that it can be built by composing business functions spanning across domains. In SOA terminology these functions can also be known as services. The services being leveraged could be readily available asset, or indigenously built or external service component. Business process solutions form the backbone of many modern enterprises, linking vital systems and business processes with real-time data interchange (Schiefer, J., et. al., 2007).

The objective of functional testing is to validate if the system works as per the end user expectation. In traditional computer systems of automated testing at each build phase where system components are developed in-house and tested within the local environment. Whereas in the case of BPM with SOA is a totally different ball game. Functional testing for a process can be difficult as a lot of dynamics come into play like the different domains, configurations and rules, etc.

The scope of testing BP is different in each testing phase of the process development lifecycle. Unit Testing or Development environment is different from the Integration Testing or Staging environment which in turn will be different from the System Testing or Production environment where the live services are being accessed from external entities or organization. Figure 3 depicts the different environment for different phases of process creation lifecycle.

Development Phase

A business process can talk to different services lying either in the same domain or external to the organization. If the process is using services external to the organization then at Unit Testing stage the services exposed by the partner organization may not be available for testing since it is a service in production. The process in consideration might also talk to other processes using different data exchange patterns. There is no control over the external process or services during the development phase. One approach to handle this issue is to create service or process stub that mimics the interfaces of the actual service or process. The development environment test will involve the process testing with stubs created by the development team. Optionally, if you are using a BP testing system and if the service can act as a downstream system then that feature can be useful in this kind of scenario.

Staging Phase

Unlike the development environment, the staging area will have an updated version of the process running with some test services or processes from other domains. In Figure 3, staging area depicts the communication of the process in consideration with other test services in other domain. If the test services are not available for integration testing then need to simulate the behavior of external processes or services.

Production Phase

Because of the dynamic environment involved, process architecture mandates some amount of testing in the production environment with dummy data. The dynamic configurations, policies, distributed protocols, integration environments, etc. are some of the reasons for testing business processes in production environment. In this environment, the various services and data communication is executed following all policies and standards agreed upon by parties.

For example, consider a collaborative supply chain process that leverages services from different applications or accessing services out of an online Customer Relationship Management (CRM) solution. The scope of testing the supply chain process will need to do a black box testing of the services lying out of their domain boundary. As mentioned earlier, some service testing tools in the market provides the functionality of creating dummy services given the interfaces of such services and processes. An ideal tool to select for process testing will be the one that provides features to make such seamless configuration from development to production environments without a lot of developer's effort.

FUTURE WORK

In this chapter we have tried to provide an introduction to BP testing. We have also discussed testing of BPs based on V-Model. But there is a lot of work can be done on defining this process more clearly for business processes. The next step to this chapter could be development of a more specific process or a methodology for testing BP. This can be based on an existing model like the V-Model or a completely new methodology. Also, in this chapter we have mentioned some of the aspects to test in a BP but as a next step some kind of template or checklist could be developed to comprehensively cover the different aspects of BP testing.

CONCLUSION

In this chapter we have discussed how BPs are different from traditional applications and the challenges that are faced in testing them because of these characteristics. We also took the V-Model of software development and testing and applied it to BP development and testing. Although all the phases in this model remain the same, the aspects that need to be tested for a BP are different than traditional software. We discussed the different abilities that the BP testing environment should have. Although we have mentioned some features here, it is not an exhaustive list of features. This list is just meant to serve as a reference list of basic features. Finally we discussed the different scopes of BP testing. Through this chapter we hope to have covered BP testing to some depth so that it can provide basic information to the BP testing development and testing teams.

REFERENCES

ACORD Insurance Domain standard (2002). *ACORD home page*. Retrieved March 10, 2008, from http://www.acord.org/home/home.aspx

Business Process Execution Language. (2006). *The OASIS Site*. Retrieved April 11, 2008, from http://docs.oasis-open.org/wsbpel/2.0/wsbpel-specification-draft.pdf

Business Process Modeling Language. (2002). *BPML Specification*. Retrieved April 14, 2008, from http://xml.coverpages.org/BPML-WD-200206.pdf

Business Process Modeling Notation. (2006). *BPMN home page*. Retrieved April 14, 2008, from http://www.bpmn.org/

eXtensible Markup Language (2001). *XML Specification*. Retrieved February 10, 2008, from http://www.w3.org/XML/

Financial Information eXchange (2005). *FIX home page*. Retrieved on April 21, 2008, from http://www.fixprotocol.org/

Parnas, D. (1994). Software aging. *International Conference of Software Engineering* (pp. 279-287). IEEE Computer Society Press.

Perry. W. E (1995). *Effective methods for software testing*. John Wiley & Sons.

Schema, X. M. L. (2001). *XML Schema Specification*. Retrieved February 10, 2008, from http://www.w3.org/XML/Schema

Schiefer, J., Roth, H., Suntinger, M., & Schatten, A. (2007). Simulating business process scenarios for event based systems. *Schatten Personal web site*. Retrieved February 20, 2008, from http://www.schatten.info/pub/ecis/ecis2007.pdf

Service Component Architecture Home. (2007). *Open Service Oriented Architecture Site*. Retrieved March 10, 2008, from http://www.osoa.org/display/Main/Service+Component+Architecture+Home

Service Oriented Architecture. (2008). *The wikipedia.org site*. Retrieved March 10, 2008, from http://en.wikipedia.org/wiki/Service-oriented_architecture

Simple Object Access Protocol. (2007). *The w3.org site*. Retrieved March 22, 2008, from http://www.w3.org/TR/soap/

Society for Worldwide Interbank Financial Telecommunication. (2008). *Bitpipe.com site*. Retrieved March 14, 2008, from http://www.bitpipe.com/tlist/SWIFT.html

Web Services. (2004). *Web services tutorial*. Retrieved February 17, 2008, from http://www.w3schools.com/webservices/default.asp

Web Services Description Language. (2007). *WSDL specification*. Retrieved March 22, 2008, from http://www.w3.org/TR/wsdl

KEY TERMS AND DEFINITIONS

Business Process Execution Language: A specification for defining business process in a standard XML notation.

Business Process Implementation: The representation of BP in a form that the computer can understand and execute.

Business Process Implementation Testing: Testing the execution of the business process to make sure that it does whatever that it is required to do.

Business Process Modeling Language: A specification for defining business process in standard XML notation. It is a predecessor to the BPEL specification.

Business Process Modeling Notation: A specification for defining business process in a standard visual notation.

Service Component Architecture: A specification built on SOA principles for creation of components and applications from components.

Service Oriented Architecture: An architecture style that allows definition of reusable components as services and states that new applications can be built by assembling exiting reusable services.

Simple Object Access Protocol: A specification used for exchange of data in web services.

V-Model for Testing: A software development and testing approach that states that each development phase should to a corresponding testing phase for easy and comprehensive software testing.

Web Services: A set of specifications that allows a functionality to be deployed over the internet or intranet so that it is accessible in an interoperable manner

Web Services Description Language: A specification used describing web services.

Chapter 21
Identifying Batch Processing Features in Workflows

Jianxun Liu
Hunan University of Science and Technology, China

Yiping Wen
Hunan University of Science and Technology, China

ABSTRACT

The employment of batch processing in workflow is to model and enact the batch processing logic for multiple cases of a workflow in order to optimize business processes execution dynamically. Our previous work has preliminarily investigated the model and its implementation. However, it does not figure out precisely which activity and how a/multiple workflow activity(s) can gain execution efficiency from batch processing. Inspired by workflow mining and functional dependency inference, this chapter proposes a method for mining batch processing patterns in workflows from process dataflow logs. We first introduce a new concept, batch dependency, which is a specific type of functional dependency in database. The theoretical foundation of batch dependency as well as its mining algorithms is analyzed and investigated. Based on batch dependency and its discovery technique, the activities meriting batch processing and their batch processing features are identified. With the batch processing features discovered, the batch processing areas in workflow are recognized then. Finally, an experiment is demonstrated to show the effectiveness of our method.

INTRODUCTION

The aim of batch processing in workflow is to improve the execution efficiency of business processes by modeling and enactment of batch logic for multiple workflow cases, i.e. vertically combining multiple *workflow activity* (hereafter activity) cases together and submitting for execution according to batch logics. In our previous literatures(Liu 2005, Liu 2007), we proposed a dynamic batch processing scheduling model and discussed the design and implementation of dynamic batch processing in WfMSs.

DOI: 10.4018/978-1-60566-669-3.ch021

However, there are still many problems need to be investigated. The following three problems are not solved yet: 1) determination of which *activity merits batch processing* (hereafter batch-efficient activity); 2) if it is a batch-efficient activity, how the multiple cases of the activity are batch-processed; and 3) the setting of the batch processing areas (batch processing patterns). In fact, just like the definition of workflow models, the design and modeling of batch-efficient activities as well as batch processing areas are also a time-consuming and error-prone task. They can be easily influenced by the perception of *business process designer* (hereafter designer). Moreover, designers may not know exactly which activity deserves batch processing (batch efficient activities) at workflow building time since there is no real data at that time to let us make a right decision. Even more designers may ignore these kinds of batch processing features due to their unconsciousness about the existence of batch efficiency in tasks. To optimize business processes, therefore, it is important to explore a way to identify and model both batch-efficient activities and batch processing areas automatically.

Inspired by data mining and workflow mining, this chapter proposes a method for identification of batch-efficient activities and their batch processing features as well as recognition of batch processing areas of a workflow from workflow logs. The basic idea of this method is to employ the control and relevant data in workflow logs to automatically discover the batch-efficient activities and their batch processing features, which is one or a set of input parameters of an activity and on which activities are batch-processed. To solve this problem, we introduce a new concept, batch dependency, which is a specific type of functional dependency in database. With the batch-efficient activities and their batch processing features, batch processing areas in workflow can be recognized and can be set automatically then. It is shown from the simulation experiments that our method works effectively.

The remainder of this chapter is organized as follows. First, in Section II we give an introduction of the background knowledge, notations, concepts and the problem itself for simplicity and clarification in identification and recognition algorithms. Section III is the theoretical foundation of our method, in which the batch dependency and its mining algorithm is introduced and investigated. In Section IV, we design two algorithms, one for identification of batch-efficient activities as well as recognition of their batch processing features and another for recognition of batch processing areas. Simulation experiments are done in Section V. Section VI is the review of related work. Our contribution is also pointed out here. Finally, Section VII concludes this chapter and points out some future directions.

PROBLEM DEFINITION

In this section we will give a brief introduction to what batch processing in workflow is, what data we will employ and how mining steps start and proceed.

Concept of Batch Processing in Workflow

Figure 1 is an example of processes with batch deserving activities (Liu 2007). It consists of six activities: "Application", "Examination and Approval", "Denial Informing", "Renting Car", "Informing", and "Charging". Table 1 shows the dataflow logs of activity "Renting Car" of the process in Figure 1. Let every car for renting with the same car type, e.g. Honda Civil, and can accommodate up to 4 passengers each time. In Table 1, tuple t_1, t_3, t_5 and t_8 are with the same destination, *Changsha*, and almost

Figure 1. A car sharing renting process

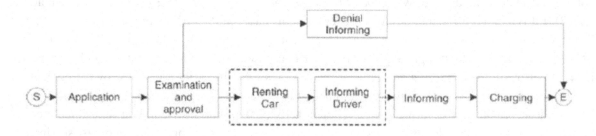

the same departure time, about *2005.10.13, 9:00AM*, but with different number of passengers, 1,1,4,3 and different cost (unit: Chinese RMB Yuan), 100, 100, 130, 120.

From these data in Table 1, we observed the fact that the cost of each application case (instance) increases less than proportional to the number of passengers when the value of the number of passengers increases. For instance, the number of passengers of t_6 doubles that of t_1, but the cost of t_6 only increases by 10% when compared with that of t_1. We call this kind of activity as batch deserving activity. It means that if a car can accommodate more than one passenger and there are several instances of the activity, "Renting Car", which have the same destination and departure time, the car can run once but serves several cases of the process, which can save much money for customers (applicants). In other words, several activity cases from multiple instances of the same workflow can be grouped vertically by certain rules, and it is the group being submitted for execution instead of each activity case. This is the concept of batch processing in workflow as we proposed in (Liu 2005, Liu 2007). Here activity parameters, such as destination, departure time, and number of persons as well as the car-renting fare, are batch processing

Table 1. The dataflow log of activity "Renting Car"

Workflow Instance Identifier	Application	...	Renting Car							...
			Input Parameters			Output Parameters				
			Departure time	destination	No. of passengers	driver' name	Duration (Unit: minute)	Cost (Unit: Yuan)		
t_1	...	...	2005.10.13, 8:30AM	Changsha	1	D1	50	100		...
t_2	...	...	2005.10.13, 8:30AM	Hengyan	2	D1	200	600		...
t_3	...	...	2005.10.13, 8:30AM	Changsha	1	D2	50	100		...
t_4	...	...	2005.10.13, 8:40AM	Zhouzhou	1	D6	45	90		...
t_t	...	...	2005.10.13, 8:40AM	Changsha	4	D2	50	130		...
t_6	...	...	2005.10.13, 9:20 AM	Changsha	2	D4	50	110		...
t_7	...	...	2005.10.13, 9:30AM	Zhouzhou	1	D5	45	90		...
t_8	...	...	2005.10.13, 9:30 PM	Changsha	3	D4	50	120		...
t_9	...	...	2005.10.13, 9:40AM	Zhouzhou	3	D3	45	110		...

Figure 2. Different patterns in workflow

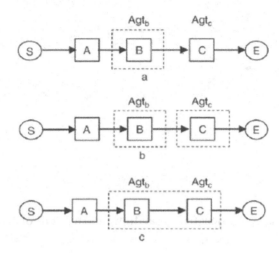

features, in which destination and departure time is the conditional features and the number of persons as well as the car-renting fare is the real batch processing functional features.

Definition 2.1 An activity A is batch-efficient in respect to an output parameter y if the value of y is a function of the input parameter x which represents the number of objects processed in a batch, and y increases less than proportional to x when the value of x increases, that is, if the *Condition-1* formally defined in Section 3.2 (III-B) is satisfied.

We have also defined three types of batch processing pattern in workflow (Liu 2007), which are shown in Figure 2. For simplicity and clarification, let us suppose there are only three activities A, B and C in a workflow W. The area encircled by dotted line is called BPA (Batch Processing Area), which means that the activities there are batch-efficient activities. The words shown above those activity boxes stand for agents that execute the corresponding activities. Supposing W has two instances, W1 and W2. In Figure 2a, only activity B is batch-efficient activity. In Figure 2b, both activity B and C are batch-efficient activity. But they are independent of each other, i.e., they possess different batch processing features. Situation in Figure 2c is different from that in Figure 2b. Activities B and C in W will employ the same grouping strategies, i.e., they have the same batch processing features.

Data and its Structure

Just like workflow mining, mining of batch processing features in workflow also starts from pure workflow logs. It can also start from transaction logs of information system using transactional and embedded workflow systems such as ERP (Enterprise Resource Planning), CRM (Customer Relationship Management). However, what we need to emphasize is that here we only consider the situation that the WfMS which has not deployed batch processing mechanism, e.g. the logs shown in Table 1. As for the situation where the WfMS which has deployed batch mechanism, the logs will be different to that of Table 1. The mining method is different and it is investigated in another paper. The following definitions illustrate the data elements as well as its structure we will employ.

Figure 3. An example workflow process: ProcA

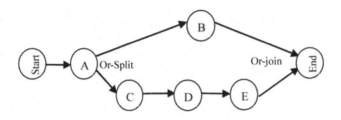

Definition 2.2: The relevant data (denoted as dataflow) and the control data (denoted as control flow) of a process, which are used or generated by workflow enactment, are available in workflow logs.

According to (Aalst 2004), control data of a process, i.e. Event logs, is in workflow logs. According to WfMC, input and output data of workflow activities are all workflow relevant data and execution provenances of work-flow activities such as execution sequence and so on are all workflow control data. Therefore, the dataflow and control flow can be obtained from workflow logs.

To illustrate the principle of batch pattern mining from workflow log, we take the process, namely *ProcA*, in Figure 3 as an example. The data in workflow logs we will employ is shown in Table 2, and Table 3. Table 2 shows some of the workflow control data, i.e. control flow and Table 3 shows the workflow relevant data, i.e. dataflow. This log contains 10 cases of *ProcA*. The log shows that for 9 cases (1,2,3,4,5,6,7,8,9), the task *A, C, D, E* has been executed. For the tenth case, only two tasks are executed: tasks *A, B*. For simplicity, we only show part of the dataflow of *ProcA* in Table 2.3, i.e. task *C, D, E*. In Table 2.3, x_i, y_i represents the input and output parameters of an activity respectively. There are 4 input parameters and 3 output parameters in Activity *C*, 3 and 1 in Activity *D* and 2 and 1 in Activity *E*. The Dataflow for activity *C, D, E* of the first 9 cases (1,2,3,4,5,6,7,8,9) are with concrete data while that of the tenth case (10) is null, denoted by "-", in Table 3. The input parameters x_1 and x_2 of activity *C*, denoted as $C.x_1, C.x_2$, is the same as that of activity *D*, i.e. $D.x_1 D.x_2$ is functional dependent on $C.x_1 C.x_2$ (Abiteboul 1995, Yao 2008).

Outline of Our Solution

Based on the concept and patterns of batch process model of workflow in (Liu 2005, Liu 2007) and the data set described in Section 2.2 (II-B), without losing generality, the idea of our solution is to mine and recognize the batch-efficient activities, their features and batch processing areas of the process in Figure 3 from the data set with schema shown in Table 2 and Table 3. Figure 4 shows the entire framework of our solution. First, we need to exploit current existing workflow mining algorithms to obtain workflow models from workflow control flow logs as shown in Table 2. We refer to the reader to W.M.P van der Aalst et al (Aalst 2004) for a thorough discussion of this algorithm. Then, we identify batch-efficient activities and their batch processing features from workflow relevant data in dataflow logs as shown in Table 3 by employing batch dependency mining algorithms, which are newly developed mining algorithms similar to that of mining functional dependencies from data (Yao 2008, Huhtala 1999). They are the core algorithms of our approach and the theoretical foundation will be illustrated in Section III.

Table 2. The Control Flow log of ProcA in Figure 3

Process case identifier	Activity case identifier	Process case identifier	Activity case identifier
Case 1	Activity A	Case 5	Activity D
Case 1	Activity C	Case 6	Activity D
Case 2	Activity A	Case 8	Activity A
Case 3	Activity A	Case 4	Activity D
Case 1	Activity D	Case 4	Activity E
Case 3	Activity C	Case 9	Activity A
Case 4	Activity A	Case 5	Activity E
Case 1	Activity E	Case 7	Activity C
Case 2	Activity C	Case 6	Activity E
Case 3	Activity D	Case 8	Activity C
Case 4	Activity C	Case 9	Activity C
Case 2	Activity D	Case 7	Activity D
Case 2	Activity E	Case 8	Activity D
Case 3	Activity E	Case 10	Activity A
Case 5	Activity A	Case 7	Activity E
Case 6	Activity A	Case 8	Activity E
Case 5	Activity C	Case 9	Activity D
Case 6	Activity C	Case 10	Activity B

Based on batch-efficient activities and their batch processing features, batch processing areas and batch processing patterns in workflow models are discovered finally.

Table 3: The Dataflow log of ProcA in Figure 3

Workflow case identifier	Activity A	Activity C					Activity D				Activity E			Activity B
		Inputs			Outputs		Inputs			Output	Inputs		Output	
		x_1	x_2	x_4	y_1	y_2	x_1	x_2	x_3	y_2	x_1	x_2	y_1	
t_1	...	A1	B1	1	50	100	A1	B1	1	10	C1	1	150	...
t_2	...	A2	B2	2	200	600	A2	B2	2	60	C3	2	250	...
t_3	...	A1	B1	1	50	100	A1	B1	1	10	C2	2	250	...
t_4	...	A1	B3	1	45	90	A1	B3	1	9	C1	4	500	...
t_5	...	A3	B1	4	50	130	A3	B1	4	13	C3	6	700	...
t_6	...	A2	B1	2	50	110	A2	B1	2	11	C5	4	500	...
t_7	...	A1	B3	1	45	90	A1	B3	1	9	C7	6	700	...
t_8	...	A3	B1	3	50	120	A3	B1	3	12	C8	3	350	...
t_9	...	A1	B3	3	45	110	A1	B3	3	11	C9	1	150	...
t_{10}	AI	-	-	-	-	-	-	-	-	-	-	-	-	BI

Figure 4. The basic idea of mining batch processing patterns in workflow

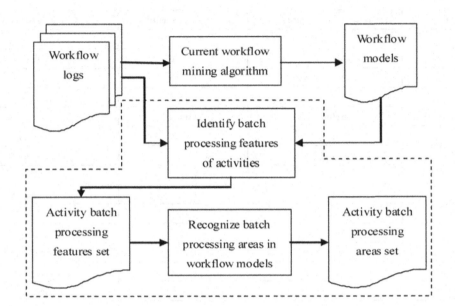

THEORETICAL FOUNDATION

To identify batch-efficient activities and their batch processing features from workflow relevant data in dataflow logs, we introduce a specific type of functional dependency, namely batch dependency. The theoretical foundation as well as its mining algorithms will be analyzed and investigated at below. It likes that of discovering functional dependencies in databases.

Functional Dependency

Functional dependencies are relationship between attributes of a database relation: a functional dependency states that the value of an attribute is uniquely determined by the values of some other attributes. Given a relation R, the attribute B is said to be functionally dependent on attribute A if at every instant of time each value of A has no more than one value of B associated with it. More formally, if two rows in R agree no the A column, they must agree on the B column. For example, in an address database, zip code is determined by city and street address. The discovery of functional dependencies from relations has received considerable interest (Abiteboul 1995, Yao 2008, Huhtala 1999).

Table 4. A relation r on XY={$x_1, ..., x_n, y_1, ..., y_m$}

	x_1	x_2	...	x_n	y_1	y_2	...	y_m
	$t_1(x_1)$	$t_1(x_2)$	...	$t_1(x_n)$	$t_1(y_1)$	$t_1(y_2)$	...	$t_1(y_n)$
$r =$	.	.	.	.	.	.	.	.
	$t_k(x_1)$	$t_k(x_2)$	...	$t_k(x_n)$	$t_k(y_1)$	$t_k(y_2)$	...	$t_k(y_n)$

Definition 3.1 (Huhtala 1999) Let *r(U)* be a relation and $X, Y \subseteq U$. A *functional dependency (FD)* is a constraint, denoted $X \rightarrow Y$. The *FD* $X \rightarrow Y$ is satisfied by *r(U)* if every two tuples $t_i, t_j \in r(U)$ that $t_i[X] = t_j[Y]$ also have $t_i[Y] = t_j[Y]$. In a FD $X \rightarrow Y$, we refer to X as the *antecedent* and *Y* as the *consequent*.

Batch Dependency

Let *Y = F(X)* be a function, where *X* be a set of discrete variables called *inputs*, $X = (x_1, x_2, ..., x_n)$, *Y* be a set of variables called *outputs*, $Y = (y_1, y_2, ..., y_m)$ and *F* is a mapping relation from *X* to *Y*. The union $X \cup Y$ is sometimes simply denoted as *XY*. Each inputs or outputs has a finite domain, denoted *dom(x_i)*, *dom(y_j)*, representing the values that x_i, y_i can take on respectively. For a subset $D = (x_i, ..., x_j)$ of *X*, we write *dom(D)* for the Cartesian product of the domains of the individual inputs in *X*, namely, $dom(D) = dom(d_i) \times ... \times Dom(d_j)$. For a subset $V = (y_i, ..., y_j)$ of *Y*, we write *dom(V)* for the Cartesian product of the domains of the individual inputs in *Y*, namely, $dom(V) = dom(v_i) \times ... \times Dom(v_j)$. A relation *r* on *XY*, written *r(XY)*, is a finite set of mapping $t \in r(XY)$, $t[x_i]$ must be in *dom(x_i)*, $1 \le i \le n$, $t[y_j]$ must be in *dom(y_j)*, $1 \le j \le m$, where $t[x_i], t[y_j]$ denotes the value obtained by restricting the mapping *t* to x_i, y_j. A relation *r* on $XY = \{x_1, x_2, ..., x_n, y_1, y_2, ..., y_m\}$ is depicted in Table 4. Each mapping *t* is called a tuple and $t[x_i]$ and $t[y_j]$ are called the x_i-value, y_j-value of *t* respectively. To simplify notation, we may write the singleton set $\{x_i\}$, $\{y_j\}$ as the single attribute x_i, y_i and the set of attributes $\{x_1, ..., x_i\}$, $\{y_1, ..., y_j\}$ as $x_1, ..., x_i, y_1, ..., y_j$.

Definition 3.2 Let *r(XY)* be a relation and $x \in X, y \in Y$. A batch *dependency (BD)* is a constraint, denoted *BD* $x \rightarrow y$. The *BD* $x \rightarrow y$ is satisfied by *r(XY)* if every two tuples $t_i, t_j \in r(XY)$, that have *Condition 1* satisfied. In a *BD* $x \rightarrow y$, we also refer to *x* as the *antecedent* and *y* as the *consequent*.

$$Condition\ 1 = \begin{cases} t_i[y] / t_j[y] > t_i[x] / t_j[x], & t_i[x] < t_j[x]; \\ t_i[y] = t_j[y], & t_i[x] = t_j[x]; \end{cases}$$

Definition 3.3 Let *r(XY)* be a relation and $x \in X, y \in Y, D \subseteq X - x$. A *conditional batch dependency (CBD)* is a constraint, denoted *CBD* $x\big|_D \rightarrow y$. The *CBD* $x\big|_D \rightarrow y$ is satisfied by *r(XY)* if every two tuples $t_i, t_j \in r(XY)$, $t_i[D] = t_j[D]$ that have also *Condition 1* satisfied on *r(XY)*. We refer attribute set *D* as the batch dependency condition, i.e., if t_i, t_j agree on attribute set *D*, *Condition 1* will be satisfied on *r(XY)*.

Theorem 3.1 Let $x \in X, y \in Y, D \subseteq X - x$. If $x \rightarrow y$ then $x\big|_D \rightarrow y$.

Proof. By $x \rightarrow y$, we have, for every two tuples $t_i, t_j \in r(XY)$, that have *condition 1*. Then for every two tuples $t_i, t_j \in r(XY)$, if $t_i[D] = t_j[D]$, we also have *condition 1*, which gives $x\big|_D \rightarrow y$.

Example 3.1 Consider the example relation *r(XY)* shown in Table 5. We have *BD* $x_3 \rightarrow y_3$ and *CBD* $x_4\big|_{x_1 x_2} \rightarrow y_2$.

Definition 3.4 Let $v \in XY$, the attribute *v* is called numerical type, denoted *Numerical*, if *dom(v)* is a numerical and can be computed mathematically. Otherwise, *v* is called Label type, denoted *Label*, if *v* is not a numerical attributes.

Table 5. An example relation

TID	x_1	x_2	x_3	x_4	y_1	y_2	y_3
t_1	A1	B1	1	1	50	100	15
t_2	A2	B2	2	2	200	600	25
t_3	A1	B1	2	1	50	100	25
t_4	A1	B3	4	1	45	90	50
t_5	A3	B1	6	4	50	130	70
t_6	A2	B1	4	2	50	110	50
t_7	A1	B3	6	1	45	90	70
t_8	A3	B1	3	3	50	120	35
t_9	A1	B3	1	3	45	110	15

Example 3.2 Take Table 5 as an example. The attributes x_1, x_2 is with type *Label* and x_3,x_4,y_1,y_2,y_3 is with type *Numerical*.

The BD_Mine Algorithm

In this section, the BD_Mine algorithm for finding BDs from data is described. Algorithm 3.1 shows the BD_Mine Algorithm. In Algorithm 3.1, *obtainBD()* is to decide for $x_i \in X, y_j \in Y$ that whether $x_i \rightarrow y_j$ is satisfied by *r(XY)* or not. The *r(S)* in Algorithm 3.1 is the projection of x_i, y_j on relation *r(XY)*.

Algorithm 3.1: BD_Mine(r(XY))

```
Input: A relation r(XY) over XY ={ x₁,x₂,…,xₙ, y₁,y₂,…,yₘ}
Output: A set BF of batch dependencies over r(XY).
BF =∅; r(S) =∅;
For each Numerical type x₁∈ X         // We only consider the numerical type of attributes
    For each Numerical type yⱼ∈ Y
        r(S) = π_{xi,yi}r(XY);        // r(S) is the projection of x₁, yⱼ on relation r(XY)
        if obtainBD(r(S)) is true     // S = {x₁, yⱼ}
            BF = BF ∪ xᵢ → yⱼ;
        Endif
    Endfor
Endfor
Return (BF);
```

Algorithm 3.2 shows the *obtainBD()* algorithm, which uses *condition 1* as the criteria to judge if $x \rightarrow y$ is satisfied on r(S). The time complexity of Algorithm 3.2 is $O(l^2)$. So that of Algorithm 3.1 is $O(m \times n \times l^2)$, where *n* is the number of input attributes, *m* output attributes and *l* the number of rows (records) in *r(XY)*.

Algorithm 3.2: obtainBD(r(S))

```
Input: A relation r(S) over r(S) ={x,y}
Output: the result of batch dependency of x → y. If it is satisfied, true, otherwise
false.
i = 1; j = 1;
l = the number of rows in relation r(S), i.e., in r(XY);
For (i = 1, i≤l; i++)
    For (j = 1, j≤l; j++)
        If Condition 1 is not satisfied
                Return(False);
        Endif
    Endfor
Endfor
Return (True);
```

Example 3.3: Take Table 5 as an example, the batch dependencies which are satisfied are $BDs = \{x_3 \to y_3\}$.

CBD_Mine Algorithm

In this section, the CBD_Mine algorithm for finding CBDs in data is described. To find CBDs, we need to know all the subsets of input attributes X. Let $X = \{A,B,C,D\}$, the power set of X, denoted as $P(X)$, is that shown in Figure 5. $P(X) = \{A, B, C, D, AB, AC, ..., ABCD\}$. We need first compute and get the partition of every s in $P(X)$ over $r(XY)$, denoted as $\prod_s$. For example, in Table 5, $\prod_{x_1} =\{\{t_1,t_3,t_4,t_7,t_9\}, \{t_2, t_6\}, \{t_5,t_8\}\}$, $\prod_{x_2} =\{\{t_1,t_3,t_5,t_6,t_8\}, \{t_2\}, \{t_4,t_7,t_9\}\}$, $\prod_{x_1 x_2} =\{\{t_1,t_3\}, \{t_2\}, \{t_4,t_7,t_9\}, \{t_5,t_8\}, \{t_6\}\}$. Algorithm 3.3 shows the CBD_Mine Algorithm. When computing each $x_i \to y_j$, it first uses pruning algorithm, *Prune()*, to delete the unnecessary conditions to reduce the search space. Then for each condition, we partition the relation $r(XY)$ according to this condition into a partition set $\prod$. The *CalculatePartition* algorithm accesses the relation to calculate the actual partition of $r(XY)$ on px. We refer to the reader to Huhtala et al (Huhtala 1999) for a thorough discussion of this algorithm. Finally, we compute if in every equivalence class the batch dependency is satisfied. If it is true, we have the result, *CBD* $x_i\big|_{px} \to y_j$.

Algorithm 3.3: CBD_Mine(*r(XY), BF*)

```
Input:  A relation r(XY) over XY ={x_1,x_2,...,x_n, y_1,y_2,...,y_m}, a set of batch-dependencies on r(XY).
Output: A set CBF of conditional batch dependencies over r(XY).
CBF  =∅ ; r(S) =∅ ; PX=PS=∅ ;
For each Numerical type x_i ∈ X        // We only consider the numerical type of attributes
    For each Numerical type y_j ∈ Y
        PX = Prune(P(X), BF, x_i, y_j);        //P(X) is the set of all the subset of X
```

```
For each px ∈ PX
        PS = calculatePartition(px, r(XY));        // PS = ∏px
        CBD_Flag = True;
        For each ps ∈ PS                // ps is one of the equivalence class in PS
            r(S) = πxi,yi σps r(XY);
```

// π, σ represents projection and selection from a relation respectively. r(S) is the projection of x_i, y_j on //relation r(XY) whose tuples belong to ps

```
                If (Not obtainBD(r(S)))        // Get batch dependency status in the
                equivalence class ps
                    CBD_Flag = False;
                        //The batch dependency in the equivalence in ps is
                        not satisfied.
                    Exit for; // Exit from this For loop
                Endif
        Endfor
        If (CBD_Flag)
            CBF = CBF ∪ xi|px → yj;
                        // yj is batch dependent on xi at condition px on r(XY)
        Endif
    Endfor
  Endfor
Endfor
Return (CBF);
```

Algorithm 3.4 shows the prune algorithm. Function *antecedent()* and *consequence()* are used to get the antecedent and consequence of a *BD*. Let s = $x \rightarrow y$, the result of *consequence(s)* is y and antecedent(s) is x. Line 2 to Line 7 in Algorithm 3.4 is to get the attributes need to be deleted from *P(X)*. Line 2 is to delete the current computing attribute in *X*. Line 3 to Line 7 is to delete the attributes according to

Figure 5. A set containment lattice for X={A,B,C,D}

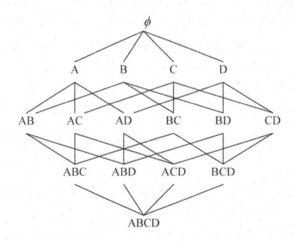

Theorem 3.1. Line 8 to Line 12 is to delete all the subsets of X who stem from any attributes in S.

Algorithm 3.4: Prune(P(X), BF, x,y)

```
Input: all the subset of X, P(X), a set of batch-dependencies, BF, on r(XY) and the cur-
rent dependency being computed, .
Output: the pruned subset of X.
1   PX = P(X); px =∅ ;
2   PruneS = { x }; // x is the antecedent of the dependency currently computed.
3   For each s ∈ BF
4       If(consequence(s)=y) //Let s=x → y,the result of consequence(s) is y and
        antecedent(s) is x.
5               S = S ∪ antecedent(s) //According to Theorem 1.
6       Endif
7   Endfor
8   For each px ∈ P(X)
9       If (Not empty (S ∩ px))
10              PX = PX - px //delete px from PX
11      Endif
12  Endfor
13  Return (PX);
```

Example 3.4: Take Table 5 as an example, the batch dependencies which are satisfied are $BDs = \{ x_3 \rightarrow y_3 \}$. When computing $x_4 \rightarrow y_2$, we only need to compute the pruned $PX = \{x_1, x_2, x_3, x_1x_2, x_1x_3, x_2x_3, x_1x_2x_3\}$. And the conditional batch dependencies which are satisfied are $CBDs = \{ x_4 \mid_{x_1x_2} \rightarrow y_2 \}$.

MINING OF BATCH PROCESSING PATTERNS IN WORKFLOW

As stated before, our solution consists of two main phases. They will be elaborated in Section 4.2 (IV-B) to 4.3 (IV-C). For simplicity and clarity, we first give out the formal definitions of related notations and concepts in Section 4.1(IV-A).

Basic Definitions

Definition 4.1 (Workflow model): A workflow model (type) W is a four-tuple, $W=<T, E, s, F>$, in which T is a set of activities, $E \subseteq (T - F) \times (T - \{s\})$ the set of their relations, $s \in T$ the starting activity, $F \subseteq T$ the set of its ending activities.

Definition 4.2 (Activity trace): Workflow activity trace, *WAT*, is a three-tuple, *WAT*=<t, RD, CD>, where t stands for activity name; *RD* dataflow trace schema of t, i.e. the input and output parameters of t, *RD* = *{Inputs; Outputs}*; *CD* control flow trance schema of t and *CD* =*{ st, et}*, in which *st* and *et* stands for the starting time and ending time of t respectively.

Definition 4.3 (Workflow trace): Workflow trace schema, *WT*, is a tuple, *WT* = *<insW, S_WAT>*, where *insW* stands for the workflow instance number, *S_WAT* the set of *WAT* of activities in *W*.

Definition 4.4 (Workflow log): Let *m* is a workflow model in an organization, *P(m*)* is all the possible workflow traces, *WAT*, of *m*, we name *L(m)*, $L(m) \subset P(m^*)$, a workflow log and use $L(m,t)$ to represent all the activity traces pertain to activity, *t*, in $L(m)$.

For example, the log of *ProcA*, *L(ProcA)*, is like that shown in Table 3 and the *L(ProcA, C)* is like the columns $x_1, x_2, x_3, x_4, y_1, y_2, y_3$ of activity *C* in Table 3.

Definition 4.5 (Batch-efficient activity): Activity *t* is a batch-efficient activity on *L(m,t)* if $\exists x \in t.Inputs, y \in t.Outputs, D \subset t.Inputs$ such that *BD* $x \to y$ or *CBD* $x|_D \to y$ is satisfied on *L(m,t)*, where *t.Inputs, t.Ouputs* stand for the input and output parameters of activity *t* respectively.

Definition 4.6 (Batch processing features): Let *t* be batch-efficient activity of a workflow model *m*. The batch processing features schema, *BF*, of *t*, is a three-tuple, *BF=<x, D, y>*, where *x*, *y* stand for the antecedent and consequence of a *BD* $x \to y$ or *CBD* $x|_D \to y$ on *L(m,t)* respectively. D is the batch dependency condition in *CBD* $x|_D \to y$ or *D ={Inputs − x}* if $x \to y$.

According to the definition of batch dependency or conditional batch dependency, the meaning of definition 4.5 is that if an activity *t* of workflow *m* is batch-efficient activity, then for any two activity traces (cases), $P_i, P_j \in L(m,t)$, execution cost of batch-processing of these two cases should be less than sum of the cost of two cases executed independently. This is the strict selection criteria for identification of batch-efficient activities. In practice, one can design or construct his/her own selection criteria for recognition.

In order to recognize batch processing areas and patterns in workflow model, we need to distinguish logical relations between batch-efficient activities, which is shown in Definition 4.7.

Definition 4.7 (Relations between workflow activities (Aalst 2007)**):** Let T is a set of workflow activities, $\sigma \in T^*$ is the activity sequence, $L(T^*)$ is the set of all the activity sequences in workflow log L. Let $a, b \in T$, we define the following expressions for identification algorithm:

1) $a >_w b \ \exists \sigma = t_1 t_2 ... t_n$ satisfying $\sigma \in L(T^*), t_i = a, t_{i+1} = b,$ in which $i \in \{1, ..., n\}$;
2) $a \to_w b$ if $a >_w b$ and $b \not>_w a$;
3) $a \#_w b$ if $a \not>_w b$ and $b \not>_w a$;
4) $a \|_w b$ if $a >_w b$ and $b \not>_w a$;
5) $a \mapsto_w b$ if $a \to_w b$ and only a in T satisfying $a \to_w b$.

In Definition 4.7, relations 1)-4) are basic ordering relations between activities. Relation 5) is used to differentiate sequence ordering activity from splitting ordering activity. Because if there is a relation $a \to_w b$ between activity *a* and activity *b*, $a \to_w c$ may also holds. That is, activity *a* is a splitting ordering activity, but sequence ordering activities are needed in batch processing area.

Definition 4.8 (Batch processing area): Let *BF(t)* denotes the set of all batch processing features of activity *t*, *TB=<$T_1, T_2, ..., T_n$>* ($n \geq 1$) is a batch processing area if:

1) $\forall T_i, T_{i+1} \in TB, T_i \mapsto_w T_{i+1}$;
2) $\forall T_i \in T, BF(T_i) \neq \varnothing$;
3) $\forall T_i, T_j \in TB, BF(T_i) \cap BF(T_j) \neq \varnothing$;

4)   If $\exists t \notin T, t \mapsto_w T_1$, then $BF(t) \cap BF(T_1) = \varnothing$;

5)   If $\exists t \notin T, T_n \mapsto_w t$, then $BF(t) \cap BF(T_n) = \varnothing$.

In definition 4.8, conditions 4) and 5) ensure there is no common batch features between an activity and a batch processing area.

Corollary 4.1: If workflow activity t is a batch-efficient activity in workflow m, then t belongs to and only belongs to a batch processing area of m.

Moreover, according to the three different dynamic batch processing patterns (referring (Liu 2007) for more details), it is easy to infer that a batch processing area itself is a batch processing activity, just like that a composite web service itself is a web service. The batch processing features of a batch processing area is the same features of the batch-efficient activities within this area. Thus, we redefine batch processing area mentioned in (Liu 2007) as Definition 11.

Definition 4.9 (Batch processing activity): Activity batch processing area is a three-tuple, *BPA=<m, T, F>*, in which m is the number of workflow model, T a batch processing area and F the set of all batch processing features of T.

Definition 4.10: Let *BF(t)* denotes set of all batch processing features of activity t, if $TB=<T_1, T_2, ..., T_n>$ ($n \geq 1$) is a batch processing area, then $BF(T_1) \cap BF(T_2) \cap ... \cap BF(T_n)$ is the set of all batch processing features of it.

Since $\forall T_i, T_j \in T$, $BF(T_i) \cap BF(T_j) \neq \varnothing$, so $BF(T_1) \cap BF(T_2) \cap ... \cap BF(T_n)$ is the set of common batch processing features of activities in T. That is, each activity in T can be batch processed according to certain feature in the set, so $BF(T_1) \cap BF(T_2) \cap ... \cap BF(T_n)$ is the set of all batch processing features of T.

Mining of Activity Batch Processing Features

Activity batch processing features are mainly inferred from the dataflow in workflow logs. According to Definition 4.5 and 4.6, if we can find out batch processing data parameters of an activity and identify an activity which deserves batch processing, we can then obtain its batch processing features. Algorithm 4.1 is designed to discover activity batch processing features.

Algorithm 4.1: Mine_BatchFeatures(L(m))

```
//Pseudo code for recognition of activity batch processing features
Input:  L(m)                // L is the log of workflow model m.
Output: F(L)                // F(L) is a set of batch processing features for each
batch-efficient activity in m, which is inferred from L(m).
F(L) =∅;
For(each activity t in m)
    BDs(t) =∅;
    Get the record set L(m,t) refer to activity t in L(m);
    L(m,t) = preprocess(L(m,t));   // delete the empty records
    Get Output data item set t.Outputs refer to activity t;
```

```
      Get Input data item set t.Inputs refer to activity t;  // get the batch dependencies
      on L(m,t)
      BDs(t) = BD_Mine(t.Inputs, t.Ouputs, L(m,t));          // get the conditional batch
      dependencies on L(m,t)
      BDs(t) = BDs(t) ∪ CBD_Mine(t.Inputs, t.Outputs, L(m,t));
      If (not empty BDs(t))    // denotes that activity t is batch-efficient activity
      according to definition 4.5
          F(L) = F(L) ∪ obtainBatchFeatures(BDs(t)); // Obtain batch Features of activity t
      Endif
End for
Return F(L);
```

$$x_3 \mid_{x_1 x_2} \to y_2 \; x_3 \mid_{x_1 x_2} \to y_1 \; x_3 \mid_{x_1 x_2} \to y_2 \; x_3 \mid_{x_1 x_2} \to y_1 \; x_2 \mid_{x_1} \to y_1 \; x_3 \mid_{x_1 x_2} \to y_1 \; x_2 \mid_{x_1} \to y_1$$

Example 4.1 Take Figure 3 and the data in Table 3 as an example, the batch-efficient activities discovered are {C, D, E}. The batch dependencies for each activity and their batch processing features are shown in Table 6.

Recognition of Batch Processing Areas in Workflow

Based on the results of Section 4.2, it is easy to find out the batch processing activities, i.e, if batch processing features of an activity returned by Algorithm 4.1 are not empty, it is batch-efficient activity. Batch processing areas can also be easily obtained. Thus, batch processing areas mentioned in Section 2.1(II-A) can be set automatically. Algorithm 4.2 shows the recognition approach.

Algorithm 4.2: Find_BPA(m, L(m), F(L))

```
//Pseudo code for recognition of batch processing areas in workflow
Input:  L(m), m, F(L)       // M is a set of workflow models, L is a workflow log. F(L)
is the set obtained from Algorithm 4.1.
Output: T(L)                // T(L) is the set of all batch processing areas in M in-
ferred from L and F(L).
Infer batch processing activity set mSet from m and F(L);
```

$$X = \{(A,B) | A \subseteq mSet \land B \subseteq mSet \land \forall a \in A \forall b \in B$$
$$a \to_w b \land \forall a_1, a_2 \in A a_1 \#_w a_2 \land \forall b_1, b_2 \in B b_1 \#_w b_2\};$$
$$Y = \{(A,B) | (A,B) \in X \land \forall b \in (mSet - \{A\}) b \not\to_w B\}; //\text{that is,}$$
$$Y = \{(A,B) | (A,B) \in X \land A \mapsto B\}$$

Table 6. The batch dependencies discovered

Activity	Is batch-deserved?	Batch dependencies discovered		Batch Features		
		No	Batch dependencies	Antecedent	Condition	Consequence
A	No	0	-	-	-	-
B	No	0	-	-	-	-
C	Yes	1	CBD $x_3\big|_{x_1 x_2} \to y_2$	C.x_3	C.x_1C.x2	C.y_2
D	Yes	1	CBD $x_3\big|_{x_1 x_2} \to y_1$	C.x_3	D.x_1D.x_2	D.y_1
E	Yes	1	CBD $x_2\big|_{x_1} \to y_1$	E.x_2	E.x_1	E.y_1

```
S = mSet;
For (each activity t in S)
    OS = Create_Orded_Set(t); //create an ordered set OS to represent a batch processing area
    S = S - {t};
    Get the batch processing features set F(t) of t;
    TF = F(t);  //TF represent a batch processing features set
    Do while
```
$$\left(\exists a \in S \wedge (a,t) \in Y\right)$$
```
        Get the batch processing features set F(a) of a;
        If
```
$$\left(TF \cap F(a) \neq \varnothing\right)$$
$$TF = TF \cap F(a);$$
```
        OS = Left_Insert_OS (OS, a); // insert an activity into OS and it becomes the
        leftmost item of OS
        S = S - {a}; t = a;
    End if
    End do
    Do while
```
$$\left(\exists b \in S \wedge (t,b) \in Y\right)$$
```
        Get the batch processing features set F(b) of b;
        If
```
$$\left(TF \cap F(b) \neq \varnothing\right)$$
$$TF = TF \cap F(b);$$
```
        OS = Right_Insert_OS (OS, b);   //insert an activity into OS and it becomes the
        rightmost item of OS
        S = S - {b}; t = b;
        End if
    End do
    Tm = Create_Batch_Area(m,OS,TF);   // create a batch processing area
```
$$T(L) = T(L) \cup \{Tm\};$$
```
End for
```

Explanation: Supposing input parameters of *L, m, F(L)* is available and workflow model *m*, which is the workflow shown in Figure 4, when applying Algorithm 4.2 to them, we get the following example steps.

Batch-efficient activity set of *m* can be inferred from *F(L)* and relations between activities can be described in set *X* and *Y*. To get all the batch processing areas in *m*, we construct an initial batch processing area with a single batch-efficient activity firstly, which can be denoted by *OS*. If there are some batch-efficient activities satisfied the requirements of the batch processing area, *OS*, i.e., they have the same batch processing features, all of them are added to *OS* orderly according to relations between them, which can be found in set *Y*. After that, if there are batch-efficient activities which do not belong to *OS*, we construct an initial batch processing area again. This process repeats until all batch-efficient activities have been added to one of the batch processing areas. Then all the batch processing areas in workflow model *m* are found out. So are the rest of workflow models in *M*. Therefore, all batch processing areas in workflow log *L* can be recognized.

SIMULATION EXPERIMENTS

Algorithms introduced above were demostrated by simulation experiments. All experiments were done on a Personal Computer with 3 GHz CPU of Pentium 4, 512 MB memory and 80 GB hard disk. All algorithms were implemented by Visual Basic. All data sets for experiments were obtained by means of system simulation and stored in a Microsoft SQL Server 2000 DBMS. No optimizations such as parallel processing, multithreading, caching files, or compression were used in the following tests.

Simulation Data Sets

To test the validity of our approach, we simulate the car sharing renting process mentioned in Figure 1. Figure 6 shows the simulation model.

We apply Visual Basic 6.0 and Microsoft SQL Server 2000 to implement this simulation model. Based on the simulation model, the runtime data of activities (workflow log) are obtained through simulation operation and are exported to a SQL Server 2000 database. In our implementation, there are some assumptions while taking the simulation. 1) The arrival rate of sharing-car application obeys Poisson distribution with parameter λ ; 2) the maximum number of passengers of cars are equal, i.e., the accommodation difference of cars is ignored; 3) the number of cars is equal for each destination. Each destination has and only has a car and the renting application is denied if the car has set out for the destination; 4) the departing time is ignored, i.e., only a car is available, one can depart out. Besides, for passengers preferring to share cars, at least two passengers are required to set off a car and for passengers preferring to ride a car exclusively, they can depart out whenever a car is available; 5) riding time and renting fare are respectively set by function *f1 =A*f(destination)* and function *f2=B*f(destination)-C*batched*f(destination)*, where function *f(destination)* is to transform the name of destination to a OoS value of distance so as to be convenient for computation. The initial data settings of our experiments are as follows:

1) the value of parameter λ refers to application arrival: 0.5
2) the number of workflow cases: 500, 1000, 2000, 4000, 8000

Figure. 6. Simulation model for the car sharing renting process

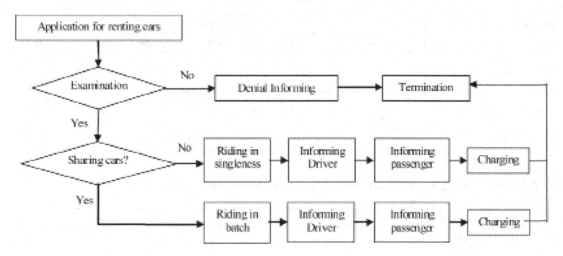

3) the number of destinations: 8
4) the maximum number of passengers in cars: 4
5) the value of parameter A in function $f1$: 0.1 second
6) the value of parameter B in function $f2$: 10 dollars
7) the value of parameter C in function f2: -0.2, -0.4, 0, 0.2, 0.4
8) function $f(destination)$: $f=1+ random()\ mod\ 10$
9) the destination distribution in passenger's renting applications: $1 + random()\ mod\ 8$
10) passengers' willingness of sharing a car in the renting applications: $random()\ mod\ 2$

Experiments Analysis

With these simulation data sets generated in 5.1, Algorithm 4.1 and 4.2 can be verified and evaluated by experiments. Workflow model of renting cars is assumed to be available for simplifying the experiment. The evaluation function for the execution cost of "Renting Car" activity in Figure 1 considers both the riding time and riding fare, while those of the rest activities in Figure 1 are all set as E = 1, i.e., their execution cost are equal.

Experiment 1: Identifying activity batch processing features

Table 6 shows the execution time of Algorithm 4.1 when simulated workflow cases and riding fare parameter, C, are under a certain level. The number of batch processing features recognized by Algorithm 4.1 and that of actual batch processing features are shown in Table 7. It is shown from the experiments that batch processing features being recognized by Algorithm 4.1 are not exact equal to the actual ones when the number of workflow cases in workflow log is small, e.g., when the number of workflow cases is 100 and C = -0.2, Algorithm 4.1 did not find out a batch processing feature. However, when the number of workflow cases increase, we can find out all batch processing features.

Experiment 2: Recognition of batch processing areas in workflow

Table 8 describes execution time of Algorithm 4.2 when Algorithm 4.1 has been executed and its outputs are available. Table 9 describes number of batch processing areas recognized by Algorithm 4.2 and that of actual batch processing areas. It is shown from the experiments that Algorithm 4.2 runs fast

Table 7. Execution time of Algorithm 4.1 (Time unit: second)

Riding fare parameter, C	The number of workflow cases				
	100	1000	2000	4000	8000
-0.4	10.3	38.8	109.4	192.8	286.4
-0.2	9.4	41.3	115.3	204.4	304.9
0	9.9	40.9	108.5	188.5	297.7
0.2	26.4	129.5	438.2	1355.7	4011.2
0.4	27.1	133.2	429.9	1387.1	4004.9

Table 8. Count of workflow batch processing features obtained by Algorithm 4.1

Riding fare parameter, C		-0.4	-0.2	0	0.2	0.4
Number of actual batch processing features		1	1	1	2	2
Number of batch processing features recognized by Algorithm 4.1	100	1	1	1	2	2
	1000	1	1	1	2	2
	2000	1	1	1	2	2
	4000	1	1	1	2	2
	8000	1	1	1	2	2

when the number of batch process features is small. Although the speed of Algorithm 4.2 is affected by the number of workflow cases a lot, it can still find out all batch process areas in a workflow model effectively.

RELATED WORK

The idea of batch processing can be traced back to operating systems. Traditional workflow model does not support batch processing. Our previous work (Liu 2005, Liu 2007) introduce it into the field of workflow for the first time. In (Liu 2005, Liu 2007), three types of workflow batch processing patterns are identified and implementation of batch processing in workflow is investigated. Van der Aalst mentions the workflow batch processing in his latest paper (Georgakopoulos 1995), too. However, those work did not consider the automatic identification of batch-efficient activities, their batch processing features as well as the type of batch processing patterns in workflow.

A strictly related but quite different data mining problem in WfMS context is workflow mining. It is a novel modeling method, which can automatically derive workflow model from workflow logs or from transaction logs of information system using transactional systems such as ERP, CRM. With workflow mining, we can obtain an objective workflow model without misunderstanding from perceptions or normative behaviors of different designers. Moreover, workflow mining can provide us a good understanding of existed processes.

Table 9. Executing time of Algorithm 4.2 (Time unit: second)

Riding fare parameter, C	Number of batch processing features recognized by Algorithm 4.1	The number of workflow cases			
		1000	2000	4000	8000
-0.4	1	0.013	0.016	0.014	0.014
-0.2	1	0.015	0.013	0.011	0.017
0	1	0.010	0.014	0.017	0.015
0.2	2	1.19	2.16	4.13	7.15
0.4	2	1.08	2.13	3.73	6.81

Table 10. Count of workflow batch processing areas obtained by Algorithm 4.2

Riding fare parameter, C		-0.4	-0.2	0	0.2	0.4
Number of batch processing features obtained from Algorithm 1		1	1	1	2	2
Number of actual batch processing features		1	1	1	1	1
Number of batch processing areas recognized by Algorithm 4.2	1000	1	1	1	1	1
	2000	1	1	1	1	1
	4000	1	1	1	1	1
	8000	1	1	1	1	1

The idea of process mining was first investigated in field of software development (Cook 1998). Since Agrawal et al (Agrawal 1998) first considered mining of workflow models in 1998, a lot of work on the workflow mining has been done and a number of workflow mining approaches have been proposed. Some typical ones are α algorithm based on WF-net (workflow-net) in (Aalst 2004), induction algorithm based on SAG (stochastic activity graph) and approach of multi-stage procedure based on block- structured workflow model in (Herbst 2004) and so on. However, because batch processing is not offered in traditional workflow model, current workflow mining approaches do not consider it yet.

The discovery of functional and conditional functional dependencies and from relations has received considerable interest (Yao 2008, Huhtala 1999, Bravo 2007, Bohannon 2007). Batch dependency, to some extent, is like the functional and conditional functional dependencies, but with different criteria, meaning and purposes. The research results of inferring functional and conditional functional dependencies from relation are helpful for batch dependency discovery.

The first contribution of our work is that we observed the batch processing recognition problem in workflow. The second contribution of this work is that we proposed a new kind of functional dependency, batch dependency, and designed effective and efficient algorithms to automatically mine these batch dependencies. Using batch dependency inference system, we can finally mine batch-efficient activities, their batch processing features as well as batch processing areas from control and relevant data in workflow logs so as to improve the efficiency of business processes.

CONCLUSION AND FUTURE WORK

The application of batch processing workflow systems in reality need to model and set batch process parameters and batch processing areas. This chapter has presented the question of identifying workflow batch processing features and batch-deserved activities and recognizing batch processing areas from workflow as well as other MIS execution logs automatically. Based on functional dependency inference system, this chapter proposes a new and specific kind of functional dependency, batch dependency and investigates the theoretical foundations as well as inference algorithms. After using the existing workflow mining approaches to mining out the process models, this chapter has proposed a method for recognition of batch processing features in workflow, which consists of two algorithms. One is an algorithm for identification of activity batch processing features via batch dependency inference algorithm and another is for recognition of batch processing areas. Their effectiveness is demonstrated by the simulation experiments. This new method will benefit the application of workflow systems in support of batch processing and improve its performance so as to optimize business processes.

With these contributions, we are planning to optimize the algorithms for efficiency and handling logs with noises (such as incorrect, incomplete, or exceptions) and to integrate the quality of batching processing service and into our method so that it can support user requirements of quality of service.

ACKNOWLEDGMENT

We would like to thank Dr. Jinmin Hu, Dr. Jinjun Chen and Dr. Jun-Lian Wang for his helpful comments and suggestions. This work was supported by National Basic Research Program of China, 973 Plan, under grant no: 2003CB317007, Natural Science Foundation of China, under grant no: 60673119.

REFERENCES

Abiteboul, S., Hull, R., & Vianu, V. (Eds.). (1995). Foundations of databases: The logical level. Boston, MA: Addison-Wesley Longman Publishing Co., Inc.

Agrawal, R., Gunopulos, D., & Leymann, F. (2008). Mining process models from workflow logs. In *Proceedings from EDBT'08: The Sixth International Conference on Extending Database Technology* (pp. 469-483).

Bohannon, P., Fan, W. F., Geerts, F., Jia, X. B., & Kementsietsidis, A. (2007). The conditional functional dependencies for data cleaning. In *Proceedings from ICDE '07: The IEEE 23rd International Conference on Data Engineering*. CA: IEEE Computer Society Press.

Bravo, L., Fan, W. F., & Ma, S. (2007). Extending dependencies with conditions. In *Proceedings from VLDB'07: The 33rd international Conference on Very Large Data Bases (Vienna, Austria, September 23 - 27, 2007). Very Large Data Bases. VLDB Endowment* (pp. 243-254).

Cook, J. E., & Wolf, A. L. (1998). Discovering models of software processes from event-based data. *ACM Transactions on Software Engineering and Methodology, 7*(3), 215–249. doi:10.1145/287000.287001

Georgakopoulos, D., Hornick, & Sheth, A. (1995). An overview of workflow management: From process modeling to workflow automation infrastructure. *Distributed and Parallel Databases, 3*(2), 119–153. doi:10.1007/BF01277643

Greco, G., Guzzo, A., Manco, G., & Sacca, D. (2005). Mining and reasoning on workflows. *IEEE Transactions on Knowledge and Data Engineering, 17*(4), 519–534. doi:10.1109/TKDE.2005.63

Herbst, J., & Karagiannis, D. (2004). Workflow mining with InWoLve. *Computers in Industry, 53*(3), 245–264. doi:10.1016/j.compind.2003.10.002

Huhtala, Y., Karkkainen, J., Porkka, P., & Toivonen, H. (1999). TANE: An efficient algorithm for discovering functional and approximate dependencies. *The Computer Journal, 42*(2), 100–111. doi:10.1093/comjnl/42.2.100

Liu, J. X., & Chen, H. Y. Hu, & J. M. (2005). A study on batch processing model in workflow. In *Proceedings from SKG '05: The 1th International Conference on Semantics, Knowledge and Grid, Beijing, CA*. IEEE.

Liu, J. X., & Hu, J. M. (2007). Dynamic batch processing in workflows: Model and implementation. *Future Generation Computer Systems, 23*(3), 338–347. doi:10.1016/j.future.2006.06.003

Luo, H. B., Fan, Y. S., & Wu, C. (2000). An overview of workflow. [in Chinese]. *Chinese Journal of Software, 11*(7), 899–907.

Pinar, S., & Ismail, H. T. (2005). An architecture for workflow scheduling under resource allocation constraints. *Information Systems, 30*, 399–422. doi:10.1016/j.is.2004.03.003

Schimm, G. (2004). Mining exact models of concurrent workflows. *Computers in Industry, 53*(2), 265–281. doi:10.1016/j.compind.2003.10.003

van der Aalst, W. M. P., Dongen, B. F., Herbst, J., Maruster, L., Schimm, G., & Weijters, A. J. M. M. (2003). Workflow mining: A survey of issues and approaches. *Data & Knowledge Engineering, 47*(1), 237–267. doi:10.1016/S0169-023X(03)00066-1

van der Aalst, W. M. P., Hofstede, A., Kiepuszewski, B., & Barros, A. P. (2003). Workflow patterns. *Distributed and Parallel Databases, 14*(3), 5–51. doi:10.1023/A:1022883727209

van der Aalst, W. M. P., Michael, R., & Marlon, D. (2007). Deadline-based escalation in process-aware information systems. *Decision Support Systems, 43*, 492–511. doi:10.1016/j.dss.2006.11.005

van der Aalst, W. M. P., Weijters, T., & Maruster, L. (2004). Workflow mining: Discovering process models from event logs. *IEEE Transactions on Knowledge and Data Engineering, 16*(9), 1128–1142. doi:10.1109/TKDE.2004.47

Yao, H., & Hamilton, H. J. (2008). Mining functional dependencies from data. *Data Mining and Knowledge Discovery, 16*, 197–219. doi:10.1007/s10618-007-0083-9

KEY TERMS AND DEFINITIONS

Batch Dependency: A batch dependency is a constraint of a relation, which holds if there is a pair of attribute or attribute set of the relation satisfies some conditions.

Batch Processing Area: A batch processing area is a set of sequence ordering activities in workflow, in which activities have common batch processing feature and sequence ordering relation holds between them.

Batch Processing Feature: A batch processing feature is one or a set of input parameters of an activity in workflow, on which activities can be batch-processed.

Data Mining: Data mining is the nontrivial extraction of implicit, previously unknown, and potentially useful information from data. It is a science of extracting useful information from large data sets or databases.

Functional Dependency: Functional dependencies are relationship between attributes of a database relation: a functional dependency states that the value of an attribute is uniquely determined by the values of some other attributes.

Workflow: A workflow is a partial or total automation of a business process. More abstractly, a workflow is a pattern of activity enabled by a systematic organization of resources, defined roles and mass, energy and information flows, into a work process that can be documented and learned.

Workflow Mining: Workflow mining is a novel modelling method, which can automatically derive workflow model from workflow logs or from transaction logs of information system using transactional systems such as ERP, CRM.

Section 5
Business Process Management in Practice

Chapter 22
Developing Efficient Processes and Process Management in New Business Creation in the ICT–Sector

Arla Juntunen
Helsinki School of Economics, Finland

ABSTRACT

In this study, a Finnish telecommunication company is analyzed from 1990-2007. Discussing the major developments in technology, society and firm-level decisions, this study focuses on the R&D process development and changes due to these exogenous and endogenous factors that have occurred. These factors have also caused changes in the company's competitive advantage, organizational structure, product- and service portfolio. It has required adaptation skills and capabilities to manage change in order to survive in a rapidly changing competitive environment. This chapter will describe the changes in the R&D process from the in-house development to a multi-partner R&D network. Information and Communication Technology (ICT) can be considered both a strategic catalyst and enabler of business process reengineering (BPR). In summary, the chapter discusses how a competitive advantage in mobile and multimedia business was created by efficient process changes and network management capabilities.

INTRODUCTION

Over and above the managerial challenges inherent in a business creation and development, high-tech companies face unique challenges due to technology-driven services and markets. These firms need to cope with exceptionally short product life-cycles in the face of fast changing technology and need to be able to adapt to rapidly evolving or collapsing markets (cf. McGrath 1995, 4). In high-tech and knowledge-intensive industries, R&D-partnerships, alliances and coalitions are often used for creating new technological platforms and dominant solutions (cf. e.g. Blomqvist, 2002; Möller and Rajala, 1999).

DOI: 10.4018/978-1-60566-669-3.ch022

Recent years have shown an exceptional growth in demand for inter-organizational partnerships (Achrol and Kotler, 1999; Brandenburger and Nalebuff, 1996; Gulati, 1998; Gulati et al, 2000; Hagedoorn, 1990, 1995; Spekman et al., 2000) resulting from the rapid pace of technology development along with the dispersion of knowledge and technological resources. Partnering is a process where a customer firm and supplier form strong and also broad social, economic, service and technical ties over time (Anderson and Narus, 1999). To be competitive and survive in a network economy, organizations need efficient business processes within and between the partner-organizations that are creating services or products together. In this chapter, the concept efficiency describes the efficient use of resources available and tuning business processes so that there are no overlapping tasks. Effectiveness refers to a capability to produce more innovations from R&D-process or new product versions from the product maintenance process into the commercialization process. Moreover, the capability view requires also the explanation of how processes and capabilities are linked, for example, Eisenhardt and Martin (2000, 1107) defined dynamic capabilities as the firm's "processes to integrate, reconfigure, gain and release resources," to match and even create market change.

This chapter describes a new business development based on technologies, like broadband, Internet and mobile in Finland. In addition, a pioneering actor as the case organization in this study was, it had to develop specific managerial capabilities in order to be able to fine-tune the existing processes to adjust to new demands and market changes, to launch new services and to advance from the development of basic technologies to the commercialization and marketing of information and communication technology (ICT)-solutions and home commerce (HC)-services. The business development and success was based on adaptive and adjusting R&D process and business process development. In other words, the purpose of this paper is to describe how the ability to develop efficient process management was a critical condition for success.

BACKGROUND

The case organization is Elisa. It is a leading Finnish information and communication technology (ICT) solutions company offering a comprehensive range of communications services, including voice and data services, connections to the internet, customised ICT-solutions and network operator services. Elisa is a forerunner of new mobile and content services (Elisa's annual report 2006). Its core business areas are fixed network mobile network including internet-based services (Juntunen 2005). Elisa's organization was integrated from several subsidiaries of different names into one Elisa in 2003. Elisa continued its corporate restructuring in 2006: Tikka Communications Oy and Jyväsviestintä Oy merged with Elisa. Saunalahti Group became a wholly-owned subsidiary of Elisa, and Lounet company was also acquired. Elisa's mission is to offer its customers fast, effective and secure communication telecommunication services. Its vision is to be the most attractive and effective operator. Elisa operates in Finland and in carefully selected international market areas, and provides international services in association with its partners, Vodafone and Telenor .(Elisa's annual report 2006) It seems that Elisa's customers have adopted smartphones and mobile broadband to productive use both in the home market and internationally through the Vodafone partnership. In 2007, its revenue in 2007 increased by 3.3 per cent to EUR 1,568 million. Its mobile subscription base increased by almost seven percent, that is about 170,000 subscriptions, on the previous year. CEO Veli-Matti Mattila stated on February 12th 2008: "*Customer subscription churn decreased by more than one percentage point on the previous year to approximately*

12 per cent. Elisa's market position has strengthened further, particularly with regard to 3G services and broadband. The expansion of mobile Internet was boosted by extending 3G network coverage and introducing consumer-friendly pricing and new Internet devices. Elisa also strengthened its market position in corporate customers and public sector." A major investment in 2007 was the construction of the 3G network that enables faster mobile broadband. By the end of 2007, Elisa's 3G network covered 75 per cent of Finland's population and was the best network in terms of coverage and reception. Elisa has an approximate market share of 50 per cent of 3G users. The fact that Elisa exceeded the limit of one million 3G customers proved that allowing bundling had a positive effect on Elisa's overall market development. The amount of personnel was 3,000 in 2007. (Elisa's annual report 2007)

The basic figures, i.e. turnover and the number of employees, of the case corporation changed during the timeframe of 1990-2007. The amount of employees in 1990 was approximately the same as in 2007. However, in 1990, the turnover was roughly 800 M€[1] when in 2007 the turnover was about 1,57 billion. The highest amount of employees were in the year 2000 about 8000 employees and the turnover in 2000 was about 1,500 M€. This shows the hype of ICT-sector in the middle and late 1990s and the burst of the "IT-bubble" in early 2000s with the decrease in the number of employees.

This study is originally based on a longitudinal study in 1990-2003 made in the case organization (see Juntunen, 2005). However, an additional study was made for this chapter to update the facts. In order to capture the creation dynamics of a new business and processual changes, a longitudinal study was required in a field that is characterized by technological and commercial change and uncertainty. The ICT-sector was seen to match well the requirements of both technological and commercial turbulence. A longitudinal qualitative study was chosen as the research strategy. The focal business and managers were studied over a ten year period. This time span helped to capture the evolutional and intentional development of managerial capabilities in collaborative networks leading to new business development. Research documentation in this case study consists of both information about the telecommunication industry and the case corporation, Elisa, and HCB's development during the period under study. About twenty persons representing various business units and subsidiaries of Elisa and cooperating partners were interviewed during the period of 1999-2006. The interviews concerned the R&D processes and business networking. Data gathered consists of articles, project documents, e-mails between members of the projects, memorandums concerning strategy and business plans and annual reports from the years 1990-2006. Even if majority of the material came from HCB-based sources, this does not diminish the value of the conceptualized findings, however. It can be claimed that the conceptualized findings have more general relevance, particularly for firms operating in dynamic, rapidly changing fields characterized by several interlinked technologies. It is also claimed that this relevance reaches beyond the limited historical period. Of the research method and research design, see e.g. Miles and Huberman, 1994, and Yin, 1994.

This study describes a new business and process development and changes over the years based on technologies, like broadband, Internet and mobile, and how the business group called the Home Commerce Business Group (HCB) developed their business processes, collaborative networks and organized their business. HCB launched several industry projects with its network partners to develop user interface technologies, modular technology platforms, design platforms for wireless products, service platforms for broadband technologies, 4G systems and system concepts, hardware for wireless data gathering, as well as software and for managing digital content.

The most important success factor contributing to their success in a new business development in a networked environment was the efficient management and operation of the business processes and

Figure 1. Organization of the chapter's sections.

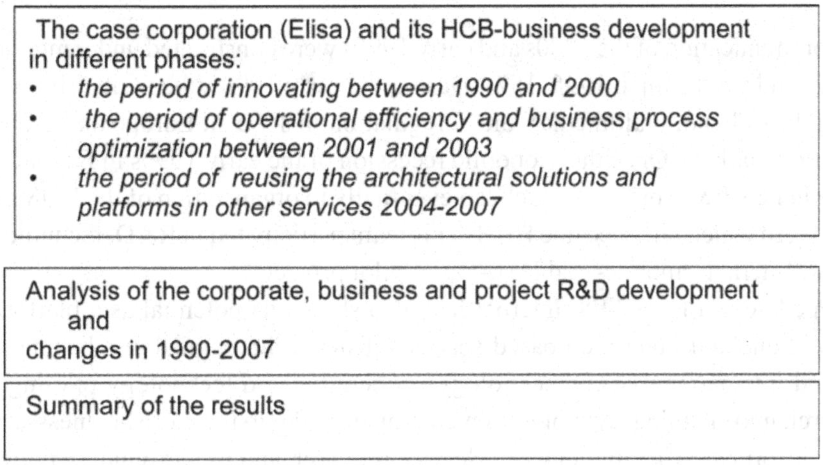

The case corporation (Elisa) and its HCB-business development in different phases:
- *the period of innovating between 1990 and 2000*
- *the period of operational efficiency and business process optimization between 2001 and 2003*
- *the period of reusing the architectural solutions and platforms in other services 2004-2007*

Analysis of the corporate, business and project R&D development and changes in 1990-2007

Summary of the results

linkages and contribution of customers in business service development In addition, to survive in the fast-changing environment the HCB as "an adaptive organization" (Hewlett Packard 2005, Radjou, et al., 2006) were more like a shifting "constellation" (Mintzberg, 1979; Toffler, 1985) that had linkages (Pinfield et al. 1974) with its decentralized organizational units. These linkages were for example linked organizational groups like functional teams, cross-functional teams, special task forces or project teams (Edgelow, 2006). The adaptive organization in this chapter is a networked organization with internal and external partners and flexible decision processes (Larraine, 2002; Möller et al. 2005; Juntunen, 2005).

BUSINESS DEVELOPMENT AND COMMERCIALIZATION

In order to answer the three research objectives, the paper will next describe the development of HCB, an Internet-driven business group within the case corporation, between 1990 and 2007. It will concentrate on the capability and business network development in the R&D process. In order to facilitate the analysis of rich, complex material the era under study was first divided into the following periods from the perspective of the development of the HCB: 1) *the period of innovating between 1990 and 2000* which described the emergence of HCB and also illustrated the developmental process of business networks and 3) *the period of operational efficiency and business process optimization between 2001 and 2003*, which described the achievement of HCB in terms of top products and profitability, and 4) *the period of reusing the architectural solutions and platforms in other services 2004-2007*. This periodization was based on the qualitatively different characteristics of the identified phases. It was also supported by Ghauri et al's (2003) suggestion that the developmental process of business networks can generally be divided into different phases.The following Figure 1 will describe the organization of the following sections in this chapter.

After the brief description of the HCB business development in different phases, this study will discuss of the R&D process development and changes in corporate, business and project levels.

Finally, the results and conclusions are made.

The Period of Innovating 1990 – 2000

European telecommunication of the 1980s and early 1990s were constructed under monopoly conditions (Beardsley, Bray and van Rooijen 1995, 157). During the early 1990s, the main drivers of change were technology (e.g. broadband, multimedia), the deregulation in 1995 in Europe and globalization of the telecommunication markets. Once the economic recession of the early 1990s in Finland was over, Elisa began investing in new R&D projects which led eventually to organization of the MuMe-team (this was the Multimedia team which later became HCB. This team participated in R&D, technology assessments and multimedia-, Internet-, mobile- and DSL-based pilot projects.

In the "e-hype" years of 1997-98, Internet had also shown its potential as a platform for telecommunication, telephone and other web-based services. Both technological and business visions drove both national and international R&D technology-cooperation and technology piloting. The results of this wider research into enabling technologies were transferred into the more business-oriented strategic dyad with a key Information Technology and Service provider, and its surrounding network, for further development.

The R&D processes were not linked with each others and each project was managed by a different project manager. There were also several concurrent researches going on in different business units. The business units were not always aware of what was researched or innovated in the other business units. The case corporation noted the waste of resources and decided to collaborate on corporate level by creating a R&D technology management group which was an internal network consisting of R&D employees and managers of different business units and also later on of different subsidiaries. The network discussed and prioritized of new R&D ideas and technologies. The competition at a business level was still ongoing and sometimes hindered the collaboration and revealing or establishing a joint-development group for a new multi-technology service idea.

The interdependency of the business and technology was also shown in the way that the corporation had several technologies tested, and in use and also different versions of same technologies. This was due to the fact that the investments of older technologies wanted to be kept for as long as possible if they were still usable and efficient. However, the newer technologies and versions were tested to see what would be the next evolution of technology architecture. Not all information systems or platforms were changed at once.

Developments in the previous period of 1990-98 resulted in the creation of a technological platform of enabling Internet and broadband technologies, which could be used in a more business-oriented development of the home-commerce business area. In Finland, this coincided with the deregulation of the telecommunication sector in 1998. During the period 1998-2000, the IT boom and rapid changes in competitive environment caused organizational changes, while new business and related projects received a higher proportion of resources and investments than they had before. R&D projects completed in 1990-2000 provided insight and direction suggesting the types of new knowledge, resources and capabilities required when constructing architecture based on the new enabling technologies.

In the case corporation, it was clearly understood that gaining competitive advantage in the new Internet- and multimedia-driven business required additional technology, business and managerial capabilities. This capability gap was perceived to be growing wider until Elisa's top management decided in 1998 to start building capabilities by establishing a product/service-oriented business unit (that later became HCB) and provided funding for further network projects. Also, it was noted that the previous information systems and processes created for them were not adequate or functional for the new technologies. Therefore, the case corporation started to renew the information systems that were created for billing and product maintenance in order to be able to maintain and sell the new technology-based products and services to their customers.

The first 'real' business network aimed at new multimedia-technology-based business was Arenanet. The driving vision behind Arenanet, a coalition of culture and technology triggered by the City of Helsinki, European Cultural City of 2000 project, was to offer broadband-based services to every single home in Finland (Lehmus, 1999). The ambitious objectives of "Helsinki Arena 2000" were: to create a virtual Helsinki, a next generation multimedia network environment for Finland's capital city, to provide a forum for citizens, and a place where culture and business could meet (Salmi, 1999; Tenhovuori, 1996). By joining this network, the case corporation was aiming to create competitive advantage in this area of e-business, to strengthen both its role and its image, and to expand its customer base. It was a deliberate strategic move to combine new technological knowledge with new business development. Learning new technologies, integrating and implementing them into a business context underlay the main learning race within the ICT-sector during the 1990s. The capabilities developed around these new technologies and the businesses based on them were the source for HCB's competitive advantage. After this Arenanet-business network, the new business group (HCB) started several other ones during 1998-2003 with growing success rate and customer count.

A key technology alliance in the development of the platforms and R&D process development was made with Nokia in 1999-2000. It assisted the case corporation to identify the capabilities needed in process development and how to organize the concurrent R&D projects. A particular goal in the alliance was to fine-tune product concepts generated from earlier R&D projects. These ideas related to educational platforms in the Internet, self-learning in the Internet, home automation, data security issues, and VOIP-technology[2]. The case corporation's project group also tried to establish a best practice method, with which the case corporation could manage either several concurrent R&D processes in different business units or concurrent R&D projects, concerning multiple products and services, within the case corporation (Hölttä 2000). Elisa's subprojects in the alliance were not only related to the learning and transferal of technology but also the integration of multiple technologies and platforms. As part of these projects, several technologies were tested: data security, in particular PKI[3], VOIP-technology, Gigabit-Ethernet network technology, and e-learning environments which led to the establishment of Efodi in 2000. Efodi was "the e-learning space" and Elisa's e-learning platform (Hölttä, 1999). Also, the initial Home Commerce business platform ideas were developed during this time. Mainly because of these Silicon Hill alliances and their subprojects, resource allocation and product development in the case corporation shifted from separate sequential to parallel R&D processes.

Concurrent R&D processes were seen in various research-lines, sets of R&D projects in a common area, including: *Billing in the Internet and e-payment, multimedia*-technology-related and *Home networks and service.* In these research lines, there was both parallel progress as well as sequential continuity in R&D projects during the years 1998 to 2000 (see Figure 2). The results-based management style of the case corporation insisted on tuning processes and a certain number of product-launches per year, both of which caused resultant pressure on strategic business units' R&D.

Besides the R&D synchronization within the case corporation and with the business goals, the Figure 2 also shows the interdependency development of the R&D projects especially also in different business and technology areas.

*Figure 2. R&D process change in 1990-2003 © [2005] [**Arla Juntunen**]. Used with permission.*

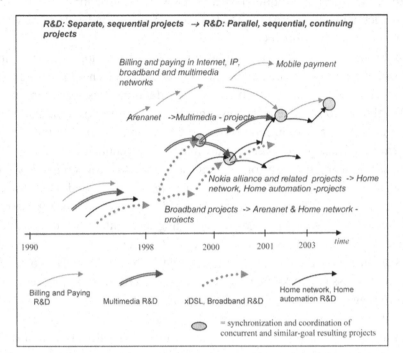

The Stabilization Phase in 2001-2003

The years 1998-2000 were time of the 'IT-boom' and "e-hype" in Finland as well as in Europe. During that time, the case corporation's R&D was allowed to test and fine-tune their products to be perfect in every way possible. However, the years 2000-2003, showed unpredictable economic situation in the ICT-sector, and R&D- investments were expected to have a short pay-back time and there was no extra time to spend in perfectionism in product designs. The years 2001 to 2003 showed the impact of exogenous factors, such as the burst of the "IT-bubble" and associated declining profits in the ICT-sector, in the case corporation in many ways. The impacts seen included:

- *at a business level:* termination of unpredictable business, concentration on core and profitable products and services, the pruning of non-core business, the analysis of future business possibilities and the investment in promising technological and business areas,
- *at the organizational level:* the retrenchment of employees, the restructuring of the organization, and
- *customer service* was considered to be more important than in the years of rapid growth and expansion seen during 1998 to 2000.

The reduction of investment in R&D affected HCB to the extent that the new product development was terminated and HCB instructed to concentrate on their core business and key products like ADSL and Kotiportti™. Processes and interfaces of services underwent tuning to increase efficiency. Senior management's key motivation in investing in the new Home Commerce related business projects was because they saw these as a way to enhance current businesses and create new business opportunities. Organizational restructuring affected so that a couple of new emerging businesses were merged to HCB.

The formation of internal networks to focus on certain R&D-areas of the business had changed within the case corporation. Whereas, in the 1990s, R&D was focusing on single technology pilots, in 2001-2003, the focus was on business issues, and technologies related to that business.

Reuse of the Architectural Solutions and Platforms in 2004-2007

In 2004-2007 the reuse of the architectural solutions and platforms were the main focus, thus, saving innovating resources and allowing the new services and products a faster development to commercialization time. The amount of employees were decreasing to the level of 1990s. At the same time, the corporate profitability was growing. The new services required faster mobile networks, new bundled services and reuse of existing solutions and architectural designs. It resulted to decreasing customer churn and growing number of subscriptions in mobile network.

The Analysis of the Corporate R&D and Process Changes in 1990-2003

The corporate R&D process (Maanavilja, 2001) is described in Figure 3. It illustrates the Research Center's role as a key member in corporate R&D helping business units to put new ideas into practice.

The Research Center studied future trends, convergence issues and the restructure of the markets. It undertook R&D trials in conjunction with business units. R&D-pilots were carried out with a customer-centric focus. The R&D process followed the corporate vision and strategy. Business units obeyed their own business strategies and objectives in their own R&D. The results of the corporate R&D included the creation of new products or businesses.

Figure 4 describes the process from the project point of view. During the 1980 and early 1990s, the R&D –process remained in-house. The following paragraphs will describe the phases of the process illustrated in the figure 4. This model can be compared to the stage-gate model of different managerial decisions in each phase (cf. product development institute and stage-gate model).

1. Idea and innovation -collection and processing included a detailed description of an idea. The outcomes from this phase included potential R&D-project ideas but also were ideas, which while not exactly suitable for R&D-projects, might for example be related to business process tuning or increasing production efficiency.

Some ideas were left on hold due to the fact that technology was either not yet 'mature', that is sufficiently developed. In many cases it was deemed too expensive in light of the commercialization process or R&D-funds available to start to research on a particular idea.

2. The initial research phase included both an appraisal of the possibilities and a market study of the specific idea/innovation. This phase included the investigation of patents, an evaluation of technology, assessment of marketing possibilities and an estimation of how this idea would fit into the existing product portfolio. The outcome of this phase was a formal report detailing market possibilities, target customers, a preliminary estimation of the costs of the project, resource allocation

*Figure 3. The corporate R&D -process in the late 1990s © [2005] [**Arla Juntunen**]. Used with permission.*

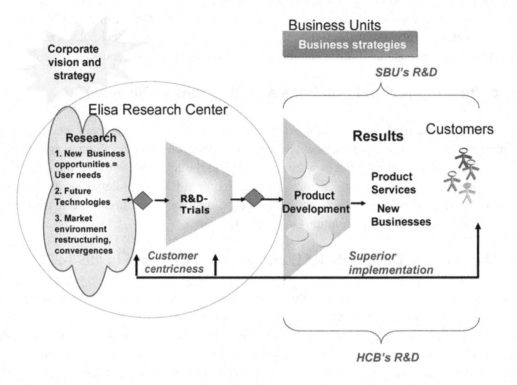

Figure 4. In-house R&D -process in the late 1980s to the early 1990s in Elisa.

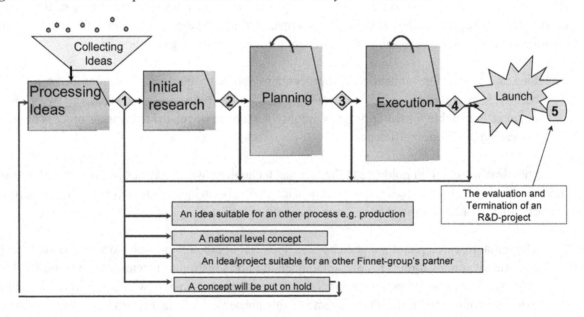

requirements and a proposed timeline of the project. However, if there was found to be an existing patent, the idea was considered unsuitable for further processing. This phase could also expose any unclear marketing and technology issues that might make the project too expensive or ultimately unprofitable.

3. The project planning phase's outcome was a detailed R&D project plan, complete with an accurate resource allocation. It contained suggestions as to who should be on the management board of the project. It also detailed the description of the proposed billing for the new product/service, a description of the order, details of production and delivery process and an implementation and an integration plan with regard to the existing architecture and fixed-line network[4].

The business design component of this phase included the commercialization of the product/service and the development of a detailed planning business plan, mapping out the proposed nature of the future business.

4. The project execution phase included testing of network changes, programs related to telephone centers and information systems related to order, billing and delivery. The project had certain set milestones at which the project's management board reviewed the current status of the project. At any milestone, the board had the possibility to terminate the project or to put it on hold.

Following the assessment of the outcomes of the project and testing of the various parts that were developed or maintained in terms of the information systems (IS) and systems architecture, pilot customers were chosen among the case corporation. The pilot group was responsible for testing the new product/service and to make suggestions as to what changes were needed. The pilot group consisted of both customers and developers. They looked for errors and determined if the product was suitable, interesting, and easy-to-use by any potential customer defined in the initial project plan.

5. The launch –phase included approving the new product/service in terms of the existing product portfolio and informing the sales and marketing departments of the new product. Inclusive in the sales and marketing information was training in regard of the new product to provide the necessary basic information needed to market and sell the product. During this phase the product development unit delivered the new product to the product maintenance unit, teaching them its architecture and the maintenance. The actual launch process of the new product was divided into internal and external. The internal launch process incorporated the communicating information regarding the new product within the case corporation and its subsidiaries, whereas the external launch process related to the media and external customers. After the launch phase, the R&D-process was terminated. This was done by writing a memorandum detailing all the phases and associated outcomes of the projects. In this document, the project manager assessed the completed project along with suggestions for future projects and products. Once the development project was finished, the management board evaluated and terminated the project.

During the 1980 and early 1990s, the R&D –process remained in-house but, due to networking and outsourcing activities, that process changed. HCB's R&D process (see Figures 4, 5) describes part of the corporate R&D process in detail, starting from product development. This is undertaken in conjunction with the Research Center if necessary. Figure 6 illustrates the process from the project point of view. The

*Figure 5. HCB's R&D -process in the late 1990s © [2005] [**Arla Juntunen**]. Used with permission.*

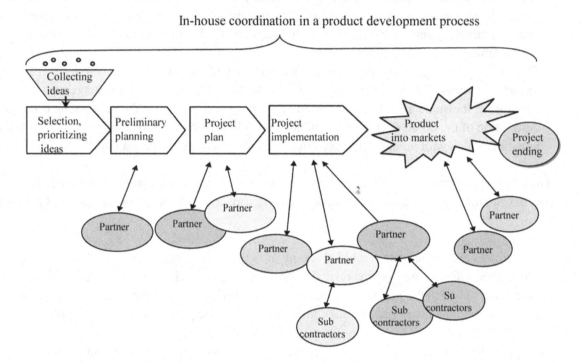

In-house coordination in a product development process

collection and selection of ideas and their prioritization remained within HCB. It was difficult to divide these activities between because HCB wanted to orchestrate the operations of the actors and guide the business networks created towards their goals. In other activities, there could be several parties performing a distinct role. Innovations and ideas were sometimes gathered from outside the business. HCB could not construct its architecture without additional parties as they needed diverse industry-based knowledge and information for solution formulation. Moreover, their in-house resources and capabilities were not sufficient to build the whole complex architecture and solutions by themselves. The integration of different services or technologies was carried out either by HCB or by partners that HCB coordinated.

Figure 6 describes the connection between the technical R&D process and the commercial process. For example, ADSL was transferred from HCB to the product maintenance department in the way described in Figure 4. Once the ADSL product was technically ready, it was transferred to the commercial process. The commercial process planned the timing of the product launch, checked the order and billing information systems and verified that the necessary information was available for both customer service and installation of the new product. The commercial process also incorporated packaging where several products needed to be coupled and sold together. The commercial process also planned the advertising campaign and schedule. After the launch of a new product, the product was transferred to the to the product maintenance process, which made new versions of the product, corrected errors detected and was responsible for preparing documentation for the product.

In 2000, it was clear that there were some critical issues affecting product development, management and maintenance. These issues not only related to the capabilities of the employees but also to hierarchical organizational structures and the competition between and within different business areas. In addition, problems concerned the time taken for a new product and service to be implemented in the

Figure 6. HCB's technical R&D –process and commercial product development process in the late 1990s © [2005] [Arla Juntunen]. Used with permission.

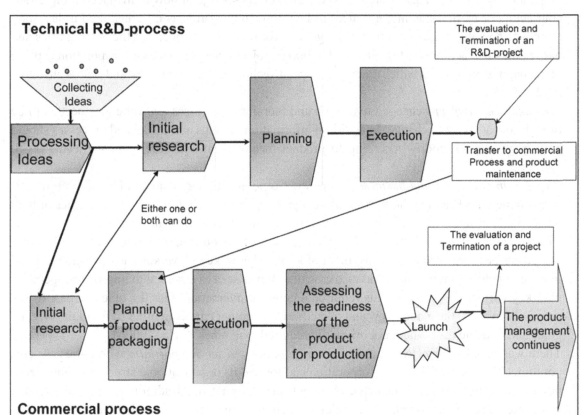

existing legacy systems, and the times required for training the customer service department to install and use the new services, as well as advise the customers. (PCS, 2000a, 2000b) The critical issues targeted for improvement in the following year 2001 included the management of process and projects as well as the motivation of personnel. It was acknowledged that multiple capabilities and knowledge were required in R&D projects. However, such persons could not be sourced directly from school or the employment market because such skills took time to acquire. Therefore, it was suggested that the career development of R&D personnel from a junior to a senior position should include several steps. As a junior, the person could do more routine tasks, and later, when he had learnt business and organization rules and built a network of contacts, he could take on more demanding tasks. (PCS 2000b) Some lessons learned during the R&D-process served to highlight the endogenous factors that can affect the process are introduced in the following:

- *Organizational changes*: new organizational structures affected information flows and processes. It took time to reorganize business processes, contacts inside the organization as well as the responsibilities and duties of each party involved.
- *Result-based management* in units or subsidiaries restricts or hinders joint projects (PCS 2000a)

- *Project management*: the change from in-house development to projects involving multiple participants was not easy. There were no experiences or knowledge of how to manage multiple subcontractors or participants in the project-or how to maintain projects on schedule. Furthermore, there was no knowledge of contract management for the differing needs of the various roles and participants in a net. It took time to develop into a project manager in a large corporation capable of managing projects in which there are several technologies, businesses and actors involved (PCS, 2000b)

- *Customer target groups* changed over time and therefore, processes and functions needed to be flexible and adaptive to change. In addition, information systems and associated processes should have been easy to modify according to product management and developments needs. (PCS, 2000a)

- *Changes in corporate and business strategies*: Corporate strategy change affected both investments in new R&D and in the start-up of new projects; changes in the business strategies of both the strategic business areas influenced how projects and ideas were prioritized.

- *Changes in relationships and partners*: management of relationships, management of resources and capabilities was needed, management of knowledge of key players in the business field and in the competitive environment was also essential. It was seen as essential to improve cooperation with key partners in projects. This required a constant interaction with the other parties. It was necessary to "sell" the global view and objectives to the other parties in order to fulfill the original goals and to avoid diversified, not originally required, outcomes. (PCS, 2000b)

- There was a *lack of knowledge of the existing product and service portfolio* within the case corporation (PCS, 2000b). The case corporation had formed its organizational structure around technology-based businesses, for example, Kolumbus had Internet- and Radiolinja had mobile-related businesses. Yet the integration of technologies with existing platforms, services and products was essential for the further development of the case corporation. The various subsidiaries and business areas were independent, with their individual responsibilities and organizational boundaries explicitly defined However, this was not only related to organizational structure but was also a consequence of rapid growth within the business and the organization as a whole. Besides the structural changes in the case corporation, the rapid growth in the number of employees from the early 1996 to 2000 was another reason why it was difficult to locate the correct contact persons and knowing where to find information. There were more employees recruited during 1998-2000 than what had been done during the early 1990s.

SUMMARY

What were the benefits of R&D in the case corporation, in particular of a small R&D group as exemplified by HCB in the late 1990s? When considering size as defined by financial resources or the number of employees, HCB was still considered a small group. Large, diversified firms were seen to benefit from positive spillovers between various research projects, economies of scope in R&D, and the returns from R&D were seen to be higher when the innovator had a large volume of sales over which to spread the fixed costs of innovation, economies of scale in R&D. Perhaps one of the key factors underlying HCB's success for can be found among arguments against R&D in large organizations such as the bureaucratization of inventive activity in large organizations. The core HCB team was allowed to innovate with the direct support of the senior management of the case corporation. In addition, they were able to see both the successes and the failures of their efforts in putting technological innovations into business use, as well as in forming relationships with manufacturers, content providers, service providers and other actors in their business area.

Through this kind of analytical process it was identified that the development of a new business involved different kinds of collaborative forms, including various technology development forums, R&D projects with various actors and, finally, intentionally built business networks with actors from several industries. These forms were interlinked, that is, they influenced each others. They were also cumulative in a sense that the established relationships and their governance forms guided the development of the next phase cooperative forms and their management solutions. The study revealed that the evolution of a new business represented co-evolution of breakthrough technologies and capabilities within a business context, and a learning process within the focal actor's organization.

Another major result was the observation that such a pioneering actor as the HCB had to develop specific interorganizational relationship, process and network management capabilities in order to be able to advance from the development of basic technologies to the commercialization and marketing of ICT solutions and home commerce services. It should also be noted that each service application examined during the period of 1990-2007 required a collaborative net of actors for both its R&D platform development and commercialization. In other words, the ability to develop efficient network and process management capabilities as well as partner portfolio was seen critical for success.

The coordination within the partner network plays a key role in this new business development. Performance and efficiency of a business or an R&D network depends largely on efficient coordination of the activities of the partners (cf. Schneeweiss et al., 2004). Coordination is needed to guarantee both the accurate flow of information and of materials. To succeed in coordination, network partners need to agree on common governance mechanisms to manage the flow of information or materials. These governance mechanisms support the processes and structure the relationships that exist between the participants of the network.

As a summary, the contribution of this study to the previous research is to the discussion of fast paced technology development and network and relationship management as well as how the technology can change the business processes and also business models. Technology can also modify the strategies and firm evolution creating competitive advantage. By joining the next generation multimedia network, the company can strengthen its role and image and to expand its customer base and continue expanding it through the following ten years. The basis for the success seems to be capabilities of the management of the business networks and partners. The partner portfolio was developed also during the years of 1997-2000 when the networks, processes and partnerships were forming. The portfolio considers the value of different partners based on their impact on current or future business goals.

Also, another important success factor was the vision of where the ICT-sector and technology development was going within the next 5-10 years.

As a summary, the contribution of this paper to the previous research is to the discussion of fast paced technology development and network and relationship management as well as how the technology can change the business processes and also business models. Technology can also modify the strategies and firm evolution creating competitive advantage.

In the empirical analysis, this study described the business development in 1990-2007 as well as analyzed the R&D development from the viewpoints of corporate R&D, business and project level. It seems that societal and technological changes drove the business development further whilst the success in partnering further assisted in creating competitive advantage. The ability to manage multiple

*Figure 7. Partner portfolio © [2005] [**Arla Juntunen**]. Used with permission.*

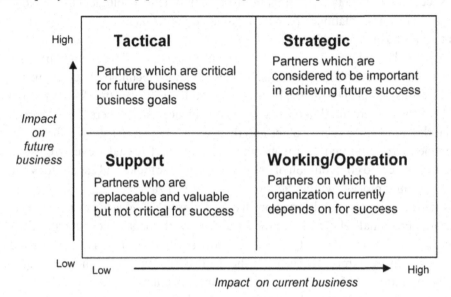

projects and actors in networks assisted in business development. The ability to adapt in changes and take an advantage of new, emerging technologies and previous R&D projects also assisted in creating knowledge base of new technologies and resources that were able to learn and adapt the new technologies into the business context.

FUTURE TRENDS

The tendency of multinational teams in ICT solutions -development (cf. Nokia or other telecommunication companies) creates a network of many cultures and backgrounds. Technology itself is not a component of a single country's culture. Many firms employ internationally, and thus, R&D processes and innovations become global faster than ever before. Considering R&D process management, managers would be able to better avoid the common pitfalls in long-run R&D management if more research was conducted on the role of managerial cognition of network management in an international context and in balancing between exploration and exploitation of external and internal resources. This analysis already discovered potential ways of how managers need creative thinkers and network management capabilities in surviving and gaining competitive advantage in a turbulent competitive environment. Also, it seems that adaptability and ceasing opportunities in new business areas is important and that it can contribute to the company's future success in other business areas as well. However, the increasing dependence in external partners instead of using internal resources may contribute the fear of external partners' opportunistic behavior, the extent of coordination costs, and the complexity of the relationship coordination with multiple partners.

CONCLUSION

Rapid innovations and imitations are prompting an increasing number of organizations to concentrate on their R&D processes and partnerships to remain competitive. Improving and developing business processes and R&D from product ideas to commercialization are related and interdependent tasks. Improving and developing business processes and R&D from product ideas to commercialization are related and interdependent tasks. This case also described the challenges of the new business creation in the fast paced, networked environment. Moreover, the broadness of the research approach of this paper suggests several types of new research possibilities, like for example, the relatedness of the processual development and network management, and the managerial capabilities. Overall, this study has highlighted the fact that coevolution of R&D and managerial capabilities takes place in a new business development and that this should be taken into account in the development of R&D –networks and partner management.

REFERENCES

Achrol, R. S., & Kotler, P. (1999). Marketing in the network economy. *Journal of Marketing, 63*, 146–163. doi:10.2307/1252108

Anderson, J. C., & Narus, J. A. (1999). *Business market management: Understanding, creating and delivering value*. Prentice Hall.

Beardsley, S. C., Bray, W. D., & van Rooijen, M. C. W. (1995). The great European multimedia gamble. *McKinsley Quarterly* 1995/3.

Blomqvist, K. (2002). *Partnering in the dynamic environment: The role of trust in asymmetric technology partnership formation*. Lappeenranta University of Technology.

Brandenburger, A. M., & Nalebuff, B. J. (1996). *Co-opetition*. New York: Doubleday.

Edgelow, C. (2006). *Helping organizations change*. Sundance Consulting Inc.

Eisenhardt, K. M., & Martin, J. A. (2000). Dynamic capabilities: What are they? *Strategic Management Journal, 21*(10/11), 1105–1121. doi:10.1002/1097-0266(200010/11)21:10/11<1105::AID-SMJ133>3.0.CO;2-E

Elisa (2006). *Annual report*.

Elisa (2007). *Presentation*.

Ford, D., Gadde, L.-E., Håkansson, H., Lundgren, A., Snehota, I., Turnbull, P., & Wilson, D. (2002). *Managing business relationships*. IMP Group. Wiley.

Frels, J. K., Shervani, T., & Srivastava, R. K. (2003). The integrated networks model: Explaining resource allocations in network markets. *Journal of Marketing, 67*, 29–45. doi:10.1509/jmkg.67.1.29.18586

Ghauri, P., Lutz, C., & Tesform, G. (2003). Using networks to solve export-marketing problems of small and medium-sized firms from developing countries. *European Journal of Marketing, 37*(5/6), 728–752. doi:10.1108/03090560310465125

Gulati, R. (1998). Alliances and networks. *Strategic Management Journal, 19*(4), 293–317. doi:10.1002/(SICI)1097-0266(199804)19:4<293::AID-SMJ982>3.0.CO;2-M

Gulati, R., Nohria, N., & Zaheer, A. (2000). Strategic networks. *Strategic Management Journal, 21*, 203–215. doi:10.1002/(SICI)1097-0266(200003)21:3<203::AID-SMJ102>3.0.CO;2-K

Hagedoorn, J. (1990). Organizational modes of inter-firm co-operation and technology transfer. *Technovation, 10*(1), 17–30. doi:10.1016/0166-4972(90)90039-M

Hagedoorn, J. (1995). Strategic technology partnering during the 1980s: Trends, networks and corporate patterns in non-core technologies. *Research Policy, 24*(2), 207–231. doi:10.1016/0048-7333(94)00763-W

Håkansson, H., & Snehota, I. (Eds.). (1995) *Developing relationships in business networks*. London: Routledge.

Hewlett Packard. (2005, February). *Adaptive enterprise at work* [White paper]. Hewlett Packard.

Hölttä, P. (1999). Verkko-opetushankkeiden eteneminen HPY:ssä. HPY Research 10/1999.

Hölttä, P. (2000). Piimäki 2000: Laajakaistaisen alueverkon uudet palvelut. tuotekehityshakemuksen liite 2. Tutkimus- ja kehitysprojektisuunnitelma TEKESin 'Tietoliikenteellä maailmalle' teknologiaohjelmaan. HPY Tutkimuskeskus.

Juntunen, A. (2005). *The emergence of a new business through collaborative networks: A longitudinal study in the ICT sector*. Acta Universitatis Oeconomicae Helsingiensis. HSEPrint. A-series no 256.

Kogut, B., & Zander, U. (1997). Knowledge of the firm, combinative capabilities, and the replication of technology. In N.J. Foss (Ed.), *Resources, fims and strategies – A reader in the resource-based perspective*. Oxford: Oxford University Press.

Larraine, S. (2002). *Dynamic leader adaptive organization: Ten essential traits for managers*. Wiley.

Lehmus, P. (1999). *Strategiasuunnitelma 2000-2003: Arena*. Helsingin Puhelin Oyj, Liiketoimintaprojektit. 14.4.1999. Helsinki, Finland.

McGrath, M. E. (1995). *Product strategy for high-technology companies: How to achieve growth, competitive advantage, and increased profits*. McGraw-Hill.

Miles, M. B., & Huberman, A. M. (1994). *Qualitative data analysis: An expanded sourcebook* (2nd Ed.). Thousand Oaks, CA: Sage Publications, Inc.

Mintzberg, H. (1979). *The structuring of organizations*. Englewood Cliffs. NJ: Prentice-Hall.

Möller, K., & Rajala, A. (1999). Organizing marketing in industrial high-tech firms: The role of internal marketing relationships. *Industrial Marketing Management, 28*(5), 521–535. doi:10.1016/S0019-8501(99)00059-0

Möller, K., Rajala, A., & Svahn, S. (2005). Strategic business nets – Their types and management. *Journal of Business Research*, 1274–1284. doi:10.1016/j.jbusres.2003.05.002

Nalebuff, B. J., & Brandenburger, A. M. (1996). *Co-opetition*. London: Harper Collins.

PCS (2000a). WS3-dokum-Tuotekeh-mita-pitaa-muuttua. March 30th 2000. Hämeenkylän kartano.

PCS (2000b). Jatkotoimenpiteet. April 17th 2000. Hämeenkylän kartano.

PCS (2001). tuotehommaa 0307. PCS, Elisa Communications July 3rd 2001.

Pinfield, L. T., Watzke, G. E., & Webb, E. J. (1974). Confederacies and brokers: Mediators between organizations and their environments. In H.Leavitt, L. Pinfield & E. Webb (Eds.), *Organizations of the future: Interaction with the external environment* (pp.83-110). New York: Praeger.

Product Development Institute Inc. Stage-Gate Model. 1996-1998.

Radjou, N., Daley, E., Rasmussen, M., & Lo, H. (2006). The rise of globally adaptive organizations. The world isn't flat till global firms are networked, risk-agile, and socially adept. In *Balancing risks and rewards in a global tech economy*. Forrester.

Salmi, P. (1999). *Helsinki Arena 2000 -esittelymateriaali*. Helsingin Puhelin Oyj. Helsinki, Finland.

Schneeweiss, C., Zimmer, K., & Zimmermann, M. (2004). The design of contracts to coordinate operational interdependencies within the supply chain. *International Journal of Production Economics*, *92*(1), 43–59. doi:10.1016/j.ijpe.2003.10.005

Spekman, R. E., Isabella, L. A., & MacAvoy, T. C. (2000). *Alliance competence: Maximizing the value of your partnerships*. New York: John Wiley & Sons.

Tenhovuori, T. (1996). *Helsinki Arena 2000 – palveluverkko. Tavoitesuunnitelma Helsinki Arena 2000*. Helsingin Puhelin Oyj. 2.12.1996. Helsinki, Finland.

Toffler, A. (1985). *The adaptive corporation*. New York: McGraw Hill.

Yin, R. K. (1994). *Case study research: Design and methods* (2nd Ed.). Thousand Oaks, CA: Sage Publications.

KEY TERMS AND DEFINITIONS

Actor: is a firm or an individual that perform activities and control resources and create value via transformation of resources. Actors refer to the business network participants.

Capabilities: The difference between resources and capabilities in a firm is that capabilities deploy or coordinate different resources, and therefore, capabilities are involved in the activities of the whole value chain of the company. Capabilities can be defined as intangible knowledge resources, and physical and non-physical resources as tangible and intangible assets

Endogenous: i.e. they may occur within the organization or within the net itself (i.e. personnel changes, changes in organizational structure or changes in business, marketing or business strategies as well as acquisitions or partner-switching)

Exogenous: i.e. they may arise from the overall business environment and include changes in technology, industrial structure and economic recession.

ICT Sector: includes both the Information Technology (IT) and telecommunication sector. The latter includes both the service and the manufacturing industry. The previous includes all the software and hardware manufacturing and developing companies.

Network: Networks can be seen as markets, groupings of firms or organizations. Vertical networks can also be called as marketing channel networks that efficiently promote, modify and move goods to markets. Horizontal networks often include cooperation among competitors, they can be partially competitive and partially cooperative, that is, coopetitive networks. The business network context is structured in the three dimensions: actors, activities and resources

Partner: is an actor that is associated with another or others in an activity or a sphere of common interest, especially a member of a business partnership.

R & D (Research and Development): Discovering new information and knowledge about products, services, and processes and then applying that knowledge to create new and improved products, services, and processes that fill market needs.

ENDNOTES

[1]   Finland used Finnish marks in 1990-2000.

[2]   VOIP: *Voice over IP*, a VoIP-device and -service to send and to receive IP-voice. Internet telephone refers to communication services – voice, facsimile, and/or voice-messaging applications – that are transported via the Internet, rather than the *public switched telephone network* (PSTN). The basic steps involved in originating an Internet telephone call are conversion of the analog voice signal to digital format and compression/translation of the signal into *Internet protocol (IP) packets* for transmission over the Internet. The process is reversed at the receiving end. (www.iec.org.online/tutorials/int_tele)

[3]   PKI: *Public Key Infrastructure*; a security service which is divided into two keys: public and secret with which the data security can be guaranteed in transfer.

[4]   This process was implemented at a time when mobile network and businesses were still a new innovation and a growing business. Therefore, the process evaluated innovations based on fixed-line network.

Chapter 23
Operational Process Management in the Financial Services Industry

Diana Heckl
Frankfurt School of Finance & Management, Germany

Jürgen Moormann
Frankfurt School of Finance & Management, Germany

ABSTRACT

The financial services industry faces significant competitive pressures. Economic and political influences, incessant regulation, and fast changing markets make for a highly complex and dynamic environment. Thus, banks and insurance companies are forced to permanently improve their performance – raising process performance represents one of the biggest levers for success. This chapter analyses the challenges of operational process management for banks and insurance companies. The involvement of customers in service processes of financial institutions make these not as easy to manage as production processes. In response to these challenges, cornerstones for a general framework for operational management of service processes will be developed. The aim of this chapter is to present a framework for structuring service processes which allows combining influences by customers and an operational process management. The concept is based on the modularisation approach and will be demonstrated using a loan process as an example.

INTRODUCTION

Today, service companies like hotel chains, tour operators, insurance companies, and banks have to deal with tough competition in their respective markets. To survive in this situation the companies' business models, cost reduction initiatives, and efforts for increasing revenues require continuous adjustments. Otherwise, these companies might fall prey to the ongoing consolidation process. Due to its extremely dynamic and complex environment, the financial services industry is particularly affected. Therefore,

DOI: 10.4018/978-1-60566-669-3.ch023

management has to continuously search for new strategic and operational solutions (e.g. Staikouras & Koutsomanoli-Fillipaki, 2006).

Meanwhile, managers of banks and insurance companies are trying to adopt ideas from other industries. Particularly, the manufacturing industry is considered as a best practice example for financial service providers. For instance, loans or insurance contracts should be "produced" as efficiently as cars. Therefore, more and more banks and insurers are relying on this approach to improve the efficiency of their processes.

A close look at the loan business, the cornerstone of traditional banking services, reveals its increasingly competitive nature and the resulting approaches to finding solutions for long-term success in this market. In particular, industry members continuously analyze opportunities for insourcing and outsourcing business processes, implementing such measures if feasible, in order to gain scale advantages and to be in a position to offer lower-cost loans. Industry members aim to reduce loan processing times and the associated costs through the introduction of process management techniques in combination with workflow management systems. These efforts result in an increased level of standardisation and automation. Managers' desired end-state for loan processing would thus resemble assembly line processing, irrespective of which process steps are performed by each partner in the process chain (e.g. Wigand, Steinfield & Markus, 2005). However, is it really possible to transfer – one to one – the concept of a production management system of a car manufacturer to the processes of service providers?

To manage an "industrialised" service process a business process management system analogous to that of car manufacturer is necessary. Therefore, this chapter's objective is to review the requirements and constraints and to develop the cornerstones of a *framework for operational process management* that is appropriate for the financial services industry. The procedure for setting up such a system on management level is shown using an end-to-end loan process as an example.

This chapter is organised as follows: Section 2 discusses the differences between manufacturers' and service providers' business processes. On this basis, the authors derive the requirements for a service process management framework (Section 3). Section 4 presents the concept of process modularisation which will be used for constructing the framework. The service process management framework will be demonstrated using as an example the loan process in banks. The following section describes further steps for setting up an operational process management system and shows the potential for further research in this field. Finally, the authors draw conclusions related to this topic in Section 6.

CHARACTERISTICS OF SERVICE PROCESSES IN THE FINANCIAL SERVICES SECTOR

The assembly line concept represented the genesis of the idea to regard the activities of an enterprise as processes. Processes are thus viewed as sets of activities with the logical internal relationship that they result in a product or service demanded by a customer (Hammer & Champy, 1993). The process therefore begins and ends with the customer. Processes exist irrespective of the functional structure of the organisation. According to this view, the loan process, for example, encompasses sub-processes such as sales, loan application processing, loan approval/rejection, customer service, risk management, and workout (end-to-end process). In order to continuously enhance process performance, the process has to be viewed and managed in its entirety as an end-to-end process. In doing so, the special characteristics of services and service processes have to be considered.

Physical Goods Production in Comparison to Service Production

The final result of a (business) process can be generally characterised with the term *output*. Yet, this term is highly heterogeneous, as there are vastly different outputs such as physical goods and services, and since the term output can be applied at different levels of specificity.

Bullinger, Fähnrich & Meiren (2003) define physical goods as raw materials, capital goods, production materials, and durable and non-durable consumer goods. Material physical goods can be therefore quite easily defined: they include raw materials, parts and components, and finished products. The industrial production of a physical good involves utilisation of various production factors. These include basic productive factors such as production facilities and equipment, human labour, raw materials, as well as logistical factors such as planning, organising, and control. The customer receives the physical good once it has been manufactured and is not involved in the actual production process (Wright & Race, 2004).

The question of what constitutes a service cannot be answered as easily. Besides intangibility, many authors cite the aspect of inseparability, i.e. the customer's involvement in the actual service delivery process, as a second distinguishing feature of services (Zeithaml, Parasuraman & Berry, 1985). A patient, for example, has to be physically present at the physician's office in order to receive an immunisation shot. Similarly, business consultants rely heavily on information their customers provide. Customers' involvement entails providing external production factors, also referred to as external factors or object factors. Very often customers provide more than just one external production factor (e.g. information and material goods) (Wright & Race, 2004). Unlike internal production factors, such external production factors are available to the service provider on a limited timely basis and are then integrated with the internal production factors into the service delivery process.

Thus, a service is – in contrast to a physical good – characterised by the involvement of the customer in the actual output process ("integration of the external factor"). Due to this customer involvement, the entire process that results in the actual service output is termed *integrative output delivery* (Wright & Race, 2004).

Handling Service Processes with Heterogeneous Integrativity

The vast differences between services become evident when comparing the service offer "loans" with other financial services such as investment services, securities purchases, and handling account transactions, or when looking at non-banking services such as haircuts or healthcare services. This heterogeneous nature of services necessitates the development of service classifications in order to conduct focused and detailed managerial analyses and to reach decisions specific to the service in question (Silvestro, Fitzgerald, & Johnston, 1992). Based on the varying definitions for services and the specific classification purpose, there are different criteria to classify services. Therefore, it is necessary to develop a classification methodology suited to the particular research question at hand.

This chapter focuses on management of processes, including their sub-processes and associated activities, and thus applies as a service classification approach a process-oriented view. Accordingly, services are produced in multiple steps, whereby the required activities are bundled in the form of processes (Stauss & Weinlich, 1997). In doing so, it is critically important to integrate external factors. External factors include the service recipient (e.g. the customer at the hairdresser's), who is involved in the service delivery process either personally or by providing information, or a service recipient's physical good (e.g. a car brought to the mechanic for servicing/repair). Without integrating the external factors, the service cannot be produced, and therefore these factors have to be considered in planning and managing the service production process (Wright & Race, 2004).

Integration of the external factor "customer" differs decidedly based on the type of service. For example, mail delivery services require integration of the external factor merely at the beginning and at the end of the service process, whereas tax consulting services require on-going and repeated contact with the external factor "customer". Consequently, the integration of the customer in the service delivery process has to be further differentiated according to additional criteria such as contact frequency or intensity, the degree of customisation, the level of differentiation, or the types of external factors that have to be integrated (Kasper et al., 1999). With respect to planning and managing the service delivery process, the customer's involvement in the actual service delivery is critically important. In the German literature this is referred to as *integrativity* (Engelhardt & Freiling, 1995). This term will be used in this chapter to refer to the customer's involvement in the service process.

Customer involvement plays a highly important role for the service provider, especially in cases when it limits the provider's options as to how, when, and where to deliver which service or service combination. A limitation of service provisioning options and thus the process itself is linked especially to information provided by the customer during the service delivery process. The customer provides such information, also referred to as external process information, for a very specific purpose, namely to obtain a service output. Two types of information have to be distinguished (Kleinaltenkamp & Haase, 1999):

- *External non-impacting process information* is processed, changed, and utilised during the service delivery process (e.g. information an insurance policy holder provides concerning items that he wishes to insure; financial statements an entrepreneur submits for the determination of his credit-worthiness).
- *External process-impacting information* includes customer information that exerts a direct influence on service provisioning, including the service provider's activities and processes. Examples include specification requirements provided to a consultancy or customer expectations related to the timely completion of a repair contract. Any subsequent activities and processes are dependent on whether or not such process-impacting information is indeed provided.

The degree of integrativity in a service process therefore depends on the extent of external process-impacting information and indicates how deeply the customer gets involved in the service delivery process, thus determining the relationship between autonomous and integrative service delivery. Moreover, the degree of integrativity is closely linked to the degree of customisation of a particular service, since external process-impacting information often relates to customer needs. If individual customer needs and requirements, thus external process-impacting information, differ significantly from one another, then the type of service will exhibit a high degree of customisation. Conversely, if individual customer needs and requirements resemble each other, then the service can be standardised, thus allowing for a standardisation of the underlying service delivery processes as well (Kasper et al., 1999).

The organisation of a service company and the design of processes for service delivery therefore depend on an understanding of the extent of customer involvement. Service delivery processes exhibiting little integrativity can thus be developed autonomously by the business and can be autonomously rearranged. Service delivery processes with a high degree of integrativity, however, have to be strongly based on customer requirements, preventing the service provider from designing service delivery processes autonomously. An understanding of this basic framework and its consequences for operational

Figure 1. An integrativity perspective of a service process and its respective process steps

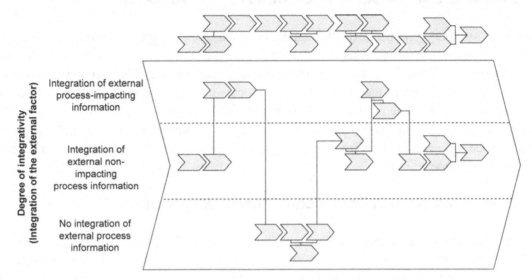

management activities and process performance is particularly important when considering options for process management. Services can entail a multi-step delivery process, in which the individual delivery phases and processes may exhibit different degrees of integrativity (Figure 1).

Therefore a service classification according to the number of service steps in combination with integrativity will serve as an approach to characterise the service delivery process and to subsequently define effective management of a service process. There are, for example, service delivery processes within the financial services industry that do not require integration of external information in any of their sub-processes (e.g. generation of an account statement at a bank). In such cases, the output of the production process is generally a physical (tangible) product. Other production processes require capturing the customer's need at the outset, but such process information may have a non-impacting character. Subsequent activities and sub-processes can therefore be performed autonomously and without integrating external process information. An example of this is meeting a customer's desired deadline through on-time completion of a maintenance or repair job at a service station or by a mechanic.

In addition, there are service delivery processes that exhibit *different degrees of integrativity* in their individual sub-processes, for example processing a loan application for a home mortgage. This process starts with consultancy and advice related to different types of mortgages and the terms and conditions. This process phase integrates external process-impacting information provided by the customer, i.e. depending on the desired mortgage and terms and conditions, additional activities within the overall service delivery process will be required. The next step involves checking the customer's credit-worthiness and conducting an economic feasibility analysis, which requires obtaining information about the customer's financial situation and the property in question (integration of external non-impacting information). An approval of the application triggers payment of the loan amount and the required refinancing activities. These process steps are typically conducted autonomously by the service provider and do not integrate external process information from the customer. Hence, the loan process can be viewed as a service process with *heterogeneous customer involvement* or integrativity.

3 OPERATIONAL MANAGEMENT OF SERVICE PROCESSES

Management's primary responsibility is to achieve an organisation's objectives through planning, organising, directing and controlling. This includes management of the processes underlying "the production of services". A distinction has to be made between normative, strategic, and operational process management. A description of these three different process management levels will be followed by a discussion on how to manage service processes at an operational level. In a last step, this section will discuss the need in the financial services industry for having a framework for the operational management of service processes with heterogeneous customer involvement. The loan process in banks will be used as an example.

Normative, Strategic, and Operational Process Management

In general, management is defined as influencing the behaviour of a system towards the accomplishment of a certain objective (Drucker, 1980). In a business organisation, the senior management team assumes responsibility for the goal-oriented direction of the business. Business objectives are, however, not determined on the basis of exogenous factors. Top management has discretion and flexibility when formulating a vision, setting objectives, and developing plans. Within this context, Ulrich (1981) refers to these activities as the *normative management* of a business, and as a function of providing normative direction, top management defines the business objectives. Based on the types of activities and measures management can select in order to change its presently unsatisfying situation, one can differentiate between strategic and operational management (Figure 2).

The purpose of *strategic management* is the establishment of long-term oriented decision frameworks that provide the parameters for *operational management*. Managers develop the strategies to achieve the stated objectives and determine the general structure and framework for the business, including the development of the organisation structure, management systems, and the process organisation. Operational management is concerned with the implementation of strategies through short-term activities that have

Figure 2. Three-loop control system

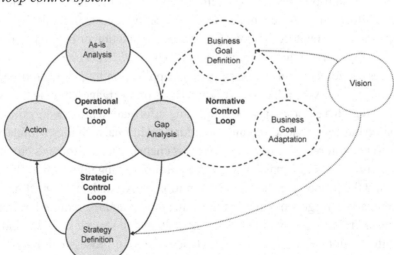

an immediate impact on the performance process. The business objectives serve as the starting point. If business objectives are considered to be instruments at the disposal of management, then a third control cycle can be identified.

For managing business processes, literature suggests implementing an integrated concept of leadership, organisation and control (Davenport & Short, 1990). Thereby, it is intended to set up a target-oriented control system of business processes. The entire company should be aligned with the requirements of its clients and other stakeholders. Within a systematic business process control concept, process targets have to be defined for every single process. Every process manager's aim should be the successful holistic control of the process. Basically, the control of a process can be classified into categories of operational, strategic, and normative process control:

- Process targets are the starting point of process control. The targets have to be verified within the normative control cycle (Zairi & Sinclair, 1995).
- In terms of Double Loop Learning (Argyris, 1999), the control of processes also refers to strategic control aspects. Hence, it may be necessary to reconsider and change the strategy with respect to the process model design. If the level of target achievement appears to be out of reach, it would be essential to develop a completely new or an improved process organisation – in radical (Hammer & Champy, 1993) as well as in evolutionary aspects (Pande, Neumann & Cavanagh, 2000). There are numerous concepts available for process optimisation (e.g. Business Process Redesign, Six Sigma) to improve the process and to broaden the spectrum of short-term improvements within the operational control.
- Within the scope of the operational control, the processes should be successfully managed to achieve the efficiency goals. Therefore, the process manager measures the current state of the process performance. In comparison with the process targets, he would analyse the level of target achievement (Neely, Gergory & Platts, 2005). In case of a deviation beyond a defined bandwidth, the process manager searches for short-term improvements that immediately influence the process performance results. These improvement activities have to be aligned with the predetermined process strategy, which is also the basis for the company's operational and organisational structure (Kueng & Kawalek, 1997).

This chapter focuses on the operational management of processes. The process objectives serve as a starting point. Moreover, the basic framework and conditions for operational management processes will be critically reviewed.

Operational Management of Service Processes with Heterogeneous Integrativity

Management of a service process requires consideration of the type of service output. Management measures and activities may yield their desired success if the process is clearly understood and if the cause-and-effect relationships within a process are known. The discussion in this chapter thus far has demonstrated that not all service delivery processes are equal. The degree of integrativity of the external factor and process diversity can differ markedly, even if a service process results in the same output. The integration of external process-impacting factors in the service delivery process exerts a strong influence on the process flow and the process output, requiring management to consider this aspect when designing processes and process management systems: the features and characteristics of the service delivery process have to be based on the process-impacting information. Decisions have to be made related to the range of optional service components as part of the service offer and variable service bundle attributes (*output dimension*). Similarly, decisions may deal with capabilities and abilities to provide a service (*potential dimension*). If different process options exist, an appropriate option has to be selected (*process dimension*).

Within the service process for loans, sub-processes exhibit heterogeneity with respect to the involvement of the external factor "customer." Depending on the sub-process, either external impacting or external non-impacting or even no external process information whatsoever may be required. Since financial services providers pursue different strategies with respect to their process design, differences pertaining to integrativity can be observed when looking at the design of loan processes. Some institutions, for example, strive to implement standardised processes, in which customers' involvement is limited to providing external non-impacting process information. Other service providers, however, aim for customer-orientation and therefore allow customers to become actively involved in the service delivery process by providing process-impacting information. Consequently, operational process management has to consider the detailed design of the loan process as well as the cause-and-effect relationships between operational management measures and the type of sub-process.

To engage in operational management of the loan process – a service process with heterogeneous integrativity – it is therefore necessary to attribute the business objectives to the specific processes in order to determine specific performance targets (Figure 3). As a next step, target measures have to be established within the operational management process to determine the level of goal attainment. Process control entails conducting comparisons between actual and planned performance. If the planned targets have not been reached during the service production process, specific actions have to be identified to improve performance levels. This requires an analysis of the activity parameters, i.e. the range of possible courses of action that can be taken and their potential influence on the level of goal attainment. The scope of the activity parameters is dependent on the design of the service delivery process in response to the degree of integrativity within the sub-processes. Finally, in case of plan deviations, the process manager has to select and implement corrective measures within the bounds of the activity parameters in order to increase process efficiency.

In addition, if plan deviations are detected, a process analysis should be conducted in order to determine whether the entire service process, i.e. the loan process, is still in alignment with the objectives (effectiveness). Depending on the analysis, modifications to the process model or modifications to the process design (e.g. changing the degree of integrativity) may be required. Moreover, the activity parameters, which provide the process manager with the scope of possible measures and activities that can be implemented, may have to be expanded or modified.

In order to conduct operational management of the service delivery process for loans, which is characterised by heterogeneous customer involvement, the following question has to be addressed: Which dependencies exist between process-related short-term activities as well as the long-term measures and process efficiency in the service delivery process for loans? In order to address this question, it is necessary to set up a *process laboratory*, i.e. a simulation laboratory. A process simulation represents a goal-oriented, experimental, computer-aided execution of process models. Such a process simulation facilitates anticipation of the characteristics of processes while they are running and provides insights into planned processes without having to actually run the process in practice. Experiments within actual process systems are often impossible, time consuming, risky, or too expensive (Bratley, Fox & Schrage,

Figure 3. Management and control cycle structure for service processes with heterogeneous integrativity

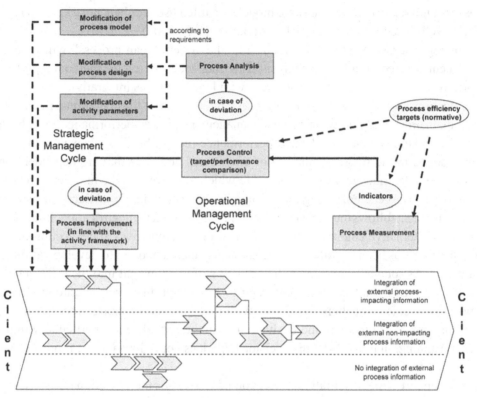

1987). A simulation, however, allows for the application of alternative approaches and solutions in different scenarios. Moreover, simulation models can be used for goal-oriented process designs and for the explanation of processes.

Necessity of a Framework for Process Management of Services with Heterogeneous Integrativity

The complexity of systems, such as the system "business enterprise" or the system "process", and the limited rational capacities of humans render it impossible to fully comprehend a system with all its cause-and-effect relationships. The reductionist approach proposes to divide the entire system into subsystems in order to reduce complexity. The holistic approach meanwhile advocates that systems have to be understood in their entirety and therefore have to be analysed in a holistic fashion. Regardless of the approach, it is impossible to experiment with the real existing (sub-) system in order to analyse the cause-and-effect relationships of the (sub-) system. This can only be done through the development of models, which incorporate a process view and a large variety of performance measures. Within this context, one has to distinguish between static models and dynamic models. In process management, process modulation models can be regarded as static models. Examples include: Architecture for Integrated Information Systems (ARIS), Unified Modelling Language (UML), Concept Mapping and Data Flow Diagrams. The following examples represent dynamic models within the area of process management:

Petri Nets, Systems Dynamics and Workflow Simulation. Static models are obviously less complex than dynamic models, since they contain less information and fewer effect dependencies. Both types of models possess high relevance – while static models are often used for benchmarking, dynamic models are especially well-suited for scenario analyses (Barber et al., 2003).

The following discussion serves to explain how the system "loan process" will be analysed and which instruments are required for the analysis. This entails describing the methodology for setting up a framework for process management of services with heterogeneous integrativity.

This chapter aims to analyse the system "process" and focuses on the operational management of the process system. In order to engage in operational management, process performance has to be determined in a first step. Deviations from the planned performance require business decisions to reach process performance targets in the future. A number of operational activities that are dependent on strategic measures are available. Management has to decide which measures to take in order to reach the stated process performance targets. Following the typology of critical and rational decision-making (Brim et al., 1962), management follows the decision-making process: problem identification, information search, determination of alternative courses of action, evaluation of alternatives and selection of one alternative. Once a problem has been identified, information is gathered in order to develop various alternative courses of action. As soon as management has gained sufficient insight into the different alternatives, management evaluates the alternatives according to a predetermined set of criteria. The alternative with the most favourable evaluation is selected. Within this decision-making process, phases three and four – determination of alternatives and evaluation – can be considered as particularly important and, often, time-consuming. In most cases, the decision path does not follow a linear progression, but rather represents an iterative process.

In order to support critical and rational decision processes for the operational service management of the loan process, with its heterogeneous customer involvement, an analysis of the interdependencies between different courses of action and attainable performance is required. In day-to-day business, such an analysis cannot be performed in an iterative fashion through continuous testing of alternative options, thus necessitating a process analysis model. Due to the dynamic interdependencies between the alternative courses of action and process performance, a dynamic model has to be developed, as such a model allows for an analysis of the interdependencies. However, the model cannot be applied to all financial services providers, as they may pursue different business objectives and may therefore have different processes. Hence, there is no such thing as "the" optimal process design. Instead, dependencies between process performance and different courses of action have to be analysed for an individual financial services provider (scenario analysis).

A model is not suitable to adequately address this business issue; one should rather develop a framework: "A [conceptual] framework provides a technical language system, a set of interpretative principles and important benchmarks for guiding thought. [...] A researcher's [conceptual] framework is likely to have been developed within a particular professional culture and internalised in such a way that the members of that culture can easily communicate with each other, share a common evaluative structure and routinely frame research questions and possible ways of finding answers" (Fleury & Fleury, 2007, p. 951).

Specifically, the framework aims to serve as a procedural model that allows for the identification of efficiency problems within the loan process. At the same time, approaches for information search, the identification of appropriate actions, and the evaluation of the identified courses of action will be presented, in order to be in a position to select a course of action that results in increased process efficiency. The framework has to be designed to serve as a systemisation instrument. Therefore a process structure which allows to combine influences by the customers on the one hand and an operational process management on the other hand is presented. A financial services provider can utilise this framework to structure and set up its operational process management in accordance with the framework.

The framework incorporates the notion of the above mentioned dynamic model (depiction of the analysed process), since reference will be made to iterative decision-making processes. The static process model does not sufficiently support an analysis of interdependencies between process performance and different courses of action. In general, there is agreement in the field of research that dynamic model description and analysis have to be integral elements of studies related to systems. Dynamic modelling, specifically simulation, can be regarded as an essential element of process modelling. The term "Business Process Simulation," for example, entails developing dynamic models for the purpose of analysing and evaluating business processes. Within this context, a number of different attempts to integrate static and dynamic process models have been undertaken – with different success rates (Barber et al., 2003). Process simulation thus provides a more differential means of evaluating different measures for increasing process efficiency, particularly since mutual dependencies and effects can be analysed based on their chronological sequence. In summary, the objective is to develop a *simulation-based framework*.

This requires the design of a framework that can provide direction for operational service process management for any loan process, regardless of how the process has been designed. The operational management cycle consists of three phases: process measurement, process control and analysis, and implementation of process improvement activities. The process subject to the operational management cycle is the loan process, a service process with heterogeneous integrativity.

Multiple research studies have already discussed and examined the aspects of process measurement, process analysis, and measures for process modifications (Neely, Gregory & Platts, 2005). The unique aspect of the framework that will be developed here lies in the interaction of these three aspects from an operational perspective. The simulation-based framework aims to enable process managers to measure, analyse and manage processes in day-to-day business. This means that a process manager has to be able to select and implement from the available portfolio of possible actions the appropriate course of action to achieve an improvement in process performance. In order to do this effectively, the process manager must have access to instruments that place him in a position to continuously measure the existing process, to compare different process variations, and to implement the selected course of action within the process flow. As a result, the following critical issues have to be addressed when designing the framework:

1. **Management of object "process"**: The system "loan process" has to be identified and structured. The depiction, design, and structure of the process have to be performed in such a way to allow for operational management of the process. Consequently, process measurement, process analysis, and process adaptations have to be made possible in the day-to-day management of the process.

2. **Management of the options ("activity framework")**: Having defined and structured the management object, the process manager's activity framework has to be evaluated. This entails describing to what extent the process manager is permitted to change input, throughput, and output of the process through corrective courses of action. Thus, the range of design options for the process is defined.

3. **Management of measurement**: The process manager is capable of taking action, since the management object and the activity framework have been defined. However, taking corrective action serves to improve process performance and process target attainment. Therefore, definitions are

required of how to evaluate the management object and the activity framework. Consequently, process indicators and measurements have to be defined.

4. **Management of decision**: If the process manager detects any deviations from the target perfor-mance, he has to make decisions concerning an appropriate corrective measure. He has the measures defined in the activity framework at his disposition. The selection of the "correct" measure requires an analysis and comparison of the different design options within the range of possible variations. Finally, the optimal decision specific to the situation at hand has to be made.

The decision is thus based on a comparison of design options and the selection of the situation-specific optimal process design. The comparison of design options can be described as the benchmarking of process variations. The process laboratory aims to support such benchmarking efforts. The starting point for the development of a process laboratory is the management object "loan process." The following explanations are therefore limited to the first critical issues identified above, namely the modularisation of the object "loan process."

MODULARISATION OF SERVICE PROCESSES AS A STARTING POINT FOR A FRAMEWORK

Modularisation represents a means to disaggregate business processes ideally into completely independent process modules. The primary objective is to reduce the complexity of processes. This is necessary for service processes in financial institutions, because they are – as shown in Section 2 – characterised by heterogeneous integrativity of customers. In addition, modularisation aims to integrate different process flows within one process model. This section starts with an explanation of the modularisation concept. This is followed by a description of the specific methodology for the modularisation of business pro-cesses. Finally, modularisation will be illustrated, using the loan process as an example.

Modularisation Concept

The objective pursued with modularisation is to better understand and manage a complex system. A complex system consists of a multitude of components that interact with one another (Simon & Cilliers, 2005). In order to reduce the complexity, the components are combined in clusters (also referred to as modules), resulting in a decrease in the number of system components that interact with each other.

Hence, a modular system consists of individual component clusters, the modules. Ideally, these mod-ules do not exhibit any dependencies between each other; i.e. they can exist independently. The system, however, only functions as an integrated whole. The components within a module interact strongly with each other. In order to reduce complexity, the interactions between the individual units are, however, no longer examined. In looking at the development of a modular system, Baldwin and Clark (2000) therefore distinguish between visible and hidden construction parameters for the system. On the one hand, the hidden construction parameters represent module-inherent information on the interaction of the units within the module and which do not influence the system as whole. The visible construction parameters, on the other hand, describe the configuration of the system and thus the interaction of the modules. They influence the system configuration and can be distinguished in three categories:

- *Architecture:* The architecture describes which modules are part of the entire system and with which properties (i.e. functions) they should be endowed.
- *Interfaces:* The module interfaces describe in detail how the modules interact and how they have to be adapted to and combined with each other.
- *Norms:* Using norms, the modules can be tested for system conformity. Norms also provide the basis for determining the relative performance of the modules.

The objective of developing a modular system is to minimise the interdependencies between the units within a system or between the modules that are to be developed. The system should be divided into its components in a comprehensible manner.

If the modularisation approach is pursued, then, according to Camuffo (2000), attention must be paid to three perspectives: modularity in product architecture, modularity in process (production) architecture, and modularity in organisational architecture. When thinking of a product or service, attention has to be given from the very beginning to the independent units. The individual modules and their interfaces have to be defined. Based on this, the production process has to be thought through. Independent modules can be simultaneously developed, produced, and tested. In such a case, the opportunity exists to engage a cooperation partner in the module production. Including external partners in the production of the individual modules may result in scale economies (increase in efficiency). Moreover, flexibility in meeting individual customer requirements may rise, since the modules can be assembled according to the specific customer requirements (Feitzinger & Lee, 1997). When the definition of modules is completed, the modules have to be combined and tested for their functionality. Additionally, the whole organisation has to be compatible with the modularisation concept. Organisational processes, governance structures, as well as marketing and sales structures, have to be aligned with the modular approach.

In the optimal case, the resulting structure resembles that recommended by Baldwin and Clark (2000) and depicted in Figure 4. In the first production step, a *Basis Process Module* consisting of interdependent activities is created. The outputs of the basis module represent impacting information (inputs) for subsequent process modules. Impacting information includes, for example, the property definitions of the product or service that has to be produced. The individual module outputs are produced through the *Process Modules* on the basis of the impacting information. The process modules themselves consist of mutually dependent activities. However, there are no dependencies between the individual process modules, except for a visible dependency between the basis module and the individual process modules. The information derived from the basis modules serves to combine the individual module outputs in the last production step, the *End Design*, to result in the finished product or service.

A disadvantage of this methodology is that the design of the modular architecture depends on a substantial amount of information needed to evaluate the dependency criteria, and not all companies may have access to the required information. Access to sufficient information that meets certain quality standards is unavoidable. Furthermore, this methodology carries the risk of introducing bias, particularly in the evaluation of the dependency criteria (Gershenson et al., 2004).

An appropriate design and the successful implementation of the module architecture can provide for a significant reduction in the complexity of the process model. Process managers can then align potential modules in parallel, exchange modules, or eliminate and/or add new modules (Feitzinger & Lee, 1997). In order to determine whether the module architecture supports such activities, the six-stage model "process module architecture maturity" developed by Tu et al. (2004) can be applied. According to this model, the next higher stage can only be reached if the requirements for the stages below have been met.

Figure 4. Schematic modularisation of a service process

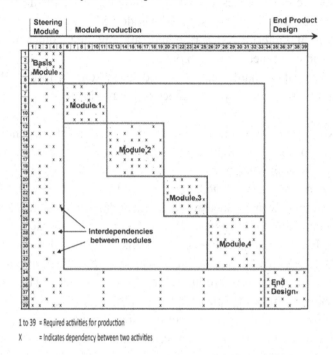

Once the highest stage is met, standardised and customised process modules can be arranged in such a way that selected standardised process modules can be performed by cooperation partners within a cross-organisational network structure. The maturity of the process module architecture thus determines opportunities for cooperation models and for the management of the production process.

Methodology for the Modularisation of Service Processes with Heterogeneous Integrativity

The module concept serves as a basis for the development of a loan process model. The process manager's operational management task is therefore only related to the configuration and design of the process modules and at the same time takes into consideration the interdependencies between the process modules. The inherent dependencies between activities within a single process module are only considered to the extent that operational management also entails initiating a check of the process module and the activities within the module. Management of the individual activities within a process module and of the inherent dependencies should not be performed. This ensures focus of the management task on a limited number of process modules. The process manager is therefore able to measure and analyse the process efficiency of clearly delineated process modules. Consequently, the process manager can evaluate measures to increase process efficiency. When identifying the "correct" measure, the process manager has to merely consider the interdependencies between the modules.

A question remains, however, pertaining to the specific methodology of building the process modules. Ideally, such activities that are highly dependent on one another are combined in one process module.

The dependency between the individual process modules should be zero or as minimal as possible.

However, service processes such as the loan process exhibit dependencies beyond processes alone. A service process is also dependent on the external factor "customer" and the information provided by customers, namely external non-impacting process information and external process-impacting information. External non-impacting process information is processed, used, and changed during the provisioning process (e.g. the loan applicant provides information on the home that serves as collateral). Such information, however, does not impact the process flow but is merely used to provide the final service offer itself. Very often such information is also needed to tailor the service offer to the customer's desired service attributes (e.g. information related to desired early payment options). External process-impacting information refers to customer information that impacts the service provider's service delivery flexibility, the specific activities and processes. For example, if a customer desires a home financing loan, different service delivery processes and process flows will be required than for a personal loan. The request for a home loan necessitates activities related to the assessment of the collateral and agreements on the encumbrance of the property, whereas these activities are not required for a personal loan.

Ideally, customers' external process-impacting information should be collected and compiled at the very beginning of the service delivery process in order to enable the process manager to understand, from the outset, the dependencies on such impacting information and to eliminate any potential unknown factors. As recommended in the Baldwin and Clark model, such impacting information could be integrated into the basis process module. External non-impacting information, however, does not necessarily have to be known at the outset of the service delivery process but rather can be introduced during the actual process flow. Still, it appears sensible that not all modules are created in such a way that they are dependent on non-impacting information. Bundling non-impacting information in clearly defined process modules appears highly appropriate to reduce complexity. Following Baldwin and Clark, the loan process can be divided into three phases:

1. The first phase encompasses the sub-processes sales/application preparation and loan decision, i.e. all activities until the bank achieves a decision whether or not to approve a loan and to engage in the business. At the beginning of this phase, all information pertaining to the attributes of the desired service offer constitutes impacting information.

2. The second phase starts with the processing of the loan documentation and making the loan amount available. Besides on-going servicing, this phase includes monitoring debt payments and risk management (sub-processes loan processing/servicing and risk management including monitoring). This phase is dependent on the impacting information related to the desired service offer, the loan decision, as well as the loan acceptance by the customer or any changes the customer wishes to make to the requested loan.

3. The third phase entails the service provider's methods, procedures, and activities in cases of customers who may default on their loans (sub-process workout). These activities are dependent on customer information, his financial situation, and his payment ability.

Figure 5 illustrates the concept of the three-phase loan process model. Each phase starts with a basis process module into which the customer's external impacting information enters.

The external impacting information is an input factor – without this information none of the subsequent activities during this phase can be performed. The customer's external impacting information ultimately determines the selection of the required process modules within the basis process module as well as the

Figure 5. The three-phase loan process model

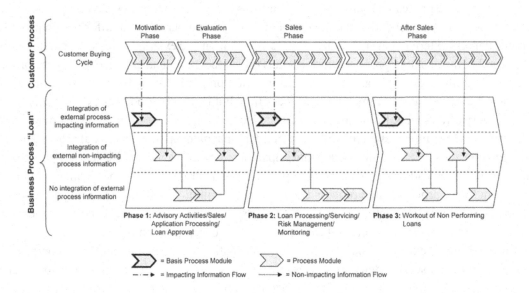

sequence of the modules within that phase. All available modules of a bank or of its network are considered (i.e. the bank and its cooperation partners). External non-impacting information is considered as well, but such information merely impacts the service attributes (e.g. loan decision, interest conditions, payment terms), and it does not influence process module selection or process module sequence. The design of the process model should therefore combine *in each phase* within the basis process module those activities that depend on external impacting customer information. All other activities should be combined in process modules on the basis of their degree of interdependence on one another. The process modules should be as independent from each other as possible, while the activities within a module should exhibit a degree of interdependence that is as high as possible. Activities that require external non-impacting customer information should be preferably combined within a small number of process modules in each phase.

Modularisation of the Loan Process – a Process with Heterogeneous Integrativity

In the following, the modularisation methodology will be demonstrated by depicting the management object "loan process" as a modularised process model. Figure 6 depicts the results of the modularisation of Phase 1 "Sales/Application Preparation and Loan Decision." The phase is divided into "Steering Module Design," "Module Production," and "End Product Design."

The "Steering Module Design" phase includes establishing contact with the customer and developing an initial offer that is tailored to the customer's requirements. The offer includes the loan and additional required products. The determination of the modules required for the provisioning of the loan occurs during the last sub-process within "Steering Module Design." The other products within the overall service package will not be examined in this process model. While preparing the offer and determining the modules, those customer requirements and pieces of information are gathered that at this point

Figure 6. Sub-processes of phase 1 "Sales/Application Preparation and Loan Decision"

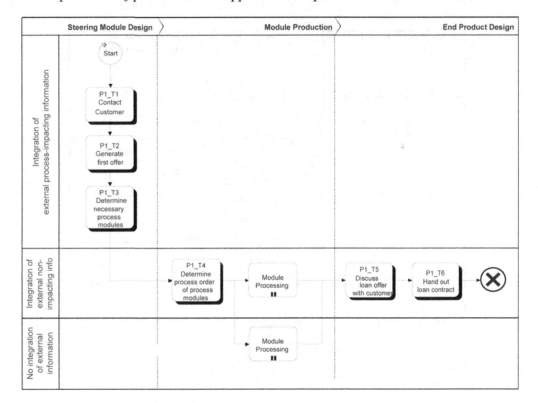

exert a steering impact on the process flow. As the process moves into the "Module Production" phase, impacting influence by the customer is no longer permitted.

The identified modules that are required to deliver the requested service (e.g. liquidity analysis, credit-rating report, financing decision, collateral evaluation, back-office financing decision) are completed during the "Module Production" phase. The individual service components are produced in the respective modules. Some modules require for this customer information, which, however, does not have an impact on the process flow. Moreover, the chronological sequence of the modules has to be defined in more detail, even though there is an opportunity for operational intervention at this point.

The outputs of the modules are combined in the "End Product Design" phase. In addition, a decision is made during this phase about whether the loan service can actually be offered to the customer. If the decision is negative, the customer will receive a rejection notification. If the decision is positive, a final loan offer with terms and conditions is developed and discussed with the customer. The loan contract is handed to the customer with the request for signature.

Phase 1, "Sales/Application Preparation and Loan Decision," ends at this point. If the customer decides to accept the loan offer and signs the loan contract, the process transitions to Phase 2, "Loan Processing/Servicing and Risk Management." Figure 7 summarises the required sub-processes during Phase 1 and for each sub-process the available process modules.

The modularisation of processes ensures a clear-cut process flow and sequence. Moreover, it is clearly defined when process-impacting information is permitted to enter the process flow and as of which point in time such impacting customer information is no longer desired. A further significant advantage of process modularisation is increased flexibility concerning the sequence and flow of the

Figure 7. Sub-processes and available modules in phase 1

Sub-process		Module	
P1_S1	**Establish Contact with Customer**	P_C01	Process Customer's Appointment Request
		P_C02	Process Customer's Product Request
		P_C03	Process Customer's Request for Offer
		P_C04	Prepare Customer Meeting
		P_C05	Reject Application
P1_S2	**Develop Initial Offer**	P_C06	Document Decline of Offer
P1_S3	**Determine Process Modules to Be Used**	P1_C01	Create Customer Record
		P1_C02	Check Loan Criteria
		P1_C03	Obtain Credit Rating
		P1_C04	Make Initial Loan Decision
		P1_C05	Conduct Back-Office Loan Decision
		P1_C06	Inspect Property
		P1_C07	Solicit References, Obtain Company Information
		P1_C08	Analyse Financial Records
		P1_C09	Make Final Loan Decision
		P1_C10	Escalate Decision
		P1_C11	Check Debts on Collateral
		P1_C12	Check Other Collateral
		P_C05	Reject Application
		P_C06	Document Decline of Offer
P1_S4	**Determine Sequence of Loan Decision Process**	Determine Process Modules from P1_S3 That Have to Be Used	
P1_S5	**Discuss Loan Offer**	P_C05	Reject Application
		P_C06	Document Decline of Offer
P1_S6	**Deliver Loan Contract**	P_C06	Document Decline of Offer
		P1_C13	Delete Loan Application

P = Phase
S = Sub-process
C = Centrally Available Process Module

process modules. The process manager has the possibility to change the module sequence during module production. At the same time, he has more flexibility in resource allocation. Operational management of the service process "loan" with its heterogeneous customer involvement is thus made possible thanks to the modularisation of the management object. Building on this, the framework for operational process management can be developed.

FUTURE DEVELOPMENTS OF OPERATIONAL PROCESS MANAGEMENT FOR SERVICE PROCESSES WITH HETEROGENEOUS INTEGRATIVITY

The development of a framework for operational process management of the service process "loan" with its heterogeneous customer involvement necessitates a discussion of the phases depicted in Figure 3: process measurement, process control and process improvement. As previously discussed, much academic research has been dedicated to these topics. However, the relationship between the individual phases has not been examined very closely. In the future, more attention has to be paid to the relationship between the three phases and the implications of the results of each individual phase. This requires at the analytical level a discussion of the management object "process," the management options, the management of measurement, and the management of the decision. A simulation-based framework supports the analysis of these issues. The framework does not offer a pre-packaged solution for real-life problems within the operational management of loan processes – instead, it provides direction for the development of operational process management for individual situations.

The starting point to address the management problem is the definition of the management object. This entails describing the process flow for the service process "loan," a process with heterogeneous integrativity. Thus far, this chapter has described the activities required to provision a loan from end-to-end. It became evident that the customer's direct involvement results in high service process complexity and constrains the ability to manage the process. In order to reduce complexity and to increase opportunities for process modifications during the operational flow, the modularisation approach was applied to the process model. The result was a manageable end-to-end loan process model.

Once the management object has been defined, the management options can be determined in a next step. Consequently, general courses of action for process performance improvement have to be outlined. Based on this, the courses of action applicable for the service process "loan process" have to be developed, keeping the heterogeneous customer involvement in mind. This results in a variety of different possible process designs. The management object and the activity framework for operational management have thus been defined, and the operational management process can be developed from here.

CONCLUSION

The financial services industry is characterized by intense competition. In order to succeed in such a competitive environment, industry members continuously search for solutions that fit their specific situation. In particular, banks and insurance companies attempt to apply classic process management approaches from manufacturing industries to the service sector. However, this chapter has highlighted marked differences between the production process for a physical good and the production process for services. Services, in contrast to physical goods, are characterised by the involvement of the customer in the production process (integration of the external factor). When comparing different types of services, it becomes evident that there are significant differences as well, in particular concerning the degree of customer involvement. The degree of such integrativity serves as an indicator of how strongly a customer impacts the service delivery process of the service provider and thus determines the relationship between autonomous and integrative service delivery.

This chapter has pointed out that the degree of integrativity has to be considered particularly in the operational management of service processes. In addition, this chapter has stressed the necessity of developing a simulation-based framework, for the operational management of service processes with heterogeneous integrativity. Such a framework provides direction for service processes of any kind. The starting point for the development of a framework is the definition of the management object "process" as well as the determination of the activity options or parameters for management decisions. In accordance with the management object, the system "service process" has to be identified and structured. This entails selecting a design, configuration, and structure of the process, all of which enable operational process management. Using a service process, specifically the loan process, as an example, this chapter has illustrated how the management object has to be structured in order to engage in operational management. The authors have used the modularisation approach to accomplish this. Using modularisation, the process model was divided into process components and process modules that were as independent from one another as possible. This resulted in a reduction in the complexity of the process model. Modularisation also enables the integration of different process flows within one process model.

A modularised process model supports the development of activity parameters for the operational management of the process. These can then be compared within the simulation model, providing the process manager with the opportunity to select and implement the optimal course of action.

REFERENCES

Argyris, C. (1999). *On organizational learning* (2nd ed.). Oxford: Blackwell.

Baldwin, C. Y., & Clark, K. B. (2000). *Design rules: The power of modularity*. Cambridge, MA: MIT Press.

Barber, K. D., Dewhurst, F. W., Burns, R. L. D. H., & Rogers, J. B. B. (2003). Business-process modelling and simulation for manufacturing management. A practical way forward. *Business Process Management Journal, 4*(9), 527–542. doi:10.1108/14637150310484544

Bratley, P., Fox, B. L., & Schrage, L. E. (1987). *A guide to simulation* (2nd ed.). New York: Springer.

Brim, O. G., Class, D. C., Lavin, D. E., & Goodman, N. E. (1962). *Personality and decision process – Studies in the social psychology of thinking*. Stanford, CA: Stanford University Press.

Bullinger, H.-J., Fähnrich, K.-P., & Meiren, T. (2003). Service engineering – Methodical development of new service products. *International Journal of Production Economics, 3*(85), 275–287. doi:10.1016/S0925-5273(03)00116-6

Camuffo, A. (2000). *Rolling out a "World car." Globalization, outsourcing and modularity in the auto industry*. Venice, Italy: Ca´ Foscari University, Department of Business Economics and Management.

Davenport, T. H., & Short, J. E. (1990). The new industrial engineering. Information technology and business process redesign. *Sloan Management Review, 4*(31), 11–27.

Drucker, P. (1980), *Managing in turbulent times*. New York: Harper & Row.

Engelhardt, W. H., & Freiling, J. (1995). Die integrative Gestaltung von Leistungspotentialen. *Zeitschrift für betriebswirtschaftliche Forschung, 10*(47), 899–918.

Feitzinger, E., & Lee, H. L. (1997). Mass customization at Hewlett-Packard. The power of postponement. *Harvard Business Review, 1*(75), 116–121.

Fleury, A., & Fleury, M. T. (2007). The evolution of production systems and conceptual frameworks. *Journal of Manufacturing Technology Management, 8*(18), 949–965. doi:10.1108/17410380710828271

Gershenson, J. K., Prasad, G. J., & Zhang, Y. (2004). Product modularity: Measures and design methods. *Journal of Engineering Design, 1*(15), 33–51. doi:10.1080/0954482032000101731

Hammer, M., & Champy, J. (1993), *Reengineering the corporation: A Manifesto for business revolution*. New York: Harper Business.

Kasper, H., van Helsdingen, P., & de Vries, W. (1999). *Services marketing management. An international perspective*. New York: John Wiley.

Kleinaltenkamp, M., & Haase, M. (1999). Externe Faktoren in der Theorie der Unternehmensführung. In H. H. Albach (Ed.), *Die Theorie der Unternehmung in Forschung und Praxis* (pp. 167-194). Berlin: Springer.

Kueng, P., & Kawalek, P. (1997). Goal-based business process models: Creation and evaluation. *Business Process Management Journal, 1*(3), 17–38. doi:10.1108/14637159710161567

Neely, A., Gregory, M., & Platts, K. (2005). Performance measurement system design: A literature review and research agenda. *International Journal of Operations & Production Management, 12*(25), 1228–1263. doi:10.1108/01443570510633639

Pande, P. S., Neumann, R. P., & Cavanagh, R. (2000). *The six sigma way.* New York: McGraw-Hill.

Silvestro, R., Fitzgerald, L., & Johnston, R. (1992). Towards a classification of service processes. *International Journal of Service Industry Management, 3*(3), 62–75. doi:10.1108/09564239210015175

Simon, H., & Cilliers, P. (2005). The architecture of complexity. *Emergence: Complexity & Organization, 3/4*(7), 138–154.

Staikouras, C. K., & Koutsomanoli-Fillipaki, A. (2006). Competition and concentration in the new European banking landscape. *European Financial Management, 3*(12), 443–482. doi:10.1111/j.1354-7798.2006.00327.x

Stauss, B., & Weinlich, B. (1997). Process-oriented measurement of service quality. *European Journal of Marketing, 1*(31), 33–55. doi:10.1108/03090569710157025

Tu, Q., Vonderembse, M. A., Ragu-Nathan, T. S., & Ragu-Nathan, B. (2004). Measuring modularity-based manufacturing practices and their impact on mass customization capability. A customer-driven perspective. *Decision Sciences, 2*(35), 147–168. doi:10.1111/j.00117315.2004.02663.x

Ulrich, H. H. (1981). Die Bedeutung der Management-Philosophie für die Unternehmensführung. In H.H. Ulrich (Ed.), *Management-Philosophie für die Zukunft* (pp. 11-24). Bern, Stuttgart: Haupt.

Wigand, R. T., Steinfield, C. W., & Markus, M. L. (2005). Information technology standards choices and industry structure outcomes: The case of the U.S. home mortgage industry. *Journal of Management Information Systems, 2*(22), 165–191.

Wright, J., & Race, P. (2004). The management of service operations (2nd ed.). London: Thomson.

Zairi, M., & Sinclair, D. (1995). Business process reengineering and process improvement. A survey of current practice and future trends in integrated management. *Management Decision, 3*(33), 3–16. doi:10.1108/00251749510085021

Zeithaml, V. A., Parasuraman, A., & Berry, L. L. (1985). Problems and strategies in services marketing. *Journal of Marketing, 2*(49), 33–46. doi:10.2307/1251563

KEY TERMS AND DEFINITIONS

Financial Services Industry: Commercial banks, investment banks and insurance companies comprise the major share of the financial services sector. The work is performed by central banks, stock exchanges and regulatory authorities.

Framework: A framework is an instrument to identify relevant variables and the relationship between them for a specific practical question. It consists of a combination of deductive models and inductive based case studies. A framework needs to be adapted to many different situations and therefore delivers a set of alternatives.

Heterogeneous Integrativity: The necessity of involving the customer ("external factor") in service production constitutes a major difference from mass production of physical goods. The degree of customer integration within a service process differs with respect to the dependence on the information needed and on the type of service.

Loan Process: This is considered to be one of the core business processes in banking. The loan process comprises the following sub-processes: advisory and sales, processing of the application, loan approval/rejection, loan processing and servicing, risk management and monitoring, and workout.

Modularisation: The concept of modularisation is used for reducing the complexity of a system. This system (e.g. business process, organisational structure, IT application) is deconstructed into more or less independent units ("modules"). The modules should be able to exist independently from each other, but the system as a whole can only function as an integrated structure.

Operational Process Management: As part of a comprehensive business process control structure, operational process management consists of three phases: process measurement, process control, and process improvement.

Service Process: As compared to manufacturing, a service process results in the delivery of non-physical goods. Thus, there is no assembly line, and machinery usually plays a minor role. However, intensive involvement of human resources and information technology is crucial.

Chapter 24
Knowledge Flow Networks and Communities of Practice In Business Process Management

Rajiv Khosla
La Trobe University, Australia

Mei-Tai Chu
La Trobe University, Australia

Shinichi Doi
NEC Corporation, Japan

Keiji Yamada
NEC Corporation Japan

Toyoaki Nishida
Kyoto University, Japan

ABSTRACT

Business process management (BPM) is a common approach used in dynamic and complicated environ-ment throughout the organizations' operation. Knowledge Flow Networks (KFN) and Communities of Practice (CoPs), especially that resulting from innovation needs, is regarded as a BPM issue. It involves both personal and organizational aspects, and is an iteration of the transmission between explicit and tacit knowledge. We discuss business process management in the context of Knowledge Management (KM) and knowledge flow networks. KFN, unlike workflow, can often transcend organizational bound-aries and are distinct and different than workflow models. In this chapter, we develop, implement, and analyze a CoPs Centered KFN model in a multinational organization. The CoPs Centered KFN model is underpinned in a CoPs model built around four organization performance evaluation dimensions and sixteen criteria. Many criteria and clusters need to be taken into consideration while establishing a CoPs model. For this purpose, fuzzy multi-criteria decision making and cluster analysis techniques for evaluation of the CoPs Centered KFN model are employed in this chapter. A Dynamic Knowledge Flow Activity Analysis Model is also defined as part of our ongoing and future work.

DOI: 10.4018/978-1-60566-669-3.ch024

INTRODUCTION

Organizations today exist in the knowledge era as against the information era of 1980 and 1990`s. They compete with each other on the basis of knowledge and innovation (OECD 1996, 1999). Thus organizational innovation through knowledge creation and flow is an important means of surviving as well as thriving in a highly competitive business environment. In pursuit of knowledge organizations of the future will not be constrained by traditional boundaries. Thus this research envisions organizations as a set of Knowledge Flow Networks (KFN) which can extend outside organizational boundaries as against conventional work flow networks. Human nodes used in workflow are not necessarily the same as nodes used in knowledge flow in an organization.

KFN not only falls within the scope of managers, information technologists and knowledge workers but involves Communities of Practice (CoPs) in an organization (Lesser, 2001). Most of the existing work on knowledge flow networks has centered around linking people based on organization structure, tasks, and knowledge compatibility (Zhuge, 2006). Existing research does not throw adequate light on the need that knowledge flow occurs between knowledge workers outside traditional organizational structure, business functions and organizational boundaries. In this chapter, the authors propose to enhance in design of KFN by modeling them based on CoPs in an organisation. In CoPs, like in KFN, people with a common goal come together to create, learn, process and share knowledge based on best practices. In this research, a CoPs model has been defined, which constitutes 16 criteria along four performance measurement dimensions. These criteria and dimensions are used to identify common interaction factors (beliefs and attitudes) which link and facilitate effective knowledge sharing between knowledge workers in a KFN. These factors and the CoPs model have been validated using a large multinational organization as a case study. Given that, knowledge flow is dynamic phenomena in an organization, we also define a dynamic model for analysing knowledge flow activities like knowledge sharing, knowledge discovery, and knowledge creation.

The chapter is organized as follows. Section 2 covers the theoretical considerations underpinning the definition and construction of KFN model. Section 3 describes implementation and Techniques of KFN model based on survey of R&D personnel in a multinational organization. Section 4 presents results and findings of the survey based on the fuzzy multi criteria decision making and cluster analysis techniques. Section 5 suggests the future research and trend. Section 6 concludes the chapter with future research directions.

THEORETICAL UNDERPINNINGS OF KFN MODEL

In this section we construct KFN model based on CoPs. We assume in this research that design of KFN is driven by the need to develop effective knowledge sharing and knowledge management (KM) mechanisms in order to enable organizations to compete in a knowledge based economy. In this context we, firstly, define a CoPs model, the criteria and dimensions it is based and the business strategies or benefits which can be evaluated using the model. We follow this with definition of CoPs centered KFN model which is used for implementation and analysis in our case study.

Communities of Practice

Despite the rise of technology-based Knowledge Management tools, implementations often fail to realize their stated objectives (Ambrosio 2000). It is envisaged that 70% of existing knowledge management tools have failed to achieve the anticipated business performance outcomes they had been designed for (Malhotra 2004). One of the primary reasons identified for the failure of existing KM tools has been that existing Knowledge Management tools and research have primarily been designed around technology-push models as against strategy-pull models (Malhotra 2004). The technology-push model which is based on application of information technologies on historical data largely produce pre-specified meanings/ knowledge and pre-specified outcomes which are useful in predictable and stable business environments. On the other hand, strategy-pull model turns the technology-push model on its head and drive the construction and creation of knowledge and related actions based on business strategy and performance driven outcome rather than somehow find a business strategy fit for the pre-specified knowledge and outcomes produced by technology-push models.

In an era where organizations are undergoing rapid, discontinuous and turbulent change it is imperative that KM systems and organizational entities like CoPs which facilitate KM and organizational transformation are more closely aligned with business strategies and goals of an organization. This would enable organizations to respond more quickly to changing business environments and business process and corresponding change in their KM needs from time to time.

Wenger (1998) first proposed CoPs in the Harvard Business Review, who believes CoPs is an informal group sharing knowledge, points out CoPs is composed by three critical elements (mutual engagement, joint enterprise, shared repository). Allee (2000) thought knowledge should include and utilize CoPs to create organizational knowledge. Besides, CoPs are distinguishing from other organizational groups such as formal divisions, project teams and informal network (Cohendet & Meyer-Krahmer, 2001; Allee, 2000; Wenger et al., 2002). CoPs can enable member interaction, knowledge sharing, organization learning, and open innovation simultaneously; it emphasizes more on facilitating, extracting and sharing tacit knowledge to maximize KM value. Many world class companies have taken CoPs as a new central role in the value chain (Chu et al, 2007).

As outlined by Chu et al., (2007) the benefits of CoPs can be distinguished by organization performance and operation mode as the matrix as shown in Figure 1. Mostly, some firms are likely to emphasize how to reduce costs or increase profits instead, while some companies tend to focus on group learning or reuse intellectual asset (IA) more. The first two factors (cost down and revenue up) can be categorized into organizational performance axle, and the latter two factors (group learning and reuse IA) can be grouped into operation mode axle in the matrix.

While CoPs emphasize competency and efficiency enhancement, their organization performance tends to cost down effectively. But when CoPs focus on innovation and responsiveness, which would aim at create new value or revenue up. Furthermore, this research points out that the operation mode residing in CoPs leads to behavioral changes, which in turn results in different preference on organizational performance. On one hand, when CoPs prefer explicit knowledge content, the operation mode may focus on reuse IA, and emphasize the storage, access, and reusing of knowledge. This sort of CoPs tends to pursue organizational performance on business strategies like **Enhanced Working Efficiency** and **Promoted Responsiveness** through getting warning through analysis and classification of knowledge. On the other hand, when CoPs prefer tacit knowledge, the operation mode may stress to create grouping learning, providing experts to exchange, interact, sharing best practices. This sort of CoPs tends to pursue

Figure 1. CoPs Benefit Matrix

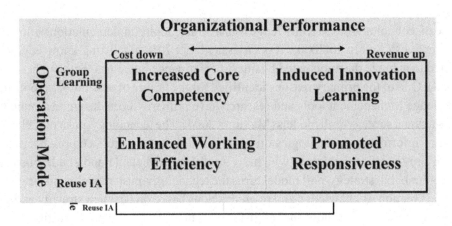

the organizational performance on business strategies like **Increased Core Competency** and **Induced Innovation Learning** through raising the capability via cross-domain exchange.

Acknowledging that CoPs can link with organizational performance very well, CoPs are essential to overcome the inherent problems of a slow-moving traditional hierarchy in a fast-moving knowledge economy. Therefore, this research uses the four CoPs benefits or business strategies **Induce Innovation Learning**, **Promote Responsiveness**, **Increase Core Competency**, and **Enhance Working Efficiency** to develop the CoPs model. These four CoPs business strategies need to be well defined and then pursued, because they will influence the KM achievements and the community's resources allocation direction.

The first benefit is to **Induce Innovation Learning.** The specific characteristics include cross-domain sharing to support new idea and creation according to common interests through group learning. The CoPs under this strategy often provide a safe or low-cost infrastructure for try and error attempts freely to facilitate new thinking and innovation.

The second benefit is to **Promote Responsiveness** by collecting and classifying knowledge objects. CoPs can directly obtain the problem-oriented solution, because the colleagues with similar working experiences are easy to find. They can help other members who are facing same questions based on the common language and shared foundations which lead to promote responsiveness.

The third benefit is to **Increase Core Competency.** Members can promote skill by shifting the best knowledge practices. It will be efficient to figure out who are domain-experts, how to enable insight exchange between senior and junior members. The organization principals can be established and increase core competency.

The fourth benefit is to **Enhance Working Efficiency.** CoPs members can reuse existing intellectual property invented by others in a well structured database easily, access related documents and authors' information quickly. The entire productivity will be improved and working efficiency will be enhanced in a disciplined way.

CoPs Model and its Components

In order to realize the four business benefits or strategies the CoPs model is defined and evaluated along four performance dimensions and sixteen criteria as outlined in Chu et al, (2007). The hierarchy of the

Figure 2. CoPs Centered Evaluation Hierarchy Model

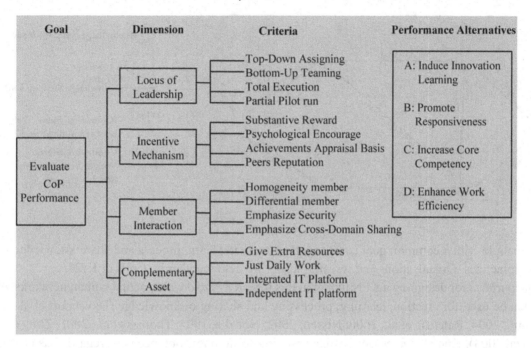

four dimensions and sixteen criteria is shown in Figure 2 (Chu et al, 2007). The four dimensions are explained as follows respectively:

- Locus of Leadership: relates to enforcement or volunteer, wholly or partially adoption
- Incentive Mechanism: relates to award or punishment
- Member Interaction: relates to sharing or security
- Complementary Asset: relates to infrastructure and resource

The **Locus of Leadership** dimension contains four criteria: Top-Down Assigning, Bottom-Up Teaming, Total Execution, and Partial Pilot run. The **Incentive Mechanism** dimension contains: Substantive Reward, Psychological Encourage, Achievements Appraisal Basis, and Peers Reputation. The **Member Interaction** contains: Homogeneity of members, Differential members, Emphasize security, and Emphasize cross-domain Sharing. The **Complementary Asset** dimension contains: Give Extra Resources, Just Daily Work, Integrated IT Platform, and Independent IT platform.

CoPs Centered Knowledge Flow Network Model

In the preceding section the ground related to definition and construction of CoPs model has been outlined. In this section we use the CoPs cantered parameters to define the components and terminologies of the knowledge flow network model. The KFN includes quantitative implications of the human and social factors like beliefs and attitudes for interaction between knowledge workers derived from the CoPs model (Thomas et al., 2001). These interaction beliefs and attitudes for knowledge sharing are based on the sixteen criteria used by the CoPs model. KFN can also be considered as CoPs in an organization

Figure 3. Knowledge Flow Network Model

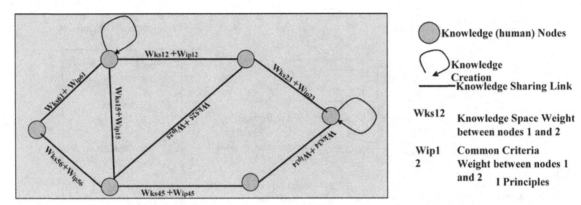

where people with a common goal come together to create, learn, process and share knowledge based on best practices. Organisations and research teams are held together by CoPs or KFN.

The purpose for designing a KFN model in this research is to develop actual human networks which can then be used for creation, learning, processing and sharing of knowledge (Davenport et al., 2004; Malhotra, 2004; Ratcliffe et al., 2000; Nissen, 2002; Nonaka, 1994; Thomas et al., 2001; Zhuge, 2003; Desouza, 2003). Knowledge especially that resulting from innovation needs, is regarded as an organizational transformation issue. It involves transmission of explicit, tacit and embodied knowledge in an iterative manner through KFN.

A KFN model as shown in Figure 3 consists of knowledge nodes (human or knowledge portal or process), knowledge links and weight which help to specify the strength of the knowledge link. With the definition of CoPs and existing research, knowledge workers share knowledge based knowledge compatibility as well as a set of interaction principles and beliefs which define their underlying knowledge sharing philosophy (Thomas et al., 2001). Although these interaction principles are not a determining factor for knowledge sharing they do influence the effectiveness and efficiency of knowledge sharing between two knowledge workers. These interaction principles and beliefs are defined based on the 16 criteria defined in CoPs model.

To draw an analogy, consider a situation for recruitment of sales person for selling computers. On one hand the recruitment panel will determine the knowledge compatibility of the sales person in the domain of computers. On the other hand, they will also study or analyse (based on range of criteria) how this sales person will interact with a customer in an actual selling situation. Similarly, knowledge level and space of a knowledge worker or a researcher can be determined based on their experience, CV, etc. However, to what extent they actually engage in knowledge sharing (especially, tacit knowledge) may be influenced by the 16 criteria for knowledge sharing and management. Other factors which can influence knowledge sharing can be trust and psychological profiles of the cooperating knowledge workers. However, the latter factors can be extended based on this research.

Therefore in Figure 3 we consider two types of weights, knowledge space weight and interaction principles weight. The knowledge space weight can vary between 0-1 and can be specified by the group or network leader based on knowledge and experience of the two knowledge workers, between discussions and consensus to calculate the impact of interaction principles on the overall effectiveness and efficiency of the knowledge link between two human nodes. Thus knowledge link weight between two

Figure 4. Knowledge flow and Workflow

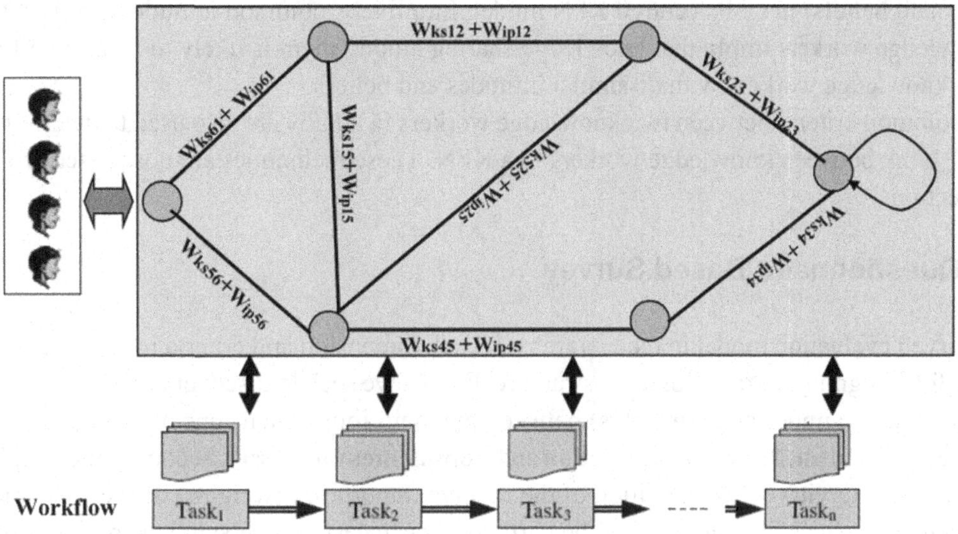

human nodes is calculated as follows:

$$KLW_{mn} = KSW_{mn} + \sum_{i=1}^{i=16} CCW_{mni}$$

Where KLW_{mn} is the knowledge link weight between nodes m and n, KSW_{mn} is the knowledge space weight between nodes m and n, and CCW_{mni} is the common criteria weight of criteria i between nodes m and n. The criteria weight are normalised between 0-1. The criteria with weight 0.1 or above may be added to determine CCW_{mn}. Figure 4 shows the difference between a knowledge flow network and work flow network. The workflow in Figure 4 is between various project tasks as shown. However, the knowledge flow pattern is different than work flow and may or may not follow the same pattern or path as the work flow.

KFN model can also assist in formation and growth of knowledge flow teams for R&D organizations as well as identification of high and low knowledge energy nodes. The human node in Figure 3 with the highest number of links is the node with highest knowledge energy as it represents knowledge sharing and interaction potential of the node.

TECHNIQUES AND IMPLEMENTATION OF COPS CENTERED KFN MODEL

In this section the authors describe the techniques used for construction of CoPs Centered knowledge flow network model in a large multinational organization. These techniques include a CoPs question-naire based survey of knowledge workers. The survey is used to evaluate the importance attributed by knowledge workers to 16 CoPs criteria of knowledge workers along four business performance evaluation dimensions. Fuzzy MCDM (Multi-Criteria Decision-Making) techniques are used to calculate the importance attributed to each dimension and each criterion by the knowledge worker participating in the survey. Finally clustering technique is used to connect knowledge workers with common criteria (attitudes and beliefs) in CoPs centred KFN model. Intuitively, common attitudes and beliefs between two knowledge workers imply that knowledge sharing among them is likely to be more effective than between knowledge workers with dissimilar attitudes and beliefs.

The common criteria between two knowledge workers in a KFN are also used to determine strength of CCW_{mn} link between knowledge workers in a KFN. These techniques are now described in the rest of this section.

CoPs Questionnaire Based Survey

The observed evaluation model in the hierarchy of each dimension and criteria in Figure 2 are used as a template for designing the questionnaire structure. Firstly, we seek to discover the participants' recognition of the relative importance (weights) between the main four dimensions of **Locus of Leadership**, **Incentive Mechanism, Member Interaction** and **Complementary Asset**. Secondly, the template is used to find out the interviewee's recognition of the relative importance (weights) of the evaluation criteria below each dimension. Therefore, all of the participants can easily understand the problem and analyze the relationship between each evaluation criteria. This result can reflect the true aspect of each opinion towards the relative importance of the evaluation criteria in the questionnaire. Thirdly, the definition of linguistic expression range and preferred business strategies are required to show the viewpoints by each participant. This result can collect the final value towards different business strategy alternatives, namely, **Induce Innovation Learning**, **Promote Responsiveness**, **Increase Core Competency**, and **Enhance Work Efficiency**.

Although many scholars assert that CoPs create organization value, there has been relatively little systematic and quantitative study on the linkage between community outcomes and the underlying functional structure, the majority of paper focuses on individual and subjective viewpoints, this research attempts to determine these insufficiencies, and aims at debatable criteria for future analysis. The questionnaires were designed to reveal the perspectives of each researcher in five laboratories of our case. The questionnaires were also designed to weight their comparative importance of business strategies. The questionnaire was distributed to a broad sampling of researchers, to seek their views and calculate their final values. The aim is to provide a valuable reference when choosing suitable CoPs business strategies. Thirty nine valid questionnaires out of seventy were collected with a response rate at 55.7%.

Fuzzy MCDM Techniques

When establishing CoPs model, many different aspects can be taken into consideration. There are numerous evaluation indexes. Moreover, their structures are hierarchical (Kerzner, 1989). Many scholars and experts have adopted the Analytic Hierarchy Process (AHP) (Saaty, 1977 & 1980) method to evaluate the problems of relative level factors of hierarchy and to provide a more complete depiction of the structural and functional aspects of whole system. For instance, Hwang & Yoon (1981) discussed multi-attribute decision methods and application, In addition, Mon et al. (1994) evaluated weapon system by AHP, Tsaur et al. (1997) analyzed tourist risk using fuzzy perspectives, and Tang & Tzeng (1999) researched e-business promotion strategy for information service industry. In the questionnaire, dimensions were measured by pairwise comparison; participants are easier to decide dimension A is more important than B dimension instead of dimension A versus B is 5 to 1.

In a pure environment or simplified appraisal, the method such as cost minimization, profit maximization, or cost effect analysis to evaluate different plans can be used. However, a complex situation with multi-goals has too many interdependent variables to analyze. The traditional analysis method is not suitable to find the solution (Tzeng, et al., 1992; Tzeng & Teng, 1994; Tsaur et al., 1997; Tang et al., 1999). Recently some scholars used Fuzzy AHP (Buckley, 1985) to handle linguistic scale problems, which is more convenient to help participants to express opinion and concept precisely. The inconsistent environment is due to the multi dimension. During the process, all participants' linguistic opinion is not absolute and unique. Therefore this research used fuzzy MCDM to evaluate four CoPs benefits, and adopts fuzzy linguistic cognition to capture varying degree of value by each participant. The following sections explain the related procedures and steps.

Relative Weight by Pairwise Comparison

The evaluation of the related hierarchy system and weight comes from a pairwise comparison of AHP method; each factor's importance within the hierarchy is determined by their weights (Saaty, 1977 & 1980). When there are evaluation criteria/objectives, decision makers must carry out a pairwise comparison. In the process of comparison, a certain degree of inconsistency is allowed. Saaty used this to depict a scale to come up with the main Eigenvector of the pairwise comparison matrix. The same scale was used to find different comparative weights of different standards.

The following is a mathematical formula given to compare standard set with n standards, according to its relative importance (weights). Suppose the standard for comparison is $c_1, c_2 \dots c_n$, and the weights of each is $w_1, w_2 \dots w_n$ and assuming $w = (w_1, w_2, \dots, w_n)^t$, then the pairwise comparison can be represented by formula of matrix A'

$$(A - \lambda_{max} I)\, w = 0$$

Formula (1) shows how A is a pairwise comparison matrix sorted in order by instinct and judgment. In order to come up with the priority Eigenvector, we must satisfy the Eigenvector of every w of $Aw = \lambda_{max} w$, the λ_{max} is the maximum eigenvalue of A. The sorting judgment of the order of pairwise comparison is observed and examined for consistency because an $n \times n$ matrix A includes n independent feature$*_j$; moreover, $j=1,2 \dots n$, also ranks aspects in order according to dimension (the same as the concept of main component analysis), $\sum_{j=1}^{n} \lambda_j$ is the Diagonal Element of matrix A and $\sum_{j=1}^{n} \lambda_j = tr(A)$ is the total. The diagonal factor line of matrix A is 1, so the total of the diagonal line factor of matrix A is n, therefore, only one $\lambda_j = 0$ ($\lambda_j \neq \lambda_{max}$) from the middle of $C.I. = (\lambda_{max} - n)/(n-1), (C.I.)$. The latter deviation value is what evaluates consistency. As an example: C.I.$= (\lambda max - n)/(n-1), (C.I.)$ is close to the consistency index, so it's deemed consistent. Generally speaking, only a value smaller than 0.1, can satisfy our judgment.

Constructing a Multi-Criteria Decision-Making System

The aim of this section is to build a multi-objective and multi-standard evaluation system for evaluating CoPs model. The three steps in building the system are:

a. Describe the situation
b. Establish the multi-goals construction and correlation tree shape structure
c. Evaluate the results

The method and concept of PATTERN (Planning Assistance through Technical Evaluation of Relevance Number) (NASA PATTERN, 1965; Tzeng, 1977; Tzeng & Shiau, 1987; Tzeng, et al., 1992; Tzeng & Teng, 1994; Tang, et al., 1999) was used to establish an CoPs centered evaluation model as the following section. The process of this research is to use fuzzy MCDM method to identify the dimensions and criteria priority as well as measure the four benefits of CoPs.

Non-Fuzzy Performance

This research uses the fuzzy AHP method proposed by Buckley in 1985. This work also employs triangle fuzzy theory to value the four business strategies in view of sixteen criteria. Participants have chosen a fuzzy value region in their questionnaire to show their priority setting. Center of Area (COA) solutions were used to transfer fuzzy linguistic expression (very high, high, fair, low, and very low) to Best Non-fuzzy Performance (BNP). These BNP represent the participant's comment on the quantity criteria value regarding the four kinds of business strategies and sixteen criteria. These effective values form this participant's effective matrix, and U participants represent the 1st participant's effectiveness matrix.

Clustering Techniques

Clustering Techniques can find groups with similarities or common elements (Fowlkes & Mallows, 1983). This technique is applied to solve theoretical and practical problems (Clatworthy et al, 2005). It is a data reduction process and an entire data set can be represented by a small numbers of clusters. All the clusters divide a data set so that records with similar content are in the same group, and groups are as different as possible from each other. Since the categories are unspecified, this is also known as unsupervised classification which can be useful in predictive modeling. In this research, researchers could be clustered into homogenous groups based on their responses. Then a network can be built to predict the cluster membership according to more easily obtained input variables.

One of the most widely used clustering techniques is the K-means clustering algorithm (Huang, 1998; Mackay, 2003). K-means clustering algorithm uses properties of k-nearest neighbors to justify what classes a new instance belongs to. The implementation of K-means clustering algorithm firstly needs to train the available examples as follows:For each training example<*x, f(x)*>, add the example to the training set *f(x)* is of the form *f: $R^n \rightarrow V$, where V* is the finite class set $\{v_1, v_2 \dots v_s\}$.

For a new instance x_q, computing the distance among the new instance and every trained data using the following Euclidean distance formula:

$$d(x_i, x_j) = \sqrt{\sum_{p=1}^{n} (a_p(x_i) - a_p(x_j))^2}$$

Then, for *K* nearest neighbors $(x_1, x_2 \dots x_k)$ found in the last step, the following formula can help to find the class of x_q:

$$\hat{f}(x_q) \leftarrow \arg\max_{v \in V} \sum_{i=1}^{k} \delta(v, f(x_i))$$

where $\delta(a,b)=1$ if $a=b$, and $\delta(a,b)=0$ otherwise.

K-means clustering algorithm is a least-squares partitioning method that divide available data into K partitions, in which data within same partition are mutually nearest and data in different partition are mutually farthest apart. The k-means clustering algorithm works as follows: The dataset is firstly partitioned into K clusters and the data points are randomly assigned to the clusters resulting in clusters that have roughly the same number of data points. For each data point, calculate the distance from the data point to each cluster. If the data point is closest to its own cluster, leave it where it is. If the data point is not closest to its own cluster, move it into the closest cluster. Repeat the above step until a complete pass through all the data points' results in no data point moving from one cluster to another. At this point the clusters are stable and the clustering process ends. The algorithm for partitioning (or clustering) N data points into K disjoint subsets S_j containing N_j data points so as to minimize the squared-error criterion

$$E = \sum_{i=1}^{k} \sum_{n \in S_j} \left| x_n - \mu_j \right|^2$$

where x_n is a vector representing the nth data point and μ_j is the geometric centroid of the data points in S_j ($\mu_j = \dfrac{1}{N_j} \sum_{i=1}^{N_j} x_i$).

RESULTS, ANALYSIS AND FINDINGS

The software of AHP, EXCEL, and SPSS were used to analyze the questionnaires, which were collected at different stages of the hierarchy and for different types of calculations. This section addresses the computation of dimension, criteria and benefits.

Relative Priority by Participants of Each Dimension and Criteria

In this section, relative importance or priority of each dimension and criteria rated by participants from case study is discussed. The relative importance or priority is expressed in the form of weight. The total weight of 4 dimensions and 16 criteria is normalized to 1.

Particularly, the priority result of all participants (shown in Table 1) displayed the top weighting order in dimension as **Member Interaction** with a high score of 0.344. Nevertheless, **Complementary Asset** is the least highlighted dimension. As to the aspect of weight within criteria, the top ranked criteria is **Bottom-Up Teaming** in **Locus of Leadership** Dimension, **Psychological Encourage** in **Incentive Mechanism** Dimension, **Emphasize Cross-Domain Sharing** in **Member Interaction** Dimension, and **Give Extra Resource** in **Complementary Asset** Dimension. Meanwhile, the weight cross criteria reveal they focus on **Emphasize Cross-Domain Sharing** as the highest among 16 criteria, **Independent IT**

Table 1. Dimension and Criteria Weight of All Participants

Weight Dimension/Criteria	Weight of Each Dimension	Weight within Criteria	Weight cross Criteria (Ranking)
Locus of Leadership	0.264		
Top-Down Assigning		0.271 (2)	0.071 (05)
Bottom-Up Teaming		**0.305 (1)**	0.080 (03)
Total Execution		0.164 (4)	0.043 (12)
Partial Pilot run		0.260 (3)	0.069 (06)
Incentive Mechanism	0.246		
Substantive Reward		0.177 (4)	0.044 (11)
Psychological Encourage		**0.312 (1)**	0.077 (04)
Achievements Appraisal Basis		0.252 (3)	0.062 (08)
Peers Reputation		0.259 (2)	0.064 (07)
Member Interaction	**0.344**		
Homogeneity member		0.135 (3)	0.046 (09)
Differential member		0.361 (2)	0.124 (02)
Emphasize Security		0.103 (4)	0.035 (15)
Emphasize Cross-Domain Sharing		**0.401 (1)**	**0.138 (01)**
Complementary Asset	0.147		
Give Extra Resource		**0.303 (1)**	0.045 (10)
Just Daily Work		0.256 (3)	0.038 (13)
Integrated IT Platform		0.260 (2)	0.038 (13)
Independent IT platform		0.181 (4)	0.027 (16)

Table 2. Example of Importance of Fuzzy Expression of Participants

Participant Number	Very High	High	Fair	Low	Very Low
1	(0, 10, 20)	(20, 30, 40)	(40, 50, 60)	(60, 70, 80)	(80, 90, 100)
2	(0, 05, 10)	(15, 25, 40)	(35, 50, 65)	(60, 75, 90)	(90, 95, 100)
…	…	…	…	…	…
39	(0, 15, 25)	(20, 35, 45)	(40, 50, 65)	(55, 70, 85)	(75, 90, 100)

Table 3. Average Utility Values towards Four Strategies of All Participants

Four Strategies (Benefit Preference)	Average Utility Values	Ranking
A. Induce Innovation Learning	60.38	2
B. Promote Responsiveness	**61.21**	**1**
C. Increase Core Competency	58.24	3
D. Enhance Work Efficiency	54.70	4

Table 4. Overview of Average Utility Values/Ranking

Labs/ Benefit Preference	Induce Innovation Learning (Average Utility Values/ Ranking)	Promote Responsiveness (Average Utility Values/ Ranking)	Increase Core Competency (Average Utility Values/ Ranking)	Enhance Work Efficiency (Average Utility Values/ Ranking)
1	58.98 (02)	**60.75 (01)**	58.88 (03)	57.76 (04)
2	58.21 (02)	**60.10 (01)**	55.72 (03)	54.17 (04)
3	**62.73 (01)**	59.27 (03)	60.43 (02)	51.84 (04)
4	62.26 (02)	**63.07 (01)**	59.34 (03)	54.13 (04)
5	64.93 (02)	**66.04 (01)**	58.33 (03)	54.88 (04)
All Labs	60.38 (02)	**61.21 (01)**	58.24 (03)	54.70 (04)

Platform as the lowest rank instead. Other various dimensions and criteria priority are listed in Table 1.

Utility Value Matrix

Each participant used fuzzy language to express five types of effectiveness boundaries. These rankings are very high, high, fair, low, and very low. The example is as shown in Table 2.

Average Utility Value and Ranking

The cross dimension weights derived from Table 1 = (0.071, 0.080, 0.043, 0.069, 0.044, 0.077, 0.062, 0.064, 0.046, 0.124, 0.035, 0.138, 0.045, 0.038, 0.038, 0.027) was used to calculate the average utility value and ranking by multiplying U_i. Each participant's utility value for four business strategies is derived. The averages of the all-participant utility values for four business strategy can be seen in Table 3. From this score, it is obvious that all researchers would rather **Promote Responsiveness** than others. In addition, the overview of average utility value and ranking comparison among laboratories can be found in Table 4.

Cluster Analysis

The attribute analyses of KFN Model for CoPs designs can determine the characteristic of each cluster and identify suggestions for effective linkage. This KFN model adopted cluster analysis to be the basis of attribute analysis. Based on the differences of each participant, a hierarchical cluster diagram is generated. The similarity degree increased gradually from top down; the lower the knowledge workers are on the hierarchy, the more unique they appear to be (Pellitteri, 2002; Akamatsu et al., 1998; OECD, 1996).

The cluster analysis contains several steps. First, we input the factor scores to the model of cluster analysis. Second, we divided five clusters among all the participants. Third, we calculated the mean value and variable number of score of factor for each knowledge worker so as to explain their differences and characteristics. This research divided into five groups after the analysis results and actual discussions about the features towards CoPs beliefs

Figure 5. Sample Knowledge Flow Network for Number 5.

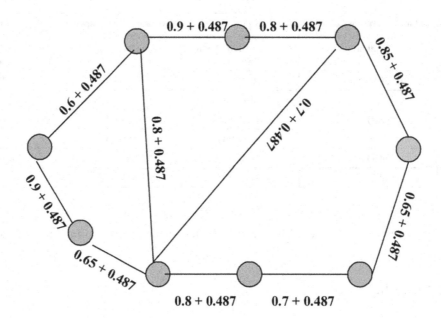

Knowledge Flow Network Analysis

In order to illustrate the application of knowledge link weight, a KFN of the case study is shown in Figure 5. The knowledge flow network has been constructed using the CoPs Centred model designed in previous section. The CoPs model was used to design a questionnaire involving four dimensions, sixteen criteria, and four business strategies or performance preferences. The sixteen criteria represent among other aspects, represent beliefs and interaction principles of knowledge workers for knowledge sharing and management.

The feedback from 39 participants was used to compute the weight or relative importance assigned to each criterion by a participant. The weight values were than used to cluster the weighted responses from 39 participants. The purpose of clustering was to determine the similarities in relative importance of sixteen criteria among 39 participants. The clustering technique was derived from SPSS software (Zadeh, 1981). Five clusters or groups of researchers were identified. Each group or cluster in this research is considered to be eligible to form a knowledge flow network.

Table 5 shows the KFN group number and number of knowledge workers in each KFN. Table 6 shows

Table 5. Participants in each Knowledge Flow Network

Knowledge Flow Network Number	No. of People
1	9
2	7
3	5
4	9
5	9

similar weight values for various criteria allocated by members of 5 KFN. The weight values above 0.1 are highlighted in bold. These are used to calculate the Common Criteria Weight (CCW) between two members in a KFN. As illustration KFN for network number 5 is shown in Figure 5. The criteria weights for criteria differential member and cross-domain sharing are added up. The values based on experience of members/researchers in a related knowledge domain have been used for illustration purpose only.

Figure 6. Common Criteria Weight and Knowledge Flow Network Number

Variables	Cluster Group				
	1	**2**	**3**	**4**	**5**
Top-Down Assigning	**0.156**	0.060	0.022	0.052	0.043
Bottom-Up Teaming	**0.101**	**0.132**	0.063	0.044	0.066
Total Execution	0.085	0.043	0.021	0.038	0.020
Partial Pilot Run	**0.126**	0.076	0.025	0.038	0.060
Substantive Reward	0.044	0.083	0.062	0.036	0.019
Psychological Encourage	0.059	0.077	**0.214**	0.039	0.071
Achievement Apprasial Basis	0.051	**0.122**	0.094	0.045	0.038
Peers Reputation	0.048	0.079	**0.182**	0.035	0.043
Homogeneity Member	0.031	0.054	0.027	0.047	0.062
Differential Member	0.053	0.077	**0.121**	**0.142**	**0.207**
Empahasize Security	0.028	0.034	0.023	0.049	0.035
Emphasize Cross-Domain Sharing	0.080	0.068	0.087	**0.126**	**0.280**
Give Extra Resources	0.041	0.024	0.019	**0.101**	0.014
Just Daily Work	0.031	0.024	0.012	0.077	0.023
Integrated IT Platform	0.034	0.019	0.013	0.092	0.011
Independent IT Platform	0.031	0.030	0.014	0.040	0.009

FUTURE RESEARCH AND TRENDS

Actually, knowledge flow and sharing in a project is a dynamic activity (Nissen, 2002; Zhuge 2003). Our ongoing work includes construction of Dynamic Knowledge Flow Activity Analysis Model (DKFAAM). We intend to use DKFAAM to visualise the knowledge flow activity in a given project and determine the bottlenecks for knowledge management, knowledge sharing and knowledge creation.

In Dynamic Knowledge Flow Activity Analysis Model (DKFAAM), the dynamic components and terms are defined to model and analyse the dynamic flow of knowledge between two knowledge nodes. This model can help in visualising knowledge flow and modelling knowledge sharing between knowledge nodes and determining knowledge bottlenecks related to certain project task in a given time interval. Dynamic analysis of a knowledge flow activity in a knowledge flow network can assist in determining state of the knowledge flow network at particular instant of time, identify knowledge bottlenecks, visualise knowledge flow activity in a research group or network and determine correlations between intelligent activity monitored through various sensors and actual knowledge flow activity (Nissen, 2002; Zhuge, 2003).

A node in KFN can be considered as a social agent. Thus from a software design and implementation perspective it is useful to do a dynamic analysis of the knowledge flow activity in a KFN. A dynamic knowledge flow activity analysis model is shown in Figure 6.

The above model is extension of the original Petri Net developed by Petri (Petri, 1966; Genrich & Lautenbach, 1981; Jensen, 1981). A Petri net is a particular kind of directed graph with two types of nodes, namely, the places (graphically depicted as circles) and transitions (graphically depicted as bars). The basic structure of a Petri Net consists of a set of places, a set of transitions and a set of directed arcs, which connect the transitions and places. The presence of token/s in the input place causes the transition to fire, leading to the removal of the token/s from input place and deposition of token/s in the output place of the transition. The pattern of placement of tokens through the net at a particular time is called the marking of the net. A given marking corresponds to a state of the net.

A knowledge node in the dynamic knowledge flow activity analysis model is represented as a place. In order for the network state to change the transitions (shown as vertical bars in Figure 6) need to fire. There are three types of transitions shown in Figure 6. These are knowledge sharing transition, knowledge creation transition and resource node knowledge transition. Transitions are fired to represent events occurring.

The places are taken to represent the states of knowledge nodes with tokens variable extensions and transitions represent categories of elementary changes in variables in the place. These variables may be parts of a token. A token in a place denotes the fact that the predicate corresponding to that place is true for that particular instantiation of variables contained in the token.

The net result of a transition firing is the exchange of token from places to places and a new marking or state of the knowledge flow network. The different types of tokens shown in place i in Figure 6 are:

- **New Knowledge Token** - representing a new algorithm developed by a knowledge worker represented by the knowledge node and place i
- **Action Token** - representing different activities leading to knowledge creation or knowledge sharing
- **Control Token** - representing the node or place in which knowledge activity is taking place in time instant t_i. It can also be used to determine where knowledge activity is held up or stuck.

Figure 7. Dynamic Knowledge Flow Activity Analysis Model

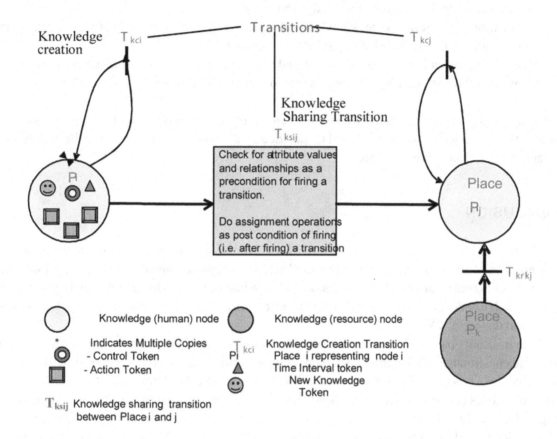

- **Time Interval Token** - The time interval token represents the fact that certain knowledge creation, knowledge sharing or knowledge discovery activity needs to be completed in a certain time interval (corresponding to a project or workflow related task) otherwise the benefits of knowledge creation, sharing or discovery may be limited to the organization/group.

A knowledge flow activity in the model shown in Figure 7 can be represented by firing of a transition. The event representing firing of a transition could be a knowledge creation event, knowledge sharing event or a resource nodded based knowledge discovery event.

The transition enabling conditions can refer to both tokens in input places and to data referenced as preconditions in the inscribed transition structure (e.g., the box in Figure 7 representing the knowledge sharing transition). A knowledge sharing transition $\mathbf{T_{ksij}}$ is enabled when

- **Abduction condition is true:** knowledge of node or place *i* enable node or place *j* to prove some new hypothesis or goal.
- **Association condition is true:** knowledge of node or place *i* enables node or place *j* to create new knowledge through some association with existing knowledge index.
- **Induction condition is true:** knowledge of node or place *i* enable node or place *j* to induce or generalize new knowledge through examples.

- **Deduction condition is true:** knowledge of node or place *i* enables node or place *j* to deduce new knowledge using their existing knowledge index.
- **Integration Condition is true:** knowledge of node or place *i* enables node or place *j* can be integrated with existing knowledge to produce new knowledge.
- **Hybrid Condition is tru**e: knowledge of node or place *i* enables node or place *j* to produce new knowledge through some hybrid combination of above conditions.

A knowledge sharing transition will be fired when any one of the above conditions is true, knowledge sharing takes place within the time interval t_{ij} specified by the time interval token, and the control taken is changes place from place *i* to place *j*.

CONCLUSION

Organisations in this research are viewed as KFN involved in knowledge creation, knowledge sharing and innovation. This is in contrast to the traditional view that organisations consist primarily of workflow networks. KFN consist of knowledge nodes, knowledge links and knowledge link weight respectively. The knowledge nodes are primarily human nodes but also can be resource nodes (e.g., robot, knowledge portals, databases, WWW).

The significant goal of this research is to study how CoPs can help to synergize the existing collaboration and construction of KFN in an open innovation infrastructure. The KFN are constructed based on actual study of CoPs in one large multinational R&D organization. The knowledge link weight between two human nodes consists of Knowledge Space (or compatibility) Weight (KSW) and Common Criteria Weight (CCW). KSW between two human nodes is determined by a manger or group leader based on CV, experience of the two human nodes and their knowledge compatibility. The 16 criteria along four Performance evaluation dimensions (Locus of leadership, Member interaction, Incentive mechanism and Complementary asset) in the CoPs questionnaire, among other aspects, can be considered to provide information on the interaction attitude and beliefs of researchers for cooperation and knowledge sharing. These interaction principles although, not a determining factor for knowledge sharing, can improve or enhance the effectiveness of knowledge sharing, creation and innovation. The feedback on the CoPs questionnaire, among other aspects, is used for clustering the researchers in knowledge flow network group. In this research 39 participants have been clustered into five KFN. Fuzzy MCDM techniques and tools have been used to compute the data from questionnaire feedback, such as AHP, Fuzzy AHP and SPSS.

While attempting to create a beneficial and valuable infrastructure to connect knowledge owners in a KFN is crucial, the results in the study show concentration on **Member Interaction** the most compared to the other three dimensions. Overall, the opinions from five laboratories surveyed are similar, even though there is slight difference in some criteria and dimensions. Among the sixteen criteria, they emphasize **Bottom-Up Teaming, Psychological Encourage, Emphasize Cross-Domain Sharing** and **Give Extra Resource** in each dimension respectively. In particular, **Emphasize Cross-Domain Sharing** gets the highest rank among 16 criteria. As to the preferred business strategy, the case study shows the tendency to view **Promote Responsiveness** as the first priority relatively. It is likely researchers' expectations are considering to promote responsiveness as a business strategy seriously, and solve problems to enable open innovation rapidly, so that they can justify strategy by getting more support from top management to deal with conflicts between current and expected situation. For example, organization can implement CoPs as a major approach to outline the future roadmap by frequent member interaction. During the development, psychological encouragement could be the best reward for knowledge sharing between researchers to respond to changing customer needs. Thus findings of this research can promote performance and can facilitate allocation of organizational resources for knowledge sharing and innovation among the participants

REFERENCES

Allee, V. (2000). Knowledge networks and communities of practice. *OD Practitioner Online, 32*(4).

Ambrosio, J. (2000). *Knowledge management mistakes.*

Buckley, J. J. (1985). Ranking alternatives using fuzzy number. *Fuzzy Sets and Systems, 15*(1), 21–31. doi:10.1016/0165-0114(85)90013-2

Chu, M. T., Shyu, J. Z., Tzeng, G. H., & Khosla, R. (2007). Comparison among three analytical methods for knowledge communities group-decision analysis. *Expert Systems with Applications, 33*(4), 1011–1024. doi:10.1016/j.eswa.2006.08.026

Chu, M. T., Shyu, J. Z., Tzeng, G. H., & Khosla, R. (2007). Using non-additive fuzzy integral to assess performance of organization transformation via communities of practice. *IEEE Transactions on Engineering Management, 54*(2), 1–13. doi:10.1109/TEM.2007.893987

Clatworthy, J., Buick, D., Hankins, M., Weinman, J., & Horne, R. (2005). The use and reporting of cluster analysis in health psychology: A review. *British Journal of Health Psychology, 10*, 329–358. doi:10.1348/135910705X25697

Cohendet, P., & Meyer-Krahmer, F. (2001). The theoretical and policy implications of knowledge codification. *Research Policy, 30*, 1563–1591. doi:10.1016/S0048-7333(01)00168-8

Davenport, T. H., Jarvenpaa, S. I., & Beer, M. C. (2004). Improving knowledge work process. *Sloan Management Review, 34*(4), 53–65.

Desouza, K. C. (2003). Facilitating tacit knowledge exchange. *CACM, 46*(6), 85–86.

Fowlkes, E. B., & Mallows, C. L. (1983). A method for comparing two hierarchical clusterings. *Journal of the American Statistical Association, 78*(383), 553–584. doi:10.2307/2288117

Genrich, A., & Lautenbach, K. (1981). System modelling with high level Petri nets. *Theoretical Computer Science, 35*, 1–41.

Huang, Z. (1998). Extensions to the K-means algorithm for clustering large datasets with categorical values. *Data Mining and Knowledge Discovery, 2*, 283–304. doi:10.1023/A:1009769707641

Hwang, C. L., & Yoon, K. (1981). *Multiple attribute decision making: Methods and applications.* New York: Springer-Verlag.

Jensen, K. (1981). Colored Petri nets and the invariant method. *Theoretical Computer Science, 14*, 317–336. doi:10.1016/0304-3975(81)90049-9

Kerzner, H. (1989). *Project management: A system approach to planning scheduling and controlling* (pp. 759-764).

Lesser, E. L., & Storck, J. (2001). Communities of practice and organizational performance. *IBM Systems Journal, 40*(4).

Lyons, M. J., Akamatsu, S., Kamachi, M., & Gyoba, J. (1998). *Coding facial expressions with Gabor wavelets.* In *Proceedings of the Third IEEE International Conference on Automatic Face and Gesture Recognition* (pp. 200-205).

MacKay, D. J. C. (2003). *Information theory, inference, and learning algorithms.* Cambridge University Press.

Malhotra, Y. (2004). Why knowledge management systems fail? Enablers and constraints of knowledge management in human enterprises. *American Society for Information Science and Technology Monograph Series* (pp. 87-112).

Mon, D. L., Cheng, C. H., & Lin, J. C. (1994). Evaluating weapon system using fuzzy analytic hierarchy process based on entropy weigh. *Fuzzy Sets and Systems, 61*, 1–8. doi:10.1016/0165-0114(94)90279-8

Nissen, M. E. (2002). An extended model of knowledge flow dynamics. *CACM, 8*, 251–266.

Nonaka, I. (1994). A dynamic theory of organizational knowledge creation. *Organization Science, 5*(1), 14–37. doi:10.1287/orsc.5.1.14

OECD. (1996). The knowledge based economy. *Science, Technology and Industry Outlook.* Paris.

OECD. (1999). *Measuring knowledge in learning economies and societies.* Draft Report on Washington Forum.

Pellitteri, J. (2002). The relationship between emotional intelligence and ego defence mechanisms. *The Journal of Psychology, 136*, 182–194.

Petri, C. (1966). *Communication in automata* (Tech Rep RADC-TR-65-377, 1). Rome Air Development Center, Griffths Air Base, USA.

Ratcliffe-Martin, V., Coakes, E., & Sugden, G. (2000). Knowledge management issues in universities. *Vine Journal, 30*, 14–19. doi:10.1108/eb040770

Saaty, T. L. (1977). A scaling method for priorities in hierarchical structures. *Journal of Mathematical Psychology, 15*(3), 234–281. doi:10.1016/0022-2496(77)90033-5

Saaty, T. L. (1980). *The analytic hierarchy process.* New York: McGraw-Hill.

Tang, M. T., & Tzeng, G. H. (1999). A hierarchy fuzzy MCDM method for studying electronic marketing strategies in the information service industry. *Journal of International Information Management, 8*(1), 1–22.

Thomas, J. C., Kellog, W. A., & Erickson, T. (2001). The knowledge management puzzle: human and social factors in knowledge management. *IBM Systems Journal, 40*(4), 863–884.

Tsaur, S. H., Tzeng, G. H., & Wang, K. C. (1997). Evaluating tourist risks from fuzzy perspectives. *Annals of Tourism Research, 24*(4), 796–812. doi:10.1016/S0160-7383(97)00059-5

Tzeng, G. H. (1977). A study on the PATTERN method for the decision process in the public system. *Japan Journal of Behavior Metrics, 4*(2), 29–44.

Tzeng, G. H., Shian, T. A., & Lin, C. Y. (1992). Application of multicriteria decision making to the evaluation of new energy-system development in Taiwan. *Energy, 17*(10), 983–992. doi:10.1016/0360-5442(92)90047-4

Tzeng, G. H., & Shiau, T. A. (1987). Energy conservation strategies in urban transportation: Application of multiple criteria decision-making. *Energy Systems and Policy, 11*(1), 1–19.

Tzeng, G. H., & Teng, J. Y. (1994). Multicriteria evaluation for strategies of improving and controlling air-quality in the super city: A case of Taipei city. *Journal of Environmental Management, 40*(3), 213–229. doi:10.1006/jema.1994.1016

U.S. Department of Commerce. (1965). *National Technical Information Service*, NASA, PATTERN Relevance Guide, 3.

Wenger, E. (1998). *Communities of practice*. Cambridge University Press.

Wenger, E., McDermott, R. A., & Snyder, W. (2002). *Cultivating Communities of practice*. Boston: Harvard Business School Press.

Zadeh, L. A. (1981). *A definition of soft computing*.

Zhuge, H. (2003). Component-based workflow systems design. *Decision Support Systems, 35*(4), 517–536. doi:10.1016/S0167-9236(02)00127-6

Zhuge, H. (2006). Knowledge flow network planning and simulation. *Decision Support Systems, 42*, 571–592. doi:10.1016/j.dss.2005.03.007

KEY TERMS AND DEFINITIONS

Business Process Management: (BPM): Business Process Management is a field of management focused on aligning organizations with the wants and needs of clients. It is a holistic management approach that promotes business effectiveness and efficiency while striving for innovation, flexibility and integration with technology.

Communities of Practice (CoPs): community of practice refers to the process of social learning that occurs and shared sociocultural practices that emerge and evolve when people who have common goals interact as they strive towards those goals.

Knowledge Flow: knowledge flow is the passing of knowledge between nodes according to certain rules and principles.

Knowledge Space: knowledge space is a combinatorial structure describing the possible states of knowledge of a human learner.

Multi-Criteria Decision-Making (MCDM): Multi Criteria Decision Making is a discipline aimed at supporting decision makers who are faced with making numerous and conflicting evaluations. MCDA aims at highlighting these conflicts and deriving a way to come to a compromise in a transparent process.

Chapter 25
Designing Complex Organizations Computationally

Carl L. Oros
Lt. Col., Naval Postgraduate School, USA

Mark E. Nissen
Naval Postgraduate School, USA

ABSTRACT

Business process management is recognized increasingly as a critical factor in organizational success, leaders and managers seek to cope with increasingly complex and dynamic environments, and traditional approaches to process management become increasingly inadequate due to their lack of flexibility and adaptability. Alternatively, an organizational form receiving considerable current focus is the Edge, which distributes knowledge and power to the "edges" of organizations, and which enables organizational members and units to self-organize and self-synchronize their activities. The dynamics of such self-organization and self-synchronization, however, are extremely complex, and balancing the flexibility and adaptability inherent in the Edge with sufficient control to avoid chaos is very challenging. We employ the state-of-the-art POWer environment for dynamic organizational representation and emulation to develop and experiment with models of competing organizational forms, and to inform our understanding of complex organizational design and management—thereby making an important contribution to theory, research methodology, and practice.

INTRODUCTION

Business process management is recognized increasingly as a critical factor in organizational success: a factor that helps to improve organizational processes, to reduce operational costs, and to promote real-time visibility into performance (Al-Mudimigh, 2007; Shaw, Holland, Kawalek, Snowdon, & Warboys, 2007). In recent years, organizational processes have been becoming increasingly complex and dynamic,

DOI: 10.4018/978-1-60566-669-3.ch025

as leaders and managers seek to cope with increasingly complex and dynamic environments (Chen, Zhang, & Zhou, 2007; J. E. Scott, 2007).

Indeed, Nissen and Leweling (Nissen & Leweling, 2008) explain how numerous organizational scholars (Chaharbaghi & Nugent, 1994; Donaldson, 1987; Tung, 1979) note widely that the contingency contexts of many modern organizations can change rapidly and unpredictably (Romanelli & Tushman, 1994), due to multiple factors such as globalization (Raynor & Bower, 2001), technology (Adner & Levinthal, 2002; Rahrami, 1992), hypercompetition (D'Aveni, 1994; Hanssen-Bauer & Snow, 1996), knowledge-based innovation (Jelinek & Schoonhoven, 1990), explicit linking of organizational structures to strategies (Sabherwal, Hirschheim, & Goles, 2001; Venkatraman & Prescott, 1990; Zajac, Kraatz, & Bresser, 2000), mounting competition from co-evolutionary firms (Barnett & Sorenson, 2002), high-velocity environments that are in perpetual flux, and the kinds of nonlinear, dynamic environmental patterns that never establish equilibrium (Eisenhardt & Tabrizi, 1995). Traditional approaches to process management are becoming increasingly inadequate in such dynamic environments due to their lack of flexibility and adaptability (Küng & Hagen, 2007; Ramesh, Jain, Nissen, & Xu, 2005; Vanderhaeghen & Loos, 2007).

Alternatively, an increasing number of scholars are viewing organizations as complex adaptive systems, which are designed, managed and redesigned iteratively to fit and adapt to complex, unpredictable and constantly shifting environments (Brown & Eisenhardt, 1997; Burgelman & Grove, 2007). One such organization receiving considerable current focus is the Edge (Alberts & Hayes, 2003), which distributes knowledge and power to the "edges" of organizations (e.g., where they interact directly with their environments and other players in the corresponding organizational field (W. R. Scott, 1995)), and which enables organizational members and units to self-organize and self-synchronize their activities. Key to Edge performance is decentralization, empowerment, shared awareness and freely flowing knowledge required to push power for informed decision making and competent action to the edges.

As an organizational form, the Edge shares almost no similarities with the Hierarchy, the latter of which represents the predominant form today (Nissen, 2007), and which is notably rigid, inflexible and slow to adapt to change. Indeed, well over a hundred, diverse organizational forms (e.g., M-Forms, see (Chandler, 1962); Clans, see (Ouchi, 1980); Virtual, see (Davidow & Malone, 1992)) have been proposed over the past several decades as contrasts to the Hierarchy (Nissen, 2005). We focus here on the Edge, because it is designed explicitly to be flexible and adaptable, and to address the kinds of unpredictable, dynamic environments noted above. Also, the Edge provides a vivid contrast with the predominant Hierarchy. Additional examination of other organizational forms via the approach described in this chapter is certainly merited, and represents a useful avenue for future research along these lines.

The dynamics of Edge self-organization and self-synchronization, however, are extremely complex and challenging. Without the traditional hierarchy to provide guidance, structure and stability, many people find it difficult to organize themselves effectively. The apparent disarray of many social movements and ad-hoc groups provide a couple of easily identifiable examples, and team-based approaches (e.g., cross-functional teams, matrix organizations) require sufficient buffering and management support (Thompson, 1967) that is provided generally by the traditionally hierarchical organizations within which such teams operate. Moreover, without well-established organizational routines and well-practiced communication patterns, many people find it difficult to synchronize their activities. This is particularly the case where people are dispersed geographically. Further, balancing the flexibility and adaptability inherent in the Edge with sufficient control to avoid chaos is very challenging. As Nissen and Leweling (Nissen & Leweling, 2008) explain, "maneuverability" (e.g., via flexibility and adaptability) is inherently at odds with "stability" (e.g., both static and dynamic). Notwithstanding the putative benefits of flexible, adaptable and maneuverable organizations such as the Edge, where a complex organization is sufficiently unstable in its dynamic environment, it risks spiraling quickly into chaos (Brown & Eisenhardt, 1997; Osborn & Hunt, 2007).

The emerging field of Complex Adaptive Systems (CAS) offers considerable promise to examine and understand complex, dynamic and adaptable organizations through methods and tools associated with computational modeling and experimentation (J. Miller & Page, 2007). Indeed, computational modeling of and experimentation on organizations enable us to investigate the dynamic structures and behaviors of the Edge and other organizational forms (Gateau, Leweling, Looney, & Nissen, 2007), and to learn to understand the kinds of organizational design and management techniques required to develop, control and adapt such organizations in practice. Although myriad, diverse applications are available to support business process modeling and simulation, we are interested specifically in the ability to model and simulate different organizational forms, knowledge, information and work flows, personnel compositions and capabilities, and technologies—*together*, as an integrated design problem (Leavitt, 1965). Very few such applications are capable of supporting such integrated analysis. Further, because we seek high degrees of external validity for our simulations—arguing that organizational structures and behaviors that we model and simulate should reflect the kinds of structures and behaviors of corresponding operational organizations in the field—applications benefiting from extensive external validation are important. This limits the field of applications tremendously.

Toward this end, in this chapter we employ the state-of-the-art environment for dynamic organizational representation and emulation called POWer to develop and experiment with models of Edge and competing organizational forms, and we use knowledge developed through examination of such models to inform our understanding of organizational design and management. We explain how POWer satisfies our demanding requirements from above (e.g., integrated analysis, external validation). Further, we ground these models in an operational organization in the field, and discuss how theoretical and empirical results can be generalized and employed in practice, along with future trends elucidated through this research. This work makes an important contribution to theory, to research methodology, and to practice.

BACKGROUND

In this section we draw heavily from (Gateau et al., 2007), first outlining background information pertaining to computational modeling in general, and then describing the POWer modeling environment in particular.

Computational Modeling

Computational Organization Theory (COT) and Computational Social Science (CSS) are multidisciplinary fields that integrate aspects of artificial intelligence, organization studies and system dynamics/simulation (K. M. Carley & Prietula, 1994). Most research in this developing field involves computational tools, which are employed to support computational experimentation and theorem proving through executable models developed to emulate the behaviors of physical organizations (Burton, Lauridsen, & Obel, 2002; K. M. Carley & Lin, 1997).

Several distinct classes of models have evolved for particular purposes, including: descriptive models, quasi-realistic models, normative models, and man-machine interaction models for training (Burton, Obel, & Keeshan, 1995; K. J. Cohen & Cyert, 1965). More recent models have been used for purposes such as developing theory, testing theory and competing hypotheses, fine-tuning laboratory experiments and field studies, reconstructing historical events, extrapolating and analyzing past trends, exploring basic principles, and reasoning about organizational and social phenomena (K. Carley & Hill, 2001).

Our research in this area builds upon the planned accumulation of collaborative work over almost two decades to develop rich, theory-based models of organizational processes (Levitt, 2004). Using an agent-based representation (G. P. Cohen, 1992; Kunz, Christiansen, Cohen, Jin, & Levitt, 1998), micro-level organizational behaviors have been researched and formalized to reflect well-accepted organization theory (Levitt, Thomsen, Christiansen, & Kunz, 1999). Extensive empirical validation projects (Christiansen, 1993; Thomsen, Levitt, Kunz, Nass, & Fridsma, 1999) have demonstrated the representational fidelity, and shown how the qualitative and quantitative behaviors of our computational models correspond closely with a diversity of enterprise processes in practice.

This research stream continues by developing new micro-organization theory, and embedding it in software tools that can be used to design organizations in the same way that engineers design bridges, semiconductors or airplanes—through computational modeling, analysis and evaluation of multiple virtual prototypes. Virtual prototypes also enable us to move well beyond relying upon the kinds of informal and ambiguous, natural-language descriptions that comprise the bulk of organization theory today. In addition to providing textual description, organization theory is imbued with a rich, time-tested collection of micro-theories that lend themselves to computational representation and analysis. Examples include Galbraith's (Galbraith, 1977) information processing abstraction, March and Simon's (March & Simon, 1958) bounded rationality assumption, and Thompson's (Thompson, 1967) task interdependence contingencies. Drawing on such micro-theories, we employ symbolic (i.e., non-numeric) representation and reasoning techniques from established research on artificial intelligence to develop computational models of theoretical phenomena. Once formalized through a computational model, the symbolic representation is "executable," meaning it can be used to emulate organizational dynamics.

Notwithstanding critiques focused on the imprecision of qualitative variables and relationships (cf. the precision offered by numerical models), our computational models are semi-formal (e.g., most people viewing the model can agree on what it describes), reliable (e.g., the same sets of organizational conditions and environmental factors generate the same sets of behaviors) and explicit (e.g., much ambiguity inherent in natural language is obviated). Particularly when used *in conjunction with* the descriptive natural language theory of our extant literature, this represents a substantial advance in the field of organizational analysis and design, and offers direct application to research and practice associated with complex dynamic process management.

Additionally, when modeling aggregations of people, such as work groups, departments, or firms, one can augment the kind of symbolic model from above with certain aspects of numerical representation. The distribution of skill levels in an organization can be approximated—in aggregate—by a Bell Curve; the probability of a given task incurring exceptions and requiring rework can be specified—organization wide—by a distribution; and the irregular attention of a worker to any particular activity or event (e.g., new work task or communication) can be modeled—stochastically—to approximate collective behavior. Also, specific organizational behaviors can be simulated hundreds of times—such as through Monte Carlo techniques—to gain insight into which results are common and expected versus rare and exceptional.

Figure 1. Model Elements and Descriptions adapted from (Orr & Nissen, 2006)

Model Element	Element Description
Tasks	Abstract representations of any work that consumes time, is required for project completion and can generate exceptions.
Actors	A person or a group of persons who perform work and process information.
Exceptions	Simulated situations where an actor needs additional information, requires a decision from a supervisor, or discovers an error that needs correcting.
Milestones	Points in a project where major business objectives are accomplished, but such markers neither represent tasks nor entail effort.
Successor links	Define an order in which tasks and milestones occur in a model, but they do not constrain these events to occur in a strict sequence. Tasks can also occur in parallel. POWer offers three types of successor links: finish-start, start-start and finish-finish.
Rework links	Rework links connect one task (called the *driver* task) with another (called the *dependent* task), and indicate that the dependent task depends on the success of the driver task. If the driver fails, some rework time is added to all dependent tasks linked to the driver task by rework links.
Task assignments	Show which actors are responsible for completing direct and indirect work resulting from a task.
Supervision links	Show which actors supervise which subordinates. In POWer, the supervision structure (also called the *exception-handling hierarchy*) represents a hierarchy of positions, defining who a subordinate would go to for information or to report an exception.

Further, this approach enables us to *integrate* the kinds of dynamic, qualitative behaviors emulated by symbolic models with quantitative metrics generated through discrete-event simulation, and hence to move beyond the extant array of numerical simulation techniques used to represent the structures and behaviors of organizations today (Law & Kelton, 1991). Through such integration of qualitative and quantitative models—bolstered by reliance on sound theory and empirical validation—our approach diverges most from extant research methods, and offers new insight into organizational dynamics.

POWer Computational Modeling Environment

POWer (i.e., Projects, Organizations and Work for Edge Research; see (Gateau et al., 2007), the computational modeling environment used in this research, consists of the elements described in Figure 1. This environment has been developed directly from Galbraith's information processing view of organizations. This view of organizations (see (Jin & Levitt, 1996) for details), has three key implications: 1) ontological, 2) computational, and 3) validational.

Ontologically, we model knowledge work through interactions of *tasks* to be performed; *actors* communicating with one another, and performing tasks; and an *organization structure* that defines actors' roles, and constrains their behaviors. Figure 2 illustrates this view of tasks, actors and organization structure. As suggested by the figure, we model the organization structure as a network of reporting relations,

Figure 2. Information Processing View of Knowledge Work (adapted from (Nissen & Levitt, 2004)

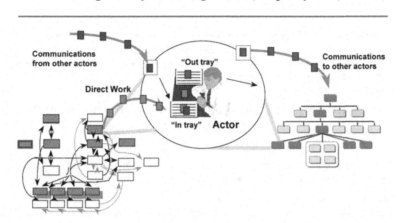

which can capture micro-behaviors such as managerial attention, span of control, and empowerment. We represent the task structure as a separate network of activities, which can capture organizational attributes such as expected duration, complexity and required skills. Within the organization structure, we further model various *roles* (e.g., marketing analyst, design engineer, manager), which can capture organizational attributes such as skills possessed, levels of experience, and task familiarity. Within the task structure, we further model various sequencing constraints, interdependencies, and quality/rework loops, which can capture considerable variety in terms of how knowledge work is organized and performed.

As suggested by the figure also, each actor within the intertwined organization and task structures has a queue of information tasks to be performed (e.g., assigned work activities, messages from other actors, meetings to attend) and a queue of information outputs (e.g., completed work products, communications to other actors, requests for assistance). Each actor processes such tasks according to how well the actor's skill set matches those required for a given activity, the relative priority and complexity of the task, the actor's work backlog (i.e., queue length), and how many interruptions divert the actor's attention from the task at hand.

Computationally, *work volume* is modeled in terms of both *direct work* (e.g., planning, design, manufacturing) and *indirect work* (e.g., decision wait time, rework, coordination work). Measuring indirect work enables the quantitative assessment of (virtual) process performance (e.g., through schedule growth, cost growth, quality).

Validationally, the computational modeling environment has been validated extensively, over a period spanning almost two decades, by a team of more than 30 researchers (Levitt, 2004). This validation process has involved three primary streams of effort: 1) internal validation against micro-social science research findings and against observed micro-behaviors in real-world organizations, 2) external validation against the predictions of macro-theory and against the observed macro-experience of real-world organizations, and 3) model cross-docking experiments against the predictions of other computational models with the same input data sets (Levitt, Orr, & Nissen, 2005). As such, ours is one of the few, implemented, computational organization modeling environments that has been subjected to such a thorough, multi-method trajectory of validation.

Much has been written about POWer and its predecessors (e.g., VDT, SimVision) over the past two decades, including considerable detail pertaining to the application (G. P. Cohen, 1992; Jin & Levitt, 1996; Kunz et al., 1998; Levitt et al., 1999), validation (Christensen, Christiansen, Jin, Kunz, & Levitt, 1999;

Levitt et al., 2005; Thomsen et al., 1999) and usage (Cheng & Levitt, 2001; Horii, Jin, & Levitt, 2004; Mahalingam, Levitt, & Scott, 2005). The interested reader is directed to such references for details.

RESEARCH DESIGN

In this section we summarize the computational experimentation research design. We first identify a suitable organization in the field to serve as our focus of modeling and experimentation, and we formulate a POWer computational model of such organization to serve as a baseline for experimentation. Then we outline a set of experimentation manipulations designed to test alternate organizational designs, and explain the kinds of measures used to assess comparative organizational performance.

Field Organization

We state above our interest in seeking to cope with increasingly complex and dynamic environments, and in viewing organizations as complex adaptive systems, which can be designed, managed and redesigned iteratively to fit and adapt to such environments. We state also the putative benefits of flexible, adaptable and maneuverable organizations such as the Edge—particularly when compared to the Hierarchy—to perform and adapt well to complex, unpredictable and constantly shifting environments. Hence we identify an organization that exemplifies a typical Hierarchy today, that suffers from inadequacy in terms of both performance and adaptation, and that offers potential for insight into computational experimentation and analysis as CAS.

A very suitable organizational instance can be found in the US Marine Corps. This, stereotypically hierarchical organization reflects hundreds of years of tradition, doctrine development and refinement to perform well in the kinds of missions and environments it has encountered throughout its storied history. However, some aspects of its current mission-environmental context reveal problems with the organization as designed currently. In particular, its participation in the Global War on Terror (GWOT) is presenting many, persistent challenges, especially when faced with terrorist and insurgent adversaries in confined urban areas as opposed to uniformed armies in open-field battles. This environment has forced commanders to operate on "larger *frontages* and [in] complex areas of operation with potentially fewer forces conducting operations." Additionally, forces operating in these complex urban and rural environments may experience isolation even though they are not geographically separated. These emergent battlefield attributes (esp. threat diversity and relative isolation) have created the "need for autonomy of decision-making and tactical action" (Amos, 2007).

For specific instance, when a particular Marine unit comes under fire in the open, traditional battlefield, it can call in fire support (i.e., using larger, more lethal weapons) from multiple sources (e.g., mortars, artillery, fixed-wing and rotary-wing aircraft, naval gunfire) using pre-established and well-understood organizational routines and communication patterns. In such cases, members of the Marine unit remain reasonably close to one another, and relatively easy to differentiate from enemy combatants. Hence support from artillery, air bombing, naval gunfire or other sources can be directed with relative ease, precision and confidence toward adversaries and away from the Marine unit. Alternatively, in urban guerrilla warfare, many opposite conditions can obtain: members of the Marine unit become geographically dispersed; Marines fight in very close proximity to enemy combatants and unarmed civilians; and it becomes very difficult to differentiate friendly from enemy combatants and noncombatants. Hence support from artillery, air bombing, naval gunfire or other sources becomes very difficult to direct with confidence. The result is markedly less effective organizational performance in this urban combat environment than in the open battlefield, with much of the cause appearing to stem from the Marine organization itself, which remains quite rigid, inflexible and slow to adapt.

POWer Organizational Model

Here we use the POWer computational modeling environment to represent the Marine organization summarized above. Such model becomes the baseline for comparison with alternate organizational designs to be assessed via computational experimentation. We begin with description of the focal organization and its POWer computational model representation, and then summarize the corresponding model parameterization.

Model Description

Figure 3 displays a POWer screenshot of the baseline organization. Doctrinally, six warfighting functions encompass all military activities: 1) Command and Control (C2), 2) Maneuver, 3) Fires, 4) Intelligence, 5) Logistics, and 6) Force Protection. Our principal focus in this chapter is on Fires, which involves the employment of firepower against the enemy's air, ground, and sea targets in order to delay, disrupt, degrade, or destroy the enemy capabilities, forces, facilities, or will to fight. We focus further on the operation of a company sized force through the fires lens to model, analyze and understand its associated organizational structure and dynamics.

Specifically, the model depicted in Figure 3 represents such company sized force set within its Marine infantry battalion organizational structure as modeled in POWer. Instantiation of the model is guided by Fleet Marine Force Manual (FMFM 6-4), *Marine Rifle Company/Platoon*, Marine Corps Warfighting Publication (MCWP 3-11.5) *Marine Infantry Battalion* [Draft], and (MCWP 3-16) *Fires Support Coordination in the Ground Combat Element*. Additionally, one of the authors has operational military experience with such operational Marine organizations in the field. The battalion is the smallest unit that combines intelligence, fires, maneuver, and sustainment under a single commander (labeled "BN CO" at the top of the figure). Hence it is relatively self-sufficient, whereas the company and lower level organizations depend heavily upon the battalion for guidance and support at present. For instance, the Commander of our focal organization A Company (labeled "A-Co Cdr" in the figure) reports to the battalion commander, along with other battalion-level leaders (e.g., "S-2" and "S-3", which handle battalion intelligence and operations, respectively). The battalion is also the lowest level of command with an executive staff. This connotes the typical, hierarchical and bureaucratic organizational form predominant throughout the Military.

The model represents a notional "day in the life" of a company-sized force that maneuvers to an objective. During the day, an event occurs (e.g., detect enemy), which causes the company to respond with its own weaponry, call in support fires, or both. Although not all depicted in the figure, a battalion consists of a headquarters element, a service support element, three infantry companies, and one weapons company. Our A Company focal organization represents one of three infantry companies. For simplicity, and to reduce clutter in the model, we do not represent the other two infantry companies. The weapons company provides the battalion its "organic" (i.e., self-contained) firepower, and battalions typically have tanks, amphibious assault vehicles, air defense assets, and other supporting arms elements

Figure 3. Baseline Company Organization

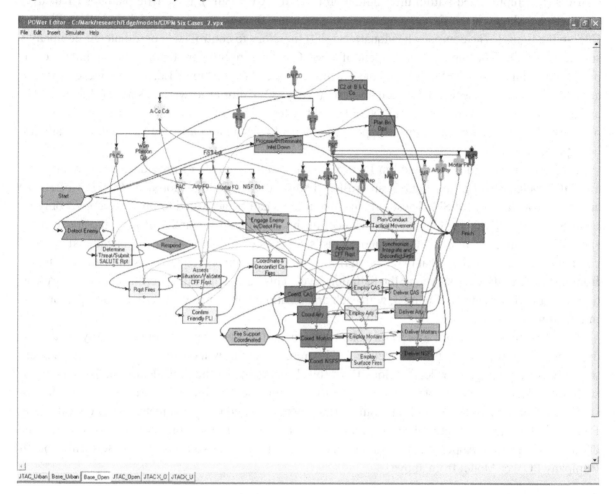

at their disposal. Although we focus principally on the company level, our inclusion of the battalion is important, for some of its organizational elements and functions may have potential to be pushed closer to the edges of this organization.

One such organization is the battalion fire support coordination center (FSCC), which is organized under Operations (i.e., S-3 in the figure). This organization coordinates communications and personnel for all forms of fire support, and hence is central to our view through the Fires lens. The FSCC monitors and receives all fire support requests originating within the battalion (e.g., at the company level). The battalion FSCC ensures that supporting arms are integrated with other units' movements (termed *maneuver*), and that friendly forces are not endangered. To coordinate with other organizations capable of supporting battalion missions through fires, the FSSC maintains several specialized functions performed by specialist personnel, including, for instance, the Fire Support Coordinator (labeled "FSC" in the figure), artillery liaison officer ("Arty LNO"), air officer ("AirO"), naval gunfire liaison officer ("NGLO"), and the 81mm mortar platoon representative ("Mortar Rep").

Our focal organization (A Company) depicted in the figure represents a classic Marine rifle company, which is the principal maneuver element of the infantry battalion. It is comprised of a company headquarters (i.e., represented within the single icon labeled "A-Co Cdr"), three rifle platoons (maneuver elements, not shown in the figure), and a weapons platoon (fire support element, labeled "Wpn Platoon Cdr" in the figure). The company headquarters (HQ) functions to control and coordinate the company's subordinate units. The company equivalent of a FSCC is the Fire Support Team (FiST), which is comprised of a company-level FSC (usually the executive officer, labeled "FiST Ldr" in the figure), forward air controller ("FAC"), artillery forward observer ("Arty FO"), mortar forward observer ("Mortar FO"), and a naval gunfire forward observer ("NGF FO"). The term *forward observer* connotes that these units maneuver integral to the company, as opposed to their FSCC counterparts that stay with the battalion headquarters.

The other organizations depicted in Figure 3 include units capable of providing fire support from aircraft (labeled "Air" in the figure), an artillery battery ("Arty Btry"), mortar platoon ("Mortar Plt) and naval warships ("NSFS"). These organizational units can be activated to provide support only by request from the Battalion Commander. Hence, in this traditional hierarchy, if A Company requires such fire support, the Company Commander must send all such requests up the organizational chain of command, and any conflicts that may obtain from multiple companies requesting simultaneous support from the same units are resolved at the battalion level. This completes our description of the organization structure represented in Figure 3, with each organizational unit or role represented by a person icon in the figure.

Also depicted in this figure are several tasks, decisions and events, which are represented by rectangles, diamonds and irregular shapes, respectively. This represents the work structure of the organization, which we discuss in greater detail below. Dark (black) links depict the precedence and sequencing of such tasks, decisions and events, and light (green) links represent reciprocal interdependence (Thompson, 1967) between certain tasks that require close interaction and mutual adjustment for coordination. Finally, light (blue) links interrelate the organization structure with the work structure to complete the diagram. We include Appendix A to summarize definitions for the key positions described in our A Company POWer Model from above.

Model Parameterization

Building upon substantial prior modeling work in the military domain (Gateau et al., 2007; Nissen, 2005; Orr & Nissen, 2006), parameter settings for the baseline model replicate very closely those reported previously. The interested reader can consult this prior work for discussion of and rationale for the parameter settings. The important point is that we have considerable basis for both theoretical and empirical grounding of the model parameters and settings, and the baseline model is specified from both doctrine and experience with such operational Marine organizations in the field. Hence the reader can have good confidence in the model and its results.

Figure 4 summarizes the key model variables and corresponding parameter settings for the baseline organization described above. Building again upon the prior work noted above, this tabular summary links all POWer model parameters to the organization studies literature, with specific connection to the most applicable Mintzberg design factors (Mintzberg, 1979) and three structural factors (i.e., organization, communication, work). Parameter settings for this baseline, hierarchical organization are taken principally from the Machine Bureaucracy Archetype discussed in (Gateau et al., 2007). The interested reader can refer to this and related prior work for details, and we include Appendix B to summarize the

Figure 4. Key Model Variables and Parameters

Structural Factor	Mintzberg Design Factor	Model Parameter	Baseline
Organization Structure	Decentralization	Centralization	High
	Formalization of behavior	Formalization	High
	Vertical specialization	Hierarchy Set-Up	3-level
	Training	Skill Level	Med
	Indoctrination	App. Experience	Med
		Team experience	Med
Communication Structure	Liaison Devices	Communication Links	Few
	"	Information Exchange	0.3
	Planning & Control Systems	Formal Meetings	none
	"	Matrix Strength	Low
Work Structure		Number of Operational Tasks	22
		Degree of Concurrency	Parallel, 2 Phase
		Interdependence	Med
		Rework Links	Few
		Rework Strength	0.3
	Environment - Complxity	FEP/PEP	0.1

rationale for parameter settings. The authors verified this baseline model and its parameter settings with military leaders familiar with the field organization.

Experimentation Manipulations

In terms of experimentation, we utilize the inherent control offered through computational models. Most notably, in a computational modeling environment, *everything remains constant—and hence controlled— unless changed specifically*. Hence, model after model, experiment after experiment, remains the same except for those specific model parameters that we manipulate in each experimentation run. This offers a degree of internal validity that is unmatched in laboratory experimentation involving people, and affords orders of magnitude greater control—and hence internal validity—than can be achieved through field experiments. Such is a long demonstrated advantage of computational experimentation (Nissen & Buettner, 2004).

Additionally, as noted above, the POWer modeling environment has undergone extensive, empirical, external validation, demonstrating that organizational structures and behaviors represented in computational models are reflective of their counterparts in operational organizations in the field. This offers a degree of external validity that is unmatched in laboratory experimentation involving small groups of people, and affords orders of magnitude greater external validity—and hence generalizability—than can be achieved through mathematical and analytical modeling. The computational experiment described in this chapter examines two alternate organizational designs across two contrasting mission-environmental settings. Building upon the baseline model discussion above, here we first discuss the mission-environmental manipulations, and then summarize the alternate organizational design.

Figure 5. Mission-Environmental Manipulations

Model Parameter	Open Battlefield	Urban Combat
Soln. Complexity	Med.	High
Requirement Complexity	Med.	High
Uncertainty	Med.	High
FEP	0.1	0.2
PEP	0.1	0.2
App. Experience	Med.	Low
Noise	0.1	0.3

Mission-Environmental Manipulations

The baseline model described and parameterized above reflects "business as usual" for the Marine Corps: maneuver in the open battlefield. As noted above, however, many of the current and important operations are conducted today with different missions in an urban combat environment, which imposes numerous and demanding constraints upon the organization. Hence we subject this baseline model to a different set of model parameter settings to reflect the contrasting mission-environmental context. Figure 5 depicts such contrasting contexts. "Open Battlefield" reflects the conditions long established with the kinds of Marine missions and environments examined here. "Urban Combat" reflects a very different kind of mission-environmental context. Parameter differences are summarized in the table in terms of seven settings: higher (solution and requirement) complexity and uncertainty, higher (functional and project) error probabilities (i.e., FEP, PEP), lower application experience (i.e., experience with this mission-environmental context), and greater noise combine to specify a considerably more uncertain and difficult environment than the open battlefield. See (Gateau et al., 2007; Nissen, 2005; Orr & Nissen, 2006) for elaboration of these variables and parameters.

Succinctly, the "open" environment is characterized by increased freedom of movement, greater force dispersion, and improved line of sight conditions (enemy and friendly). These combined factors suggest nominal (i.e., "medium") levels of task complexity and uncertainty, as well as nominal FEP and PEP. Application experience is assessed as "medium" also, due to the fact that this environment is most common, both from training and traditional operational employment perspectives, and the nominal noise setting (i.e., 0.1) suggests nothing out of the ordinary. As noted above, such nominal parameter settings are consistent with hierarchical organizations in general and the Machine Bureaucracy in particular, and they reflect the focal field organization examined here.

In contrast, the "urban" manipulation subjects the organization to challenges and complexities of military operations in urban terrain. Forces operating in this environment experience significantly degraded communications, and tend to become more isolated from one another. Additionally, the close nature of this combat setting places a premium on friendly position information, precise targeting, and accurate weaponeering in order to avert fratricide. These environmental attributes are reflected in part by the "high" solution and requirement complexity levels, "high" uncertainty, and increased FEPs and PEPs. Task experience is set as "low" to further contrast the uniqueness of this extremely chaotic operational environment, and the increased noise level (0.30) reflects degraded communication links in such demanding environment. Examining performance of the baseline organization in these two, contrasting contexts represents one key thrust of this computational experiment.

Organizational Design Manipulations

The other thrust involves examining an alternate organizational form across the same, contrasting, mission-environmental contexts, and evaluating the comparative performance of the different organizational designs. Hence we have a full-factorial, 2 x 2 computational experiment (i.e., 2 organizational designs x 2 mission-environmental contexts). This alternate organizational form derives from an operational concept called "Marine Corps Operations in Complex and Distributed Environments," (Amos, 2007) which involves distributed operations (e.g., with some Edge characteristics) at the company level and below. Hence it fits with our company-level organizational focus very well, and suggests an appealing alternate organizational form that is characterized by the Military as a promising response to its new threat environment.

Figure 6 depicts the "Enhanced Company" model corresponding to such promising alternate organizational form, which is set within its battalion organizational context as above. This organizational design involves one key change: it integrates a platoon-level position for a Joint Terminal Attack Controller (JTAC, labeled "JTAC" in the figure). The JTAC provides a capability to summon close air support (CAS; e.g., aerial bombing) directly from the platoon level (i.e., below the company level). Recalling the baseline model from above, such capability resides traditionally within the company FiST. As a result, enhanced company platoons have greater authority to affect their combat environments via air CAS, but they must also assume greater responsibility to coordinate and prevent conflicting air and surface fire missions. Since the JTAC is not an aviator (cf. the baseline case described above), this position's skill is "low" in both the open and urban manipulations. This contrasts with the baseline model above, in which the corresponding CAS-coordination and –conduct tasks are performed by the AirO with "high" skill and the FAC with "medium" skill, respectively. Hence this organization trades off the disadvantage of lower skill for the potential advantage of a more responsive, distributed organization. As with the baseline organizational design above, we examine this Enhanced Company alternate across the same two, contrasting, mission-environmental contexts: open battlefield and urban combat.

Performance Measures

Each of the six experimentation settings is run 100 times via Monte Carlo scheme, and average performance values are reported for each of the seven dependent variables explained in Figure 7: time, direct work, rework, coordination work, decision wait time, maximum backlog, and project risk. This provides the basis for evaluating comparative performance across the two organizational designs and two mission-environmental contexts.

Figure 6. Enhanced Company Organization

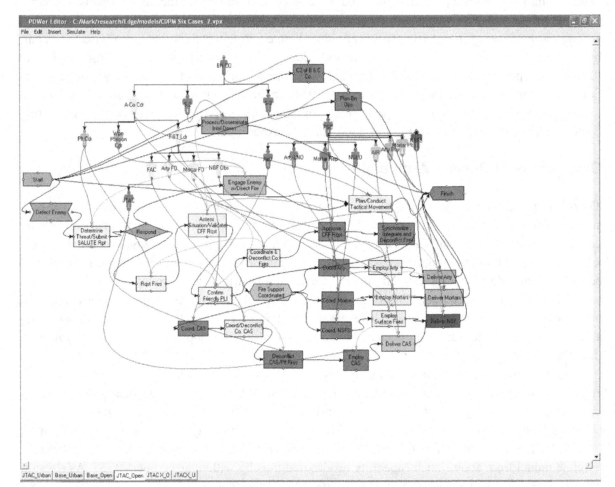

RESULTS

In this section, we describe the experimentation results produced using the computational models and 2 x 2 experimentation design outlined above. Specifically, here we evaluate emulated organizational performance for the baseline and alternate organizational design, under both Open Battlefield and Urban Combat conditions. Results are summarized in Figure 8.

For the two organizational forms shown in Figure 8, results are summarized across the seven performance measures from above. For the baseline under the Open Battlefield conditions, the mission requires 36 elapsed hours to complete all of the tasks depicted in Figure 2 above. Direct work of 78 person-hours, rework of 6 person-hours, coordination of 2 person-hours and wait time of 0.5 person-hours reflect relatively streamlined work. Additionally, the PRI of 0.22 is considerably lower than risk levels reported from prior models of hierarchical organizations in familiar environments (Gateau et al., 2007; Nissen, 2005; Orr & Nissen, 2006). Alternatively, with maximum backlog of roughly four hours (i.e.,

Figure 7. Dependent Variables

Dependent Variable	Parameter Description
Time	*Time* (hours) is the predicted time to complete a mission, in hours, which includes both direct and indirect (i.e. coordination, rework and decision latency) work.
Direct Work	*Direct work* measures the amount of time, in person-hours, that all actors in a mission spend completing direct functional or technical activities – excluding rework, coordination work, and decision wait time – related to the completion the project.
Rework	*Rework* measures the amount of time, in person-hours, that all actors in a mission spend redoing tasks that have generated exceptions.
Coordination Work	*Coordination work* measures the amount of time, in person-hours, that all actors in a mission spend attending to meetings and processing information requests from other positions.
Decision Wait Time	*Decision wait time* measures the amount of time, in person-hours, that all actors in a mission spend waiting for information and responses about how to handle exceptions.
Maximum Backlog	*Maximum Backlog* measures the number of hours' work that an organizational actor has backlogged; that is, it measures the degree to which an actor is behind schedule. A backlog of one hour would represent an actor that is fully busy but not behind.
Project risk (PRI)	*Project risk index* (PRI) measures the risk to quality arising from mission exceptions. PRI represents the likelihood that all of the planned work components will not be integrated well by mission completion, or that the integration will have residual defects based on incomplete rework and exception handling. Numerically, PRI is calculated as the fraction of effort needed to process ignored and quick-fixed mission exceptions normalized by the total effort to rework all predicted mission exceptions.

for the Company Commander), this hierarchical organization highlights a bottleneck at the company level. Notwithstanding such bottleneck, this performance reflects an organization that knows how to do what it does best, and serves as a baseline for comparison.

This same baseline organization does not perform as well under the Urban Combat conditions. Mission time (64 hours) nearly doubles, both rework (26 person-hours) and coordination effort (8 person-hours) quadruple in this more challenging mission-environmental context, and wait time (1.4 person-hours) nearly triples in magnitude. Moreover, the maximum backlog doubles to 8 hours (again, for the Company Commander), reflecting a commander who is overwhelmed; that is, one hour of backlog represents an comfortable level, in which an actor can accomplish all of its assigned work tasks each day. Alternatively, risk (0.18) decreases slightly.

Results for the enhanced company are similar to those for the baseline organization. Indeed, mission time (36) is unchanged in the open battlefield cases, and both rework (7) and coordination (3) are only slightly higher here than in the baseline case. Further, wait time (0.3) is a bit lower in this enhanced company case, suggesting that tactical decisions are being made more quickly, and that actors are spending less time waiting for important mission information. Also, maximum backlog (3) is less than in the baseline case, indicating that the company commander is not quite as burdened; however, being three

Figure 8. Comparative Organizational Performance

		Open Field	Urban Combat	% Change
Baseline	Time (hours)	36	64	78%
	Direct Work (p-hours)	78	75	-4%
	Rework (p-hours)	6	26	333%
	Coordination (p-hours)	2	8	300%
	Decision Wait (p-hours)	0.5	1.4	180%
	Max Backlog (hours)	4	8	100%
	PRI	0.22	0.18	-18%
Enhanced Company	Time (hours)	36	65	81%
	Direct Work (p-hours)	79	84	6%
	Rework (p-hours)	7	26	271%
	Coordination (p-hours)	3	8	167%
	Decision Wait (p-hours)	0.3	1.4	367%
	Max Backlog (hours)	3	8	167%
	PRI	0.15	0.20	33%

hours behind in a nominal day represents a substantial leadership challenge nonetheless. Notice how risk (0.15 PRI) decreases in this enhanced company case. Overall, the enhanced company appears to perform marginally better in the open battlefield than its baseline counterpart does, which lends empirical support for and credibility to the operational field organizations represented by our computational models; that is, the Marine Corps is moving toward such enhance company as an operational organizational structure, and results suggest that such movement is appropriate.

Likewise, as in the baseline case, performance in the urban environment is worse than that in the open battlefield. It appears that neither organizational form performs as well in the urban environment as it does in the open field. This is not a surprise, for, as noted above, the organization has been refined to operate effectively in the open battlefield for centuries if not millennia. Notice that some of the percentage increases are not as large as those summarized for the baseline organization, however. For instance, rework (271% vs. 333%) and coordination (167% vs. 300%) do not increase as much in percentage terms for the enhanced company as for the baseline organization. This suggests that the enhanced company is somewhat more robust to shifts toward urban combat than the baseline organization is. Alternatively, the increase in wait time (367% vs. 180%) and backlog (167% vs. 100%) is greater in percentage terms for the enhanced company than for the baseline. Notice that risk (PRI of 0.20) increases for the enhanced company, whereas risk corresponding to the baseline organization decreases when transition from open battlefield to urban combat. This will require additional research to understand better.

CONCLUSION

Business process management is recognized increasingly as a critical factor in organizational success: a factor that helps to improve organizational processes, to reduce operational costs, and to promote real-time visibility into performance. In recent years, organizational processes have been becoming increasingly complex and dynamic, as leaders and managers seek to cope with increasingly complex and dynamic environments. Traditional approaches to process management are becoming increasingly inadequate due to their lack of flexibility and adaptability.

Alternatively, an increasing number of scholars are viewing organizations as complex adaptive systems, which are designed, managed and redesigned iteratively to fit and adapt to complex, unpredictable and constantly shifting environments. One such organization receiving considerable current focus is the Edge, which distributes knowledge and power to the "edges" of organizations, and which enables organizational members and units to self-organize and self-synchronize their activities. Key to Edge performance is decentralization, empowerment, shared awareness and freely flowing knowledge required to push power for informed decision making and competent action to the edges.

The dynamics of such self-organization and self-synchronization, however, are extremely complex, and balancing the flexibility and adaptability inherent in the Edge with sufficient control to avoid chaos is very challenging. Without the traditional hierarchy to provide guidance, structure and stability, many people find it difficult to organize themselves effectively, and without well-established organizational routines and well-practiced communication patterns, many people find it difficult to synchronize their activities.

The emerging field of Complex Adaptive Systems offers considerable promise to examine and understand complex, dynamic and adaptable organizations through methods and tools associated with computational modeling and experimentation. Indeed, computational modeling of and experimentation on organizations enable us to investigate the dynamic structures and behaviors of the Edge and other organizational forms, and to learn to understand the kinds of organizational design and management techniques required to develop, control and adapt such organizations in practice.

In this chapter, we employ the state-of-the-art environment for dynamic organizational representation and emulation called POWer to develop and experiment with models of competing organizational forms. POWer is very well-grounded in micro-theories from Organization Studies, and it has been subjected to a lengthy and rigorous regimen of validation. Hence results are reliable, generalizable and trustworthy.

Further, we ground these models in an operational organization in the field—the Marine Corps infantry company—and discuss how the baseline organization performs across two, contrasting mission-environmental contexts: the open battlefield and urban combat. Such organizational instance and comparison are particularly germane, as the organization reflects a classic hierarchy, appears to be quite rigid and inflexible, and the transition from open battlefield to urban combat is exposing serious weaknesses and inadequacies in current field organizations reflecting this design.

We also examine the performance of an alternate, more Edge-like organizational design—the Enhanced Company—across these same two contexts. This comparison is particularly relevant, as the Enhanced Company is designed specifically to address the challenges and demands of the modern mission-environmental context, and it realizes some Edge-like properties by pushing authority for coordinating key fire-support tasks down closer to the edges of the company.

Results reflect a mix of confirming expectations and support. In terms of confirming expectations, both organizational forms perform worse in the urban combat environment than in the open field, and our seven-dimensional performance comparison reveals several subtleties and nuances associated with such comparative performance. In terms of support, the alternate organizational design performs marginally better than its baseline counterpart does, which lends some empirical support for and credibility to the operational field organizations represented by our computational models; that is, the Marine Corps is moving toward such enhanced company as an operational organizational structure, and results suggest that such movement is appropriate. Indeed, if such marginal performance improvements can be effected via the relatively minor organizational change reflected in the Enhanced Company, then the Marine Corps may benefit even further by pushing other tasks and decisions toward the edges in similar fashion. This represents a topic for future research.

In terms of theory, one can see readily that the Enhanced Company reflects a relatively minor design change to the classic hierarchical company, and hence does not incorporate the kinds of revolutionary changes associated with Edge organizations. Indeed, the relatively minor changes reflected in the Enhanced Company serve to alter organizational performance only marginally, and do not extend sufficiently far to secure benefits of Edge organization. Thus, reflecting a "quantum view" of organizations (D. Miller & Friesen, 1984), results suggest that even relatively modest changes to well-designed organizations may improve performance only marginally, and hence that large-scale, coherent design changes (e.g., transformation from Hierarchy to Edge) may be required for complex organizational adaptation and performance improvement. This helps to make an important contribution to theory regarding the management of complex dynamic processes.

In terms of empirical results, we offer multidimensional performance comparisons, generated through a controlled, 2 x 2, computational experimentation design, to support the quantum view, and to suggest that the Marine Corps should continue to push for more revolutionary yet coherent design changes to its infantry organizations. Using computational experimentation as a research method, we provide empirical evidence to support a theoretically motivated position, and we offer insight into the computational models to help organizational designers to understand which design aspects influence comparative performance most substantially. This makes an important contribution to research methodology as well as practice regarding the management of complex dynamic processes, and highlights an agenda for continue research along the lines of this investigation.

This research also helps to elucidate important future trends. First, as suggested in the introduction, classic organizational designs appear to be increasingly anachronistic, particularly as their environments become increasingly dynamic and unpredictable. Future leaders and managers will thus become increasingly concerned with organizational designs, and will become increasingly charged to transform organizations where designs fail to fit well with shifting mission-environmental contexts. Second, the power of computational experimentation demonstrated through this chapter suggests that future leaders and managers may turn increasingly to such computational methods and tools to guide and facilitate their design and transformation activities. Indeed, quite analogous to the manner in which designers of airplanes, bridges, computers and other physical artifacts rely extensively upon computational models and performance simulators to envision, evaluate and compare multiple, alternate, virtual product designs before committing to any specific designs or redesign decisions, future leaders and managers can use computational tools such as POWer to evaluate multiple, alternate, virtual organizational designs before committing to any specific designs or transformation decisions. This offers promise to revolutionize business process management as we know it today.

REFERENCES

Adner, R., & Levinthal, D. A. (2002). The emergence of emerging technologies. *California Management Review, 45*(1), 50.

Al-Mudimigh, A. S. (2007). The role and impact of business process management in enterprise systems implementation. *Business Process Management Journal, 13*(6), 866. doi:10.1108/14637150710834604

Alberts, D. S., & Hayes, R. E. (2003). *Power to the edge: Command and control in the information age.* Washington, DC: Command and Control Research Program.

Amos, J. F. Lieutenant General, USMC, (2007). *Marine Corps operations in complex and distributed environments.* Marine Corps Combat and Development Command, Quantico, VA.

Barnett, W. P., & Sorenson, O. (2002). The red queen in organizational creation and development. *Industrial and Corporate Change, 11*(2), 289–325. doi:10.1093/icc/11.2.289

Brown, S. L., & Eisenhardt, K. M. (1997). The art of continuous change: Linking complexity theory and time-paced evolution in relentlessly shifting organizations. *Administrative Science Quarterly, 42*(1), 1. doi:10.2307/2393807

Burgelman, R. A., & Grove, A. S. (2007). Let chaos reign, then rein in chaos - repeatedly: Managing strategic dynamics for corporate longevity. *Strategic Management Journal, 28*(10), 965. doi:10.1002/smj.625

Burton, R. M., Lauridsen, J., & Obel, B. (2002). Return on assets loss from situational and contingency misfits. *Management Science, 48*(11), 1461. doi:10.1287/mnsc.48.11.1461.262

Burton, R. M., Obel, B., & Keeshan, N. (1995). *Strategic organizational diagnosis and design: Developing theory for application.* Boston: Kluwer Academic Publishers.

Carley, K., & Hill, V. (2001). Structural change and learning within organizations. In A. Lomi, & E. R. Larsen (Eds.), *Dynamics of organizational computational modeling and organization theories.* Cambridge, MA: MIT Press.

Carley, K. M., & Lin, Z. (1997). A theoretical study of organizational performance under information distortion. *Management Science, 43*(7), 976. doi:10.1287/mnsc.43.7.976

Carley, K. M., & Prietula, M. J. (1994). *Computational organization theory.* Hillsdale, N.J: Lawrence Erlbaum Associates.

Chaharbaghi, K., & Nugent, E. (1994). Towards the dynamic organization. *Management Decision, 32*(6), 45. doi:10.1108/00251749410065132

Chandler, A. D. (1962). *Strategy and structure: Chapters in the history of the industrial enterprise.* Cambridge, MA: MIT Press.

Chen, M., Zhang, D., & Zhou, L. (2007). Empowering collaborative commerce with Web services enabled business process management systems. *Decision Support Systems, 43*(2), 530. doi:10.1016/j.dss.2005.05.014

Cheng, C. H. F., & Levitt, R. E. (2001). Contextually changing behavior in medical organizations. In *Proceedings of the 2001 Annual Symposium of the American Medical Informatics Association,* Washington, DC.

Christensen, L. C., Christiansen, T. R., Jin, Y., Kunz, J., & Levitt, R. E. (1999). Modeling and simulating coordination in projects. *Journal of Organizational Computing and Electronic Commerce, 9*(1), 33. doi:10.1207/s15327744joce0901_3

Christiansen, T. R. (1993). *Modeling efficiency and effectiveness of coordination in engineering design teams.* Department of Civil and Environmental Engineering, Stanford University.

Cohen, G. P. (1992). *The virtual design team: An object-oriented model of information sharing in project teams.* Department of Civil Engineering, Stanford University.

Cohen, K. J., & Cyert, R. M. (1965). Simulation of organizational behavior. In J. G. March (Ed.), *Handbook of organizations.* Chicago, IL: Rand McNally.

D'Aveni, R. A. (1994). *Hypercompetition: Managing the dynamics of strategic maneuvering.* New York: Free Press.

Davidow, W. H., & Malone, M. S. (1992). *The virtual corporation: Structuring and revitalizing the corporation for the 21st century* (1st ed.). New York: Edward Burlingame Books/HarperBusiness.

Donaldson, L. (1987). Strategy and structural adjustment to regain fit and performance: In defence of contingency theory. *Journal of Management Studies, 24*(1), 1. doi:10.1111/j.1467-6486.1987.tb00444.x

Eisenhardt, K. M., & Tabrizi, B. N. (1995). Accelerating adaptive processes: Product innovation in the global computer industry. *Administrative Science Quarterly, 40*(1), 84. doi:10.2307/2393701

Galbraith, J. R. (1977). *Organization design.* Reading, MA: Addison-Wesley.

Gateau, J. B., Leweling, T. A., Looney, J. P., & Nissen, M. E. (2007). Hypothesis testing of edge organizations: Modeling the C2 organization design space. In *Proceedings International Command & Control Research & Technology Symposium,* Newport, RI.

Hanssen-Bauer, J., & Snow, C. C. (1996). Responding to hypercompetition: The structure and processes of a regional learning network organization. *Organization Science, 7*(4), 413. doi:10.1287/orsc.7.4.413

Horii, T., Jin, Y., & Levitt, R. E. (2005). Modeling and analyzing cultural influences on project team performance. *Computational & Mathematical Organization Theory, 10*(4), 305. doi:10.1007/s10588-005-6283-1

Jelinek, M., & Schoonhoven, C. B. (1990). *The innovation marathon: Lessons from high technology firms.* Cambridge, MA: B. Blackwell.

Jin, Y., & Levitt, R. E. (1996). The virtual design team: A computational model of project organizations. *Computational & Mathematical Organization Theory, 2*(3), 171–195. doi:10.1007/BF00127273

Joint Chiefs of Staff. (2003). Joint Publication JP 3-09.3, *Joint Tactics, Techniques, and Procedures for Close Air Support (CAS),* Washington, DC.

Joint Chiefs of Staff. (2008). Joint Publication JP 1-02, *Department of Defense Dictionary of Military and Associated Terms,* Washington, DC.

Küng, P., & Hagen, C. (2007). The fruits of business process management: An experience report from a Swiss bank. *Business Process Management Journal, 13*(4), 477. doi:10.1108/14637150710763522

Kunz, J. C., Christiansen, T. R., Cohen, G. P., Jin, Y., & Levitt, R. E. (1998). The virtual design team. *Communications of the ACM, 41*(11), 84–91. doi:10.1145/287831.287844

Law, A. M., & Kelton, D. (1991). *Simulation modeling and analysis* (2nd ed.). New York: McGraw-Hill.

Leavitt, H. J. (1965). Applying organizational change in industry: Structural, technological and humanistic approaches. In J. March (Ed.), *Handbook of organizations* (pp. 1144-1170). Chicago: Rand McNally.

Levitt, R. E. (2004). Computational modeling of organizations comes of age. *Computational & Mathematical Organization Theory, 10*(2), 127. doi:10.1023/B:CMOT.0000039166.53683.d0

Levitt, R. E., Orr, R. J., & Nissen, M. E. (2005). *Validating the virtual design team (VDT) computational modeling environment.* Stanford, CA

Levitt, R. E., Thomsen, J., Christiansen, T. R., & Kunz, J. C. (1999). Simulating project work processes and organizations: Toward a micro-contingency theory of organizational design. *Management Science, 45*(11), 1479. doi:10.1287/mnsc.45.11.1479

Mahalingam, A., Levitt, R. E., & Scott, W. R. (2005). Cultural clashes in international infrastructure development projects: Which cultures matter? Las Vegas, NV.

March, J. G., & Simon, H. A. (1958). *Organizations.* New York: Wiley.

Miller, D., & Friesen, P. (1984). *Organizations: A quantum view.* Englewood Cliffs, NJ: Prentice-Hall.

Miller, J., & Page, S. (2007). *Complex adaptive systems: An introduction to computational models of social life.* Princeton, NJ: Princeton University Press.

Mintzberg, H. (1979). *The structuring of organizations: A synthesis of the research.* Englewood Cliffs, N.J: Prentice-Hall.

Nissen, M. E. (2005). Hypothesis testing of edge organizations: Specifying computational C2 models for experimentation. In *Proceedings International Command & Control Research Symposium,* McLean, VA.

Nissen, M. E. (2007). Computational experimentation on new organizational forms: Exploring behavior and performance of edge organizations. *Computational & Mathematical Organization Theory, 13*(3), 203. doi:10.1007/s10588-006-9011-6

Nissen, M. E., & Buettner, R. R. (2004). Computational experimentation with the virtual design team: Bridging the chasm between laboratory and field research in C2. In *Proceedings Command and Control Research and Technology Symposium,* San Diego, CA.

Nissen, M. E., & Levitt, R. E. (2004). Agent-based modeling of knowledge dynamics. *Knowledge Management Research & Practice, 2*(3), 169. doi:10.1057/palgrave.kmrp.8500039

Nissen, M. E., & Leweling, T. A. (2008). Conceptualizing dynamic organizational fit in multicontingency contexts. In *Proceedings Academy of Management Conference,* Anaheim, CA.

Orr, R. J., & Nissen, M. E. (2006). Computational experimentation on C2 models. In *Proceedings International Command and Control Research and Technology Symposium,* Cambridge, UK.

Osborn, R. N., & Hunt, J. G. (2007). Leadership and the choice of order: Complexity and hierarchical perspectives near the edge of chaos. *The Leadership Quarterly, 18*(4), 319. doi:10.1016/j.leaqua.2007.04.003

Ouchi, W. G. (1980). Markets, bureaucracies, and clans. *Administrative Science Quarterly, 25*(1), 129. doi:10.2307/2392231

Rahrami, H. (1992). The emerging flexible organization: Perspectives from Silicon Valley. *California Management Review, 34*(4), 33.

Ramesh, B., Jain, R., Nissen, M., & Xu, P. (2005). Managing context in business process management systems. *Requirements Engineering, 10*(3), 223. doi:10.1007/s00766-005-0005-6

Raynor, M. E., & Bower, J. L. (2001). Lead from the center: How to manage divisions dynamically. *Harvard Business Review, 79*(5), 92.

Romanelli, E., & Tushman, M. L. (1994). Organizational transformation as punctuated equilibrium: An empirical test. *Academy of Management Journal, 37*(5), 1141. doi:10.2307/256669

Sabherwal, R., Hirschheim, R., & Goles, T. (2001). The dynamics of alignment: Insights from a punctuated equilibrium model. *Organization Science, 12*(2), 179. doi:10.1287/orsc.12.2.179.10113

Scott, J. E. (2007). Mobility, business process management, software sourcing, and maturity model trends: Propositions for the IS organization of the future. *Information Systems Management, 24*(2), 139. doi:10.1080/10580530701221031

Scott, W. R. (1995). *Institutions and organizations.* Thousand Oaks, CA: Sage.

Shaw, D. R., Holland, C. P., Kawalek, P., Snowdon, B., & Warboys, B. (2007). Elements of a business process management system: Theory and practice. *Business Process Management Journal, 13*(1), 91. doi:10.1108/14637150710721140

Thompson, J. D. (1967). *Organizations in action; social science bases of administrative theory.* New York: McGraw-Hill.

Thomsen, J., Levitt, R. E., Kunz, J. C., Nass, C. I., & Fridsma, D. B. (1999). A trajectory for validating computational emulation models of organizations. *Computational & Mathematical Organization Theory, 5*(4), 385. doi:10.1023/A:1009624719571

Tung, R. L. (1979). Dimensions of organizational environments: An exploratory study of their impact on organization structure. *Academy of Management Journal (Pre-1986), 22* (000004), 672.

US Marine Corps. (1978). Fleet Marine Force Manual (FMFM) 6-4, *Marine Rifle Company/Platoon,* Marine Corps Combat Development Command, Quantico, VA

US Marine Corps. (2001). Marine Corps Warfighting Publication 3-16, (2001). *Fire Support in the Ground Combat Element,* Marine Corps Combat Development Command, Quantico, VA

US Marine Corps. (2008). Marine Corps Warfighting Publication 3-11.5, [Draft], *Marine Infantry Battalion,* Marine Corps Combat Development Command, Quantico, VA

Vanderhaeghen, D., & Loos, P. (2007). Distributed model management platform for cross-enterprise business process management in virtual enterprise networks. *Journal of Intelligent Manufacturing, 18*(5), 553. doi:10.1007/s10845-007-0060-6

Venkatraman, N., & Prescott, J. E. (1990). Environment-strategy coalignment: An empirical test of its. *Strategic Management Journal, 11*(1), 1. doi:10.1002/smj.4250110102

Zajac, E. J., Kraatz, M. S., & Bresser, R. K. F. (2000). Modeling the dynamics of strategic fit: A normative approach to strategic change. *Strategic Management Journal, 21*(4), 429. doi:10.1002/(SICI)1097-0266(200004)21:4<429::AID-SMJ81>3.0.CO;2-#

KEY TERMS

Computational Experimentation: The use of computational models—combined with experimentation protocols for controls, manipulations and measurements—to conduct experiments on virtual representations of entities.

Computational Organization Theory: A multidisciplinary field that integrates aspects of artificial intelligence, organization studies and system dynamics/simulation.

Close Air Support: Air action by fixed- and rotary-wing aircraft against hostile targets that are in close proximity to friendly forces and that require detailed integration of each air mission with the fire and movement of those forces. Also called CAS. (JP 1-02)

Doctrine: Explicit articulations and teachings pertaining to military organizations and processes.

Edge Organization: A relatively novel organizational form that distributes knowledge and power to the "edges" of organizations, and that enables organizational members and units to self-organize and self-synchronize their activities.

Fires: The effects of lethal or nonlethal weapons in a military combat context. (JP 1-02)

Organizational Design: A rational view of organizing, through which managers purposefully consider and effect changes to organizational structure in order to improve fit with changing environmental, technological, strategic and like characteristics.

POWer: A state-of-the-art environment for dynamic organizational representation and emulation, which is used to develop and experiment with models of alternate organizational forms.

Validation: An activity focused on ensuring that the structures and behaviors of computational models match those of the real-world entities represented by such models.

APPENDIX A: ORGANIZATIONAL MODEL DEFINITIONS

In this appendix we include definitions for the key positions described in our A Company POWer Model from above.

Battalion Level Positions Modeled

See Marine Corps Warfighting Publication (MCWP) 3-11.5 (draft) and MCWP 3-16 Fires Support Coordination in the GCE.

Intelligence Officer (S-2). The S-2 officer is the commander's intelligence assistant and is responsible for the production and dissemination of intelligence, counterintelligence, graphic intelligence aids, and intelligence training. The S-2 officer also serves as the Scout-Sniper platoon commander. **Operations officer (S-3).** The S-3 staff officer (operations officer) is responsible for planning, coordinating, and supervising the tactical employment of the battalion's units, and the integration of fires and maneuver. **Battalion FSC.** The fire support coordinator organizes and supervises the FSCC under the staff cognizance of the G-3/S-3 (Operations). The weapons company commander is also appointed as the battalion FSC and in this capacity serves as the special staff officer in addition to command responsibilities. **Artillery LNO.** The artillery LNO serves in the FSCC and is the senior battalion artillery officer. **AirO:** The AirO is an aviator and qualified Forward Air Controller (FAC). He is also the special staff officer to the battalion commander in regard to all aviation matters. He works within the FSCC as the air representative and coordinates air support with the FACs assigned to the battalion's infantry companies. **Mortar Rep.** The mortar rep is assigned to the battalion FSCC and is sourced from the organic 81mm mortar platoon. **NGLO.** The NGLO is assigned to the battalion FSCC and is responsible for coordinating naval gunfire fire (NGF).

Company Level Positions Modeled

See Fleet Marine Force Manual (FMFM) 6-4, Joint Pub 3-09.3, and Joint Pub 1-2.

FAC. An officer (aviator/pilot) who is a member of the tactical air control party, and who, from a forward ground or airborne position, controls aircraft in close air support of ground troops. (Joint Publication. **Joint Terminal Attack Controller (JTAC).** A joint terminal attack controller (JTAC) is a qualified (certified) service member who, from a forward position, directs the action of combat aircraft engaged in CAS and other air operations. **Platoon Commander.** Responsible to the company commander for everything the platoon does or fails to do in combat. **Weapons Platoon Commander.** Exercises direct control over his platoon and provides direct fires (60 mm mortars/heavy machine guns) in support of the platoon. **Company FSC.** Typically the company's weapons platoon commander is assigned the duty as company FSC, or FiST leader: responsible for synchronizing and de-conflicting company artillery, air, and surface fire support. **Company AirO.** FAC assigned to the rifle company. The company FAC is responsible for planning, coordinating, and employing FW/RWCAS in support of the company's maneuver. **Arty FO.** Responsible for coordinating company artillery fires. **Mortar FO.** Responsible for coordinating company organic and inorganic mortar fire support. **NGF FO.** Responsible for coordinating naval surface fire support (NSFS) in support of the company maneuver. Due to the limited range of naval gunfire, typical naval surface fires are only employed in a littoral environment and in close proximity to supporting naval shipping.

Fire Support Assets

Air. Represents the aircraft delivering close air support to the company. **Arty Battery.** Represents the artillery battery providing fire support to the battalion's companies. **Mortar Platoon.** Represents the 81mm mortar platoon provided by the weapons company and organic to the battalion. **NSFS.** Represents the naval vessel(s) providing naval surface fire support.

APPENDIX B: MODEL PARAMETERIZATION

For reference, we include Figure 3 from above here, relabel it Figure 9, and elaborate the underlying organizational features that are addressed by and reflected in our model parameterization settings. As noted above, these settings are predicated predominantly on prior research along these lines.

Organization structure. Centralization is considered High in the Baseline Organization due to the reservation of decision rights to high levels of the organization. While Centralization is concerned with the allocation of decision rights, Formalization deals with the formalization of job descriptions and means of communications within an organization. The baseline is set to High Formalization to reflect the highly defined jobs and structured communications patterns exhibited by these forms. Most jobs have formal, written descriptions and standards, and most communication occurs along prescribed lines and with structured documents. Vertical specialization here refers to the number of hierarchical levels included in the model. We include three such levels here, focusing on those most involved with and impacted by the kinds of organizational changes considered in this study. Consistent with prior models also, the skill level is set to medium as a baseline, as is application experience. However, we diverge a bit from such prior work, and set team experience to Medium; this reflects the greater amount of time that applicable Marine units spend training and working together as integrated teams.

Communication structure. Consistent with the Machine Bureaucracy, the baseline organization modeled here includes relatively few communication links, which are representative of communications constrained to supervisory links (the chain of command). However, because of the specific organization and processes represented here, we increase the information exchange parameter, which represents a percentage likelihood that communication will occur between two actors, modestly (i.e., from 0.1 to 0.3), and we include no formal meetings for the same reason. Matrix strength is intended to be reflective of the amount of cross-functional management in an organization. As the baseline organization is organized primarily by function, with little cross-functional coordination by the workers, they are rated as Low.

Work structure. With parameters in this set, we summarize the nature of work tasks, indicating a total count of 22 as depicted in the figures above. As depicted also, such tasks are organized into two, parallel work paths that progress in two phases. Because interdependence between units in this organization is more intensive than in the archetypal Machine Bureaucracy, we indicate the level as Medium here (as opposed to Low in archetypal models), which corresponds to the combination of sequential and reciprocal interactions. The few rework links pertain to a limited set of tasks. The value of 0.3 for rework strength means that when a rework link is activated, each hour of rework in the original task results in 0.3 hours of rework in the dependent task. Finally, environmental complexity refers to how likely an organization is to experience exceptions. The baseline organization has this parameter value set at the same level as the archetypal Machine Bureaucracy (i.e., 0.1).

Figure 9. Model Formulation: Baseline Organization

Structural Factor	Mintzberg Design Factor	Model Parameter	Baseline
Organization Structure	Decentralization	Centralization	High
	Formalization of behavior	Formalization	High
	Vertical specialization	Hierarchy Set-Up	3-level
	Training	Skill Level	Med
	Indoctrination	App. Experience	Med
		Team experience	Med
Communication Structure	Liaison Devices	Communication Links	Few
	"	Information Exchange	0.3
	Planning & Control Systems	Formal Meetings	none
	"	Matrix Strength	Low
Work Structure		Number of Operational Tasks	22
		Degree of Concurrency	Parallel, 2 Phase
		Interdependence	Med
		Rework Links	Few
		Rework Strength	0.3
	Environment - Complxity	FEP/PEP	0.1

Compilation of References

Aberdeen, D., & Baxter, J. (2002). Scaling internal-state policy-gradient methods for POMDPs. In *Proceedings of the 19th international conference on machine learning* (Vol. 2, pp. 3-10). Sydney, Australia: Morgan Kaufmann.

Abiteboul, S., Hull, R., & Vianu, V. (Eds.). (1995). Foundations of databases: The logical level. Boston, MA: Addison-Wesley Longman Publishing Co., Inc.

Abul, O., Polat, F., & Alhajj, R. (2000). Multiagent reinforcement learning using function approximation. In *IEEE transactions on systems, man, and cybernetics, part c* (Vol. 30, p. 485-497).

Achrol, R. S., & Kotler, P. (1999). Marketing in the network economy. *Journal of Marketing, 63,* 146–163. doi:10.2307/1252108

ACORD Insurance Domain standard (2002). *ACORD home page.* Retrieved March 10, 2008, from http://www.acord.org/home/home.aspx

Adams, M. (2007). *Facilitating dynamic flexibility and exception handling for workflows.* PhD thesis, Queensland University of Technology.

Adams, M., Edmond, D., & ter Hofstede, A. H. (2003). The application of activity theory to dynamic workflow adaptation issues. In *Proceedings of the 2003 Pacific Asia Conference on Information Systems (PACIS 2003)* (pp. 1836–1852). Adelaide, Australia.

Adams, M., ter Hofstede, A., Edmond, D., & van der Aalst, W. M. P. (2006). Worklets: A service-oriented implementation of dynamic flexibility in workflows. In *Proc. Coopis'06* (pp. 291-308).

Adner, R., & Levinthal, D. A. (2002). The emergence of emerging technologies. *California Management Review, 45*(1), 50.

Agostini, A., & De Michelis, G. (2000). Improving flexibility of workflow management systems. In W. van der Aalst & J. Oberweis (Eds.), *BPM: Models, techniques, and empirical studies* (pp. 218-234). Springer Verlag.

Agostini, A., & de Michelis, G. (2000). A light workflow management system using simple process models. *Computer Supported Cooperative Work, 9*(3-4), 335–363. doi:10.1023/A:1008703327801

Agrawal, R., Gunopulos, D., & Leymann, F. (2008). Mining process models from workflow logs. In *Proceedings from EDBT'08: The Sixth International Conference on Extending Database Technology* (pp. 469-483).

Aiello, M., Papazoglou, M., Yang, J., Carman, M., Pistore, M., Serafini, L., et al. (2002, August). A request language for Web-services based on planning and constraint satisfaction. In *Proceedings of the VLDB Workshop on Technologies for E-Services.*

Aiken, A. Widom, J., & Hellerstein, J. M. (1992). Behavior of database production rules: Termination, confluence, and observable determinism. In *Proceedings of the ACM SIGMOD Conference on Management of Data* (pp. 59-68).

Aktas, Z., & Cetin, S. (2006). We envisage the next big thing. *IDPT-2006 Integrated Design and Process Technology Conference* (pp. 404-411). San Diego, California.

Alamri, A., Eid, M., & El Saddik, A. (2006). Classification of the state-of-the-art dynamic web services composition techniques. *International Journal of Web and Grid Services, 2*(2), 148–166. doi:10.1504/IJWGS.2006.010805

Alberts, D. S., & Hayes, R. E. (2003). *Power to the edge: Command and control in the information age.* Washington, DC: Command and Control Research Program.

Allee, V. (2000). Knowledge networks and communities of practice. *OD Practitioner Online, 32*(4).

Al-Mudimigh, A. S. (2007). The role and impact of business process management in enterprise systems implementation. *Business Process Management Journal, 13*(6), 866. doi:10.1108/14637150710834604

Alonso, G., Kamath, M., Agrawal, D., El Abbadi, A., Günthör, R., & Mohan, C. (1994). Failure handling in large scale workflow management systems. *TR RJ9913, IBM Almaden Research Center.*

Alonso, G., Mohan, C., Günthör, R., Agrawal, D., El Abbadi, A., & Kamath, M. (1995). Exotica/ FMQM: Persistent message-based architecture for distributed workflow management. In *Proc. IFIP Working Conf. on Inf. Syst. for Decentralized Organisations*, Trondheim, Norway.

Altintas, N. I. (2007). *Feature-based software asset modeling with domain specific kits.* Doctoral dissertation, Middle East Technical University, Department of Computer Engineering. Ankara, Turkey. Retrieved from http://etd.lib.metu.edu.tr/upload/12608682/index.pdf

Altintas, N. I., & Cetin, S. (2005). Integrating a software product line with rule-based business process modeling. *TEAA-2005 Trends in Enterprise Application Architecture Workshop, VLDB-2005 Conference* (LNCS 3888, pp. 15-28).

Altintas, N. I., & Cetin, S. (2008). Managing large scale reuse across multiple software product lines. *ICSR-2008 10th International Conference on Software Reuse* (LNCS 5030, pp. 166-177). Beijing, China.

Altintas, N. I., Cetin, S., & Dogru, A. (2007). Industrializing software development: The "factory automation" way. *TEAA-2006 2nd Trends in Enterprise Application Architecture Conference* (LNCS 4473, pp. 54-68).

Altintas, N. I., Cetin, S., & Surav, M. (2008). OCTOPODA: Building financial gateways family system using domain specific kits. *ICONS-2008 Third International Conference on Systems* (pp. 85-92). Cancun, Mexico. DOI 10.1109/ICONS.2008.57

Alves de Medeiros, A. K., Pedrinaci, C., van der Aalst, W. M. P., Domingue, J., Song, M., Rozinat, A., et al. (2007). An outlook on semantic business process mining and monitoring. In *OTM 2007 Workshops* (pp. 1244-1255). New York: Springer.

Alves de Medeiros, A. K., van der Aalst, W. M. P., & Pedrinaci, C. (2008). *Semantic process mining tools: Core building blocks.* Paper presented at the 16th European Conference on Information Systems, Galway, Ireland.

Amato, C., Bernstein, D. S., & Zilberstein, S. (2006). Solving POMDPs using quadratically constrained linear programs. In *Proceedings of the fifth international joint conference on autonomous agents and multiagent systems* (pp. 341-343). New York: ACM Press.

Ambler, S. W. (1998). *Process patterns.* Cambridge University Press/SIGS Books.

Ambrosio, J. (2000). *Knowledge management mistakes.*

Amos, J. F. Lieutenant General, USMC, (2007). *Marine Corps operations in complex and distributed environments.* Marine Corps Combat and Development Command, Quantico, VA.

Anderson, J. C., & Narus, J. A. (1999). *Business market management: Understanding, creating and delivering value.* Prentice Hall.

Andersson, T., Andersson-Ceder, A., & Bider, I. (2002). State flow as a way of analyzing business processes – Case studies. *Logistics Information Management, 15*(1), 34–45. doi:10.1108/09576050210412657

Andrieux, A., Czajkowski, K., & Dan, A. (2004, June). *Web services agreement specification* (WS Agreement).

Argyris, C. (1999). *On organizational learning* (2nd ed.). Oxford: Blackwell.

Arkin, A., Askary, S., Fordin, S., Jekeli, W., Kawaguchi, K., Orchard, D., et al. (2002, August). *Web service choreography interface.*

Armistead, C., & Rowland, P. (1996). *Managing business processes: BPR and beyond.* New York: John Wiley and Sons.

Aversano, L., De Canfora, G., Lucia, A., & Gallucci, P. (2002). Integrating document and workflow management tools using XML and Web technologies: A case study. In *Proceedings of Sixth European Conference on Software Maintenance and Reengineering* (pp. 24-33).

Bae, H., Hur, W., Yoo, W., Kwak, B., Kim, Y., & Park, Y. (2004). Document configuration control processes captured in a workflow. *Computers in Industry, 53*(2), 117–131. doi:10.1016/j.compind.2003.07.001

Bae, J., Bae, H., Kang, S.-H., & Kim, Y. (2004). Automatic control of workflow processes using eca rules. *IEEE Transactions on Knowledge and Data Engineering, 16*(8), 1010–1023. doi:10.1109/TKDE.2004.20

Bajaj, S., Box, D., Chappell, D., Curbera, F., Daniels, G., Hallam-Baker, P., et al. (2006, March). *Web services policy framework (WS-Policy).*

Baldwin, C. Y., & Clark, K. B. (1997). Managing in an age of modularity. *Harvard Business Review, 75*(5), 84–93.

Baldwin, C. Y., & Clark, K. B. (2000). *Design rules: The power of modularity.* Cambridge, MA: MIT Press.

Baligh, H. H., Burton, R. M., et al. (1990). Devising expert systems in organization theory: The organizational consultant. In M. Masuch (Ed.), *Organization, management, and expert systems* (pp. 35-57). Berlin, Germany: Walter de Gruyter.

Banerji, A., Bartolini, C., Beringer, D., Chopella, V., Govindarajan, K., Karp, A., et al. (2004, March). *Web service conversation language (WSCL).*

Barbará, D., Mehrotra, S., & Rusinkiewicz, M. (1996). *INCAs:* Managing dynamic workflows in distributed environments. *Journal of Database Management, 7*(1), 5–15.

Barber, K. D., Dewhurst, F. W., Burns, R. L. D. H., & Rogers, J. B. B. (2003). Business-process modelling and simulation for manufacturing management. A practical way forward. *Business Process Management Journal, 4*(9), 527–542. doi:10.1108/14637150310484544

Bardram, J. E. (1997). I love the system - I just don't use it! In *Proceedings of the International ACM SIGGROUP Conference on Supporting Group Work (GROUP'97),* (pp. 251-260). Phoenix, AZ: ACM.

Barish, G., Di Pasquo, D., Knoblock, C. A., & Minton, S. (2002). A dataflow approach to agent-based information management. In *Proceedings of the 2000 International Conference on Artificial Intelligence (ICAI-2000),* Las Vegas, Nevada, USA.

Barnett, W. P., & Sorenson, O. (2002). The red queen in organizational creation and development. *Industrial and Corporate Change, 11*(2), 289–325. doi:10.1093/icc/11.2.289

Barthelmess, P., & Wainer, J. (1995). Workflow systems: A few definitions and a few suggestions. In *Proceedings of the ACM Conference on Organizational Computing Systems (COOCS'95),* (pp. 138-147). Milpitas, CA: ACM.

Bass, L., Clement, P., & Kazman, R. (1998). *Software architecture in practice.* Reading: Addison-Wesley.

Bassil, S., Keller, R., & Kropf, P. (2004). A workflow-oriented system architecture for the management of container transportation. In *Proc. BPM'04* (LNCS 3080, pp. 116-131).

Basten, A. (1998). *In terms of nets, system design with petri nets and process algebra.* Unpublished doctoral dissertation, Department of Mathematics and Computing Science.

Basu, A., & Kumar, A. (2002). Research Commentary: Workflow management systems in e-business. *Infor-*

mation Systems Research, 13(1), 1–14. doi:10.1287/isre.13.1.1.94

Bauer, T., & Dadam, P. (1997). A distributed execution environment for large-scale workflow management systems with subnets and server migration. In *Proc. CoopIS'97* (pp. 99-108).

Bauer, T., & Dadam, P. (1999). Efficient distributed control of enterprise-wide and cross-enterprise workflows. In *Proc. GI-Workshop on Enterprise-wide and Cross-enterprise Workflow Management: Concepts, Systems, Applications* (pp. 25-32). Paderborn, Germany.

Bauer, T., & Dadam, P. (2000). Efficient distributed workflow management based on variable server assignments. In *Proceedings CAiSE'00* (pp. 94-109). Stockholm, Sweden.

Bauer, T., & Reichert, M. (2004). Dynamic change of server assignments in distributed workflow management systems. In *Proc. ICEIS'04* (pp. 91-98). Porto, Portugal.

Bauer, T., Reichert, M., & Dadam, P. (2001). Effiziente Übertragung von prozessinstanzdaten in verteilten workflow-management-systemen. *Informatik - Forschung und Entwicklung, 16*(2), 76-92.

Bauer, T., Reichert, M., & Dadam, P. (2003). Intra-subnet load balancing for distributed workflow management systems. *International Journal of Cooperative Information Systems, 12*(3), 295–323. doi:10.1142/S0218843003000760

Beardsley, S. C., Bray, W. D., & van Rooijen, M. C. W. (1995). The great European multimedia gamble. *McKinsley Quarterly* 1995/3.

Berens, P. (2005). *The FLOWer case handling approach: Beyond workflow managment*, (pp. 363-395).

Berfield, A., Chrysanthis, P. K., Tsamardinos, I., Pollack, M. E., & Banerjee, S. *(2002).* A scheme for integrating e-services in establishing virtual enterprises. *Paper presented at the Research Issues in Data Engineering.*

Bergstra, J., & Klop, J. (1985). Algebra of communicating processes with abstraction. *Theoretical Computer Science, 37*(1), 77–121. doi:10.1016/0304-3975(85)90088-X

Bergstra, J., Ponse, A., & Smolka, S. (2001). *Handbook of process algebra.* Elsevier.

Besembel, I., Hennet, J. C., & Chacon, E. *(2002).* Coordination by hierarchical negotiation within an enterprise network. *Paper presented at the 8th International Conference on Concurrent Enterprising, Rome, Italy.*

Bézivin, J., Hammoudi, S., Lopes, D., & Jouault, F. (2004). *An experiment in mapping Web services to implementation platforms* (Tech. Rep. LINA, University of Nantes).

Bider, I. (2005). Masking flexibility behind rigidity: Notes on how much flexibility people are willing to cope with. In J. Castro & E. Teniente (Eds.), *Proceedings of the CAiSE'05 Workshops*, vol. 1, (pp. 7-18). Porto, Portugal: FEUP Edicoes.

Blomqvist, K. (2002). *Partnering in the dynamic environment: The role of trust in asymmetric technology partnership formation.* Lappeenranta University of Technology.

Bloomberg, J. (2006). Composing services into enterprise mashups – Empowering business users with enterprise Web 2.0. Retrieved from http://www.zapthink.com

Bødker, S., & Greenbaum, J. (1993). Design of information systems: Things versus people. In E. Green, J. Owen, & D. Pain (Eds.), *Gendered by design? Information technology and office systems* (pp. 53-63). London: Taylor and Francis.

Bohannon, P., Fan, W. F., Geerts, F., Jia, X. B., & Kementsietsidis, A. (2007). The conditional functional dependencies for data cleaning. In *Proceedings from ICDE '07: The IEEE 23rd International Conference on Data Engineering.* CA: IEEE Computer Society Press.

Boley, H. (2000). Markup languages for functional-logic programming. In *Proceedings of 9th WFLP 2000*, Benicassim, Spain.

Boley, H., Tabet, S., & Wagner, G. (2001). Design rationale of RuleML: A markup language for Semantic Web rules. In *Proceedings of SWWS'01*, Stanford.

Booch, G., Brown, A., Iyengar, S., Rumbaugh, J., & Selic, B. (2004). An MDA Manifesto. *Business Process Trends - MDA Journal*. Retrieved from http://www.bptrends. com/publicationfiles/05-04%20COL%20IBM%20Manifesto%20-%20Frankel%20-3.pdf

Booch, G., Rumbaugh, J., & Jacobson, I. (1998). *The unified modeling language user guide*. Addison-Wesley.

Bordbar, B., & Staikopoulos, A. (2004). Modelling and transforming the behavioural aspects of web services. In *Third Workshop in Software Model Engineering (WiSME2004) at UML, Lisbon, Portugal.*

Bordbar, B., & Staikopoulos, A. (2004). On behavioural model transformation in Web services. In *Conceptual Modelling for Advanced Application Domain (eCOMO)* (pp. 667-678). Shanghai, China.

Borgida, A., & Murata, T. (1999). Tolerating exceptions in workflows: A unified framework for data and processes. In *Proceedings of the International Joint Conference on Work Activities, Coordination and Collaboration (WACC'99)* (pp. 59-68). San Francisco, CA: ACM Press.

Boutilier, C. (1996). Planning, learning and coordination in multiagent decision processes. In *Proceedings of the 6th conference on theoretical aspects of rationality and knowledge* (pp. 195-210). San Francisco: Morgan Kaufmann Publishers Inc.

Bowers, J., Button, G., & Sharrock, W. (1995). Workflow from within and without: Technology and cooperative work on the print industry shopfloor. In *Proceedings of the Fourth Conference on European Conference on Computer-Supported Cooperative Work* (pp. 51-66).

Bowling, M., & Veloso, M. (2001). Rational and convergent learning in stochastic games. In *International Joint Conferences on Artificial Intelligence* (p. 1021-1026).

BPEL. (2003). *Business process execution language for Web services (BPEL4WS). Version 1.1*.Retrieved from http://www-128.ibm.com/developerworks/library/specification/wsbpel

BPEL. (2004). *BPEL: Business process execution language*. Retrieved March 30, 2008, from http://bpel. xml.org/.

BPEL4WS (n.d.). *Specification: Business process execution language for Web services* (Version 1.1). Retrieved from http://www-128.ibm.com/developerworks/library/ws-bpel/.

BPML. (2002). *BPML: Business Process Modeling Language*. Retrieved April 12, 2008, from http://www. ebpml.org/bpml.htm.

BPMN. (2004). *BPMN: Business Process Modeling Notation*. Retrieved March 12, 2008, from http://www. bpmn.org/.

Brahe, S. (2007). BPM on top of SOA: Experiences from the financial industry. In G. Alonso, P. Dadam, & M. Rosemann (Eds.), *BPM2007* (LNCS 4714, pp. 96-111).

Brahe, S. (2008). *An experiment on creating enterprise specific BPM languages and tools* (Tech. Rep. ITU-TR-2008-102). IT University of Copenhagen.

Brahe, S., & Bordbar, B. (2006). A pattern-based approach to business process modeling and implementation in Web services. In D. Georgakopoulos (Ed.), *ICSOC 2006* (LNCS 4652, pp. 161-172).

Brahe, S., & Østerbye, K. (2006). Business process modeling: Defining domain specific modeling languages by use of UML profiles. In A. Rensink & J. Warmer (Eds.), *ECMDA-FA 2006* (LNCS 4066, pp. 241-255).

Branchaud, M., & Flinn, S. (2004). xTrust: A scalable trust management infrastructure. In *Proceedings of the 2nd Annual Conference on Privacy, Security and Trust.* (pp. 207-218). Fredericton, New Brunswick, Canada, 14-15 October.

Brandenburger, A. M., & Nalebuff, B. J. (1996). *Co-opetition*. New York: Doubleday.

Bratley, P., Fox, B. L., & Schrage, L. E. (1987). *A guide to simulation* (2nd ed.). New York: Springer.

Bravo, L., Fan, W. F., & Ma, S. (2007). Extending dependencies with conditions. In *Proceedings from VLDB'07:*

The 33rd international Conference on Very Large Data Bases (Vienna, Austria, September 23 - 27, 2007). Very Large Data Bases. VLDB Endowment (pp. 243-254).

Bresciani, P., Giorgini, P., Giunchiglia, F., Mylopoulos, J., & Perini, A. (2004, May). Tropos: An Agent-oriented software development methodology. *Autonomous Agents and Multi-Agent Systems, 8*(3), 203–236. doi:10.1023/B:AGNT.0000018806.20944.ef

Brim, O. G., Class, D. C., Lavin, D. E., & Goodman, N. E. (1962). *Personality and decision process – Studies in the social psychology of thinking.* Stanford, CA: Stanford University Press.

Brooks, F. P. (1987). No silver bullet: Essence and accidents of software engineering. *Computer, 20*(4), 10–19. doi:10.1109/MC.1987.1663532

Brown, S. L., & Eisenhardt, K. M. (1997). The art of continuous change: Linking complexity theory and time-paced evolution in relentlessly shifting organizations. *Administrative Science Quarterly, 42*(1), 1. doi:10.2307/2393807

Buckley, J. J. (1985). Ranking alternatives using fuzzy number. *Fuzzy Sets and Systems, 15*(1), 21–31. doi:10.1016/0165-0114(85)90013-2

Budinsky, F., Steinberg, D., Merks, E., Ellersick, R., & Grose, T. J. (2003). Eclipse Modeling Framework: A Developer's Guide. Addison Wesley.

Bullinger, H.-J., Fähnrich, K.-P., & Meiren, T. (2003). Service engineering – Methodical development of new service products. *International Journal of Production Economics, 3*(85), 275–287. doi:10.1016/S0925-5273(03)00116-6

Burgelman, R. A., & Grove, A. S. (2007). Let chaos reign, then rein in chaos - repeatedly: Managing strategic dynamics for corporate longevity. *Strategic Management Journal, 28*(10), 965. doi:10.1002/smj.625

Burmeister, B., Steiert, H. P., Bauer, T., & Baumgärtel, H. (2006). Agile processes through goal- and context-oriented business process modeling. *DPM-2006 Dynamic Process Management Workshop at Business Process Management 2006 Conference* (LNCS 4103, pp. 217-228).

Burton, R. M., Lauridsen, J., & Obel, B. (2002). Return on assets loss from situational and contingency misfits. *Management Science, 48*(11), 1461. doi:10.1287/mnsc.48.11.1461.262

Burton, R. M., Obel, B., & Keeshan, N. (1995). *Strategic organizational diagnosis and design: Developing theory for application.* Boston: Kluwer Academic Publishers.

Business Process Execution Language. (2006). *The OASIS Site.* Retrieved April 11, 2008, from http://docs.oasis-open.org/wsbpel/2.0/wsbpel-specification-draft.pdf

Business Process Modeling Initiative. (2002, June). *Business process modeling language.*

Business Process Modeling Language. (2002). *BPML Specification.* Retrieved April 14, 2008, from http://xml.coverpages.org/BPML-WD-200206.pdf

Business Process Modeling Notation. (2006). *BPMN home page.* Retrieved April 14, 2008, from http://www.bpmn.org/

Camuffo, A. (2000). *Rolling out a "World car." Globalization, outsourcing and modularity in the auto industry.* Venice, Italy: Ca´ Foscari University, Department of Business Economics and Management.

Carley, K. M., & Lin, Z. (1997). A theoretical study of organizational performance under information distortion. *Management Science, 43*(7), 976. doi:10.1287/mnsc.43.7.976

Carley, K. M., & Prietula, M. J. (1994). *Computational organization theory.* Hillsdale, N.J: Lawrence Erlbaum Associates.

Carley, K., & Hill, V. (2001). Structural change and learning within organizations. In A. Lomi, & E. R. Larsen (Eds.), *Dynamics of organizational computational modeling and organization theories.* Cambridge, MA: MIT Press.

Carmel, D., & Markovitch, S. (1996). Learning models of intelligent agents. In *Proceedings of the thirteenth national conference on artificial intelligence* (Vol. 2, pp. 62-67). Portland, Oregon.

Casati, F. (1998). A discussion on approaches to handling exceptions in workflows. In *Proceedings of the CSCW Workshop on Adaptive Workflow Systems*. Seattle, WA.

Casati, F., & Shan, M. (2001). Dynamic and adaptive composition of e-services. *Information Systems, 26*(3), 143–163. doi:10.1016/S0306-4379(01)00014-X

Casati, F., & Shan, M. C. *(2001).* Models and languages for describing and discovering e-services (Tutorial). *Paper presented at the International Conference on ACM SIG on Management of Data, Santa Barbara, USA.*

Casati, F., Ceri, S., Paraboschi, S., & Pozzi, G. (1999). Specification and implementation of exceptions in workflow management systems. *ACM Transactions on Database Systems, 24*(3), 405–451. doi:10.1145/328939.328996

Casati, F., Ceri, S., Pernici, B., & Pozzi, G. (1996). Deriving active rules for workflow enactment. In *Proceedings of 17 Int'l Conference on Database and Expert Systems Applications* (pp. 94-110).

Casati, F., Ceri, S., Pernici, B., & Pozzi, G. (1998). Workflow evolution. *Data & Knowledge Engineering, 24*(3), 211–238. doi:10.1016/S0169-023X(97)00033-5

Casati, F., Grefen, P., Pernici, B., & Pozzi, H. & Sánchez. G. (1996). *WIDE: Workflow model and architecture* (CTIT Technical Report 96-19). University of Twente, The Netherlands.

Casati, F., Ilnicki, S., Jin, L., Krishnamoorthy, V., & Shan, M. (2000). *Adaptive and dynamic service composition in eFlow* (Tech. Rep. No. HPL-2000-39). HP Lab.

Casati, F., Sayal, M., & Shan, M. C. *(2001).* Developing e-services for composing e-services. *Paper presented at the International Conference on Advanced Information Systems Engineering.*

Casati, F., Shan, E., Dayal, U., & Shan, M. (2003). Business-oriented management of Web services. *Communications of the ACM, 46*(10), 55–60. doi:10.1145/944217.944238

Cassandra, A., Littman, M., & Zhang, N. (1997). Incremental pruning: A simple, fast, exact method for partially observable Markov decision processes. In *Proceedings of the 13th annual conference on uncertainty in artificial intelligence* (p. 54-61). San Francisco: Morgan Kaufmann.

Castelfranchi, C., & Tan, Y. H. (Eds.). (2001). *Trust and deception in virtual societies*. Norwell, MA: Kluwer Academic Publishers.

Cetin, S., & Altintas, N. I. (2008). An integration model for domain specific kits. *IDPT-2008 Integrated Design and Process Technology Conference.*

Cetin, S., Altintas, N. I., & Sener, C. (2006). An architectural modeling approach with symmetric alignment of multiple concern spaces. *ICSEA'06 International Conference on Software Engineering Advances* (pp. 48-57), Tahiti, French Polynesia. DOI 10.1109/IC-SEA.2006.261304

Cetin, S., Altintas, N. I., & Solmaz, R. (2006). Business rules segregation for dynamic process management with an aspect-oriented framework. *DPM-2006 Dynamic Process Management Workshop at Business Process Management 2006 Conference* (LNCS 4103, pp. 191-202).

Cetin, S., Altintas, N. I., & Tufekci, O. (2006). Improving model reuse with domain specific kits. *MoRSe'06 Model Reuse Strategies Workshop* (pp. 13-16). Warsaw, Poland.

Cetin, S., Altintas, N. I., Oguztuzun, H., Dogru, A., Tufekci, O., & Suloglu, S. (2007). A mashup-based strategy for migration to service-oriented computing. *ICPS'07 IEEE International Conference on Pervasive Services* (pp. 169-172). Istanbul, Turkey.

Cetin, S., Altintas, N. I., Oguztuzun, H., Dogru, A., Tufekci, O., & Suloglu, S. (2007). Legacy migration to service-oriented computing with mashups. *ICSEA'07 International Conference on Software Engineering Advances* (pp. 21-30), Cap Esterel, France. DOI 10.1109/ICSEA.2007.49

Cetin, S., Tufekci, O., Buyukkagnici, B., & Karakoc, E. (2006). Lighthouse: An experimental hyperframe for multi-model software process improvement. *Euro-SPI²-2006 European software process improvement and innovation conference*. Joensuu, Finland.

Chaharbaghi, K., & Nugent, E. (1994). Towards the dynamic organization. *Management Decision, 32*(6), 45. doi:10.1108/00251749410065132

Chalkiadakis, G., & Boutilier, C. (2003). Coordination in multiagent reinforcement learning: a Bayesian approach. In *Proceedings of the second international joint conference on autonomous agents and multiagent systems* (pp. 709-716). New York: ACM Press.

Chandler, A. D. (1962). *Strategy and structure: Chapters in the history of the industrial enterprise*. Cambridge, MA: MIT Press.

Chen & Minder. (1999). BPR methodologies: methods and tools. In D. J. Elzinga, T. R. Gulledge, & C. Lee (Eds.), *Business process engineering: Advancing the state of the art*. (pp. 187-212). Norwell, MA: Kluwer Academic Publishers.

Chen, G., Li, Z., Cheng, Z., Zhao, Z., & Yan, H. (2005). A fuzzy trust model for multiagent systems (LNCS 3612, pp. 444-448.

Chen, H., & Finin, T. & Joshi. A. (2003) *Using OWL in a pervasive computing broker*. Paper presented at the Workshop on Ontologies in Agents Systems.

Chen, L., Li, M., & Cao, J. (2006). ECA Rule-based workflow modeling and implementation for service composition. *IEICE Transactions on Information and Systems . E (Norwalk, Conn.), 89-D*(2), 624–630.

Chen, M., Zhang, D., & Zhou, L. (2007). Empowering collaborative commerce with Web services enabled business process management systems. *Decision Support Systems, 43*(2), 530. doi:10.1016/j.dss.2005.05.014

Cheng, C. H. F., & Levitt, R. E. (2001). Contextually changing behavior in medical organizations. In *Proceedings of the 2001 Annual Symposium of the American Medical Informatics Association*, Washington, DC.

Cheung, S. C., Chiu, D. K. W., & Till, S. (2003). A data-driven methodology to extending workflows across organizations over the Internet. In *Proceedings of 36ᵗʰ Hawaii International Conference on System Sciences (HICSS36)*. IEEE Computer Society Press.

Chiu, D. K. W., & Hung, P. C. K. (2005). Privacy and access control in financial enterprise content management. In *Proceedings of the 38ᵗʰ Hawaiian International Conference on System Sciences (HICSS38)*, Big Island, Hawaii. IEEE Press.

Chiu, D. K. W., Cheung, S. C., Kafeza, E., & Leung, H.-F. (2003). A three-tier view methodology for adapting m-services. *IEEE Transactions on System, Man and Cybernetics . Part A, 33*(6), 725–741.

Chiu, D. K. W., Choi, S. P. M., Wang, M., & Kafeza, E. (2008). Towards ubiquitous communication support for distance education with alert management. *Educational Technology & Society, 11*(2), 92–106.

Chiu, D. K. W., Karlapalem, K., Li, Q., & Kafeza, E. (2002). Workflow view based e-contracts in a cross-organizational e-services environment. *Distributed and Parallel Databases, 12*(2-3), 193–216. doi:10.1023/A:1016503218569

Chiu, D. K. W., Li, Q., & Karlapalem, K. (1999). A meta modeling approach for workflow management system supporting exception handling. *Information Systems, 24*(2), 159–184. doi:10.1016/S0306-4379(99)00010-1

Chiu, D. K. W., Li, Q., & Karlapalem, K. (2000). Facilitating exception handling with recovery techniques in ADOME workflow management system. *Journal of Applied Systems Studies, 1*(3), 467–488.

Chiu, D. K. W., Li, Q., & Karlapalem, K. (2001). Web interface-driven cooperative exception handling in ADOME workflow management system. *Information Systems, 26*(2), 93–120. doi:10.1016/S0306-4379(01)00012-6

Chiu, D.K.W., Yueh, Y.T.F., Leung, H.-f., Hung, P.C.K. (2008b). Towards ubiquitous tourist service coordination and process integration: A collaborative travel agent system with semantic Web services. *Information Systems Frontier*. DOI: 10.1007/s10796-008-9087-2

Christensen, E., Curbera, F., Meredith, G., & Weerawarana, S. (2001, March). *Web service description language.*

Christensen, L. C., Christiansen, T. R., Jin, Y., Kunz, J., & Levitt, R. E. (1999). Modeling and simulating coordination in projects. *Journal of Organizational Computing and Electronic Commerce, 9*(1), 33. doi:10.1207/s15327744joce0901_3

Christiansen, T. R. (1993). *Modeling efficiency and effectiveness of coordination in engineering design teams.* Department of Civil and Environmental Engineering, Stanford University.

Christophides, V., Hull, R., Kumar, A., & Simeon, J. (2000). Workflow mediation using VorteXML. *Bulletin of the IEEE Computer Society Technical Committee on Data Engineering, 24*(1), 40–45.

Chu, M. T., Shyu, J. Z., Tzeng, G. H., & Khosla, R. (2007). Comparison among three analytical methods for knowledge communities group-decision analysis. *Expert Systems with Applications, 33*(4), 1011–1024. doi:10.1016/j.eswa.2006.08.026

Chu, M. T., Shyu, J. Z., Tzeng, G. H., & Khosla, R. (2007). Using non-additive fuzzy integral to assess performance of organization transformation via communities of practice. *IEEE Transactions on Engineering Management, 54*(2), 1–13. doi:10.1109/TEM.2007.893987

Cibran, M. A., & D'Hondt, M. (2006). High-level specification of business rules and their crosscutting connections. *Aspect-Oriented Workshop at AOSD-2006,* Bonn, Germany.

Cichocki, A., Georgakopoulos, D., & Rusinkiewicz, M. (2000). Workflow migration supporting virtual enterprises. In *Proceedings BIS'00* (pp. 20-35), Poznán, Poland.

Clark, A., & Thollard, F. (2004). PAC-learnability of probabilistic deterministic finite state automata. *Journal of Machine Learning Research, 5,* 473–497.

Clatworthy, J., Buick, D., Hankins, M., Weinman, J., & Horne, R. (2005). The use and reporting of cluster analysis in health psychology: A review. *British Journal of Health Psychology, 10,* 329–358. doi:10.1348/135910705X25697

Claus, C., & Boutilier, C. (1998). The dynamics of reinforcement learning in cooperative multiagent systems. In *Proceedings of the fifteenth national/tenth conference on artificial intelligence/innovative applications of artificial intelligence* (pp. 746-752). Menlo Park: American Association for Artificial Intelligence.

Cohen, G. P. (1992). *The virtual design team: An object-oriented model of information sharing in project teams.* Department of Civil Engineering, Stanford University.

Cohen, K. J., & Cyert, R. M. (1965). Simulation of organizational behavior. In J. G. March (Ed.), *Handbook of organizations.* Chicago, IL: Rand McNally.

Cohendet, P., & Meyer-Krahmer, F. (2001). The theoretical and policy implications of knowledge codification. *Research Policy, 30,* 1563–1591. doi:10.1016/S0048-7333(01)00168-8

Colombo, E., Francalanci, C., & Pernici, B. *(2002).* Modeling coordination and control in cross-organizational workflows. *Paper presented at the DOA/CoopIS/ODBASE.*

Committee, A. T. Q. S. (1992). *Benchmarking: focus on world-class practices.* Indianapolis, IN: AT&T Bell Laboratories.

Compton, P., & Jansen, B. (1988). Knowledge in context: A strategy for expert system maintenance. In J. Siekmann (Ed.), *Proceedings of the 2nd Australian Joint Artificial Intelligence Conference* (LNCS 406, pp. 292-306). Adelaide, Australia: Springer-Verlag.

Cook, J. E., & Wolf, A. L. (1998). Discovering models of software processes from event-based data. *ACM Transactions on Software Engineering and Methodology, 7*(3), 215–249. doi:10.1145/287000.287001

COSA. (2005). COSA BPM product description. Retrieved March 13, 2008, from http://www.cosa-bpm.com/project/docs/COSA_BPM_5_Productdescription_eng.pdf

Crowston, K. G. (1991). *Towards a coordination cookbook: Recipes for multi-agent action*. Ph. D. Thesis, MIT Sloan School of Management.

Curbera, F., Goland, Y., Klein, J., Leymann, F., Roller, D., Thatte, S., et al. (2002, July). *Business process execution language for Web services.*

Curtis, B., Kellner, M., & Over, J. (1992). Process Modeling. *Communications of the ACM, 35*(9), 75–90. doi:10.1145/130994.130998

Cushman, R. (1996). Information and medical ethics: Protecting patient privacy. *IEEE Technology and Society Magazine, 15*(3), 32–39. doi:10.1109/44.536299

D'Aveni, R. A. (1994). *Hypercompetition: Managing the dynamics of strategic maneuvering*. New York: Free Press.

d'Inverno, M., Luck, M., Georgeff, M. P., Kinny, D., & Wooldridge, M. (2004). The dMARS architecture: A specification of the distributed multi-agent reasoning system. *Journal of Autonomous Agents and Multi-Agent Systems, 9*(1-2), 5–53. doi:10.1023/B:AGNT.0000019688.11109.19

Dadam, P., & Reichert, M. (1998). The ADEPT WfMS Project at the University of Ulm. In *Proc. 1st European Workshop on Workflow Management, Zurich, Switzerland.*

Dadam, P., & Reichert, M. (Eds.). (1999). Enterprise-wide and cross-enterprise workflow management: Concepts, systems, applications. In *CEUR Workshop Proceedings, Vol. 24.*

Dadam, P., Reichert, M., & Kuhn, K. (2000). Clinical workflows - The killer application for process-oriented information systems? In *Proc. 4th Int'l Conf. on Business Information Systems (BIS'00)* (pp. 36-59), Poznan, Poland.

Daneva, M. (2000). Reuse measurement in the ERP requirements engineering process. In *Proceedings of the 6th International Conference on Software Reuse: Advances in Software Reusability* (LNCS 1844).

Dastani, M., Riemsdijk, B. v., Dignum, F., & Meyer, J.-J. C. (2003). A programming language for cognitive agents goal directed 3APL. In *Programming Multi-Agent Systems* (pp. 111-130). Springer Verlag.

Date, C. J. (2000). *What not how: The business rules approach to application development*. Addison Wesley Longman Inc.

Davenport, T. H., & Perez-Guardado, M. A. (1999) Process ecology: A new metaphor for reengineering-oriented change. In D. J. Elzinga, T. R. Gulledge, & C. Lee (Eds.) *Business process engineering: Advancing the state of the art* (pp. 25-44). Norwell, MA: Kluwer Academic Publishers.

Davenport, T. H., & Short, J. E. (1990). The new industrial engineering. Information technology and business process redesign. *Sloan Management Review, 4*(31), 11–27.

Davenport, T. H., & Stoddard, D. B. (1994). Reengineering, business change of mythic proportions? *MIS Quarterly, 18*(2), 121–127. doi:10.2307/249760

Davenport, T. H., Jarvenpaa, S. I., & Beer, M. C. (2004). Improving knowledge work process. *Sloan Management Review, 34*(4), 53–65.

Davidow, W. H., & Malone, M. S. (1992). *The virtual corporation: Structuring and revitalizing the corporation for the 21st century* (1st ed.). New York: Edward Burlingame Books/HarperBusiness.

Dearden, R., Friedman, N., & Andre, D. (1999). Model-based Bayesian exploration. In *Proceedings of the 15th annual conference on uncertainty in artificial intelligence* (pp. 150-15). San Francisco: Morgan Kaufmann.

Deiters, W., & Gruhn, V. (1998). Process management in practice. Applying the FUNSOFT net approach to large-scale processes. *Automated Software Engineering, 5*(1), 7–25. doi:10.1023/A:1008654224389

Deiters, W., Goesmann, T., & L'offeler, T. (2000). Flexibility in workflow management: Dimensions and solutions. *International Journal of Computer Systems Science and Engineering, 15*(5), 303–313.

Deloitte & Touche (2000). *E-commerce security: A global status report*. Rolling Meadows II: Information Systems Audit and Control Foundation.

Desouza, K. C. (2003). Facilitating tacit knowledge exchange. *CACM, 46*(6), 85–86.

Dijkman, R., & Dumas, M. (2004). Service-oriented design: A multi-viewpoint approach. *International Journal of Cooperative Information Systems, 13*(4), 337–368. doi:10.1142/S0218843004001012

Dogac, A., et al. (1997). Design and implementation of a distributed workflow management system: METUFlow. In *Proc. NATO Advanced Study Institute on Workflow Management Systems and Interoperability* (pp. 61-91), Istanbul, Turkey.

Donaldson, L. (1987). Strategy and structural adjustment to regain fit and performance: In defence of contingency theory. *Journal of Management Studies, 24*(1), 1. doi:10.1111/j.1467-6486.1987.tb00444.x

Dou, W., Chueng, S. C., Chen, G., Wang, J., & Cai, S. J. (2005). A hybrid workflow paradigm for integrating self-managing domain-specific applications. *GCC-2005 4th International Conference on Grid and Cooperative Computing* (LNCS 3795, pp. 1084-1095). Beijing, China.

Dourish, P., Holmes, J., MacLean, A., Marqvardsen, P., & Zbyslaw, A. (1996). Freeflow: Mediating between representation and action in workflow systems. In *Proceedings of the 1996 ACM Conference on Computer Supported Cooperative Work* (pp. 190-198).

Dragos, A. M., & Johnson, R. E. (1998). A proposal for a common infrastructure for process and product models. In *Proc. OOPSLA Mid-year Workshop on Applied Object Technology for Implementing Lifecycle Process and Product Models* (pp. 81-82). Denver, Colorado.

Drake, B., & Beydoun, G. (2000). Predicate logic-based incremental knowledge acquisition. In P. Compton, A. Hoffmann, H. Motoda, & T. Yamaguchi (Eds.), *Proceedings of the Sixth Pacific International Knowledge Acquisition Workshop* (pp. 71-88). Sydney, Australia.

Drucker, P. (1980), *Managing in turbulent times*. New York: Harper & Row.

Du, W., Davis, J., & Shan, M. C. (1997). Flexible specification of workflow compensation scopes. In *GROUP ACM*, 309-316.

Dumas, M., & Hofstede, A. H. M. (2001). UML activity diagrams as a workflow specification language. In *UML 2001* (LNCS 2185, pp. 76-90).

Dumas, M., van der Aalst, W., & ter Hofstede, A. (Eds.). (2005). *Process-aware information systems: Bridging people and software through process technology*. New York: Wiley-Interscience.

Durfee, E. H. (1999). Practically coordinating. *AI Magazine, 20*(1), 99–116.

Dustdar, S., & Schreiner, W. (2005). A survey on web services composition. *Int. J. Web and Grid Services, 1*(1), 1–30. doi:10.1504/IJWGS.2005.007545

Dutta, P. S., Dasmahapatra, S., Gunn, S. R., Jennings, N., & Moreau, L. (2004). Cooperative information sharing to improve distributed learning. In *Proceedings of the aamas 2004 workshop on learning and evolution in agent-based systems* (pp. 18-23).

ebXML Initiative.(2002, September). *Collaboration protocol profile and agreement specification*.

ebXML Initiative.(2006, April). *Business process specification schema*.

Eclipse (2008). *The Eclipse project*. Retrieved from http://www.eclipse.org

Eder, J., & Liebhart, W. (1996). Workflow recovery. In *CoopIS* (pp. 124-134).

Eder, J., & Liebhart, W. (1998). Contributions to exception handling in workflow management. In O. Burkes, J. Eder, & S. Salza (Eds.), *Proceedings of the Sixth International Conference on Extending Database Technology* (pp. 3-10).

Edgelow, C. (2006). *Helping organizations change*. Sundance Consulting Inc.

Edmond, D., & ter Hofstede, A. H. (2000). A reflective infrastructure for workflow adaptability. *Data & Knowledge Engineering, 34*, 271–304. doi:10.1016/S0169-023X(00)00018-5

Ehrler, L., Fleurke, M. K., Purvis, M., & Savarimuthu, B. T. R. (2006). Agent-based workflow management systems (WfMSs). *Information Systems and E-Business Management, 4*(1), 5–23. doi:10.1007/s10257-005-0010-9

Eisenhardt, K. M., & Martin, J. A. (2000). Dynamic capabilities: What are they? *Strategic Management Journal, 21*(10/11), 1105–1121. doi:10.1002/1097-0266(200010/11)21:10/11<1105::AID-SMJ133>3.0.CO;2-E

Eisenhardt, K. M., & Tabrizi, B. N. (1995). Accelerating adaptive processes: Product innovation in the global computer industry. *Administrative Science Quarterly, 40*(1), 84. doi:10.2307/2393701

Eisenhardt, M. K. (1989). Agency theory: An assessment and review. *Academy of Management Review, 14*(1), 57–74. doi:10.2307/258191

Eiter, T., Erdem, E., & Faber, W. (2004). Plan reversals for recovery in execution monitoring. In *10th International Workshop on Non-Monotonic Reasoning* (pp. 147-154).

El Sawy, O. A. (2001). *Redesigning enterprise processes for e-business*. Boston: Irwin/McGraw-Hill

Elfatatry, A. (2007). Dealing with changes: Components versus services. *Communications of the ACM, 50*(8), 35–39. doi:10.1145/1278201.1278203

Elisa (2006). *Annual report*.

Elisa (2007). *Presentation*.

Ellis, C. A., & Maltzahn, C. (1997). The Chautauqua workflow system. In *Proc. 30ᵗʰ Hawaii Int. Conf. on System Sciences*, Maui, Hawaii.

Emery-Montemerlo, R., Gordon, G., Schneider, J., & Thrun, S. (2004). Approximate solutions for partially observable stochastic games with common payoffs. In *Proceedings of the third international joint conference on autonomous agents and multiagent systems* (pp. 136-143). Washington, DC: IEEE Computer Society.

Endsley, M. R. (1995). Toward a theory of situation awareness in dynamic systems. *Human Factors, 37*(1), 32–64. doi:10.1518/001872095779049543

Engelhardt, W. H., & Freiling, J. (1995). Die integrative Gestaltung von Leistungspotentialen. *Zeitschrift für betriebswirtschaftliche Forschung, 10*(47), 899–918.

Erl, T. (2005). Service oriented architecture: Concepts, technology and design. Prentice Hall.

eXtensible Markup Language (2001). *XML Specification*. Retrieved February 10, 2008, from http://www.w3.org/XML/

Fakas, G. J., & Karakostas, B. (2004). A peer to peer (P2P) architecture for dynamic workflow management. *Information and Software Technology, 46*(6), 423–431. doi:10.1016/j.infsof.2003.09.015

Feitzinger, E., & Lee, H. L. (1997). Mass customization at Hewlett-Packard. The power of postponement. *Harvard Business Review, 1*(75), 116–121.

Fensel, D., McGuiness, D. L., Schulten, E., Ng, W. K., Lim, E. P., & Yan, G. (2001). Ontologies and electronic commerce. *IEEE Intelligent Systems, 16*(1), 8–14. doi:10.1109/MIS.2001.1183337

Financial Information eXchange (2005). *FIX home page*. Retrieved on April 21, 2008, from http://www.fixprotocol.org/

Finnie, G., & Sun, Z. (2003). A logical foundation for the CBR Cycle. *International Journal of Intelligent Systems, 18*(4), 367–382. doi:10.1002/int.10093

Finnie, G., & Sun, Z. (2007). Negotiation, trust and experience management in e-supply chains. In Q. Zhang (Ed.), *E-Supply chain technologies and management* (pp. 172-193). Hershey, PA: Idea Group Inc.

Finnie, G., Sun, Z., & Barker, J. (2005). Trust and deception in multiagent trading systems: A logical viewpoint. In *Proceedings of the 11th Americas Information Systems* (AMCIS2005). The Association for Information Systems, Aug 11-14, 2005 (pp. 1020-1026) Omaha, NE, USA.

FIPS (1993, December). *Standard for integration definition for function modeling (IDEF0)*. National Institute of Standards and Technology (NIST). FIPS publication, 183.

Fischer, F., Rovatsos, M., & Weiss, G. (2004). Hierarchical reinforcement learning in communication-mediated multiagent coordination. In *Proceedings of the third international joint conference on autonomous agents and multiagent systems* (pp. 1334-1335). Washington, DC: IEEE Computer Society.

Fitoussi, D., & Tennenholtz, M. (2000). Choosing social laws for multi-agent systems: Minimality and simplicity. *Artificial Intelligence, 119*(1-2), 61–101. doi:10.1016/S0004-3702(00)00006-0

Fleury, A., & Fleury, M. T. (2007). The evolution of production systems and conceptual frameworks. *Journal of Manufacturing Technology Management, 8*(18), 949–965. doi:10.1108/17410380710828271

Flynn, D., Vagner, J., & Vecchio, O. D. (1995). Is CASE technology improving quality and productivity in software development? *Logistics Information Management, 8*(2), 8–21. doi:10.1108/09576059510084966

Ford, D., Gadde, L.-E., Håkansson, H., Lundgren, A., Snehota, I., Turnbull, P., & Wilson, D. (2002). *Managing business relationships*. IMP Group. Wiley.

Forum, T. M. (1998). *NGOSS Business Process Framework – eTOM*. Retrieved May 29, 2008, from http://www.tmforum.org/BestPracticesStandards/NGOSSBusinessProcess/1648/Home.html

Fowler, M. (2002). *Patterns of enterprise application architecture*. Addison-Wesley.

Fowler, M. (2005). *Language workbenches: The killer-app for domain specific languages?* Retrieved from http://martinfowler.com/articles/languageWorkbench.html.

Fowlkes, E. B., & Mallows, C. L. (1983). A method for comparing two hierarchical clusterings. *Journal of the American Statistical Association, 78*(383), 553–584. doi:10.2307/2288117

Frankel, D. S. (2003). Model driven architecture: Applying MDA to enterprise computing. OMG Press.

Frels, J. K., Shervani, T., & Srivastava, R. K. (2003). The integrated networks model: Explaining resource allocations in network markets. *Journal of Marketing, 67*, 29–45. doi:10.1509/jmkg.67.1.29.18586

Fudenberg, D., & Levine, D. K. (1998). *The theory of learning in games*. Cambridge, MA: MIT Press.

Gaaloul, W., Bhiri, S., & Godart, C. (2004 October). Discovering workflow transactional behavior from event-based log. In *On the Move to Meaningful Internet Systems 2004: CoopIS, DOA, and ODBASE* (pp. 3-18). Springer.

Galbraith, J. R. (1977). *Organization design*. Reading, MA: Addison-Wesley.

Garud, R., & Kumaraswamy, A. (2003). Technological and organizational design for realizing economies of substitution. In R. Garud, A. Kumaraswamy, & R.N. Langlois (Eds.), *Managing in the modular age: Architectures, networks, and organizations* (pp. 45-77). Blackwell Publishing Limited.

Gasser, L. (1992). *HITOP-A: Coordination, infrastructure and enterprise integration*. Paper presented at the AAAI-92 Workshop on AI in Enterprise Integration.

Gateau, J. B., Leweling, T. A., Looney, J. P., & Nissen, M. E. (2007). Hypothesis testing of edge organizations: Modeling the C2 organization design space. In *Proceedings International Command & Control Research & Technology Symposium*, Newport, RI.

Gazzotti, D., Palmirani, M., & Paganelli, P. *(2001)*. WHALES: A project life-cycle management application for extended organisations. *Paper presented at the 7th International Conference on Concurrent Enterprising, Bermen, Germany*.

Genrich, A., & Lautenbach, K. (1981). System modelling with high level Petri nets. *Theoretical Computer Science, 35*, 1–41.

Georgakopoulos, D., Hornick, & Sheth, A. (1995). An overview of workflow management: From process modeling to workflow automation infrastructure. *Distributed and Parallel Databases*, *3*(2), 119–153. doi:10.1007/BF01277643

Georgakopoulos, D., Hornick, M. F., & Manola, F. (1996). Customizing transaction models and mechanisms in a programmable environment supporting reliable workflow automation. *IEEE Transactions on Knowledge and Data Engineering*, *8*(4), 630–649. doi:10.1109/69.536255

Georgakopoulos, D., Hornick, M., & Sheth, A. (1995). An overview of workflow management: From process modelling to workflow automation infrastructure. *Journal of Distributed and Parallel Databases*, *3*(2), 119–153. doi:10.1007/BF01277643

Georgeff, M., & Pyke, J. (2003). *Dynamic process orchestration* [White paper]. Staffware PLC.

Geppert, A., & Tombros, D. (1998). Event-based distributed workflow execution with EVE. In *Proc. IFIP Int. Conf. on Distributed Systems Platforms and Open Distributed Processing* (pp. 427-442).

Gershenson, J. K., Prasad, G. J., & Zhang, Y. (2004). Product modularity: Measures and design methods. *Journal of Engineering Design*, *1*(15), 33–51. doi:10.1080/0954482032000101731

Ghauri, P., Lutz, C., & Tesform, G. (2003). Using networks to solve export-marketing problems of small and medium-sized firms from developing countries. *European Journal of Marketing*, *37*(5/6), 728–752. doi:10.1108/03090560310465125

Ghosh, A. K. (1998). *E-commerce security: Weak links, best defenses*. New York: John Wiley & Sons, Inc.

Ghosh, A. K. (2001). *Security and privacy for e-business*. New York: John Wiley & Sons, Inc.

GMF. (2008). *Graphical Modeling Framework project*. Retrieved from http://www.eclipse.org/gmf.

Goh, A., Koh, Y.-K., & Domazet, D. S. (2001). ECA rule-based support for workflows . *Artificial Intelligence in Engineering*, *15*(1), 37–46. doi:10.1016/S0954-1810(00)00028-5

Golani, M. (2008). Workflow search space reduction – A model driven approach. [IJPAM]. *International Journal of Pure and Applied Mathematics*, *44*(2), 265–280.

Golani, M., & Gal, A. (2005). Flexible business process management using forward stepping and alternative paths. In *Proceedings of the 3rd Business Process Management International Conference, BPM 2005* (LNCS 3649, pp. 48-63).

Golani, M., & Gal, A. (2006). Optimizing exception handling in workflows using process restructuring, In *Proc. BPM'06* (LNCS 4102, pp. 407-413).

Golani, M., & Pinter, S. S. (2003). Generating a process model from a process audit log. In M. Weske, W. van der Aalst, & A. ter Hofstede (Eds.), *Proceedings of the Business Process Management International Conference, BPM 2003* (LNCS 2678, pp. 136-151).

Gray, J., & Reuter, A. (1993). *Transaction processing: Concepts and techniques*. San Francisco: Morgan Kaufmann.

Greco, G., Guzzo, A., Manco, G., & Sacca, D. (2005). Mining and reasoning on workflows. *IEEE Transactions on Knowledge and Data Engineering*, *17*(4), 519–534. doi:10.1109/TKDE.2005.63

Greenfield, J., Short, K., Cook, S., & Kent, S. (2204). *Software factories: Assembling applications with patterns, models, frameworks, and tools*. Wiley.

Greenstein, M., & Vasarhelyi, M. (2002). *Electronic commerce: Security, risk management, and control (2nd ed.)*. Boston: McGraw-Hill Irwin.

Grefen, P. W. P. J., Aberer, K., Ludwig, H., & Hoffner, Y. (2001). CrossFlow: Cross-organizational workflow management for service outsourcing in dynamic virtual enterprises. *A Quarterly Bulletin of the Computer Society of the IEEE Technical Committee on Data Engineering*, *24*(1), 52–57.

Grefen, P. W. P. J., Aberer, K., Ludwig, H., & Hoffner, Y. (2001). CrossFlow: Cross-organizational workflow management for service outsourcing in dynamic virtual enterprises. *A Quarterly Bulletin of the Computer Society of the IEEE Technical Committee on Data Engineering,* *24*(1), 52–57.

Grefen, P., Aberer, K., Hoffner, Y., & Ludwig, H. (2000). Crossflow: Cross-organizational workflow management in dynamic virtual enterprises. *International Journal of Computer Systems Science & Engineering, 15*(5), 277–290.

Greiner, U., Ramsch, J., Heller, B., Löffler, M., Müller, R., & Rahm, E. (2004). Adaptive guideline-based treatment workflows with Adapt-Flow. In K. Kaiser, S. Miksch, & S. Tu (Eds.), *Proceedings of the Symposium on Computerized Guidelines and Protocols (CGP 2004)* (pp. 113-117). Prague: IOS Press.

Griffel, F., Boger, M., Weinreich, H., Lamersdorf, W., & Merz, M. *(1998).* Electronic contracting with COSMOS - How to establish, negotiate and execute electronic contracts on the Internet. *Paper presented at the 2nd Int. Enterprise Distributed Object Computing Workshop.*

Grimson, J., Stephens, G., Jung, B., Grimson, W., Berry, D., & Pardon, S. (2001). Sharing health-care records over the Internet. *IEEE Internet Computing, 5*(3), 49–58. doi:10.1109/4236.935177

Griss, M. L., & Wentzel, K. (1994). Hybrid domain specific kits for a flexible software factory. In *Proceedings of the Annual ACM Symposium, Applied Computing* (pp. 47-52). Phoenix, Arizona.

Gronemann, B., Joeris, G., Scheil, S., Steinfort, M., & Wache, H. (1999). Supporting cross organizational engineering processes by distributed collaborative workflow management - The MOKASSIN approach. In *Proc. 2nd Symposium on Concurrent Multidisciplinary Engineering*, Bremen, Germany.

Grosof, B. N., & Labrou, Y. (1999). An approach to using XML and a rule-based content language with an agent communication language. In *Proceedings of the IJCAI-99 Workshop on Agent Communication Languages (ACL-99)*. Stockholm, Sweden.

Gross, T. (2003). Security analysis of the SAML single sign-on browser/artifact profile. In *Proceedings of the*

19th Annual Computer Security Applications Conference (pp. 298- 307).

Grover, V., & Kettinger, W. J. (Eds.). (1995). *Business process change: Concepts, methodologies and technologies.* Hershey, PA: Idea Group Publishing.

Gulati, R. (1998). Alliances and networks. *Strategic Management Journal, 19*(4), 293–317. doi:10.1002/(SICI)1097-0266(199804)19:4<293::AID-SMJ982>3.0.CO;2-M

Gulati, R., Nohria, N., & Zaheer, A. (2000). Strategic networks. *Strategic Management Journal, 21*, 203–215. doi:10.1002/(SICI)1097-0266(200003)21:3<203::AID-SMJ102>3.0.CO;2-K

Gulla, J. A., Borch, H. O., & Ingvaldsen, J. E. (2006). Unsupervised keyphrase extraction for search ontologies. In *Natural Language Processing and Information Systems* (pp. 25-36). New York: Springer.

Gunasekaran, A., & Ngai, E. W. T. (2004). Information systems in supply chain integration and management. *European Journal of Operational Research, 159*(2), 269–295. doi:10.1016/j.ejor.2003.08.016

Guntama, E., Chang, E., Jayaratna, N., & Pudhota, L. (2003). Extension of activity diagrams for flexible business workflow modeling. *International Journal of Computer Systems Science & Engineering, 18*(3), 137–152.

Günther, C. W., Reichert, M., & van der Aalst, W. M. P. (2008a). Supporting flexible processes with adaptive workflow and case Handling. In *Proceedings WETICE'08, 3rd IEEE Workshop on Agile Cooperative Process-aware Information Systems*, Rome, Italy.

Günther, C. W., Rinderle, S., Reichert, M., & van der Aalst, W. M. P. (2006). Change mining in adaptive process management systems. In *Proc. 14th Int'l Conf. on Cooperative Information Systems (Coopls'06)* (LNCS 4275, pp. 309-326).

Günther, C. W., Rinderle-Ma, S., Reichert, M., van der Aalst, W. M. P., & Recker, J. (2008). Using process mining to learn from process changes in evolutionary systems. *Int'l Journal of Business Process Integration and Management, 3*(1), 61–78. doi:10.1504/IJBPIM.2008.019348

Guth, V., Lenz, K., & Oberweis, A. (1998). Distributed workflow execution based on fragmentation of Petri nets. In *Proc. 15th IFIP World Computer Congress: Telecooperation - The Global Office, Teleworking and Communication Tool* (pp. 114-125).

Hadfield, W. (2007), Tesco standardizes IT for global expansion. Retreived May 20, 2008, from http://www.computerweekly.com/Articles/2007/04/24/223408/tesco-standardises-it-for-global-expansion.htm

Hagedoorn, J. (1990). Organizational modes of inter-firm co-operation and technology transfer. *Technovation*, *10*(1), 17–30. doi:10.1016/0166-4972(90)90039-M

Hagedoorn, J. (1995). Strategic technology partnering during the 1980s: Trends, networks and corporate patterns in non-core technologies. *Research Policy*, *24*(2), 207–231. doi:10.1016/0048-7333(94)00763-W

Hagen, C., & Alonso, G. (2000). Exception handling in workflow management systems. *IEEE Transactions on Software Engineering*, *26*(10), 943–958. doi:10.1109/32.879818

Håkansson, H., & Snehota, I. (Eds.). (1995) *Developing relationships in business networks*. London: Routledge.

Hallerbach, A., Bauer, T., & Reichert, M. (2008). Managing process variants in the process lifecycle. In *Proc. 10th Int'l Conf. on Enterprise Information Systems (ICEIS'08)* (pp. 154-161), Barcelona.

Hammer, M. (1990). Reengineering work: Don't automate, obliterate. *Harvard Business Review*, *68*(4), 104–112.

Hammer, M., & Champy, J. (1993), *Reengineering the corporation: A Manifesto for business revolution*. New York: Harper Business.

Hammer, M., & Stanton, S. (1999). How process enterprises really work. *Harvard Business Review*, *77*(6), 108.

Han, Y., & Sheth, A. (1998). On adaptive workflow modeling. In *Proc. 4th Int. Conf. on Information Systems Analysis and Synthesisis*, Orlando

Han, Y., Sheth, A., & Bussler, C. (1998, November). A taxonomy of adaptive workflow management. In *Proceedings of the CSCW Workshop Towards Adaptive Workflow Systems*.

Hanssen-Bauer, J., & Snow, C. C. (1996). Responding to hypercompetition: The structure and processes of a regional learning network organization. *Organization Science*, *7*(4), 413. doi:10.1287/orsc.7.4.413

Harrison, W. H., Ossher, H. L. & Tarr, P. L. (2002). *Asymmetrically vs. symmetrically organized paradigms for software composition*. IBM Research Division, Thomas J. Watson Research Center, RC22685 (W0212-147).

Hassler, V. (2001). *Security fundamentals for e-commerce*. Norwood, MA: Artech House.

Havey, M. (2005). *Essential business process modeling*. O'Reilly.

Hector, G.-M., & Kenneth, S. (1987). Sagas. *SIGMOD Record*, *16*(3), 249–259. doi:10.1145/38714.38742

Henderson-Sellers, B., & Giorgini, P. (2005). *Agent-oriented methodologies*. Hershey, PA: Idea Group Inc.

Hendriks-Jansen, H. (1996). *Catching ourselves in the act: Situated activity, interactive emergence, evolution, and human thought*. Cambridge, MA: MIT Press.

Herbst, J., & Karagiannis, D. (2004). Workflow mining with InWoLve. *Computers in Industry*, *53*(3), 245–264. doi:10.1016/j.compind.2003.10.002

Herman, G. A., & Malone, T. W. (2003) What is in the process handbook? In T.W. Malone, K. Crowston, & G.A. Herman, (Eds.), *Organizing business knowledge: The MIT process handbook*. Cambridge MA: MIT Press.

Hewlett Packard. (2005, February). *Adaptive enterprise at work* [White paper]. Hewlett Packard.

Hibbert, G. (2004, February). Unileverage. *Financial Management*, 30-31.

Hoar, J. (1996). *Reinforcement learning applied to a real robot task*. (DAI MSc Dissertion, University of Edinburgh)

Hoare, C. (1985). *Communicating sequential processes.* Prentice Hall.

Holland, J. (1995). *Hidden order: How adaptation builds complexity.* Cambridge, MA: Perseus.

Holt, A. W. (1997). *Organized activity and its support by computer.* Dordrecht: Kluwer Academic Publishers.

Hölttä, P. (1999). Verkko-opetushankkeiden eteneminen HPY:ssä. HPY Research 10/1999.

Hölttä, P. (2000). Piimäki 2000: Laajakaistaisen alueverkon uudet palvelut. tuotekehityshakemuksen liite 2. Tutkimus- ja kehitysprojektisuunnitelma TEKESin 'Tietoliikenteellä maailmalle' teknologiaohjelmaan. HPY Tutkimuskeskus.

Horii, T., Jin, Y., & Levitt, R. E. (2005). Modeling and analyzing cultural influences on project team performance. *Computational & Mathematical Organization Theory, 10*(4), 305. doi:10.1007/s10588-005-6283-1

Horsch, A., & Balbach, T. (1999). Telemedical information systems. *IEEE Transactions on Information Technology in Biomedicine, 3*(3), 166–175. doi:10.1109/4233.788578

Huang, Z. (1998). Extensions to the K-means algorithm for clustering large datasets with categorical values. *Data Mining and Knowledge Discovery, 2*, 283–304. doi:10.1023/A:1009769707641

Huckvale, T., & Ould, M. (1998). *Process modelling- Who, what and how: Role activity diagramming.* Hershey, PA: Idea Group Publishing.

Huhns, M. N. (2002). Agents as Web services. *IEEE Internet Computing, 6*(4), 93–95. doi:10.1109/MIC.2002.1020332

Huhns, M. N., & Singh, M. P. (Eds.). (1998). *Readings in agents.* San Francisco: Morgan Kaufmann Publishers.

Huhtala, Y., Karkkainen, J., Porkka, P., & Toivonen, H. (1999). TANE: An efficient algorithm for discovering functional and approximate dependencies. *The Computer Journal, 42*(2), 100–111. doi:10.1093/comjnl/42.2.100

Hung, P. C. K. (2001). *Secure workflow model.* Ph.D.Thesis, Department of Computer Science, The Hong Kong University of Science and Technology, Hong Kong.

Hung, P. C. K., & Chiu, D. K. W. (2003). Workflow-based information integration in a Web services environment. In *Proceedings of the First International Conference on Web Services (ICWS'03)*, Monte Carlo Resort, Las Vegas, Nevada, USA.

Hung, P. C. K., & Chiu, D. K. W. (2004). Developing workflow-based information integration (WII) with exception support in a Web services environment. In *Proceedings of 36th Hawaii International Conference on System Sciences (HICSS36)*. IEEE Computer Society Press.

Hung, P. C. K., Chiu, D. K. W., Fung, W. W., Cheung, W. K., Wong, R., & Choi, S. P. (2007). End-to-end privacy control in service outsourcing of human intensive processes: A multi-layered Web service integration approach. *Information Systems Frontiers, 9*(1), 85–101. doi:10.1007/s10796-006-9019-y

Hwang, C. L., & Yoon, K. (1981). *Multiple attribute decision making: Methods and applications.* New York: Springer-Verlag.

Hwang, G. H., Lee, Y. C., & Wu, B. Y. (2003). A new language to support flexible failure recovery for workflow management systems. In J. Favela & D. Decouchant (Eds.), *CRIWG* (LNCS 2806, pp. 135-150).

Hwang, S. Y., Ho, S. F., & Tang, J. (1999). Mining exception instances to facilitate workflow exception handling. In *Proceedings of the 6th International Conference on Database Systems for Advanced Applications* (pp. 45-52).

IBM. (2005). *IBM WebSphere MQ Workflow: Concepts and architecture.* Retrieved March 14, 2008, from http://publibfp.boulder.ibm.com/epubs/pdf/h1262857.pdf

Ingvaldsen, J. E., & Gulla, J. A. (2007). Preprocessing support for large scale process mining of SAP transactions. In *Business process management workshops* (pp. 30-41). New York: Springer.

Irving, D. K., & Rea, P. W. (2006). *Producing and directing the short film and video* (3rd ed.). Burlington, Oxford, UK: Focal Press.

Ishikawa, K. (2000). Health data use and protection policy: based on differences by cultural and social environment. *International Journal of Medical Informatics, 60*(2), 19–125. doi:10.1016/S1386-5056(00)00111-8

ITU-T (2002). *Specification and Description Language (SDL), Z-100, 08/2002.* Telecommunication Standardization Sector of ITU.

Jablonski, S. (1997). Architecture of workflow management systems. *Informatik . Forschung und Entwicklung, 12*(2), 72–81. doi:10.1007/s004500050076

Jablonski, S., & Bussler, C. (1996). *Workflow management - Modeling concepts, architecture and implementation.* London: Intl. Thomson Computer Press.

Jablonski, S., & Götz, M. (2007). Perspective oriented business process visualization. In *3rd International Workshop on Business Process Design (BPD) in conjunction with the 5th International Conference on Business Process Management (BPM 2007).* Brisbane, Australia.

JBoss Inc. (2006). JBoss transactions 4.2.2 transaction core programmers guide. Retrieved May 7, 2008, from JBoss Inc.: http://labs.jboss.com/jbosstm/docs/4.2.2/manuals/pdf/core/ProgrammersGuide.pdf

Jelinek, M., & Schoonhoven, C. B. (1990). *The innovation marathon: Lessons from high technology firms.* Cambridge, MA: B. Blackwell.

Jennings, N. R. (2001). An agent-based approach for building complex software systems. *Communications of the ACM, 44*(4), 35–41. doi:10.1145/367211.367250

Jennings, N. R., Faratin, P., Norman, T. J., O'Brien, P., & Odgers, B. (2002). Autonomous agents for business process management. *International Journal of Applied Artificial Intelligence, 14*(2), 145–189.

Jensen, K. (1981). Colored Petri nets and the invariant method. *Theoretical Computer Science, 14,* 317–336. doi:10.1016/0304-3975(81)90049-9

Jeston, J., & Nelis, J. (2008). *Business process management: Practical guidelines to successful implementations* (2nd ed.). Butterworth-Heinemann.

Jin, Y., & Levitt, R. E. (1996). The virtual design team: A computational model of project organizations. *Computational & Mathematical Organization Theory, 2*(3), 171–195. doi:10.1007/BF00127273

Joeris, G. (1999). Defining flexible workflow execution behaviors. In P. Dadam, & M. Reichert (Eds.), *Enterprise-wide and cross-enterprise workflow management: concepts, systems, applications* (Vol. 24 of CEUR Workshop Proceedings) (pp. 49-55). Paderborn, Germany.

Joeris, G., & Herzog, O. (1998). Managing evolving workflow specifications. In *Proceedings of the 3rd IFCIS International Conference on Cooperative Information Systems (CoopIS '98)* (pp. 310-319). New York: IEEE Computer Society.

Joeris, G., & Herzog, O. (1999, June). Towards flexible and high level modeling and enacting of processes. In *Proceedings of the 11th International Conference on Advanced Information Systems Engineering.*

Joint Chiefs of Staff. (2003). Joint Publication JP 3-09.3, *Joint Tactics, Techniques, and Procedures for Close Air Support (CAS),* Washington, DC.

Joint Chiefs of Staff. (2008). Joint Publication JP 1-02, *Department of Defense Dictionary of Military and Associated Terms,* Washington, DC.

Jones, A. J. I., & Firozabadi, B. S. (2005). *On the characterization of a trusting agent, aspects of a formal approach.* Retrieved March 28, 2008, from http://www.sics.se/spot/document/TrustingAgent.ps

Jonkers, H., Lankhorst, M., van Buuren, R., Hoppenbrouwers, S., & Bonsangue, M. (2003). Concepts for modelling enterprise architectures. In *Proceedings of the 7th IEEE International Enterprise Distributed Object Computing Conference.*

Joubert, M., Aymard, S., Fieschi, D., Volot, F., Staccini, P., Robert, J. J., & Fieschi, M. (1998). RIANE: Integration of information databases within a hospital intranet.

International Journal of Medical Informatics, 49(3), 297–309. doi:10.1016/S1386-5056(98)00084-7

Jung, H., Chen, F. F., & Jung, B. (2008). Decentralized supply chain planning framework for third party logistics partnership. *Computers & Industrial Engineering, 55*(2), 348–364. doi:10.1016/j.cie.2007.12.017

Juntunen, A. (2005). *The emergence of a new business through collaborative networks: A longitudinal study in the ICT sector.* Acta Universitatis Oeconomicae Helsingiensis. HSEPrint. A-series no 256.

Kaan, K., Reijers, H. A., & van der Molen, P. (2006). Introducing case management: Opening workflow management's black box. In *Proceedings of the 4th International Conference on Business Process Management (BPM 2006).*

Kaasbøll, J. J., & Smørdal, O. (1996). Human work as context for development of object-oriented modelling techniques. In S. Brinkkemper (Ed.) *IFIP WG 8.1/8.2 Working Conference on Principles of Method Construction and Tool Support* (pp. 111–125). Atlanta, GA: Chapman and Hall.

Kaelbling, L. P., Littman, M. L., & Cassandra, A. R. (1998). Planning and acting in partially observable stochastic domains. *Artificial Intelligence, 101*(1-2), 99–134. doi:10.1016/S0004-3702(98)00023-X

Kafeza, E., Chiu, D. K. W., Cheung, S. C., & Kafeza, M. (2004). Alerts in mobile healthcare applications: requirements and pilot study. *IEEE Transactions on Information Technology in Biomedicine, 8*(2), 173–181. doi:10.1109/TITB.2004.828888

Kamath, M., & Ramamritham, K. (1998). Failure handling and coordinated execution of concurrent workflows. In *Proc. of the 14th Intl. Conf. on Data Engineering* (pp. 334-341).

Kamath, M., Alonso, G., Günthör, R., & Mohan, C. (1996). Providing high availability in very large workflow management systems. In *Proc. EDBT'96* (pp. 427-442), Avignon, France.

Kamathy, M., & Ramamritham, K. (1996). Correctness issues in workflow management. *Distributed Systems Engineering, 3*, 213–221. doi:10.1088/0967-1846/3/4/002

Kammer, P. J., Bolcer, G. A., Taylor, R. N., Hitomi, A. S., & Bergman, M. (2000). Techniques for supporting dynamic and adaptive workflow. *Computer Supported Cooperative Work, 9*(3-4), 269–292. doi:10.1023/A:1008747109146

Kammer, P., Bolcer, G., Taylor, R., Hitomi, A., & Bergman, M. (2000). Techniques for supporting dynamic and adaptive workflow. [CSCW]. *Computer Supported Cooperative Work, 9*(3), 269–292. doi:10.1023/A:1008747109146

Kang, B. H., Preston, P., & Compton, P. (1998). Simulated expert evaluation of multiple classification ripple down rules. In *Proceedings of the 11th Workshop on Knowledge Acquisition, Modeling and Management.* Banff, Alberta, Canada.

Kasper, H., van Helsdingen, P., & de Vries, W. (1999). *Services marketing management. An international perspective.* New York: John Wiley.

Keller, A., & Ludwig, H. (2002). Defining and monitoring service level agreements for dynamic e-business. In *Proceedings of LISA '02: Sixteenth Systems Administration Conference* (pp. 189-204). Philadelphia, PA, USA.

Keller, G., & Teufel, T. (1998). *SAP R/3 process oriented implementation.* Reading, MA: Addison-Wesley.

Kerzner, H. (1989). *Project management: A system approach to planning scheduling and controlling* (pp. 759-764).

Kettinger, W. J., Teng, J. T. C., & Guha, S. (1997b). Business process change: A study of methodologies, techniques, and tools. *MIS Quarterly, 21*(1), 55–80. doi:10.2307/249742

Khomyakov, M., & Bider, I. (2000). Achieving workflow flexibility through taming the chaos. In *OOIS 2000 - 6th International Conference on Object Oriented Information Systems* (pp. 85-92).

Kim, Y., Nair, R., Varakantham, P., Tambe, M., & Yokoo, M. (2006). Exploiting locality of interaction in networked distributed pomdps. In *Proceedings of the AAAI spring symposium on "Distributed plan and schedule management"*.

Klein, M., & Dellarocas, C. (2000). A knowledge-based approach to handling exceptions in workflow systems. *Computer Supported Cooperative Work, 9*(3), 399–412. doi:10.1023/A:1008759413689

Klein, M., & Dellarocas, C. (2000). *A systematic repository of knowledge about handling exceptions* (ASES Working Paper ASES-WP-2000-03 ASES-WP-2000-03). Cambridge, MA: Massachusetts Institute of Technology.

Klein, M., Herman, G. A., Lee, J., O'Donnell, E., & Malone, T. W. (2003) Inventing new business processes using a process repository. In T.W. Malone, K. Crowston, & G.A. Herman, (Eds.), *Organizing Business Knowledge: The MIT Process Handbook*. Cambridge MA: MIT Press.

Klein, M., Rodriguez-Aguilar, J. A., & Dellarocas, C. (2003). Using domain-independent exception handling services to enable robust open multi-agent systems: The case of agent death. *Autonomous Agents and Multi-Agent Systems, 7*(1-2), 179–189. doi:10.1023/A:1024145408578

Kleinaltenkamp, M., & Haase, M. (1999). Externe Faktoren in der Theorie der Unternehmensführung. In H. H. Albach (Ed.), *Die Theorie der Unternehmung in Forschung und Praxis* (pp. 167-194). Berlin: Springer.

Koch, F. (2005). 3APL-M: Platform for lightweight deliberative agents. Retrieved 7 May, 2008, from http://www.cs.uu.nl/3apl-m/docs/3aplm-manual.pdf

Kochut, K., Arnold, J., Sheth, A., Miller, J., Kraemer, E., Arpinar, B., & Cardoso, J. (2003). IntelliGEN: A distributed workflow system for discovering protein-protein interactions. *Distributed and Parallel Databases, 13*(1), 43–72. doi:10.1023/A:1021565722755

Koehler, J., Hauser, R., Kapoor, S., Wu, F. Y., & Kumaran, S. (2003). A Model-driven transformation method. In *7th International Enterprise Distributed Object Computing Conference (EDOC 2003)* (pp. 186-197).

Koehler, J., Hauser, R., Sendall, S., & Wahler, M. (2005). Declarative techniques for model-driven business process integration. *IBM Systems Journal, 44*(1), 47–65.

Kogut, B., & Zander, U. (1997). Knowledge of the firm, combinative capabilities, and the replication of technology. In N.J. Foss (Ed.), *Resources, firms and strategies – A reader in the resource-based perspective*. Oxford: Oxford University Press.

Koskimies, M, (2006). *Composing services in SOA: Workflow design, usage and patterns*.

Koufaris, M., & Hampton-Sosa, W. (2002). *Customer trust online: Examining the role of the experience with the Web site* (CIS-2002-05). The CIS Working Paper Series, Baruch College.

Koulopoulos, T. M. (1995). *The workflow imperative: Building real world business solutions*. New York: John Wiley & Sons, Inc.

Kradolfer, M., & Geppert, A. (1999). Dynamic workflow schema evolution based on workflow type versioning and workflow migration. In *Proceedings of the 1999 IFCIS International Conference on Cooperative Information Systems (CoopIS'99)* (pp. 104-114). Edinburgh, Scotland: IEEE Computer Society.

Kroll, P., & Kruchten, P. (2003). The rational unified process made easy. In *A Practitioner's Guide to the RUP*. Addison Wesley.

Kubeck, L. C. (1995). *Techniques for business process redesign*. New York: John Wiley and Sons.

Kubeck, L. C. (1997). Techniques for business process redesign. *Interfaces, 27*(4).

Kueng, P., & Kawalek, P. (1997). Goal-based business process models: Creation and evaluation. *Business Process Management Journal, 1*(3), 17–38. doi:10.1108/14637159710161567

Kumar, A., & Wainer, J. (2005). Meta workflows as a control and coordination mechanism for exception handling in workflow systems . *Decision Support Systems, 40*(1), 89–105. doi:10.1016/j.dss.2004.04.006

Kumar, A., & Zhao, J. L. (2002). Workflow support for electronic commerce applications. *Decision Support Systems, 32*(3), 265–278. doi:10.1016/S0167-9236(01)00114-2

Kumar, K. (2001). Technology for supporting supply chain management: Introduction. *Communications of the ACM, 44*(6), 58–61. doi:10.1145/376134.376165

Kumar, K., & Narasipuram, M. M. (2006). Defining requirements for business process flexibility. In *Seventh Workshop on Business Process Modeling, Development, and Support*. CAiSE

Kumar, K., & van Dissel, H. (1996). Sustainable collaboration: Managing conflict and cooperation in inter-organizational systems. *MIS Quarterly, 20*(3), 279–300. doi:10.2307/249657

Kumar, K., van Fenema, P. C., & von Glinow, M. A. (2007). Offshoring and the global distribution of work: Implications for task interdependence theory and practice. In *First Annual Research Conference and Workshop on Offshoring*. North Carolina

Kumaran, S., Bishop, P., Chao, T., Dhoolia, P., Jain, P., & Jaluka, R. (2007). Using a model-driven transformational approach and service-oriented architecture for service delivery management. *IBM Systems Journal, 46*(3), 513–529.

Küng, P., & Hagen, C. (2007). The fruits of business process management: An experience report from a Swiss bank. *Business Process Management Journal, 13*(4), 477. doi:10.1108/14637150710763522

Kunz, J. C., Christiansen, T. R., Cohen, G. P., Jin, Y., & Levitt, R. E. (1998). The virtual design team. *Communications of the ACM, 41*(11), 84–91. doi:10.1145/287831.287844

Küster, J. M., Koehler, J., & Ryndina, K. (2006). Improving business process models with reference models in business-driven development. *BPD-2006 Business Process Design Workshop at Business Process Management 2006 Conference* (LNCS 4103, pp. 35-44), Vienna, Austria.

Kuutti, K. (1996). *Activity theory as a potential framework for human-computer interaction research* (pp. 17-44).

Lacy, L. W. (2005). *Owl: Representing information using the web ontology language*. Trafford Publishing.

Larraine, S. (2002). *Dynamic leader adaptive organization: Ten essential traits for managers*. Wiley.

Law, A. M., & Kelton, D. (1991). *Simulation modeling and analysis* (2nd ed.). New York: McGraw-Hill.

Leavitt, H. J. (1965). Applying organizational change in industry: Structural, technological and humanistic approaches. In J. March (Ed.), *Handbook of organizations* (pp. 1144-1170). Chicago: Rand McNally.

Ledeczi, A., Maroti, M., Bakay, A., Karsai, G., Garrett, J., Thomason, C., et al. (2001). The generic modeling environment. In *Workshop on Intelligent Signal Processing*. Budapest, Hungary. Retrieved from http://www.isis.vanderbilt.edu/Projects/gme/GME2000 Overview.pdf.

Lee, J. J., & Holt, R. (2006). *The producer's business handbook* (2nd ed.). Burlington, Oxford, UK: Focal Press.

Lee, J. K., & Son, M. M. (2003). The eXtensible Rule Markup Language. *Communications of the ACM, 46*(5), 59–64. doi:10.1145/769800.769802

Lee, J., & Pentland, B. T. (2000). *Grammatical approach to organizational design*. Cambridge, MA: MIT Sloan School of Management. M+agazine, C. (1992). Back support for benchmarkers. *CIO Magazine June: 16*.

Lehmus, P. (1999). *Strategiasuunnitelma 2000-2003: Arena*. Helsingin Puhelin Oyj, Liiketoimintaprojektit. 14.4.1999. Helsinki, Finland.

Lenz, R., & Reichert, M. (2007). IT support for healthcare processes – Premises, challenges, perspectives. *Data & Knowledge Engineering, 61*, 82–111. doi:10.1016/j.datak.2006.04.007

Leontiev, A. (1974). The problem of activity in psychology. *Social Psychology, 13*(2), 4–33.

Leslie, D. (2004). *Reinforcement learning in games*. Unpublished doctoral dissertation, University of Bristol.

Lesser, E. L., & Storck, J. (2001). Communities of practice and organizational performance. *IBM Systems Journal, 40*(4).

Levitt, R. E. (2004). Computational modeling of organizations comes of age. *Computational & Mathematical Organization Theory, 10*(2), 127. doi:10.1023/B:CMOT.0000039166.53683.d0

Levitt, R. E., Orr, R. J., & Nissen, M. E. (2005). *Validating the virtual design team (VDT) computational modeling environment.* Stanford, CA

Levitt, R. E., Thomsen, J., Christiansen, T. R., & Kunz, J. C. (1999). Simulating project work processes and organizations: Toward a micro-contingency theory of organizational design. *Management Science, 45*(11), 1479. doi:10.1287/mnsc.45.11.1479

Leymann, F. (2001) *Web services flow language (WSFL 1.0).* IBM Corporation.

Leymann, F. (2006). Workflow-based coordination and cooperation in a service world. In R. Meersman, & Z. Tari (Eds.) *Proceedings of the 14th International Conference on Cooperative Information Systems (CoopIS'06)* (LNCS 4275, pp. 2-16). Montpellier, France: Springer-Verlag.

Leymann, F., & Roller, D. (2000). *Production workflow: Concepts and techniques.* Prentice Hall.

Leymann, F., & Roller, D. (2002). Using flows in information integration. *IBM Systems Journal, 41*(4), 732–742.

Leymann, F., Roller, D., & Schmidt, M. T. (2002). Web services and business process management. *IBM Systems Journal, 41*(2), 198–211.

Li, C., Reichert, M., & Wombacher, A. (2008). Discovering reference process models by mining process variants. In *Proc. 6th Int'l IEEE Conference on Web Services (ICWS'08)* (pp. 45-53), Beijing.

Liang, W.-Y., & Huang, C.-C. (2006). Agent-based demand forecast in multi-echelon supply chain. *Decision Support Systems, 42*(1), 390–407. doi:10.1016/j.dss.2005.01.009

List, B., & Korherr, B. (2005). A UML 2 profile for business process modelling. In *Perspectives in Conceptual Modeling, ER 2005 Workshops* (LNCS 3770, pp. 85-96).

Littman, M. L. (1994). Markov games as a framework for multi-agent reinforcement learning. In *Proceedings of the 11th international conference on machine learning* (pp. 157-163). New Brunswick, NJ: Morgan Kaufmann.

Liu, C. T., Long, A. G., Li, Y. C., Tsai, K. C., & Kuo, H. S. (2001). Sharing patient care records over the World Wide Web. *International Journal of Medical Informatics, 61*(2-3), 189–205. doi:10.1016/S1386-5056(01)00141-1

Liu, J. X., & Chen, H. Y. Hu, & J. M. (2005). A study on batch processing model in workflow. In *Proceedings from SKG '05: The 1th International Conference on Semantics, Knowledge and Grid, Beijing, CA.* IEEE.

Liu, J. X., & Hu, J. M. (2007). Dynamic batch processing in workflows: Model and implementation. *Future Generation Computer Systems, 23*(3), 338–347. doi:10.1016/j.future.2006.06.003

Liu, L., & Pu, C. (1997, November). ActivityFlow: Towards incremental specification and flexible coordination of workflow activities. In *Proceedings of the 16th International Conference on Conceptual Modeling.*

Liu, R., & Kumar, A. (2005). An analysis and taxonomy of unstructured workflows. *Third International Conference on Business Process Management (BPM 2005)* Nancy, France (LNCS 3649, pp. 268-284).

Liu, R., Bhattacharya, K., & Wu, F. Y. *(2007).* Modeling business contexture and behavior using business artifacts. *Paper presented at the 19th International Conference on Advanced Information Systems Engineering, Trondheim, Norway.*

Liu, R., Kumar, A., & Aalst, W. (2007). A formal modeling approach for supply chain event management. *Decision Support Systems, 43*(3), 761–778. doi:10.1016/j.dss.2006.12.009

Louwerse, K. (1998). The electronic patient record; the management of access—Case study: Leiden University

Hospital. *International Journal of Medical Informatics, 49*(1), 39–44. doi:10.1016/S1386-5056(98)00008-2

Lucia, A. D., Francese, R., & Tortora, G. (2003). Deriving workflow enactment rules from UML activity diagrams: A case study. In *Proceedings of IEEE Symposium on Human Centric Computing Languages and Environments* (pp. 211-218).

Luo, H. B., Fan, Y. S., & Wu, C. (2000). An overview of workflow. [in Chinese]. *Chinese Journal of Software, 11*(7), 899–907.

Ly, L. T., Rinderle, S., Dadam, P., & Reichert, M. (2005). Mining staff assignment rules from event-based data. In *Proc. Workshop on Business Process Intelligence (BPI)* (LNCS 3812, pp. 177-190).

Lyons, M. J., Akamatsu, S., Kamachi, M., & Gyoba, J. (1998). *Coding facial expressions with Gabor wavelets.* In *Proceedings of the Third IEEE International Conference on Automatic Face and Gesture Recognition* (pp. 200-205).

Ma, Z., Wetzstein, B., Heymans, S., & Anicic, D. (2007). Semantic business process repository. In *Proceedings of the International Workshop on Semantic Business Process Management (SBPM 2007)*, CEUR Proceedings.

MacKay, D. J. C. (2003). *Information theory, inference, and learning algorithms.* Cambridge University Press.

Mahalingam, A., Levitt, R. E., & Scott, W. R. (2005). Cultural clashes in international infrastructure development projects: Which cultures matter? Las Vegas, NV.

Maidantchik, C., Rocha, A. R. C., & Xex'eo, G. (1999). Software process standardization for distributed working groups. In *Proceedings of the 4th IEEE International Symposium and Forum on Software Engineering Standards.*

Malhotra, Y. (2004). Why knowledge management systems fail? Enablers and constraints of knowledge management in human enterprises. *American Society for Information Science and Technology Monograph Series* (pp. 87-112).

Malone, T. W., & Crowston, K. (1994). The interdisciplinary study of coordination. *ACM Computing Surveys, 26*(1), 87–119. doi:10.1145/174666.174668

Malone, T. W., Crowston, K., & Herman, G. A. (2003). *Organizing business knowledge: The MIT process handbook.* Cambridge MA: MIT Press.

Malone, T. W., Crowston, K., Lee, J., & Pentland, B. (1999). Tools for inventing organizations: Toward a handbook of organizational processes. *Management Science, 45*(3), 425–443. doi:10.1287/mnsc.45.3.425

Malone, T. W., et al. (2003). Tools for inventing organizations: Towards a handbook of organizational processes. In T.W. Malone, K. Crowston, & G.A. Herman, (Eds.). *Organizing business knowledge: The MIT process handbook.* Cambridge MA: MIT Press.

Manago, M. V., & Kodratoff, Y. (1987). Noise and knowledge acquisition. In *Proceedings of the Tenth International Joint Conference on Artificial Intelligence* (Vol. 1, pp. 348-354). Milano, Italy: Morgan Kaufmann.

Manrod, K. B., & Vitasek, K. (2004). Global process standardization: A case study. *Journal of Business Logistics, 25*(1).

March, J. G., & Simon, H. A. (1958). *Organizations.* New York: Wiley.

Marecki, J., Gupta, T., Varakantham, P., & Tambe, M. (2008). Not all agents are equal: Scaling up distributed POMDPs for agent networks. In *Proceedings of the Seventh International Joint Conference on Autonomous Agents and Multiagent Systems.*

Margherita, A., & Klein, M. (2007). An e-handbook for designing and implementing a benchmarking project. *International Journal of Process Management and Benchmarking, 2*(1), 10–28. doi:10.1504/IJPMB.2007.013315

Margherita, A., Klein, M., & Elia, G. (2007). Metrics-based process redesign with the MIT process handbook. *Knowledge and Process Management, 14*(1), 46–57. doi:10.1002/kpm.269

Marsh, A. (1997). EUROMED - the creation of a telemedical information society. In *Proceedings of the IEEE*

Symposium on Computer-Based Medical Systems (pp. 86-91).

Marsh, A. (1998). The creation of a global telemedical information society. *International Journal of Medical Informatics, 49*(2), 173–193. doi:10.1016/S1386-5056(98)00039-2

Mayer, R. J., Painter, M. K., & Menzel, C. P. Perakath, deWitte, B.P.S., & Blinn, T. (1995). *Information integration for concurrent engineering (IICE) IDEF3 process description capture method report*. Knowledge Based Systems, Inc. Retrieved from http://www.idef.com, 1995.

McCormack, K. P., & Johnson, W. C. (2001). *Business process orientation: Gaining the e-business: Competitive advantage*. St. Lucie Press.

McGrath, M. E. (1995). *Product strategy for high-technology companies: How to achieve growth, competitive advantage, and increased profits*. McGraw-Hill.

McKnight, D. H., Choudhury, V., & Kacmar, C. (2002). The impact of initial customer trust on intentions to transact with a website: A trust building model. *The Journal of Strategic Information Systems, 11*, 297–323. doi:10.1016/S0963-8687(02)00020-3

McNair, C. J., & Leibfried, K. H. J. (1992). *Benchmarking: A tool for continuous improvement*. New York: Harper Business.

MDAGuide. (2003). *MDA Guide Version 1.0.1*. Retrieved from http://www.omg.org/docs/omg/03-06-01.pdf.

Melão, N., & Pidd, M. (2000). A conceptual framework for understanding business processes and business process modeling. *Information Systems Journal, 10*(2), 105–129. doi:10.1046/j.1365-2575.2000.00075.x

Méndez, A., Bonfill, A., Espuña, A., & Puigjaner, L. (2006). Rigorous approach to coordinate production and transport scheduling in a multi-site system. *Computer Aided Chemical Engineering, 21*(2), 2171–2176. doi:10.1016/S1570-7946(06)80370-6

Mernik, M., Heering, J., & Sloane, A. M. (2005). When and how to develop domain-specific languages. *ACM Computing Surveys, 37*(4), 316–344. doi:10.1145/1118890.1118892

Mi, P., & Scacchi, W. (1993). *Articulation: An integrated approach to the diagnosis, replanning and rescheduling of software process failures*. Paper Presented at the 8th International Conference on Knowledge-Based Software Engineering.

Mi, P., & Scacchi, W. (1996). A meta-model for formulating knowledge-based models of software development. *Decision Support Systems, 17*(4), 313–330. doi:10.1016/0167-9236(96)00007-3

Michelis, G. D. (1999). Net theory and workflow models. In *Proceedings of the 20th International Conference in Application and Theory of Petri Nets*, viii+423.

Miles, M. B., & Huberman, A. M. (1994). *Qualitative data analysis: An expanded sourcebook* (2nd Ed.). Thousand Oaks, CA: Sage Publications, Inc.

Miller, D., & Friesen, P. (1984). *Organizations: A quantum view*. Englewood Cliffs, NJ: Prentice-Hall.

Miller, J., & Page, S. (2007). *Complex adaptive systems: An introduction to computational models of social life*. Princeton, NJ: Princeton University Press.

Milner, R. (1990). *Operational and algebraic semantics of concurrent processes*. Elsevier.

Minor, M., Schmalen, D., Koldehoff, A., & Bergmann, R. (2007). Structural adaptation of workflows supported by a suspension mechanism and by case-based reasoning. In *Proc. WETICE'07* (pp. 370-375), Paris.

Mintzberg, H. (1979). *The structuring of organizations: A synthesis of the research*. Englewood Cliffs, N.J: Prentice-Hall.

Mitchell, R. L. (2006). *Exxon gets power from IT standardization*. Retrieved May 20, 2008, from http://www.computerworlduk.com/management/it-business/it-organisation/case-study/index.cfm?articleid=377

Möller, K., & Rajala, A. (1999). Organizing marketing in industrial high-tech firms: The role of internal marketing relationships. *Industrial Marketing Management, 28*(5), 521–535. doi:10.1016/S0019-8501(99)00059-0

Möller, K., Rajala, A., & Svahn, S. (2005). Strategic business nets – Their types and management. *Journal of Business Research*, 1274–1284. doi:10.1016/j.jbusres.2003.05.002

Mon, D. L., Cheng, C. H., & Lin, J. C. (1994). Evaluating weapon system using fuzzy analytic hierarchy process based on entropy weigh. *Fuzzy Sets and Systems, 61*, 1–8. doi:10.1016/0165-0114(94)90279-8

Montagut, F., & Molva, R. (2007). Enforcing integrity of execution in distributed workflow management systems. In *IEEE Conf. on Services Computing (SCC'07)* (pp. 1-8).

Mouráo, H., & Antunes, P. (2007). Supporting effective unexpected exceptions handling in workflow management systems. In *Proc. SAC'07* (pp. 1242-1249).

Mowshowitz, A. (1997). Virtual organization. *Communications of the ACM, 40*(9), 30–37. doi:10.1145/260750.260759

Müller, D., Herbst, J., Hammori, M., & Reichert, M. (2006). IT support for release management processes in the automotive industry. In *Proc. 4th Int'l Conf. on Business Process Management (BPM'06)* (LNCS 4102, pp. 368-377).

Müller, D., Reichert, M., & Herbst, J. (2007). Data-driven modeling and coordination of large process structures. In: *Proc. 15th Int'l Conf. on Cooperative Information Systems (CoopIS'07)*, Vilamoura, Portugal, (LNCS 4803, pp. 131-149).

Müller, D., Reichert, M., & Herbst, J. (2008) A new paradigm for the enactment and dynamic adaptation of data-driven process structures. In *Proc. 20th Int'l Conf. on Advanced Information Systems Engineering (CAiSE'08)* (LNCS 5074, pp. 48-63).

Muller, R., Greiner, U., & Rahm, E. (2004). AgentWork: A workflow system supporting rule-based workflow adaptation. *Data & Knowledge Engineering, 51*(2), 223–256. doi:10.1016/j.datak.2004.03.010

Mumford, L. (1963). *Technics and Civilization.* Harcourt Brace Jovanovich, New York.

Murata, T. (1989). Petri nets: Properties, analysis and applications. *Proceedings of the IEEE, 77*(4), 541–580. doi:10.1109/5.24143

Muth, P., Weissenfels, J., Gillmann, M., & Weikum, G. (1999). Integrating light-weight workflow management systems withinexisting business environments. In *Proceedings of 15th International Conference on Data Engineering* (pp. 286-293).

Muth, P., Wodtke, D., Weißenfels, J., Kotz-Dittrich, A., & Weikum, G. (1998). From centralized workflow specification to distributed workflow execution. *Journal of Intelligent Information Systems, 10*(2), 159–184. doi:10.1023/A:1008608810770

Mutschler, B., Bumiller, J., & Reichert, M. (2006). Why process-orientation is scarce: An empirical study of process-oriented information systems in the automotive industry. In *Proc. 10th IEEE Int. Conf. on Enterprise Computing (EDOC '06)* (pp. 433-440), Hong Kong, China.

Mutschler, B., Reichert, M., & Bumiller, J. (2008). Unleashing the effectiveness of process-oriented information systems: problem analysis, critical success factors and implications. [Part C]. *IEEE Transactions on Systems, Man, and Cybernetics, 38*(3), 280–291. doi:10.1109/TSMCC.2008.919197

Mutschler, B., Weber, B., & Reichert, M. (2008). Workflow management versus case handling: results from a controlled software experiment. In *Proc. 23rd Annual ACM Symposium on Applied Computing (SAC'08)* (pp. 82-89), Fortaleza, Ceará, Brazil.

Nagappan, R., Skoczylas, R., & Sriganesh, R. P. (2002). *Developing Java Web Services: Architecting and developing secure Web services Using Java.* Wiley.

Nagi, K. (2001). *Transactional agents: Towards a robust multi-agent system.* Berlin, Heidelberg: Springer-Verlag.

Nalebuff, B. J., & Brandenburger, A. M. (1996). *Co-opetition.* London: Harper Collins.

Nardi, B. A. (1996). *Activity theory and human-computer interaction* (pp. 7-16).

Nardi, B. A. (Ed.). (1996). *Context and consciousness: Activity theory and human-computer interaction.* Cambridge, MA: MIT Press.

National Research Council. (2005). *Summary of a workshop on using information technology to enhance disaster management.* National Academies Press.

Neely, A., Gregory, M., & Platts, K. (2005). Performance measurement system design: A literature review and research agenda. *International Journal of Operations & Production Management, 12*(25), 1228–1263. doi:10.1108/01443570510633639

Nguyen, G., & Vernadat, F. (1994, May). Cooperative information systems in integrated manufacturing environments. In *Proceedings of the 2nd International Conference on Cooperative Information Systems.*

Nielsen, M. & Krukow, K. (2004). On the formal modelling of trust in reputation-based systems (LNCS 3113, pp. 192-204).

Nilsson, N. J. (1998). *Artificial intelligence: A new synthesis.* San Francisco: Morgan Kaufmann Publishers.

Nissen, M. (1998). Redesigning reengineering through measurement-driven inferences. *MIS Quarterly, 22*(4). doi:10.2307/249553

Nissen, M. E. (1999). A configuration-contingent enterprise redesign model. In D. J. Elzinga, T. R. Gulledge, & C. Lee (Eds.) *Business process engineering: Advancing the state of the art.* (pp. 145-186). Norwell, MA: Kluwer Academic Publishers.

Nissen, M. E. (2002). An extended model of knowledge flow dynamics. *CACM, 8*, 251–266.

Nissen, M. E. (2005). Hypothesis testing of edge organizations: Specifying computational C2 models for experimentation. In *Proceedings International Command & Control Research Symposium,* McLean, VA.

Nissen, M. E. (2007). Computational experimentation on new organizational forms: Exploring behavior and performance of edge organizations. *Computational & Mathematical Organization Theory, 13*(3), 203. doi:10.1007/s10588-006-9011-6

Nissen, M. E., & Buettner, R. R. (2004). Computational experimentation with the virtual design team: Bridging the chasm between laboratory and field research in C2. In *Proceedings Command and Control Research and Technology Symposium,* San Diego, CA.

Nissen, M. E., & Levitt, R. E. (2004). Agent-based modeling of knowledge dynamics. *Knowledge Management Research & Practice, 2*(3), 169. doi:10.1057/palgrave. kmrp.8500039

Nissen, M. E., & Leweling, T. A. (2008). Conceptualizing dynamic organizational fit in multicontingency contexts. In *Proceedings Academy of Management Conference,* Anaheim, CA.

Nonaka, I. (1994). A dynamic theory of organizational knowledge creation. *Organization Science, 5*(1), 14–37. doi:10.1287/orsc.5.1.14

oAW. *openArchitectureWare.* Retrieved from http://www. openarchitectureware.org.

Oberweis, A. (2005). *Person-to-application processes: Workflow management* (pp. 21-36).

Object Modeling Group. (2003, June). *MDA Guide 1.1.*

OECD. (1996). The knowledge based economy. *Science, Technology and Industry Outlook.* Paris.

OECD. (1999). *Measuring knowledge in learning economies and societies.* Draft Report on Washington Forum.

Olsson, O. (2002). Trust in eCommerce: the ontological status of trust. In B. Wiszniewski (Ed.), *Proceedings of ECOM-02- Electronic Commerce - Theory and Applications* (pp. 89-96), Gdansk.

OMG. (2007). *OMG Unified Modeling Language (UML), Superstructure, V2.1.2.* Object Management Group.

Orr, R. J., & Nissen, M. E. (2006). Computational experimentation on C2 models. In *Proceedings International Command and Control Research and Technology Symposium,* Cambridge, UK.

Orriëns, B. (Ed.). (2007). *On the adaptive development and management of business collaborations* (No. 194). CentER.

Osborn, R. N., & Hunt, J. G. (2007). Leadership and the choice of order: Complexity and hierarchical perspectives near the edge of chaos. *The Leadership Quarterly, 18*(4), 319. doi:10.1016/j.leaqua.2007.04.003

Osborne, M. A., Rogers, A., Ramchurn, S., Roberts, S. J., & Jennings, N. R. (2008, April). Towards real-time information processing of sensor network data using computationally efficient multi-output gaussian processes. In *International conference on information processing in sensor networks* (pp. 109–120).

Osterle, H., Fleisch, E., & Alt, R. *(2001)*. Business networking - Shaping collaboration between enterprises. *Springer Verlag.*

Ouchi, W. G. (1980). Markets, bureaucracies, and clans. *Administrative Science Quarterly, 25*(1), 129. doi:10.2307/2392231

Pacific Knowledge Systems. (2003). *Products: Rippledown.* Retrieved April 23, 2002, from http://www.pks.com.au/products/validator.htm

Palmer, N. (2007). A survey of business process initiatives. Retrieved April 4, 2008, from http://wfmc.org/researchreports/Survey_BPI.pdf

Pande, P. S., Neumann, R. P., & Cavanagh, R. (2000). *The six sigma way.* New York: McGraw-Hill.

Pandya, Vinodrai, K., & Nelis, S. (1998). Requirements for process redesign tools. *International Journal Of Computer Applications in Technology, 11*(6), 409–418.

Pang, C., Eschinger, C., Dharmasthira, Y., & Motoyoshi, K. (2007). *Market share: ERP software, worldwide, 2006.* Gartner report.

Paquet, S., Tobin, L., & Chaib-draa, B. (2005). An online POMDP algorithm for complex multiagent environments. In *Proceedings of the Fourth International Joint Conference on Autonomous Agents and Multiagent Systems* (pp. 970-977). New York: ACM Press.

Parnas, D. (1994). Software aging. *International Conference of Software Engineering* (pp. 279-287). IEEE Computer Society Press.

Pavlou, P. A. (2003). Customer acceptance of electronic commerce: Integrating trust and risk with the technology acceptance model. *International Journal of Electronic Commerce, 7*(3), 135–161.

PCS (2000). WS3-dokum-Tuotekeh-mita-pitaa-muuttua. March 30th 2000. Hämeenkylän kartano.

PCS (2000). Jatkotoimenpiteet. April 17th 2000. Hämeenkylän kartano.

PCS (2001). tuotehommaa 0307. PCS, Elisa Communications July 3rd 2001.

Pedrinaci, C., & Domingue, J. (2007). Towards an ontology for process monitoring and mining. In *Proceedings of the Workshop on Semantic Business Process and Product Lifecycle Management (SBPM-2007), CEUR-WS*

Pellitteri, J. (2002). The relationship between emotional intelligence and ego defence mechanisms. *The Journal of Psychology, 136,* 182–194.

Peltz, C. (2003, January). *Web services orchestration: A review of emerging technologies, tools, and standards.*

Pentland, B. T. (1995). Grammatical models of organizational processes. *Organization Science, 6*(5), 541–556. doi:10.1287/orsc.6.5.541

Perjons, E., Bider, I., & Andersson, B. (2007). Building and exploiting a business process model for lobbying: Experience report. [CIIMA]. *Communications of the IIMA, 7*(3), 1–14.

Perry, D. E., Romanovsky, A., & Tripathi, A. (2000). Current trends in exception handling. *IEEE Transactions on Software Engineering, 26*(10), 921–922. doi:10.1109/TSE.2000.879816

Perry. W. E (1995). *Effective methods for software testing.* John Wiley & Sons.

Pesic, M., & van der Aalst, W. (2006). A declarative approach for flexible business processes. In J. Eder, & S. Dustdar (Eds.), *Proceedings of the First International Workshop on Dynamic Process Management (DPM 2006)* (LNCS 4103, pp. 169-180).

Pesic, M., & van der Aalst, W. M. P. (2006). A declarative approach for flexible business processes management. *DPM-2006 Dynamic Process Management Workshop at Business Process Management 2006 Conference* (LNCS 4103, pp. 169-180), Vienna, Austria.

Pesic, M., Schonenberg, M., Sidorova, N., & van der Aalst, W. M. P. (2007). Constraint-based workflow models: change made easy. In *Proc. CoopIS'07* (LNCS 4803, pp. 77-94).

Petri, C. (1966). *Communication in automata* (Tech Rep RADC-TR-65-377, 1). Rome Air Development Center, Griffths Air Base, USA.

Petrie, C. J., & Bussler, C. (2003). Service agents and virtual enterprises: A survey. *IEEE Internet Computing, 4*, 68–78. doi:10.1109/MIC.2003.1215662

Pinar, S., & Ismail, H. T. (2005). An architecture for workflow scheduling under resource allocation constraints. *Information Systems, 30*, 399–422. doi:10.1016/j.is.2004.03.003

Pineau, J., Gordon, G., & Thrun, S. (2003, August). Point-based value iteration: An anytime algorithm for POMDPs. In *International Joint Conference on Artificial Intelligence* (pp. 1025 -1032).

Pinfield, L. T., Watzke, G. E., & Webb, E. J. (1974). Confederacies and brokers: Mediators between organizations and their environments. In H.Leavitt, L. Pinfield & E. Webb (Eds.), *Organizations of the future: Interaction with the external environment* (pp.83-110). New York: Praeger.

Poupart, P., Vlassis, N., Hoey, J., & Regan, K. (2006). An analytic solution to discrete Bayesian reinforcement learning. In *Proceedings of the 23rd International Conference on Machine Learning* (pp. 697-704). New York: ACM.

Pressman, R. S. (2001). *Software engineering: A practitioner's approach* (5th Ed.). Boston: McGraw-Hill Higher Education.

Product Development Institute Inc. Stage-Gate Model. 1996-1998.

Radjou, N., Daley, E., Rasmussen, M., & Lo, H. (2006). The rise of globally adaptive organizations. The world isn't flat till global firms are networked, risk-agile, and socially adept. In *Balancing risks and rewards in a global tech economy*. Forrester.

Rahrami, H. (1992). The emerging flexible organization: Perspectives from Silicon Valley. *California Management Review, 34*(4), 33.

Ramamohanarao, K., Bailey, J., & Busetta, P. (2001). Transaction oriented computational models for multi-agent systems. In *Proceedings of 13th IEEE International Conference on Tools with Artificial Intelligence (ICTAI)* (pp. 11-17). IEEE Computer Society, Washington, DC, USA.

Ramamritham, K., Stankovic, J. A., & Zhao, W. (1989). Distributed scheduling of tasks with deadlines and resource requirements. *IEEE Transactions on Computers, 38*(8), 1110–1123. doi:10.1109/12.30866

Ramchurn, S. D., Huynh, D., & Jennings, N. R. (2004). Trust in multiagent systems. *The Knowledge Engineering Review, 19*(1), 1–25. doi:10.1017/S0269888904000116

Ramesh, B., Jain, R., Nissen, M., & Xu, P. (2005). Managing context in business process management systems. *Requirements Engineering, 10*(3), 223. doi:10.1007/s00766-005-0005-6

Rao, A. S., & Georgeff, M. P. (1995, June 12-14, 1995). BDI agents: From theory to practice. In *Proceedings of the First International Conference on Multiagent Systems* (pp. 312-319), San Francisco, California, USA.

Rao, J., & Su, X. (2004). A survey of automated web service composition methods. In *Proceedings of the First International Workshop on Semantic Web Services and Web Process Composition (SWSWPC 2004)*, California. Springer-Verlag.

Rao, J., Kungas, P., & Matskin, M. (2006). Composition of semantic Web services using linear logic theorem proving. *International Journal of Information systems, 31*(4-5), 340-360.

Ratcliffe-Martin, V., Coakes, E., & Sugden, G. (2000). Knowledge management issues in universities. *Vine Journal, 30*, 14–19. doi:10.1108/eb040770

Raynor, M. E., & Bower, J. L. (2001). Lead from the center: How to manage divisions dynamically. *Harvard Business Review, 79*(5), 92.

Reichert, M. (2000). *Dynamische Ablaufänderungen in Workflow-Management-Systemen.* PhD thesis, University of Ulm (in German).

Reichert, M., & Bauer, T. (2007). Supporting ad-hoc changes in distributed workflow management systems. In *Proc. CoopIS'07* (LNCS 4803, pp. 150-168).

Reichert, M., & Dadam, P. (1997). A framework for dynamic changes in workflow management systems. In *Proceedings of the 8th International Workshop on Database and Expert Systems Applications(DEXA 97)*, (pp. 42-48). Toulouse, France: IEEE Computer Society Press.

Reichert, M., & Dadam, P. (1997, September). A framework for dynamic changes in workflow management systems. In *Proceedings of the 8th International Conference on Database and Expert Systems Applications.*

Reichert, M., & Dadam, P. (1998). ADEPTflex - Supporting dynamic changes of workflows without losing control. *Journal of Intelligent Information Systems, 10*(2), 93–129. doi:10.1023/A:1008604709862

Reichert, M., Bauer, T., & Dadam, P. (1999). Enterprise-wide and cross-enterprise workflow management: challenges and research issues for adaptive workflows. In *Proc. Workshop Informatik '99, CEUR Workshop Proceedings, Vol. 24* (pp. 56-64), Paderborn, Germany.

Reichert, M., Dadam, P., & Bauer, T. (2003). Dealing with forward and backward jumps in workflow management systems. *Software and Systems Modeling, 2*(1), 37–58. doi:10.1007/s10270-003-0018-x

Reichert, M., Hensinger, C., & Dadam, P. (1998). Supporting adaptive workflows in advanced application environments. In *Proc. EDBT Workshop on Workflow Management Systems* (pp. 100-109), Valencia, Spain.

Reichert, M., Rinderle, S., & Dadam, P. (2003). On the common support of workflow type and instance changes under correctness constraints. In *Proc. 11th Int'l Conf. Cooperative Information Systems (CoopIS '03)* (LNCS 2888, pp. 407-425).

Reichert, M., Rinderle, S., & Dadam, P. (2003) ADEPT workflow management system - Flexible support for enterprise-wide business processes. In *Proc. 1st Int'l Conf. on Business Process Management (BPM '03)* (LNCS 2678, pp. 371-379).

Reichert, M., Rinderle, S., Kreher, U., & Dadam, P. (2005) Adaptive process management with ADEPT2. In *Proc. Int'l Conf. on Data Engineering (ICDE'05)* (pp. 1113-1114), Tokyo.

Reichert, M., Rinderle, S., Kreher, U., & Dadam, P. (2005). Adaptive process management with ADEPT2. In *Proceedings of the 21st International Conference on Data Engineering (ICDE'05)*, (pp. 1113-1114). Tokyo, Japan: IEEE Computer Society Press.

Reijers, H. A., & van der Aalst, W. M. P. (2005). The effectiveness of workflow management systems: Predictions and lessons learned. *International Journal of Information Management, 25*(5), 458–472. doi:10.1016/j.ijinfomgt.2005.06.008

Reijers, H. A., Rigter, J., & van der Aalst, W. M. P. (2003). The case handling case. *International Journal of Cooperative Information Systems, 12*(3), 365–391. doi:10.1142/S0218843003000784

Resources, S. O. A. (n.d.). Retrieved from http://www.peterindia.net/SOA.html

Rhee, S. -H., Cho, N., & Bae, H. (2007). A more comprehensive approach for enhancing business process efficiency (LNCS 4558, pp. 955-964).

Rhee, S.-H., Bae, H., & Choi, Y. (2007). Enhancing the efficiency of supply chain processes through Web Services. *Information Systems Frontier: Special Issue on from Web Services to Services Computing, 9*(1), 103–118.

Richen, A., & Steinhorst, A. (2005). *Standardization or harmonization? You need both.* Retrieved September 26,

2008, from http://www.bptrends.com/publicationfiles/11-05-ART-StandardizationorHarmonizationv-Ricken-Steinhorst.pdf

Rinderle, S., Reichert, M., & Dadam, P. (2003) Evaluation of correctness criteria for dynamic workflow changes. In *Proc. 1st Int'l Conf. on Business Process Management (BPM '03)* (LNCS 2678, pp. 41-57).

Rinderle, S., Reichert, M., & Dadam, P. (2004). Correctness criteria for dynamic changes in workflow systems - A survey. *Data & Knowledge Engineering, 50*(1), 9–34. doi:10.1016/j.datak.2004.01.002

Rinderle, S., Reichert, M., & Dadam, P. (2004a). Flexible support of team processes by adaptive workflow systems. *Distributed and Parallel Databases, 16*(1), 91–116. doi:10.1023/B:DAPD.0000026270.78463.77

Rinderle, S., Reichert, M., & Dadam, P. (2004). Disjoint and overlapping process changes: challenges, solutions, applications. In *Proc. 11th Int'l Conf. on Cooperative Information Systems (CoopIS'04)* (LNCS 3290, pp. 101-121).

Rinderle, S., Reichert, M., & Dadam, P. (2004). On dealing with structural conflicts between process type and instance changes. In *Proc. 2nd. Int'l Conf. Business Process Management (BPM'04)* (LNCS 3080, pp. 274-289).

Rinderle, S., Reichert, M., Jurisch, M., & Kreher, U. (2006). On representing, purging, and utilizing change logs in process management systems. In *Proc. 4th Int'l Conf. on Business Process Management (BPM'06)* (LNCS 4102, pp. 241-256).

Rinderle, S., Weber, B., Reichert, M., & Wild, W. (2005). Integrating process learning and process evolution - A semantics based approach. In *Proc. 3rd Int'l Conf. on Business Process Management (BPM'05)* (LNCS 3649, pp. 252-267).

Rinderle, S., Weber, B., Reichert, M., & Wild, W. (2005). Integrating process learning and process evolution a semantics based approach. In W. van der Aalst, B. Benatallah, F. Casati, & F. Curbera (Eds.) *Proceedings of the 3rd International Conference on Business Process*

Management (BPM'05) (LNCS 3649, pp. 252-267). Nancy, France: Springer Verlag.

Rinderle, S., Wombacher, A., & Reichert, M. (2006) Evolution of process choreographies in DYCHOR. In *Proc. 14th Int'l Conf. on Coop. Inf. Sys.* (LNCS 4275, pp. 273-290).

Rinderle-Ma, S., & Reichert, M. (2007). A formal framework for adaptive access control models. *Journal on Data Semantics IX* (*LNCS 4601*, pp. 82–112).

Rinderle-Ma, S., & Reichert, M. (2008). Managing the life cycle of access rules in CEOSIS. In *Proc. of the 12th IEEE Int'l Enterprise Computing Conference (EDOC'08)* (pp. 257-266), Munich, Germany.

Rinderle-Ma, S., Reichert, M., & Weber, B. (2008). Relaxed compliance notions in adaptive process management systems. In *Proc. 27th Int'l Conf. on Conceptual Modeling (ER'08)* (LNCS 5231, pp. 232-247).

Rinderle-Ma, S., Reichert, M., & Weber, B. (2008). On the formal semantics of change patterns in process-aware information systems. In *Proc. 27th Int'l Conference on Conceptual Modeling (ER'08)* (LNCS 5231, pp. 279-293).

Riss, U., Rickayzen, A., Maus, H., & van der Aalst, W. (2005). Challenges for business process and task management. *Journal of Universal Knowledge Management, 0*(2), 77-100. Retrieved January 27, 2007, from http://www/jukm.org/jukm_0_2/riss

Roget's (1995). *Roget's II: The new thesaurus* (3rd ed.). Houghton Mifflin Company. (Accessed September 26, 2008)

Romanelli, E., & Tushman, M. L. (1994). Organizational transformation as punctuated equilibrium: An empirical test. *Academy of Management Journal, 37*(5), 1141. doi:10.2307/256669

RosettaNet. (2006). *RosettaNet Standards*.

Ross, R. (2003). *Principles of the business rule approach*. Addison-Wesley.

Ross, S., Chaib-draa, B., & Pineau, J. (in press). Bayes-adaptive POMDPs. In *Neural information processing systems.*

Roy, N., & Gordon, G. (2002, December). Exponential family PCA for belief compression in POMDPs. In S. Becker, S. Thrun, & K. Obermayer (Eds.), *Advances in neural information processing* (p. 1043-1049). Vancouver, Canada.

Rule, M. L. (2004). *RuleML: Rule markup language.* Retrieved April 15, 2008, from http://www.ruleml.org

Rumbaugh, J. (1991). *Object-oriented modeling and design.* Englewood Cliffs, N.J.: Prentice Hall

Russell, N., ter Hofstede, A. H. M., van der Aalst, W. M. P., & Mulyar, N. (2006). *Workflow control-flow patterns: A revised view.* BPM Center Report BPM-06-22. Retrieved from http://www.BPMcenter.org

Russell, N., van der Aalst, W., & ter Hofstede, A. (2006). Workflow exception patterns. In E. Dubois, & K. Pohl (Eds.) *Proceedings of the 18th International Conference on Advanced Information Systems Engineering (CAiSE 2006)* (pp. 288-302). Luxembourg: Springer.

Saaty, T. L. (1977). A scaling method for priorities in hierarchical structures. *Journal of Mathematical Psychology, 15*(3), 234–281. doi:10.1016/0022-2496(77)90033-5

Saaty, T. L. (1980). *The analytic hierarchy process.* New York: McGraw-Hill.

Sabherwal, R., Hirschheim, R., & Goles, T. (2001). The dynamics of alignment: Insights from a punctuated equilibrium model. *Organization Science, 12*(2), 179. doi:10.1287/orsc.12.2.179.10113

Sadiq, S., Marjanovic, O., & Orlowska, M. E. (2000). Managing change and time in dynamic workflow processes. *International Journal of Cooperative Information Systems, 9*(1-2), 93–116. doi:10.1142/S0218843000000077

Sadiq, S., Sadiq, W., & Orlowska, M. (2001). Pockets of flexibility in workflow specifications. In *Proc. ER'01* (pp. 513-526).

Sadiq, S., Sadiq, W., & Orlowska, M. (2005). A framework for constraint specification and validation inflexible workflows. *Information Systems, 30*(5), 349–378. doi:10.1016/j.is.2004.05.002

Salam, A. F., Iyer, L., Palvia, P., & Singh, R. (2005). Trust in e-commerce. *Communications of the ACM, 48*(2), 73–77. doi:10.1145/1042091.1042093

Salancik, G. R., & Leblebici, H. (1988). Variety and form in organizing transactions: A generative grammar of organizations. In N. DiTomaso & S. B. Bacharach (Eds.), *Research in the Sociology of Organizations.* Greenwich, CT: JAI Press.

Salmi, P. (1999). *Helsinki Arena 2000-esittelymateriaali.* Helsingin Puhelin Oyj. Helsinki, Finland.

Sanchez, R., & Mahoney, J. T. (2003). Modularity, flexibility, and knowledge management in product and organization design. In R. Garud, A. Kumaraswamy, & R.N. Langlois (Eds), *Managing in the modular age: Architectures, networks, and organizations* (pp. 362-389). Blackwell Publishing Limited.

SAP. (2006). *SAP advanced workflow techniques.* Retrieved March 17, 2008, from https://www.sdn.sap.com/irj/servlet/prt/portal/prtroot/docs/library/uuid/82d03e23-0a01-0010-b482-dccfe1c877c4

Scacchi, W. (1998). Modeling, integrating, and enacting complex organizational processes. In K. Carley, L. Gasser, & M. Prietula (Eds.), *Simulating organizations: Computational models of institutions and groups* (pp. 153-168). MIT Press.

Schael, T. (1998). *Workflow management systems for process organizations* (LNCS 1096).

Schank, R. C., & Abelson, R. P. (1977). *Scripts, plans, goals and understanding.* Lawrence Erlbaum Associates.

Scheer, A. (1992). *Architecture of Integrated Information Systems: Foundations of enterprise modelling.* Springer.

Scheffer, T. (1996). Algebraic foundation and improved methods of induction of ripple down rules. In *Proceedings of the 2nd Pacific Rim Workshop on Knowledge Acquisition,* (pp. 279-292). Sydney, Australia.

Schema, X. M. L. (2001). *XML Schema Specification*. Retrieved February 10, 2008, from http://www.w3.org/XML/Schema

Schiefer, J., Roth, H., Suntinger, M., & Schatten, A. (2007). Simulating business process scenarios for event based systems. *Schatten Personal web site*. Retrieved February 20, 2008, from http://www.schatten.info/pub/ecis/ecis2007.pdf

Schill, A., & Mittasch, C. (1996). Workflow management systems on top of OSF DCE and OMG Corba. *Distributed Systems Engineering, 3*(4), 206–233. doi:10.1088/0967-1846/3/4/005

Schilling, M. A. (2003). Towards general modular systems theory and its application to interfirm product modularity. In R Garud, A. Kumaraswamy, & R.N. Langlois (Eds.), *Managing in the modular age: Architectures, networks, and organizations* (pp. 172-216). Blackwell Publishing Limited.

Schillo, M., Funk, P., & Rovatsos, M. (1999). Who can you trust: Dealing with deception. In R. Falcone (Ed.), *Proceedings of Workshop on Deception, Fraud and Trust of the Autonomous Agents Conference*, Seattle, WA. Retrieved April 2, 2008, from http://www7.in.tum.de/~rovatsos/publications.shtml.

Schillo, M., Rovatsos, M., & Funk, P. (2000). Using trust for detecting deceitful agents in artificial societies. *Applied Artificial Intelligence Journal, 14*(8), 825–848. doi:10.1080/08839510050127579

Schimm, G. (2004). Mining exact models of concurrent workflows. *Computers in Industry, 53*(2), 265–281. doi:10.1016/j.compind.2003.10.003

Schmidt, S., Steele, R., Dillion, T. & Chang, E. (2005). Applying a fuzzy trust model to e-commerce systems (LNAI 3809, pp. 318-329).

Schneeweiss, C., Zimmer, K., & Zimmermann, M. (2004). The design of contracts to coordinate operational interdependencies within the supply chain. *International Journal of Production Economics, 92*(1), 43–59. doi:10.1016/j.ijpe.2003.10.005

Schneider, G. (2006). *Electronic commerce* (6th Ed.). Australia: Thomson Course Technology.

Schneiderman, B. (2000). Designing trust into online experiences. *Communications of the ACM, 43*(12), 57–59. doi:10.1145/355112.355124

Schuster, H., Neeb, J., & Schamburger, R. (1999). A configuration management approach for large workflow management systems. In *Proc. Int. Conf. on Work Activities Coordination and Collaboration*, San Francisco, 1999.

Scott, J. E. (2007). Mobility, business process management, software sourcing, and maturity model trends: Propositions for the IS organization of the future. *Information Systems Management, 24*(2), 139. doi:10.1080/10580530701221031

Scott, W. R. (1995). *Institutions and organizations*. Thousand Oaks, CA: Sage.

SEI (2005). *SMART: The service-oriented migration and reuse technique* (CMU/SEI-2005-TN-029).

SEI. (2006). CMMI® for Development, Version 1.2 (CMU/SEI-2006-TR-008). Retrieved May 27, 2008, from http://www.sei.cmu.edu

Seo, Y. (2006). Controlling general multi-echelon distribution supply chains with improved reorder decision policy utilizing real-time shared stock information. *Computers & Industrial Engineering, 51*(2), 229–246. doi:10.1016/j.cie.2006.02.005

Service Component Architecture Home. (2007). *Open Service Oriented Architecture Site*. Retrieved March 10, 2008, from http://www.osoa.org/display/Main/Service+Component+Architecture+Home

Service Oriented Architecture. (2008). *The wikipedia.org site*. Retrieved March 10, 2008, from http://en.wikipedia.org/wiki/Service-oriented_architecture

Shani, G., Brafman, R. I., & Shimony, S. E. (2005). Model-based online learning of POMDPs. In *European Conference on Machine Learning* (p. 353-364).

Shaw, D. R., Holland, C. P., Kawalek, P., Snowdon, B., & Warboys, B. (2007). Elements of a business process management system: Theory and practice. *Business Process Management Journal, 13*(1), 91. doi:10.1108/14637150710721140

Shegalov, G., Gillmann, M., & Weikum, G. (2001). XML-enabled workflow management for e-services across heterogeneous platforms. *The VLDB Journal, 10*(1), 91–103.

Sheng, O. R. L., & Chen, G. H. M. (1990). Information management in hospitals: An integrating approach. In *Proceedings of Annual Phoenix Conference* (pp. 296-303).

Sheth, A., & Kochut, K. J. (1997). Workflow applications to research agenda: scalable and dynamic work coordination and collaboration systems. In *Proc. NATO Advanced Study Institute on Workflow Management Systems and Interoperability* (pp. 12-21), Istanbul, Turkey.

Sheth, A., & Larson, J. (1990). Federated database systems. *ACM Computing Surveys, 22*(3), 183–236. doi:10.1145/96602.96604

Shi, X., Han, W., Huang, Y., & Li, Y. (2005). Service-oriented business solution development driven by process model. *CIT-2005 Fifth International Conference on Computer and Information Technology* (pp. 1086-1092). Shanghai, China.

Silvestro, R., Fitzgerald, L., & Johnston, R. (1992). Towards a classification of service processes. *International Journal of Service Industry Management, 3*(3), 62–75. doi:10.1108/09564239210015175

Simon, H. A. (1977). *The new science of management decision.* Englewood Cliffs, N.J.: Prentice-Hall

Simon, H. A. (1981). *The sciences of the artificial.* Cambridge, MA: MIT Press.

Simon, H. A. (2003). The architecture of complexity. In R Garud, A. Kumaraswamy, & R.N. Langlois (Eds), *Managing in the modular age: Architectures, networks, and organizations* (pp. 15-44). Blackwell Publishing Limited.

Simon, H., & Cilliers, P. (2005). The architecture of complexity. *Emergence: Complexity & Organization, 3/4*(7), 138–154.

Simple Object Access Protocol. (2007). *The w3.org site.* Retrieved March 22, 2008, from http://www.w3.org/TR/soap/

Skogan, D., Grønmo, R., & Solheim, I. (2004). Web service composition in UML. In *Eighth IEEE International Enterprise Distributed Object Computing Conference (EDOC'04)* (pp. 47-57).

Slyke, C. V., Belanger, F., & Comunale, C. L. (2004). Factors influencing the adoption of web-based shopping: The impact of trust. *The Data Base for Advances in Information Systems, 35*(2), 32–49.

Smith, A. J. (2002). *Dynamic generalisation of continuous action spaces in reinforcement learning: A neurally inspired approach.* (Ph.D. thesis, Division of Informatics, Edinburgh University, UK.)

Smith, H., & Fingar, P. (2003). *Business process management: The third wave.* Meghan-Kiffer Press.

Sneed, H. M. (2000). Encapsulation of legacy software: A Technique for reusing legacy software components. *Annals of Software Engineering, 9*, 293–313. doi:10.1023/A:1018989111417

Society for Worldwide Interbank Financial Telecommunication. (2008). *Bitpipe.com site.* Retrieved March 14, 2008, from http://www.bitpipe.com/tlist/SWIFT.html

Souchon, F., Dony, C., Urtado, C., & Vauttier, S. (2004). Improving exception handling in multi-agent systems. In *Software Engineering for Multi-Agent Systems II (Lecture Notes in Computer Science Vol. 2940)* (pp. 167-188). Springer Verlag.

Spekman, R. E., Isabella, L. A., & MacAvoy, T. C. (2000). *Alliance competence: Maximizing the value of your partnerships.* New York: John Wiley & Sons.

Spring. (2003). *The Spring Framework.* Retrieved April 19, 2008, from http://www.springframework.org/.

Staffware (2003). *Server Administration Guide*. Tool Documentation.

Stahl, T., Völter, M., Bettin, J., Haase, A., & Helsen, S. (2006). *Model-driven software development: technology, engineering, management*. Wiley.

Staikouras, C. K., & Koutsomanoli-Fillipaki, A. (2006). Competition and concentration in the new European banking landscape. *European Financial Management*, *3*(12), 443–482. doi:10.1111/j.1354-7798.2006.00327.x

Stauss, B., & Weinlich, B. (1997). Process-oriented measurement of service quality. *European Journal of Marketing*, *1*(31), 33–55. doi:10.1108/03090569710157025

Stein, L. A. (1999). Challenging the computational metaphor: Implications for how we think. *Cybernetics and Systems*, *30*(6). doi:10.1080/019697299125073

Stoddard, D., & Jarvenpaa, S. (1995). Business process reengineering: Tactics for managing radical change. *Journal of Management Information Systems*, *12*(1), 81–108.

Suh, B., & Han, I. (2002). Effect of trust on customer acceptance of Internet banking. *Electronic Commerce Research and Applications*, *1*, 247–263. doi:10.1016/S1567-4223(02)00017-0

Suh, B., & Han, I. (2003). The impact of customer trust and perceptions of security control on the acceptance of electronic commerce. *International Journal of Electronic Commerce*, *7*(3), 135–161.

Sun, Z., & Finnie G. (2005). MEBRS: A multiagent architecture for an experience based reasoning system (LNAI 3681, pp. 972-978).

Sun, Z., & Finnie, G. (2004). *Intelligent techniques in e-commerce: A case-based reasoning perspective*. Berlin, Heidelberg: Springer-Verlag.

Sun, Z., & Finnie, G. (2004). Experience based reasoning for recognizing fraud and deception. In *Proceedings of International Conference on Hybrid Intelligent Systems* (HIS 2004). (pp. 80-85), December 6-8, Kitakyushu, Japan. IEEE Press.

Sun, Z., & Finnie, G. (2007). A fuzzy logic approach to experience based reasoning. *International Journal of Intelligent Systems*, *22*(8), 867–889. doi:10.1002/int.20220

Sun, Z., & Huo, H. (2006). The engineering of experience. In *Proceedings of 6th Intelligent Systems Design and Applications*, vol. 2. (pp. 1114-1117), Jinan, China, 16-18 Oct. IEEE Press.

Sun, Z., Li, Y., & Zhao, S. (in press). Trust, deception and security in e-commerce. In B.K. Nescott (Ed.), *E-commerce coming into its own*. New York: Nova Science Publishers.

Sun, Z., Lu, S., Han, J., & Finnie, G. (2007). Experience-based trust in e-commerce. In W. Wang, Y. Li, Z. Duan, H. Li, & X. Yang (Eds.), *Integration and Innovation Orient to E-Society*. New York: Springer.

Supply-Chain Council. (2008). *Supply-chain operations reference-model*. Retrieved May 29, 2008, from http://www.supply-chain.org/galleries/public-gallery/SCOR%209.0%20Overview%20Booklet.pdf

Sutton, R. S., & Barto, A. G. (1998). *Reinforcement learning: An introduction*. Cambridge, MA: MIT Press.

Swithinbank, P., Chessell, M., Gardner, T., Griffin, C., Man, J., Wylie, H., & Yusuf, L. (2005). *Patterns: model-driven development using IBM rational software architect*. IBM Redbooks. Available at http://www.redbooks.ibm.com/abstracts/sg247105.html?Open.

Symon, G., Long, K., & Ellis, J. (1996). The coordination of work activities: cooperation and conflict in a hospital context. *Computer Supported Cooperative Work*, *5*(1), 1–31. doi:10.1007/BF00141934

Szyperski, C. (2002). *Component software: Beyond object-oriented programming*. Bosoton: Addison-Wesley Professional.

Taivalsaari, A. (1996). On the notion of inheritance. *ACM Computing Surveys*, *28*(3), 438–479. doi:10.1145/243439.243441

Takeda, H., Matsumura, Y., Kuwata, S., Nakano, H., Sakamoto, N., & Yamamoto, R. (2000). Architecture for networked electronic patient record systems. *International Journal of Medical Informatics, 60*(2), 161–167. doi:10.1016/S1386-5056(00)00116-7

Tambe, M., Adibi, J., Alonaizon, Y., Erdem, A., Kaminka, G. A., & Marsella, S. (1999). Building agent teams using an explicit teamwork model and learning. *Artificial Intelligence, 110*(2), 215–239. doi:10.1016/S0004-3702(99)00022-3

Tan, C. W., & Goh, A. (1999). Implementing ECA rules in an active database. *Knowledge-Based Systems, 12*(4), 137–144. doi:10.1016/S0950-7051(99)00028-3

Tan, J. K. H. (2001). *Health management information systems: Methods and practical applications* (2nd ed.). Aspen Publication.

Tan, Y. H., & Thoen, W. (2001). Toward a generic model of trust for electronic commerce. *International Journal of Electronic Commerce, 5*(2), 61–74.

Tang, M. T., & Tzeng, G. H. (1999). A hierarchy fuzzy MCDM method for studying electronic marketing strategies in the information service industry. *Journal of International Information Management, 8*(1), 1–22.

Teacy, W. T. L., Chalkiadakis, G., Rogers, A., & Jennings, N. R. (2005). Sequential decision making with untrustworthy service providers. In Padgham, Parkes, Müller & Parsons (Eds.), *Proc. of 7th Int. Conf. on Autonomous Agents and Multiagent Systems* (AAMAS 2008) (pp.755–762), May, 12-16., 2008, Estoril, Portugal.

Tenhovuori, T. (1996). *Helsinki Arena 2000 – palveluverkko. Tavoitesuunnitelma Helsinki Arena 2000.* Helsingin Puhelin Oyj. 2.12.1996. Helsinki, Finland.

Ter Beek, M., Bucchiarone, A., & Gnesi, S. (2007). Web service composition approaches: From industrial standards to formal methods. In *Proceedings of the Second International Conference on Internet and Web Applications and Services.* IEEE.

Thatte, S. (2001). *XLANG - Web services for business process design.* Microsoft Corporation.

Thomas, J. C., Kellog, W. A., & Erickson, T. (2001). The knowledge management puzzle: human and social factors in knowledge management. *IBM Systems Journal, 40*(4), 863–884.

Thompson, J. D. (1967). *Organizations in action; social science bases of administrative theory.* New York: McGraw-Hill.

Thomsen, J., Levitt, R. E., Kunz, J. C., Nass, C. I., & Fridsma, D. B. (1999). A trajectory for validating computational emulation models of organizations. *Computational & Mathematical Organization Theory, 5*(4), 385. doi:10.1023/A:1009624719571

TIBCO. (2006). *TIBCO iProcess Suite* [White paper]. Retrieved March 13, 2008, from http://www.staffware.com/resources/software/bpm/tibco_iprocess_suite_whitepaper.pdf

Toffler, A. (1985). *The adaptive corporation.* New York: McGraw Hill.

Tolvanen, J.-P., & Rossi, M. (2003). MetaEdit+: Defining and using domain-specific modeling languages and code generators. In OOPSLA '03: Companion of the 18th annual ACM SIGPLAN conference on Object-oriented programming, systems, languages, and applications (pp. 92-93). New York: ACM.

Tombros, D. (1999). *An event- and repository-based component framework for workflow system architecture.* Doctoral dissertation, University of Zurich. Retrieved February 22, 2008, from http://www.ifi.uzh.ch/archive/diss/Jahr_1999/thesis_tombros.pdf.

Traverso, P., Pistore, M., Roveri, M., Marconi, A., Kazhamiakin, R., Lucchese, P., et al. (2004, December). Supporting the negotiation between global and local business requirements in service oriented development. In *Proceedings of the 2nd International Conference on Service Oriented Computing.*

Trewin, D. (2004). *Television, film and video production in Australia* (publication 8679.0). Australian Bureau of Statistics. Retrieved April 13, 2008, from http://www.ausstats.abs.gov.au/ausstats/subscriber.nsf/0/14F1A528655E8486CA256EDE00782780/File/86790_2002-03.pdf

Tripathi, A., & Miller, R. (2001). Exception handling in agent-oriented systems. In *Advances in exception handling techniques* (LNCS 2022, pp. 128-146).

Tsaur, S. H., Tzeng, G. H., & Wang, K. C. (1997). Evaluating tourist risks from fuzzy perspectives. *Annals of Tourism Research*, 24(4), 796–812. doi:10.1016/S0160-7383(97)00059-5

Tu, Q., Vonderembse, M. A., Ragu-Nathan, T. S., & Ragu-Nathan, B. (2004). Measuring modularity-based manufacturing practices and their impact on mass customization capability. A customer-driven perspective. *Decision Sciences*, 2(35), 147–168. doi:10.1111/j.00117315.2004.02663.x

Tufekci, O., Cetin, S., & Altintas, N. I. (2006). How to process [business] processes. *IDPT-2006 Integrated Design & Process Technology Conference* (pp. 624-631). San Diego, California.

Tung, R. L. (1979). Dimensions of organizational environments: An exploratory study of their impact on organization structure. *Academy of Management Journal (Pre-1986), 22* (000004), 672.

Turing, A. (1936). On computable numbers, with an application to the entscheidungsproblem. *Proceedings of the London Mathematical Society*, 2(42), 230–265.

Tweedale, J., & Cutler, P. (2006). Trust in multiagent systems (LNCS 4252, pp. 479-485), Berlin Heidelberg: Springer-Verlag.

Tzeng, G. H. (1977). A study on the PATTERN method for the decision process in the public system. *Japan Journal of Behavior Metrics*, 4(2), 29–44.

Tzeng, G. H., & Shiau, T. A. (1987). Energy conservation strategies in urban transportation: Application of multiple criteria decision-making. *Energy Systems and Policy*, 11(1), 1–19.

Tzeng, G. H., & Teng, J. Y. (1994). Multicriteria evaluation for strategies of improving and controlling air-quality in the super city: A case of Taipei city. *Journal of Environmental Management*, 40(3), 213–229. doi:10.1006/jema.1994.1016

Tzeng, G. H., Shian, T. A., & Lin, C. Y. (1992). Application of multicriteria decision making to the evaluation of new energy-system development in Taiwan. *Energy*, 17(10), 983–992. doi:10.1016/0360-5442(92)90047-4

U.S. Department of Commerce. (1965). *National Technical Information Service*, NASA, PATTERN Relevance Guide, 3.

Ulrich, H. H. (1981). Die Bedeutung der Management-Philosophie für die Unternehmensführung. In H.H. Ulrich (Ed.), *Management-Philosophie für die Zukunft* (pp. 11-24). Bern, Stuttgart: Haupt.

Unruh, A., Bailey, J., & Ramamohanarao, K. (2004). Managing semantic compensation in a multi-agent system. In *International Conference on Cooperative Information Systems* (LNCS 3290).

US Department of Defense Dictionary of Military and Associated Terms. (2005). Retrieved September 26, 2008, from http://handle.dtic.mil/100.2/ADA439918

US Marine Corps. (1978). Fleet Marine Force Manual (FMFM) 6-4, *Marine Rifle Company/Platoon*, Marine Corps Combat Development Command, Quantico, VA

US Marine Corps. (2001). Marine Corps Warfighting Publication 3-16, (2001). *Fire Support in the Ground Combat Element*, Marine Corps Combat Development Command, Quantico, VA

US Marine Corps. (2008). Marine Corps Warfighting Publication 3-11.5, [Draft], *Marine Infantry Battalion*, Marine Corps Combat Development Command, Quantico, VA

Uslaner, E. M. (2004). Trust online, trust offline. *Communications of the ACM*, 47(4), 28–29. doi:10.1145/975817.975838

van der Aalst W. M. P., ter Hofstede A. H. M., Kiepuszewski B., & Barros A. P. (2000). Advanced workflow patterns (LNCS 1901, 18-19).

van der Aalst, W. (1998). The application of petri nets to workflow management. *Journal of Circuits . Systems and Computers*, 8(1), 21–66.

van der Aalst, W. (2001). Exterminating the dynamic change bug: A concrete approach to support workflow change. *Information Systems Frontiers*, *3*(3), 297–317. doi:10.1023/A:1011409408711

van der Aalst, W. M. P. (2001). How to handle dynamic change and capture management information: An approach based on generic workflow models. *Int. Journal of Computer Systems, Science, and Engineering*, *16*(5), 295–318.

van der Aalst, W. M. P. (2001). Exterminating the dynamic change bug: a concrete approach to support workflow change. *Information Systems Frontiers*, *3*(3), 297–317. doi:10.1023/A:1011409408711

Van der Aalst, W. M. P., & Basten, T. (1999). *Inheritance of workflows: An approach to tackling problems related to change* (Tech. Rep.). Eindhoven: Eindhoven University of Technology.

van der Aalst, W. M. P., & Basten, T. (2002). Inheritance of workflows: An approach to tackling problems related to change. *Theoretical Computer Science*, *270*(1-2), 125–203. doi:10.1016/S0304-3975(00)00321-2

van der Aalst, W. M. P., & ter Hofstede, A. (2000). Verification of workflow task structures: A Petri-net-based approach. *Information Systems*, *25*(1), 43–69. doi:10.1016/S0306-4379(00)00008-9

van der Aalst, W. M. P., & van Hee, K. M. (2002). *Workflow management: Models, methods, and systems*. Cambridge, MA: MIT Press.

van der Aalst, W. M. P., & Weijters, A. J. M. M. (2005). Process mining. In M. Dumas, W.M.P. van der Aalst & A.H.M ter Hofstede (Ed.), *Process aware information systems* (pp. 235-255). Wiley Interscience

van der Aalst, W. M. P., Barthelmess, P., Ellis, C. A., & Wainer, J. (2000). Workflow modeling using Proclets (LNCS 1901, pp. 198-209).

van der Aalst, W. M. P., Dongen, B. F., Herbst, J., Maruster, L., Schimm, G., & Weijters, A. J. M. M. (2003). Workflow mining: A survey of issues and approaches. *Data & Knowledge Engineering*, *47*(1), 237–267. doi:10.1016/S0169-023X(03)00066-1

van der Aalst, W. M. P., et al. (2000). Advance workflow patterns. In O. Etzion & P. Scheuermann (Eds.), *Cooperative Information Systems, 8th International Conference, CoopIS 2000* (LNCS 1901, pp. 18-29).

van der Aalst, W. M. P., Michael, R., & Marlon, D. (2007). Deadline-based escalation in process-aware information systems. *Decision Support Systems*, *43*, 492–511. doi:10.1016/j.dss.2006.11.005

van der Aalst, W. M. P., Reijers, H. A., Weijters, A. J. M. M., van Dongen, B. F., Alves de Medeiros, A. K., Song, M., & Verbeek, H. M. W. (2007). Business process mining: An industrial application. *Information Systems*, *32*(1), 713–732. doi:10.1016/j.is.2006.05.003

van der Aalst, W. M. P., ter Hofstede, A. H. M., Kiepuszewski, B., & Barros, A. P. (2003). Workflow Patterns. *Distributed and Parallel Databases*, *14*(3), 5–51. doi:10.1023/A:1022883727209

van der Aalst, W. M. P., van Dongen, B. F., Günther, C. W., Mans, R. S., Alves de Medeiros, A. K., Rozinat, A., et al. Verbeek H. M. W., & Weijters, A. J. M. M. (2007). ProM 4.0: Comprehensive support for real process analysis. In *Petri Nets and Other Models of Concurrency – ICATPN 2007* (pp. 484-494). New York: Springer.

Van der Aalst, W. M. P., Van Dongen, B. F., Herbst, J., Maruster, L., Schimm, G., & Weijters, A. (2003). Workflow mining: A survey of issues and approaches. *Data & Knowledge Engineering*, *47*(2), 237–267. doi:10.1016/S0169-023X(03)00066-1

van der Aalst, W. M. P., Weijters, T., & Maruster, L. (2004). Workflow mining: Discovering process models from event logs. *IEEE Transactions on Knowledge and Data Engineering*, *16*(9), 1128–1142. doi:10.1109/TKDE.2004.47

van der Aalst, W. M. P., Weske, M., & Grunbauer, D. (2005). Case handling: A new paradigm for business process support. *Data & Knowledge Engineering*, *53*(2), 129–162. doi:10.1016/j.datak.2004.07.003

van der Aalst, W., & Basten, T. (2002). Inheritance of workflows: An approach to tackling problems related to change. *Theoretical Computer Science, 270*(1-2), 125–203. doi:10.1016/S0304-3975(00)00321-2

van der Aalst, W., & Berens, P. (2001). Beyond workflow management: Product-driven case handling. In S. Ellis, T. Rodden, & I. Zigurs (Eds.), *Proceedings of the International ACM SIGGROUP Conference on Supporting Group Work*, (pp. 42–51). New York: ACM Press.

van der Aalst, W., & ter Hofstede, A. (2005). YAWL: Yet another workflow language. *Information Systems, 30*(4), 245–275. doi:10.1016/j.is.2004.02.002

van der Aalst, W., & van Hee, K. (2004). *Workflow management: Models, methods and systems.* Cambridge, Massachusetts: The MIT Press.

van der Aalst, W., & Weske, M., & Gräunbauer, D. (2005). Case handling: A new paradigm for business process support. *Data & Knowledge Engineering, 53*(2), 129–162. doi:10.1016/j.datak.2004.07.003

van der Aalst, W., Aldred, L., Dumas, M., & ter Hofstede, A. (2004). Design and implementation of the YAWL system. In A. Persson, & J. Stirna (Eds.), *Proceedings of The 16th International Conference on Advanced Information Systems Engineering (CAiSE 04)* (LNCS 3084, pp. 142-159). Riga, Latvia: Springer Verlag.

van der Aalst, W., ter Hofstede, A., & Weske, M. (2003, June). On the application of formal methods to process-aware information systems. In *Proceedings of the International Conference on Business Process Management.*

van der Aalst, W., ter Hofstede, A., Kiepuszewski, B., & Barros, A. (2003). Workflow patterns. *Distributed and Parallel Databases, 14*(3), 5–51. doi:10.1023/A:1022883727209

Van Hoof, J. (2007). SOA and EDA: Using events to bridge decoupled service boundaries. *The SOA Magazine.* Retrieved from http://www.soamag.com/I4/0207-2.asp

Vanderhaeghen, D., & Loos, P. (2007). Distributed model management platform for cross-enterprise business process management in virtual enterprise networks. *Journal of Intelligent Manufacturing, 18*(5), 553. doi:10.1007/s10845-007-0060-6

Venkatraman, N., & Prescott, J. E. (1990). Environment-strategy coalignment: An empirical test of its. *Strategic Management Journal, 11*(1), 1. doi:10.1002/smj.4250110102

Verbeek, E., & Aalst, W. van der. (2000, June). Woflan 2.0 - A Petri-net-based workflow diagnosis tool. In *Proceedings of the 21st International Application and Theory of Petri Nets.*

Verhagen, T., Meents, S., & Tan, Y. H. (2006). Perceived risk and trust associated with purchasing at electronic marketplaces. *European Journal of Information Systems, 15*, 542–555. doi:10.1057/palgrave.ejis.3000644

Vernadat, F. (1992). CIMOSA - A European development for enterprise integration (Part 2): enterprise modeling. Pergamon Press Inc.

Vissers, C. A., Lankhorst, M. M., & Slagter:, R. (2003). Reference models for advanced e-services. Paper presented at the 3rd IFIP Conference on E-Commerce, E-Business, E-Government, São Paulo, Brazil.

Volberda, H. W. (1999). *Building the flexible firm: How to remain competitive.* Oxford University Press

von Halle, B. (2002). *Business rules applied: Building better systems using the business rule approach.* John Wiley & Sons Ltd.

Vu, T., Powers, R., & Shoham, Y. (2006). Learning against multiple opponents. In *Proceedings of the fifth international joint conference on autonomous agents and multiagent systems* (pp. 752–759). New York: ACM.

Wagealla, W., Carbone, M., English, C., Terzis, S., & Nixon, P. (2003). A formal model for trust lifecycle management. In *Proceedings of Workshop on Formal Aspects of Security and Trust (FAST2003) as part of the 12th Formal Methods Europe Symposium (FM2003).* Retrieved April 23 2008, from http://www.cis.strath.ac.uk/research/publications/papers/strath_cis_publication_213.pdf.

Wagner, G. (2002, June). How to design a general rule markup language? In *Proceedings of the Workshop XML Technologies for the Semantic Web.*

Wang, F. (2002). Self-organising communities formed by middle agents. In *Proceedings of the first international joint conference on autonomous agents and multiagent systems* (pp. 1333-1339). New York: ACM Press.

Wang, M., & Kumar, K. (2008). Developing flexible business process management systems using modular computing technologies. In *Proceedings of Eighth Global Conference on Flexible Systems Management (GlOGIFT-08)*. Hoboken, NJ.

Wang, M., & Wang, H. (2002). Intelligent agents supported flexible workflow monitoring system. In *Proceedings of the14th International Conference on Advanced Information Systems Engineering (CAiSE'02)* (LNCS 2348, pp. 787-791).

Wang, M., & Wang, H. (2005). Intelligent agent supported business process management. In *Proceedings of 38th Hawaii International Conference on System Sciences (HICSS-38)*. IEEE Computer Society Press.

Wang, M., & Wang, H. (2006). From process logic to business logic - A cognitive approach to business process management. *Information & Management, 43*(2), 179–193. doi:10.1016/j.im.2005.06.001

Wang, M., Cheung, W. K., Liu, J., Xie, X., & Lou, Z. (2006). E-Service/process composition through multi-agent constraint management. *International Conference on Business Process Management (BPM 2006)* (LNCS 4102, pp. 274-289).

Wang, M., Liu, J., Wang, H., Cheung, W., & Xie, X. (2008b). On-demand e-supply chain integration: A multi-agent constraint-based approach. *Expert Systems with Applications, 34*(4), 2683–2692. doi:10.1016/j.eswa.2007.05.041

Wang, M., Wang, H., & Xu, D. (2005). The design of intelligent workflow monitoring with agent technology. *Knowledge-Based Systems, 18*(6), 257–266. doi:10.1016/j.knosys.2004.04.012

Wang, Y., & Singh, M. P. (2007). *Formal trust model for multiagent systems*. Retrieved April 28 2008, from http://www.csc.ncsu.edu/faculty/mpsingh/papers/mas/ijcai-07-trust.pdf.

Web Services Description Language. (2007). *WSDL specification*. Retrieved March 22, 2008, from http://www.w3.org/TR/wsdl

Web Services. (2004). *Web services tutorial*. Retrieved February 17, 2008, from http://www.w3schools.com/webservices/default.asp

Weber, B., & Reichert, M. (2008b). Refactoring process models in large process repositories. In *Proc. CAiSE'08* (LNCS 5074, pp. 124-139).

Weber, B., Reichert, M., & Rinderle-Ma, S. (2008). Change patterns and change support features - Enhancing flexibility in process-aware information systems. *Data & Knowledge Engineering, 66*(3), 438–466. doi:10.1016/j.datak.2008.05.001

Weber, B., Reichert, M., & Wild, W. (2006). Case-base maintenance for CCBR-based process evolution. In *Proc. 8th European Conf. on Case-Based Reasoning (ECCBR'06)* (LNCS 4106, pp. 106-120).

Weber, B., Reichert, M., Rinderle, S., & Wild, W. (2006). Towards a framework for the agile mining of business processes. In *BPM'05 Workshop Proceedings* (LNCS 3812, pp. 191-202).

Weber, B., Reichert, M., Wild, W., & Rinderle, S. (2005) Balancing flexibility and security in adaptive process management systems. In *Proc. 13th Int'l Conf. on Cooperative Information Systems (CooplS '05)* (LNCS 3760, pp. 59-76).

Weber, B., Reichert, M., Wild, W., & Rinderle-Ma, S. (2009). Providing integrated life cycle support in process-aware information systems. *Int'l Journal of Cooperative Information Systems (IJCIS), 18*(1), 115-165.

Weber, B., Rinderle, S., & Reichert, M. (2007). Change patterns and change support features in process-aware information systems. In *Proc. 19th Int'l Conf. on Advanced Information Systems Engineering (CAiSE'07)* (LNCS 4495, pp. 574-588).

Weber, B., Rinderle, S., Wild, W., & Reichert, M. (2005 a). CCBR-driven business process evolution. In *Proc. 6th Int'l Conf. on Case-Based Reasoning (ICCBR'05)* (LNCS 3620, pp. 610-624).

Weber, B., Wild, W., & Breu, R. (2004). CBRFlow: Enabling adaptive workflow management through conversational case-based reasoning. In P. Funk, & P. A. Gonzalez Calero (Eds.), *Proceedings of the 7th European Conference for Advances in Case Based Reasoning (ECCBR'04)* (LNCS 3155, pp. 434-448). Madrid, Spain: Springer.

Weerawarana, S., Curbera, F., Leymann, F., Storey, T., & Ferguson, D. F. (2005). *Web services platform architecture: SOAP, WSDL, WS-Policy, WS-Addressing, WS-BPEL, WS-reliable messaging, and more.* Prentice Hall.

Weikum, G., & Schek, H.-J. (1992). Concepts and applications of multilevel transactions and open nested transactions. In *Database transaction models for advanced applications* (pp. 515-553). San Francisco: Morgan Kaufmann Publishers, Inc.

Weiss, G. (Ed.). (1999). *Multiagent systems: A modern approach to distributed artificial intelligence.* Cambridge, MA: MIT Press.

Weissenfels, J., Muth, P., & Weikum, G. (1998). Flexible worklist management in a light-weight workflow management system. In *Proceedings of EDBT Workshop on Workflow Management Systems, Valencia.*

Welch, G., & Bishop, G. (1995). *An introduction to the Kalman filter* (Tech. Rep.). Chapel Hill, NC: University of North Carolina at Chapel Hill.

Wenger, E. (1998). *Communities of practice.* Cambridge University Press.

Wenger, E., McDermott, R. A., & Snyder, W. (2002). *Cultivating Communities of practice.* Boston: Harvard Business School Press.

Weske, M. (1998). Flexible modeling and execution of workflow activities. In *Proc. 31st Hawaii Int. Conf. on Sys Sciences* (pp. 713-722), Hawaii.

Weske, M. (1998). Object-oriented design of a flexible workflow management system. *2nd East-European Symposium on Advances in Databases and Information Systems* (LNCS 1475, pp. 119-130).

Weske, M. (1999). Workflow management through distributed and persistent CORBA workflow objects. In *Proc. CAiSE'99* (pp. 446-450), Heidelberg, Germany.

Weske, M. (2001). Formal foundation and conceptual design of dynamic adaptations in a workflow management system. In *Proc. HICSS-34.* Maui, Hawaii

Weske, M. (2007). *Business process management: Concepts, methods, technology.* Springer.

WFMC-AD. (1998). *Workflow management coalition 1998. Interface 5 - Audit data specification* (Tech. Rep. wfmc-tc-1015 issue 1.1). workflow management coalition.

WFMC-RM (1995). Workflow management coalition. *The workflow reference model* (wfmc-tc-1003).

WfMC-TC00-1003 (1995). *The workflow reference model.* Workflow Management Coalition, Lighthouse Point, FL.

White, S. (2006). *Business process modeling notation* (Version 1.0). Available at http://www.bpmn.org/Documents/OMG-02-01.pdf.

White, T. E., & Fischer, L. (1995). *New tools for new times: The workflow paradigm.* Future Strategies Inc.

Wiederhold, G. (1992). Mediators in the architecture of future information systems. *IEEE Computer, 25*(3), 38–49.

Wigand, R. T., Steinfield, C. W., & Markus, M. L. (2005). Information technology standards choices and industry structure outcomes: The case of the U.S. home mortgage industry. *Journal of Management Information Systems, 2*(22), 165–191.

Wild, W., Wirthenson, R., & Weber, B. (2006). Dynamic engines - A flexible approach to the extension of legacy code and process-oriented application development. *WETICE-2006 Proceedings of the 15th IEEE International Workshops on Enabling Technologies: Infrastructure for Collaborative Enterprises* (pp. 279-284). Manchester, UK

Windsor, J. (1986). Are automated tools changing systems analysis and design? *Journal of Systems Management*, *37*(11), 28–33.

Wingreen, S. C., & Baglione, S. L. (2005). Untangling the antecedents and covariates of e-commerce trust: Institutional trust vs. knowledge-based trust. *Electronic Markets*, *15*(3), 246–260. doi:10.1080/10196780500209010

Winograd, T., & Flores, F. (1986). *Understanding computers and cognition: A new foundation for design.* Addison-Wesley, Norwood, NJ.

Wohed, P., Aalst, W. M. P., Dumas, M., & Hostede, A. H. M ter (2003). Analysis of Web services composition languages: The case of bpel4ws. In Song et al. (Eds.), *Conceptual Modeling - ER 2003 - 22nd international Conference on Conceptual Modeling* (LNCS 2813, pp. 200-215).

Wolters, N. J. (2002). *The business of modularity and the modularity of business.* PhD Thesis, Erasmus Research Institute of Management, Rotterdam

Wong, J. Y. Y., Chiu, D. K. W., & Mark, K. P. (2007). Effective e-Government process monitoring and interoperation: A case study on the removal of unauthorized building works in Hong Kong. In *Proceedings of the 40th Hawaii International Conference on System Science (HICSS40)*. IEEE Press.

Wooldridge, M. (2002). *An introduction to multi-agent systems.* Wiley.

Wooldridge, M., & Jennings, N. R. (1999). Software engineering with agents: Pitfalls and pratfalls. *IEEE Internet Computing*, *3*(3), 20–27. doi:10.1109/4236.769419

Workflow Management Coalition. (1995, January). *The workflow reference model.*

Workflow Management Coalition. (2002). *Introduction to workflow.* Retrieved November 14, 2004, from http://www.wfmc.org/introduction_to_workflow.pdf

World Wide Web Consortium. (n.d.). *WSDL Specification: Web services description language (WSDL) version 2.0.* Retrieved from http://www.w3.org/TR/wsdl.

Worthen, B. (2002). Nestle's enterprise resource planning (ERP) odyssey. Retreived May 20, 2008, from http://www.cio.com/article/31066

Wright, J., & Race, P. (2004). The management of service operations (2nd ed.). London: Thomson.

WS-BPEL 2.0. (2007). *WS-BPEL 2.0: Web services for business process execution language.* Retrieved April 25, 2008, from http://docs.oasis-open.org/wsbpel/2.0/OS/wsbpel-v2.0-OS.html.

WS-CAF. (2003). *Web services composite application framework (WS-CAF).* Retrieved July 28, 2007, from http://www.oasis-open.org/committees/tc_home.php?wg_abbrev=ws-caf

Wullenweber, K., & Weitzel, T. (2007). An empirical exploration of how process standardization reduces outsourcing risks. In *Proceedings of the 40th Hawaii International Conference on System Sciences – 2007.*

Wyner, G., & Lee, J. (2001). *Defining specialization for process models* (Tech. Rep. # 4159). Boston: MIT Sloan School of Management.

Xiong, L., & Liu, L. (2002). Building trust in decentralized peer-to-peer electronic communities. In *Proceedings of International Conference on Electronic Commerce Research* (ICECR-5), Montreal, Canada, October.

Xiu, D., & Liu, Z. (2005). A formal definition for trust in distributed systems (LNCS 3650, pp. 482-489).

Yan, J., Yang, Y., & Raikundalla, G. (2004). Towards incompletely specified process support in SwinDeW - A peer-to-peer based workflow system. In W. Shen, Z. Lin, J. Barthμes, & T. Li (Eds.), *Proceedings of the 8th International Conference on Computer Supported Cooperative Work in Design (CSCWD 2004)* (LNCS 3168, pp. 328-338). Xiamen, China: Springer.

Yao, H., & Hamilton, H. J. (2008). Mining functional dependencies from data. *Data Mining and Knowledge Discovery*, *16*, 197–219. doi:10.1007/s10618-007-0083-9

Yeh, R. T. (1991). System development as a wicked problem. *International Journal of Software Engineering and Knowledge Engineering, 1*(2), 117–130. doi:10.1142/S0218194091000123

Yin, R. K. (1994). *Case study research: Design and methods* (2nd Ed.). Thousand Oaks, CA: Sage Publications.

Yoder, W., & Razavi, R. (2000). Adaptive object-models, *Conference on Object-Oriented Programming Systems Languages and Applications* (pp. 81-82). Minneapolis, Minnesota.

Zachman, J. (1987). A framework for information systems architecture. *IBM Systems Journal, 26*(3), 276–292.

Zadeh, L. A. (1981). *A definition of soft computing.*

Zairi, M., & Sinclair, D. (1995). Business process reengineering and process improvement. A survey of current practice and future trends in integrated management. *Management Decision, 3*(33), 3–16. doi:10.1108/00251749510085021

Zajac, E. J., Kraatz, M. S., & Bresser, R. K. F. (2000). Modeling the dynamics of strategic fit: A normative approach to strategic change. *Strategic Management Journal, 21*(4), 429. doi:10.1002/(SICI)1097-0266(200004)21:4<429::AID-SMJ81>3.0.CO;2-#

Zeithaml, V. A., Parasuraman, A., & Berry, L. L. (1985). Problems and strategies in services marketing. *Journal of Marketing, 2*(49), 33–46. doi:10.2307/1251563

Zeng, L., Benatallah, B., Lei, H., Ngu, A., Flaxer, D., & Chang, H. (2003). Flexible Composition of enterprise Web services. *Electronic Markets - The International Journal of Electronic Commerce and Business Media, 13*(2), 141-152.

Zhang, S., Lu, D., & Yang, Y. (2004). A fuzzy set based trust and reputation model in P2P networks (LNCS 3177, pp. 211-217).

Zhao, S., Liu, H., & Sun, Z. (2008). Scalable trust in multi-agent e-commerce system. In *ISECS 2008*, August 3-5, Guangzhou, China, (pp.990-993). IEEE Computer Society.

Zhao, X., & Liu, C. (2006). Supporting relative workflows with Web services. *Paper presented at the the 8th Asia Pacific Web Conference, Harbin, China.*

Zhao, X., Liu, C., & Yang, Y. (2005). An organisational perspective of inter-organisational workflows. *Paper presented at the 3rd International Conference on Business Process Management.*

Zhao, X., Liu, C., & Yang, Y. (2006). Supporting virtual organisation alliances with relative workflows. *Paper presented at the 3rd Asia-Pacific Conference on Conceptual Modelling Hobart, Australia.*

Zhao, X., Liu, C., Sadiq, W., & Kowalkiewicz, M. (2008). Process view derivation and composition in a dynamic collaboration environment. *Paper presented at the 16th International Conference on Cooperative Information Systems, Monterrey, Mexico.*

Zhao, X., Liu, C., Yang, Y., & Sadiq, W. (2007). Handling instance correspondence in inter-organisational workflows. *Paper presented at the 19th International Conference on Advanced Information Systems Engineering, Trondheim, Norway.*

Zhuang, H., Wongsoontorn, S., & Zhao, Y. (2003). A fuzzy-logic based trust model and its optimization for e-commerce. Retrieved May 2 2008, from http://www.eng.fau.edu/conf/fcrar2003/papers/FuzzyTrustModel21.pdf.

Zhuge, H. (2003). Component-based workflow systems design. *Decision Support Systems, 35*(4), 517–536. doi:10.1016/S0167-9236(02)00127-6

Zhuge, H. (2006). Knowledge flow network planning and simulation. *Decision Support Systems, 42*, 571–592. doi:10.1016/j.dss.2005.03.007

Ziemann, J., Leyking, K., Kahl, T., & Dirk, W. (2006). Enterprise model driven migration from legacy to SOA. *Software Reengineering and Services Workshop.*

Zimmermann, H. J. (1996). *Fuzzy set theory and its applications.* New York: Kluwer Academic Publisher.

zur Muehlen, M. (2004). *Workflow-based process controlling. Foundation, design, and implementation of workflow-driven process information systems.* Berlin: Logos.

About the Contributors

Minhong Wang is an Assistant Professor of Information &Technology Studies at the Faculty of Education, The University of Hong Kong. She received her PhD in Information Systems from City University of Hong Kong in 2005. Her current research interests include business process management, workflow systems, knowledge management, information systems, and e-learning. She has published papers in *Information & Management, Expert Systems with Applications, Knowledge-based Systems, Engineering Applications of Artificial Intelligence, Journal of Educational Technology and Society, International Journal of Intelligent Information Technologies, International Journal of Internet & Enterprise Management, International Journal of Technology and Human Interaction,* and presented papers at international conferences, including CAiSE, BPM, HICSS, AMCIS, ICEIS, PRICAI, CEC/EEE, ICELW among others. She is the Editor-in-Chief of *Knowledge Management & E-Learning: an International Journal (KM&EL),* and *The Handbook of Research on Complex Dynamic Process Management: Techniques for Adaptability in Turbulent Environments.* She is the Guest Editor of *International Journal of Internet & Enterprise Management.* She also serves on the Editorial Board for a number of international journals.

* * *

Wil van der Aalst is a full professor of Information Systems at the Technische Universiteit Eindhoven. Currently he is also an adjunct professor at Queensland University of Technology working within the BPM group there. His research interests include workflow management, process mining, Petri nets, business process management, process modeling, and process analysis. Many of his papers are highly cited (he has an H-index of more than 50 according to Google Scholar) and his ideas have influenced researchers, software developers, and standardization committees working on process support. For more information about his work visit: www.workflowpatterns.com, www.workflowcourse.com, www.processmining.org, www.yawl-system.com, www.wvdaalst.com.

Michael Adams is a senior researcher within the BPM group at the Queensland University of Technology in Brisbane, Australia, and was awarded his PhD in 2007. He is currently directly responsible for the ongoing development and maintenance of the YAWL project. He designed, developed and implemented two core YAWL services: the Worklet Service; and the Resource Service, which provides for resource allocation and task routing, integrating a built-in worklist handler and administration tools. He is additionally responsible for improvements to the YAWL Engine and Process Editor, and is the primary developer of YAWL Release 2.0.

Mair Allen-Williams did her first degree at the University of Cambridge, studying computer science. After a year as a research assistant investigating a distributed programming language, she moved to Edinburgh for a Masters in informatics. She is currently working on a PhD in distributed agent learning at the University of Southampton.

N. Ilker Altintas has received his B.Sc., M.Sc. and Ph.D. degrees from the Department of Computer Engineering at Middle East Technical University. He has worked as a research assistant at the same university during 1992-1998 where he participated actively in many research and industrial projects. Then, he joined Cybersoft in 2000 and worked as a project manager in banking and financial projects. He still works as Projects Coordinator in Istanbul where he is managing the banking product family. His technical interests include large scale software development, software product line engineering, software architectures and software development methodologies.

Hyerim Bae is an associate professor in the Industrial Engineering Department at Pusan National University (PNU), Korea. He received PhD, MS, and BS degrees from the Industrial Engineering Department at Seoul National University, Korea. He had been a manager for information strategic planning at Samsung Card Corporation before he joined PNU. He is interested in the areas of Business Process Management (BPM), process-based B2B integration, and ubiquitous business computing. His current research activities include analysis of business process efficiency, controlling of logistics processes with context awareness, convenient modeling of business processes, and inter-organizational workflow process.

Thomas Bauer has been a senior researcher at the Daimler Research Centre in Ulm, Germany since 2002. Focus of his work is on advanced issues related to process support in the automotive domain. Until 2001 he worked for the Institute of Databases and Information Systems at the University of Ulm where he finished his PhD thesis on the efficient management of enterprise-wide workflows in 2001. Current research areas include management of business process variants, business process visualization, integration of workflows with human tasks, and integration of process management technology with service-oriented architectures.

Jyoti Bhat leads the Business Process Management Research group within the Software Engineering and Technology Labs (SETLabs) of Infosys. Her current research interests include Process monitoring, simulation, process innovation, BPM governance and BPM-SOA methodologies. She has 15 years of industry experience in software delivery, research and process consulting. She has expertise in several areas of Process Management, change management, software engineering including Object Oriented Analysis and Design, Requirements Analysis and Business Process Management. Jyoti has been the Program Manager for Infosys Strategic Initiatives, Metrics Program and several Process Improvement initiatives. She program managed the creation of the Business process repository and project management platform for Infosys. She is a certified CMMI Assessor and ISO Auditor. She has several publications on Process Management, Requirements Engineering and software engineering. One of the papers she co-authored titled "Measuring and Improving Process Capabilities – Best Practices" was awarded the Best practice paper in the SEPG conference APAC 2002.

Ilia Bider is Director R&D and co-founder of IbisSoft. He is an active proponent of Douglas Engelbart's vision that the aim of a computer system is to enhance human intellect, rather than substitute it, or turn humans into slaves. Dr. Bider has combined experience of over 30 years of research and practical work in five countries. He is the inventor of the state-oriented business process modeling technique, and the author of over 50 research papers, as well as a considerable number of articles for practitioners. He frequently holds tutorials at international conferences, and he sits on the editorial board of several academic journals.

Steen Brahe is an innovation specialist at Danske Bank, Denmark. He has a master of science in engineering and holds a PhD degree in computer science from the IT University of Copenhagen, where he researched in Model Driven Development and Business Process Management. He has worked within the software industry for several years, particularly with SOA, MDD and BPM. Currently, Steen works with technological oriented innovation with focus on software development tools.

Semih Cetin has received B.Sc., M.Sc. and Ph.D. degrees from the Department of Computer Engineering at Middle East Technical University. He has previously worked as a software engineer, consultant, R&D and project manager at the beginning of his career. In 1995, he has co-founded Cybersoft Information Technologies and still works in the company as a managing partner mainly responsible for improving the technology base. His technical interests include software development methodologies, software process management, object orientation, aspect orientation, software architectures, and middleware technologies. He gives lectures in Computer Engineering departments at Middle East Technical University and Cankaya University.

Pethuru Raj Chelliah (www.peterindia.net) has been working as a senior consultant in business integration stream of Wipro Technologies, Bangalore, India for the last two years. Before that, he worked in a couple of research assignments in leading Japanese universities. He has 10 years of IT industry experiences after the successful completion of his UGC-sponsored PhD in formal language theory / fine automata in the year 1997. He worked as a CSIR research associate in the department of computer science and automation (CSA), Indian institute of science (IISc), Bangalore for 14 memorable months. He has been authoring research papers for leading journals and is currently involved in writing a comprehensive and informative book on Next-Generation Service Oriented Architecture (SOA).

Jinjun Chen received the BS degree in Applied Mathematics and ME degree in Communication and Information Systems from XiDian University, China, in 1996 and 1999 respectively. He received the PhD degree in Computer Science and Software Engineering from Swinburne University of Technology, Australia, in 2007. He is currently a lecturer in Faculty of Information and Communication Technologies at Swinburne University of Technology. His research interests include scientific workflow management and applications, software verification and validation in workflow systems, and service oriented computing. He is a member of the IEEE and the IEEE Computer Society.

Dickson K.W. Chiu received the B.Sc. (Hons.) degree in Computer Studies from the University of Hong Kong in 1987. He received the M.Sc. (1994) and the Ph.D. (2000) degrees in Computer Science from the Hong Kong University of Science and Technology, where he worked as a Visiting Assistant Lecturer after graduation. He also started his own computer company while studying part-time. From

2001 to 2003, he was an Assistant Professor at the Department of Computer Science, the Chinese University of Hong Kong. He was a Visiting Assistant Professor in 2006 at the Computing Department, Hong Kong Polytechnic University for teaching M.Sc. courses. With his solid industrial experience and cross-disciplinary research, he has taught a wide range of subjects at various levels. His research interests are in information systems, information technologies, service computing, and e-/m-business with a cross-disciplinary approach, involving Internet technologies, agents, workflows, software engineering, information system management, security, and databases. His research results have been published in over 100 papers in international journals and conference proceedings, including practical results of many master and undergraduate projects. He received a best paper award in the 37th Hawaii International Conference on System Sciences (HICSS) in 2004. He serves as Associate Editor of the Engineering Letters and Editorial Board Member of the International Journal of Web Service Research, and International Journal of Software Architecture. He co-founded several international workshops and co-edited several special issues in journals. He also served as a mini-track co-chair in the Decision Technologies track of HICSS, a theme (Service Intelligence and Service Science) co-chair in the International Conference of Machine Learning and Cybernetics, and program committee member in many international conferences. Dr. Chiu is a Senior Member of the ACM, a Senior Member of the IEEE, and a life member of the Hong Kong Computer Society.

Mei-Tai Chu is a sessional lecturer of School of Business, La Trobe University. Her PhD thesis is Communities of Practice Driven Knowledge Management. She has published over 20 journal articles, referred conference papers and book chapters. She received Master's degree in Technology of Management from Chaio-Tung University, Taiwan. Her current research interests include communities of practice, knowledge management, multiple criteria decision making, enterprise business intelligence, e-business systems and project management. She has received the Outstanding Conference Paper Award of the Chinese Association of Value of Taiwan and Best Master Thesis Award Certificate of Chinese Society of Technology of Management of Taiwan. She has engaged with KM consultancy in several organizations including universities on knowledge management projects.

Peter Dadam has been full professor at the University of Ulm and director of the Institute of Databases and Information Systems since 1990. Before he started his work at the University of Ulm he had been director of the research department for Advanced Information Management (AIM) at the IBM Heidelberg Science Center (HDSC). At HDSC he managed the AIM-P project on advanced database technology and applications. Current research areas include distributed, cooperative information systems, workflow management and database technology as well as their use in advanced application areas. Peter was PC Co-chair of the BPM'07 conference in Brisbane, Australia. Together with Manfred Reichert he will be General Co-chair of the BPM'09 conference in Ulm.

Terance Bernard Dias is a member of the Web Services/SOA Center of Excellence in SETLabs, the technology research division at Infosys Technologies, India. He has substantial experience in publishing papers, presenting papers at conferences, and defining standards for SOA and Web services. His fields of interest include SOA enabling technologies like ESB, web services interoperability and grid computing.

Shinichi Doi received the B.A. from College of Arts and Sciences, University of Tokyo in 1985 and the M.A. from Department of General Systems Studies, Graduate School of Arts and Sciences, University of Tokyo in 1987. In 1990, he joined C&C information Technology research laboratories, NEC Corporation. From 1996 to 1997, he was a visiting researcher at Human Communication Research Centre, University of Edinburgh. Now, he is a principal researcher of C&C Innovation Research Laboratories, NEC Corporation. His research areas are human communication, natural language processing and social interaction.

Dong Dong is an associate professor in Computer Science and Technology at College of Mathematics and Information Science, Hebei Normal University, China. His research interests include software engineering, information systems and intelligent computing. He has a BSci from Hebei Normal University, a MEng from Beijing University of Technology, a MSci from Asian Institute of Technology. He is a member of the China Computer Federation.

Jude Fernandez leads research projects within the BPM Research Center at the Software Engineering & Technology Labs (SETLabs) in Infosys. He has been instrumental in developing Infosys' BPM viewpoint and his current research interests include exploring distributed work patterns in addition to other related BPM areas. Jude has about 15 years of experience in the Process arena both as an internal and external consultant. He was a key member of the Corporate Quality team at Infosys and was the change agent for initiatives including Malcolm Baldrige assessments for Infosys, 6 Sigma-based BPR projects, Annual Customer Satisfaction Survey amongst others. Jude's consulting experience covers different areas including Balanced Scorecard, Process Analysis and Improvement, BPR etc. He was the chairperson of the first International Workshop on BPM Governance (held in Sept 2007 co-located with BPM 2007).

Mati Golani is a staff member in the software engineering department at Ort Braude college, Israel. He holds a Ph.D. in Information Management Engineering from the Technion - Israel Institute of Technology. Current research involves workflow systems and modeling, especially in aspects of dynamic and ad-hoc changes. It also includes several papers, published in various conferences, and journals, as well as membership in several program committees. Research interests also include rule management systems, databases, software design, and information systems analysis. Before completion of his Ph.D. and Joining Braude College, Mati held a position as a research staff member in the IBM research laboratories in Israel since 2000. He worked in the Active middleware technologies department on new technologies/tooling development. In the recent two decades, Mati also provides consulting and integration services for the industry, especially in ERP environment and business process related topics in various projects.

Jon Atle Gulla is professor of Information Systems at the Norwegian University of Science and Technology (NTNU) since 2002. He received his M.Sc. in 1988 and his Ph.D. in 1993, both in Information Systems at the Norwegian Institute of Technology. Gulla also has a M.Sc. in Linguistics from the University of Trondheim from 1995 and a M.Sc. of Management (Sloan fellow) from London Business School from 2003. He has previously worked as the general manager of Elexir Sprachtechnologie in Munich and as a senior consultant and project leader for Norsk Hydro in Brussels. His research interests include text mining, information retrieval, semantic web, ontologies, conceptual modeling and large-scale enterprise systems.

Jun Han is now an associate professor in School of Computer Science and Engineering, Beihang University, Beijing, China. Upon graduation from the Department of Automatic Control at Beijing Institute of Technology in 1990, Jun Han was employed by the Institute of Automation of HLJ Provincial Academy of Science in China. After having worked there for 5 years as an engineer, he was promoted to be head of the Department of Product Development. In 1996, he took up the post of vice general manager and chief engineer of Huajie Electronic Company. He commenced his study as a research student at Bond University in Australia in 1999 and was awarded the degree of PhD in 2003. His current research interests include network synthesis, operations research and intelligent systems.

Diana Heckl is research associate and postgraduate at the research centre ProcessLab at Frankfurt School of Finance & Management. Born in 1981, she studied Business Administration at the University of Cooperative Education Mannheim (Bachelor of Arts). Then, she graduated from Frankfurt School of Finance & Management (Master of Arts). Next to her studies, she worked at the DZ BANK AG (2000 - 2005): two-year training education, two-year referee work with varied projects concerning questions of principle, customer relation management (CRM), SAP and process problems, and one year of referee work at the management board.

Arthur ter Hofstede received his PhD in Computer Science from the University of Nijmegen in The Netherlands in 1993. Currently he works as a Professor at Queensland University of Technology in Brisbane, Australia, where he is co-leader of the BPM group. His main research interests are in the conceptual and formal foundations of workflow. He is involved in both the Workflow Patterns Initiative (www.workflowpatterns.com <http://www.workflowpatterns.com/>) and the YAWL (Yet Another Workflow Language) Initiative (www.yawl-system.com <http://www.yawl-system.com/>).

Haiyang Hu received the BS, MS, and PhD degree from Nanjing University, Nanjing, China, in 2000, 2003 and 2006, respectively. He is currently an Associate Professor in the College of Computer Science and Information Engineering, Zhejiang Gongshang University, Hangzhou, China. His current research interests include mobile computing, and software engineering. He has published about 20 research papers in international journals and conferences. Dr. Hu has served as the PC members in conferences and workshops (NASAC'08, MBC'09, WCMT'09). He is a senior member of CCF.

Hua Hu received the BS, MS, and PhD degree from Zhejiang University, Hangzhou, China, in 1987, 1990 and 1998, respectively. He is currently a full Professor at the College of Computer Science and Information Engineering, Zhejiang Gongshang University, Hangzhou, China. He was also a visiting professor at the State Unversity of New York, USA. His current research interests include distributed computing, software agents, and workflow technology. He has published more than 60 research papers in international journals and conferences. Dr.Hu has served as the general chair in the MBC'09 and WCMT'09 international workshops.

Patrick Hung is an Associate Professor and IT Director at the Faculty of Business and Information Technology in UOIT and an Adjunct Faculty Member at the Department of Electrical and Computer Engineering in University of Waterloo. Patrick is currently collaborating with Boeing Phantom Works (Seattle, USA) and Bell Canada on security- and privacy-related research projects, and he has filed two US patent applications on "Mobile Network Dynamic Workflow Exception Handling System." Patrick is also cooperating on Web services composition research projects with Southeast University in China. Recently he is working on a mobile healthcare project with the Hong Kong Red Cross with the Chinese University of Hong Kong. He is an executive committee member of the IEEE Computer Society's Technical Steering Committee for Services Computing, a steering member of EDOC "Enterprise Computing," and an associate editor/editorial board member/guest editor in several international journals such as the IEEE Transactions on Services Computing (TSC), International Journal of Web Services Research (JWSR) and International journal of Business Process and Integration Management (IJBPIM). He has been published more than 100 research and technical articles in International journals, conferences and workshops.

Jon Espen Ingvaldsen is a PhD student at the Norwegian University of Science and Technology. His research interest is in the border areas of business intelligence, unstructured data and business process management.

Nicholas R Jennings is Professor of Computer Science in the 5*-rated School of Electronics and Computer Science at Southampton University, where he carries out research in agent-based computing and complex adaptive systems. He is Associate Dean (Research and Enterprise) for the Faculty of Engineering Science and Maths, Head of the Intelligence, Agents, Multimedia Group (which consists of some 120 research staff and postgraduate students), Director of the BAE Systems / EPSRC Strategic Partnership on Decentralised Data and Information Systems, and the Chief Scientific Officer for Lost Wax. He was previously the Deputy Head of School for Research (2001-08).

Arla Juntunen PhD in Marketing at the Helsinki School of Economics (HSE), Marketing and Management Department, Finland and a Master's degree in Administrative Information Systems at the University of Helsinki. She is a post-doc researcher at the University of Helsinki, researcher at the HSE and a Senior Advisor in Finland's Supreme Command of the Police. Her research interests focus on strategic management, innovation and business networks, and Management Information Systems (MIS).

Rajiv Khosla holds degrees in Engineering (B.E. Electrical Eng), Management (M. Tech Management and Systems), and Computer Science (M.Sc. and Ph.D.). He has published 10 books, and over 100 research papers in intelligent systems, soft computing, e-business, emotional intelligence, management, software engineering, and power systems. He is the director of BSKM Research Laboratory at La Trobe University, Melbourne Australia. His research interests include knowledge management, e-business, intelligent systems, management information systems, Context-aware emotion-based systems, human-centered systems, agent-orient software engineering, soft computing agents, and data mining. He is on the editorial board of five international journals in Intelligent Informatics, Intelligent Manufacturing, Pattern Recognition, Cognitive Systems Research and Knowledge-based Engineering Systems.

Mark Klein is a Principal Research Scientist at the MIT Center for Coordination Science, and an Affiliate at the MIT CS and AI Lab (CSAIL) as well the New England Complex Systems Institute. His research is in the domain of coordination science, with the goal of developing methods and tools that support more effective coordination in groups with humans and/or computer-based agents. Mark has published over 90 papers in these areas, and has developed systems for conflict management, design rationale capture, exception handling, negotiation, process retrieval, and knowledge management. He also sits on the editorial boards for CERA, AI EDAM and CSCW.

Kuldeep Kumar is a professor of IS at Florida International University. He is also a visiting professor in the Department of Information Systems at the City University of Hong Kong. He received his PhD in Management Science and Information Systems from McMaster University. His research interests include IT-enabled collaboration and cooperation, methodology engineering, and management of information systems. He has published papers in *MIS Quarterly, Communications of ACM, Information Systems, IEEE Transactions on Software Engineering,* among others. He is also a Guest Editor of *Communications of ACM.*

Krishnendu Kunti is working as a Technical Architect with SETLBAS SOA Center of excellence, Infosys technologies LTD. Krishnendu has extensively published in leading journals, conferences and books. He had worked across a gamut of projects involving SOA, starting from setting up SOA center of excellence to architecting solutions based on SOA across multiple platforms. He has also lead the development of Infosys SOA testing framework "ACCORD SOA Solution" and has been involved in formulation of go to market strategy. His areas of interest includes SOA, Data services and application architecture in general, he can be reached at krishnendu_kunti@infosys.com

Chengfei Liu is an associate professor of Faculty of Information and Communication Technologies, Swinburne University of Technology, Australia. He is also the leader of Web and Data Engineering program of Centre for Information and Technology Research. His research interests cover XML data integration, advanced database systems, workflows, and transaction management for collaborative business processes. Liu has a Ph.D in Computer Science from Nanjing University, China.

Jianxun Liu was born in 1970, received his MS and PhD degree in computer science from Central South University of Technology in 1997 and Shanghai Jiao Tong University in 2003, respectively. He is now a professor and vice dean of School of Computer Science and Engineering, Hunan University of Science and Technology. His current interests include workflow management systems, service computing, semantic and knowledge grid. He has published about 40 academic papers in technical journals, books, international journal and conference proceedings.

Bijoy Majumdar is a member of the SOA and Web Services group of SETLabs, research arm of Infosys Technologies, a global IT consulting firm and has substantial experience in publishing papers, presenting papers at conferences, and defining solutions for SOA and Web services. Bijoy works as a technical architect in designing enterprise solutions with leading-edge technologies. For the past couple of years, he anchors the design, development and evangelization of Infosys BPM product PEAS. He can be reached at bijoy_majumdar@infosys.com.

Jürgen Moormann, Professor of Banking Head of ProcessLab. Since 1995 Professor of Banking with Frankfurt School of Finance and Management. Areas of teaching and research are Bank Strategy, Business Process Management, and IT Management in banks. 2005 foundation of ProcessLab - a research center focussing on bank-related process management. Visiting Professor at the University of Colorado/USA, at the University of New South Wales, Sydney, Australia, and at the Queensland University of Technology, Brisbane, Australia. Member of the advisory boards of comdirect private finance AG, Quickborn, and Karis AG, Griesheim, and Liaison Tutor of the Friedrich-Naumann-Foundation, Berlin.

John Mylopoulos earned a PhD degree from Princeton University in 1970 and has been professor of Computer Science at the University of Toronto since that year. His research interests include conceptual modelling, requirements engineering, data semantics and knowledge management. Mylopoulos is a fellow of the Association for the Advancement of Artificial Intelligence (AAAI, aka American Association for Artificial Intelligence) and the Royal Society of Canada (Academy of Sciences). He has served as programme/general chair of international conferences in Artificial Intelligence, Databases and Software Engineering, including IJCAI (1991), Requirements Engineering (1997), and VLDB (2004). He is currently serving as series co-editor of the Lecture Notes in Business Information Processing (LNBIP) series published by Springer-Verlag. Since September 2005 Mylopoulos holds a distinguished professorship (chiara fama) of Science at the University of Trento.

Toyoaki Nishida is a professor of Department of Intelligence Science and Technology, Graduate School of Informatics, Kyoto University. He received the Doctor of Engineering degree from Kyoto University in 1984. His research centers on Social Intelligence Design and Conversational Informatics. His representative work is Nishida (ed.) Conversational Informatics -- An Engineering Approach, Wiley, 2007. He was appointed an associate member of the Science Council of Japan, a vice-president of JSAI (Japanese Society for Artificial Intelligence), and a member of the board of directors of IPS (Information Processing Society) of Japan, in 2008.

Mark Nissen is Chair Professor of Command & Control, Information Science and Management at the Naval Postgraduate School. He focuses on dynamic knowledge and organization for competitive advantage. He views work, technology and organization as an integrated design problem, and had his second book, entitled *Harnessing Knowledge Dynamics: Principled Organizational Knowing & Learning* (IRM Press 2006), published recently. Mark's extensive publications span information systems, project management, organization studies, knowledge management, counterterrorism and related fields. Before his information systems doctoral work at the University of Southern California, he acquired over a dozen years' management experience in the aerospace and electronics industries.

Lieutenant Colonel Carl Oros, United States Marine Corps, is a member of the faculty in the Information Sciences Department of the Naval Postgraduate School where he teaches courses in Information Operations and wireless networking. Carl views the organization as a dynamic interaction of people, their tasks, technology, and associated organizational structure. His interests lie in understanding and architecting the "infostructure" essential to the organization's mission. He has published papers in the International Command & Control Research Technology Symposium (ICCRTS) and has previously spoken on this topic as a key note at the World Wide Consortium of the Grid (W2COG) inaugural conference and recently at the Armed Forces Communications Electronics Association (AFCEA) George Mason University's conference on Critical Issues in C4I."

Bart Orriëns is an experienced researcher in the domain of information management. His interests lie in the area of business rules and composition of automated services with a specific interest to develop theories, techniques and methodologies that can supports business collaborations. He has considerable expertise in the domains of Service Oriented Architectures, Web Services technology as well as business process modeling, constraint analysis, rule specification and management, and (formal) rule driven model generating. Moreover, he is well skilled in the entirety of software development from the initial phase of requirements analysis to actual prototyping.

Erik Perjons is a Univ. lecturer at Royal Institute of Technology (KTH). He teaches and does his research in the areas of information and process modeling, workflow management systems, service-oriented architecture and computing, model driven development, system integration, e-cooperation and business intelligence. He has many-years of experience of national and international research projects with and without participation of the industrial partners. He has also a background in journalism and experience of working for daily press, as well as media intelligence companies.

Claudio Petti is Assistant Professor at the e-Business Management Section of the Scuola Superiore ISUFI – University of Salento. His research interests spans in the fields of Strategic Management and ICT-enabled Innovation and is regularly involved in teaching such topics in graduate and executive programs. He has been and is currently involved in applied research projects related with digital and organizational innovation issues mainly at the Mediterranean level (Morocco, Tunisia and Jordan) where he is coordinating initiatives for the diffusion of ICTs and e-Business culture and practices in Small and Medium Enterprises.

Kotagiri Ramamohanarao (Rao) received the ME degree from the Indian Institute of Science in 1974, and the PhD degree from Monash University in 1980. He is a professor in computer science in Melbourne University, Australia. He is on the Editorial Boards for Universal Computer Science, the Journal of Knowledge and Information Systems, IEEE TKDE and VLDB Journal. He is also a steering committee member of IEEE ICDM, PAKDD and DASFAA. Rao is a fellow of the Institute of Engineers Australia, Australian Academy Technological Sciences and Engineering and Australian Academy of Science. Rao has research interests in database systems, agent oriented systems, data mining and machine learning.

Manfred Reichert has been full professor at the University of Ulm since January 2008. From 2005 to 2007 he worked as Associate Professor at the University of Twente (UT) where he was coordinator of the strategic research initiatives on E-health (2005 - 2006) and Service-oriented Computing (2007). At UT he was also member of the Management Board of the *Centre for Telematics and Information Technology* which is the largest ICT research institute in the Netherlands. Manfred has worked on advanced issues related to process management technology and service-oriented computing for ten years. Together with Peter Dadam he pioneered the work on the ADEPT process management system, which currently provides the most advanced technology for realising flexible process-aware information systems. Manfred was PC Co-chair of the BPM'08 conference in Milan and will be General Co-chair of the BPM'09 conference in Ulm.

Hajo Reijers is an assistant professor with the Information Systems group of Eindhoven University of Technology. In 2002, he got his PhD in Computer Science from Eindhoven University of Technology, while he worked as a manager for Deloitte Consulting. His research interests are in business process modeling, workflow management technology, and discrete event simulation. He published on these and other topics in Information Systems, Journal of Management Information Systems, Omega, International Journal of Cooperative Information Systems, Computer Supported Cooperative Work, and other scholarly journals.

Nick Russell has 20 years' experience in the IT industry in a variety of technical and senior management roles. During this time, he has led a number of high-profile systems integration and product development initiatives for organizations in the financial and retail sectors. He completed his PhD at Queensland University of Technology and is currently conducting postdoctoral research at the Technische Universiteit Eindhoven in the Netherlands. Over the past five years, he has been the driving force for the extension of the workflow patterns to the data, resource and exception handling perspectives and the development of the newYAWL business process modeling reference language.

Zhaohao Sun received a PhD in information technology from Bond University, Australia. Currently, Currently, he is a senior lecturer in Information Systems at Graduate School of Information technology and Mathematical Sciences, University of Ballarat, Australia, after working as a full professor of computer science and technology and the Head of the School of Computer Science and Technology at Hebei Normal University, China for two years (2007-2009). He previously held academic positions at Hebei University, China; RWTH Aachen, TU Cottbus, Germany; Bond University and the University of Wollongong, Australia. He has two books and more than 80 research publications of national and/or international journals, book chapters and conference proceedings. His monograph (co-authored with Prof Gavin Finnie): Intelligent Techniques in E-Commerce was published by Springer Verlag, Berlin Heidelberg, Germany in 2004. He has lectured more than 20 different subjects for computing undergraduate and postgraduate students in China and Australia. His current research interests include algorithm analysis and design, e-commerce and e-business, intelligent techniques in e-commerce and e-services, case-based/experience-based reasoning, multiagent systems, web intelligence and web engineering, intelligent computing, knowledge/experience management. He is a member of the AIS and the IEEE.

Thomas Trojer received the BS degree from University of Innsbruck, Austria, in 2007 and is currently doing his Master studies in Computer Science. He is working for the Research Group Quality Engineering headed by Profesor Ruth Breu in Innsbruck and is collaborating with Patrick C.K. Hung (University of Ontario Institute of Technology, Canada) in his research fields of interest, namely, service computing, security in service computing, data privacy and access control. Thomas gathered project experience during his work on several projects in the fields of inter-organisational workflow security, privacy-aware access control in healthcare systems and mobile healthcare systems.

Ozgur Tufekci has graduated from Industrial Engineering Department of Middle East Technical University in 1995. She has received her M.Sc. degree in 1997 from the Industrial Engineering Department at Bilkent University while working as a research assistant in the same department. Later, she moved to industry and started working in R&D Department of ASELSAN Communications Division. She has joined Cybersoft in 1998 and still works as Projects Coordinator responsible from Ankara Branch. Mrs. Tufekci is a Ph.D. candidate in Informatics Institute at Middle East Technical University.

Amy Unruh received the BS degree from UC Santa Barbara in 1984 and the PhD degree in computer science from Stanford University in 1993. She was a research fellow in the Department of Computer

Science and Software Engineering at the University of Melbourne. Her research interests include web technologies, multi-agent systems, information integration, distributed control and event detection, and planning.

Mingzhong Wang received the ME degree from Northwestern Polytechnical University, China, in 2005. At present he is a PhD candidate of the Department of Computer Science and Software Engineering at the University of Melbourne, Australia. His research interests include robust agent systems, parallel and distributed systems, and workflow systems. He is a member of the IEEE, the IEEE Computer Society and the ACM.

Yiping Wen received his MS degree in computer science from Hunan University of Science and Technology in 2008. During his studies he participated in research projects in the areas of workflow. He is now working at Hunan University of Science and Technology. His research interests include workflow, data mining and service computing.

Keiji Yamada received the B.E., the M.E., and the Dr. Eng degrees in information science from Kyoto University in 1982, 1984, and 1987. In 1987, he joined C&C information Technology research laboratories, NEC Corporation. From 1990 to 1991, he was a visiting scholar of Computer Science and Engineering Department, University of California at San Diego. Now, he is a general manager of C&C Innovation Research Laboratories, NEC Corporation. His research interest covers knowledge processing and human communication based on pattern recognition, computer vision, artificial neural network, machine learning, human interaction, and intelligent network.

Jian Yang is an associate professor at Department of Computing, Macquarie University. She received her PhD distributed systems area from The Australian National University in 1995. Before she joined Macquarie University, she worked as an associate professor at Tilburg University, Netherlands, a senior research scientist at the Division of Mathematical and Information Science, CSIRO, and as a lecturer at Dept of Computer Science, The Australian Defence Force Academy. Her main research interests are: business process modeling and management, web service technology; interoperability issues in digital libraries and e-commerce; query languages and query optimization; materialized view design and data warehousing.

Shuliang Zhao received the PhD degree from Bejing University of Technology, Beijing in 2006. He is an associate professor in computer science and technology at College of Mathematics and Information Science, Hebei Normal University. He has published more than 30 research papers. His research interests include multiagent system and business intelligence.

Xiaohui Zhao is a postdoctoral research fellow of Faculty of Information and Communication Technologies, Swinburne University of Technology, Australia. Zhao's research interests include business process management and service-oriented architecture. Zhao has a Ph.D in Information Technology from Swinburne University of Technology, Australia.

Yi Zhuang was a recipient of IBM Ph.D Fellowship 2007-2008, participating in the study of an optimal hybrid storage model based on DB2 as a research intern in IBM China Research Lab. His research interests include database systems, index techniques, parallel computing and multimedia retrieval and indexing. He is currently an Associate Professor at the College of Computer & Information Engineering in Zhejiang Gongshang University. He obtained his PhD degree in computer science from Zhejiang University in 2008. Dr. Zhuang is currently a member of ACM, a member of IEEE, and senior member of CCF. Dr. Zhuang has served as PC co-chairs in the MBC'09 and WCMT'09 international workshops as well as PC members and reviewers for some top technical journals and leading international conferences such as TMM, TKDE, ACM MM'08, ICDE'08,'09, MMM'05,'06, WAIM'05,'08. Dr. Zhuang has published more than 20 papers including IEEE International Conference on Distributed Computing Systems (ICDCS'08), ACM Trans. on Asian Language Information Processing (TALIP), Journal of Computer Science and Technology (JCST), Science in China (E: Information Science), etc. Dr. Zhuang has also co-authored two books and received 3 patents.

Index